SELECTIONS FROM THE SMUTS PAPERS

VOLUME VII

SELECTIONS FROM THE
SMUTS PAPERS

VOLUME VII

AUGUST 1945–OCTOBER 1950

BIOGRAPHICAL NOTES AND INDEX

EDITED BY

JEAN VAN DER POEL

CAMBRIDGE
AT THE UNIVERSITY PRESS

1973

Published by the Syndics of the Cambridge University Press
Bentley House, 200 Euston Road, London NW1 2DB
American Branch: 32 East 57th Street, New York, N.Y. 10022

Library of Congress Catalogue Card Number: 64–21586

ISBN: 0 521 08604 3

Printed in Great Britain
at the University Printing House, Cambridge
(Brooke Crutchley, University Printer)

CONTENTS OF VOLUME VII

PART XVIII: THE LAST FIVE YEARS

27 AUGUST 1945–17 OCTOBER 1950

PART XVIII

THE LAST FIVE YEARS

27 AUGUST 1945–17 OCTOBER 1950

THE LAST FIVE YEARS

For almost three of the last five years of his life Smuts continued to bear, without respite, the responsibilities of a prime minister and leading statesman. After his defeat at the election of May 1948 he went once more into active opposition until struck down by the illness of which he died. His private papers for this period remain voluminous and the best of his own letters remain perceptive and forceful.

The end of the war did not decrease his anxieties about the state of the world nor ease his difficulties in his own country. The mood of his letters is more and more one of disillusionment, disappointment, almost despair. He soon saw that the attempts to conclude peace treaties were futile (**681, 687, 706–8, 715**). U.N.O., he feared, would prove a 'broken reed' (**720, 745, 754, 757**) and he was shaken at the harshness with which it impugned his South African policies (**720, 729–31, 733, 735, 738, 742**). He dreaded a future of atomic power rivalry between Russia and the United States (**697, 699, 710, 720, 744**) and hoped that 'a third grouping based on Europe' would emerge though he gave up the idea that Great Britain might lead it (**757, 760, 774, 881, 882**). When N.A.T.O. and 'the very great move' of the Marshall plan appeared they seemed to him 'foundation stones of the future world structure'. But West Germany must, he insisted, be 'integrated' and not remain 'a fatal vacuum in Europe' (**754, 816, 822, 824, 844, 845, 847, 868**). Other matters that engaged his thought and moved him to such action as he could take were the weakening Commonwealth (**760, 792**), the anomalous position of India within it (**842, 843, 846–9**), the prospects of the restored monarchy in Greece (**706, 735, 774, 823, 832**), the hazardous birth of the state of Israel (**693, 708, 747, 749, 789, 791, 801, 863**). The statesmen to whom he most often wrote were Churchill, L. S. Amery, Weizmann and Wavell. Attlee and General Marshall were also approached and there were some sharp exchanges with Nehru.

In his latter years as prime minister of South Africa Smuts was chiefly occupied with 'racial conundrums', particularly with that bugbear—the Indian question in Natal and the Transvaal. He made a last considerable effort to reach a fair settlement in a situation where 'both sides are unreasonable'. His measures were rejected by the South African Indians and castigated by the Asian Indians at U.N.O. (**696, 700–5, 726, 750, 755**). For the Africans in the Union he saw that the 'trusteeship' he had undertaken to provide was not enough and that the conditions of life of the urban African would have to be radically changed. The Native Laws commission was appointed to find out how this was to be done (**720, 740, 743, 764**). But the Native Representative Council rejected all compromise in advance (**717, 724, 726**) and the advent of the National party government killed the creative proposals of the commission.

Smuts hardly hesitated to move once more into 'the cold shades of opposition' although he would gladly have retired (**797, 798, 819**). At first he thought that his party would soon return to power and rejected advice to seek a coalition with the 'liberal' Nationalists (**812–14**). But the government grew stronger (**827, 838, 850, 853**) and Smuts fought a losing battle against its colour policies (**810, 833, 834, 840, 843, 857, 858, 872, 885**).

His personal life at this time was beset by adversity (**818–20, 829, 830**) but also sweetened by the conferment of notable honours (**738, 774, 776, 777, 800, 801, 817**). Botany and palaeontology remained lively interests; Shakespeare studies provided a new one. And almost to the end he found time for such extras as a tribute to Campbell-Bannerman (**779, 780**); eulogy of an Afrikander hero (**782**); a philosophy programme for U.N.E.S.C.O. (**758**); criticism of a MS on reincarnation by an old college friend (**752**); carefully considered forewords to deserving books (**884**) and a special journey to London to speak in praise of Weizmann (**862, 863**).

678 To M. C. Gillett — Vol. 77, no. 259

Doornkloof
[Transvaal]
27 August 1945

A letter from you and another from Arthur—both welcome delightful chats. You write of...Aston in its last stages,[1] of a visit to the Murrays, with a short side glance at politics. Arthur writes of politics and the election, and other high stuff. It was amusing to see his reflections on the change, and its high promise. May he be right. It is and remains a grim world, whoever is in charge. We are all so helpless before such forces as the world war has let loose. We can but pray for those who have to control those forces. I saw what the last war led to; I shall not see what this one will lead to. But already I can hear the wail which goes up from large portions of Europe. In fact I am beginning to skip certain parts of the news, as one finds it very difficult to read without asking what has come to Europe, what is happening in the world in this twentieth century. I feel inclined to look the other way and pass on, like that Pharisee.[2] Why endure what one cannot cure.[3] The feeling of helplessness is so demoralizing. It is better not to know what is happening. But

[1] The Gilletts gave up their cottage at Aston when they moved to Street.

[2] *St Luke* x.30–1.

[3] 'What cannot be cured were best endured' (*Optimum est pati, quod emendare non possis*). Seneca, *Epistulae ad Lucilium*, cvii, sec. 9.

I may not continue in this strain—it is no use, and it only lacerates your feelings also. I can understand what you say about Gilbert Murray's dread of Russia. The Europeans are so pitiless. The mercy of God has not visited their souls. They are cruel and pitiless beyond the African savages, or the beasts of the field, who kill and tear for food, but not like Europeans for mental satisfaction.

A real kettle of fish has been served up by Truman in the sudden repeal of lease-lend.[1] I claim no particular foresight, but by 1944 already I had got my suspicion about lease-lend and informed the Yanks that I preferred to pay in cash; and at the beginning of this year I squared all accounts, and since then have paid in cash for everything. They began by asking us to keep no accounts so as to destroy the dollar sign in this war[2] and leave no debts between Allies. Then they asked us to keep and render accounts—for satisfying the congress. Then they asked us what things and services we could render in return for lease-lend. Then they suggested that they should have a claim on our 'raw materials'. I did not know what that meant and how far it might go—minerals, wool, gold, diamonds: all were raw materials. I then became uneasy and since then asked for the privilege to pay in cash, which eventually was conceded. It is not a pleasant story, but at least I have not been completely surprised at a most awkward moment, like the English. I hope some arrangement will soon be come to,[3] or otherwise a feeling may grow up between the two countries far worse than that created by our default in the old post-war years. Britain could not be hit harder than by this sudden change at this stage; and then to be asked for the surrender of the markets which are essential to her life as a people. It sounds like an outrage, although one knows it is not meant as such. One misses the hand of Roosevelt who was a big human, and not a dollar man.

Last week I spent some days in Natal where Durban and Pietermaritzburg gave me tumultuous receptions—really unbelievable functions. It was an expression of the pent-up feelings of the people after six years of war. This week I shall be at Johannesburg for its welcome and thanks. I suppose it will be the same. I shall

[1] *See* vol. VI, p. 353, note 1.

[2] When Roosevelt first put forward the idea of lend-lease he told reporters that he was merely trying to get rid of the 'silly, foolish, old dollar sign' (J. N. Burns, *Roosevelt, the Lion and the Fox*, p. 457).

[3] On 7 December 1945 British negotiators in Washington arrived at an agreement by which the United States would lend Great Britain 3,750 million dollars at an interest of 2 per cent, the capital being repayable in fifty annual instalments from 31 December 1951. In addition the net lend-lease liability of Great Britain was reduced from over 31,260 to 650 million dollars, to be repaid simultaneously and on the same terms.

be as good as dead when it is all over. For Cape Town and other big coastal centres are still to follow. After the long and almost unendurable strain of the war effort one has to undergo this emotional ordeal, so kindly meant, but in effect so pitiless as to leave one almost more dead than alive. It will be my last war; in all three I have had this emotional aftermath, although it has varied in every case: dumb misery after the Boer War; the despair of disillusion after the last war; the gratitude and deep poignancy of this war. What a drama, what a tragedy of history, far surpassing anything one finds in books. For me this will be the last; may it be so for this much tried race of man. Perhaps fear will do what high hope could not do—the atomic bomb may at last *frighten* man into more sensible ways of settling his disputes...

679 From C. R. Attlee Vol. 76, no. 25

10 Downing Street
Whitehall
31 August 1945

My dear Field Marshal, I have given much thought to the message which you sent me through the South African high commissioner here in reply to my personal telegram of 1 August supplementing the final report of the Berlin conference. Needless to say, I welcome this expression of your views on a subject on which you are so well qualified to speak, and I am glad that you have given us such a clear exposition of the anxieties which you feel and which, to some extent, we naturally share.

I do not disagree with your diagnosis of the threatening situation in Europe, more particularly in the eastern countries. The growth of Anglo-Russian antagonism on the Continent, and the creation of spheres of influence, would be disastrous to Europe and would stultify all the ideals for which we have fought. But I think we must at all costs avoid trying to seek a cure by building up Germany or by forming blocs aimed at Russia. It is of course true that to depress the level of Germany's industry and standard of living below a certain point would do harm to Europe as a whole and to ourselves. We shall do everything in our power to prevent this, but any suspicion—and the Russians are not slow to form suspicions—that we were trying to deal softly with Germany, or to build her up, would be such an obvious threat to Russia that we could thereby harden the Soviet government's present attitude in eastern Europe and help to give actual shape to our fears.

I think that whether Europe remains 'unbalanced, lop-sided and depressed' is first of all an economic question. As you know, supply is short and distribution is difficult. But we are not blind to the vital necessity of finding a solution which will bridge over the danger period until next year's harvests are gathered in. Secondly, it is a question of restoring confidence among the liberated peoples and though we and the Americans may be able to assist in this by giving sound advice to their governments, the problem is very largely dependent on the re-establishment of a wholesome economy. Thirdly, it is a matter of allowing time for wounds to heal.

We believe that the only road to safety lies in the maintenance of trust and understanding between the great powers which will give some opportunity for the successful establishment and functioning of the world organization on which our hopes for the future are based. It is true that 'an effort to reach an accord between the present conflicting interests of the Allies and their partisans', if such an effort were to mean the sacrifice of a principle, would not suffice. It is also true that Russia's idea of 'sober realism' differs from our own and that during the Berlin conference, and the meetings of the reparations commission, we have not received the consistent and resolute American support for which we had hoped. Nevertheless, I think you will agree that the maintenance of Allied unity is of paramount importance. Subject to this, we for our part shall certainly do all we can to exercise a moderating influence in pursuit of the objectives that you and we both have in view.

I am sorry you cannot come to London during the meeting of foreign ministers. Your great experience in these matters and the reliance which we have always been able to place on your advice lead me to hope that you may find an opportunity during the next few months to pay us a visit here, giving us the benefit of your counsel. The coming of the atomic bomb means that we have got to consider from a new angle most of the problems of foreign policy and defence and that many principles hitherto accepted as axiomatic will have to be amended or discarded. For such discussions your presence among us would indeed be welcome. With all good wishes, Yours sincerely,

C. R. Attlee

680 From L. S. Amery Vol. 76, no. 17

112 Eaton Square
S.W.1
5 September 1945

My dear Smuts, Our good American friends have brought us up with a pretty round turn over lend–lease.[1] The amusing thing is the way in which genuine breadth of view and generosity in intention gets whittled down to meet the more selfish outlook of congress. That applies not only to the immediate short-term question of some sort of tapering off of lend–lease, but even more to economic policy generally.

I have no doubt that Cordell Hull and Roosevelt were quite sincerely, though mistakenly, thinking they were acting for the good of the world as well as for that of the United States when they tried to tie us down in the lend–lease agreement to what they called non-discrimination i.e. the enforcement of the most favoured nation clause and the abolition or whittling away of imperial preference.[2] When it comes to practice, however, what we shall be confronted by, if we agree to that policy in return for immediate financial help, is a tremendous American export and external investment push with no correspondingly adequate increase of American imports, which will create for the world at large all the dangers and difficulties of the great depression of fifteen years ago, and incidentally prove disastrous, not only to the United Kingdom, but to the economic expansion of the whole of the British Empire.

The fundamental mistake in the American outlook is to think that trade as such is expansion. What is really expansion is production, and the unregulated flow of trade may be as disastrous to the steady development of production in individual countries, and indeed in the world as a whole, as the unregulated flow of water. Soil erosion and deep-cut dongas can be economic as well as physical consequences of leaving things to immediate individual interest. For many reasons international trade, whether actually conducted by the state or by individuals, will be governed by considerations of national policy. That does not necessarily mean a rigid autarky, but it does mean that economic concessions will tend to be given for good value either bilaterally, or in nation groups. And they will naturally be given most readily within a group whose members have wider reasons for being interested in each other's welfare and strength than purely economic ones.

I enclose a copy of an article I scribbled for the *Sunday Times*

[1] *See* **678**.

[2] *See* vol. v, p. 193, note 1.

on the subject[1] which may interest you. I am also sending a copy to Hofmeyr, in answer to a letter in which he very kindly congratulated me on my C.H. Yours ever,

Leo Amery

681 To L. S. Amery Vol. 77, no. 192

Prime Minister's Office
Pretoria
27 September 1945

My dear Amery, I have two very interesting letters from you, as usual full of matter for thought and discussion—for which, alas, there is so little time. I note your interesting point about non-discrimination and most favoured treatment. Unfortunately the position is much complicated by the master agreement under lease-lend,[2] by which we are pledged to these principles. The only line left us now is to argue for effective scaling down of American tariffs, which also is covered by that agreement. Unless American markets are effectively opened to British and Dominion exports, we shall no doubt stand pat on our existing *status quo*.

I am deeply perturbed over the doings of the Council of Foreign Ministers,[3] and especially the way the Mediterranean position and the Italian colonies are being dealt with. With *international* mandates over the Italian colonies, other powers get a footing across our vital communications, and I am not impressed by the argument that these concessions are merely an international organization. Russia is holding on firmly to all her conquered territory. Why should we complacently surrender colonies for which we paid so dearly? Unless we are admitted into the huge Russian enclave, we should refuse to surrender what we hold by right of conquest.

I fear this peace treaty will find the British group weakened financially, commercially, and in their essential communications. The United States of America is also holding on to her Pacific bases. Only we make the surrenders. Not merely our interest but also our prestige is involved, and the world will look upon us as no longer able to hold our own and as dominated by the greater powers.

I did not congratulate you on the C.H. which, of course, is

[1] Omitted by the editor.

[2] This was signed on 23 February 1942.

[3] Established at the Berlin (Potsdam) conference. It represented the five chief powers and was set up to prepare the peace treaties with Italy, Rumania, Bulgaria, Hungary and Finland, and to investigate other matters that might be referred to it.

a very high honour. But there is no honour too high for you to have, so why worry?

My kindest and affectionate regards to you and dear Mrs Amery. I feel most deeply with you both over the sad vagaries of your son.[1] May all come right in the end. Ever yours,

s. J. C. Smuts

682 From L. S. Amery — Vol. 76, no. 18

112 Eaton Square
S.W.1
3 October 1945

My dear Smuts, I am afraid the big power talks have arrived at a hopeless deadlock.[2] The reason is perfectly simple if only we face it. Russia never came into this war for the sake of the good of the world. She was pushed into it by Hitler's anticipating what he believed to be Russia's aggressive intentions in south-east Europe. Having won a great victory, her leaders, whose mentality is after all some centuries behind us, mean to exploit it to the full. That is all there is to it and the only thing we can do is, in the interests of the world and of our own, to decide where we call a halt and how to make the best arrangements for what is left. That, so far as we are concerned, is western Europe, Africa, the Middle East and the Indian ocean zone. So far as the Americans are concerned it is the American continents south of Canada, the northern Pacific and the Far East. As between us and Russia in Europe and between the United States and Russia in the Far East there is no reason why there should not be a peaceful adjustment, but only on the basis of a mutual recognition of each other's strength and determination. As between the British Commonwealth and the United States the partition into two effective enlarged Monroe doctrines[3] will be based on a natural division of labour.

As for the world security organization, to which you gave so much of your mind and heart, are the meetings of the Security Council likely to differ in any respect from those of the present meeting of foreign ministers? The Russian will always dig in his

[1] John Amery, born 1912, tried for high treason in 1945 and executed.

[2] The first meeting of the Council of Foreign Ministers in London in September broke up on procedural questions, that is, which powers should participate in the preparation of the various peace treaties. The Russian representative, Molotov, tried to exclude France and China.

[3] *See* vol. III, p. 639, note 2.

toes under orders from Moscow and, whatever the rights and wrongs of a question, fight for Russia's interest. To expect anything else is just to deceive ourselves.

In the political sphere Russia's interest, as she conceives it, is to keep the nations of Europe outside her immediate tributary zone as broken up and divided as possible. That is why she so noisily opposes anything like a western European grouping, though there is in fact nothing she can do to stop it if we are firm on the subject.

So much on the political side. On the economic side the United States are essentially Russian in their outlook, that is to say they are determined to expand their economic power and for that purpose object violently to any economic grouping on the part of anybody else, whether by way of empire preference, or of mutual preferences among other groups of nations. There again they can do nothing if we go about our own business, except—and that is of course a serious matter for the time being—to refuse further assistance to this country. To my mind there is no other possible answer than to say that we cannot take this assistance if it means depriving us of our economic liberty. If we do so we shall no doubt have to keep our belts tightened for a while longer. For the rest of the Empire, at any rate the sterling area, it will mean a more rapid expansion of production and export.

You may be interested to read the enclosed address[1] which I delivered a few days ago to the Institute of Export. I am sure we shall only be up against another world disaster if we commit ourselves to trying to set the humpty-dumpty of nineteenth century economic internationalism on his wall again. Yours ever,

Leo Amery

683 To A. B. Gillett Vol. 77, no. 262

Doornkloof
[Transvaal]
9 October 1945

I have just had a welcome air letter from you, arriving together with another by air mail from Margaret. I am glad you are now out of the Oxford bank and can give attention to some of your hobbies and beloved interests. When shall I be able to do likewise? Life is too much of a toil, instead of being that free and loving devotion to our dear hobbies. What does one care about distant

[1] Omitted by the editor.

countries and insoluble financial problems; yet they eat up all one's little remaining time. The world is full of difficulties, now more than ever; yet I agree with you that there is also more human good will and understanding among private people than ever before. Unfortunately the concentration of the press on the things that go wrong creates a wrong perspective and helps to make a world of friction and irritation—so different from the true picture.

I hope you will find some consolation in Beveridge.[1] I am so afraid that we shall drift into a world of easiness and, in the end, laziness. I believe in the sweat of the brow and of the brain. Sweets are not good for our spiritual digestion. But then I have the habits of a slave, in a world longing for the good things!

Russia has extracted vast power and resources for the state from the labour of the people, whose standards must be simply awful from all one hears from the present occupied countries. Indeed their general standard must be below that of African Natives if one is to believe the reports which come from people not hostile to the Soviet.

The failure of the Council of Foreign Ministers[2] is sad and causes deep foreboding. Things are taking a course which was never contemplated at San Francisco, where great power unity was assumed as basic for future United Nations activity. It almost looks as if Europe has been smashed, and Russia is stepping into the liquidated position. What the consequences of such a development may be no one can foresee, but I am full of anxiety. There is the old saying of the frying pan and the fire!

Cato [Clark] will have told you all the local news. It was very sweet having her here and the effect on Isie was very marked. Of Bancroft we saw little as he was always on business moves and travels.

Your news from the family appears very good. You will now be able to see more of them and indulge your grandfatherly instincts to your heart's content. Jan, I suppose, will soon be home again. He has had a hard time in the East.

All goes well here, but the political grind is pretty severe, especially as I have had no respite and see no sign of it. Such is our lot in this world. Dear love to you and Margaret.

Jan

[1] *See* vol. VI, p. 414, note 2.

[2] *See supra*, p. 10, note 2.

684 To M. C. Gillett Vol. 77, no. 263

Doornkloof
[Transvaal]
15 October 1945

I write on Monday evening having missed the week-end for writing. As a matter of fact I had a lot of official writing to do, and your weekly letter got squeezed out. Then the summer rains began last night and what a joy it was to listen to that music of pattering on the iron roof. It has been a long and exceptional drought, as in so many other countries, and our food position has become precarious. In the Transkei about 50 per cent of the cattle have died, and we are largely feeding the Natives, there and elsewhere. However, we can rejoice once more. The wrath is never too long on us. But what a wrath on mankind! Have you ever read of a period in history in which there was such piled up human agony as today? One turns to the newspapers with a feeling of aversion. The war and its mechanical horrors were bad enough. But this milling round of millions of people in all lands, homeless, foodless, hopeless, rotten with disease and drifting like flotsam before the wrath—is a picture of misery more than one can bear, even to read of, let alone actually experience or witness. It is the religion of pity which we are most in need of today. It is curious that this most primitive of kindly feelings is the one most lacking today. 'Have pity on us, O Lord' seems to be the prayer rising from millions of hearts to a pitiless heaven. Man's inhumanity to man[1] finds more dreadful expression today than in the most barbarous periods of which one reads. This morning there was the protest from poor Austria that a million homeless refugees are on her frontiers and threatening to rush in and bring typhus and venereal and what not with them. I dare not think of all that is going on, and think the hardest of all to witness is perhaps not the misery of the sufferers so much as the cruelty and devilry of those who push them on and out to utter ruin. If this is vengeance for what has gone before how much greater will be the vengeance which will revenge it! What an era of history the new generation is moving into! One can read of these dreadful things in the old books, but to think all this is happening in this age when human sensitiveness has been developed to a maximum which increases the moral and physical suffering to an unbearable limit. When I think of the

1 Man's inhumanity to man
Makes countless thousands mourn!
Robert Burns, *Man was made to Mourn.*

suffering I have seen in my day and which I looked upon as the limit I can realize how comparatively trivial it was compared to what is now taking place, and on a scale never seen before in history.

And yet, and yet—there is so much that is good and godlike in man. God himself so loved the world that He sent his only Son to redeem it and save it.[1] He would not have done it for a godless robot world of men. There is so much that is divine in us, so near is man to God, that it only increases the pain and the horror of this tragedy beyond all comprehension. One can but bow one's head before this revelation of evil, of the evil in us and in our human arrangements. No devil could have conceived something worse than what is our human handiwork. And yet, God so loved the world! That is the enigma, the mystery of both evil and good. No wonder that our forefathers could understand it in terms of both God and the Devil. *It is both*, and no philosophy can argue away this deep-seated duality in human nature.

But you will say I am not writing a letter but the atomic bomb! I shall not go on, and feel better for having got this off my chest as they say. This week I have to go to Port Elizabeth but shall be back before the week-end. It is a great tax on one's strength and time to have to make these distant visits, even with a fast aeroplane. One is exhausted by the effort and returns to a host of problems which require close attention. It is really a dreadful thing in these times to be the government of *any* country, even so good a country as South Africa. But think of the government in Britain which, in addition to all these tangled problems, have also to face unreason and irresponsibleness in the form of strikes at ports and in essential services.[2] My only consoling thought is that these visitations don't last long. They work themselves out fairly rapidly, and people then return to the normal again, and behave decently once more. It is really funny to think of your Labour government having to use the military to do the job which their labour supporters refuse to do. We have made it a crime to strike in essential services.[3] But who cares about the law? At Cape Town a bakery strike is in full swing since yesterday, and one and all have to go without bread for days until this strike is over. And the reason for it was that the workers refuse to do a night shift in baking! I thought that

[1] 'For God so loved the world, that he gave his only begotten Son...that the world through him might be saved.' *St John* iii.16–17.

[2] An extended strike of over 40,000 dock-workers occurred from 25 September to 14 December when an increased wage was agreed upon. The strike was unofficial and was prolonged in defiance of the orders of trade union officials.

[3] By the Industrial Conciliation Act of 1924.

all baking was done the night before so that the bread can be fresh the next morning.

Is this not a cheerful letter? I suppose I must have had a bad day in office to take this revenge on innocent you. Forgive me. I hope to be in better letter form next time. But it is hard, very hard to control oneself amid all these vagaries of mankind, today more fit for a sanatorium or an asylum than the nice sweet homes we dreamt of after the war. God bless you, dear children, and forgive my ravings.

Jan

685 To M. C. Gillett Vol. 77, no. 256

Doornkloof
[Transvaal]
25 October 1945

Another welcome letter from you. Your letters are a great comfort to me. It tells of your visit to Nico [Gillett], and how happy it made you and how restored and well he is. All very good news. And it tells of your reading and interpretation of *John* iii and xvii. By the way, you will remember how puzzled I was to find where the saying comes from: 'In the world but not of it'. Well, it is nowhere put in that short form anywhere in the Bible, but it is taken from two verses in *John* xvii. The whole prayer of Jesus is for his own who are in the world, though they are not of it. The quotation is a condensation of what he said, and how neatly and finely it expresses a great spiritual truth. So the new and higher evolves from the lower but is also beyond it, and immanence and transcendence meet. Of course the concept of space is really inappropriate in such matters, and we speak in a metaphor. To me John's Gospel is a curious phenomenon. It is no longer Jewish and breathes another spirit, as of the later Gentile Church. And yet there is more of the real spirit one senses in Jesus in it than in the older Gospel narratives.

The spiritual insight and felicity of expression of these writers are really most astonishing to me. I dare say the expression follows from the marvellous insight. It is curious how it is all based on family experience and the life of the family. The new spiritual vision is that of the common family life, but raised to a new higher level. God is the father, men are brothers, and the Holy Spirit is that which unconsciously pervades the family group. It is this realism and appeal to our common human experience which makes the Gospel such a powerful force. Our more abstract philosophical or theological formulations don't touch this utter simplicity and appeal.

I have again had a very busy week, what with administration and public meetings and functions which take up so much time. Next week I shall be in Cape Town for similar functions and business. When you receive this you will have seen that van Zyl [G.B.], the Cape administrator, has been appointed governor-general. It is the best I could recommend under very difficult circumstances, and I can't hope to have given universal satisfaction. I am glad that this tangle is at last off my mind. Then the Labour party have decided to leave my coalition government and Madeley is going in a friendly spirit next week. I had hoped to keep them with me for much longer, and I fear their going will in due course force them once more into an unholy pact with the Nationalists.[1] We have had no quarrel and they part on the principle of private enterprise! I should say we came as near to state socialism as any country in the world. But the general Leftist movement in the world, the example of Britain, and the general inspiration of Moscow's example have proved too much for my Labour friends. So my difficulties will continue to grow. South Africa has been singularly free from labour strife and strikes. But this may not continue. In any case we could not be worse than Britain or the United States at this moment. I do hope that Labour will be able to restore discipline to the rank and file. Otherwise the resulting resentment and chaos of unrest and an undefined longing for change may give great shocks to an already deeply shattered society. Victory and all its fruits seem to be endangered in the hour of triumph.

I hope we shall avoid an economic and trade clash with the United States. Such a development would be worst of all, even worse than the misunderstandings already existing with Russia. There is so much confusion and friction at the moment that I am for going slow and for avoiding sudden decisions which may lead us in a wrong direction. The moment is unpropitious for solutions which require a different atmosphere. That atmosphere may come, but not in these noises and confusions. I believe that the essential character of this epoch is that of transition, one of the great passages in history. One holds firmly to essentials of our civilization and our ethical outlook but hesitates to venture too much in these uncertainties. I hope things will improve and the conditions for solutions and new directives will also improve. But at present it

[1] *See* vol. v, p. 224, note 3.

is a case of Mr Holdfast or Standfast according to Bunyan's story.[1]

In spite of all this troubled scene there is so much that is good in man. Never has human nature shown itself better than in these terrible times. I meet goodness everywhere in human relationships today. So why despair of the future? The Light will shine again outside as it already shines inside.

No more. Perhaps I am only whistling to keep my courage up. All best wishes. Ever yours,

Jan

686 To M. C. Gillett — Vol. 77, no. 266

Doornkloof
[Transvaal]
2 November 1945

Two very good and welcome letters from you and Arthur after your visit to Eastbourne. It was all very good news that both of you reported from that small family.[2] Arthur went on to refer to finance, but it is clear that he is as much at sea as I am, and that comforts me. I had grown up with the idea that money is a big thing, spelt with a big G like God, and my respect for money was in inverse proportion to my possession of it. Nowadays it is considered nothing and only a thing to be juggled with. But I still think it represents or ought to represent *work*, and if it does not, our economic arrangements all hang in the air. Grandiose security schemes and the like mean to me work, and we can only have so much social security as we have earned. Money is or ought to be the symbol or expression of this earned security. Then you write of your visits to the aged. Well, remember that not only on Boars Hill[3] but in South Africa there are some aged friends who long to see you both. I also love old people, especially old women, in whom the spirit has found expression in a peace and calm which often is more than of this world. I think old women more lovely than young women, whose attraction is often so disturbing. And how beautiful a lovely old woman, with plenty of soul in her, can be!

I note what you say about the U.N.A.[4] meeting. The U.N.A. has once more elected me to vice-presidency which I much appreciate. May U.N.O. prove more successful than its predecessor.

[1] Mr Standfast in *Pilgrim's Progress*.

[2] The family of Jan Gillett.

[3] Gilbert and Mary Murray lived there.

[4] United Nations Association.

But it cannot move much in advance of public opinion—that hydra-headed, brainless monster which rules all our affairs nowadays. What a pass we have come to at the end of this war, with all our squabbling and self-seeking! It is only one's faith in the good and in God that saves one from despair in this mad world, where even the most dreadful experience teaches us so little. You may be right, and even the atomic bomb may not be enough to give us peace. It becomes a rivalry as to who can make the most dreadful and destructive atomic bomb. And so we muddle on to the edge of the volcano.

I am amused at your suggested parallel between Grey Cardinal Eminence and J.C.S.! What an idea, even though the Eminence is a far-distant relative of mine.[1] And yet one never knows oneself. I am certain you know me much better than I know myself, and I continue a painful puzzle to myself. But Grey Eminence as depicted by Huxley was the most glaring case of dual personality one has read about. And in me it is not a case of dual personality, but of that battle in the one personality or soul, which St Paul has painted with such fidelity and insight in *Romans* vii. It is the warfare in the soul, and not between two souls, that is mine. Paul evidently had it, otherwise he could not have described it so accurately. If I may say so, I belong to the family of Paul and not of the Grey Cardinal! But, unlike Paul, I remain self-defeated, whereas he emerged victorious, with a faith which has guided the yearning soul of our civilization these two thousand years. My vision of holism, of the soul that is whole, of the personality that is completely integrated, is derived from that inner consciousness of struggle which is always with me and still remains unachieved. O miserable sinner that I am!

I returned yesterday from Cape Town where I spent two tumultuous days and nights. I had a reception which kings might envy me. And through it all I felt how little worthy I was of all that praise. But I know that in a terrible struggle I had shown South Africa the way, and could understand the gratitude. But as a matter of fact it was the cause itself which provided the momentum to win through, and my work was but to press the button and let the cause work its own way to success. The pity is that in our international cause there is no such inner momentum, and even the best planning is of no avail. The steam is not in the

[1] A reference to *Grey Eminence* (1942) by Aldous Huxley—a study of Cardinal Richelieu's confidant, Joseph le Père (François Leclerc du Tremblay). In saying that du Tremblay was 'a far-distant relative' Smuts seems to have confused him with Richelieu (Armand-Jean du Plessis) for Jean Prieur du Plessis, who came to the Cape in 1688, was an ancestor of Smuts's mother.

engine, however well devised and constructed it is. How to mobilize that inner subtle spirit, that Holy Spirit, which lies within all great causes; that is the problem. And it is largely a problem of human personality. Jesus could do it. Paul in a large measure did it. In a base, degraded way even Hitler could do it and prove the Pied Piper to lead his people to utter destruction. But few have that supreme gift of genius or personality which works miracles.

Hutchinson has just written me that his book is finished[1] and that a copy is being sent me by South Africa House. He sounds very happy. I am glad of his success. He is such a good soul and so deserving of success.

I am reading some of the literature you sent me. But unfortunately I am worked to death, and have never felt cheaper while still preserving the deceptive appearance of vitality and alertness. My political troubles are very considerable. Of course I have no illusions and expect to get my dismissal as the other actors on the stage have got already. But one likes to make a clean job of one's work before the end. Ever yours,

Jan

687 To M. C. Gillett — Vol. 77, no. 267

Doornkloof
[Transvaal]
9 November 1945

...Hofmeyr just back tells me he saw you but not Arthur. I have had only a few minutes with him and have still to hear his news in detail. As a matter of fact I am so busy these days that I can find little time for consulting my colleagues. Deputations are my special plague. Tomorrow I have two of them on the Indian question in Transvaal and Natal.[2] They are enough to waste a whole day. And besides I have to receive the van Zyls here and to get three cabinet ministers sworn in on a reshuffle of the cabinet. Colin Steyn goes to labour (vice Madeley resigned), Lawrence goes to justice vice Steyn, and a new man Dr [H.] Gluckman gets public health. It is a slight improvement on the old arrangement which put too heavy a burden on Lawrence. Health now gets a medical man who is really interested. My main trouble remains Indians for whom I have neither a man nor a solution. And my

[1] *See* vol. VI, p. 505, note 4.

[2] The deputation from the Natal Indian Congress presented a memorandum for which *see* the *Cape Argus*, 10 November 1945.

work is so heavy that I really have no time for these insoluble, tiresome racial conundrums. I sometimes ask with Isie: why did the good Lord create colours and languages? The Dutch are now also in dire trouble in Java, like the English in India. The upshot will be that both will be booted out in spite of the magnificent work they have done, and both Indians and Indonesians will be unhappy ever after. It reminds me of what must have been the experience of the Britons in England after they had wiped the Romans out and their conditions reverted to the prior barbarism. But of course people prefer to govern themselves badly rather than be well governed by others. I have heard you say that liberty is better than good government, and the sentiment is quite proper for an old Liberal. Whether you still think so as a Socialist I rather doubt, as the new creed apparently places less emphasis on liberty. There certainly is not much in latter day trade-unionism.

I was much interested in your statement about the continuance of your Friends schools. I really was under the impression that, subject to government inspection, they *did* get government subsidies. That is our South African system. Our Jew and Anglican schools and the like get their government grant subject to government supervision. I don't see how your Friends schools can continue under present taxation without government assistance. And my impression is that government schools are now quite good, though perhaps not select enough for Quakers! All our children have been (like their parents) to government schools.

I had a letter from Hamburg University[1] last mail to ask whether they may translate my *Holism* into Spanish for use in Spain and South America. It was translated into German before the war, but banned by the Nazis during the war.[2] Now it is once more being taught in the university. Professor Meyer[3] says the interest in the subject is increasing all the time on the Continent. So my friend Princess Frederica may yet be right when she says it is going to be the basis of the future religion. But I don't wish to give permission for the Spanish translation as so much of the scientific part is really obsolete. The advance of physics and biology in the last twenty years has really been phenomenal, and my earlier chapters read like pre-scientific. I wish I could find time to write my second volume, and let the first become antiquarian as it is practically antiquated. But affairs and politics choke my life and almost choke my soul in these end-of-the-age times. Whatever is going to happen to the world? I have just been reading the brief

[1] Smuts Collection, vol. 77, no. 6.

[2] *See* vol. VI, p. 126.

[3] Professor Adolf Meyer-Abich (q.v.).

cabled reports of the foreign office debate in the commons on the eve of Attlee's flight to Truman to discuss the atom bomb. Foreign relations are apparently in chaos, and the world, or much of Europe, is drifting to famine and anarchy. The Red Cross reports from Europe are shocking, and even what a hard-boiled fellow like Montgomery says is enough to startle me. The reports in the Belgian papers are ten times worse than anything I see in the English press. How can you think of abstract questions when this storm is raging in the world? I did my best at San Francisco, but building a peace structure for such a world is worse than building on sand. 'I and my Father are one'[1] keeps ringing in my mind, as you read it in *John* xvii. Is there any other way out except this union of the human and the divine? Is the world not saved by the divine at the heart of it, and can our economic scientific society be saved without a new deeper religious outlook? Is it the Man of Galilee or another like him born from our distressful conditions who will point the way out of this darkness in which we are milling round? I myself cannot see my way through our social tangle, and somehow no Hand seems stretched out to us at present. Will holism do without the holistic Personality? Best wishes. Ever yours,

Jan

P.S. Send me Seward's *Geology for Everyman* (Cambridge University Press 1943). Includes much palaeobotany.

688 To W. S. Churchill — Vol. 77, no. 210

Prime Minister's Office
Pretoria
10 November 1945

My dear Winston, The Avro York which carries [G.B.] van Zyl, the governor-general designate, to London, will also bring you a case of our brandy and another of our sherry as a token of affection from me. South Africa House will see to its delivery.

I have not written you before as I thought you would prefer not to be bothered with correspondence and would rather learn the taste of the grass to which the old war horse had been put. But now I may express to you that the elections have been one of the major surprises of my life. Nothing I knew or had heard from the best sources had prepared me for this shock. But there it is, and

[1] 'That they all may be one; as thou, Father, art in me, and I in thee, that they also may be one in us.' *St John* xvii.21.

what cannot be prevented had better be enjoyed! And so I hope you are making the best of the new life, as no doubt you will.

What continues to trouble me is the waste of it. The problem of waste has always, with me, been one of the great enigmas of life. What purpose does it serve in a universe largely dominated by purposefulness? How much appears to be sheer waste. What a small, almost infinitely small, part is not wasted and is materially and socially effective! It seems all so senseless and chaotic.

At this moment when all is at stake for Britain, and her future is at the mercy of vast, almost uncontrollable forces, she drops the one man who could have provided leadership and a measure of insurance for herself. No doubt the people were desirous for a change from the Conservative policies, but dropping the pilot in mid storm!

I am full of troubles of my own. Perhaps the worst is the Indian question which, like most of our present world problems, seems almost insoluble in the present temper. To you it will appear small.

I send you and dear Clemmie my deep affection. God bless you both, as well as the dear daughters. Ever yours,

J. C. Smuts

689 From L. S. Amery — Vol. 76, no. 19

112 Eaton Square
S.W.1
20 November 1945

My dear Smuts, Having heard a rumour that you might be in London in December I asked Heaton-Nicholls to sound you as to whether you would in that case come as my guest to the annual dinner of the Alpine Club of which I am president. I remember a splendid talk you gave on the whole subject of mountaineering on the occasion of the unveiling of the memorial to the members of the Cape Town Club who fell in the last war, and even a few words from you would cheer our members enormously.

In that connection I seem to remember seeing an admirable photograph of yourself, seated I think, on a great block of rock on the summit of Table mountain. I am bringing out shortly a sequel to my *Days of Fresh Air* in the shape of memoirs of climbing and travelling between the two wars. Among the climbs I mention is my climb of Table mountain when I was in South Africa in 1927 and I should greatly like to illustrate that by the photograph of yourself if you have a copy that you can spare.

As regards the general situation, Bevin has spoken straightforwardly and courageously and I imagine that is about the only way in which Russia can be dealt with. But the situation is not improving. Both in Persia and in Manchuria the Russians look very much like trying to set up puppet states of their own and the attitude of ourselves and the Americans over the atomic bomb hasn't helped matters—not that I disagree with it.

The right line for us to take, I am sure, is to make up our minds as to what we must accept from the Russians in the way of hegemony on their borders, and where we must draw the line. West of that we ought to go right ahead with building up the unity of Europe. As you know, that is a matter on which I have been a very strong advocate for the last twenty years, believing that it means much more for the peace of the world than any world organization. I was therefore very pleased when Winston delivered himself at Brussels the other day of the following sentence:

> I see no reason why, under the guardianship of a world organization, there should not arise a United States of Europe which would ultimately unify this continent in a manner never known since the fall of the Roman Empire, and within which all its peoples may dwell together in prosperity, in justice and in peace.

According to the press this met with quite a remarkable ovation, and I believe Europe, or at least western Europe, is ripe for the building up of something in the nature of a commonwealth on the British model. If it comes into being I am by no means certain that a good many countries now in the Russian zone will not swing back to Europe in the next few years.

I cannot see, however, that you can have an effective European commonwealth without thoroughgoing economic co-operation, i.e. preferential arrangements of every kind and disregard of the most favoured nation clause as at present interpreted by the United States. The trouble is that just as Russia objects to any political grouping outside herself, so American export interests object to any economic grouping. In both cases it seems to me that the only answer is, not to appease, but to go ahead straightforwardly justifying our policy in the interests of the world as well as our own. I am delivering a lecture to the University on that theme next week and will send you a copy as soon as it is printed.

You mention in your last letter[1] that the master agreement under lend–lease does involve us in considerable difficulties. That is of course true. At the same time that master agreement refers back

[1] 681.

at the end to the Atlantic Charter which explicitly confirmed our right to imperial preference under the heading of 'existing obligations'. There is also the further fact that non-discrimination in international trade is not defined, nor apparently was it ever seriously argued. Yet for nearly fifty years we have in every commercial treaty, confirming the most favoured nation clause internationally, directly excluded inter-imperial trade and I should have thought that we had a very strong case for continuing to maintain that position. After all, even if we committed ourselves to what I believe to be the wild goose chase of lowering tariffs all round, that might be an argument for each country in the Empire lowering its tariff to the outside world if America and other countries give the lead, but should have nothing to do with any further lowering of tariffs inter-imperially.

The position is really made quite absurd by the fact that while the present American interpretation (dating only since 1922) of the most favoured nation clause excludes partial preference, it accepts the view that there can be a hundred per cent preference in the shape of a customs union. More than that, in the last commercial treaty between the United States and the Argentine the former accepted the right of the Argentine to make preferential arrangements with other South American countries on the slender ground that a South American customs union was ultimately contemplated.

I enclose a couple of recent productions of my own[1] which it may interest you to read. I did give one of them to Hofmeyr in roneo form which he may have shown you, but you will find it easier to read it in print. Yours ever,

Leo Amery

690 To N. M. Butler — Vol. 77, no. 221

Telegram

From: secretary for external affairs, Pretoria

To: South African legation, Washington

Dated 20 November 1945

Following for President Nicholas Murray Butler of Columbia University from Field Marshal Smuts. Begins: Thank you for your invitation to me to make suggestions for future activities of Carnegie Endowment. I would suggest that Endowment contracts to more

[1] Not attached to the document in the Smuts Collection.

special purposes the assistance hitherto so generously given to wide variety of social purposes. The world is moving into new era when mankind will have to become more closely knit under aegis of the World Charter. All available resources should be devoted to this great purpose which is vital to future peace and progress of the race. Funds should therefore be used to promote international intercourse and understanding and building up the international community. Travel and education scholarships should be available for this purpose. Selected future political leaders should mix with those of other countries. Dissemination of international ideals among intelligentsia should be promoted. Journalists and press leaders should be encouraged to visit and study conditions in other countries. Men of wide spiritual leadership and appeal should be enabled to do missionary work on world-wide basis, as Paul preached the Gospel to the Gentiles. The Endowment might in this way become the mechanism for spreading the new message for which mankind is waiting.

Above all suggest the basic idea in my mind, and its detailed application might perhaps deserve earnest consideration of Endowment which has already established such a high record of human service.

All kind regards and good wishes. Ends.

691 To A. B. Gillett — Vol. 77, no. 269

Pretoria
21 November 1945

I have a few moments before lunch in which to thank you for yours of 14 November from your club. It was a comfort to note your good spirits, whether due to that good claret or to the after effects of the Quantocks[1] or the speeches of Attlee I don't know. But it is good to hear you say: 'I am full of hope about the world.' If one can say this in this dark hour, there must be some good ground for it, and I take heart from your inspiration.

I note what you say about Russia and her suspicions or fears. I watched her closely at San Francisco and was much intrigued by her hesitations and strange unforthcoming ways. I asked myself—'Is it not mostly a sense of strangeness, of her feeling herself pulled into a strange world, from which she had been excluded for a long generation, and which now made the same impression on her which a man feels who is being drawn into deep

[1] A range of hills in north-west Somersetshire.

water and is unable to swim.' Is it this hesitation springing from strangeness and fear of an unknown world into which she is being pulled? Or is there something deeper and more sinister? Time only can show. We must be patient and wise. We are all at the parting of the ways in our forward movement. A false step may send the world into decades of unrest and suffering. Russia is a strange case, perhaps a psychical case at the moment, in any case an enigma with her combination of East and West. I am for going slow, not hurrying and hustling like our American friends, and soon finding ourselves in a horrible mess. Patience, time, generosity are the words.

This letter must serve as my weekly letter to you and Margaret. I am at present working at full stretch, with Party congresses here and next week in Cape Town and week thereafter in Bloemfontein. In between I sandwich in a St Andrew's banquet at Bulawayo and reviews of troops both there and at Salisbury, with all the air flights all this will involve. Meanwhile the wheels of office and correspondence and incidental troubles go on. You will agree that it is not as agreeable as the Quantocks or the other dreamlands in which we have dwelt awhile. But slaves are not free men, and must behave themselves. You suggest Hofmeyr as the way out. It may yet be my luck, but not now. I have a high opinion of his great ability and high character. But he has been our finance minister in war and has had to tax heavily, far too heavily for the taste of our people, who, unlike the English, hate taxation. His popular appeal is therefore not of the best at present. And so I must be the stopgap and keep the way open for him at a more opportune moment. You see the plan? It may not work, but it is the plan at present.

I am sad to hear of Gilbert Murray's mishap.[1] If you see him give him and her my warm affection. He has done grand work, which at last may come into its own if there is not some other undisclosed mishap. I love him not only for his international work but more for being the greatest Greek among us, who has brought to our tumultuous times the great message of Greek poetry and philosophy. God bless him. Ever yours,

Jan

[1] He had fallen down a small flight of steps and injured his spine.

692 To I. Olsvanger Vol. 77, no. 220

Pretoria
[November 1945]

Dear Dr Olsvanger, I have your letter of 16 November[1] and have read it with deep and poignant interest. As the whole matter is now *sub judice* before the Anglo-American commission whose appointment has just been announced, it would not be proper for me to enter upon it at this stage.[2] I have already expressed in public my earnest wish and that of South Africa that the commission may see its way to recommend the maximum immigration into the national home. In view of the present international situation as a whole I think the joint commission may prove to be a fair and proper tribunal to advise the governments and to guide world opinion. I hope its findings will justify our hopes. Nothing should be said at this stage which would still further exacerbate the widespread excitement on both sides, and everything should be done to urge and fortify the Jewish claims before the commission to the fullest extent. With all good wishes, Yours sincerely,

J. C. Smuts

693 Statement (1946) Vol. 80, no. 81A

It is not known exactly when Smuts submitted this statement to the Anglo-American committee of inquiry into Jewish immigration into Palestine. The report of the committee was published on 30 April 1946.

As the one surviving member of the war cabinet of the last war, and one who in 1917 took an active part in the planning of the Balfour declaration, I submit the following statement to the Anglo-American committee of inquiry on the question of Jewish immigration into Palestine and elsewhere. I shall have no opportunity to give oral evidence before the committee, but consider it right and proper to clear up one point, which I consider of great importance, for the information of the committee.

That point is the question whether the declaration was at its inception meant to be a mere temporary expedient out of a present difficulty, or was intended to be a declaration of long-range policy for the future. It must be important for the committee to know

[1] Smuts Collection, vol. 77, no. 49.

[2] The appointment of the Anglo-American committee of inquiry into the question of Jewish immigration into Palestine was made public on 13 November. *See also* **693**.

whether, in the minds of the original authors of the declaration, it was planned as a firm policy for the future, or merely as a temporary plan to deal with an existing problem of a passing nature. Clarity on this point must have a close bearing on the question of a large-scale revision, or even abandonment, of the plan embodied in the declaration. It is this particular point on which I wish to make the following statement of my clear impression and understanding of the scope and intention of the Balfour declaration.

Now I am quite clear that the declaration was meant to be a statement of long-range policy for the future. Of course all human policies are subject to change of circumstances, and to revision in the light of such change. But there is no doubt in my mind that the declaration was meant to affect permanently the future course of events in Palestine, and was so conceived by those who took part in its formulation. It was no mere temporary expedient in view of some pressing and passing problem of the time. It was a policy for the future intended to shape that future. In that sense I have always understood the declaration and repeatedly declared it to be the expression of a permanent policy to be carried out through the course of the years.

When the declaration was made in 1917 there was no sudden emergency calling for an executive plan. There was no problem of large-scale Jewish persecution at that time calling for such a plan. Jewish persecution in its intense form is a phenomenon of post-war developments. The concept of nationality was coming very much to the fore, and in the subsequent peace treaty led to the recasting of the political map of Europe. The Jews were considered a people who had been expatriated from their homeland and scattered over the world. In that sense they were a homeless people, and historic justice demanded a policy of their return to the ancient homeland. That land was at the time under the domination of an enemy power, the Turkish Empire, from which every effort was being made to expel the Turk. The situation was therefore ripe for a declaration about the future of Palestine, and the Balfour declaration emerged as a statement of policy whereby the Jews would be provided after the war with a national home in their historic homeland, from which they had been expelled by Romans and Turks in the course of the centuries. The declaration in its very essence aimed at a long-range national plan for the future.

It provided for a national home in Palestine and not for a Jewish state of Palestine, of which all Jews would become nationals. This was due partly to the small Jewish population of Palestine (then under 100,000) and to the fear of many prominent Jews that the declaration of a Jewish Palestine state might endanger their nationality in their present countries of residence, which they valued very highly. The question of the political status of the future Jewish Palestine was a matter of time, dependent no doubt on the increase of the Jewish population by immigration and otherwise. The question of a Jewish state was therefore deliberately left over for the future.

Nor was the declaration conceived in a spirit of hostility to the Arabs. On the contrary, at the very time of the declaration, Britain was busy in freeing the Hedjaz from Turkish domination, and every assistance was being given the Arabs through Lawrence to secure their liberation from the Turks. In the end three independent Arab kingdoms (Hedjaz, Iraq, Transjordania) were established through the Allied victory, and two more independent Arab states (Syria and Lebanon) have since arisen. It was naturally assumed that large-scale immigration of Jews into their historic homeland could not and would not be looked upon as a hostile gesture to the highly favoured Arab people who, largely as a result of British action, came better out of the Great War than any other people. Neither large-scale persecution of the Jews elsewhere, nor hostility towards Arabs had anything to do with the inception of the declaration, which was based on humanitarian considerations, on concepts of nationality and justice, and meant to be a long-range policy for future implementation by the promotion of a policy of Jewish immigration and the re-establishment of the Jewish people in a homeland of their own and of their ancient race. It was also assumed, perhaps in too high a spirit of idealism and optimism, that Jewish immigration would not be resented by Arabs, especially as the religious, cultural, and civic rights of Arabs in Palestine were expressly safeguarded in the declaration.

The Balfour declaration was assented to by the governments of the United States of America and France, and subsequently, at the peace conference, where the mandate system was evolved and applied to the conquered German and Turkish territories, it was embodied in the mandate for Palestine. The policy thus received universal assent and became part of the public law of the world. In view of all the facts it is difficult to believe that the Balfour declaration was intended as a temporary experiment and not rather as a permanent long-range policy, to be carried out in the course of the years. Whether in the end the national home would develop to the status of an independent Jewish state, like the neighbouring Arab states of Syria and Lebanon, was left an open question to be solved by the course of future developments. The embodiment of the

Balfour declaration into the international mandate, so far from detracting from its essentially indefinite character, actually strengthens it, and gives it a wider validity than it might have had merely as a declaration by one great power confirmed by two others. If there had been any intention to change the policy and to limit its scope, that should have been expressed in the terms of the mandate. No such limitation was made in the mandate, which thus gave added validity to the policy of the declaration in its full generality.

The White Paper of 1938,[1] which purports to limit the immigration policy under the mandate, by a term of years and a limit by numbers, was merely the unilateral act of the British government and—it seems to me—in conflict with the real character of the mandate. I do not think that it can be used as an argument in the interpretation either of the declaration or the mandate. The joint committee, in inquiring into the original intention of the declaration and the mandate, should therefore not be influenced by the White Paper. The correct view, I submit, is that both of them embodied a general immigration policy unlimited either as regards time or numbers.

This, of course, does not dispose of the whole matter. It is undoubted that difficulties have turned up in the execution of the immigration policy which were not envisaged, or not clearly envisaged, in 1917 or 1920. The Arabs in Palestine have in the course of time developed a fear complex, with regrettable consequences for good order in the country. The neighbouring Arab peoples now threaten to take a hand in the quarrel. The situation with which the British government is now faced is a much more obscure and difficult one than that which existed at the end of the last war or for years thereafter. It may be that the execution of the immigration policy has to be fitted into the new situation which has arisen since then. That is the problem with which the committee of inquiry has to deal. It will be for the committee to decide, after hearing the evidence and considering the case as a whole, whether any fair and reasonable compromise is called for. It would be wrong for me to express any views in the absence of the evidence or the facts. All I wish to emphasize in this statement is that the Balfour declaration made by the British government, assented to by the American and French governments, and subsequently solemnly confirmed in the mandate by the nations of the League, is a solemn and sacrosanct document, embodying a long-range

[1] Smuts wrote '1938' but the reference is to the notorious White Paper of 1939 (Cmd. 6019). *See* C. Sykes, *Cross Roads to Israel* (Mentor edition 1967), pp. 206–8.

policy of Jewish immigration into Palestine, that it should be treated with respect as such, and that the fundamental rights thereby assured to the Jewish people should not be abridged or tempered with more than is absolutely necessary under all the circumstances of the case. If the United Nations Organization steps into the shoes of the League of Nations, it should respect with scrupulous regard both the character of the original declaration and the rights thereby pledged to a people who, beyond all others and beyond all measure, have suffered in this war, and whose desperate plight now forms an additional ground for not taking away what was so nobly and generously given them in the Great War.

J. C. Smuts
F.M.

694 To J. Hutchinson — Vol. 77, no. 230

Doornkloof
Transvaal
8 December 1945

My dear Hutchinson, I am reading your *Botanist in Africa*[1] with great enjoyment and absorbed interest. It is indeed a fascinating work, primarily phytogeographical, but written in the form of a personal narrative of travel which gives it a great additional interest. I am sure the book will interest a wide public, and is indeed a new way of making botany popular and accessible to the general public.

Incidentally I am interested in your chapter on phylogeny, in which I see you make much more of the distinction between *lignosae* and *herbaceae* than has been done before. Indeed you erect two phylla on the distinction. As you are apparently going to publish a new work in which this development will be further applied, I add the following remarks which occur to me and which you no doubt have had in your own mind. You will no doubt have to make out a strong case for this new departure. And the question will be asked whether the difference between the two groups is really so important as you make it out to be.

Woody structure is of course a biological development intended to give strength in case of height, weight or other stresses from physical nature. Where there are no such stresses or urges the fibrous structure is mere surplusage. And you will have to consider the physical basis for the new phylla you create in botany.

[1] *See* **645**.

Years ago when I read Bews's book on Plant Forms[1] and the light they throw on our South African flora, I was much struck by the stress he laid on the fact that, apart from the flora of the western Cape, our South African flora was of northern or tropical descent, and the plant forms had adapted themselves to the new climatic conditions as they travelled south from the tropics. They became smaller, and gradually became transformed from the large, powerful, tropical forms to the smaller, frailer, more herbaceous types in the south. You know of course all the evidence which bears this out. In case of the *Gramineae*, for instance, you have the tropical bamboos and arundinarias in the tropics, the tall cymbopogon types as you travel south to the subtropics, until finally you come to the small herbaceous panicums and other grasses in the south. The luxuriant urge diminishes, and the fibrous structure therefore becomes unnecessary with the smaller size and weight. It is thus mostly a matter of climate and physical factors. Some of the tropical trees, no longer requiring the strong structure above ground, keep up only an underground fibrous storage for water, e.g. *Dichapetalum cymosum*, and *Erythrina zeyheri*, and others. The difference between lignous and herbaceous structure thus becomes more a matter of physical, climatic conditions than of genetic character. And there is apparently no good ground for erecting different plant phylla on such variable and varying physical factors. I do not say that you are not right, and I am much impressed by your instances of parallelism, such as *Araliaceae* and *Umbelliferae*, but I hope you will not base this parallelism on grounds which might not be defensible.

How long have plants been lignous or fibrous? How much is it their *nature* or only the result of their changing habitats? Flowers, we agree, are intrinsically genetic, and their structure points to their nature and are good grounds for fundamental phylogenetic classification. But is their stem structure as lignous or herbaceous of equal value for their genetic classification?

I have no time or even the information to guide me in these matters. But I attach great value to your phylogenetic work, and should like you to go carefully into the question of the genetic and permanent *basis* of the new developments you propose. I simply raise the matter for your consideration in case you have not yet given it fundamental thought.

I hope you will by this time have seen Pole-Evans's statement on your book. I think it good and fair and likely to be helpful to your publicity. We are all most desirous of the success of this

[1] J. W. Bews, *Plant Forms and their Evolution in South Africa* (1925).

work, which is a powerful contribution to our botanical literature and to popular interest in it. I think it is quite equal to Burchell,[1] and it has even more of a topical, personal, popular interest.

With all good wishes for the new year from all of us and the whole Doornkloof circle. Ever yours,

s. J. C. Smuts

695 To Lord Wavell Vol. 77, no. 236

Pretoria
14 December 1945

My dear Wavell, I have two welcome letters from you to answer (19 July and 27 November).[2] Both were written round an exchange of photos. I am pleased with yours and you are pleased with mine! They will be mementoes of the times and occasions when our paths have crossed in life. And what times they have been! May I add with how much pleasure I have constantly read and enjoyed your anthology,[3] so different in contents and in conception from the usual anthology. My copy was a gift from you and therefore doubly precious to me.

You refer to the new situation arising in India after the elections.[4] I must admit that I am far from happy about that situation. India is determined to go her own way, but there is grave risk that the removal of the British control—the steel framework of the Indian structure—may mean the collapse of the whole vast system.

Indian leaders have not been trained for heavy responsibility and do not appear to face up to all it means. And India itself may be in grave danger. With Muslims aiming at Pakistan, the bigger states may desire also to go on their own, and a break-up may result which will put India back to where it was before the British Raj which first united the sub-continent. In fact all Asia seems to be on the move to get rid of its European guides, and it may wander in the dark into dangerous paths. And beyond that lies the issue of East and West, and all it may mean for our human future.

Your immediate task after the elections is likely to become much more difficult. You will have a government consisting of party representatives looking at the problem of government from their

[1] *See* vol. VI, p. 505, note 4.
[2] Smuts Collection, vol. 77, nos. 323, 324.
[3] *Other Men's Flowers* (1944).
[4] The elections for the central and provincial legislatures preparatory to convening a body to frame a constitution for a self-governing India.

party points of view. Your own authority may be correspondingly affected and your task complicated. Nobody will envy you the job of liquidating the old system which has done so much for the advance of India and inaugurating a new system intended to reduce British influence to a minimum. Even so, however, one hopes that enough will remain as a precious tradition and asset for the India of the future. You have my best wishes in the difficult work before you. There is this to be said for your handling the case: that your long training and experience among men of different races and outlooks gives you a good background for this new adventure, greater than any of your previous career.

What I told you in London after your appointment still holds. Keep your eye not only on India but also on London. Your difficulties may be as much in the one as in the other. And you will be in the position of an honest impartial broker between these two vast interests.

My wife has been poorly these last couple of years, from sheer overwork in the war. We are keeping her quiet, and our youngest daughter, who is a doctor, is keeping an eye on her to prevent her from indulging in too much public activity. With kind regards and best wishes to both you and Lady Wavell, Ever yours sincerely,

s. J. C. Smuts

P.S. I am sending you a separate letter on Indian matters in the Union.[1]

696 To Lord Wavell — Vol. 77, no. 235

Pretoria
14 December 1945

My dear Wavell, You will be interested to have my views on the present Indian situation in the Union. I promised before to let you know how my mind was moving towards a solution of this problem, but my long absence at San Francisco and many conferences since my return with the various sections of opinion have prevented me from being in a position to write to you sooner.

It has not been easy to see a way through this welter of differences and prejudices. Indeed, in many ways the position has worsened since the Pretoria Agreement, which failed largely because of my absence from the country. Differences have become more accentuated. The Indians have moved more to the left and have emphasized

[1] 696.

their standpoint more forcibly. The Europeans have become panicky for their future in Natal. The Indian congress has elected a new executive of a more uncompromising character who have pressed for their maximum programme—equal rights, equal franchise on a common roll, and all the other economic items of their programme. The break-up of the coalition government has also made the position more difficult, as both Labour and Dominion parties are inclined to exploit the Indian question in their own interests. My United party is naturally in a difficult position with Natal opinion so excited and panicky. I refer to these matters to make you realize the political difficulties of the situation.

On the passing of the Pegging Act the Broome commission[1] was appointed to work out plans for a permanent settlement of the Natal Indian question. This commission has proved singularly unfruitful,[2] and its final recommendation was for a joint conference between India and South Africa to explore a solution. I do not favour such a joint conference as it may be as much of a failure as was the previous conference.[3] This time a failure would be more serious. In the present excited temper the intrusion of India into this matter might be resented and make a solution even more difficult as an intervention from outside, and any unpopular recommendations would be blamed on the Indian influence in the joint conference. I therefore think the wiser course is to deal with the matter with our own resources of wisdom, at least in the first instance, and to avoid the appearance of an extraneous influence on the proposals to be submitted to parliament.

My idea is to introduce legislation into the Union parliament which will give Indians in Natal and the Transvaal representation in both houses of parliament and in the provincial councils of those provinces. I also wish to take further measures, mostly administrative, for India participating in municipal affairs, and receiving better appointments in the public and railway services and in educational and economic directions.

It is proposed in the Land Tenure Bill to provide for open or free areas in Natal, where ownership and occupancy will be open to everybody while in the rest of the province ownership and

[1] This was the third commission on Indian affairs with Judge F. N. Broome as chairman or sole member. Appointed in March 1944, it reported in June 1945. *See Interim Report of the Commission of Enquiry into matters affecting the Indian Population of the Province of Natal* (U.G. 22 of 1945).

[2] In protest against the Natal provincial legislation (*see* **646**) the two Indian members of the commission, A. I. Kajee and S. R. Naidoo, resigned and Indian organizations and individuals refused to give evidence before it.

[3] The Cape Town Agreement of 1927.

occupation will be controlled by a board composed equally of European and Indian representatives under an official chairman.[1]

The Representation Bill will give the Indians three elected members in the house of assembly for Natal and one for the Transvaal. Natal and the Transvaal together will have one elected and one nominated senator in the senate. In the Orange Free State there are no Indians, and in the Cape Province Indians have common and equal franchise with Europeans under the existing arrangements. The franchise in Natal and Transvaal will be communal and will be based on education and income or property qualifications so as to exclude the lower classes of illiterates. The question whether representation should be through European or Indian members still remains open for further examination.

On some such broad lines a comprehensive solution might perhaps be found possible, at any rate as a beginning and its elaboration will be left to the future in the light of experience.

I am not sanguine that Indians will pledge their support to such a scheme, especially as they are so wedded to a common franchise. But if once passed they may take their part in the political life of the country and be prepared to work out their salvation in common co-operation with the rest of the population.

I have in mind in all this merely to give you a general outline of what is in my mind. If it proves feasible the details can be filled in due course.

Deshmukh will bring you this letter, and I have verbally outlined my proposed plan to him without going into details. I may add that in Deshmukh I think you have an able and co-operative high commissioner whose experience and good work may prove very helpful in our mutual relations. With all good wishes, Yours ever sincerely,

s. J. C. Smuts

697 To M. C. Gillett — Vol. 80, no. 194

Groote Schuur
[Cape Town]
26 January 1946

From Arthur's letter I gather that you are either at Eastbourne now for recuperation or that you may already have returned from

[1] The Asiatic Land Tenure and Indian Representation Act (No. 28) was duly passed in 1946.

that change. I hope it has done much good and that the effects of the fever (or whatever it was) and the weakness which always follows have been shaken off...Poor Grace, to have lost her precious turkeys at such a time.[1] All this crime wave, even in most secluded spots, is very curious. Something primeval from our most hoary past seems to boil up like an epidemic; and then subsides again after the outburst. We know so little of ourselves and especially of that deposit of the animal and sub-human past in our make-up. I am always reminded of Miss Murray's (in *Witchcraft in the Middle Ages*)[2] contention that devil worship continued the suppressed religion of Europe throughout the centuries, and Christianity formed no more than a mere veneer in the popular mind. The past is still too much with us or in us, and after an upset like the war it overpowers the later overlay of culture and intelligence. We have the crime wave pretty bad in South Africa also, and a very ominous aspect is that it is affecting our Native population also, generally so law-abiding. I hope the evil will subside and pass. The element of fear is already too strong in the European mind, and it will only get worse if this undesirable visitation continues too long. I think it will pass. Owing to a combination of factors and especially the severe drought there is a very heavy influx of Natives from the rural parts to the towns where better provision for food can be made. And as you know the more the Natives invade the European centres the greater becomes the fear obsession. Fortunately the drought has broken and heavy rain is falling in most parts of the country. But the evil effects will remain. The maize harvest this year will be largely a failure; I doubt whether we shall have one-third of our average maize crop. Supplies from abroad are almost unprocurable in competition with the heavier demands from a hungry Europe and Asia, and the transport problem remains very acute. We are going to have a very bad time, and the forces making for violence and crime may receive a fresh impetus. The wheat crop is also largely a failure, but of course maize, which sustains our Native population, constitutes the greater problem. And we have so many other problems. But why should I complain, in a world of dire problems and troubles? And my experience has taught me that in the end there is always somehow a way out, not seen far in advance and at a distance. Anyway, this session of parliament is going to prove a trying one, and I shall have to make the best use of my resources to see the fight through. I sometimes

[1] Grace—wife of a farmer near Oxford who had been the Gilletts' cook. She lost a large number of valuable poultry through organized theft. (Note by M. C. Gillett.)

[2] Margaret A. Murray, *The Witch-cult in Western Europe* (1933).

feel that the physical strain is too much at my age. But at present I see no alternative but to carry on a task which sometimes seems more than this old body can carry. With the coalition dissolved and three oppositions once more busy in the house our majority is reduced to a little over twenty in a house of 153; and it is only my still strong hand and influence which can carry us through this post-war period. We have done very well with demobilization, but the final resettlement of our returned men in industry will continue to be a grave responsibility, and the housing problem is especially bad, mostly for reasons beyond our control. The Natal Indian question is once more coming up in menacing form, and I have a difficult problem with U.N.O. over South West Africa. These are all matters which call for my personal attention and influence.

...So de Gaulle has gone.[1] His limitations as a public man were very great, but he did an immortal service in helping France to get going again, and to recover her soul—if she has really recovered it. I have had the feeling, which I still partly have, that the utter failure of leadership in France after 1939 (and before) points to some deep-seated evil which it may take France time to recover from. Let us hope and pray things will continue to improve. But de Gaulle was the only man, and the events may yet prove that his departure has been a crippling blow. What feeble creatures those other French leaders were! I do not mean only Pétain and all his defeatist tribe, but the others too to whom one had looked for some greatness of spirit. But perhaps de Gaulle's work—like that of Joan of Arc—has been done, and things will slowly right themselves now.

Russia is proving very difficult. I look upon the Iran situation as the acid test, and it looks as if Russia is consciously, deliberately, defaulting on her undertakings and is once more riding the pre-war high horse.[2] I understand the need for patience and understanding on our part. But I gravely suspect that the men who rule Russian policy are still on the old road to imperialism and perhaps even Czarism, and that very difficult days are ahead for our new World

[1] De Gaulle had been head of the government since the liberation of France in August 1944. In November 1945 a constituent assembly was elected which unanimously chose him to lead the government. But he apparently found its criticisms irksome and unexpectedly resigned on 20 January 1946 to remain out of office for the next twelve years.

[2] In 1941 British and Russian forces invaded Iran to expel German agents admitted by the Shah. They were to withdraw after the war but the Russian troops remained in northern Iran where an attempt was made to set up a local Communist government. This led to a clash between the Soviet Union and the West in the United Nations Organization. Eventually the Russians withdrew.

Organization. The strike[1] and other troubles in the United States are also most aggravating, and must slow down world recovery very much. I think I have already suggested to you that we may be in the throes of a world revolution the end of which is not yet, and which may continue for many decades longer. The swing is now to the Left, but if the turmoil and suffering continue too long it may swing with equal violence to the Right. No one can foretell, and the passing of an era may take many decades besides those we have already passed through. And behind it all lies the spectre of the East, facing the West with all its glorious record of human advance. These are far speculations, but we are passing through a soul-searching epoch, and one cannot help thinking of the meaning and trend of it all. It seems almost too much for us, and almost instinctively we turn to the simple things of the personal and the domestic life which abide through all the secular changes. And especially to that fundamental faith in something basic in our human guidance which will steady us and prevent us from swaying too far from the true trend and line of advance. Ever yours,

Jan

698 To J. G. McConnell — Vol. 80, no. 52

Cape Town
3 February 1946

Dear Mr McConnell, With Mr Mackenzie King, I very much commend your enterprise and that of the *Montreal Standard* in giving prominent attention to the subject of atomic energy and enlightening the public on what surely is going to be one of the great controls of our human future. South Africa's high commissioner in Canada[2] has conveyed to me the request of the *Standard* for an expression of my views on the proposed control of atomic energy, and in particular on the question whether the steps taken by U.N.O. would be sufficient to safeguard the world against the disastrous war which would follow the use of atomic energy.

It is difficult to answer this last question, as the action proposed by U.N.O. has not yet taken final shape. So far as its use in war is concerned, atomic energy will undoubtedly be a matter for the Security Council to deal with, and the council has not yet formulated its proposals. Even when it has done so, the veto principle

[1] The most important strike was that of 700,000 to 800,000 workers in the steel industry. There was also at this time a long and costly strike in the automobile industry and another in the electrical industry.

[2] Dr P. R. Viljoen (q.v.).

which operates in the council may stop or slow down decisions, or interfere with practical action. The whole subject is therefore in a very preliminary stage and we must await further information and developments.

We are undoubtedly confronted with a problem which may affect not only future warfare, but our whole way of life as a civilized world. I still remember the speculations early in this century when the artificial splitting of the atom was effected by Rutherford, and scientists felt that we were at the beginning of something quite new, something far more novel and revolutionary than the discovery of the steam engine, the electric dynamo, or the internal combustion engine. The war use of atomic energy was then not anticipated, but it was felt by those who know that something was happening which might open an entirely new stage in our human advance, and render obsolete most of what had gone before. That anticipation has now come to pass. Atomic energy is at last released in quantity, and it will not be the same world thereafter. It is not merely the war use of the new discovery, but its shattering effect on the whole industrial mechanism of our civilization, that has to be envisaged. We have to rethink, and may have to replan, the mechanical basis on which our civilization rests.

That is how I look upon the release of this new source of energy. Grave as would be its abuse in war, terrible as is the message of Hiroshima and Nagasaki, that is only one aspect, and not the most important, of the discovery. Nor is it only a matter for U.N.O. and the Security Council, but for all of us, and all who give thought to the future of our race.

The release of this energy, so difficult and expensive as yet, may soon become much easier and cheaper. The gradual exhaustion of other sources of energy—coal, oil, and the like—which appear likely to limit our future prospects, may now be replaced by something infinitely more powerful, and quite inexhaustible in quantity. No material discovery is like this, and its effects in all directions may be no less unique.

Atomic energy is thus a subject of active concern not only for our military or political institutions, but for all. U.N.O. should not be the only organ concerned with it. Science, religion, the organs of human welfare, the irresistible force of public opinion, should all be marshalled in this great cause. Here is something infinitely dangerous, infinitely beneficial. There should be such an organization of all the forces which shape and direct human action that atomic energy may become the most beneficent aid in our human advance instead of another and greater fear.

Let us not merely look to U.N.O. Let us expect the best from that great experiment, but let us not put all our faith in it. It is only another human institution, and so may have already failed us. The future of the race cannot afford failure here. Atomic energy now becomes our greatest overall concern. Let us give thought to the way of dealing with this new opportunity. Let public opinion be mobilized as never before. Let U.N.O. be only one of the network of safeguards so that, if peradventure U.N.O. fails us or goes wrong here, we shall still prevent irreparable mischief. Let us establish controls which will control U.N.O. itself, and all the dark forces on our path. But this can only be done if an irresistible world-wide public opinion is created to control atomic energy in the right direction. The press is one of the most powerful agencies for doing this great service to mankind. And your great paper will, I am sure, do its bit. Yours sincerely,

J. C. Smuts

699 From N. H. D. Bohr — Vol. 78, no. 37

Gl. Carlsberg
Copenhagen
22 February 1946

My dear Field Marshal, I take the opportunity to send you the very best wishes through my friend Mr [E.] Torp-Pedersen, who is going to South Africa as Danish minister. During his stay in Stockholm as counsellor at the Danish legation Mr Torp-Pedersen has been a great support to the many Danes who found refuge there during the occupation of our country. Personally, I owe much to his help and advice in the critical days I spent in Stockholm on my way to London after having escaped from Denmark.

May I use this occasion also to give expression to my gratitude for all the kindness and sympathy you extended to me during our meetings in London. I need not say that the great problems which the advance of science have raised are constantly on my mind and I trust that the unique opportunities for furthering international relationships, which we discussed, will not be missed. I still hope that scientists may in some way offer help to the endeavours of the statesmen, and with the purpose of assisting in preparing, especially among scientists of all nations, a favourable attitude, I have written two small articles of which I enclose reprints.[1]

[1] Only one article is enclosed: 'A Challenge to Civilization', reprinted from *Science*, vol. 102, pp. 363–4.

Hoping that I shall sometime again have the great pleasure of meeting you, I am, in deep respect and admiration, Yours sincerely,

Niels Bohr

700 To M. C. Gillett Vol. 80, no. 198

Groote Schuur
[Cape Town]
26 February 1946

Last week I wrote to Arthur in response to two letters from him. The second was written at the time of his Eastbourne illness, and I was glad to infer from his general tone that his condition was not as bad as I had been led to suspect. I was much amused by his political change of front or party, and this also strengthened my impression that things were not too bad with him. This has reassured me and given me much pleasure.

...From now on I shall be heavily engaged on the parliamentary front, and will continue in that state until I leave at the end of April for an imperial conference and the Paris peace (!) conference thereafter. The Indian question which has flared up in one of its worst phases will keep me busy for most of March and April.[1] How deeply I had longed to be rid of this incubus, which has been with me most of my working life. But no such luck. The Indian penetration, real or imagined, has caused a panic which may easily lead to worse, and so I am once more grappling with the insoluble. It is not only here that the Indian question has come into the picture. There have just been the mutinies and riots at Bombay and Karachi; the political aspect of 'Quit India' is once more practical politics, and a British government commission has gone forth to help poor Wavell in his troubles.[2] A mission is also proceeding from here to Britain to publicize the way Indians are ill-treated in South Africa.[3] It will be a case like that of Poutsma in 1914 who said I was better than the devil at my job, and ended years after in being a firm follower and party secretary.[4] (His

[1] The Asiatic Land Tenure and Indian Representation Bill was introduced in the house of assembly on 15 March.

[2] Following a mutiny of the sailors of the Indian navy at Bombay, Karachi and other ports which involved serious riots, the British government announced on 19 February that a cabinet mission would go to India to help Indian leaders in devising a method of framing the new constitution.

[3] After unanimously declaring the proposed legislation to be unacceptable the Natal Indian Congress had decided on 12 February to send deputations to India, Great Britain and the United States.

[4] *See* vol. IV, p. 370.

daughter has been one of the brightest and best in our S.A.W.A.S.[1] war organization.) I hate these racial and colour questions, and yet it is my evil fate always at one stage or another to get deeply involved in them, and then to be looked upon as the devil of the piece. These are among my unpleasant duties and I ask for no sympathy in their performance. But the process is always most distasteful to me.

At the coming conference we shall once more have to deal with the vexed questions of Germany and Italy, which troubled us twenty-six years ago at Paris, and now in much worse form. I am for making war when war is on, and for making peace when peace is on. But so many people cannot distinguish between the two, and look upon peace as a continuance of war. Where all this is going to end it is most difficult to foresee. I had this morning a talk with high representatives of the Geneva International Red Cross who gave me a most harrowing description of the millions of disabled, displaced and homeless, countryless people, wandering about Europe in the most pitiable plight imaginable. Literally millions of them, just milling around in indescribable sufferings and privations. I think the human levels are sinking everywhere, and no one can foresee the end of this nameless horror. Pity has perished from the face of the earth. It is no use talking of liberty and all the other high idealisms, when people have sunk to a level below that of the beasts of the field. And the scale of this misery is so vast that one scarcely knows how to set about it. It is a world which can only be reconstructed from the very foundations; and the foundations themselves are not to be found in these quicksands. The international scene is dark enough, but this *human* scene is something far worse. One cannot even bear to look at it or to think about it.

I do not know why I should plague you with these dark and desperate matters, except that they occupy so much space in one's thoughts. The Light will shine again but I don't know where to look for it. Our compasses seem to give us no direction. Ever lovingly yours,

Jan

[1] South African Women's Auxiliary Services.

701 To M. C. Gillett Vol. 80, no. 199

Groote Schuur
[Cape Town]
3 March 1946

This is Sunday morning and I am spending the morning at home in order to finish papers and correspondence. In all other respects it is a most beautiful day. The wind has shifted to the north-west which shows that we may expect rain tomorrow. But it is cool and pleasant and the sun shines bright. All morning since I awoke I have been enjoying the bits of cloud floating across the mountain. The doves sing, the squirrels chase each other in their fun and love affairs, the Belladonna lilies are out among the ancient graves higher up. There is a brooding of the spirit on this bright Sunday morn, and I feel the goodness of the world surrounding me in a sort of affectionate embrace. I might have gone for a bathe but a cold hanging on to me makes that risky, and so I read and write and rummage through papers—in that pleasant unstrenuous way which is itself a form of rest and relaxation. Isie and the rest of the household are all busy downstairs—I suppose in letter writing and reading, while I enjoy my own company upstairs...

I myself shall in all probability leave here towards the end of April to attend conferences in London and Paris and may be away till late in June. It is an inconvenient time for me to be away, but the business in London and Paris may be important and justify my absence from pressing duties here. I must confess I do not look forward to this visit, now perhaps less than ever before. These absences from South Africa are harmful here, and I always have the feeling that nothing of any consequence can be or is done by my missions abroad. Events are shaping the course of history beyond our power of control, and one has a painful sense of frustration at the apparent or real failure. I am not in real sympathy with present world tendencies, and have only a real sense that my intervention is of no use. Still, one cannot arbitrarily pull out of the responsibility, small as it may be, and so one drifts along like a bit of wreckage on a stormy current. Just at present the Big Three are sparring with each other and using language such as has seldom been heard in public diplomacy. Russia is going her way imperturbably, with little regard for the feelings and protests of her partners. The United States is involved in a cyclone of strikes, with inflation in prospect. And Britain (in spite of [E.] Bevin) is timidly cooing in diplomatic language, without apparently having much influence on decisions. Even Egypt thinks fit to use insulting or defiant language towards her. I do not see what effect such as I could possibly produce in such a disorderly scene; and so I feel that my presence in these quarrels may be not only no use but even unwelcome, as I don't agree with any of the parties in their approach to the problems before us. Central Europe is the heart of our problem—the future is definitely being made there—and yet we are endlessly quarrelling over other things which are of comparatively minor importance.

Meanwhile I have troubles of my own in South Africa. The inconvenient Indian nuisance has once more shown its ugly head here;[1] and the problem of South West Africa is coming up at the next U.N.O. meeting in New York. Both of them will put us out of gear with the general trend of world opinion, and make poor South Africa once more appear more reactionary than she really is. It is all a great pity, but I suppose part of that impish element in history which makes fools of us when we think ourselves specially wise or right! Besides all this, the party fight in South Africa is on in all its usual violence; several bye-elections are pending which are like straws to show the direction of the wind. My absence will not be helpful in these circumstances. I am anxious to hand over a good going concern when I leave eventually, and I cannot afford to saddle my successor with a rather rickety political situation. That is my trouble, and you will understand how it troubles me amidst the larger troubles which affect us in common with the rest of the world. Public affairs are not a bed of roses in these perverse tumultuous times, and old age becomes querulous in such circumstances! Dear child, why should I be inflicting all this on you? Still, you would not like me to avoid what is unpleasant to both of us. Let us curse our times and that evil spite which proved too much even for Hamlet.

I hope this finds Arthur fully restored to health and vigour. Owing to letters arriving at wrong dates there has been a great deal of misunderstanding about his illness and his process of recovery. Really he now appears to have been much weaker than I had inferred from the correspondence. All the more reason for him now to go quietly, and first get himself into good form again. This sort of thing happened to him before at the end of the Great War. Now at the end of this he is once more out of action, a sort of war casualty, almost a shell-shock case! But just as before he had a complete recovery and was a fitter man thereafter than he had been before, so now, too, I hope a complete recovery is possible, and *will* be made if he just rests and vegetates and takes

[1] *See supra*, p. 42, note 3.

time for the purpose. I notice that scratches and wounds on me now take a much longer time to heal. It is all the slow pace of old age. Let Arthur be patient with himself—as patient as he is with his wife and his friend! And then he will once more be his old self, and perhaps flourish long after either or both of us have departed this scene for a better country! My dear Arthur, you must follow this good advice, and just be content to do nothing till you have once more a clean bill of health. So there, be a good boy, and humour the anxiety of your old friend.

All the rest of you seem to be getting on well now, except perhaps yourself, dear Margaret. I don't know what particular medicine is good for you. I sometimes feel you overdo your educational and other Quakerly activities, but I can't really judge. I only know that time is passing and that we must slow down in order still to do the few things which we are capable of doing. St Paul has written that wonderful ode on the change from childhood to manhood (1 *Corinthians* xiii), but there is another stage (still unsung), which carries us from maturity to old age. It is a wonderful stage—it is *our* stage. Let us make a success of it. Or did Browning describe it in *Rabbi Ben Ezra*? However, though we cannot sing it, we can *live* it. So do! Ever yours,

Jan

702 To M. C. Gillett — Vol. 80, no. 200

Groote Schuur
[Cape Town]
9 March 1946

This is Saturday morning and I sit quite alone in this house. Isie left two days ago and must have arrived at Doornkloof this morning in company with Louis [MacIldowie]. Today the other members of the family will be gathering there and they are certain to have a good week-end. So far so good, although the result here is that I sit in solitary state in this house and can only occupy myself with letters and with official work of which there is no end. I am waiting for a conference here this morning, and occupy the time meanwhile in writing to you...

So far I had written when my conference over Natal Indians took place.[1] It is all a tough business. While I have my serious difficulties with Indian and world opinion, I am up against Natal opinion also, and the struggle therefore continues on more than

[1] *See* **703**.

one front. Both sides are unreasonable and press their case too far and too violently. Both suffer from a form of hysteria, and the path of the peace-maker who labours for reasonable solutions under most difficult circumstances is therefore a very rough one. In the end Natal may curse me as much as Indians do. I find, however, that the position is becoming a dangerous one and unless dealt with now by some one with sufficient authority to do so it may never be dealt with at all—with consequences which I shudder to contemplate. In the last resort I take sides with the European and what he stands for on this continent. India will not bring healing to Africa and has not done so in the hundreds of years of her intrusion into or contact with Africa. The European with all his faults carries a message for Africa which India does not. Tanganyika and Kenya are rapidly falling a prey to India. Natal should be saved from that fate.

So far this morning, and in the afternoon I took a long walk along the mountain slopes from Constantia Nek to Skeleton ravine. A bath thereafter and a good meal have greatly added to my refreshment. Here I write upstairs alone in this house, surrounded with peace and silence, and content to be alone for the present. From tomorrow I shall have company and very acceptable company too.

I have a letter from you since you left Eastbourne and another from May [Hobbs] who saw you after your arrival at Oxford. She continues to write cheerfully, and...judging from what both you and she write I fear you are having a heavy task with all your packing and general winding up for the move to Street. I am sorry that all this burden should fall on you at a time of accumulated anxieties and worries, and only hope you are not overdoing it in your own feeble physical condition. Arthur has clearly overstrained his resources, and I hope you have both learned a lesson. I preach like the physician who does not heal himself.[1] But in my case there is no choice. The burden and the strain are imposed by uncontrollable circumstances, and while I occupy the position I must carry on the duties which belong to it. I have seldom, if ever, had more constant trouble, and would gladly get out of it if I could do so with a fair conscience. But while I am held to the post, I must also carry the post, hard as it is. However, I don't complain. Compared to other government leaders elsewhere my troubles are not exceptional: slavery is the badge of all our tribe[2] in these days. And

[1] *St Luke* iv.23.

[2] 'For sufferance is the badge of all our tribe.' Shakespeare, *The Merchant of Venice*, I.iii.111.

they become more and more clouded with international and national problems. We must just recognize that we have struck a bad patch and do the best we can about it. But I do sometimes feel terribly tired, and fit only for bed when I get home in the evening.

The food position has eased somewhat. The very good rains over most of the country have improved the crop prospects, and the good pastures mean that our meat, butter and milk difficulties are in a fair way towards solution. The wheat position continues critical, and much will depend on what can be done for us by the combined Food Board at Washington.[1] The world position—in Europe, India, and China—is so critical and the menace of famine so grave that the Board will find it difficult to apportion its supplies.

You will see from this arid letter that I have a drought of the soul. One feels not only tired but parched and empty spiritually. I suppose we have to be patient and 'wait on the Lord' as the older generation said. We evidently cannot do all that is called for in this terrible world situation, and patience and forbearance and a spirit of understanding are above all needed in so difficult and perplexing a situation. I have seen the last couple of days the speeches of Churchill in the U.S.A. in which he pleads for a spirit of 'fraternal association' in the English-speaking world, and asks whither Russia is moving. I am not sure that, with the best intentions, more harm than good is not done by these speeches. But then what should public speakers say? Surely they cannot merely preach appeasement with Russia in her strange doings in Europe and Asia. One cannot in a responsible position simply remain silent. What lead can one give in so perplexing a world situation? I agree that clear, definite, plain outspokenness of the Bevin type is necessary. But more than that is necessary. There should be closer private confidential contacts which will enable leaders to understand each other's minds and points of view. I wonder whether such contacts are being kept. I fear not. There is plain speaking at arm's length, but not also confidential exchanges which would take the asperity and poison and misunderstanding out of the apparent public brawling. If the Security Council could become such a constant round-table for confidential friendly contacts and exchanges much progress could be made where now one sees only a retreat from understanding.

I had a long talk today with Sir Ernest Oppenheimer—our gold and diamond king—just returned from London and the Continent. He says there is too much austerity in England. People should be

[1] The Food and Agriculture Organization (F.A.O.) set up on 16 October 1945 as a special agency of the United Nations.

cheered up instead of hearing only austerity. Let the women have silk stockings, the men do some gambling and the workers get beer etc. etc. Is this nonsense or worldly wisdom? He says Brussels and other places are kept going—fairly well—on the black market, which is quite helpful for morale! I listened with much interest to all this worldly talk. Perhaps we are all too morally earnest! Think it over, my good Quakers! Ever lovingly and unforgettingly yours,

Jan

703 From J. H. Hofmeyr — Vol. 79, no. 28

'Woolsack'
[Cape Town]
9 March 1946

My dear General, I am sorry that I am still not well enough to attend the meeting you are to have with Mitchell [D. E.] about the Asiatic Bill.[1] I therefore write to set my views briefly before you.

It seems to me that in the property clauses of the bill we are making a surrender to European prejudice in Natal which I for one shall find it difficult to justify. In sticking to the colour bar as far as concerns Indian representation in assembly and senate we shall be making a further surrender. To impose in respect of the Natal provincial [council] a colour bar which does not exist today is yet one more surrender. I regard it as the last straw breaking the camel's back, and I cannot be a party to it.

If the pressure from Natal is going to be too strong on this point, I suggest that you abandon the communal franchise proposal and go back to the Broome scheme of a loaded franchise on a common roll. That would be a substantial concession to the Indian point of view, and I think one could in that event justify the colour bar as far as representatives is concerned.

Failing that, I can only suggest that in the legislation we confine ourselves to the ratification of the Pretoria Agreement, and do no more. I am sorry I am unable to set forth my views more fully, but am still feeling rather 'played out'. Yours sincerely,

Jan H. Hofmeyr

P.S. Since writing this, I have had a talk with Mitchell. As a result the suggestion has emerged that, in order to overcome the discrimination argument, the bill should provide that there *will* be

[1] *See supra*, p. 36, note 1; also **696**.

an Indian representative in the Transvaal provincial council, but only when the total number of Indian qualified voters has reached the European quota. This will of course take a long time to attain, and our Transvaal supporters might be got to support it. In any case it seems to me to be well worth exploring.

J. H. H.

704 From M. K. Gandhi Vol. 78, no. 157

Telegram

From: M. K. Gandhi

To: Field Marshal Smuts, Cape Town

Dated 18 March 1946

Your Asiatic policy requires overhauling. It ill becomes you. Least you should do is to withdraw threatened land and franchise measure[1] and call advisory round-table conference at least of Union, British and Indian governments and if possible of all associate powers to consider Asiatic, African and general colour policy arising from Asiatic Bill. This is not for publication unless you so wish. Your and South Africa's sincere friend.

705 To M. K. Gandhi Vol. 80, no. 80

Telegram

From: Smuts

To: Mahatma Gandhi

Dated 21 March 1946

I much appreciate your interest and your kind message of friendship which is warmly reciprocated. Indian difficulties in Natal have become much more acute in recent years and now have to be urgently dealt with to prevent deterioration from which Indians may be greatest sufferers. Repeated local conferences with Indian organizations have produced no solutions and round table conference with outside powers is not politically feasible. As regards proposed legislation, conferment of political status on Indians has become highly expedient and is great step forward even though representation is by Europeans under South Africa Act. To allay fears of further penetration bill proposes demarcation of free areas in Natal where

[1] *See supra*, p. 36, note 1.

Indians and others can buy and occupy land freely and question of Indian segregation does not arise. Demarcation to be made by joint boards on which Indians adequately represented. Although bill curtails rights of Indians to buy and occupy anywhere in Natal it is essentially not unfair in intention or effect and will provide workable basis for Indian development and racial peace for many years. As such I commend it to you who know how great are the difficulties in maintaining harmony among South Africans of all races. I assure you of the friendly spirit in which I am acting in a situation which may easily get out of control. This is for your information and not for publication. I see no harm however in statement that you and I have been personally in communication over this matter if you consider it desirable.

706 To S. M. Smuts — Vol. 80, no. 93

South Africa House
Trafalgar Square
London, W.C.2
13 Mei 1946

Liefste Mamma, Ek begin nou my derde week in Londen, en nog kan ons nie sien wanneer die Parys Konferensie sal begin nie. Die Foreign Ministers is nog besig om to verskil en kan nie hul voorloopige aanbevelings in orde kry nie. Ons eie werk in Londen is voorloopig klaar en ons wag nou vir die aankoms van Mackenzie King van Canada aan die end van hierdie week. As dinge so bly sloer sal ek in oorweging moet neem of ek nie maar liewer vir eers na Suid Afrika terug sal keer en dan later weer terugkom na Parys. As die Konferensie uitgestel word tot Juli sal dit seker die beste wees want dit is nie goed vir my so lang van S. Afrika afwesig te wees nie. Ek voel nie gerus oor die loop van sake daar nie. Ek het alles in goeie orde in die Volksraad gelaat, maar nou lyk dit vir my of sake weer in die war begin raak. Dit is swaar vir Jantjie sy eie werk en ook myne te doen, en sy gesondheid is nie van die beste nie. Ek sal seker aanstaande week moet besluit wat bes is te doen. Hier in Londen wil ek nie onnoodig bly nie. Die voedsel posisie in S. Afrika en oor die heele wereld word al moeilikker [*sic*]—so moeilik ook hier dat die Regeering Morrison na die Ver. State gestuur het om te sien of daar nie meer kos uit die Ver. State te kry is nie. Die rapporte van Duitsland en elders word baie onrusbarend. Die volgende paar maande sal die gevaarlikste van almal wees. Daar word gepraat van hongersnood op grooter skaal as ooit tevore in die geskiedenis en van millioene mense omkom. Dit is seker 'n oordrywing, maar dit dui ten minste aan dat die nood verskriklik hoog steig. In India sê hul is dit nog baie erger. Die werelddroogte en misoeste kan een van die groot rampe word, nog erger as die oorlog self. Ons doen alles wat ons kan om voorsiening vir Suid-Afrika te maak, maar die nood is oneindig erger in baie ander lande. Morrison sal darem ons saak ook te Washington bepleit.

Laaste week was Arthur en Margaret eenige dae in Londen en het ons taamlik van hul gesien. Saterdag had ek hier vir lunch hul en die Hutchinsons van Kew en ook Jo Moore. Toe is ons na lunch na Kew om die blomme op hul bes in mooi weer te sien. Dit was waarlik 'n baie aangename besoek en almal het dit baie geniet tot op die finale tee en koek van Mrs H. Hutch self sien daar goed uit en stuur groete. Gister (Sondag) was ons stil en alleen in ons Hotel en het ek kan lees en skrywe na hartelus. Ek is bly as daar so 'n stille tydjie opdraai waar die gedurige besoek nie so druk is nie. Hierdie week is vol van bestellings. Vandag sal ons Joy en die Athlones sien en vaarwel sê aan Joy wat op punt staan terug te keer. Ons sal ook Queen Mary gaan besoek ensovoort. Ons is nog nie na Cato nie om nie in die pad daar te wees nie, voor dat sy weer op en wel is. Bancroft en Margaret sê dit is 'n allerliefste klein dogter en dat sy pragtige oë het—seker soos Ouma! Ek sal hierdie week ook besluit of daar kans is na Duitsland te gaan om dinge daar te bekyk. Dan is daar uitnoodigings na baie plekke vir Freedoms wat ek nog nie aangeneem het nie.

Ek sien hier nou ooral die boekie *Ouma Smuts* en ons het ook een wat Japie nou lees. Ek self het nog nie kans gehad om dit te lees nie. Ek hoop dit is in goeie gees geskrywe en Japie sê my dit is in orde van daardie oogpunt. Hul oordrywe darem almal dat jy en ek so danig anti-Engels was in die jare na die Boere oorlog, en oordryf die saak baie. Ons het ons maar min oor die Engelse bekommer in daardie jare van kommer en smart.

Churchill het 'n verbasende ontvangs in Holland gehad—'n koninklike ontvangs. Hy sal hierdie week terug wees, dan sal ek seker alles van hom verneem. Die Hollandse ambassadeur was hier om my ook namens die Koningin en regering uit te nooi, maar ek het gesê dit moet 'n beetje wag totdat ek eers kan sien hoe my tydtafel staan. Ek sal graag wil gaan as daar opening kom. Die Griekse Regering het my uitgenooi en dieselfde antwoord gekry. Die koninklike terugkeer sal nou in orde kom en by Sep. sal die Koninklike familie na Athene gaan. Wat sal Palo en Freddie nie bly wees nie! Hy was taamlik siek maar is nou vinnig aan herstel.

Ek was bly die liewe kinders te Alex te sien, en die klein Irene was nie van my weg te kry nie. Vreeslik oulik en lief.

Baie dankie vir jou liewe brief. Ek was bly oor die besoek na Rooikop te lees. Baie liefde van

Pappa

TRANSLATION

South Africa House
Trafalgar Square
London, W.C.2
13 May 1946

Dearest Mamma, I am now starting my third week in London, and we still cannot see when the Paris conference[1] will begin. The foreign ministers are still at loggerheads and cannot get their preliminary recommendations settled.[2] Our own work[3] in London is for the time being done and we are now waiting for the arrival of Mackenzie King from Canada at the end of this week. If things drag on like this I shall have to consider whether I shall not first return to South Africa and come back to Paris later. If the conference is postponed until July, that would be the best course because it is not desirable for me to be so long away from South Africa. I do not feel easy about the way things are going there. I left everything in good order in the house, but it seems to me now that things are again falling into confusion. It is hard for Jantjie[4] to do his own work as well as mine and his health is not of the best. I shall probably have to decide next week what had best be done. I do not want to stay here in London unnecessarily.

The food position in South Africa and throughout the world is becoming more and more difficult—so difficult here as well that the government has sent Morrison [H. S.] to the United States to see if more food cannot be got from America. Reports from Germany and elsewhere are very disquieting. The next few months will be the most dangerous of all. People talk of famine on a bigger scale than ever before in history and of millions of people dying. That is probably an exaggeration but at any rate it indicates that distress is growing terribly fast. In India, they say, it is much worse.

[1] The Paris peace conference.

[2] The second meeting of the Council of Foreign Ministers was held in Paris from 25 April to 16 May. Its discussions revealed sharp divergencies between the United States and Great Britain on the one hand and the Soviet Union on the other while France tried to steer a middle course.

[3] Smuts was in London for the conference of Commonwealth prime ministers.

[4] J. H. Hofmeyr.

The world-wide drought and crop failures may become one of the great disasters, still worse than the war itself. We are doing all we can to make provision for South Africa, but the need is infinitely greater in many other countries. However, Morrison will plead our cause at Washington as well.

Last week Arthur and Margaret [Gillett] were in London for a few days and we[1] saw them quite often. On Saturday I had them here to lunch and also the Hutchinsons of Kew and Jo Moore. After lunch we went to Kew to see the flowers at their best in fine weather. It was really a very pleasant visit and everyone enjoyed it very much right up to Mrs Hutchinson's final tea and cake. Hutch himself looks well and sends greetings. Yesterday (Sunday) we were quiet and alone in our hotel and I could read and write to my heart's content. I am glad when such a quiet time turns up when constant visiting is not so pressing. This week is full of appointments. Today we shall see Joy [van der Byl][2] and the Athlones and say good-bye to Joy who is about to return. We shall also go to see Queen Mary—and so on. We have not yet been to Cato's so as not to be in the way before she is again up and well. Bancroft [Clark] and Margaret [Gillett] say it is a most sweet little girl[3] and that she has lovely eyes—like Ouma! I shall also decide this week whether there is a chance of going to Germany to have a look at things there. There are also invitations to many places to get Freedoms which I have not yet accepted. I have been seeing here everywhere the little book *Ouma Smuts*[4] and we have one which Japie is now reading. I have not yet had a chance to read it. I hope it is written in a good spirit; Japie tells me it is in order from that point of view. But they all exaggerate your and my being so very anti-English in the years after the Anglo-Boer War and make too much of it. We were very little concerned about the English in those years of trouble and sorrow.

Churchill has had an astonishing reception in Holland—a kingly reception. He will be back this week and I shall then no doubt hear all about it from him. The Netherlands ambassador has been here to invite me also on behalf of the queen and the government, but I said it would have to stand over for a while until I can see what my time-table is. I should like to go if there is an opening. The Greek government has invited me and has received the same answer. The return of the king will now take place and by September

[1] Smuts was accompanied by his elder son, J. D. Smuts.

[2] Born Joy Clare Fleming; married P. J. van der Byl in 1922.

[3] Sarah Clark, born 5 May 1946.

[4] T. MacDonald, *Ouma Smuts; the First Lady of South Africa* (1946).

the royal family will go to Athens.[1] How glad Palo and Freddie will be! He was rather ill but is now recovering fast. I was glad to see the dear children at Alexandria and little Irene could not be prised away from me—most cute and sweet.

Many thanks for your dear letter. I was glad to read about the visit to Rooikop. Much love from

Pappa

707 To S. M. Smuts — Vol. 80, no. 94

South Africa House
Trafalgar Square
London, W.C.2
20 Mei 1946

Liefste Mamma, Ek skryf weer met my ou dik pen, wat vir baie maande weg was en wat Japie weer in my studeer kamer tuis gevind het. (Ek het op die oomblik drie of vier vulpenne hier—een in goud van Frederica om die Vredesverdrag mee te teken!)

Japie en ek is gister van Duitsland terug gekom na drie dae aldaar te wees—te Berlin, Hamburg en naby Hanover waar die hoofkwartier van die Engelese leër is. Sat. 18 Mei was ons op Schloss Marienburg naby Hanover om Frederica's ouers en broers te sien. Ons kon hul al die nuus van die koninklike Grieke gee en had daar 'n aller aangenaamste halfdag. Die Prinses is soos jy weet 'n dogter van die Kaiser en ek moet sê dat ek haar biesonder lief en aangenaam gevind het. Haar pa is ook 'n sagte liewe man en haar drie broers eerste klas flukse seuns, twee waarvan die stryd van Stalingrad deurgemaak het, waar een swaar gewond was. Haar 4de broer is so pas getroud en was nie op die Schloss nie. Japie skrywe seker alle biesonderhede sodat jy dit van Kitty sal verneem.

Ons had 'n biesonder leersame besoek ook te Berlin en Hamburg waar ons al die ongelooflik verwoesting kon sien en onderhoud hê met baie leidende persone—Duitsers ingeslote. Die kos toestande is verskriklik sleg en gevaarlik in die groot stede, nie so seer op die platteland waar mense minder van kos invoer afhanklik is. Levensgevaar is daar op baie groot skaal en ons sal swaar moet werk om hongersnood te voorkom. Ek het skole besoek om na die kinders te kyk, die vernielde agterbuurtes om na die armes te kyk. Toestande is werklik totaal onbeskryflik. Dit lyk tog nou of die Ver. State

[1] At popular elections on 31 March 1946 the royalists won 231 of the 354 seats in the chamber. Tsaldaris, leader of the Popular party, formed a government and ordered a plebiscite on the monarchical issue to be held on 1 September.

meer koring gaan stuur en daar is dus op die oomblik beetje meer hoop. Maar my moed was byna gebreek om te sien wat die daadwerklike toestande in die verwoeste Duitse stede is. Die Britse outoriteite was ons baie mooi behulpsaam met vervoer en ontvangs, en ons het die uitstappie baie geniet.

Hierdie week sal ons weer met moeilike vraagstukke in ons Konferensie besig wees. Daarna hoop ek Street en Cambridge te besoek—miskien ook tyd vind vir 'n paar ander besoeke. Ek sal hier bly om die Victory Parade op 8 Junie by te woon en dan huiswaarts keer. Die sogenaamde Vredes konferensie te Parys waarvoor ek oorgekom het het op niks uitgeloop, en daar is nou sprake van dit in Nov. te hou. Intussen sal ek begin van Sep. te New York moet wees vir die vergadering van die UNO, waar die kwestie van S. W. Afrika miskien beslis sal word. Jy sien dus hoe moeilik my tydtafel word met alles wat voorlê, beide in S. Afrika en in die buiteland. Ek weet waarlik nie hoe ek deur dit alles sal kom nie—en dan nog die Koning se besoek en die gelyktydige Parlements sitting. Geen rus vir die goddeloose! Te Berlin het ek verneem dat ons manne baie informasie inwin omtrent die optree van ons Afrikaanse verraaiers gedurende die oorlog. Dit kom alles uit die geheime stukke van die Duitsers. Jammer dat hul so voorbarig was met die Malan ondersoek in die parlement.

Ek hoef nie te sê dat ons hier baie besig is en maar min tyd vir bysake het. Japie is my weer tot groot hulp en troos. Die Hollandse regeering het my na Holland uitgenooi maar ek vrees daar sal nie tyd voor wees nie. Churchill had daar 'n verbasende ontvangs, die grootste van sy lewe. Mens kan dit ook begryp. Vir my sal dit natuurlik op kleine skaal wees, maar ek vrees die tyd daarvoor sal nie te vinde wees as ek dadelik na 8 Juni huiswaarts moet keer.

Jou briewe kom gereeld—al twee aangekom—en is baie lief en welkom. Al jul nuus lyk goed, en ek hoop die ryp sal die mielieoes geen skade aandoen nie, want die kos kwestie gaan ons nog baie moeite en verdriet gee. Ek was viral bly om van jou rit na Rooikop te verneem. Ek hoop dit gaan jul ooral baie goed. Gee my groete en liefde aan al die familie en soentjies en beste wense vir jouself. Alles van die beste.

Pappa

TRANSLATION

South Africa House
Trafalgar Square
London, W.C.2
20 May 1946

Dearest Mamma, I am again writing with my old thick pen which was lost for many months and found again by Japie [Smuts] in my room at home. (I have three or four fountain-pens here at the moment—one of gold from Frederica with which to sign the peace treaty!)

Yesterday Japie and I returned from Germany after being there three days—in Berlin, in Hamburg and near Hanover where the headquarters of the British army are. On Saturday, 18 May, we were at Schloss Marienburg near Hanover to see Frederica's parents[1] and brothers. We could give them all the news of the royal Greeks and spent a most pleasant half day there. The princess is, as you know, a daughter of the Kaiser and I must say that I found her particularly sweet and agreeable. Her father also is a kind, good-natured man and her three brothers first-class fine boys two of whom went through the battle of Stalingrad where one was seriously wounded. Her fourth brother has just been married and was not at the Schloss. Japie will probably write all the details so that you can hear them from Kitty.

We also had a most instructive visit to Berlin and Hamburg where we could see the incredible destruction and have interviews with many leading persons—including Germans. Food conditions are terribly bad and dangerous in the big towns—not so much in the countryside where fewer people are dependent on imported food. Life is endangered on a very large scale and we shall have to work hard to prevent famine. I visited schools to see the children and the wrecked slums to see the poor. Conditions are really altogether indescribable. It does now look as if the United States is going to send more wheat so there is at the moment a little more hope. But I was almost reduced to despair to see what the actual conditions in the devastated German cities are. The British authorities were very helpful with transport and reception and we enjoyed the trip very much.

This week we shall again be busy with difficult problems in our conference. After that I hope to visit Street and Cambridge—and perhaps find time for a few other visits. I shall stay here to attend the victory parade on 8 June and then make for home. The so-called

[1] *See* vol. VI, p. 379, note 2.

peace conference in Paris for which I came over has come to nothing and there is now talk of holding it in November.[1] In the meantime I shall have to be in New York at the beginning of September for the meeting of U.N.O. where the question of South West Africa may be decided. So you see how difficult my time-table is becoming with all that lies ahead both in South Africa and abroad. I really do not know how I shall get through it all—and in addition the king's visit[2] and the simultaneous parliamentary session. No rest for the wicked!

In Berlin I learned that our men are collecting a lot of information about the conduct of our Afrikander traitors during the war. All of this comes from German secret documents. A pity that the Malan inquiry in parliament[3] was so premature.

I need not say that we are very busy here and have little time for side-issues. Japie is again a great help and comfort to me. The government of the Netherlands has invited me to go there but I am afraid there will not be time for that. Churchill had an astonishing reception there—the greatest in his life. One can understand it. For me, of course, it would be on a small scale but I fear no time can be found for it if I must return home immediately after 8 June.

Your letters come regularly—two have already arrived—and are very dear and welcome. All your news seems good and I hope the frost will not damage the maize crop for this food question is going to cause us much trouble and sorrow. I was specially glad to hear of your drive to Rooikop. I hope all goes well with you. Give my greetings and love to all the family and kisses and best wishes for yourself. With every good wish,

Pappa

[1] After inconclusive discussions the Council of Foreign Ministers went into recess on 16 May without completing the preparatory work for the peace conference.

[2] The projected visit of George VI to the Union of South Africa.

[3] On 7 May 1946 the minister of justice, quoting captured German documents, raised the question of treasonable connections between Dr D. F. Malan and Nazi agents in 1940. Malan admitted meeting such persons but denied collusion and said he had been sure they were Union government agents sent 'to trap me'. A select committee appointed to inquire into the matter unanimously exonerated Malan. (*See House of Assembly Debates*, vol. 57, cols. 6947–7318, 10207, 10586–607, and S.C. 5 of 1946.)

708 To M. C. Gillett Vol. 80, no. 205

Doornkloof
[Transvaal]
23 June 1946

I write on Groote Schuur paper but actually I am at Doornkloof where I arrived yesterday by air from Cape Town. I had spent a very busy week there at the end of the parliamentary session, flying there immediately after my arrival from Cairo. My flight from London to Rome, Cairo and Cape Town was uneventful, and was as hurried as business would allow—a day and two nights at Rome, the same at Cairo, the same at Pretoria, and then straight into parliament at Cape Town. At Rome and Cairo much necessary work was done. I actually was at Rome when Umberto left and instead of seeing him, as my appointment was, I saw the prime minister de Gasperi [A.] who was acting for him. At Cairo I saw the king[1] (who gave me his highest order) and the military and diplomatic authorities. Montgomery was also there and we had a pleasant time together, and I hope useful. I did my best to be helpful over the treaty business. The high commissioner (Alan Cunningham) flew over from Jerusalem to consult me about the Jewish trouble. I gave him such advice as I still thought appropriate in the awful mess we are in over the Anglo-American report.[2] One cannot help feeling deeply sorry for the British government over the Middle East situation in which they find themselves. The dilemma is very great and has now been deepened by the appearance of the Mufti at Farouk's palace.[3] Great Britain is once more in a sea of trouble, and only firmness and courage and decision can help her in this situation. Let there be the appearance of strength even where the reality is lacking! But I sympathize with the government over the position they are in and only hope they will not be minded simply with a feeling of getting out of it anyhow. That way disaster lies.

At Cape Town I made a general statement over the peace question and the European position generally which was as restrained and moderate as possible. But I could not avoid showing my feeling that the position is most dangerous and critical and

[1] Victor Emmanuel III (q.v.).

[2] The report of the Anglo-American committee of inquiry was published on 30 April 1946. Its recommendations were never implemented but they exacerbated Anglo-American differences, particularly on the inflammable question of immigration.

[3] The Mufti of Jerusalem, Haj Amin El Husseini (q.v.), escaped from France, where he had been imprisoned since the end of the war, and reached Cairo at the end of May.

reinforcing what I had said in my broadcast on 31 May. With Europe in confusion, Asia in revolt, and the United States fast moving towards inflation, the scene is set for one of the major disasters in the world, unless we act with decision and as speedily as possible. I can get no comfort from the skimpy reports of the foreign ministers' doings at Paris,[1] and fear a peace conference will soon have to be called. I note that Byrnes [J. F.] has proposed it for 1 August, but that Russia demurs. However inconvenient, I shall have to do my best to attend as the occasion is bound to be one of far-reaching importance. It is most awkward for me to be so often and so long away from South Africa, where great tasks are before us and my colleagues are overworked. But what can one do? And the bitter memories of 1919 in Paris make a revisit on a similar mission in 1946 most distasteful to me. But one has no option. The soldier goes into battle, however uncertain of the issue and his own fate. The course of recent events is such that I for one see small chance of doing better or even as well as we did in 1919. We are in a business which evidently seems too much for us, and the best one could hope for is that the door for the future may not be closed; that an opening, however small, may be left through which mankind could escape from the clutches of the past and eventually reach a more satisfactory settlement than is now possible. Britain has no longer the strength which she could exert in 1919, and American leadership has been mortally struck by the going of Roosevelt. Russia is more of a riddle than she has been since the days of Napoleon, and one cannot see what her trend is—whether back towards Czarist imperialism or forward to international Communism. Both views are at present tenable, and both may be wrong. But what is the right view of her policy? Does even Russia know, or are we once more being driven forward blindly by a fate which we cannot fathom.

We have so longed for some day of rest after our heavy labours, some respite after the sorrows and agonies we have passed through. How pitiable today is the lot of man! Perhaps more so than ever before in history. We seem to be passing through a blackout—a night in which only the distant stars cast a dim light. We are so small, so helpless in the face of such forces as are now driving us on through the night. And yet we dare not lose hope or heart or faith.

I am reminded of a certain verse which Joan [Boardman] copied out for me from the English hymn book, which seems to express

[1] The Foreign Ministers' Council had reconvened in Paris on 15 June.

this mood of faith and steadfastness in the times which we are now passing through. I quote them for you who probably know them quite well. But they strengthen my weak fainting spirit.

> But the slow watches of the night
> No less to God belong!
> And for the everlasting Right
> The silent stars are strong.[1]

How small we are, how great God is! In that knowledge and the faith that springs from it, we can take courage and pass on.

This is Sunday night and you can see that the time and the occasion have carried me to a Sunday mood. Tomorrow I shall be in office again, grappling with our local problems. We can at least cultivate our own garden as the wise Frenchman has remarked,[2] even where we cannot move the world or the stars in their courses.

I hope 'Portway House'[3] is getting on famously, that at least that garden is gradually taking shape, and that in our small corners of the world we are not neglecting the duty which lies to hand. Love and loving thoughts to you and Arthur. Ever yours,

Jan

709 To M. C. Gillett Vol. 80, no. 207

Doornkloof
[Transvaal]
14 July 1946

I am under the impression that I did not write to you last week. This is just to put you wise in case you expect a missing letter. I have been abnormally busy getting abreast of official business and it is possible that your letter got lost in the pressure! But *your* letter to me duly arrived, giving the intimate details which are more welcome than more general remarks on a situation which no one really comprehends. We long for a co-operative attitude among the great ones at a time when the framework of our world organization is strained to the limits. We fear for the future in view not only of these differences among great powers but because of the intensive effort now being devoted everywhere to planning and trying out new weapons of destruction. The differences at

[1] The hymn, by F. L. Hosmer, in *Songs of Praise* begins:
Thy kingdom come, on bended knee
The passing ages pray.

[2] Voltaire, *Candide*, chapter 30.

[3] The Gilletts' house at Street, formerly called 'Askew'.

Paris have to be taken in conjunction with the doings at Bikini,[1] Peenemünde[2] (where Russia appears to be continuing the German research into new far-reaching methods of warfare) and curious developments in the Balkans, in China, and in other parts of the world. Appearances are all in the wrong direction, and one does not feel certain that they are not realities in the relations of the nations. One hopes and prays that all these developments are but a passing phase due to persistence of old fears and misunderstandings. But one cannot be certain that they are not the manifestations of a new international policy which may once more disrupt the world and lead to another cataclysm—not today—but in another generation. And so the suspense continues, and the sense of general defeatism and hopelessness continues. It is difficult to speak about these matters in public because of the extreme sensitiveness of people and the danger of inflaming the feelings which one hopes will subside with time. Patience is perhaps the best policy, and a continuous effort to take no unnecessary offence, but at the same time not to follow a policy of appeasement or of peace for the sake of peace, which we know by experience may be the most dangerous of all. These are very dangerous and fateful times, and whatever is done or said must be done or said with open eyes, with sincerity and frankness, and with every effort to avoid giving unnecessary offence.

The peace conference is now fixed for 29 July, and the U.N.O. meeting for 23 September. I have to attend both, but as regards the first, it is impossible for me to be at the opening and I shall not be able to attend till the third week of August. I hope minor business will keep the conference going the first two weeks so that I could be in at the moment of real business. I have to unveil the Botha monument at the Union Buildings on 15 August and I have to do a great deal of other very necessary and important work during the interim. My continued absence from the country is not in its interest, and I don't think it is right for a prime minister to spend so much of his time abroad. He is the leader of the government and the people, and his place is in his own country. So that is that! How long the peace conference will continue I don't know, but I sincerely hope that I shall be able to spend some time in South Africa between the peace and the U.N.O. conferences. I fear the latter will also be a tedious and disappointing affair

[1] Uninhabited atoll, one of the Marshall Islands in the central Pacific, where atom bomb tests were made by the United States in 1946.

[2] On the Baltic coast of Germany from which the first rocket bombs were launched during the Second World War. After the war it was occupied by the Russians.

just as was the San Francisco conference. These big conferences lead to much irresponsible talk and self-advertising, especially among the irresponsible minor elements. I shall not receive much sympathy in connection with Indian troubles and the incorporation of South West Africa into the Union...

710 To M. C. Gillett Vol. 80, no. 209

Pretoria
24 July 1946

I have just read a beautiful letter from you, written on Bastille day,[1] and ruminating over the far reach of the commotions which have been set going in the world by single great events. No doubt you are right that we are once more passing through a similar phenomenon of vast change set going from the smashing of the old nineteenth century imperialism. The waves of change are still spreading, and will continue to spread and influence our human lot long after the times have passed. It all depends on our correct understanding and appreciation of what is happening—how much of it is really new, and how much merely a harking back to the past. In regard to Russia, for instance, do we see a new Slav world emerging and struggling towards the light, or is it merely a return of the Tzarist outlook and expansion and reaching out to world power? Hitlerism no doubt was a return to the past; is Sovietism not a similar phenomenon? Who can say? But we can be patient and helpful and do our best to tide the world over the present dangerous phase. Our destiny seems to hang on a thread, and we must do nothing which may precipitate us into the abyss which yawns before us. I hate the atomic bomb and all it means, and I deplore the present secretiveness in its handling. But I must frankly admit that until Russian policy becomes more clarified I would prefer the United States to keep the secret of its manufacture and use. It might be fatal to entrust the secret to so ruthless and immature a power as Russia before we know where we are. The Americans after all are less likely to make a fatal abuse of it for power ends. But what a pass we have come to! I knew about the bomb since 1943 and did my best to prevent its secrecy becoming a new source of division and strife. But I feel now more inclined to be cautious, until we know where exactly we are. In the end the bomb will have to go, if a sufficiently tight control over its use could be established.

[1] The attack on the Bastille prison in Paris on 14 July 1789 is taken to mark the beginning of the French Revolution. The day is kept as a national holiday.

I love to think of you enjoying your days of rest in the garden. Yes, I envy you. But I remain so absurdly well that no excuse is given for dropping out of the ranks and stretching my limbs on the roadside. So on it goes—on and on.

Last week-end I spent a glorious day at Rooikop with Sylma [Coaton] and Jannie [Smuts]. What a day it was, tramping over the veld in perfect spring weather. I found there *Bronte Poems* given me by dear Alice [Clark] in 1919, and now appropriated by Sylma. I read Emily's poems once more. There is one of them, 'Remembrance', which moved me beyond expression. I don't know whether you have read it. It is one of the perfect gems in English literature, evidently written from the heart and as it were with heart's blood, but camouflaged as a 'Gondal' poem.[1] What that soul must have suffered and how she moved me! Just a hundred years ago! Ever yours,

Jan

711 To R. Broom — Vol. 80, no. 104

Pretoria
24 July 1946

My dear Broom, Clark's article is indeed a feather in your cap, and an indication of the great work you have been doing not only in palaeontology but also in human palaeontology.

As a layman interested in any human and prehuman fact I congratulate you and look forward to more! Ever yours,

J. C. Smuts

712 Address (1946) — Box L, no. 212

This address was delivered on 15 August 1946 at the unveiling of the statue of General Botha in the grounds of the Union Buildings in Pretoria.

We are gathered here today on one of the special occasions in our history—to honour the memory of one of our truly great men. For the name of Louis Botha remains one of the very greatest in our national story. This great gathering round this monument from all parts of the country is proof that all sections of our people regard this function as one of memorable and outstanding sig-

[1] Emily Brontë and her sister Anne invented an elaborate story about 'the Gondals'. Most of Emily's poems are part of the Gondal saga in which she and Anne lived imaginary lives.

nificance. We meet here to acclaim a great national hero and to pay his memory our tribute of praise, love and gratitude.

To all of you I extend a most hearty welcome. Specially do I thank their excellencies the governor-general and Mrs van Zyl for honouring the occasion with their presence. I also welcome the many representatives of foreign governments whose presence here today is a tribute to Louis Botha as not merely a national but also an international figure. And lastly, and above all, I welcome the many old veterans, comrades of Louis Botha in our bygone wars, who have come here today, many in their old age, once more to warm their hearts round his memory, and to feel once more the inspiration he was to them when they were young. To all of us he is the great man, the great national and international figure, but to those old war veterans he was the leader whom they followed through bright and dark days, even through mortal dangers, in the greatest experience of their lives. We rejoice to have them today with us when we honour their and our leader in a fitting manner.

Louis Botha passed away from us twenty-seven years ago, and many of us here today still remember that moment of great sorrow and that sense of bitter loss which overwhelmed us when we buried him shortly after his return from the peace conference at the end of the last war. Deeply as we felt the loss then, we would have felt it even more if we had foreseen what lay ahead of us—the ups and downs of a stormy era of history, ending in the greatest tragedy of all history. I then at his burial called him happy in the moment of his death, in the hour of victory.[1] We would have called him even happier if we could have known what lay ahead, and if we could have guessed the sad fate of the world in the generation that was to follow his going. He was fortunately spared that disillusion which turned our vast hopes after that victory into Dead sea fruit.[2]

Memorials went up in his honour, at Durban and Cape Town and elsewhere, but we delayed the erection of this national memorial to quieter and happier times, when the bitter memories of war and civil strife would have passed away. Little did we expect that there were worse days ahead for us. And so we waited for twenty-seven years, and even now the end is not yet. But we can wait no longer, otherwise none of us, his old friends and companions, would be alive to discharge this last debt of honour which we owe to his service and his memory, and which we, the living, so deeply

[1] *See* vol. IV, p. 288.

[2] The 'apples of Sodom', said to grow on the shores of the Dead sea. Beautiful to the eye, they are bitter to the taste.

feel his due from us. And so—what with the long delay and the impact of new troubles—it comes about that this memorial is erected at the conclusion of another and greater world war, when peace itself has not yet been concluded. Bitter indeed has been our passage through life in our generation. But the long delay has at least helped us to value more highly his message of good will and conciliation in a world now torn even more by the hatred and passions of war than was our own country at the end of the South African war. His message, his appeal, is even more opportune today than it was in his own lifetime and at his passing. To that message I shall come back just now.

But first let me point out some other aspects of his great and abiding services to South Africa and the world. Dying at the comparatively early age of fifty-seven he left a record seldom if ever equalled by any other South African. Without the advantage of education or scholarship and without a background of culture, he rose from his simple Boer beginnings through the hard and exacting life of the veld to be one of the commanding figures, one of the leaders of men, of his time. But he had the native endowment of courage, sound sense, and a fine sense of justice and humanity, to which experience added a power of decision and command which enabled him to make the most of the ample opportunities which came his way. His trials as a young farmer, his part in the Native troubles and turbulent events of his early life made him even then conspicuous among his associates. Then, unexpectedly, came the greatest of his opportunities in the South African war, which he had opposed to the best of his power as a member of the old Volksraad. Suddenly, by his charm and magnetism of personality, his military insight and power of leadership, he rose in a matter of months from a very junior staff position to be our commander-in-chief in the field. The rise was spectacular—sudden and rapid enough to turn the head of any smaller man. To him it came as the call to all that was best and finest in him, and in spite of all the immense ups and downs, the victories and defeats, he retained his position and continued to rise in the estimation of his fellows to the very end. When that bitter end came he showed up, if possible, to even greater advantage, and rose from commander-in-chief of our armies to the greater leader of our people. From commandant-general he became the sagacious and far-sighted statesman, if indeed the two are not really the same in fact. He planned and pursued peace as he had planned and fought the war—with results which form perhaps the great turning-point in the history of South Africa. What might have been a soured, frustrated and embittered people took its place in the forward march and finally achieved victories it could never—even with the wildest good fortune—have won on the field of battle. There was that greatness in him which could outmatch defeat. There was a greatness of soul in him which expressed and completed all his other great qualities, and which endeared him to his fellows and secured for him their loyalty and devotion, and finally inspired thousands who never knew him in person. I do not minimize his intellectual qualities—his massive intelligence, his intuitive insight, his sure and faultless judgment. But in a truly remarkable degree he had those qualities of sympathy and understanding, of kindness and compassion, which made him perhaps the most sensitive and lovable among the great men I have known. And there was nothing small in him, and his essential greatness tended rather to repel and sour others who in their smallness could not help envying and even hating him. Such is human nature at a lower level, which he did not always understand, and which deeply wounded his sensitive spirit. All these qualities of mind and heart were combined in him in a most attractive personality—which outwardly was perhaps his most striking feature. You could not meet him without being deeply struck by him at first sight. I had opportunity to see the deep impression he made not only on simple men of the veld (who are often very shrewd judges of men) but also on those very distinguished statesmen whom he met at the end of the Great War in London and in Paris at the peace conference, men of wide experience who were able to recognize a great man when they saw him. Many of them have recorded their impression of him and placed him very high among the world-leaders of their time. He was indeed a prince among men, and they felt it.

Such was Louis Botha. Of the great South Africans I have known I put Paul Kruger and Louis Botha in a class by themselves, although as types, as personalities, they were poles apart. To this class English-speaking South Africa added Cecil Rhodes, who again was a personal type utterly unlike either of the other two. A country so small as ours that can produce such men, cannot itself be lacking in greatness. And so let us hope that in future our people, our united South African people to be, may not fail to produce other types of like dimensions. May South Africa, so dangerously placed in the world, never be lacking in high leadership in whatever crisis may be her lot.

At the conclusion of the South African war forty-four years ago the country was at its parting of the ways. There were indeed no defined ways yet in a scene of disaster and confusion such as always follows great wars. But there were, so to say, two signposts pointing to the future, at right angles to each other on racial lines. At this psychological moment Louis Botha the statesman appeared, quietly took both signposts down, and put up another, intermediate between the two. He called it the path of conciliation, conciliation among the sections of our Afrikaans people, hopelessly split by the long agony of the war; and again conciliation between the war opponents, English and Afrikaans. This was his new lead, his vision, his inspiration for the future, his message to his people for the future. It sounded unbelievable and hopelessly impracticable. It ran stark against all the deep passions and sense of injury at the end of a terrible conflict in which great wrongs had been suffered. It was against the grain and seemed bound to fail. And yet it appealed to something deep down in the hearts of South Africans of both races, who are bad haters, even of each other. It appealed to the sound commonsense in both of them. It appealed with the inevitability of history after the great judgment of war. And the appeal came from one who wielded great authority and enjoyed in a special measure the trust and confidence of all sections of our people. The great warrior became the great peace-maker, and brought peace to this war-torn land.

And so the impossible happened. Louis Botha's direction was accepted and followed. There he rendered South Africa his greatest service of all. His signpost became for us the finger of our destiny. He set us on our course at the most critical moment of our history, and on the whole South Africa has now for about half a century followed this course, although not without deviations, twists and turns. In a real sense the Botha signpost has become the magnet for our course as a people. It is the pole on which our progress turns through the years and which leads us to our greater destiny. This is his supreme achievement. Others have shared his insight and vision, others have stood by him and marched with him. But it is his influence, his commanding authority, his greatness of soul which have guided us in the path we are going and shall continue to go. In honouring Louis Botha today we pay homage to our own national destiny. We salute not the dead, but the living, aye the future South Africa, born of the travail of his great soul.

I shall not mention in detail how far we have already travelled on the Botha road. I need only say that that road led to early self-government in the Transvaal and Orange Free State, to the National convention, to a united South Africa, to our free association with the Commonwealth as an equal sovereign state, and to our membership of the United Nations. It is a wonderful record, and indeed a great romance of recent history, and the name of Louis Botha is inseparably linked with the earlier and decisive phases of it.

So far I have spoken of the major permanent achievements and successes of Louis Botha. But the high lights were not without their deep shadows. The first phase of his brilliant military career in the Boer War ended in defeat and surrender. I still remember how deeply moved he was after signing the Vereeniging peace. It took him months to recover from that deep sorrow which he shared with his people. In the second phase his brilliant campaign in German West Africa (one of the model desert campaigns in the history of warfare) was preceded by the rebellion in the Union, which cut more deeply into his soul and caused him more personal anguish than probably any other event of his life. Both duty and honour compelled him to take the field personally to restore order and keep the pledged word of his country. But he had to fight not an enemy but his old Boer War friends and comrades. It was a cruel fate from which he did not shrink, but which cut him to the quick. But I know how deeply he suffered at that time of national tragedy, and I have no doubt that it shortened his life. The Vereeniging surrender did not touch the honour of his people or the reputation of his brave commandos. But the rebellion, whatever the underlying motives, moved him to his very depths and alienated old comrades to whom he had been deeply attached. To a man of his extremely sensitive nature the personal anguish was unspeakable, and the wound never healed. When, after some years of absence from South Africa, I saw him again in London and Paris at the peace conference I saw a physically changed man, and as the event showed the hand of death was already on him. The rebellion had taken him into the valley of the great shadow. It is therefore a mistake to look upon Louis Botha as a darling of fortune. Fate lavished on him her full measure both of joys and of sorrows. He suffered deeply, and the very greatness of the qualities which secured his successes also made him all the more sensitive to the harsh blows which he had to endure. Of lesser troubles, many of a political nature, he had his full share. But the effect adversity had on him was only to make him more humble and patient. He was a man of deep religious faith, although we did not often discuss religious questions. To his friends he was a friend beyond compare, and he sought in faith and friendship and hard work, as well as in the affections of his family, the relief which his sympathetic spirit craved for. Great men are often disagreeable characters; but here was a great man whose beautiful character matched his other brilliant qualities. Not only in his far-sighted leadership but also in his life and character he remains a shining light for the generations to come. Old age did not touch him or dim his faculties. He passed away at the height of his powers and his career, leaving behind a record of achievement to which there is no parallel in the history of our country. The new South Africa is largely his work, and his fame will last as long as the land he so largely created will endure. It will outlast this monument which we are dedicating to him today.

So far I have spoken of the past, and necessarily so, as Louis Botha died twenty-seven years ago. But standing here today at his monument and from it viewing the world around us, our minds are involuntarily carried forward from the past to the present and the future. We see a world around us not so different to that from which Louis Botha departed, only in a deeper gloom and more desperate plight. A great victory has once more been won in a war even far more destructive than the Great War. We have again to write a peace after this greater world war.

How would Louis Botha have approached it if he had still been alive? Has he no message for us in this peace-making also? Would we be far wrong if we say that the message he gave his people after the Boer War and which he repeated to the world after the Great War would still be his message to the world today in its dire distress? He would once more be the apostle of conciliation. He would bind the wounds of the nations—victims and defeated—and in a spirit of justice and moderation[1] would heal their differences in a world divided, disrupted, stricken, and suffering almost to death. He would write the peace in terms of humanity. Humanity would be his key word, rather than retaliation, vengeance and hatred. He would once more be the great human, and on a foundation of human understanding and reconciliation build the new world as he builded the new South Africa.

Hitler, with Versailles on his lips and world domination in his heart, dragged his own people and many others to the brink of destruction. Following Botha's lead let us rather leave vengeance to God and to His eternal law of cause and effect, and temper our justice with moderation and humanity, which is part of the concept of justice. Let us be concerned with the future more than with the past. The past with all its wrongs and injustices and shames is beyond human remedy. The past is with God—leave it there. Rather is it for us to save the precious human stuff which can still be saved from the wreck and to turn it from the darkness

[1] *See* vol. I, p. 519.

to the light. There is a vast emptiness in Europe—physical, ethical, spiritual. Fill it up once more with the human, with the spirit of our ethical civilization, lest worse devils enter and complete the ruins of war.

It is not for us to go into details. But in general such a message of human conciliation and constructive peace-making would be in the spirit of Louis Botha. In this way the torch which he lighted could be kept flaming in a world today plunged in darkness and despair.

Here today at this monument we thank God for Louis Botha, for his work, and for his legacy to us and the world.

713 To M. C. Gillett — Vol. 80, no. 211

Paris
23 August 1946

I have now had two letters from you since I arrived a week ago—so I consider myself specially favoured. Indeed this is the only favour which has so far been vouchsafed to me. The conference is just wasting time, and my attention is kept busy with minor problems and the constant thought how little wisdom goes to the running of our human affairs. No progress—rather small increments of further trouble all the time. What a waste of time international conference machinery is! It makes one despair of democracy and its ways. Give me a little more leadership and rather less democratic talk!

Perhaps this sounds an unhappy mood. But how could it be otherwise, after all these years and memories of twenty-seven years ago? There is an air of madness over it all for me. I seem to have survived from one shipwreck long ago only to be thrown into another a generation after. Paul had, I believe, three shipwrecks, but they must all have happened in a short time, and in the last a kind fate rescued him from the viper's poison.[1] But what kind fate can save one from this sense of frustration and almost despair over the course of affairs? The plight of the world is today far, far worse than it was twenty-seven years ago. And wisdom has not increased correspondingly, if at all. But so much is hidden from us that it would be a mistake to rush to conclusions and to think that this is a lost generation. Somehow, somewhere in the hidden paths salvation may be awaiting or preparing for us. So let us keep up heart and struggle on.

[1] *See Acts* xxviii.1–6.

This is Saturday morning. I left Doornkloof at 9 p.m. on Friday the 16th and was next morning at Kisumu for breakfast and later at Cairo for tea. Sunday I stayed over there for consultations and, leaving Cairo at 9 p.m., I was here at 11 a.m. on Monday. McIldowie[1] came with me as A.D.C. and Cooper [H. W. A.] as private secretary —Japie and Jannie [Smuts] were too much wrapt up in their mining tasks. I left all well at home—well and cheerful. The Thursday, 15 August, we had the unveiling of the Botha monument below the Union Buildings—a great affair where I had to make the speech,[2] as I had to do twenty-seven years ago at his grave.[3] My speech then was better than my address now. But I suppose I am no longer what I was twenty-seven years ago! Here I have been continuously busy with the conference work, without the satisfaction of any real progress being made as I have already said. I find large numbers of people coming to me and appealing to me for one thing and another. Some really think I can help and do things. How pathetic their faith in one who can do almost nothing in this jam and crush of affairs. But at least I am kept very busy and have thus no time to contemplate my own failures. Whilst I was writing this I had to listen to a deputation from the South Tyrol where a bad mistake was made in 1919[4] which today is almost beyond repair. Time itself is a fact and a factor and makes the future run of things irreversible.

I have not referred to your news, but it is all so good and cheering. Only I do continue to protest against your return to your old activities instead of quietly enjoying Portway. I hope these educational and other tasks will not once more upset your apple cart. Go slow. Think of Anno Domini. Keep a good reserve fund, like a wise banker's wife. One never knows what calls the future may bring. And now my dear love to you both and all the dear Street circle.

J.C.S.

714 To J. H. Hofmeyr — Vol. 80, no. 112

Hotel Claridge
Paris
29 August 1946

My dear Jantjie, Just a line to keep touch with you. We have now been here for more than a week, but very little progress indeed

[1] Denis McIldowie, son-in-law of Smuts.

[2] **712**.

[3] Vol. IV, no. **1066**.

[4] The South Tyrol, a former Austrian territory, was annexed by Italy in 1919. The northern part of the region contained a considerable German-speaking population.

has been made in the conference. There is great concern over the failure of the conference and the endless quarrels, especially with Russia and her following. It would almost look as if below the surface of friction and frustration the lines of the future are forming and the world is already beginning to divide into two camps. This is the real danger and this conference has brought it to the surface, so to say. The Americans are dismayed and their opinion is hardening that Russia is the enemy. I myself think this rather premature. Our fears may be right and again they may prove to be wrong. For conditions in the world are fluid and changing and the situation of today may not be that of tomorrow. The part of wisdom is therefore vigilant watchfulness and firm handling of situations as they arise, but a determined avoidance of the worst, as if the world has already begun to move to the next war. So much may happen in Russia, in the world, in the march of events which we witness today. My influence here has been to strike this note of caution and reserve, and I think it has not been without its effect.

I have not taken part in the work of the commissions[1] in which we are fairly well represented. We have a talk every morning in the South African delegation to discuss the day's programme, and the tedious movement of the conference does not call for my presence. Theron is doing well. I shall have to depart for New York in a couple of weeks and Theron's leadership had therefore best continue uninterrupted. The full conference is not likely to meet while the commissions are busy with their work. It is quite possible that on my return from New York I may still be in time for the completion of the peace treaties in full conference. The idea at present is *not* to postpone U.N.O., but to carry on both conferences *pari passu*.

I am seeing most of the leaders of the delegations and have useful contacts in this way. My unique position as the only survivor here of the last peace is duly appreciated and useful from many points of view. The general attitude of South Africa is also favourably noted. We have kept out of all the squabbles in which Evatt [H.V.] and the other Australians have involved themselves. An attitude of wise reserve and good temper and helpfulness serves our cause and the general interest much better. The Americans especially seem to like us and the line we take. The smaller European delegations evidently look to us as a humane and moderating influence.

[1] The machinery of the conference included a general commission, a military commission, a legal and drafting commission, two economic commissions, and five political commissions—one for each of the five proposed treaties.

Next week-end I shall spend with Churchill at Geneva. He has invited me and I think it useful to keep touch. The king has invited me to Balmoral where I shall be the following week-end. The third will find me on my way to New York.

I have seen a good deal of the Greek delegation here and have been helpful to them in their dealings with the United Kingdom. The crown prince and princess were here in touch with their delegation and have returned to Egypt on the way to Athens, where all expect their return after the plebiscite.

What a confused world Paris is—far more so than twenty-seven years ago. The caravan is still moving, but how much more chaotically than after the Great War. All good wishes. Ever yours,

J. C. Smuts

I am so glad that your news from South Africa continues favourable.

715 To S. M. Smuts — Vol. 80, no. 115

[Parys]
3 September 1946

Liefste Mamma, Kyk na die datum—3 September wat my herinner aan daardie Sondag in 1939 toe ons die toekoms en ons deelname in die oorlog in die koalisie kabinet moes uitveg. Hoeveel is nie sedert gebeur nie—hoe 'n verskriklike geskiedenis, hoe 'n oorweldigende oorwinning. En tog is die einde van ons moeilikhede nie daar nie. Maar tog ook het ons geen rede te wanhoop nie.

Gister aand is Dennis en ek terug gekom van Geneva van 'n motor besoek aan Churchill wat my dringend en herhaaldelik daarheen uitgenooi het. Hy is daar op 'n besoek en wou sake met my bespreek. Ons had geen vliegtuig van hier en is per auto gegaan. Van daar het die Switzer regering my 'n Dakota vir die terugkeer aangebied maar ek het dit beter geag dit nie aan te neem nie. Dus daarheen en terug per auto—Saterdag en Maandag, en Sondag daar. Beide ritte het ons omtrent 12 uur geneem maar moes veel minder wees. Maar daar was baie oponthoud met petrol en ander motor moeilikhede wat Denis seker sal beskrywe. Alles is darem goed gegaan en ons is gistraand (Maandag) veilig in Parys teruggekeer. Die rit was deur pragtige wêreld en viral die van die Jura berge voor ons by Geneva gekom het was uitermate skoon. Op en af, en bo en onder vir 'n 50 of meer myl deur die berge—in mooi weer so dat mens alles kon sien. Sondag by die villa Choisi—20 myl van Geneva—was dit aanhoudend reën so dat ons binnenshuis moes bly. Maar daar ek meestal vir besprekings gegaan het was dit, vir my ten minste, nie so erg nie. Ons kon die heele Sondag gesels en wereldsake bespreek. Hy (Churchill) was erg begaan oor die gevaar van 'n spoedige oorlog maar ek kon hom kalmeer en ek [is] oortuig dat die gevaar daarvan nie 'n werklikheid is nie. Niemand, selfs nie die dolste, wil vandag of in die nabye toekoms weer in oorlog gedompel wees nie. Ons moet nie slaap nie maar ook nie ons deur drome laat skrik nie. Ons plig is om sake so te reël dat die oorlog in die toekoms nie 'n praktiese kwestie sal word nie. Viral het ons die kwestie van 'n Unie van Europa of Wes Europa taamlik ernstig bespreek.

My koms was baie welkom en die vloere was te koud vir Denis en my. Clemmie en al 3 dogters was daar—Diana, Mary (Nee, Sarah was nie daar nie). Hul wou ons langs die meer na die ooste neem maar die reent het dit verhinder. Hul is baie opgenome met hul reis na Suid-Afrika *na* die koning, en kyk met gretigheid daarna uit. Die Botha funksie is ook baie bespreek daar hy Botha baie lief had. Ek gaan 'n krans met my vir die monument meebreng met my terugkeer.

Toe ek gistraand laat hier aankom was daar weer 'n brief van jou—die twede sedert my aankoms. Baie dankie vir al die nuus wat ons natuurlik baie interesseer. Die briewe van jou en Louis gee ons 'n volledige verhaal van alles wat gaande is, en dit is vir ons natuurlik lief om dit alles te hoor. Ek sal voortgaan om 'n weeklikse brief te skrywe. Jy sal natuurlik verstaan dat my tyd verbasend in beslag geneem word en min tyd vir private korrespondensie oorlaat. Ek verskyn nie op die Kommissies nie, waar my jongspan en staf die donkey werk kan doen. Maar daar is gedurige konferensies en onderhoude en reëlings wat moet gemaak word. Die Konferensie self met al sy getwis en gekyf interesseer my minder. Daar is ook aanhoudende telegram wisseling met Pretoria oor kwesties waarin my leiding noodig is. So bly my hande taamlik vol. Ek hoor die Grieke het die volkstelling gewen. Hul sal nou seker spoedig na Athene terugkeer, en 'n einde sien van die lange ballingskap. Palo en Freddie is vol daarvan laaste week van Parys weg. Miskien sal ek hul nog te Athene op my terugreis sien. Nou genoeg. Hier alles wel. Gesondheid goed, en Denis kyk uitstekend goed na my en doen alles wat hy kan om my pad skoon te hou. Liefde aan jul almal.

Pappa

TRANSLATION

[Paris]
3 September 1946

Dearest Mamma, Look at the date—3 September—which reminds me of that Sunday in 1939 when we had to fight out the question of our future and our participation in the war in the coalition cabinet. How much has not happened since—what a terrible history, what an overwhelming victory. And yet the end of our troubles is not yet. But again, we have no reason to despair.

Yesterday evening Denis [McIldowie] and I returned from Geneva from a visit by motor-car to Churchill who had urgently and repeatedly invited me. He is on a visit there and wished to discuss matters with me. We had no aircraft from here and went by car. There the Swiss government offered me a Dakota for the return journey but I considered it better not to accept. So, there and back by car on Saturday and Monday, spending Sunday there. Both trips took us about twelve hours and should have taken far less but there were all sorts of delays for petrol and other car trouble which Denis will no doubt describe. However all went well and we reached Paris safely yesterday evening (Monday). The drive took us through lovely country—the region of the Jura mountains in particular, before we reached Geneva, was exceptionally beautiful. Up and down, over and under through the mountains for fifty miles and more—in fine weather so that one could see everything. Sunday at the Villa Choisi, twenty miles from Geneva, it rained incessantly so that we had to stay indoors. But, since I had gone chiefly for discussions, it was not so bad—for me at least. We could talk the whole of Sunday and discuss world affairs. He (Churchill) was most concerned about the danger of an early war but I was able to calm him; I am convinced that this danger is not real. Nobody, not even the maddest, wishes to be plunged into war now or in the near future. We must not go to sleep but also not be frightened by dreams. Our duty is so to arrange things that war will be impracticable in future. In particular we had a pretty serious discussion on the question of a Union of Europe or of Western Europe.

My arrival was very welcome and nothing was too good for Denis and me. Clemmie and all three daughters were there—Diana,[1] Mary[2]—no, Sarah[3] was not there. They wanted to take

[1] Born 1909; married Duncan Sandys (q.v.) in 1935; divorced 1960; died 1963.

[2] Married Rt. Hon. Christopher Soames in 1947.

[3] Born 1914; actress; married Vic Oliver in 1936; divorced 1945; married Anthony Beauchamp in 1949 and after his death Lord Audley.

us eastwards along the lake but the rain prevented that. They are very pleased about their visit to South Africa *after* the king's and are eagerly looking forward to it. The Botha function was also much discussed for he loved Botha very much. When I go back I am to take a wreath for the monument with me.

When I arrived here late last evening there was again a letter from you—the second since my arrival. Many thanks for all the news which, of course, interests us very much. Your letters and Louis' give us the full story of what goes on and of course it is lovely for us to hear it all. I shall continue to write a weekly letter. But you will understand that my time is surprisingly taken up and leaves me little for private correspondence. I do not take part in the commissions where my young people and staff can do the donkey work. But there are constant conferences and interviews and arrangements to be made. The conference itself with all its quarrelling and bickering interests me less. There is also a continual exchange of telegrams with Pretoria about matters in which my guidance is needed. So my hands remain fairly full.

I hear that the Greeks have won the plebiscite.[1] They will now probably soon return to Athens and see the end of a long exile. Palo and Freddie left Paris last week full of it. Perhaps I shall see them in Athens on my return journey. And now enough. All well here. Health good, and Denis looks after me excellently and does all he can to keep my way clear. Love to you all.

Pappa

716 To S. M. Smuts — Vol. 80, no. 116

Parys
7 September 1946

Liefste Mamma, Weer 'n brief van jou wat baie welkom is. Die possak en mail briewe kom op dieselfde tyd aan en jy kan dus pos soos jy wil, maar na Amerika is dit bes na South Africa House Trafalgar Sq. Londen te stuur vir versending.

Ons vertrek a.s. Saterdag 14 September na Londen en dieselfde namiddag van daar na Balmoral waar ons Sondag dan sal oorbly en Maandag terug na Londen om dieselfde week na New York per Constellation te vlie. Die York sal in Engeland vir nuwe engines bly. Dis nog onseker of ons lang of kort in New York sal vertoef. Miskien kom ons Suid Afrikaanse twee kwesties nie op en dan kom ek terug na Parys om die week hier te voltooi

[1] In the plebiscite, held on 1 September, 69 per cent voted for the monarchy.

voor terugkeer na S.A. Die plan is om die programma vir New York te beperk tot noodsaaklike administratiewe reëlings van UNO en ander werk te laat oorstaan. Maar daar is nog geen sekerheid op hierdie punt nie. Die Groot Vier kan oor niks besluit omdat Rusland hardnekkig haar eie aparte paadjie volg en met niemand saamstem nie. Wat kan ons doen? Niemand kan hier uitmaak wat Rusland in die mou het nie, en tyd alleen sal ons leer. Maar niemand weet ook nie wanneer die verdaagde vergadering van UNO dan gehou sal word nie. Dit kan wees as die koning in S.A. is of die parlement sit, en dan sal dit vir my onmoontlik wees by te woon. En wat word dan van ons werk by UNO? Dit is alles baie lastig en vervelig, maar alles is duister en ons moet maar geduld uitoefen.

Verder alles goed. Piet Nel was na Cairo om die Griekse vriende en andere daarheen te neem en sy machine te toets. Hy sal vandag hier terug wees. Die Griekse plebiscite het pragtig afgeloop en ek vermoed dat die koning en ons vrinde nog hierdie maand in Athene sal wees. Ek het hul beloof te Athene af te kom op my pad terug. Die vlug gaan oor Athene en die Griekse volk het my uitgenooi vir eerbewys vir al my hulp en steun in hul saak. Freddie is seker al gek van vreugde oor die loop van sake. Maar ek vrees hul gaan nog swaar kry met die Grieke, daar die inwendige toestande, viral finansieel, vir my maar leelik lyk. Ek bly hier in noue aanraking met die Griekse afvaardiging.

Denis en ek neem nog gereeld ons wandelinge in die groot bosse romdom Parys. Die ou paleise soos St Cloud, St Germain, Versailles ens. is omring deur groot houtbosse waar jy tot hartelus kan wandel en perde oefening neem. So neem ons dan ook een uur of meer ieder namiddag of ander namiddag. Die weer bly nog goed en die reën dreig maar selde, viral in die namiddae. Ons neem gereeld 'n polisie wag met ons mee. Ek woon maar min die Kommissies by wat gewoonlik in die namiddae sit, dus is daar kans vir oefening. Hierdie naweek het ons geen plan om ver af te gaan nie, en sal ek maar stil my gewone koers tuis bly volg. Daar is altyd veel te lees en besoek deur andere is daar ook altyd volop.

Gesondheid bly biesonder goed. Slaap, eet en dergelyk gaan soos gewoonlik in die ouderdom voort. Maar ek sou baie liewers tuis wil wees!

Jul nuus is en bly goed en dit gee my baie tevredenheid. Nou dat die koue dae oor is en die somer snel nader sal jul seker nog lekkerder hê. Ek hoor niks slegte nuus van S.A. nie en dit lyk of dinge hul normale loop neem. Daar is 'n geweldige drang in Europa vir verhuising na S.A. en Heaton Nicholls sê my dat daar in Engeland alleen 'n 40,000 is wat al ingeskrywe is vir immigrasie so gou as daar skeepsvaart is. Die toestande is dan hier ook sodanig dat mens dit kan begryp. Nou is ons kans as ons meer blankes wil hê om ons klein getalle aan te vul. Ek sien die Nat koerante raas en skree dat ek die Afrikaner element wil 'inploe'. My doel is om hul te red en die land van gewisse ondergang in die verre toekoms te red. Nou is ons kans—wat ons miskien nie gou weer in so'n mate sal kry nie. Die syfers wat ek noem geld net vir Brittanje. Maar jy kan begryp wat dit vir heel Europa moet wees. Almal ooral praat maar net van vlug uit Europa, en dit lyk of S.A. nou die uitverkose toevlugsoord is. Mag die armes nie bedroë word nie! Dis snaaks. Ek word van alle kante meegedeel dat die beste immigrante van al sal die Balte wees wat uit die Baltiese state van die Russe gevlug het. Van Duitse afkoms, protestante, in karakter en ontwikkeling baie hoogstaande, is hul nou in die interneer kampe in Duitsland as landloose bevolking (Displaced Persons, DPs).

Nou genoeg. My innige liefde en gedurige gedagte is by jou en jul almal. Soentjies aan almal van

Pappa

TRANSLATION

Paris
7 September 1946

Dearest Mamma, Again a very welcome letter from you. The diplomatic bag and mail letters arrive at the same time so you can post as you wish, but for America it will be best to address to South Africa House, Trafalgar Square, London, for despatch.

We leave next Saturday, 14 September, for London and the same afternoon from there for Balmoral where we shall stay over on Sunday and return to London on Monday in order to fly by Constellation that week to New York. The York will stay in England for new engines. It is still uncertain whether we shall stay long or briefly in New York. Perhaps our two South African questions will not come up in which case I shall come back to Paris to finish the week here before returning to South Africa. The intention is to limit the New York programme to essential administrative arrangements for U.N.O. and to let other work stand over. But there is no certainty yet on this point. The Big Four can make no decisions because Russia stubbornly follows her own road and agrees with no one. What can we do? Nobody here can make out what Russia has up her sleeve and time alone will tell us. Again, no one knows when, in that case, the adjourned meeting of U.N.O. will be held. It may be when the king is in South Africa or when parliament is in session and then it will be impossible for me to attend. And what will become of our work at U.N.O.? It is a great nuisance and a bore, but all is obscure and we can but have patience.

For the rest all is well. Piet Nel has been to Cairo to take the Greek friends and others there and to test his aircraft. He will be back here today. The Greek plebiscite went off beautifully and I expect that the king and our friends will be in Athens this month. I have promised them to land in Athens on my way back. The flight is via Athens and the Greek people have invited me in order to do me honour for all my help and support in their cause. Freddie is probably mad with joy at the way things have worked out. But I fear they are going to have a hard time with the Greeks as internal conditions, especially financial conditions, look ugly to me. Here I remain in close touch with the Greek delegation.

Denis [McIldowie] and I now regularly take our walks in the great woods round Paris. The old palaces like St Cloud, St Germain, Versailles, etc. are surrounded by huge woods when one can walk or ride to one's heart's content. And so we do—an hour or more every afternoon or every other afternoon. The weather remains good and there is seldom a threat of rain, especially in the afternoons. We regularly take a police guard along. I seldom attend the commissions which usually meet in the afternoons, so there is an opportunity for exercise. We have no plan to go far this week-end and I shall quietly follow my usual routine at home. There is always much to read and visits by others are also plentiful.

My health remains particularly good. Sleeping, eating and such go on as is usual at my age. But I would much rather be at home!

Your news is and remains good and that gives me much satisfaction. Now that the cold days are over and summer is near you will have a better time than ever. I hear no bad news from South Africa and it looks as if things are taking their normal course. There is a tremendous urge in Europe to emigrate to South Africa and Heaton Nicholls tells me that in England alone some 40,000 have registered for immigration as soon as there is shipping. Conditions here are such that one can understand it. Now is our chance if we want more whites to augment our small numbers. I see that the Nat newspapers fulminate and scream to the effect that I want to 'plough the Afrikander element under'. My object is to save them and to rescue the country from inevitable decline in the far future. Now is our chance—which we may not perhaps have again in such measure. The figures I mention refer only to Britain. But you can understand what they must be for the whole of Europe. Everyone everywhere is talking of fleeing Europe and it looks as if South Africa is now the chosen place of refuge. May the poor things not be deceived! It is strange—I am told on all sides that the best immigrants of all would be the Balts who have fled from the Russian Baltic states. Of German descent, Protestants, of very high character and development—they are now in the internment camps in Germany as displaced persons—D.P.s.

Well, enough. My deep love and constant thoughts are with you and with all. Kisses to everyone from

Pappa

717 From J. H. Hofmeyr Vol. 79, no. 30

Pretoria
8 September 1946

My dear General, Thank you for your letter which, of course, I read with very much interest. The whole situation at Paris seems to be a ticklish one, and it must be difficult to remain patient. It appears that a final decision will be come to today about the U.N.O. meeting. This may have some effect on your plans.

Here things have been going quite well, and no difficulties of any consequence have arisen. All but one of the United party (Transvaal) conferences have now taken place. Those that I attended—at Pretoria, Rustenburg and Johannesburg, went very well, and the same applies I believe, also to those at Klerksdorp, Nelspruit, and Ermelo. There was, however, in these cases, very strong speaking against [A.M.] Conroy's Land Settlement Act.[1] It is clear that we are facing a very difficult position in this regard. We shall no doubt hear a good deal more about the matter at the Transvaal congress on 1, 2 and 3 October.

Things are pretty quiet now on the food front, and it seems probable that we shall be able to escape coupon rationing of cereals. Wheat crop prospects are still on the whole promising, but a good deal will depend on whether rain falls in the Orange Free State this month. The weather indications seem to be working up that way. Northern Natal and parts of the eastern Transvaal have already had fair rains—also the East London area and the northern Karroo. We shall probably be short of meat again at the

[1] This act (No. 42 of 1944) placed retrospective restrictions on the use and resale of land acquired by settlers under the Land Settlement Act of 1912.

end of the year, and the sugar position, because of the drought, is by no means good.

Housing is still our chief immediate difficulty, although the building material position seems to be improving. The press continues to attack us on the point of divided control of building matters. There is an undercurrent of friction between Mushet [J.W.] and Gluckman which may cause trouble.

All is quiet as far as the gold mines are concerned. The mine-workers dispute is still before the courts, and it looks as if some time will elapse before anything definite emerges.[1] Meantime the Chamber of Mines has given an extra 1*s*. 6*d*. a day allowance to its Europeans,[2] which seems to have gone quite well.

The Native mine-workers are working quite well, I am told, but as Oppenheimer points out, nothing has really been settled. We shall undoubtedly have to set up machinery for the consideration of disputes affecting them.

What to my mind is even more serious is the attitude of the Native Representative Council.[3] It means that the hitherto moderate intellectuals of the Professor [Z.K.] Matthews type are now committed to an extreme line against colour discrimination, and have carried the chiefs with them. We can't afford to allow them to be swept into the extremist camp, but I don't see what we can do to satisfy them, which would be tolerated by European public opinion. The Native Representation Council was, however, a vital part of the 1936 legislation, and if it cannot be made to function, far-reaching questions will arise.

We went out to Irene this afternoon and found all well there. Tant Isie was in particularly good form. With all good wishes from us both, Yours sincerely,

Jan H. Hofmeyr

[1] Following a serious strike by African mine-workers from 12 to 16 August in which the strikers clashed with the police, the trial of over fifty persons charged with the infringement of War Measure 145 began in Johannesburg on 26 August.

[2] White miners at the Blyvooruitsig mine were also on strike at this time.

[3] The Native Representative Council was discussing a resolution to adjourn *sine die* in protest against the Native policy of the government and had called upon it 'forthwith to abolish all discriminatory legislation affecting non-Europeans'. *See also* **724**.

718 To J. H. Hofmeyr — Vol. 80, no. 124

Telegram

From: Smuts

To: J. H. Hofmeyr

Dated 20 September 1946

Your letter of 12 September[1] re Kakamas Bill. Please give following message to Senator Conroy from me begins: Situation re Kakamas Bill gives me great concern.[2] Last year you readily accepted my request that bill should stand over for 1947 session. Subsequently I undertook to see deputation of Dutch Reformed Church before introduction of bill. Unforeseen postponement of U.N.O. meeting prevents my return till late in November or in December and thus seeing deputation in time for bill to be published as hybrid measure.[3] In view of my undertaking and serious view church takes of matter I must ask you again to postpone publication which means introduction of bill next session. You will appreciate my personal difficulty as I am sure my other colleagues will also, quite apart from importance church attaches to matter. Postponement will also give opportunity to consult caucus as we are bound to do. Publication now will put me in false position and party in great difficulty. Under circumstances I count on your acquiescence in postponement.

719 To S. M. Smuts — Vol. 80, no. 125

Parys
21 September 1946

Liefste Mamma, Ek had 'n liewe lange brief van jou hierdie week, vol van nuus wat goed en welkom was. Dit lyk uit jou en ander briewe wat ek kry dat dinge taamlik normaal in Suid-Afrika is. Van Jantjie 'n brief oor die politiek, van organisasies van die party besluite van dank en waardering. Dit is natuurlik goed om dit alles te hoor. Ek vrees egter dat my lang afwesigheid nie sonder

[1] Not in the Smuts Collection.

[2] Since 1898 land had been reserved at Kakamas on the Orange river in the north-western Cape Province for the establishment of a labour colony for poor whites under the control of the Dutch Reformed (N.G.) Church. In 1945 A. M. Conroy appointed a commission of inquiry into the affairs of the colony. In 1946 he prepared a bill designed to make the Kakamas colony a state settlement controlled by a board of management. It was bitterly opposed by the church and the National party.

[3] A public bill which affects the private rights of individuals or corporate bodies. After the second reading it is referred to a select committee which hears representations from affected parties.

sy gevare is nie. Ek kan darem nie terug na S.A. voor my vertrek na New York. Ek het uitnoodigings van Holland en België aangeneem om hul 'n besoek te breng. Dit sal aanstaande maand wees. Dan moet ek weer na Londen vir noodsaaklike besprekings voor my vertrek na Amerika. Hier moet ek die finale sittings van die Konferensie bywoon. Ek sal dus vasgehou word tot die einde —en dit sal miskien nie voor die einde of begin van December in New York wees nie. Dan klaar maak vir die Parlement en die visiete van die koning. En so gaan dit maar onophoudelik voort.

Athene het my laat weet dat 'n straat nou Jan Smuts genoem is en dat ek uitgenooi word om die stad te besoek en die vrydom daarvan te ontvang as dank vir alles wat ons vir Griekeland in die oorlog en daarna gedoen het. Ek hoop dit te doen op my terugkeer as daar tyd voor kan gevind word.

Binne 'n paar dae vertrek die Griekse Koning na Athene, en Palo en Freddie sal hom op pad ontmoet om dan saam die groot intog in Athene te maak. Sy sal seker bars van die vreugde. Die kinders sal later van Alex volg. Intussen lyk dit of daar baie onluste en moeilikheid in Griekeland is, en hul sal nie na 'n roseland terug gaan nie. Die Koning het ek laaste Maandag in Londen gesien, en hy het my dit alles meegedeel. By dieselfde geleentheid het ek ook Dr Weizmann gaan besoek; hul albei stuur baie liefde en groete aan jou. Hy het 'n pynlike operasie vir cataract ondergaan, maar kan nou weer 'n beetjie sien. Die Palestina onderhandeling is aan gang en hy gaan daaraan deel neem. Ek help hul waar ek kan, maar dit gaan maar baie swaar, viral weëns die terroriste misdade van die Joodse gangs wat die Engelse baie boos maak. Dit is nie duidelik dat die Kommuniste gangs nie van buite af ondersteun en aan gang gehou word nie.

Die Indiese moeilikheid duur maar voort in Indië en gedeeltelik om die aandag daarvan af te trek verskerp die Indiese houding teen Suid-Afrika. Nehru, die nuwe Premier, het gesê dat India S. Afrika gaan bestry tot die uiterste limiete, en hul praat nou Gandhi oor om na die U.N.O. vergadering te gaan om my te beveg en getuienis teen S. Afrika af te lê! Dit sal nogal interessant vir die wêreld wees om Gandhi en my weer op ons oudag teen mekaar te sien voor 'n wêreldhof! Dit is waarlik 'n rare wêreld en tyd waarin ons lewe. In Indië self lyk dit baie of dinge na 'n burger-oorlog loop en mens kan dus verstaan dat hul die wêreld aandag van so'n leelike situatie wil wegtrek.

Op 29 Sep. saai B.B.C. 'n wêreld uitsaai van my uit oor die huidige situatie in verband met wêreld vrede. Ek hoop jul sal dit tuis goed kan hoor. Ek het dit al uitgeskrywe.

Jy kan sien dat my skrywe nie van die beste is nie. Dit is te wyte aan die weersverandering wat nou kouer word, en my hand beetjie stywer maak. Ons weer is tot dus ver pragtig gewees en ons het dit geniet, maar die herfs is daar en binne kort sal dit hier aanmerklik kouer wees. In New York sal dit natuurlik baie koud wees, maar gelukkig hoop ons daar voor die ergste weg te kom. Ons neem nog gereëld ons wandeling in die bosse, en agtermiddag (dis vandag Saterdag) hoop Dennis en ek weer 'n goeie lange oefening te kry. Hy kla van vet word maar ek sien daar niks van. Ek hou my ou gewig en voel van die beste.

Die groot tjek van oor 'n millioen en 'n kwart van die *Tribute to Britain Fund* is aangekom en ek sal dit eersdaags plegtig aan Attlee oorhandig. Soentjies en hartelike groete aan jul almal van

Pappa

TRANSLATION

Paris

21 September 1946

Dearest Mamma, I had a dear, long letter from you this week, full of news which was good and welcome. It seems from your letters and others I receive that things are fairly normal in South Africa. From Jantjie[1] I had a letter about politics, party organizations, resolutions of thanks and appreciation. Of course it is good to hear all this. But I fear my long absence is not without its dangers. However, I cannot return to South Africa before my departure for New York. I have accepted invitations from Holland and Belgium to pay them a visit—that will be next month. Then I must go to London again for essential discussions before my departure to America. Here I must attend the final sessions of the conference. So I shall be tied to the last—and that will perhaps not be until the end or the beginning of December in New York. After that preparations for parliament and the king's visit. And so it goes interminably on.

Athens has informed me that a street has now been named Jan Smuts and that I am invited to visit the city and receive its freedom as thanks for all that we did for Greece during and after the war. I hope to do this on my way back if time can be found for it.

Within a few days the king of Greece leaves for Athens and Palo and Freddie will meet him on the way to share the grand procession into Athens. She will probably be bursting with joy.

[1] J. H. Hofmeyr.

The children will follow later from Alexandria. In the meantime it seems that there are many disturbances and troubles in Greece; they will not be returning to a land of roses. I saw the king last Monday in London and he told me all this. On the same day I also visited Dr Weizmann; they both send you greetings and much love. He has undergone a painful operation for cataract but can now again see a little. The Palestine negotiations are going on and he will take part in them.[1] I help them where I can but this is very difficult, chiefly because of the terrorist crimes of the Jewish gangs which infuriate the English.[2] It is not at all clear that the Communist gangs are not supported and kept going from outside.

The Indian troubles (in India) continue and it is partly to divert attention from this that the Indian opposition to South Africa has sharpened. Nehru [J.], the new prime minister,[3] has said that India will fight South Africa to the furthest limits and they are now persuading Gandhi to go to the U.N.O. meeting to oppose me and give evidence against South Africa! The world will find it quite interesting to see Gandhi and me once more in conflict in our old age before a world court! It really is a strange world and time in which we live. In India itself it looks very much as if things are moving to civil war[4] so one can understand that they want to divert world attention from such an ugly state of affairs.

On 29 September the B.B.C. is making a broadcast of a talk by me on the present situation in connection with world peace.[5] I hope you will be able to hear it well. I have already written it out.

You will see that my handwriting is not at its best. That is due to a change in the weather which is getting colder and stiffens my hand a bit. The weather so far has been lovely and we enjoyed it but autumn has come and soon it will be noticeably colder here. Of course it will be very cold in New York but fortunately we hope to get away before the worst of it. We still take our regular

[1] Talks between Bevin and Weizmann on a compromise plan were proceeding. *See* C. Sykes, *Cross Roads to Israel* (Mentor edition 1967), pp. 317–18.

[2] In July 1946 the Irgun Tsva'i Leumi (National Military Organization) had blown up a wing of the King David Hotel in Jerusalem killing ninety-one persons and wounding forty-five.

[3] Nehru had formed an interim government pending the drawing up of a constitution for a self-governing India.

[4] The irreconcilable differences between congress and the Muslim League had led to the declaration of a Muslim hartal (general strike) on 16 August when Muslim–Hindu riots broke out in Calcutta and spread to other parts of the country. In Calcutta there were 4,700 deaths, 15,000 injured and 150,000 refugees. *See* T. W. Wallbank, *A Short History of India and Pakistan*, p. 224.

[5] *See* Smuts Collection, Box L, no. 214.

walks in the woods and this afternoon (it is Saturday) Denis [McIldowie] and I hope to have good, long exercise. He complains of getting fat but I can't see it. I stay at my old weight and feel fine.

The big cheque of over a million and a quarter for the Tribute to Britain Fund has arrived and I shall soon hand it ceremonially to Attlee. Kisses and hearty greetings to you all from

Pappa

720 To J. H. Hofmeyr Vol. 80, no. 126

Paris
23 September 1946

My dear Jantjie, Thank you for your interesting and informative letter of 8 September[1] which arrived a few days ago. I am glad that things are more or less normal on the political front.

Although I had toyed with the idea of a brief return to South Africa I have had to abandon the idea. The York's wiring system has been seriously damaged by the two blitzes and has to be redone and it will be out of action for at least two months. Flying by the Springbok service is really too arduous and uncomfortable for old age! Besides matters do turn up here which call for my direction. So I have promised Holland and Belgium a visit instead. Three more weeks here, then a few days in London for contacts and for handing over the Tribute to Britain Fund to Attlee, and then to U.N.O. The Council of Foreign Ministers are likely to remain here in order to complete the work of the conference and have the treaties ready for signature about 15 November. Whether any of them will go on to New York is still uncertain. Bevin and Bidault [G.] are not likely to go, and Molotov and Byrnes are undecided.

Our line at the conference generally has been to support Italy and Greece as friendly Mediterranean powers, but our efforts have not been actively backed up by the rest of the Commonwealth. Both of them come badly out of this conference, and their governments may suffer in consequence. Russia has successfully championed the cause of her satellites, and the comparison will not redound to British credit. Already some ill-disposed Italians say that it would have paid them better to have gone Communist! At any rate South Africa has done what it could, which amounted to very little.

[1] 717.

I am sorry there was a slip in connection with our lease–lend telegrams. An important telegram which I had drafted in reply to Holloway [J.E.] got mislaid while I was away in Scotland, and I assumed all along that it had been sent—hence another urgent appeal from you a week or more later. I shall discuss the whole position with Holloway when he comes to London next month. I have approved your and the cabinet's advice.[1] But there is no doubt that we are going to strike heavy weather on this as well as on the two other matters which concern us at U.N.O. There is a growing widespread opinion adverse to us. South Africans are getting into ill odour, owing to colour bar and wrong Native publicity, and perhaps also owing to our prosperous condition in an impoverished world. I fear our going will not be too good. As Nicholls puts it, 'South Africa will be on the spot' at New York. Our difficulties are due partly to our bad propaganda. Even South Africans do nothing but crab us. Take e.g. [J.P.] Cope's letters to the *Observer*[2]—are so bad, I understand, that they were not placed. Solly Sachs and correspondents to the *Manchester Guardian*, the *Scotsman*, and other papers, have done much harm. I sense a worsening atmosphere in many directions. Mostly, of course, the trouble is due to the South African attitude on Native political rights and the difficult structure of our social racial system. Our difficulties in this 'one world' are increasing, and I don't see clearly what can be done about it. On top of all this came the matters you mention—the difficulty with the Native Representative Council, and the question of Native trade unions and right to strike. Both of these deserve our very careful consideration. Especially the Native unions. I hope our commission on Native pass laws and Native urban matters[3] will not unduly delay their inquiry and report, as they bear closely on the very essence of our Native troubles. With the Native Representative Council we must temporize for the present, while the mines and pass laws etc., are being dealt with.

I am very glad de V. Graaff has been nominated.[4] The vacant East London seat ought to be captured by us. Perhaps we could

[1] The cabinet had advised that the limit of lease–lend payment should be 100 million dollars against the American proposal of 125 millions. *See* Smuts Collection, vol. 79, no. 31.

[2] A. Paton notes that Cope wrote to *The Times*, not the *Observer*. *See Hofmeyr*, p. 435, note 2. But no letters from Cope appear in *The Times* of 1946.

[3] The Native Laws commission appointed on 16 August 1946 to inquire into laws affecting urban Natives, the pass laws and migratory labour. The chairman was Mr Justice H. A. Fagan (q.v.). It reported on 19 February 1948 (U.G. 28 of 1948).

[4] For the bye-election in the Hottentots Holland constituency.

find a United party candidate who would not be unacceptable to our Labour friends in our party. I note our United party congress is due to meet at Bloemfontein on 27 November. I am very anxious to be at this important meeting and fear that I may not be able to get away in time from New York if the U.N.O. meeting is a long one. You and Oosthuizen [O.A.] should therefore *bear in mind* that the congress date may have to be postponed till December if this appears necessary later.

The Conroy difficulties are very tiresome. I have wired about Kakamas and trust he will fall into line.[1] If so, the Kakamas affair will not come up before parliament till after the general election in 1948. Perhaps as well. The land settlement difficulty is not so serious, though also very tiresome. I hope we shall get along with our colleagues till after the next general election when, no doubt, important changes will be made in our cabinet if we are still there!

Isie writes about your and Borrie's[2] visit which she much enjoyed. She wrote how fit and well you looked. Keep up your fitness, as great and heavy work still lies ahead. Unless some unseen misfortune overtakes us, the United party will continue to rule the country for years to come!

The world position is obscure and difficult. The English are very piano and the Labour government find the home and foreign front very difficult. France is in great confusion and even the constitutions still remain unsettled, while de Gaulle—still very influential—follows a line of his own. Italy is in a bad way—Greece is an uncertain quantity, and the king's return will not change matters much. (By the way, a street in Athens is now called after me, and the freedom of the city has also been offered me if I can come to accept it.) The German position is now becoming so dangerous that the English and Americans can wait no longer and will unite their zones economically, and to some extent politically. Russia is, in spite or perhaps because of disturbed internal conditions, very active and pushing forward in all directions. I see no danger of war in the near future; Russia knows this, and meanwhile is bluffing her way forward. Her influence and prestige are growing. Her star is rising. The Canadian spy report[3] is a most

[1] *See* **718**.

[2] Mrs Deborah Hofmeyr (q.v.).

[3] The final report of a royal commission appointed to make an investigation into espionage in Canada was tabled in the Canadian house of commons on 15 July 1946. It revealed that Canadian public officials and other persons in positions of trust had given secret information to Russian agents; that a fifth column organized by Russian agents existed in Canada and that one of the spy rings was headed by the Soviet military attaché in Ottawa.

revealing document and you must certainly read it. In the United States Byrnes's foreign policy has for the moment won, but I fear the [H.A.] Wallace sections[1] and Republican elements may now frighten the Americans with the cry of war with Russia, and thus open the way to another isolationist development. India, Indonesia, etc., are on the knees of the gods. Never has there been such international uncertainty. And U.N.O., with the arbitrary abuse of the veto, may prove a broken reed to lean upon. Fortunately there is no danger of war, otherwise the plight of the world would be simply awful. The atom bomb continues; the flying rocket from Peenemunde continues. The fear is spreading, perhaps unnecessarily. But it is all a strange world after our victory. I have faith in the human race and in a return of sanity and balance. But just at present it is not a pleasant scene to contemplate. So don't think that South Africa has an undue share of the world's troubles and the world's dangers.

My love to you and Borrie. My best wishes and regards to all my colleagues. And forgive this long letter which I hope you can decipher! Ever yours,

J. C. Smuts

721 To M. C. Gillett — Vol. 80, no. 216

Paris
24 September 1946

Thank you for sending me some pages of *The Times Literary Supplement*. Some of them interest me greatly, and at least provide bedtime reading. Recently I have taken to reading Shakespeare's tragedies at bedtime. I have thus covered *Lear*, *Anthony and Cleopatra*, *Julius Caesar*, *Cymbeline*, and am now busy with *Coriolanus*. Reading through this series I can see for myself (without any instruction) which are real Shakespeare plays and which are probably only retouched work of others. I could become a Shakespeare scholar if I had the time! But I am getting to know his style and language and thought to such an extent that I can notice (I think) where the stuff is not his. I have a collection of the tragedies you gave me—one volume in a collection of three containing all his plays.

I have arranged to be in Holland and Belgium from 9 to 13 October on the invitation of their governments. Very inconvenient

[1] Henry A. Wallace was the leader of a revived Progressive party, which was traditionally isolationist. He stood as its presidential candidate in 1948.

to be away in this last period of this conference, but I do not wish to decline their invitations. I shall probably leave here immediately after the conference ends on 15 October and spend some days in London before leaving for the States. I can only give you closer dates later on, as we are still much in the dark as to the end of this conference. We are all very sick of it. Not only the conference but U.N.O. also is in a bad way. I fear our international organization is making heavy weather. The temper is bad and owing to unmitigated publicity everything is reported and increases the sense of differences and quarrelling. Our international work is thus carried on under difficult and unfavourable conditions. It is a phase we shall have to pass through—one only hopes we shall get through it without too much damage.

I still continue to take walks in the woods round Paris for exercise as often as I can. This keeps me physically fit even where the mind is subject to strains and friction! The news from South Africa continues good, from Doornkloof specially so. So there is much to be thankful for. Ever yours,

Jan

P.S. Excuse this wretched writing, due to the paper or the pen!

722 From J. H. Hofmeyr Vol. 79, no. 32

Telegram

From: J. H. Hofmeyr

To: Smuts

Dated 26 September 1946

Have communicated message in your telegram to Conroy [A.M.] who has asked me to send you following reply. Begins: Your cable of 20th September Kakamas Bill. I accepted postponement last year on your definite written undertaking that bill would be introduced 1947. I assume your promise to meet church deputation did not commit you or imply a promise not to proceed with the bill especially in view of your emphatic assurance to me. I assure you government and party's prestige will be enhanced if bill proceeded with and permitted system prevailing there rectified. They asked for commission inquiry into bill result unanimous decision.[1] Further postponement means scrapping. If you insist my position

[1] The report of the commission of inquiry on the Kakamas Labour Colony, with Mr Justice J. E. de Villiers as chairman, stated that the Dutch Reformed Church had achieved its mission since the colony was no longer one of indigent whites. The

will be quite impossible and most humiliating. I cannot face it, my honour and prestige at stake. I appeal to you to adhere to your implicit written undertaking and let me proceed as intended. Ends.

723 To J. H. Hofmeyr Vol. 80, no. 130

Telegram

From: Smuts

To: J. H. Hofmeyr

Dated 28 September 1946

This is a pretty kettle of fish. Trouble at moment is early publication of bill before my return. Of course I did *not* undertake to church or plan that bill would not be proceeded with before seeing deputation. Correspondence must be in the office. But fact remains that trouble is serious and may be serious also in caucus. Please let me know your reaction especially if worst should happen, if you feel free to give me your view.

724 To J. H. Hofmeyr Vol. 80, no. 131

Telegram

From: Smuts

To: J. H. Hofmeyr

Dated 28 September 1946

Native Representative Council. Your letter of 16 September[1] refers. In view of outrageous and indeed insulting terms of resolution[2] and preceding speeches it would outrage public opinion if your

commission regarded the existing system of control as defective and recommended the creation of a new board of control representative of the settlers, the church and the state. It also recommended the abolition of compulsory labour, the granting of land title to settlers, the creation of credit facilities and co-operative trading.

[1] Not in the Smuts Collection.

[2] *See supra*, p. 82, note 3. The resolution was as follows: 'This council, having since its inception brought to the notice of the government the reactionary character of the Union Native policy of segregation in all its ramifications, deprecates the government's post-war continuation of a policy of Fascism which is the antithesis and negation of the letter and spirit of the Atlantic Charter and the United Nations Charter. The Council therefore, in protest against this breach of faith towards the African people in particular, and the cause of world freedom in general, resolves to adjourn this session, and calls upon the government forthwith to abolish all discriminatory legislation affecting non-Europeans in this country.'

alternative suggestions were followed. Resolution is certainly in any case going to lead to difficult debate in parliament and we would be much weakened by what would fairly be taken as a surrender to Native dictations. I myself think our Native policy would have to be liberalized at modest pace but public opinion has to be carried with us and your first suggestion would find very small public support.

I am for trying second alternative sketched in your paragraph eight but should like draft sent me before action taken. I think we shall have to accept in it recognition in principle of Native unions on separate basis on general lines of draft bill, but you must get cabinet consent. I had wished to secure this myself but my long absence makes cabinet consultation without me necessary. You may pass my views herein to my colleagues. My Cape Town speech[1] pointed to failure of segregation as solution of Native question because it had failed in its object of keeping Natives from white urban areas to which they were flocking in ever increasing numbers. Practical social policy away from politics as stated by me still holds, is being carried out, and will be so more and more as finance permits.

725 To J. H. Hofmeyr — Vol. 80, no. 136

Telegram

From: Smuts

To: J. H. Hofmeyr

Dated 6 October 1946

Have given careful consideration to whole matter and see great probability that Conroy [A. M.] may take extreme course. This in my absence should be avoided. Crisis now likely to come on in very inconvenient time of session of parliament but at least I shall be on spot either to prevent it or deal with it. In spite of coming agitation by church I therefore authorize publication of bill whose fate will be decided by caucus decision. You will please inform Conroy that I have agreed to publication but he must clearly understand that fate of bill will depend on free vote of caucus and not repeat not on coercion by government.

[1] *See* **556**.

726 From J. H. Hofmeyr Vol. 79, no. 34

Pretoria
7 October 1946

My dear General, Thank you for your letter of 23 September and for the comments on various matters which it contained.

I am sending you this by Forsyth who is due to leave in a few days time (probably the quickest way of getting to you). He will be able to post you fully as to developments here, so that there is less for me to say than would otherwise be the case.

The Transvaal congress last week passed off very well. The main snag was the land servitudes trouble. The campaign against Conroy [A.M.] had been well worked up and there was a great deal of speech-making. The spirit was, however, a good deal better than I had feared it might be, and it proved to be possible to keep the situation under control. Ultimately a unanimous resolution was passed (Conroy consenting) referring the whole matter to the consideration of the government in the light of the views which had been expressed. It seems to me that the way out is to appoint a commission to investigate the position—certainly as far as section 11 cases are concerned. To this I think Conroy would agree. A statement to this effect might be made by you at the Union congress.

I have advised you that it is possible to arrange for that congress on 18, 19 and 20 December and am now awaiting your reply. I hope you will be back by then.

About Kakamas I am also awaiting your reply. I am sorry that you have been put in such a difficult situation over it. As I cabled to you I think it would be better to grasp the nettle now—the situation is likely to become more rather than less difficult. I am quite sure that, save for a very strong appeal from you, caucus will not be found to agree to the bill, and Conroy is more likely to resign if his bill is killed at that stage than he would be if that happened now. However, I await your decision.

I have also advised you about developments in the Indian situation here. Kajee, who came to see me at his own request on Saturday, is very pessimistic and most anxious to find a way out. He tells me that unemployment is growing among the Indians in Natal because of the increasingly hostile attitude of the Europeans. There is also something of a boycott of Indian traders—in the Transvaal as well as in Natal. The Communist section is likely at elections to be held next week to get control of the congress in the Transvaal, as they already have in Natal. Kajee's own position will therefore become increasingly difficult. It is however clear that he realizes that extremism won't pay the Indian community here and must be modified. He also realizes that they can expect very little from U.N.O. It may be that at New York he will be able to help in building a bridge between yourself and the leaders of the Indian delegation.

I hope also to be able to send you with Forsyth a draft statement to be made at the Natives Representative Council meeting on 20 November. I think however that you should know that Professor Matthews came to see me a week or two ago. He was at great pains to emphasize that they did not want the council to be abolished, and hoped that we would be conciliatory. I told him that, having regard to their resolution and the speeches that led up to it, we could not do anything that would be interpreted as a surrender, and suggested that they should reconsider the position from that angle. He said that he would take steps to consult his colleagues. As a result there may be something in the nature of a climb-down, in which event I shall of course let you know. It is clear that some at least of them are now frightened as to the possible consequences of their action...

I have just heard that Willem Bezuidenhout of Heidelberg died yesterday. I shall go to the funeral tomorrow if I can manage it. All good wishes. Yours sincerely,

Jan H. Hofmeyr

727 To S. M. Smuts — Vol. 80, no. 141

Parys
14 Oktober 1946

Liefste Mamma, Vanoggend is ons terug gekom van Brussel, na ons besoek aan Holland en België. Dit was 1 uur vliegtyd die heele weg in F.M. Montgomery se machine wat aan my geleen was, daar die York nog onder reparasie is. Die besoek het 5 dae geduur en is een van die swaarste maar ook suksesvolste stukke werk wat ek ooit gedoen het. Vyf dae van aanhoudend gepraat en funksies van allerlei soort. Te Den Haag en Brussel het ek die beide parlementshuise toegespreek, te Amsterdam die Koninklike Akademie, en die publiek ooral—eindigende gister te Antwerpen waar ek heel dag besig was. My mond is seer van Afrikaans praat! Ooral kon hul my goed verstaan—die Belgiërs so goed as die Hollanders. Ooral was hul verbaas om iemand van ver af hul eie taal te hoor praat met die grootste gemak en natuurlikheid. Een dag is op

Walcheren en te Middelburg en omliggende stede en dorpe deurgebreng. Ooral het die kinders Sarie Marais en boere liedjies gesing. Dit was werklik verrassend en aandoenlik om al die entoesiasme te sien. Nooit selfs in Suid-Afrika het ek 'n heerliker ontvangs gehad—by die volk, die hoë lui, en die koninklike persone. Koningin Wilhelmina was biesonder aangenaam, so ook Juliana en die kleintjies. Klein Magriet was baie opgenome met my en het my uitgenooi met haar en Irene te kom lunch: 'Komt u met ons eten?' Amsterdam was heerlik, net soos Antwerpen. Die mense het my geneem vir 'n teruggekeerde familie lid van die jaar vroeg! Die Koningin het my die Groot Leeu van Oranje gegee—hul hoogste eerbewys. By Prins Charles te Brussel was ons te huis en was die ontvangs allerliefst. Denis het ooral 'n baie goeie indruk gemaak, en sy rokkie was die vermaak van almal, viral die vroue!

Die land ooral goed bewerk—in Holland meer koeie as voor die oorlog, maar nog 'n beetjie jong vir melkdiere. Maar jy het seker alles al in die koerante gesien, en die res in Denis se briewe. Dus sal ek jou nie verder daarmee lastig val nie.

Hier vanoggend aangekom om heel dag met onderhoude en korrespondensie besig te wees. Morre ook nog so, en dan die volgende dag (Woensdag 16 Okt.) weg na Londen waar ons 4 dae tot Sondag sal bly voor ons wegvlie na New York. In Londen sal dit baie druk gaan, en wag daar werk vir my. So baie dinge moet klaar gemaak word vir Amerika. Ek hoop darem vir Cato en die vrinde te sien. As ek tyd het sal ek van daar ook skrywe, maar miskien sal dit nie moontlik wees nie.

Ek het hier talle van telegramme viral uit Griekeland om my te dank vir alles wat ek vir hul gedoen het—die Koning sê meer as iemand anders. En die Grieke sal my seker dood maak van opgewondenheid as ek te Athene sou aanland. Freddie is natuurlik in die wolke van opgewondenheid. Die arme ding moes gister haar groot toespraak in Grieks maak, en had die bewerasie daaroor, toe sy geskrywe het.

Met gesondheid gaan dit goed. Dis net jammer dat ek so lang weg moet wees. En die trip na Amerika sal ver van aangenaam wees—met al die koue en moeilikhede wat voorlê.

Die Moores is in Londen en wil graag na Suid-Afrika, maar kan tot dus ver nie vlieg vervoer kry nie. As hul kom sal hul 'n week by jul vertoef voor hul na Groote Schuur gaan. Daaroor later.

Die Hollands-Belgies trip was werklik vir my self 'n 'eye-opener', en ek had nooit soo iets verwag. Ooral ook oor jou gevra. Toe, goeie nag. Lekker slaap!

Pappa

96

TRANSLATION

Paris
14 October 1946

Dearest Mamma, This morning we returned from Brussels after our visit to Holland and Belgium. It was one hour flying time the whole way in Field Marshal Montgomery's aircraft which was lent to me as the York is still being repaired. The visit lasted five days and is one of the hardest but also most successful pieces of work I have ever done. Five days of constant talking and functions of every sort. I addressed both houses of parliament at the Hague and Brussels, the Royal Academy at Amsterdam, and the public everywhere, finishing yesterday at Antwerp where I was busy all day. My mouth is sore from so much Afrikaans! Everywhere they could understand me well—the Belgians as well as the Dutch. Everywhere they were surprised to hear someone from a distant country speak their own language with the greatest ease and naturalness. One day was spent at Walcheren and Middleburg[1] and neighbouring towns and villages. Everywhere the children sang *Sarie Marais* and Boer songs. It was really surprising and moving to see all this enthusiasm. I have never, even in South Afrika, had a more delightful reception—by the people, the notables and the royal personages. Queen Wilhelmina was particularly nice and so were Juliana and the children. Little Margriet[2] was much taken up with me and asked me to lunch with herself and Irene:[3] 'Are you coming to eat with us?' Amsterdam was delightful, just as Antwerp was. People took me for a member of the family who had returned after many years! The queen gave me the Great Lion of Orange[4]—their highest honour. In Brussels we stayed with Prince Charles[5] and our reception was most friendly. Denis [McIldowie] made a good impression everywhere and his kilt amused everyone, especially the women!

The country is well cultivated everywhere—in Holland there are more cows than before the war, but they are still a bit young for milking. But you will already have seen all this in the newspapers and the rest in Denis's letters. So I will not bother you with any more of it.

[1] Smuts's ancestor, Michiel Cornelis Smuts, went as a colonist to the Cape from Middleburg *c.* 1692.

[2] Princess Margriet Francisca, born 19 January 1943; married Piet van Vollenhoven in 1967.

[3] Princess Irene Emma Elizabeth, born 5 August 1939; married Prince Carlos Hugo of Bourbon-Parma in 1964.

[4] Grootkruis van de Orde van de Nederlandsche Leeuw.

[5] Regent of Belgium.

Arrived here this morning and have been busy all day with interviews and correspondence. Tomorrow the same thing and the next day (Wednesday 16 October) off to London where we shall stay for four days until Sunday before we fly to New York. I shall be very busy in London where work awaits me. So many things must be prepared for America. But I hope to see Cato [Clark] and the friends. If I have time I shall write again from there but it may not be possible.

I have had numbers of telegrams here, especially from Greece, to thank me for all I have done for them—the king says, more than anyone else. And the Greeks will probably kill me with excitement if I were to land in Athens. Freddie, of course, is in the clouds with excitement. The poor thing had to make her big speech in Greek yesterday and was shaking in her shoes when she wrote.

My health is good. But it is a pity I must be away so long. And the trip to America will be far from pleasant—with all that cold and these troubles that lie ahead.

The Moores are in London and would like to go to South Africa but cannot so far find air transport. If they come they will stay with you for a week before going to Groote Schuur. More about that later.

The Holland–Belgium trip was really an eye-opener even to me—I never expected anything like it. Everywhere also I was asked about you. Now, good night. Sleep well!

Pappa

728 To J. H. Hofmeyr — Vol. 80, no. 142

Hotel Claridge
[Paris]
15 October 1946

My dear Jantjie, This is the last day of the conference and my last day of Paris. Tomorrow I shall be in London for business and intend getting away from there on Sunday the 20th.

I arrived back from Holland and Belgium yesterday. I had a most successful visit there and a reception which far exceeded anything I had anticipated. In both countries I could easily establish a personal footing and people came to regard me, not as a distinguished visitor, but one of them—a member of the family returned after a long absence! I spoke Afrikaans everywhere, except for part of my address to the Belgian parliament, and was perfectly understood everywhere. (Excuse the blot.) Afrikaans *liedjies*[1]

[1] Folk-songs.

greeted me everywhere, and politics were quite forgotten in this racial reunion, if I may call it so. I am sure the visit has been well worth while, although very arduous and exciting. Boetzelaer [C.W.van], the Dutch foreign minister, spoke to me about the prospects of a loan from South Africa. I was non-committal and left it to the discussion between the Dutch emissary and our treasury. I see great difficulties about it from several points of view, very much like you.[1]

The peace conference was fairly successful, but if Yugoslavia carries out its threat *not* to sign (no doubt with Russian backing behind it) the position will be a bad one—not only from the point of view of the present Italian peace, but more so from the ominous prospects for the future. I have adopted a conciliatory attitude throughout so as to put the onus for future dissensions wholly on Russia and to avoid giving her any excuse for making trouble. The Americans are getting fed up and in no mood to be merely onlookers —as they had no doubt originally intended to be. I don't think of war, but of continual international friction and uncertainty. Our conciliatory attitude towards, and support of, Italy and Greece were fully justified and in the end many delegations came to realize that we were right. This accounts for the slap in the face which the Big Four finally got on the plenary session over the Brazilian frontier question.

Tomorrow and the following days in London I shall take up the South African questions awaiting us in U.N.O. and Washington. Prospects look pretty bad, but I shall do what I can to reach solutions, or a decent way of postponement where solutions are not possible. I shall keep you informed how things are going. The president has invited me to stay at the White House and this may give an opening for me. With Byrnes I have established good relations. The pressure groups at New York and Washington will be extremely active and tiresome.

In London we have the *kafferboeties*[2] of the Labour Left to deal with, and they are also very troublesome

The Conroy trouble I have thought best to put off, although it means running a risk during the session. However, it may be the wiser course. I hope we shall hold Hottentots Holland and win East London which will both be good signs. I fear the U.N.O. meeting may last till the end of November and that I may be

[1] Hofmeyr wrote on 25 October that the Dutch loan was 'out of the question' as the money could not be found 'without detriment to our own interests' (Smuts Collection, vol. 79, no. 39).

[2] Colloquial Afrikaans for negrophilists.

wanted there at the end; hence my advice to go on with our congress, as it will be a mistake not to hold one this year.

I have not heard much of Waterson's work but shall be informed tomorrow. There is a great trouble to get transport for him back to the Union.

The news from South Africa continues good and this eases my mind in being forced to be away so long.

Kind regards to the colleagues and to Borrie.[1] Ever yours,

s. J. C. Smuts

729 To J. H. Hofmeyr Vol. 80, no. 144

Hyde Park Hotel
London, S.W.1
17 October 1946

My dear Jantjie, I have your letter per Forsyth and also your draft reply to the Native Representative Council. I have made some amendments for your consideration which make the answer somewhat less apologetic in tone and somewhat stiffer, as it should be!

I note the Conroy servitude clause did not raise too much trouble—thanks no doubt to your handling of the situation. May one be as lucky when the Kakamas bill comes before caucus!

Kajee will no doubt see me at U.N.O. in due course. I hope we shall get over that hurdle also. This morning I had a talk with Attlee over South West Africa—quite satisfactory so far as the United Kingdom is concerned. But we run the risk of a U.N.O. resolution for a U.N.O. inquiry on the spot, which of course we shall resist. We shall put the view of the South West Africa inhabitants before U.N.O. without asking generally for a motion of annexation which would only lead to defeat—to be avoided at all costs.

The few days in London are being spent in interviews. I am taking Holloway back with me for lease–lend and further inquiry into the Tennessee Valley Authority.[2] Lease–lend is now in a bad state, but I shall do what I can to pull it out of the present impasse.

I see you are arranging for congress to be postponed till 18 to 20 December. I may be back then, and that would be alright as far as I am concerned.

[1] J. H. Hofmeyr's mother.

[2] The independent controlling body set up on 18 May 1933 by the United States congress to integrate the development of the whole Tennessee river basin chiefly by means of a system of dams and reservoirs and also by soil conservation, the operation of power plants, social and educational activities, etc.

On Monday night I am leaving for New York with Nicholls and Forsyth, and shall therefore be at the opening with luck. With all good wishes, Ever yours,

s. J. C. Smuts

730 To M. C. Gillett Vol. 80, no. 220

Waldorf Astoria
New York
27 October 1946

A pleasant and safe flight brought us to New York at 10.30 p.m. last Tuesday, after fourteen hours in the air. Of course we gain five hours in flying west. Since then I have been very busy in conference work, being on the general or steering committee which settles the programme. Indians and South West Africa figured on the list of our discussions and it is evident that I am going to have much trouble over these items which concern South Africa. The going will be difficult. The conference as a whole, while not disliking South Africa, dislikes its colour bars and its racial outlook. Again, it is against annexation and prefers U.N.O. trusteeships. So you can see what is in store for me. I shall be entangled with minor issues which will consume my time and energy, while immense issues of our human future fail to be dealt with. I hate this entanglement and would have done anything to be free for the bigger issues. But such is fate, and as you say I have no choice. We are passing through a period in which the lines of the future will be shaping, if not actually laid down. But I am detailed for the minor features. And yet they are not minor for South Africa. We have built up a European civilization there where our Portuguese neighbours have failed. South Africa is a little epic of European civilization on a dark continent. India is threatening this noble experiment with her vast millions who have frustrated themselves and now threaten to frustrate us. All along the east coast of Africa from Mombasa to Durban and ultimately to Cape Town they are invading, infiltrating, penetrating in all sorts of devious ways to reverse the role which we have thought our destiny. East and West meet there at this moment of history and I frankly am a Westerner, although I love and respect the whole human family, irrespective of colour or race. We stand for something which will go and be lost to the world, if India gets control of eastern South Africa. So I have to fight out the issue on this apparent side issue and side-show of the conference. But often the least important turns out to be the most important, though this may be seen only after many years. I have a most difficult and invidious and distasteful job, but it happens to be my job, and I must do it—remembering at the same time the vast human background and setting of which I am fully conscious. This looks like an *apologia*, but it is just a statement of the factual position for your information.

Mrs [V.L.] Pandit, Nehru's sister, made an impressive speech, much applauded, in which she attacked South Africa, and said India was all for equality, non-discrimination, and all the other good things. But see what is actually happening in India, the greatest country of discrimination and communal disunity in the whole world. I wish to avoid pogroms and bloody clashes in Natal, hence my attempt to keep the conflicting elements apart on sound and sensible lines. But enough of this.

We are quite comfortable in this big hotel, which is like a city by itself. But it is such a distance to get out of the city that I don't see how I shall ever be able to take country exercise. Alas. Even to get to the conference takes thirty to forty minutes, and two to three hours a day of our precious time is taken up with travelling to and from the conference. The commissions will meet still farther away, a full hour I fear from the hotel. It is all a shocking waste of time, and it seems as if this is going to be the permanent situation for U.N.O. How far better Geneva was and would again have been!

I am reading that curious book on love which you gave me—a really interesting book.[1] As love is the centre of man and his world, any philosophical discussion of the subject cannot fail to be interesting. What I had not realized at first was the ecstatic erotic element in Greek philosophy and poetry—even in Plato. The Greek world view was not all rational, but in the background were the Eleusinian mysteries, the ecstatic union with the God, the absorption of the individual in the divine. It gives meaning to that curious expression—'in love with love', not with an individual, but with something beyond the individual. Christianity substituted for this vague passion of the soul, the *human* Christ, and thus applied the incarnation to this aspect of love also, and to the union of the human with the divine *soul*. For the Greeks it was ἔρως, for the Christians ἀγάπη. But in the mystics and saints there appeared a curious blend of the two. The ecstasies of the female saints have a strong element of the erotic; and why not? Is deep physical passion not as holy as anything in our being? Here the Greek and

[1] M. C. D'Arcy, *The Mind and Heart of Love* (1945).

the Christian elements of love have blended, but the Catholic Church as a rule did not quite like this blending of the elements in love. The whole subject is most interesting and D'Arcy has not said the last word on it. Ever lovingly,

J.C.S.

731 To S. M. Smuts — Vol. 80, no. 147

Waldorf Astor Hotel
New York
27 Oktober 1946

Liefste Mamma, Dinsdag oggend van Londen in die aand hier aangekom na aangename en voorspoedige vlug. 17 uur op pad, 14 in die lug, met pauses te Shannon in Ierland en Gander in Newfoundland. Ons is aangenaam gehuis in hierdie Hotel en alles is goed en in orde.

Ons werk het Woensdag begin en gaan voort—met baie gepraat. Vishinski die Rus het dadelik objeksie gemaak teen ons aanspraak op S.W.A. en die Indiër kwestie sowel as S.W.A. is na 'n reëlings kommissie verwys waar daar sterk opposisie teen Suid-Afrika ontwikkel het. Albei sake sal nou hierdie week terugkom na die Algemeene Vergadering vir bespreking. Mrs Pandit, suster van Nehru, en hoof van die Indiese delegasie het in 'n toespraak heftige beskuldigings teen S.A. gemaak—met groot applous van die Vergadering en die gallerye. Dis duidelik dat ons hier swaar gaan kry, daar die publiek gevoel teen ons kleurlyn beleid in Suid-Afrika baie sterk is, viral in 'n organisasie waar kleur sterk verteenwoordig is en baie vooroordeel teen ons op daardie beleid bestaan. Die regte stryd sal maar snel ontwikkel en ons is klaar daarvoor. Maar S.A. sal in die toekoms in die oog moet hou hoe sterk die wêreld gevoel teen haar kleur beleid is. Dit kan nog baie weeë vir ons land en volk baar. Dit is nie biesonder aangenaam vir my aan die einde van my lewe en werk in so'n stryd betrokke to geraak nie wat my min tyd vir ander dinge laat waarin ek meer belang stel. Maar ek het geen keuse nie en moet maar die mas opkom soos ek bes kan.

Ons het gelukkig nog heerlike herfs weer—nie koud nie, en ook nie warm nie, en dis moeilik om te weet watter klere te dra. Maar ek verwag spoedige verandering en vanoggend is die lug bewolk. Denis gaan vrinde buitekant N.Y. besoek maar ek sal maar stil en rustig op my kamers bly en lees. Daar is ook baie korrespondensie af te werk. Ek skryf nou aan jou voor ontbyt en selfs voor die tee gekom het. Voedsel hier volop—behalwe suiker, en ons het werklik oor niks te kla nie. Selfs die publiek is nie te lastig nie, daar daar so baie andere is om lastig te val! Ons is tweemaal by die Lamonts gewees wat baie groete en liefde en beste wense aan jou en die huisgesin stuur. Tom is baie ernstig siek gewees en ons kon hom nie by die eerste besoek sien nie, maar gister was hy op en het hy nie sleg gelyk nie. Dit is sy hart en vir 'n tyd moes hy oxygen en selfs bloedinspuiting kry. Daar is darem nou 'n keer gekom en Florence is meer hoopvol. Sy sien daar fluks en aktief uit en is so gesellig as altoos. Hul wou my graag by hul aan tuis hê, maar my werk laat dit nie toe nie, en sy toestand maak dit ook ongerieflik. Hul het baie oor alles uitgevra, die liewe vrinde, en hul hart is nog baie in Suid Afrika wat hul nou seker nooit weer sal sien nie. Seker dinge moet mens maar afskrywe soos die jare klim. Ek wonder soms wat ek nou moet begin af te skrywe! Ek voel nog fluks maar ook ver nie meer wat ek was nie. En dis verstandig om jou bedrywighede in te perk soos jy na die end gaan. Ek wens soms dat ek die swaar las van die politiek en die groot verantwoordelikheid neer kan lê. Maar die vraag is wanneer die geskikste geleentheid daarvoor kom. In elk geval moet ons die Koninklike besoek en die goue bruilof afwag, maar hoe lang nog daarna? Die tyd sal die antwoord hierop gee. Die Nattes is natuurlik baie verlangend dat ek nie langer die leier teen hul sal bly nie.

Van Freddie 'n brief ontvang waarin sy skrywe hoe heerlik en lieflik sy alles in Athene aangetref het. Lag en trane van vreugde was die orde van die dag. Sy is van plan na die Griekse kerk oor to gaan en ek keur dit goed, daar dit 'n band sal wees met die kerk van die volk en haar man en haar kinders. Die Grieke uit alle dele stuur nog dank vir my optree vir hul saak te Parys, en Athene dring daarop aan dat ek daarheen sal kom om 'n ereburger te word. 'n Straat heet al Jan Smuts. Die Griek ⟨Niarchos⟩ het ook my naam aan 'n groot skip gegee wat 18,000 ton sal weeg en onder ons vlag. Van anderkant hoor ek darem dat dinge taamlik deurmekaar is beide op politiek en finansieel gebied. Rusland stook die vuur aan.

Nuus van S.A. nie volop nie, maar dit is miskien goed. Die storm sal seker weer losbars sodra ek terugkom!

Jul tuis nuus is baie goed en jou laaste brief oor alles baie welkom. Liefde en soentjies van

Pappa

TRANSLATION

Waldorf Astoria Hotel
New York
27 October 1946

Dearest Mamma, We left London on Tuesday morning and arrived here in the evening after a good pleasant flight—seventeen hours on the way, fourteen in the air with pauses at Shannon in Ireland and Gandar in Newfoundland. We are pleasantly housed in this hotel and all is well and in order.

Our work began on Wednesday and goes on—with much talk. Vishinski [A. Y.] the Russian at once made an objection to our claim to South West Africa and the Indian question as well as South West Africa have been referred to a steering committee in which strong opposition to South Africa has developed. Both matters will now come back this week to the general assembly for discussion. Mrs Pandit, sister of Nehru and head of the Indian delegation, made violent accusations against South Africa in her speech—with loud applause from the assembly and the galleries. It is clear that we shall have a hard time here as public feeling is strongly against our colour bar policy in South Africa, particularly in an organization where colour is strongly represented and where there is much prejudice against us and that policy. South Africa will in future have to keep in view how strong world feeling against her policy is. It may yet bring forth many woes for our country and people. It is not particularly pleasant for me, at the end of my life and work, to become involved in this kind of conflict which leaves me little time for other things in which I am more interested. But I have no choice and shall have to climb the greasy pole as best I may.

Fortunately we are still having delightful autumn weather—neither cold nor warm and it is difficult to know what clothes to wear. But I expect a change soon and this morning the sky is clouded. Denis [McIldowie] is going to visit friends outside New York but I shall stay quietly and peacefully in my rooms and read. There is also a lot of correspondence to work off. I am now writing to you before breakfast, even before early morning tea. Food is plentiful here—except sugar, and we really have nothing to complain of. Even the public is not too much of a nuisance because there are so many others to worry!

We have been twice to the Lamonts who send good wishes and much love to you and the family. Tom has been very seriously ill—we could not see him on our first visit, but he was up yesterday and did not look bad. It is his heart; he had to have oxygen for a while and even a blood transfusion. Now, however, there has been a turn for the better and Florence is more hopeful. She looks alert and active and is as entertaining as ever. They wanted to have me in their home but my work does not allow of that and his condition makes it inconvenient. They asked about everything, those dear friends, and their hearts are much in South Africa which they will probably never see again.

One has to write off some things as the years advance. I sometimes wonder what I should now begin to write off! I still feel energetic but at the same time not nearly what I was. It is sensible to limit one's activities as one moves towards the end. I sometimes wish I could lay down the heavy burden of politics and the great responsibility. But the question is: when will the most suitable opportunity appear. In any case we shall have to await the king's visit and the golden wedding[1]—but how much longer after that? Time will give the answer. Of course the Nats are longing for the day when I shall no longer be the leader against them.

I have had a letter from Freddie in which she tells me how delightful and lovely she found everything in Athens. Laughter and tears of joy were the order of the day. She intends going over to the Greek Church, which I approve, because it will be a bond with the church of the people, of her husband and of her children. From all quarters Greeks are still sending me thanks for pleading their cause in Paris, and Athens insists on my going there to become a freeman of the city. A street has already been named Jan Smuts. The Greek ⟨Niarchos⟩ has also given my name to a large ship of 18,000 tons which will sail under our flag. On the other hand I hear that things are pretty chaotic both politically and financially. Russia is stoking the fires.

There is not much news from South Africa, but that may be a good thing. No doubt the storm will break as soon as I return!

Your home news is very good and your last letter about everything was very welcome. Love and kisses from

Pappa

[1] Smuts married in 1897.

732 To S. M. Smuts Vol. 80, no. 153

Waldorf Astor Hotel
New York
2 November 1946

Liefste Mamma, Ek was bly van oggend in die koerant te sien dat ons party die Munisipale eleksie in Johburg gewen het. Dit is 'n verblydende teeken en sal die Nattes 'n les leer. Die Arbeiders het so klei getrap dat mense taamlik moeg van hul moet wees. Dit lyk of ons Immigrasie beleid 'n goeie invloed op die land en die publiek het, ten spyte van al die geskree van die Nattes. Die nuus is welkom viral omdat ons maar hotagter in die Konferensie kry. Die gevoel teen ons kleur en kleurlyn beleid is baie sterk, viral in 'n Konferensie wat kleur so sterk verteenwoordig. Ek weet nie hoeveel, maar seker $\frac{2}{3}$ of meer van die mensheid is gekleur, en die meeste van hul is hier verteenwoordig. Die Indiërs het ook baie propaganda gemaak en vind meer byval as ek verwag het. Ons doen ons bes, maar dit gaan opdraand.

Een van ons moeilikhede hier is dat ons so ver van ons vergader plaas woon. Dit neem ons nou meer as 'n halfuur om by Flushing van die Hotel te kom. Nou moet ons nog verder, 'n volle uur na Lake Success. Begryp jou aan—twee vergaderings per dag beteeken dus 4 uur per motor—en die dae is nie so lang meer nie. N. York is werklik 'n onmoontlike plek vir so'n konferensie, en dit lyk nou as of dit die permanente setel van U.N.O. sal word. Ek wonder of ek ooit weer hierheen sal kom. Ek hoop ten minste nie! Mens kan ook geen oefening hier kry nie. In Londen kon ek uit my hotel in Hyde Park stap en $1\frac{1}{4}$ of $2\frac{1}{2}$ uur rondwandel sonder eenige tydverlies. Hier is dit totaal onmoontlik. Ek wonder of ek ooit eenige oefening hier sal kry. Denis en ek wil Sondag (môre) probeer met Florence na hul buite plek gaan—40 myl van hier!

Hierdie week het ek 'n vergadering bygewoon waar ek 'n goeie woord oor die Britse Gemeenebes gepraat het. Die gevoel hier is sterk dat dit net 'n uitbuitery is van ander minderwaardige volke, en sluit aan by die sterke antikleur gevoel waarin ons ook betrokke is. Dit skep kwaai bloed tussen die Engelse en die Amerikaners wat nie alleen hul maar ook ons tref. Ek het 'n goeie pers gehad en 'n pragtige uitsaai byna oor die hele land, en ek hoop dit was die moeite werd, want ek kon maar na een uur die nag na bed gaan. Alles neem hier baie tyd, en ek het werklik nie die tyd vir al sulke dinge, hoewel ek soms dink dat ek goed kan doen deur daarheen te gaan en te praat. Ek sal bly wees as ek weer op pad huistoe is, hoor! Dit sal seker maar eers in December kan wees.

Alles gaan so stadig, en ek sal miskien tot die einde hier moet bly. Dan vroeg weer na die Parlement. Die lewe word darem taamlik ondraaglik.

Jul nuus bly goed, of jul vertel ons net die goeie nuus. Ek hoor van goeie reëns, en mense is alleen bekommer oor die graansakke wat ons tot dus ver van Indië gekry het. Hierdie lande het duisendmaal meer moeilikhede en duisendmaal grooter as ons. Mens voel hier hoe 'n paradys Suid-Afrika is. O neem my terug na my paradys, waar my Isie woon, en al die ander geliefdes! Nou maar eindig—maar met innigste liefde en beste wense van

Pappa

TRANSLATION

Waldorf Astoria Hotel
New York
2 November 1946

Dearest Mamma, I was glad to see in the paper this morning that our party had won the municipal election in Johannesburg.[1] It is a hopeful sign and will teach the Nats a lesson. The Labourites have floundered about so much that people must be pretty tired of them. It looks as if our immigration policy is having a good effect on the country and the public in spite of all the fulminations of the Nats. This news is particularly welcome because we are having a difficult time at the conference. Feeling is very strong against our colour and colour bar policy, especially in a conference where colour is so heavily represented. I do not know how much of mankind is coloured but probably two-thirds or more are, and most of them are represented here. There has also been much Indian propaganda and it is proving more acceptable than I thought. We do our best but it is uphill work.

One of our difficulties here is that we live so far from our place of meeting. It takes us more than half an hour to get to Flushing from the hotel. Now we have to go still further—a full hour to Lake Success. Imagine it—two meetings a day means four hours by car, and the days are getting shorter. New York is really an impossible place for a conference and it looks as if it will now be the permanent seat of U.N.O. I wonder if I shall ever come here again. I hope not! Nor can one get any exercise here. In London I could step out of my hotel into Hyde Park and wander about for an hour and a quarter or two hours and a half without wasting

[1] The results were: United party 22, Labour party 12, National party 5, Independents 2, Communist party 1.

any time. Here it is quite impossible. I wonder if I shall ever get any exercise here. Tomorrow Denis and I want to try to go with Florence [Lamont] to their country place—forty miles away![1]

This week I attended a meeting where I could say a good word for the British Commonwealth.[2] There is a strong feeling here that it is mere exploitation of other, inferior peoples—an attitude which is linked with the strong anti-colour feeling in which we, also, are involved. It makes bad blood between the English and the Americans and this hits not only them but us as well. I had a good press and a fine nation-wide broadcast. I hope it was worth the trouble because I could not get to bed until after one o'clock. Everything here takes a long time and I really do not have the time for such things although I sometimes think I can do good by going along and speaking. I shall be glad when I am again on the way home, believe me! That will probably be only in December. Everything is so slow and I may have to stay here until the end. Then off again very soon to parliament. Life is really becoming pretty unbearable.

Your news remains good—or perhaps you tell us only the good news. I hear of good rains and people's only worry is the grain-bags that we previously got from India.[3] These countries have a thousand times more trouble than we—and a thousand times greater. One realizes here what a paradise South Africa is. O, take me back to my paradise where my Isie lives[4] and all the other loved ones! And now I had better end—but with deepest love and best wishes from

Pappa

733 To M. C. Gillett — Vol. 80, no. 223

Waldorf Astoria
New York
17 November 1946

Sunday afternoon is a good time for a moment's chat. I have been busy all morning finishing an address which I began last night—to the national manufacturers' association[5] which is one of their

[1] 'Palisades' in Rockland county, New York.

[2] On 30 October Smuts spoke on 'The British Commonwealth Pattern' to the *Herald Tribune* forum, New York. *See* Smuts Collection, Box L, no. 218.

[3] The government of India having ended trade relations with the Union of South Africa, there was a temporary shortage of jute bags formerly imported from India.

[4] A paraphrase of lines from the Afrikaans folk-song *Sarie Marais*.

[5] Entitled 'Ideologies and World Peace'; delivered to the Congress of American Industry; dated 7 December 1946 (Smuts Collection, Box L, no. 230).

most influential bodies in the States. The rough notes are finished now and will I think make a good address which will make people think. I had previously written an address for the Foreign Relations Council, another very important body, but on reflection I do not think I should deliver it as it may prove too explosive.[1] I had too much fuss over another harmless address which as you remember proved too much for people and caused me much trouble.[2] Important people (like me!) are expected to say nothing in particular!

Last Sunday I kept indoors, except for an hour's walk in the park. Today I shall not leave my rooms at all. It is a hard life and the only redeeming thing about it is that my health still stands this racket. I was in conference all Saturday (yesterday) getting home at 7 p.m. and so it goes on, world without end. I have told you that the going is very bad here. Violent opposition both on the Indian and South West Africa questions. Colour queers my poor pitch everywhere. I quite understand and can look at it all philosophically. But South Africans cannot understand. Colour bars are to them part of the divine order of things. But I sometimes wonder what our position in years to come will be when the whole world will be against us. And yet there is so much to be said for the South African point of view who fear getting submerged in black Africa. I can watch the feeling in my own family, which is as good as the purest gold. It is a sound instinct of self-preservation where the self is so good and not mere selfishness. What can one do about it when (as Isie says) the Lord himself made the mistake of creating colour! I can but bow my head and accept the blows which come my way. Don't think I complain. I am just talking to you of the fleas that bite *this* dog.[3] But of course I am considered a hypocrite, saying nice things and doing such awful things!

Now, like a silly ass, I have started talking about myself when I really wanted to ask you how that erring breastbone of yours was getting on. By now I hope all is well again and you will not continue flattened out any longer. Resting is a good thing, but one can have too much of it. Your family news sounds very good, and your grandchildren have become a real major interest to you. So should it be. We may not make the world better, but we can at least produce good offspring and so do our bit to improve it....

The conference looks like going on till near Christmas. But I must leave earlier even if my work is not finished here. Present date is 7 December. Then a day or two in London, a couple in

[1] Entitled 'The World Power Pattern'; undated (Smuts Collection, Box L, no. 219).

[2] **624**.

[3] *See* vol. v, p. 16, note 1.

Rome and Athens for my legations, and this ought to bring me home before Isie's birthday on the 22nd. Heavy tasks await me in South Africa. Many things are unsettled or have gone wrong. My own mission to U.N.O. a failure. Parliament to meet in the middle of January to work off steam before the royal family arrives. The pace remains hot, and I sometimes groan 'How long O Lord'.[1] And the road winds uphill all the way.[2] I do not complain, but I could have wished for some free time to enjoy my own company before the end. I like that funny English expression 'enjoy myself'. It sounds so good, and I have no experience of it. What is the psychology behind it in the popular mind? I know I *could* really enjoy myself when free and released from it all.

Now good-bye to you and Arthur. My love to that dear Street circle. Think of 1906 there![3] Ever yours,

J.C.S.

734 To F. Lamont — Vol. 80, no. 174

Waldorf Astoria
New York
8 December 1946

Dear Florence, Thank you for that farewell note. And yet we never say farewell to each other, except in the conventional way. Friends such as we are never do part, but are always together in the great Presence which visits them.

It was so refreshing to be repeatedly with you and Tom, to be with you at 'Palisades', to be together in the world which is beyond space and time. All too seldom however!

This refreshment has been specially good for me, as I have passed through a difficult time at New York. Doubts like clouds pass over our minds and dim the glory of the day. Heart-searchings beset us, and fears follow. Then the human presence helps, and the contacts with the simple natural scene which has carried us thus far.

I hope we shall meet again—soon, here or elsewhere, and in the meantime keep touch through the poor means of letters.

I shall take your messages to Isie who is devoted to you and Tom, especially Tom, as becomes the woman.

[1] *See* vol. III, p. 87, note 1.

[2] *See* vol. III, p. 595.

[3] Smuts first met Margaret Gillett's parents and their family in 1906 and stayed at their house in Street.

Please do not forget my message to Dorothea.[1] Tell her how sorry I am not to have found an opportunity of seeing her and her husband. She is woven into great memories of our lives.

And now good-bye, as they say. Good be with you and Tom, and may Florida be a joy and renewal of body and spirit for both of you. Lovingly yours ever,

J.C.S.

735 To M. C. Gillett — Vol. 80, no. 225

Doornkloof
[Transvaal]
26 December 1946

Note the date. Yesterday I did my best walk for many months in the happy company of Japie [Smuts] and Denis [McIldowie]. Today I shall be busy with visitors. In between I have once more read *The Tempest*—this time in the Cambridge edition you obtained for me. What glory it is! What a message of healing and forgiveness and for a sense of the spaciousness and graciousness of the world. I think this is one of the most precious impressions one derives from Shakespeare, apart from the magic of language and of high art. With him you feel in the great company and in the glory of it. You also feel the mystery of it all—'Men hither—ripeness is all.'[2] There is the pattern of the full circle with all its colour and variety of experience—and beyond it lie the mysteries.

We have had glorious rains, though late, and the magic of nature lies over the land. To tread this earth is to feel yourself carried beyond it. To me, after all I have been through in recent months, the refreshment is great and welcome indeed.

I have not written you since my departure from London. The flights were good and enjoyable except the last one from Kisumu to Pretoria, which was bumpy and unpleasant all the way for eight or nine hours. Still, I stood it, or rather lay it, without actually succumbing. An afternoon and night at Rome, where I could meet the prime minister[3] and our South African circle. Then two-and-a-half days at Athens where I had a glorious reception

[1] Dorothea Blagden, born Draper. The Blagdens had visited South Africa in 1935–6.

[2]
...Men must endure
Their going hence, even as their coming hither:
Ripeness is all.

Shakespeare, *King Lear*, v.ii.9.

[3] Alcide de Gasperi (q.v.).

from the warm-hearted Greeks who look upon me as a second Byron. I have indeed stood by them since 1941 and they know it —often alone, when they seemed neglected by their bigger allies. They have behaved so grandly, and now and for the last couple of years have had such a rough time and met with such discouragements from the Allies. I addressed the parliament, the university and the municipal council. The best show was at the university where I appeared as another Odysseus back from long wars and distant travels. It was all so good and human, and the kindness so great. It is interesting to see how these sunny people of the south can for the moment forget their troubles and set-backs and enjoy themselves in the passing show. The northerners are inclined to carry the sadness of life into their joys—the southerners do just the opposite and so get more out of life....

Isie and the rest of the family with all the Pretoria notables were at the aerodrome to receive me. Isie looked better than when I had left her, and the quiet which Louis [McIldowie] secures for her is evidently having an excellent effect. Next day I broadcasted to South Africa,[1] and the day thereafter I addressed the women of Pretoria and Johannesburg at a welcome meeting, where I gave my impressions of my visit abroad. At a lunch the same day I similarly addressed the men.

South Africa is dazed and amazed by our rebuff at New York. The refusal of South West Africa incorporation into the Union and the Indian rebuff[2] have come as a great shock to them, even more than to me, who could understand these events in their larger international setting. I did my best to calm the waters but a wound has been inflicted which will continue to be painful and hurt the pride and self-respect of the people. All this will make my task more difficult in South Africa. Tempers are more inflamed and the feeling away from U.N.O. and towards isolation will become stronger. I shall have to keep public opinion steady, otherwise something may happen which will or *may* vitally affect the future of this country in this world of growing dangers.

I am very busy indeed, dealing with heavy arrears, and with preparations for parliament next month. My colleagues are all rather tired as they don't spare themselves, and I shall have to carry a large part of the load myself. Fortunately I still feel fit and well, although no longer up to the standard of my past. But what

[1] *See* Smuts Collection, Box L, no. 234.

[2] The Indians in South Africa rejected the franchise enacted in the Asiatic Land Tenure and Indian Representation Act and the Indian delegation at U.N.O. declared it to be a violation of the United Nations Charter.

can one do? I had looked forward to quietly easing off and perhaps stepping out at this stage and after much labour. But I fear my influence is still wanted, and I must continue to give it as long as it is there to be given. I must also see the king's visit through...

736 To D. W. du Preez — Vol. 80, no. 186

Pretoria
30 Desember 1946

Waarde du Preez, In antwoord op u brief van 17 Desember kan ek alleen sê dat ek geen opening kon vind om 'n vergadering te Standerton voor my vertrek na die Parlement te hou nie. Ek vertrou my vriende sal dit verstaan, en my talm met 'n antwoord op u brief was juis daaraan te wyte om te sien of so'n ontmoeting te Standerton nie moontlik sou wees. Ek hoop Standerton te kom besoek met die visite van S.M. die Koning en daar my getroue en liewe vriende se hand te kan druk.

In tusse my beste wense aan hul almal vir die nuwe jaar. Steeds getrou die uwe,

get. J. C. Smuts

TRANSLATION

Pretoria
30 December 1946

Dear du Preez,[1] In answer to your letter of 7 December I can only say that I could find no opening to hold a meeting at Standerton before my departure for parliament. I trust my friends will understand this; indeed my delay in answering your letter was due to my wishing to see if such a meeting at Standerton would not be possible. I hope to come to Standerton at the visit of his majesty the king and to shake hands with my dear and faithful friends.

In the meantime, my best wishes to them all for the New Year. Ever yours truly,

s. J. C. Smuts

[1] Secretary of the district executive of the United party at Standerton, Transvaal, which was Smuts's constituency.

737 To C. van Riet Lowe Vol. 80, no. 189

Pretoria
31 December 1946

My dear van Riet Lowe, I saw your letter of 26 October about Dr Broom and the action of the National Monuments Commission.[1]

I would urge you and the commission not to interfere with the scientific work of Broom who has brought immense world-wide distinction on South Africa, of which I had striking evidence now again in the United States. While I see no objection to your long and large-scale planning for Kromdraai and Sterkfontein[2] research, I would ask you to leave Broom alone to visit these places and use the evidence there obtained for his purposes. He is getting very old and his work may be lost to us if now at this late stage interfered with. So please let him just carry on as usual.

You will have heard of the University of California expedition to do palaeontological work in South Africa.[3] Please give them your strong support. They are very well equipped financially and have an expert staff of unrivalled ability. Both Drs Gregory [J.T.] and Camp [C.L.] asked me to be helpful to them as they will be extremely useful to us with our vast hoard of material and shortages of man-power and finance. I promised that South Africa will not be lacking in whatever assistance we could give to so highly organized an expedition. All best wishes for the New Year. Ever yours sincerely,

s. J. C. Smuts

738 To M. C. Gillett Vol. 84, no. 191

Groote Schuur
[Cape Town]
14 January 1947

What a beautiful and dear letter you wrote me on New Year's Eve—so full of ripeness and the wisdom of the years. I do think the years and even the absence have brought us closer together in their mysterious way. And this is what I must have meant when

[1] The Historical Monuments Commission had refused to allow Broom to work individually on the Kromdraai and Sterkfontein sites and had suggested 'systematic exploration by a team of expert geologists, palaeontologists and archaeologists' (*see* Smuts Collection, vol. 79, no. 117).

[2] Prehistorical sites near Krugersdorp, Transvaal.

[3] The expedition was led by Wendell Phillips who had approached Smuts when he was in New York in November 1946.

I have written you that memory often holds more and conveys more than perception. There is a new dimension in memory, and looking back through the years there is as it were a magnification and an intensification of the deeper spiritual aspects. The physical is less obtrusive, there is a haze, and we look back through a haze of associations to the blue hills which near by appeared to us in too glaring and less attractive a light. Of course I believe in the Presence—sometimes so overwhelming. But the Absence has its own story to unfold, more subdued, more of the sense of mortality in it, more poignant and complex in its composition.

That Collard Point function[1] must have been a fine ending of the year. It reads like a sacrament of love at this distance. I am so glad that you are well enough to partake in and enjoy all this, and to feel the goodness of the world in the goodness of that dear circle surrounding you. Bless you and dear Arthur. I say that not to you but to myself as I write!

That O.M. was rather overwhelming to me. The king had mentioned it at Balmoral,[2] but somehow I never took him seriously, and it was only when the award actually came in published print that I began to realize that I had been greatly singled out for honour. I have really done or achieved little to deserve it, and usually only have the sense of how little I have really achieved of the dreams I have had through a long and busy life. So much chaff with so little corn in it. But it is never good to be retrospective or introspective, but still to look forward, as is the nature of life. And so I prefer to keep smiling even when inwardly one has little sense of being much good. There is this to be said on the other side—that we pass through a strange and baffling epoch, when achievement is more difficult than in normal times and when the scene is covered with the wreckage of high hopes and great plans. It is a terrible thing to be an idealist and spiritualist in a realist and materialist age. But such is our lot and we must make the best of it.

Parliament is once more meeting and I am full of all the trouble it means for government in these days. My failure with U.N.O. has been a bitter experience, even where I know, or perhaps more *because* I know, that essentially it is South Africa's as much as mine. The world does not know or understand us, and we feel this deeply, even when we are conscious that we are much to blame in it all. It *is* a good country, and a good people, but the world

[1] A picnic of the Clark–Gillett circle at Street where meat was roasted on open fires as at a South African *braaivleis*.

[2] Smuts had stayed there in September 1946.

sees its mistakes more clearly than its goodness or virtues. I don't despair of the future, but it will not be easy to keep South Africa steady in this avalanche of condemnation which has so suddenly and unexpectedly overwhelmed it. People simply cannot understand it and are running over with resentment. It will be my part to keep them cool, and if possible reflective, so that good may come out of this evil. The opposition naturally rejoices and puts this all to my account, and to the liberalism (!) with which I have led the world astray. Here is the author of the great preamble of the Charter, exposed as a hypocrite and a double-faced time server! They are of course all right, and so is dear South Africa. But look at this bad fellow who is responsible for it all!

I am still having my bathes, and as I wrote last week, I have even been up Table mountain again since I came down a little more than a week ago. I feel fit and well, only get more easily and sooner tired after heavy exertion. This is largely a new experience to me and perhaps a warning not to overdo it. I have good companions in Lady Moore and her daughter [D. O'Neill], who is now in her last medical year at this university. The mother will stay on till the end of February and thus witness the royal arrival. Her husband must have his hands full at Colombo where a heavy constitutional storm is blowing up, as almost everywhere in the East. How ungainly is the waking up of that giant! How upsetting to all the other continents! And what portents for the future!

17 January. Thus far I had written a couple of days ago, and since then another letter from you has arrived, full of family and Street news, including seeing Professor [D. S.] Robertson,[1] and sending your two darlings home to their mother (with another baby). I am glad that Jan is getting on well[2] and that the salary troubles don't trouble. I love these letters from you, now sounding the depths, and then quietly flowing on again on the surface of domestic news. That is how letters should be written. Thank you.

Tomorrow our parliament resumes its work and the opposition will move a vote condemning me for 'liberalism' and for my U.N.O. failures. And so the dismal fight goes on as long as there is a scrap of strength left to continue it. All so futile, and unfortunately so mischievous. We have just lost Hottentots' Holland seat in an important bye-election[3]—rather a bad defeat, as we had a first-

[1] His son married Eleanor, daughter of Roger Clark (q.v.).

[2] Jan Gillett was at this time government botanist in Baghdad.

[3] The result was: H. J. van Aarde (National party) 5,593; Sir de Villiers Graaff (United party) 4,956.

class candidate (Sir de Villiers Graaff, son of the old magnate friend[1] of General Botha). We were so certain of victory, and the enemy is now cock-a-hoop. Well, it is all in the day's march, and it is uphill most of the time. I feel very sorry for young Graaff who was nominated in 1943, would have been triumphantly elected, but instead was captured with the rest at Tobruk and spent two-and-a-half years in a German prison camp, and now when the seat is vacant again and he stands again, is again defeated—a real second Tobruk! But he will rise again, and be a cabinet minister and perhaps prime minister in time. A first-rate fellow. Well, good-night. Ever yours,

Jan

739 To S. M. Smuts — Vol. 84, no. 9

Parlement
23 Januarie 1947

Liefste Mamma, Jou brief van 20 Januarie net aangekom. Denis sal natuurlik baie welkom wees en ek verwag hom op 30 Januarie. Daar ek nie weet wanneer hy aankom (tensy hy ons laat weet) sal geen skikking vir sy afhaal by die vliegveld moontlik wees nie.

Jou brief is vol interessante nuus en dit is alles goeie nuus. Ek is ook bly dat ou Joubert weer geholpe is.

Ek glo nie, op grond van al my informasie, dat Jantjie se toespraak iets biesonder met ons nederlaag te Hottentots Holland te doen had. Dit is die aand voor die eleksie gemaak en was dus te laat om verskil te maak. Daar is baie ander redes—viral verslapping en ontevredenheid oor kontroles en ander kleiner griewe wat by mense meer weeg as die hoë politiek; de Villiers Graaff self is tevrede dat dit ander redes was.

Ek gaan Borrie met my mee neem na Paarl en Stellenbosch die dag wat ek die Koning daarheen sal vergesel. Sy sal jou plaas moet inneem!

Vir Daphne en Deirdre is plek gemaak op die funksies en hul is gelukkig hier. Bool en Lettie was een namiddag te Groote Schuur, maar ek was natuurlik weg in die Volksraad en het hul nie gesien nie. Ek is natuurlik baie besig in die Volksraad met my werk. Die V.V.O. debat is aan gang en ek het net na 'n pragtige toespraak van Jantjie geluister—die beste wat nog in the debat gemaak is. My eie toespraak was niks biesonders en ek was daar nie mee tevrede. Ongelukkig moes ek Malan volg, en dus voor die ander

[1] Sir David P. de Villiers Graaff (q.v.).

aanvalle gemaak is wat nou, soos mostert na die maaltyd, sonder antwoord van my kom.

Ek voel heelmal gesond nietteenstaande al die gewoel en gewerskaf. En ook slaap ek heelmaal goed. Vanoggend het ek die skildery tentoonstelling van Princess Patricia Ramsay (dogter van oorlede Duke of Connaught) by Maskew Miller geopen, en hul het jou 'n mooi geskenk van 'n tulp skildery gegee wat later sal afkom.

Nou weer na die Raad om die debat te volg. Met liefde en soentjies,

Pappa

TRANSLATION

Parliament
[Cape Town]
23 January 1947

Dearest Mamma, Your letter of 20 January has just come. Of course Denis [McIldowie] will be very welcome and I shall expect him on 30 January. As I do not know at what time he is arriving (unless he lets us know) no arrangement for meeting him at the airport will be possible.

Your letter is full of interesting news—and all good. And I am glad that old Joubert[1] is again all right.

I do not think, judging from all my information, that Jantjie's speech had anything to do with our defeat at Hottentots Holland. It was made the night before the election and was therefore too late to make a difference.[2] There are many other reasons—especially slackness and dissatisfaction about controls and other smaller grievances which weigh more with people than high politics. De Villiers Graaff himself is satisfied that it was due to other reasons.

I am taking Borrie[3] with me to Paarl and Stellenbosch on the day that I shall accompany the king there. She will have to take your place!

Daphne [Moore] and Deirdre [O'Neill] have been given places at the functions and they are happy here. Bool and Lettie [Smuts] were at Groote Schuur one afternoon but I was, of course, away—in parliament and did not see them. I am very busy with my parliamentary work. The U.N.O. debate is going on and I have just listened to a beautiful speech by Jantjie—the best so far in

[1] Daniel S. Joubert, an ex-foreman at Rooikop re-employed at this time at Doornkloof.

[2] In answer to a question Hofmeyr had said: 'Natives will eventually be represented in parliament by Natives and Indians by Indians.' *See* A. Paton, *Hofmeyr*, p. 443.

[3] Mrs Deborah Hofmeyr.

the debate. My own speech was nothing much and I was not satisfied with it.[1] Unfortunately I had to follow Malan [D. F.] and so had to speak before the other attacks which are now being made, like mustard after the meat, without any answer from me.

I feel quite well in spite of all the hustle and bustle. And I sleep quite well. This morning at Maskew Miller's I opened an exhibition of paintings by Princess Patricia Ramsay[2] (daughter of the late Duke of Connaught) and they have given you a nice present—a painting of a tulip—which will be sent up later.

Now back to the house to follow the debate. With love and kisses,

Pappa

740 To M. C. Gillett — Vol. 84, no. 195

Groote Schuur
[Cape Town]
1 February 1947

This is Friday night, at the end of a heavy week. And it is not the end as I shall have to spend tomorrow morning in office for interviews. But it almost felt the end as this afternoon I stole away from parliament and office and went for a bathe at Strandfontein. I could wash away all this sin and dirt that had gathered on body and soul during a hard week, and tonight I feel clean, and my nerves composed. This week I wrote a line to Arthur in reply to a note from him, and I also received a pleasant domestic letter from you about doings and comings at Street; and this now will be my response. Your news is so good, but Nicholas's [Gillett] family is down with measles. You describe the beautiful weather and the sunsets in the skies; but the papers the last few days have been full of the terrible weather now settling down on England and the Continent. What suffering this must mean in that coalless hungry world. The horror of it all; one dare not even think of it. If we were more coarsely made we would feel less pain—but also we would feel less pleasure, have less sensitiveness of mind and soul, and would live on a lower level. The pain is just the physical counterpart to this higher and intenser spiritual sensitivity. But what a price to pay for our higher grade of structure! And the mind—with all its thinking and remembering and comparing—

[1] *See House of Assembly Debates*, vol. 59, cols. 10910–27, 11087–98.

[2] Lady Victoria Patricia Helena Elizabeth Ramsay, born 1886; married the Hon. Sir Alexander Ramsay in 1919; died 1942.

makes the pain even worse. Great must be the spiritual gain to make up for such suffering.

The royal family has left today in all this cold for South Africa and I have moved for addresses of welcome in both houses. I hope they will have a smooth and safe passage by sea. The air has had so many fatal accidents the last few months that people are getting very nervous about flying. And yet it is the only way in which I can still cover the big distances in the little time at my disposal. There seems to be a real crisis on in air travel and I hope everything will be done to secure greater safety in air travel. Otherwise South Africans, already perturbed over my flying, will insist on my going by sea on these long visits to other countries...

I am very busy these days to see what can be done to improve European–non-European relations, which are definitely deteriorating. This is due not only to more difficult conditions here—rising cost of living, scarcities, higher prices with which wages do not keep pace, but also to the new wind blowing through the world. The fully publicized discussions at U.N.O. are having a great effect in all directions. We even hear about them from our domestic and farm Natives who really have nothing to complain of, but are deeply stirred by all this talk of equality and non-discrimination. I am so anxious to stay this rot and get a move on to better relations, but it is even more difficult now in view of these Native claims, which have just the opposite effect on European mentality. Both extremes are gathering strength and it is all the more difficult to find a *via media* as a solution. The old Fabian slogan of gradualness would be the best solution under the circumstances, but the extreme tempers on both sides almost rule this out. If only one could get people back into a reasonable mood, but that is the very thing that has disappeared on both sides. Still, I am anxious to try my hand at a solution. The danger is that by appearing pro-Native I may run the risk to lose the general election next year, and thus hand the Natives over to the other extreme. The time has certainly arrived when a new effort at reasonable compromise and to secure a new hope for Native advance should be opened up.

I fear I am beginning to write political letters to you which may be wearisome. But that is the element in which I am living and to which my thinking is subdued. I would so prefer to roam in the realms of thought, but my life is tied down to mundane affairs. How pleasant to fly away if one had the wings of the dove?[1] But

[1] 'Though ye have lien among the pots, yet shall ye be as the wings of a dove...' *Psalms* lxviii.13.

there is no escape from the burden and the toil—from 'life's toil and endless endeavour, and tonight I long for rest'.[1]

Thank you for the books that have come which vary my botanical diet at bedtime. I can now read Bertrand Russell and the rest, and that too is an escape from the pressure preparatory to sleep. Fortunately I remain a good sleeper and get my fair share, even if it means an hour or two of waking at night. I do not really need more than about six hours of sleep. My appetite for reading remains as good as ever, but after a day's hard work one has not the mental energy to do justice to any serious subject except botany or poetry, and they are not serious subjects but real relaxation.

We shall have a little respite the week before the king arrives. Parliament will be prorogued until he opens the new session on 19 or 20 February. I hope then to steal some days of the free week to run loose and gather fresh strength for the ordeal of the visit, which will be pretty exhausting. Good-night. Lovingly yours,

Jan

741 To M. C. Gillett — Vol. 84, no. 196

Groote Schuur
[Cape Town]
6 February 1947

I see many English visitors nowadays who come to South Africa partly for change of climate and partly no doubt for business. Sir John Chancellor and wife, Sir Charles Davis (ex lord mayor) and wife, Sir Clive Bailleu and wife, Lord Bicester (brother of Lady Buxton) and wife, Lord Brand and his nephew Tom Brand (who was at Yalta and Potsdam) and many other less distinguished figures have been entertained by me the last week. Arthur would know them all. They bring information and points of view and keep me in touch with events, while we keep them in touch with the glories and products of the Cape summer. All the time we read of the awful winter you are having, of coal shortages and industries closing down, and the general worsening of conditions in Britain and on the Continent. You do not say much of all this in your letters, I suppose to spare my feelings and not to rake your own. But things must really be pretty bad if one is to judge from the cables and the reports of these well-informed people. Arthur's letters are on the whole less pessimistic, and I sometimes wonder whether his views really reflect the situation or are coloured by

[1] H. W. Longfellow, *The Day is Done.*

his religious outlook and faith in Providence. The European scene is a bleak one and a sense of melancholy comes over one when reflecting on what is happening.

I have much to occupy my attention. This and last week I have been giving my attention to the next moves to be made in our Native and Indian questions—both at present in a jam which must be broken, if we have not to come to a definite standstill. I must meet the Native leaders and open up new outlooks and inspire new faith in their future. Similarly I must deal with the real grievances of Indians and not with those they exploited for propaganda purposes at U.N.O. The fact is that both Native and Indian leaders want *status* and not social benefits and advance. They suffer from the inferiority complex and will not be fobbed off with substantial economic or social improvements. Mrs Ballinger said the other day in parliament that in social and economic advances we have a strong case, but the Natives want *rights* and not improvements. There we bump up against the claim for equality which it is most difficult to concede except in very small doses which will not satisfy the leaders. I have so far done my best to follow the other line (of improvements) as less open to white prejudice and opposition. I must try again.

I was glad to get your *Times* cutting with the review of Bertrand Russell's *History of Philosophy*.[1] It is a searching and valuable review which coincides with my own view. The insoluble problem for Russell on his philosophy is to account for personality which I consider basic for philosophy and indeed for all knowledge of values. Russell's doctrine is really much like Hume's—he also analyses experience into its ultimate elements, but fails to show how from these elements (sense data and sensibilia) you can get to the whole (personality) of which they constitute the elements. Unless the holistic factor is introduced into this analytical situation you are left with the raw crude elements. How can you reverence the human personality—and give it the status which it occupies in the preamble of the Charter, if personality is but sense-data and sensibilia? The thing is really too absurd to be taken seriously. Yet to this the Russell philosophy essentially reduces in the last resort. Holism is the clue—exclude that, and you are left with titbits of experience which you cannot reverence or worship or indeed think of any value at all. And this applies not only to personality but to all the other concrete wholes of our experience—in fact our whole material world which forms but the enlargement of our personality. Even a physical thing is more than the electrons and protons and

[1] *A History of Western Philosophy* (1946).

the rest into which it can be analysed. Why will people not take holism seriously? But of course Russell is delightful reading, and now at bed time I have a variation—botany if I am very tired, Russell's philosophy if there is still a small spark left in me. Raven's paper I shall also read but have not yet come to it....

742 To J. G. Latham Vol. 84, no. 15

Personal

Cape Town
12 February 1947

My dear Chief Justice, It was a great pleasure to receive your letter of 23 December with the interesting cuttings enclosed.[1] I much appreciate all you so kindly say and it was good of you to write to me as you have done.

I have followed your work in Japan and also heard many details from Officer (F.K.] who was there at the same time as yourself. You were indeed fortunate to escape before the storm burst. But Tokio must have been a great experience for you and your service there was not in vain.

I had better not say anything about Australia's attitude at the U.N.O. meeting. My attitude generally was intended to serve the cause both of Australia and South Africa. In the new world now emerging both are in a somewhat precarious position. The European leadership of the world is in grave danger, if not already lost, and the European is being booted out of Asia and the Far East. What is the future of Australia going to be in that Asiatic world? Similarly what is the position of South Africa going to be if she can no longer look to European leadership as her bulwark? Some vast change is silently coming over the course of history, and the future of both of our young European communities may be hopelessly compromised if we endorse the new policies which are being favoured by U.N.O. Ours is a case for caution and going slow and giving Europe time to recover her breath after the terrible calamity that has overcome her and shifted the world balance of power so fundamentally. With kind remembrances and good wishes, Yours sincerely,

J. C. Smuts

[1] Cutting of an article on the Indian problem in South Africa in *The Bulletin* of Sydney (18 December 1946) supporting Smuts's attitude at U.N.O. (Smuts Collection, vol. 79, no. 101.)

743 To D. Moore Vol. 84, no. 22

Groote Schuur
[Cape Town]
2 March 1947

My dear Daphne, This is Sunday morning and I am in my little upstairs room looking at the mountain—clear, cloudless, sunlit, with no speck of cloud or wisp of wind. It is warm, but to me pleasantly so. The doves are cooing in the oaks, the squirrels are squirrelling, and the cicadas are singing their endless shrill song. The world is still in other respects. The house is empty except for me... I have been dealing with arrear correspondence, and with a very heavy week before me I write to you to prove that I am not quite alone—if the presence is not there, the memory takes its place. And memory is often greater and richer than the presence itself. I find something very beautiful in the gospel story in *St John*, where Jesus tells the distressed disciples that he is going but he will send the Comforter, the Holy Spirit, to make up for his going.[1] Memory is in many respects the Holy Spirit of friendship. The friend goes but the immortal memory remains. It is in some ways more effective and goes deeper than the presence itself. The presence is so absorbing, in a sense so disturbing; its emotional pull is so terrific and almost shattering. The memory is gentler, more spiritual, more of a Holy Spirit, and softens and sublimates the actualities of the presence. At bottom we are more spiritual than physical in our nature—the inmost core of our being is spirit and not body. And so in physical absence the spiritual memory comes into play, and we can ponder over things in their real meaning, undisturbed by the bodily pulls. The great meaning behind it all stands out more clearly. Here as I sit alone in this room my mind wanders back and dwells on those weeks of your sojourn in this dear house. It all sets afresh in a new setting. The glare is gone and the gentler light of the memory lightens up and brings into relief aspects of friendship which the actual presence did not make us realize so fully. We have memory the comforter, and it goes a long way, in the end perhaps a longer way than the fierce presence. So let us bless the memory of those weeks and cherish them as among our treasured possessions for ever.

I had your wire from Nairobi telling of your good flight and safe arrival, and probable departure for Ceylon on 6 March, that is, this week. May soft winds waft you home where Henry will be comforted and glad to have your companionship in his life and

[1] *St John* xiv.16–18, 26.

work. I am glad that events were so disposed that you could stay longer here for Deirdre [O'Neill] and myself. The friendship we formed in war years in Nairobi and London and South Africa has been cemented by this close living together under conditions which liberated body and soul from the pressures of our time and our society and made us understand and know each other as never before. I had understood the intellectual and critical side of you well before; now I began to sense the deeper emotional layers, and I was glad to do so. After all intellect, brilliant as it may be, is more an aspect of the surface—the emotional nature constitutes the very soul and core of us. And so you laid yourself bare and open to the friendship which surely is the greatest thing in the world—'Life's great meaning, dear my lord'.[1] I thank you for this friendship, this *richesse* of the spirit, this revelation of the deeper self. Perhaps you saw beneath my intellectual skin too, and so we have become clear to each other in life's deeper meaning. Is this in the end not all we get out of this life of ours? What else is there in it? A poor thing at best, but the key which unlocks the door of this universe, and links the human with the divine.

I continue to swim in my sea of troubles, and may yet drown in it. On one side I am a human and a humanist, and the author of the preamble to the Charter. On the other I am a South African European, proud of our heritage and proud of the clean European society we have built up in South Africa, and which I am determined not to see lost in the black pool of Africa. Recent developments have sent the two extremes farther apart, and the role of peacemaker and bridge-builder between them has become much harder. Colour in the world and in South Africa has become more intransigent because of the acclaim of human rights at U.N.O. How is the practical compromise to be found? That is the problem which confronts us in South Africa and me in particular. The world is reeling between the two poles of White and Colour. What is the future of our race going to be? And in South Africa the problem is coming to a head.

You came as a relief to this dark background. Thank you for it. With affectionate good wishes to you both, Ever yours,

J.C.S.

[1] Not traced.

744 To M. C. Gillett Vol. 84, no. 202

Natal National Park
16 March 1947

As you see I write from this veritable paradise of beauty which Isie once called the most beautiful part of South Africa. For the last three days I have accompanied the royal party to Harrismith and Ladysmith[1] in a whirlwind of receptions, and from Ladysmith we passed close by Spionkop[2] to this wonderful retreat to spend the week-end quietly and away from the public. We had planned an attack on the high mountains, but the first day was spent in a gentle walk up the lower slopes, and since then the rain has set in and continues, so that we shall leave tomorrow without any success as mountaineers. This is Sunday morning and I am keeping indoors in the rain and writing letters to my nearest and dearest. Yesterday morning during a couple of fair hours I botanized the lower forests in company with a trained botanist and found the experience most pleasant and useful. I found a number of plant forms new to me, including the only Erica found on these high mountains.

The hostel is in an amphitheatre of the high Drakensberg with peaks up to 11,500 towering above us. Immense sheer precipices with wonderful colouring and strange shapes of all patterns. It is Mont-aux-Sources from which the Orange flows west and the Tugela east—the mother of waters and of the greatest thing in this land. I could spend weeks here, the world forgetting, of the world forgotten,[3] but alas, tomorrow we pass on to Colenso and Estcourt and Maritzburg where I shall desert royalty and return to my tasks at Cape Town.

The royal family have had a wonderful reception everywhere and enjoy their visit to the full, in spite of its being strenuous as all these functions must be. Every section of our population have played their part magnificently and even politics has retired before this triumph. The queen has captured all hearts, and the king has also been very good. The princesses are full of fun and jollity. All have made the greatest and best impression. I am coming back week after next to rejoin them at Pretoria and Johannesburg and shall be there for Easter, when they return from the Kruger Park.

Apart from these frivolities our minds are dominated by conditions

[1] In the Orange Free State and Natal respectively.

[2] *See* vol. 1, p. 562, note 1.

[3] How happy is the blameless vestal's lot!
The world forgetting, by the world forgot.
Alexander Pope, *Eloisa to Abelard*, l. 207.

in England and Europe, and much more pleasantly by Truman's message to congress about Greece and Turkey—a truly momentous declaration of American policy[1] which goes much farther than any previous indication of how far the United States is prepared to go towards a world policy. Isolation will be a thing of the past if congress implements this policy. Either Communism will be halted or the world will divide into two camps—East and West—with far-reaching consequences for the future. It is difficult to foresee the new world pattern which may develop from this beginning, but it is evident that it may be Duo instead of U.N.O., and all that may follow from such a set-up. No one can dare to prophesy. My own experience at San Francisco and New York has inclined me to think that world unity is still too ambitious a move, and that some intermediate stage of international evolution would be more of a success. But a division of the world, with the United States and Russia as the two poles, opens up new dangers which one is loath to contemplate. I myself have rather thought of the restored Europe as the third in a new Trio, and I still think that would be the wiser and safer course. Neither Russia nor America fills the bill for me. The treasures of European culture and experience should balance the other two, and so bring about a new world equilibrium, at least for our time. I cannot reconcile myself to the idea that Europe is no longer a first-class factor in world progress. But the subject is much too large and deep for a casual letter discussion, and so I desist. But my first impression is to welcome Truman's policy, while not unmindful of what it may mean for this troubled human racė divine.

Cato [Clark] will be here next week I hope, and I may have the fun of flying her and her little company with me to Pretoria. Then in May I hope to have my dear Gilletts with me, and my cup will be running over. There is therefore much to cheer me up in these days, and with the psalmist I affirm that my lines are cast in pleasant places.[2] Not that we don't have very fierce problems. Not that we forget the great European world passing through its Gethsemane. But we do rejoice, and it is a poor heart that never rejoices.

Now good-bye dears. Ever my dear love, ever the pleasant thought of blessed reunions to come.

J.C.S.

[1] On 12 March 1947 Truman addressed a joint session of congress. He proposed financial and economic assistance to Greece and Turkey and support from the United States to 'peoples who are resisting attempted subjugation by armed minorities or outside pressures'. For his speech *see* L. L. Snyder, *Fifty Major Documents of the Twentieth Century*, pp. 131–7.

[2] 'The lines are fallen unto me in pleasant places.' *Psalms* xvi.6.

745 To F. Lamont Vol. 84, no. 28

Doornkloof
Transvaal
31 March 1947

My dear Florence, This silence since we parted at New York last year has lasted much too long, and you will begin to think that I have forgotten to write. But you have been constantly in my thoughts, and only the continuous strain and pressure on my time have interfered—much too long—with correspondence. The good time I had with you and Tom at 107, and with you at Palisades, has remained an oasis in a wilderness of worries and preoccupations. So please do not think that these things are forgotten—these unforgettable moments of friendship and intimate contact. Life for me has been hard these intervening months. U.N.O. gave me a bad blow, which has had its reactions in South Africa also, and my worries have been greater than usual. I can fairly say that these years of post-war peace have been in many ways a heavier burden for me to carry than the war years themselves. War is a great stimulus, and an effective answer to your opponents. Now we are back in the old pulls and divided counsels and the world of small things—and life is much more of a burden than ever before. What a blessed release it was for your *bête noire* Roosevelt to go just when he did! What good luck Winston had when an unconsidering electorate sent him about his business! But for me no such luck. I think I am now the only one of the old gang, indeed of the older gang before the most recent, still to carry on, and still to be called to account for my sins and for the greater sins of others. U.N.O. gave me my first great knock and since then others have found courage and opportunity to administer theirs also. And so it goes on and will go on to the end—which in the ordinary course can now not be far off. I regret all this—I would so love to leave no loose ends hanging about and leave our estate in good ship shape for those who will follow me. But I suppose this is too much to hope for or to expect in all fairness.

U.N.O. has been a grave disappointment to me—not only personally, but from the larger viewpoint which we have at heart. Our primary intention was to provide for world security against war. But look at the Security Council and its sorry antics! Even our old League did better. It managed world affairs with decency and fair success for ten years and only thereafter was struck by the Hitler blitz, which proved too much for it. The U.N.O. in its security arrangements is moving all wrong from the very start, and the international situation is more clouded and uncertain than ever before.

Then again U.N.O. has prematurely started on an enterprise which looks very much like world government and world reform in all directions—a task for which it is hopelessly unfitted. It is interfering with domestic affairs of other countries, which must make the already difficult task of government in an unsettled world more difficult than ever. I can only judge from its influence on government in South Africa. After all we have been a well-ordered, well-governed state; but the influence of U.N.O. policies has been profoundly disturbing and upsetting. Countries which cannot govern themselves now sit in judgment on others who have done their job fairly well in spite of all sorts of difficulties. A new machine of a most elaborate and costly character is being set going, and who is to pay for it? Few countries paid their subscriptions to the League; who will pay for the much heavier burdens of U.N.O.? All these things cause me grave anxiety. And behind it all is the far larger issue of world peace which continues to be as precarious as ever before in a world more dangerous than ever.

I have no doubt that we shall somehow pull through these dangerous times, but I wonder whether the present set-up of U.N.O. is such as to fit it for this task. Democracy without leadership is a sham, and U.N.O. seems to me a democracy without leadership, or with a leadership so divided that it is ineffective for all practical purposes. It may be that we shall soon have to face a thorough revision of the present set-up, and have something more modest, but more real and effective than this general Aeropagus[1] or talking shop, in which the incompetents and misfits rule by counting of heads.

This is my grouse and my deep doubt about U.N.O. With the United States and the Soviet Union facing each other across the world, with Europe still sinking and its leadership derelict, with Britain struck to its foundations, the world is today in a precarious and dangerous position such as has not existed since the fall of Rome. I cannot see U.N.O. leading us out of this fateful situation. This is what troubles me. Tell me what you and Tom think about it. Give me some comfort if you can.

I was so pleased to see the magnificent donation Tom had made for the restoration of Canterbury Cathedral.[2] What a gesture of American sympathy and good will! I am also pleased to see that President Truman is moving to the financial support and security

[1] *See* vol. IV, p. 21, note 1.

[2] Thomas W. Lamont had made a donation of 500,000 dollars.

of Greece and Turkey, especially the former.[1] That is at present the weakest link in our Western line of defence; if it goes the Bolshevik wave may roll over all Europe—and what will remain of the free world! Science with its inventions and the resulting aggregation of world power have created a situation of unparalleled menace for the free human spirit, and as things now are America is our best hope of stemming the flowing tide of universal despotism. The forces of good will remain but they are unorganized and impotent in the face of the new dangers.

Here at home we are happy and all goes well. The family is flourishing and all are hard at work. Isie has to keep quiet after her exhausting war labours, but is otherwise well. The two sons are very busy in the mines, the daughters in their family life. The visit of the royal family has been a great joy to South Africa, and their graciousness and kindliness have won all hearts. We sorrow for Britain in her sorrows and distresses. We sorrow for the world. And we are all the more grateful for this piece of good earth where the sun shines and the people as a whole are happy in spite of U.N.O. strictures and carpings.

All send their warm love and good wishes to you and Tom and the children and the grandchildren. We hope and pray for Tom's health and strength. And my heart remains full of affection for the dear circle at 107. God bless you all. Ever yours affectionately,

J. C. Smuts

746 From L. S. Amery — Vol. 81, no. 17

112 Eaton Square
S.W.1
9 April 1947

My dear Oubaas, I seem to have taken my Near Eastern tour a little too strenuously on top of much previous work and have been ordered a month's rest. The result is that I have been able to read some of the books that have been waiting on my desk for some time past. One of these is Crafford's life of yourself.[2] I was amused to find in it an account of our first meeting in President Kruger's room in September 1899, though he only refers to me as a press correspondent. I wonder how he got hold of the story.

He makes a great deal of the connection between your political and your philosophic outlook, but, if I may say so, misses the real point of holism. My long lost copy of your work has turned

[1] *See supra*, p. 128, note 1. [2] *See* vol. VI, p. 489, note 1.

up again and I rather think I shall refresh my mind with it during these weeks of recreation. Meanwhile my conception of your idea is not that holism means simply striving for greater wholes as such, but that a 'whole' is something complete and balanced in itself. When it lacks that balance it has to make it up by the creation of a larger whole. A salt crystal is perfectly content to remain a simple cube *ad infinitum*. A complex mass of organic matter is always in a state of unbalance and therefore requires to bring in extraneous matter, whether by absorption or combination, in order to keep going. The spider with web and poison fang has constructed a whole of its own, i.e. a cycle of life which can go on indefinitely so long as there are flies. Man, with stick and stone, books and what not, is continually unbalancing life and creating complex wholes outside himself.

So, too, in politics. The Transvaal of the Voortrekkers was a whole which might have continued for generations, but for the gold-mines and the flooding in of new population. That created an unbalanced situation which only the Union of South Africa could remedy. Even the Union was psychologically unbalanced so long as the British element could not give a whole-hearted allegiance to South Africa except as part of the British Empire and so long as the Dutch element resented being in the Empire because it seemed to involve subordination. The answer was the Commonwealth, i.e. unity based on free co-operation.

There was a case of a satisfactory whole being created, not by physical enlargement, but by a new conception. The trouble with both the League of Nations and with U.N.O. has been that the only unifying conception, viz. that of peace, has not appealed nearly enough to the interests and instincts of sovereign nations. I know you wished from the outset to have made the League a more positive thing, and it seemed easier in those days when the victors of the First World War lived, ideologically, on more or less the same plane. Today the rift in conceptions is far too deep, I fear, to make U.N.O. in any sense a whole and I think we must concentrate on creating, by the co-operation of the British Commonwealth and a United Europe, an intermediate whole between the antagonistic Russian and American wholes, in order to preserve the peace of our generation and lead up to some greater whole in the future.

Meanwhile the Americans are moving pretty solidly in the direction of a world clearly divided into two antagonistic halves and of their own duty to maintain the free half by war if necessary. I don't know whether you have ever read James Burnham's very suggestive work *The Managerial Revolution*.[1] Recently he has produced a book called *The World Struggle*, exaggerated perhaps but full of insight, in which he takes the view that the world cannot be united in order to preserve peace on any basis of voluntary coalescence, but only on the basis of what he calls empire, i.e. the domination of one supremely strong power, in other words the United States, with the British Commonwealth as junior partner. This, said with greater moderation, but with a very sound technical analysis of the problems of war is also the theme of George Fielding Elliot's latest book *Meeting the Danger*. We may come to that, though I still hope that the middle term Commonwealth plus Europe may mitigate the danger of a head-on collision. Also I am by no means sure that if world government is to be built round a single nucleus our Commonwealth isn't more suitable. For one thing its structure is so flexible that the United States could join it tomorrow with some provision for interchangeable citizenship and regular consultation, whereas the federal structure of the United States could not even absorb Canada without destroying its nationality. Our geographical distribution is also in our favour as, in a world developing regionally, we are already in every region. That is one of the reasons why I still somehow hope that India and Burma will remain in the Commonwealth orbit even if they call themselves independent.

I think you know the new king and queen of Greece intimately. I saw something of them in Athens and was impressed both by his commonsense and by her vivacious charm, intelligence and courage. They ought to make a success of the monarchy if anybody can. I am glad to see that the Americans have requested our service missions to stay on. The Greeks would have been most unhappy if they had gone and been replaced by American missions. On the other hand I fancy the Americans will take pretty complete control of the economic situation and bring Greece into the dollar area.

Here at home the collapse of the government in face of the revolt over national service[2] is, I fear, a serious blow to Bevin and will be looked upon in America as a running away from the obligations of partnership. The only sensible answer now in order to meet our oversea commitments is to build up quickly the largest possible foreign legion of Poles, Yugoslavs and others.

[1] First published in 1941.

[2] Under the National Service Bill all men between eighteen and twenty-six were to be liable for eighteen months' full-time service. At the second reading some of their supporters voted against the government which then proposed to reduce the period of service. The act, which became law in July 1947, required a period of service of twelve months.

In that connection it seems as if nothing had been thought out as to what is to be done with the 750,000 displaced persons when U.N.R.R.A. comes to an end. To hand them over to their countries of origin would in most cases be condemning them to death. This would be bad enough in itself, but made doubly worse by the fact that most of these people are our friends and will be murdered for that very reason. An unpleasant world. Yours ever,

Leo Amery

747 From C. Weizmann — Vol. 84, no. 254

Weizmann House
Rehovot
Palestine
22 April 1947

My dear General, In a few days' time the general assembly of the U.N.O. will meet at Lake Success,[1] and although I am not now on active service,[2] I feel impelled to write you a few lines on what may well be a fateful turn in our affairs.

I need hardly tell you much about conditions here; I am told that Palestine has become headline news for the English-speaking world. It is a sad distinction not of our making. One of the finest efforts of reconstruction—political, economic and psychological—which our generation has seen is being dragged into the mire of violence. All the evil consequences which Churchill and the leaders of the present government foresaw when the White Paper was enacted in 1939[3] have come true. There is no rule of law in Palestine any more; draconic emergency regulations have been enacted which vest the power over life and death in the hands of military courts not governed by judicial rules of evidence. The appeal to the civil courts and the privy council have now also been abolished. This week, four young Jews were hanged, three of them merely for the possession of arms, no charge of homicide having been preferred against them. The executions were carried out in the dead of the night. Last night two young men have blown themselves up in the condemned cell and in that way have cheated the hangman. I need hardly tell you what all this means to a community for which life has now become so precious a thing, and

[1] The British government had asked for a special session of the assembly on Palestine. This was to meet on 9 May.

[2] Weizmann had ceased to be president of the World Zionist Organization in 1946 when he was not re-elected to a position which he had held since 1935.

[3] *See* vol. VI, p. 161, note 1.

which abhors death sentences from times immemorial. Everybody now lives in trembling of what the terrorists may next do by way of retaliation, and what the authorities may then do by way of further retaliation. It is the old vicious circle from which the common man who has come here to build and not to destroy—and he forms the bulk of the community—suffers.

No one knows what U.N.O. will do. I am none too happy about the decision of the British government to refer this complex and tortuous issue to so vast an assembly of such diversified and frequently contending interests. The best that one can hope for is that they may set up a really neutral and unprejudiced fact-finding commission with instructions to prepare fully elaborated and not merely general proposals for a final solution to be considered at the September meeting of the United Nations.

The second thing for which we urgently hope, and which I regard as vital, is that a satisfactory interim scheme of administration be adopted providing for a substantial increase of the monthly immigration quota and rescission of the ruinous land regulations. Something must be done immediately to relieve the unbearable strain on the Jewish refugees in Europe, and the psychological strain which their prolonged detention in central Europe is exerting on the Jewish community here. Unless this is done, there is hardly any prospect of stopping the trend to despair and violence from which terrorism springs. You can have no idea what each boat-load of what are called 'illegal immigrants' and their forcible expulsion to Cyprus means. I am convinced that if the immigration quota were increased to, say, three to four thousand a month, the sad chapter of these boats with all their tragic attending circumstances would be speedily liquidated. We could then start again a properly ordered immigration, giving certificates as in former years to men and women who have gone through a sound agricultural or industrial training. As things are at present the most highly qualified men cannot reach Palestine except on one of these 'illegal boats' for the simple reason that no legal certificates are available for distribution. This is bad all round. The country is urgently in need of working hands both in agriculture and industry. In Europe the men and women who could meet that need, and in doing so rebuild their own shattered lives, are rotting in the areas of the dread concentration camps.

I am taking the liberty of writing at such length on this subject because it holds in my opinion the key to the solution of the present impasse. In spite of all that has happened during the past two tragic years, the Jewish community is still—as it always was

—an essentially constructive force. If the creeping paralysis which has entered the life of the country under the dispensation of the White Paper is stopped, then I am firmly convinced the future of this great effort, on which you built such high hopes and which you have helped so much to advance, is assured.

I send you and your family my affectionate regards and remain with best wishes in which Mrs Weizmann joins me, Yours,

Ch. Weizmann

748 To D. Moore Vol. 84, no. 50

Groote Schuur
[Cape Town]
18 May 1947

My dear Daphne, Sunday morning in my upstairs study. The sun shines bright, pouring into the room after a cold night, and I love to write to you in this benign warmth. I am all alone in the house and have been so since my return from the golden anniversary[1] at home. It was all a most happy family affair, with children and grandchildren all about the house, and giving great joy to the grandparents. Isie was in fine form, especially as there was not much public about...

Thank you for two letters which have arrived since I last wrote to you. It is a joy getting your letters and seeing how you are getting on and what is happening to your world. It does not look as if Dominion status is near, but safeguards for our internal communications *must* be agreed to in advance. From that point of view Ceylon is even more important than India. I shall be happy to see Henry [Moore] governor-general, but that is a small matter where the future of our Commonwealth is concerned. Henry must do all he can to get his men to guarantee our sea, air, and land communications. The rest really does not matter much, though I fear Ceylon will be a much misgoverned Dominion.

In India too things are going from bad to worse. Now that India is visibly breaking up many responsible Indians will become doubtful whether Britain should really quit, and would probably plump for the British connection if the choice was given them. I think Mountbatten's flight to London[2] may possibly have something to

[1] The golden wedding of Smuts and his wife had been celebrated some days after the proper date, 30 April, because of his parliamentary duties.

[2] He had gone to London to advise the British government that their plan to maintain the political unity of India could not be applied and to seek an alternative.

do with the new fears arising in a fateful situation. What is now happening in Punjab, Behar and Bengal[1] will tomorrow happen all over India as the mirage of independence becomes a nightmare. Poor India. Poor East, which has been asleep these thousands of years and is now having such a rude awakening. Meanwhile Nehru is keeping bombarding me with his silly correspondence and mouthing his broken agreements and human rights. At least we know how to run a country decently and in orderly fashion which Indians have never been able to do without the Raj.

Freddy[2] writes in high spirits now that the American loan to Greece has passed congress. It must be due largely to [General G.C.] Marshall who in Europe and in China has convinced himself of the inwardness of Russian designs. I see Marshall's hand in much of the new firmer policy of America. He and Eisenhower were the two great finds of Roosevelt, and both of them are making a great mark in world policies. They realize what the decline of Britain means to the world—Britain who in two world wars had to bear the brunt of the desperate struggle in its most fateful phases and is now paying the penalty.

The royal visit has had a great effect not only here but also in Britain and the Commonwealth and the world. The old show is after all not so rickety as its critics had thought. The king's speech at the Guild Hall[3] struck a new note of faith and courage which he must have derived from his South African experience. It has all been a great affair for the royal family and all they stand for. I also get some shine from reflected glory!

Dear child, we miss you here. I wonder whether we have spoiled you more than you have spoilt us. I suppose it is a mutual infection. I still have my walks, and yesterday, alone with my policeman, I had one of the best in nice cold weather. Winter is on us and the nights are cold and the days often rainy. But it is still South Africa, full of politics, full of good things, and never knuckling under. My love to you and Henry. Ever yours,

J.C.S.

[1] The Hindu–Muslim clashes which began in Calcutta (*see supra*, p. 86, note 4) spread to Behar, Bengal and the Punjab.

[2] Queen Frederica of Greece.

[3] Smuts had written the greater part of the speech (*see* Smuts Collection, vol. 84, no. 49).

749 To C. Weizmann Vol. 84, no. 56

Cape Town
29 May 1947

My dear Doctor, Your letter of 22 April[1] reached me here last week. What a sad letter, and what a sadder situation it sketches! I can imagine your anguish in a world which was so full of hope, and today has nothing but despair to show for itself.

We cannot undo the past, and can only try to find a better way to the future. As I told you in London last year I see now, at this sad stage, no escape except by way of partition. I was long for an undivided Palestine, but after all these failures and missed opportunities I see no other way out of the present impasse. Only yesterday, speaking in our parliament, I expressed myself publicly in favour of this solution—if solution it is. Palestine never was undivided in the great past, and perhaps a fair share of it for Jewry may once more be the nucleus of a national home and a Holy Land. Now that a U.N.O. commission has been appointed[2] to assemble the facts and search for recommendations my expression of opinion, as one of the original authors of the Balfour declaration, may carry some weight with the commission. At any rate it is something concrete and definite, and not another and further postponement of a decision which can brook no further delay.

It must be a heartbreaking misery for you to live amid all that scene of frustration and suffering—of lawlessness and counter lawlessness. You who have laboured so hard and so long to enter upon the Promise. I can only hope that you are keeping in fair health and spirit.

I send you and Mrs Weizmann my very warm wishes for your welfare and my ardent hope that at last the end of all this misery has come, and a new beginning will soon be made as a result of this inquiry.

I blame no one, I praise no one. I only pray that the great Mercy will once more come, and wash out even the memory of these years.

With all my heart's good wishes for both of you and the hope we share in common, Ever yours affectionately,

s. J. C. Smuts

[1] 747.

[2] A special session of the general assembly resulted in the appointment of the United Nations Special Committee on Palestine (Unscop). On 1 September 1947 they produced a 'fantastic partition scheme' (*see* C. Sykes, *Cross Roads to Israel*, Mentor edition 1967, p. 335).

750 To D. Moore — Vol. 84, no. 57

Groote Schuur
[Cape Town]
1 June 1947

My dear Daphne, Your amusing and interesting letters arrive regularly and bring a sense of glow and comfort. Thank you. I fear the same cannot be said of my erratic correspondence. But you are an understanding creature and will make allowance for a most oppressed soul, who is overwhelmed with work of all kinds and has to give to the public what is due to his friends! These last weeks of parliament have absorbed most of my time, and my correspondence is much in arrear. I look forward every day to the coming of night when sleep cancels out all. As you know I am —unlike you—a fair sleeper, and six hours of sleep generally sets me up for the following day and all it may bring. But heavy arrears of work or correspondence trouble me and almost prey on my mind...

I was concerned to hear on the radio last night of the general strike which has befallen Ceylon. It must be an awkward and bad business. The last general strike I had here was in 1922 when I called up the commandos and forcibly suppressed the Bolshevik business. But as you know I was punished at the following general election and did not again become prime minister till fifteen years later, when I was almost in my dotage. What punishment for having done one's duty only and for saving the country from disaster! That is the pretty wage of democracy, and I am a democrat. Henry [Moore] is only a public servant and cannot adopt such ruthless tactics, and I fear the general interest will suffer badly. Still, the country wants to be a Dominion, and must have its experience of how to run and save itself. Our slogans and shibboleths will not save or help us, and a hard lesson has to be learnt by those who aspire to be free and govern themselves.

When this reaches you we shall have heard how Mountbatten's message to the Indian leaders[1] has been received, and what they are going to do about it. India is in a terrible dilemma. It can only be free and independent as a much partitioned India; and even then it faces anarchy unless it maintains the British connection instead of becoming a series of independent republics fighting each other. And Britain is so sick of the business and so anxious *not* to be mixed up with the bloodshed and confusion which

[1] On 3 June, after a meeting with the Indian leaders, the viceroy announced that the ruling power in India would be transferred to two new Dominions, India and Pakistan, by about 15 August.

appears almost inevitable. A partitioned India will probably think it safe to remain in the Commonwealth and so secure the support of some outside power. But one never knows what silly politicians may do in a crisis. Perhaps we shall know before you read this. Mountbatten seems to have handled the situation much better than his predecessor[1] whom nobody heard or understood. Nehru and I still continue at loggerheads, but I cannot say that this has caused me sleepless nights. The Indians here are becoming seriously divided, and some now think the intervention of New Delhi was a bad blunder—a blunder which they themselves gave the original impetus to.[2]

We shall wind up the session this week, and in fact it is only certain final measures that remain over. The benches are getting empty and whips are hard put to it to keep a quorum. I hope to be at Doornkloof for next week-end. The Gilletts are slowly moving north and will take some weeks longer to arrive there. Then I shall have to take a hand in the political game which is livening up, with a general election coming next year. The opposition is elated with their Hottentot's Holland victory[3] and the general dislike of controls and shortages and all the post-war muddles and grievances. Our conditions are perhaps the most satisfactory in the whole world, but the heart minds its own troubles without bothering about the greater troubles of others. And so a great struggle lies ahead, and I shall have to take a hand in it, although I know there are bigger and more troublesome problems elsewhere. This is the way of democracy; which is a school for people to learn the hard lesson of self-government. Their mistakes are part of this schooling, and must therefore be accepted as inevitable. South Africa has, however, so often been right at critical moments that one should not mind smaller incidental mistakes too much. Still I am most anxious to win and not to lose the next election!... Ever yours,

J.C.S.

[1] Lord Wavell.

[2] At the conference of the South African Indian Congress in Cape Town a unanimous resolution was adopted on 12 February 1946 to send a deputation to the government of India to urge it to take diplomatic and, if necessary, economic action against South Africa.

[3] *See supra*, p. 117, note 3.

751 From L. S. Amery Vol. 81, no. 18

112 Eaton Square
S.W.1
6 June 1947

My dear Ou Baas,[1] Mountbatten may have pulled off a big thing. It was his own idea making India, whether divided or single, independent first and let it work out constitutional details later and this time the cabinet accepted it and even Winston has blessed it. When I advocated that sequence during the war, to be done on V. J. Day[2] as a gesture, not only my Conservative colleagues, but Cripps and Attlee, were horrified and the most I was allowed to do was to assure all but Dominion status for the interim government which Wavell tried to form and all but succeeded in forming in June 1945.

What is really important now is to get the Indians to realize that a partitioned India can still maintain unity on Commonwealth lines, i.e. maintaining a common citizenship, a regular standing conference etc.—the system, in fact, which we all agreed on in 1918 but which was allowed to fade away so sadly in the reaction of the post-war years. Meanwhile I am still not altogether sure that, face to face with the complications of partition, some sort of structural unity may not still be patched up.

All my gloomy prophecies as to what will face us when the American loan[3] runs out next year look like being more than fulfilled. The government are very frightened but daren't go beyond exhortation. A wages policy that might attract men into the coal-mines is vetoed by the powerful Transport and General Workers Union. A trade policy is vetoed by our pledges to America from which we shall only be released when Geneva proves a failure. What with America's 100 per cent preference to and in the Philippines, the escape clause which makes every American concession almost worthless, and now the threat to raise the wool tariff directly or indirectly, it doesn't look as if there can now be any question of preference being eliminated or even of our agreeing not to increase it. In any case I believe you in South Africa, as well as producers in every other Dominion, colony or non-dollar country, will be justified in preparing now to increase your output of consumable goods to the utmost that labour and equipment will permit.

Winston is going into hospital for three weeks or so for a slight

[1] Smuts was called the *Oubaas*, literally Old Master, by the members of his family.

[2] The day of victory over Japan, that is, 14 August 1945.

[3] *See supra*, p. 5, note 3.

operation, but has every intention to be ready to go over to Paris for a United Europe demonstration about 17 July and I shall probably go over too. I think the idea is really catching hold in Europe, but it will be a matter of a good many years. Meanwhile your old friend Bela Kun's[1] successors look like jumping the chain in Hungary with Russian help.[2] Palestine is a tragic mess, but Indian partition may possibly give a lead to the only solution there. Yours ever,

Leo Amery

752 To R. Kotze Vol. 84, no. 75

Prime Minister's Office
Pretoria
13 June 1947

My dear Kotze, I have read your *Scheme of Things*[3] with deep interest, and now write a few lines to give you my impression of it as a whole.

Your scheme is dominated by the concept of reincarnation, and in fact, the scheme stands or falls by the validity of that concept. I shall mainly confine my remarks to it.

But before doing so, I wish to compliment you on the lucidity and directness with which you have expressed your ideas, and the skill with which the argument is set out. There is little circumlocution and the reasoning is on the whole clear and logical. In certain chapters the material of other chapters is repeated to some extent, and I infer that this must be due to your having worked on some earlier draft which has left its traces in the final form. I do not say this by way of criticism, but just by the way.

I find your use of the concept of the group soul very suggestive. Your application of it to the human soul or psyche is interesting, and I am inclined to think that much more can be made of it than you have done. This also by the way! Your main object seems to be to explore the reincarnation concept, and you have therefore treated the group soul as a minor element in your argument.

Now for your use of 'reincarnation'. I must frankly confess that

[1] *See* vol. IV, p. 346.

[2] Elections in November 1945 had put the Smallholders' party, under Nagy, into power and made Hungary a democratic republic. In May 1946 two Communist ministers, Rákosi and Rajk, supported by the Soviet commander, General Sviridov, and his forces, succeeded in weakening the ruling party and reconstructing the government.

[3] Published in 1949.

the concept does not appeal to me, nor could it be expected to make any wide popular appeal. Historically it is a discarded idea, coming from the East, used by Plato to explain immortality and memory, even taken up by the early Christian Church, but finally abandoned and now more of an historical curiosity.

It is not a substitute for the Christian idea of immortality, as Paul has expounded it in 1 *Corinthians* 15, and cannot satisfy the deep longing for personal immortality which forms such a powerful appeal in Christianity. This transfer of the psyche from person to person, in which the psyche gains richer experience in an unending series of lives, makes no appeal to the individual at all. It does not satisfy 'my' sense of identity to learn that it has been the identity of A B C D and an infinite series of other unknowns. It is not mine, and has no sense or value for me. The notion of 'me' and 'mine' is quite unique, and only suffers by confusion or merger with the 'me' and 'mine' of other people through long time. It can never take the place of real individual personal identity and immortality, and one can understand why it has made no appeal to the common man of a religious bent of mind.

Nor is it a substitute for the scientific concept of evolution. In fact there is nothing in biological evolution, as scientifically understood, which warrants this flitting about of the psyche or entelechy from person to person. Genes are transmitted and produce the inheritable qualities of the scientific biologist, but whole psyches or entelechies are not thus transmitted. Your reincarnation concept must therefore appear strange and experimentally unfounded and far-fetched to the orthodox scientist.

I also have the suspicion that your ideas must inevitably lead to a weakening of the sense of personal responsibility, and therefore in the long run be harmful to the community. How can 'I' be held responsible for my actions when this 'I' was transmitted to me as the 'I' of other persons unknown to me? If the person's 'I', now in me, was a liar or a cheat, why should I be responsible for his operations in me? This reincarnated 'I' of yours is so different from the usual 'I' which is my own, my only and deepest self, that I may become indifferent about the whole matter, and tend to lose all sense of direct personal responsibility for my actions, which are on analysis found to be the actions of somebody else, or many other somebodies in me. I do not know whether I make my meaning clear, but I do sense a real difference between an 'I' and a reincarnated 'I' for whom I may be tempted to disclaim responsibility.

I raise this point because it seems to me important, and specially important in these times when there seems to be a lessened sense of personal obligation and responsibility. People are so dominated by social concepts, and are so prone to pass their shortcomings on to their society or environment, that a strong prop and support of the moral life is weakened. The sense of 'sin' has already largely disappeared, and even the more general sense of duty, obligation and responsibility is seriously weakened. People clamour only for their 'rights' and forget their duties, and a lopsided social ethical outlook is one of the weaknesses from which our society is suffering today.

This may appear a far-fetched objection to you, but it is well worth bearing in mind.

You have asked for my objective view, and here I give you my reactions to your use of the concept of reincarnation. And I hope you will not mind the directness with which I have stated my reactions. I much enjoyed reading your book, but I believe its fundamental thesis is unsound, and probably mischievous!

I think much of the concept of incarnation—of the interpretation of the divine and the human—as it is incorporated in Christianity and other mystical religions. But your idea of reincarnation of human psyches as a sort of perpetual if not eternal process, is something quite different, and makes no religious, scientific, or personal appeal or sense to me.

I return your typescript to the Rand Club. Ever yours,

J. C. Smuts

753 To G. Huggins — Vol. 84, no. 74

Pretoria
13 June 1947

My dear Huggins, I have already congratulated you on the high honour of P.C., and think it more than justified by your long and distinguished services as prime minister and your more special defence service in the recent war.

I also acknowledge your letter of 6 June enclosing copy of your important letter to Attlee.[1] Incidentally I agree with you in being doubtful about U.N.O. and in holding that we had better look to our own defences until we feel more confidence in U.N.O.

But you will allow me to say that I do not fully appreciate the argument you use in your letter to Attlee. Your letter seems to be a plea for a common authority to be responsible for the defence of the Commonwealth as a whole. You say that such an authority

[1] Not in the Smuts Collection.

was not established in 1926, when virtual independence was given the Dominions, nor has it been established since, with the result that the Dominions settle their own foreign policies and defence, and rely for Empire defence as a whole on the United Kingdom government.

In this matter there are two questions—common defence and common foreign policy. I think I state the position fairly as follows.

There never has been a common defence authority since 1926, nor is it possible with Dominion status to have such an authority. It would derogate from that status to give such authority to the United Kingdom government, and the alternative would be a super government over the whole Commonwealth, which would be equally impracticable. Neither alternatives would be agreed to by the Dominions. That frankly is the constitutional position on which we have based our practice for the last twenty years.

That practice has been for the Dominions to agree, at conferences or individually, with the United Kingdom government as to the form and size of their own defences which the Dominions can make, and any additional forces they can contribute towards general defence in an emergency. The defence services and the imperial defence committee consult with the Dominions and advise them on technical aspects of their defences. At present there is close liaison between the imperial and the Dominion defence services which is most useful all round. There are no fixed treaty obligations but there is a system of voluntary understanding and consultation about defence matters which has worked well, and under which the Dominions have made their maximum possible war effort. The Dominion contribution to their own and to general defence has been increasing all the time, but the main burden has been borne by the United Kingdom.

In future the United Kingdom may not be able to do as much as it has done hitherto, and the Dominions will be able to and will do more. There is no common defence authority with overall responsibility, but there is something better in the system of consultation, liaison, and maximum voluntary effort by the Dominions. The system works in the same practical empirical way in which the British constitution and the Dominion constitutions work.

There has always been a group in London and elsewhere who have insisted on closer, more water-tight defence and foreign policy arrangements. I don't think they are feasible, and even if they were, they will not produce better results than the existing system produced. So why worry about a central Commonwealth authority?

These matters were again discussed fairly fully at the Commonwealth conference last year, and in substance the existing policy was reaffirmed.

Of course, if the changed circumstances since the last war call for substantial changes in the defence and strategical situations, we shall meet again and discuss them in connection with Commonwealth defence as a whole. But I do not think the concept of a central authority will prove helpful in our consultations, and it may only be the occasion for unfruitful wrangling and unsettlement.

Such is my view and I believe the Canadian view also. I cannot speak for Australia and New Zealand whose approach I do not always understand clearly. Ever yours sincerely,

J. C. Smuts

754 To D. Moore — Vol. 84, no. 76

Doornkloof
[Transvaal]
14 June 1947

My dear Daphne, Your letters are most interesting, but in spite of that all the news from Ceylon continues bad. What bad luck for Henry and you that you have struck such snags just at this time, when the prospect of higher status should have put everybody in a good humour. But humour is lacking in the outlook of the Ceylonese, and good humour is even more lacking. The conditions for Dominion status as now laid down in London could and should easily be agreed to, but I wonder whether the people are really capable of running their own affairs. It is of course possible that they may be so frightened by what is now happening that they may wisely decide to stick to Henry as governor-general instead of nominating one of their own men.

India is now definitely being partitioned but the working of the mechanism of partition is probably beyond them. Still, rather what has happened and Dominion status being accepted, even if temporarily, than an immediate cutting of the painter, with fatal results.

The correspondence between Nehru and me over Indian grievances here continues. I don't expect any immediate results, and U.N.O. will probably have another opportunity of demonstrating its incompetence for world government which some so fondly expect from it. Even so I have enough trouble on my hands, and solutions are made more difficult by a general election next year, the prospect of which prevents clear-cut solutions even if they were otherwise possible. I doubt whether I shall be able to go to U.N.O. this year or indeed anywhere else abroad, when an election campaign has in fact already been started by my opposition. I may have to confine my travels to this subcontinent—South West Africa, the Congo (to meet Prince Regent Charles) and similar African trips will probably be all I could contemplate. My heart is not in this business, and sometimes I feel [that I am] wasting my time on trifles. But at present I see no way out of my troubles, not at least before a general election has been held and the country has decided on its future government.

I have mentioned India and Ceylon; but Burma, now also talking of independence, is probably as bad as either of them. The Burmese will probably prove as incompetent and unreliable in peace as they have proved in war.

By the way, the Supremo[1] is proving himself an adept political negotiator and a great improvement on Wavell. If he liquidates the British Empire successfully in India his stock will rise very high, and he may yet play a great part in Britain. His debonair ways and nonchalant attitude must be helpful in the grim situation with which he has to deal. 'Grim but gay' is Winston's phrase, and it may apply here.

Marshall's offer of lease–lend to a bankrupt Europe, if only it will work out a common economic plan, is a very great move. If successful it may be the first step to a Council of Europe such as Churchill has propagandized. But what about the East–West shadow and the Iron Curtain which darkens the European scene? I am deeply interested in these developments which are far more important than all the other questions in international life today.

Freddie[2] writes to me in a very subdued vein. She is attempting so much and working so hard but nothing happens. She feels sad and frustrated. I have counselled patience and cool courage. At any rate she is gathering her experience and enriching her own life. What after all is life but experience? We start with nothing and shall end with nothing, but in the meantime we learn our lesson and build up our character and personality. 'This world is the valley of soul-making', Keats said[3] when he was dying of T.B., and the human soul is the greatest thing in the universe. To this soul-building defeat is often just as valuable and essential as success and victory. I believe in Plato's saying that time is but the moving finger of eternity.[4] In all these temporal events and experiences

[1] Lord Mountbatten. [2] Queen Frederica of Greece.

[3] *See* vol. v, p. 32, note 4.

[4] 'Time was created as an image of eternity.' Diogenes Laertius, *Plato*, book III, sec. 73.

eternity is present and is the meaning and reality of it all. And the soul is the element of the eternal in us. Temporary success must not be overvalued.

All this you have learnt in your life which contains perhaps more defeat and frustration than success. So we pass through our school of life. But I admit it is often a very hard school. And Freddie is also learning her lesson. Ever yours,

J. C. S.

755 To Jawaharlal Nehru — Vol. 84, no. 78

The document in the Smuts Collection is a draft in Smuts's handwriting.

16 June 1947

Dear Pandit Nehru, The answer to your letter of 7 May 1946[1] has been delayed as at the time of its receipt and subsequently conversations between the government and groups of South African Indians were going on in connection with Indian questions. These groups, representing all classes of Indians in the various provinces, were dissatisfied with the conduct of their affairs by the Natal Indian Congress, whose leadership was under idealogical influences of which they disapproved and whose approach they considered harmful to Indian interests. They had consequently separated from the Natal Indian Congress and formed themselves into a new organization,[2] determined to make a new and more conciliatory approach to the government for the remedy of Indian grievances.

The government were quite willing to discuss their problems with them, and in the result a number of matters could be cleaned up. These conversations covered such matters as land areas set aside for Indians, or open to Indian acquisition under the Asiatic Land Tenure Act of 1946,[3] education, health, amenities generally for the Indian community in Durban, trading licences and inter-provincial movements. Some of these matters could be definitely settled and others were reserved for further consideration after consultation with the local authorities concerned. These Indian representatives of the new organization were rightly of the opinion

[1] Not in the Smuts Collection.

[2] The Natal Indian Organization, formed in the latter part of 1946 with A. S. Kajee as president. Its policy was that of A. I. Kajee (q.v.) but he remained outside it. It advocated negotiations between the South African and Indian governments, with representatives of the local Indians present, as against intervention by U.N.O.

[3] *See supra*, p. 36, note 1.

that a direct approach to their own government was the most hopeful method of achieving solutions of their problems.

They were, however, also deeply concerned that relations between the Union and India's governments should be regularized in their own interests, and put on a proper footing as soon as possible. They had been perturbed by reports that the Indian government had refused to send their high commissioner back to the Union, and both they and the South African Indian Congress had already made representations to the Indian government for the return of the high commissioner to the Union. They pressed the Union government very strongly not to feel rebuffed by the refusal of the Indian government, and to renew the request for his return. This the Union government promised to do, and we accordingly urge once more that the Indian high commissioner should be sent back in spite of the objections to such a course stated in your letter under reply.

I may point out that this is the proper course under international practice and under the circumstances connected with the departure of Mr Deshmukh. It was not a rupture of relations between the governments but simply a recall of the high commissioner to report to his government, while the office and the staff remained in function as before. His return to office after his long absence would therefore involve no question of prestige, and would enable the two governments to resume discussions in the usual way on the matters in issue. If the Indian government should regrettably be unwilling to do so, it would appear useless, if not improper, to devise other means of discussion. Technically we are on the footing of friendly governments, and the Union government are anxious to treat the Indian government on that footing.

You will allow me to point out that the Union government are under severe provocation to consider the attitude of the Indian government in this and in other respects less than friendly. The Indian government have severed trade relations with South Africa and unilaterally applied trade sanctions to the Union, to the great injury of South African interests, including those of its Indian inhabitants. It was, in fact, a hostile act, for which the Union government would have been justified to invoke the intervention of the Security Council. The Union government with great patience and forbearance refrained from doing so, preferring to look upon India as a fellow member of the British Commonwealth. In the same spirit the Union has favoured the rise of India to her full status of freedom and sovereignty in the most recent constitutional developments, and I have publicly welcomed this splendid achievement of Indian and British statesmanship, and wholeheartedly given it such blessing on behalf of South Africa as I can. Throughout this troubled period our attitude has been not only proper but indeed friendly, in spite of the difficult Indian problems which the Union has to face internally and the provocative attitude of the Indian government abroad. That friendly attitude we wish to maintain.

Under all these circumstances, and backed up by a considerable volume of responsible Indian opinion in South Africa, I can fairly claim that our relations should be normalized, and that the Indian high commissioner should be returned to his duties in the Union. I ask you to give serious consideration to our claim.

As you have sent copies of our previous correspondence to the secretary-general of the U.N.O., I follow for convenience sake the same course. Believe me, Yours faithfully,

[J. C. Smuts]

756 From M. E. Boyle[1] Vol. 81, no. 67

Witwatersrand University
[Johannesburg]
24 June 1947

My dear General Smuts, The Abbé asks me to tell you that he has just received a letter from Paris saying that Father Teilhard de Chardin has had a serious heart attack and that he will be unable to travel, so his journey to Africa can never take place. Father Teilhard was not well enough to write himself, though the immediate crisis is past, and there is hope of some betterment. His collapse is a great sorrow to the Abbé.

Now that Father Teilhard will not be here in July and August the Abbé would like to go to South West [Africa] in August before it is too hot. Professor van Riet Lowe has told the Abbé that he himself is too busy to go there this year, so the Abbé asks if you could arrange our transport and send word to the authorities. The Abbé would be very glad to have a little conversation with you, if you can spare the time. He thinks he would have about a month's work in South West and would be very glad to be accompanied by John Goodwin.

We had a most interesting trip of three weeks in Natal from which we returned on Sunday.

My apologies for giving your staff the bother of re-directing

[1] Secretary of the Abbé Breuil.

a letter to me. The two Frenchwomen who sent it probably thought that you controlled every detail of the administration, and that only you would know where I was.

The Abbé sends his most respectful and warmest regards, and so do I.

Mary E. Boyle

757 To F. Lamont Vol. 84, no. 99

Doornkloof
[Transvaal]
29 July 1947

Dear, dear Florence, What a lovely letter I had from you, and I have delayed so long in answering it. But I have read it several times and it has done me good. You are a cheerful, cheering spirit, and I conserved it as a cure for low spirits. Even those lines from Walter de la Mare ('Look thy last on all things lovely') which you quoted could not damp my spirits, although they express the very essence of sadness—the sadness of the last farewell. Thank you for that letter, and so much in it. Best of all was the good news about Tom's health. What a spirit he has, and it is his spirit that has pulled him right. I look upon his letter to the Archbishop of Canterbury, to whom he gave that magnificent gift for the restoration of the cathedral, as one of the finest things I have ever read. So good, so true, so finely expressed. One of my English friends told me that nothing has ever moved him so deeply as that letter.

And then you go down as Tom goes up. I do think you live too much on your reserves, and your blood pressure is only a solemn monitor of the risk you are running. You keep as lively as a cricket all the time and engage in a multiplicity of activities and interests beyond what you should really do. There is a rhythm of life, and it slows down as the years move on. Stick to that rhythm; it is foolish to force the pace. You warn me about climbing the mountains, although that is part of my religion. I warn you in return to moderate your American pace. I am glad that the English visit has done you good. And how much you saw in that brief ten days' visit! I never have your luck in these matters. My visits are generally connected with my political affairs, and so I see only the politicals who, as you know, are never the most interesting of people. Indeed, politicians are more to be pitied than most other sorts of people. *You* see the poets, the makers, the ardent spirits who walk with face toward the sun and the future. I see those who are occupied with the grievances, the frustrations, the things that go wrong and pull us wrong with them.

And how much does go wrong nowadays. I always look back to those bright Victorian years, the years of 'all things lovely' and the infinite hopes of that world of peace and optimism. And I was young and full of the ardour of thought. Life was 'all a wonder and a wild desire', to quote Browning.[1] And now? I do my best to be cheerful and to take a hopeful view of things. But what a world we have moved into! You saw the beauty of the English scene—'England's green and pleasant land'.[2] But what a different England it is from what we have known! O what a fall was there![3] To think of that land in decay, declining, unable to carry her burdens and hold her own in the world! I do not think people realize what a human set-back that is—how much it is a set-back for all the causes we have held and hold dear. Russia bestriding Europe—400 million people under her as de Gaulle has just said, and the British Empire breaking up, and Britain scarce able to feed herself and provide for her necessities. It sounds so much like Rome. And we know what followed the fall of Rome. It is a stout-hearted people and they will pull themselves together again. But in this moment of weakness how much will be lost, both for herself and mankind! And the position of Europe, civilized Western Europe, is even worse than that of Britain. Just at the moment in history when Asia is rampant and on the move and Europe has to be strong, she is down and out. Of course there is North America, and I thank God for her, for her good will, her spirit of humanity, her readiness to jump into the breach and save what can be saved. But for her the world scene would indeed be a dreary one. Marshall appeals to me as a greater man than I had thought, and he had done magnificently in wartime. America may once more produce the men, the man, and pull the world out of the pit. But you must not blame me because I am deeply concerned and feel that much, very much, is at stake for what is precious in our world. I do not expect much from U.N.O. I doubt whether it is the right set-up, and it is failing from the start—unlike the League which made at least an excellent beginning. But British and American co-operation may yet save the world—if only Britain were not so crippled in this vital hour!

I shall not attend the next U.N.O. meeting and shall therefore

[1] 'O lyric Love, half angel and half bird
And all a wonder and a wild desire.
Robert Browning, *The Ring and the Book*, book I, l. 1391.

[2] William Blake, *Milton*, preface.

[3] William Shakespeare, *Julius Caesar*, III.ii.[195].

not see you and Tom this year. This is another reason for sadness. But I must face a general election next year, a critical post-war election, and I dare not be away from South Africa at this time. So many things go inevitably wrong; there is a spirit of change about the world. All other governments have fallen in this post-war time—why should I not fall too? People get tired of you. Roosevelt told me that the people were getting tired of him even in the war, tired of his voice, his looks, his laugh and his fireside chats. Why should South Africa not have her change also? But what will that change mean for her? And so I must stick to my job, and miss seeing you.

Mind you, I am myself tired or getting tired. This job has been going on very long and without a break. And no holiday has sweetened the toil. So a kind fate may wish me well and have a last holiday for me in store. But I may not take it myself—it must be thrust on me!

No, I have just had a long week-end holiday—three days of it—in the Dongola game reserve in the northern Transvaal, which you have never seen. I prefer it to the Kruger game reserve. Three days of it with my Gillett friends. We saw heaps of game in the wildest, most eerie part of our bushveld. I tried to film a bull elephant at twenty yards and almost got trampled in the process. I saw a huge python a couple of feet away, staring with fixed, unblinking gaze at me! And so much besides. I climbed the Dongola mountain, and would have done more if there had been time. No, I had my holiday, but all too short, and not enough to make a lasting impression. The Gilletts continued on to the Victoria Falls and Northern Rhodesia, but I returned by air to the daily grind.

The family is well and Isie has written Tom all the home news I hope, so that I need not bore you with it. When I write about my work you must not think that is the whole story. There is home also—dear Doornkloof with its lovely home circle; there at nights the shadows of the day are chased away, and one can feel very near the great things of life—the things of our personal life which are so much nearer to us than the things which form the texture of our work. Here I sit tonight by the fire writing to you and hearing pleasant voices in the dining-room. What company could be better than this? After all it is these simple things of our intimate personal life that sweeten life and make up for all the irritations and frustrations that confront one in our public world. And here too I can meet the poets and the dreamers and the philosophers and all the happiness which comes through the companionship of books. And here too one can forget the world and dream the dreams which may yet come true when we are gone. Sometimes I think this dream world is our real world, the world of our inner life which means so much more than the public world in which we spend ourselves.

And would it not be happiness to get away with friends and intimates into the wilds, as we did years ago, and live the simple carefree life of the trees and the animals and of all things lovely? I fear our dream of east Africa can now never be realized, but still I love to think of it and to savour its sweetness even when I know it will never be. How good are the things we remember, the things which we imagine—even though we know they are but memories and imaginings! I think of 'Palisades', and our sitting on those benches and looking at that broad stretch of Hudson water, and a glow comes over me and a warming of the heart such as no worldly success could give.

Good-bye, dear friend. My love to you and Tom. Ever yours,

J. C. Smuts

758 To Chung-Shu Lo — Vol. 84, no. 101

Pretoria
29 July 1947

Dear Dr Chung-Shu Lo, I have your letter of 25 June with its two enclosures, and have read all with much interest. I would gladly have complied with your request to write some suggestions for U.N.E.S.C.O. in regard to the role of philosophy in the programme of U.N.E.S.C.O.'s activities. But I am so deeply and continuously engaged in my other public tasks at present that I can find no opportunity of accepting your kind invitation. I regret this all the more as I look upon U.N.E.S.C.O. as not the least important of the United Nations organs. In the intellectual, scientific, and cultural sphere there is immense scope for promoting our human advance, and much of the future of our race depends on the success of our efforts in this direction.

I find myself much in agreement with the general tenor of the address you gave at Lund,[1] and also with many of the suggestions you make at the end of your address. So far as the funds of U.N.E.S.C.O. will allow I hope that many of these suggested projects will, in time, and progressively, be carried out. Among them all I attach great value to the suggested anthology, which

[1] In Sweden.

would be the least expensive and probably the most immediately helpful as, so to say, a spiritual compass for mankind. The world does want a modern human 'Bible' today, a guide for spiritual direction and inspiration taken from all that is best in the spiritual thoughts and aspirations of our race, as expressed by the choice spirits of the nations in all ages. In its highest and noblest literary inspirations mankind will find a unifying factor of incalculable importance. With you I believe in the human race divine as a family, as an organic unity, and in the integration of the highest culture of the race in something like a new Bible, that organic unity will find its truest spiritual expression. In my book *Holism and Evolution*, written in 1924, I tried to explore the concept of the whole which I consider fundamental for science and philosophy and religion, and I consider that in the organic or rather holistic idea the solution of many of the most profound problems of our thought and life may be found. However that may be, I find myself in deep agreement with your remarks in your address on the value of the organic idea for the large human objectives which U.N.E.S.C.O. has in view.

I find your list of 'rights' in the other paper less satisfactory. Of course there is the right to live, to self-development, to self-expression, and to enjoyment. They are matters of course, but their affirmation does not take us much further.

Indeed I find our modern emphasis on 'rights' somewhat overdone and misleading. It is a modern way of expression, probably owing something to Rousseau and the French Revolution and the American Declaration of Independence. It makes people forget that the other and more important side of 'right' is 'duty'. And indeed the great historic codes of our human advance emphasized duties and not rights. The laws of Hammurabi,[1] the Roman Twelve Tables,[2] the Ten Commandments, even that highest, noblest code of man, the Sermon on the Mount of Christ—all are silent on rights, all lay stress on duties. I dare say your Chinese wisdom follows the same line. If the rule to be just and honest and kind and merciful and compassionate etc. were followed, all would be well with our human society and we shall enjoy all the life, self-development, self-expression and enjoyment which is our share in our earthly space. The 'rights' are much too individualistic and give no due recognition to that organic human and social unity

[1] Hammurabi, King of Babylonia, lived some time between 2100 and 1800 B.C. The code of laws bearing his name is extensive and developed.

[2] The earliest code of Roman law compiled *c.* 450 B.C. by ten men—*decemviri*—chosen for the purpose.

which the duties of the older codes recognized as the real rule and law and pattern of right living. I do not wish to elaborate this line of thought further, but you and your associates may, if you wish, follow it up in the interests of that finer social and ethical and spiritual advance which is U.N.E.S.C.O.'s objective. I should think the preamble to the Charter fairly expresses the fundamental objectives of our advancing human society in their most general form. If we have to be more specific we would stress justice, the rule of law, and the like. In English Magna Charta[1] and the Bill of Rights[2] are monuments along this road of advance. There are other practical principles also which are not mere slogans and vague generalities like the 'rights' to life and enjoyment and the like. I would lay much more stress on such practical and empirical concepts and formulations than on mere generalities. A bill of human rights, to be of any real value, would have to deal with such practical rules and guides of conduct, rather than with high sounding phrases which have no practical value. The most recent development of philosophy (I refer to logical positivism) deals with these pitfalls in language which have led to endless philosophical puzzles and insoluble problems. By being practical and realistic in its statement of general principles U.N.E.S.C.O. might avoid similar pitfalls in the new regime it is now setting up for our future social conduct. The snares of words and language and slogans and catchwords and tautologies have to be avoided as much as possible in what is going to be a code.

s. J. C. Smuts

759 To D. Moore — Vol. 84, no. 103

Doornkloof
Transvaal
1 August 1947

My dear Daphne, What a lovely letter that last one of yours was from the Hyde Park Hotel![3] Full of information and description of London and of politicians, not without a delightful touch of criticism here and there. It is quite clear that you have really enjoyed yourself and return refreshed to Colombo. Change is

[1] A charter of feudal rights and privileges to which the English barons forced King John to agree in 1215. By later interpretation it became a guarantee of the personal freedom of Englishmen.

[2] This statute of 1689, supplemented by the Act of Settlement of 1701, established the supremacy of the English parliament after its long struggle against the Stuart kings.

[3] *See* Smuts Collection, vol. 82, no. 206.

usually good, but in your case it was doubly good because you could rise, both appreciatively and critically, to the unnatural situation in London. And then there was Henry's remarkable success.[1] I could follow the change he brought about from my official telegrams. Of course the credit is nowhere given to him, but the change of outlook and of reaching a solution in the end was fully set out and I could supply the key from my private information. Yes, Henry will be governor-general, but of course that means he will be fixed up in that funny country and society for the next five years, and will probably retire a mental and physical wreck—not to mention his wife, who will bear the brunt of all this physical and human onset. I pity you, even while I congratulate you and him. I was much amused by your sketches of leaders now in charge of operations in what may prove one of the blizzards of history. For the financial position is really unspeakably bad. I think the leaders are really frightened beyond measure and are just waiting for something to happen, some providential escape like Dunkirk or the like. America has been draining the world of dollars, which is now the world currency. How on earth can recovery be effected, even if coal and steel production is stepped up on a large scale? The policy to establish world trade and the simultaneous policy to exact repayment of the loan are contradictory and destructive of each other. I fear by the beginning of next year the full blast will be felt, and Marshall's policy will be like Canute's broom[2] sweeping back the flood. It will be felt everywhere and not only in Britain, but there, of course, its effect will be most damaging to our position as a pillar of the new world order. I may take a jaundiced view of the situation but every bit of information coming to me alarms me more and more.

I see the royal wedding[3] is now fixed for 20 November and I assume the prime ministers are going to be invited to attend. If so, I may have to be in London then and shall see for myself how things are going. I hope my fears are exaggerated.

[1] Lady Moore had written: '...he [Sir Henry Moore] was able...to mow down the thicket of compromises, conditions and other prickly growths that the colonial office were assiduously cultivating to hide the essential fact that Ceylon is to have Dominion status...He has also managed to bring about an agreement with regard to defence...and foreign relations and to torpedo a determined effort to entrap Ceylon in a stultifying trade agreement.'

[2] Smuts has confused two stories: that of Canute the Dane, King of England (1016–35), who, to reprove flatterers, sat down on the seashore and forbade the rising tide to advance; and that of Dame Partington, who during a gale in November 1824 which drove the waves into her cottage on the shore of Sidmouth, tried to keep the water out with her mop.

[3] The wedding of Princess Elizabeth and Prince Philip, later Duke of Edinburgh.

I enjoyed what you wrote of Jo [Moore]. She must be a remarkable girl, not merely in ability, but in outlook and personality. She must really be an exceptional and curious case in that society of young people. She may yet surprise you!

Tomorrow morning early I am off to the Congo (Elizabethville) to bring my respects to the Prince Regent, Charles, who is on a visit to the Congo. It is only a courtesy call and I shall be back the following day. I stayed with him in Brussels on my visit last year and really liked him and hope to hear much useful information from him. Our royal family had a very good opinion of him.

I am now moving into the period of meetings and campaignings in the country. Politics is getting very active, and there is a current flowing against the government which has to be carefully watched—the spirit of change, which is universal and based on a good deal of grievances, just or unjust. Not that I care to continue in office, but I am for fighting if a fight there is to be. But after fifty years of this sort of thing it has no attraction for me any more. How much nicer to sit back and survey these years and try to forecast the future! I have still the power to dream; and what a time for dreaming it is now in this confused tumultuous world! But no such luck for me at present.

Now good-night. Sweet dreams for you, before the next storm arises and perhaps upsets your apple cart! Love to you both and all the success you so well deserve.

J.C.S.

760 To D. Moore — Vol. 84, no. 121

Pretoria
3 September 1947

My dear Daphne...Now I have just received your last letter (23 August) written after the Great Flood.[1] What a tragedy—twenty-seven inches in twenty-four hours is really more than I can take in! Your description of it all and of the human comedy accompanying it in connection with the elections[2] was very vivid. It must have been an exciting experience to you, and you and Henry have deserved your short retreat to Kandy. I hope you will find it a real relaxation and refreshment.

[1] *See* Smuts Collection, vol. 82, no. 209.

[2] Lady Moore had written: 'Every candidate seized on the opportunity to endear himself to potential voters by sending out vast quantities of our precious foodstuffs, marked "Vote for Buggins" or whatever the name might be, and in some districts the astonished villagers have enjoyed more good food during the past week than they have ever seen in their lives before.'

The situation in Britain must be really indescribable. We are still continuing our negotiations over the large gold loans we propose to make.[1] But there too you find the same official muddle which postpones a decision, and we are now sending some experts to clear up the difficulty—in itself quite small. I feel deeply sorry for that mighty country in this hour of great danger. Partly it is due to war exhaustion and weariness. But mixed up with it is the human factor—the inertia and perplexity and temptation to seek for solutions in slogans and catchwords and party formulas. The nation is distracted and the leadership is lacking. How poor is democracy without leadership. But that was lost in 1945 and may not be again recovered. You have the case of an insecure party majority which no war election may end, but the leadership apparently is not in that party. And without Churchill it may be in no party at all, and he is no longer what he was in England's greatest hour. The eclipse of Britain has put the whole world in darkness, and we can but wait and work and pray for the next dawn.

I shall not be able to go to U.N.O. as the political situation here is more important at the moment, but I may have to go to the wedding, and so have an opportunity to see what is really going on in Britain. U.N.O. does not matter in comparison with this tragedy in our Commonwealth. Never before in history has there been such a crisis affecting a whole world, but with courage and resolution the position may still be saved, and we may not be left with the Soviet as the only alternative in the civilization of the West. Britain was the leader but she is herself now without a leader, and the confusion all over Europe is indescribable. The wedding may bring the light touch and the saving grace into this grim scene. But I am writing too sombrely. After all, we have been through worse dangers in our day, and there is no reason to fear that we shall not pull through this stretch. But what a wreckage will be left when it is all over! When we look at what is happening today it seems like the greatest drama of all history. Your deluge is nothing compared to this greatest flood of history. Yours has passed, this will pass, and at the end people will wonder how it happened and what might have prevented it.

More and more the United States and Russia stand out above this flood of waters and tears. I had so hoped that a third peak will stand out, and I have not yet given up hope. But at the moment

[1] The amount of the loan was £80,000,000, to be repaid in three years. Part of it was to be spent on South African agricultural products. The loan agreement was signed on 9 October.

it is only the two that appear in the new picture, the one veiled in mystery, the other with a great hope written on her brow. It may be that America's destiny is to save our human world from vast dangers now looming ahead. But I should prefer our British group emerging from the present flood and once more supplying sanity and wisdom and graciousness to the times to come. Such things are truly on the knees of the gods.

Forgive this ponderous note. But I live at present in this sombre mood. My loving thoughts and all good wishes to you ever.

J.C.S.

761 From M. E. Boyle Vol. 81, no. 68

Grossherzog Hotel
Windhoek
[South West Africa]
5 September 1947

My dear General, Before we leave South West Africa tomorrow to return to Johannesburg, the Abbé [Breuil] and I would like to thank you for having made it possible for us to realize our dream and see and study 'Our Lady of the Brandberg'.[1] Though we stayed there ten days, during which the Abbé slept at her feet each night and I at the foot of another rock nearby, she still keeps all her mystery, or is perhaps more mysterious. At noon on 5 August we first stood before her and said to each other, 'It does not seem real.' She is in perfect preservation, painted on granite, the centre of a procession of most interesting figures. Immediately behind her walks a man dressed in red and brown with a feather in his hat but the face is that of a skeleton, the jaw and teeth clearly showing. Is it Death following Beauty? Far too advanced an idea for Bushmen, but then, these are strangers. She walks towards another white woman, seated, wearing a red hood like hers, but as well as having beads it is decorated with a wing. This figure also holds what seems to be a flower on a long curved black stalk to her face. She has the same red armlets, girdle, and knee-bands and her bow like all the rest, white with a red cord, has been taken by a young native boy who is moving away carrying two bows, and the feathers in the arrows on his back give him a look of Eros.

[1] The Brandberg, a range in the district of Omaruru 260 miles north-west of Windhoek, has a large number of rock paintings and engravings. The most famous painting is the 'White Lady' in the Maack cave in the Tsisab gorge. It was discovered in 1918. The origin of the 'White Lady' remains a mystery.

Like the two women he wears moccasins. Above him is a seated skeleton, arms outstretched, seated, with short cut red hair. The whole procession is led by a native with a scarlet hat and jacket and a man in white doublet slashed with red, but his head has *gemsbok* horns and the teeth of a crocodile. Behind, and perhaps of a different age, in some cases, are red-haired women archers, very faded, but the red gauntlets, girdles, knee- and arm-bands are clear and some of the white bodies. A small nude child has the same red square-cut hair and is attached to two very young girls of the same type who at a later date have been painted over in flesh pink, giving them bird heads and lengthening their legs. Several of the faces have been spoilt in the same manner, one being given a negro chin and lips added below the real chin in white paint, and a white man with flowers in his hair has been given the face of a baboon, a sort of snout, in the same manner. All are walking briskly forward except the seated woman I mentioned and, on the extreme left, a big but faded figure standing as if to receive the oncomers and wearing a yellowish scarlet turban with a brush or aigrette in front and a girdle with several tassels, the same colour. Beneath all this gaily dressed company are small older paintings of Bushman type. Dr [E.R.] Schertz, who with Dr [H.] Martin, accompanied us, took excellent photos which were shown before the local scientific society and the administrator[1] last night when the Abbé lectured.

We returned from the Brandberg on 17 August and took the opportunity of a lift in the car of a skin-buyer to go out to the Naukluft range where we were the guests of a German farmer most of the time, a Mr [R.G.] Strey, a keen botanist.[2] He drove us more than three hundred miles to paintings and one site of engravings, the hoof-prints of game, far in the Bastard[3] country. Here the paintings have nothing to compare with the Brandberg, but in one guano cave in the Baviaanskranz there are concentric circles. The only other example in Africa the Abbé knows of is in Rhodesia, though we have many in Europe. The tools associated with all the paintings are Middle Stone Age and there is a very rich site round the farmhouse of Mr Strey. The Brandberg has a white quartz industry of small tools. An official report with fuller details of the tools and of two examination trenches dug by Dr Martin, one in the Lady's cave and one in another in the Brandberg,

[1] Colonel Imker Hoogenhout (q.v.).

[2] Rudolph G. Strey also accompanied the Abbé Breuil on expeditions in 1948 and 1950. He has published articles in South African botanical journals.

[3] The Reheboth Bastards. *See* vol. III, p. 454, note 3.

will be sent to you later. This is only to let you know that the expedition was indeed worth while.

There are nineteen other known painted rocks near the Lady and we have only been not quite half-way up the ravine. The Abbé considers the Lady and her companions the most important painting in Africa and every effort should be made to protect her, for we see everywhere pieces chipped out of the centres of paintings, names cut or written across them and I fear that the publicity given to our finds will tempt many irresponsible people to visit the Brandberg. She needs a protective locked cage so that she cannot be touched or we shall see some speculator ruining this great work of art—an irreparable loss.

Dr Martin and Dr Schertz were most helpful and pleasant companions and guides and I had my birthday dinner of stewed zebra and tinned peas cooked by Dr Martin. The Southern Cross and Scorpion lit my rock room till the moonlight turned all to fairyland and then dawn tipped all the crests with pure flame. Thank you for a great experience of true beauty healing the mind and heart. With our united thanks and gratitude, Yours very sincerely,

Mary E. Boyle

762 To R. Broom — Vol. 84, no. 123

Pretoria
8 September 1947

My dear Broom, Congratulations on your ever increasing discoveries! Thank you for the latest diagram of your Sterkfontein finds.[1]

It is very handsome of the British Association to write you that appreciative letter. Good luck to you; may it continue. Ever yours,

J. C. Smuts

763 To R. Broom — Vol. 84, no. 129

Pretoria
20 September 1947

Dear Broom, I have read your note and the enclosure about what happened at the British Association[2] with deep interest. I can

[1] For Broom's letter, enclosing one from the British Association for the Advancement of Science, *see* Smuts Collection, vol. 81, no. 87.

[2] Broom's letter enclosed a report from the *Daily Telegraph* of 3 September on the meeting of the British Association at Dundee at which Professor le Gros Clark had described Broom's Sterkfontein finds as 'of surpassing importance in the study of man's evolution' (Smuts Collection, vol. 81, no. 88).

understand that you must be proud and thrilled at the recognition of your work.

The Great Gap is closing. The Anthropoid is moving up toward man. It now remains to move earliest man down, and so close the gap. If only we ever find earlier sub-human fossils. Where will they be found—in Java or China or South Africa?

That is the quest now after your great discoveries. I am thrilled to think what contribution my octogenarian friend is making in this most fascinating section of science.

Once more I say: good luck to you. Ever yours,

J. C. Smuts

764 To D. Moore Vol. 84, no. 131

Doornkloof
[Transvaal]
23 September 1947

My dear Daphne, I see from the papers that your general election has come off and that Senanayake [D. S.] has emerged the victor. He will now form his government which will build the bridge to Dominion status. Good luck to him, and thanks to Henry who has really done the work. I hope that nothing will happen hereafter to make him regret the great part he played in the switch over to Dominion status. I happen to be mildly sceptical of the political capacity of the Oriental. He is a great talker and is up to all the arts of demogogy. But democracy—the art of popular self-government—is mostly beyond him. Could anything be more terrible and terrifying than the mess the Indian and Pakistan leaders are making of their country, now that they have succeeded in ridding themselves of British government? I wonder what the world will think and say if they were to know what really has been happening in India these past months! I have seen some of the official secret accounts which may never see the light of day, and it is a story of savagery which takes you back to the darkest ages of history. At the moment there is a pause in this orgy; let us hope the pause will be a long one. If ever Gandhi's *non-violence* has proved to be a delusion and a snare it is in this awful catastrophe of bloodshed and crime which has overwhelmed India. Happily the situation is very different in Ceylon and she will be spared these horrors. But what is going to happen in Burma?

At U.N.O. the combat in the council and the assembly deepens. The language the United States and the U.S.S.R. hurl at each other in public is quite unprecedented. The United Kingdom wades in less violently but with little less sting and bite. I sometimes wonder whether mankind is ripe even for the little advances we have attempted in U.N.O. And then some people talk lightly of going still further and plunging into the chaos of world government! Are the East and the West 'one world'? And is the Far East not another, third, world? It almost looks as if in the coming together of East and West in U.N.O. we have only started new world-wide frictions and antagonisms. If two young people can't agree and abide each other is it wise to unite them in wedlock? It almost looks as if we have planned a marriage where contrariety of tempers makes a common life impossible. Perhaps if each had quietly gone his or her own way there might have been less cause for friction and antagonism. How much the world has still to learn, and how small is our fitness for real international co-operation. On the other hand, our paths in the world cross and recross, and if we go our own separate ways, there may be worse collisions than in U.N.O. So we shall continue experimenting with new forms of international relationships and co-operations, and with the grace of God we may yet hit on the right solution. We have not done so yet.

Meanwhile our Indian trouble at U.N.O. is less, and we may manage to patch up some arrangement which will look less scandalous than the quarrel which has been going on these last twelve months. Harry Lawrence is doing very well and is treading the soft pedal—so is the wily Mrs Pandit who finds the atmosphere much less favourable this year at U.N.O. I think the best attempt now being made to pull the world out of the pit into which it is sinking is the Marshall plan. If it succeeds it will not only save Europe from decay but it will be a first great step towards that unity of Europe which seems to me to be essential for the preservation of our Western civilization. The counterweight to Slavdom and its Communist ideology is a united Europe, far more than a United States hegemony. Europe herself must save herself and can only do it by uniting her scattered fragments. That will be a gigantic task but not beyond the bounds of possibility, probably far more feasible than the grandiose plan of U.N.O. which at present is no more than a paper plan—and a problem. I am all for a Greater Europe, which will be able to face Greater Russia, though not without the financial and industrial help of America in the years to come. It may look audacious and even outrageous to say all this—but 'dem is my sentiments'. It will all happen after my time, and so I can safely assume the role of prophet!

I fear this once more looks like a political letter, and I know you hate politics and political epistles from your friends. So please excuse me!

Here we are jogging along as usual. I am giving much of my attention to Native problems which are rapidly crowding in upon us. We are also dealing with the gold loan which we intend to make the United Kingdom, and which I hope will be quite a handsome thing, not unworthy of South Africa. I hope it will cheer up British folk and make them feel that there is deep sympathy and affection for her, and a hand stretched out from the Commonwealth. Our path has been made very difficult by the Anglo-American loan agreement, and we are trying to cut some of the strings attached to that ill-fated instrument. The Americans think they are clever business people, but cleverness and hard bargaining seldom pay in the great affairs of the world. Generosity between friends is the better policy. Our war effort has been a fine performance and if we can cap it now by a really great peace-time gesture, the world will not think of us so meanly as it has done recently!

I fear that we shall have some hard nuts to crack at the prime ministers' talks which will take place at the wedding. For me it will be all the more awkward as I shall have to hurry back as soon as possible to our parliamentary session in January. The financial weakness of Britain and her difficulty to face up to her heavy tasks, such as defence and the expensive Empire problems, will require very careful consideration. The danger is that in these lean and difficult years much may be lost which may never be recovered again when better times come, as come they will. So many insolvencies occur which were never necessary and which patience and wisdom might have prevented. The Labour government is a heavy burden to carry in such testing times, and one must try and prevent too much mischief resulting from this unhappy situation. I think it is possible and the attempt should be made.

And there will be the wedding to cheer our hearts and make us rejoice in a good world! Ever yours,

J.C.S.

765 To P. E. von Lettow-Vorbeck — Vol. 84, no. 147

Pretoria
31 October 1947

My dear General, I have received your letter of 23 September[1] in reference to the return of your nephew, Eduard Kurt von Bülow,

[1] Smuts Collection, vol. 84, no. 246.

to South Africa. I have given instructions to the department of the interior to give him the necessary permission, and you may inform him that he is free to return to South Africa as soon as he can make his arrangements.

Let me add that I was pleased to hear from you and to know that you are still alive. I hope you are well and that you find life not too hard in your circumstances and at your age. You have all the good wishes from me which one old warrior can send his opponent according to the rules which still prevail between those who have done their duty faithfully. All kind regards from one African to another. Yours sincerely,

s. J. C. Smuts

766 To N. Bohr Vol. 84, no. 157

Pretoria
13 November 1947

Dear Professor Bohr, Torp-Pedersen duly handed me the letter you gave him last year,[1] and I have delayed all this time answering it because I had the hope that we might meet again to discuss with each other the problem which has been so much in our minds. I shall be in London when you receive this and, as I do not expect to meet you there, I write instead this line to my old friend.

You have often been present in my thoughts during these last years of absence. Our problem still remains unsolved. It has now become mixed up with other difficult and dangerous problems in the relations of the two super powers. Perhaps an understanding between them on other issues may cover this problem too. Perhaps a great change may come over Russia internally which will give an opening to a solution. Perhaps God will have mercy on his stupid, wayward children. The whole human outlook is so black at the moment that we see nothing but insoluble problems before our society, and when the great change comes—as come it must—the whole tangle of the insolubles will disappear in a new kindlier atmosphere.

Let us hope for the best and continue to work for it.

I hope you continue well. My kind regards to you and your son in which my son Jannie warmly joins. Ever yours sincerely,

J. C. Smuts

[1] 699.

767 To K. von Neergaard[1] Vol. 84, no. 156

Pretoria
13 November 1947

Dear Professor von Neergaard, I have your interesting letter of 6 October[1] suggesting a Swiss edition of my work on *Holism and Evolution* published more than twenty years ago, with some editions since now long exhausted. I thank you for your suggestions.

I have declined repeated applications for the republication of the work in English because the scientific basis on which much of the book is founded has altered materially since 1925 and much of the book is obsolete although the fundamental conception has remained, and indeed has grown in importance. I have the feeling that holism is the next move and may supply the key to many of the great problems which trouble our science, philosophy, and religion today. It has always been my wish to follow up the effort of 1925 with a fuller and more satisfactory exploration of the central idea, but heavy problems of peace and war have occupied my time and prevented my doing so. I still hope against hope that some release and some opportunity to return to this lifelong problem of mine will come to me, although the time is now becoming very short. To republish the book now, even with the suggestions for alteration which you kindly make, will not do justice to what is really in my mind. And so I must wait for my opportunity, if ever it comes.

I am glad to notice from various influential quarters that the basic idea of the whole is being more and more realized, partly from the study of my book, and partly independently of it. Earnest men are everywhere digging for new foundations for our intellectual and spiritual life, now so shattered and almost in ruins. I am glad you are also turning your thoughts in that direction. I am therefore all the more sorry that I cannot accept your suggestion to me. With all good wishes,

s. J. C. Smuts

[1] Of the Universitäts-Poliklinik für physikalische therapie of the University of Zürich.

[2] Smuts Collection, vol. 84, no. 248.

768 From C. Weizmann Vol. 84, no. 253

Telegram

From: Chaim Weizmann, New York

To: Field Marshal Smuts, S.A. Legation, Rome

Dated 30 November 1947

At this milestone in Jewish history[1] I think with feelings of deepest gratitude of your noble friendship and unwavering support throughout the years from 1917 onward for the cause of my people. May God bless you and guard you. Affectionately.

769 To C. Weizmann Vol. 84, no. 173

Pretoria
5 December 1947

My dear Weizmann, I was deeply moved by your kind wire from New York[2] on the passing of the partition motion. I received the wire at Rome on my way back to South Africa and have had no earlier opportunity to thank you for a wire I deeply appreciate. My service in the cause has been small, but it has been whole-hearted all the way and in all weathers. The motion of partition is not the end but, as you say, a milestone in the history of Israel. The weather is not clear ahead, but that is no reason to daunt us.

With the leading people in the British cabinet I have discussed the necessity of a fair ending which will not leave Palestine in a mess. It must be an orderly and proper ending of a great chapter of history. I hope this appeal will have a good response.

Great Britain has been the friend, although sometimes a difficult friend. It has initiated the policy of the national home. It must retain Jewish friendship in the difficult chapter ahead. It is to be hoped that nothing will jeopardize that friendship.

The figure that stands out above all others in these thirty years of struggle is your own—you have laboured and you have suffered for the cause. Nothing can detract from that great record.

I enclose a message[3] which I have sent to a great Jewish gathering in Johannesburg next Sunday for your information.

With kind regards and warm affection for both you and Mrs Weizmann, Ever yours faithfully,

s. J. C. Smuts

[1] The partition plan of the United Nations special committee on Palestine (*see supra*, p. 138, note 2) was passed by the general assembly of U.N.O. at the end of November 1947.

[2] **768**. Smuts Collection, Box F, no. 95.

770 To G. G. A. Murray Vol. 84, no. 175

Pretoria
17 December 1947

My dear Murray, Your kind note about my seeing Sir Clifford Heathcote-Smith only reached me after my return to South Africa. The memorandum on refugees will be considered here.

I am looking forward to your *From League to United Nations*[1] and thank you for proposing to send it to me. It will be read with deep interest from one who took such an interest in the League. I still think it on the whole a better concept than U.N.O.

And now another vast development is taking place which may involve far-reaching changes for U.N.O. in its turn. What shape they may take after the present fissure between East and West none can foresee. I am so partial to West European ideas and outlook that I cannot but pray that the West may continue to fight on its own for its cultural stand-point. The Trotsky ideal of universal communism seems finally to have become Stalin's,[2] and its victory may mean the rebarbarization of Europe. The outlook for the Continent is already so grim that this further set-back may mean a further decline relatively to the other continents. Evidently further searching tests are being applied to our civilization: may it come through, purified and reinvigorated from this era of storm and stress.

Kind regards and affectionate Christmas and New Year greetings to you and Lady Mary. Ever yours,

J. C. Smuts

771 To M. C. Gillett Vol. 84, no. 216

Doornkloof
[Transvaal]
19 December 1947

A nice letter today from you, full of your visits and doings and the children and grandchildren. What better stuff to write about? What better element to move and live in? Certainly far better than this

[1] Published in 1948.

[2] In April 1943 Stalin, in order to impress the Allies, had abolished the Comintern, the international Communist organization. In September 1947 the growing 'Cold War' between the Soviet Union and the Western powers and a revival of nationalism among some of the satellite states caused Stalin to set up a new organ of international Communism. This was the Cominform, ostensibly an information bureau, but actually an instrument of Soviet foreign policy.

milling round in affairs which we call politics. And not only better but certainly nearer the heart of things. In domestic affairs you cannot think in *clichés* and slogans, in formulas and abstractions. You are in the concrete world, and in the familiar circle which forms the centre of our affections and interests. You never can go far wrong as you are so close to what you know and what is dear to you. It is all part of you. I suppose that is one of the reasons why Jesus took his whole conception of religion from the family circle. God as the father, we as the children, kindness and love as you see it in that intimate circle. No abstractions, no imaginary woes or unreal exaltations; all facts and familiar things. The old political economy got lost in abstractions; science too is largely a conceptual world, only a sort of substitute or *ersatz* world for that of our real perceptions and experiences. We get away from our roots and get lost in the substitute world of our own creating or imagining. The point is how to imitate the technique of Jesus in the conditions of today. You can do it in Portway House but much less so in the shoe factory. You might give your mind to these simple problems which yet lie at the root of all the troubles of our world.

And what a world of trouble it is! The Council of Foreign Ministers gone phut,[1] the German and Austrian peace once more put off, perhaps a world dividing into two, and a new chapter of dissension and confusion opened. It almost looks now as if Germany will be cut up, the east going to the Soviet, the west continuing with the Anglo-American set up. How long could this last? I see no light in the despairing speech which Bevin made in the commons yesterday. Marshall is speaking tomorrow, and may be more constructive. What of the future?

I see no hope except in a European Union, and if Eastern Germany is gobbled up by Russia and formed into another satellite state, then Western Germany must be integrated into the West European Union and become perhaps its most important unit. Then also Western Germany must be put on her feet again and restored as fast as possible—both for her own sake and for the restoration of Europe. But then a quite different policy will have to be followed from the break-down policy followed hitherto. Then our whole outlook on the German question will have to be revised. But what will the other European countries, with their bitter

[1] The Council of Foreign Ministers had, since its inception, been unable to agree on the terms of a German peace treaty. Renewed attempts to do so in January, March and November 1947 also failed, the main point of contention being Russia's reparation claims. On 15 December the council adjourned *sine die*.

memories of the two world wars say? It looks so complete a change, and so suddenly forced on us! But what other course will be left?

I think the time is rapidly coming for a far more realistic and dispassionate and objective reconsideration of the whole European question than that which has hitherto been given to it. But is the world ripe for such a change? Yet, if it is to be a divided world, how else have we to secure our Western way of life for which we have sacrificed so much? These are some of the problems passing through my mind in these days of confusion and frustration, when we seem to have lost our way and grope round in darkness. I wonder what your reaction, what Arthur's reaction is to what is happening in the world?

Here at the moment the scene is much pleasanter, and you must not think of me as lost in insoluble political enigmas. After the rains the air is cool, the veld is green, there is a feeling of freshness and exhilaration about. One is almost inclined to be an optimist, until one looks again on that far-off world scene. I have had some long walks, one once more from here to Pretoria. I have spent a week-end with Jannie [Smuts] at Rooikop, and had a good ramble through the bush there, with beautiful grass and a great variety of flowers in all directions. No, it is a goodly and a pleasant land here. Politically the situation is also generally satisfactory, and I am getting ready for the parliamentary session next month. I really have nothing at the moment to complain about. Isie is well, so are the rest. Tomorrow Japie [Smuts] and Jannie will come over with their families. Does it not all sound very good? I give you this domestic picture as the pendant to yours in your last letter.

And so I close on this happier note, and wish you and Arthur and all the other dear ones a happy, a happier, New Year. And if it is not happier, may we face it once more with faith and courage, and in health and strength. Ever yours,

Jan

772 To S. M. Smuts — Vol. 88, no. 6

Groote Schuur
16 Januarie 1948

Liefste Mamma, Net 'n lyntjie om met Sylma saam te stuur. Ek skryf voor haar vertrek, as 'n bewys van liefde, hoewel ek weet dat sy al die nuus aan jou persoonlik sal oorbreng. Haar kort verblyf hierdie week was my tot troos en groot genoë. Ek denk ook dat sy en Sybilla die kort verandering baie geniet het. Ek self is baie besig al die tyd gewees. Daar was die gaste van buite wat aangenaam was maar tyd opgeneem het. Daar was die moeilikheid in die Kabinet wat op 'n grootskaalse omruiling van portefeuilles geloop [*sic*] het en gister agtermiddag laat eers in orde kon gebreng word. Dit spyt my, maar Jantjie was gedetermineer op die verandering wat net so die vooraand van die sitting op 'n baie ongeleë oomblik kom en miskien deur die publiek nie begryp sal word nie. Ek vrees dit is Borrie daar agter wat onnoodig bevrees is vir sy gesondheid.

Dan moes ek eergister op Oos Londen deurbreng, en die reis daarheen en terug. Alles pragtig afgeloop, maar dit gaan nie in jou klere sit nie, hoor! Dit was 'n eindelose gedoente, en my ou been het maar daarvoor moet uitboet. Maar die been is tog aan beter word en hoop ek sal nou gou in orde kom. Ek hoop hierdie naweek so stil as moontlik te bly, want dit is al wat noodig is. Hier sal gelukkig niemand te G. S. wees nie en ek sal dus maar op my kamer bly soveel moontlik. Geen pyn, maar alleen nog beetje hinkende.

Die weer bly uitstekend—heerlike koele dae en lekker nagte, wat my goed laat slaap. Ek hoor dit is vreeslik warm in die noorde en dit sal seker weer baie reën meebreng. Wees maar gelukkig en wees verseker dat dit my hier goed gaan.

Ek hoor van die vreeslike ongeluk nou vir die tweede keer op die kruispad te Pinedene. Dit is werklik akelig en 'n ware 'death trap'.

Ek hoop dit gaan jul almal baie goed. Hier is niks om oor te kla nie, hoewel ek 'n warm sitting verwag. Maar ek is daarvoor klaar.

Nou 'n soentjie en baie liefde en harts groete aan jul almal. My hart is maar by jou en by jul almal.

Pappa

TRANSLATION

Groote Schuur
[Cape Town]
16 January 1948

Dearest Mamma, Just a line to send with Sylma [Coaton]. I write before her departure as a token of love although I know that she will give you all the news personally. Her brief visit this week was a great comfort and pleasure to me. And I think that she and Sybilla [Strick] enjoyed the short change very much. I myself was very busy all the time. There were the guests from outside who were pleasant but took up time. There was the trouble in the cabinet, which led to a large-scale reshuffle of portfolios and could only be settled late yesterday afternoon. I am sorry, but Jantjie was set upon the change which, just on the eve of the session, comes at a very unsuitable time and will perhaps not be understood by the public.[1] I am afraid that Borrie,[2] who is unnecessarily concerned about his health, is behind it.

I had to spend the day before yesterday at East London[3] and make the journey there and back. Everything went off beautifully, but these things leave their mark on one, believe me. It was an endless affair, and my old leg had to pay the penalty for it. However, the leg is mending and will soon be right now.[4] I hope to stay as quiet as possible this week-end because that is all that is necessary. Fortunately there will be no one here at Groote Schuur and so I shall stay in my room as much as I can. I have no pain but only limp a little.

The weather remains excellent—lovely cool days and pleasant nights that make me sleep well. I hear that it is terribly hot in the north; this will probably once more bring heavy rain. Be happy and rest assured that all is well with me here.

I have heard of the terrible accident, for the second time, on the cross-roads at Pinedene. It is really frightful and truly a death trap.

I hope you are all very well. Nothing to complain of here, although I expect a lively session. But I am ready for it.

And now a kiss, much love and greetings from the heart to you all. My heart is with you and with you all.

Pappa

[1] J. H. Hofmeyr was at this time minister of finance and of education and leader of the house of assembly. He was not well and asked Smuts on 5 January to be relieved at least of finance (*see* A. Paton, *Hofmeyr*, pp. 468–9). On 15 January Hofmeyr was made deputy prime minister and minister of mines and retained education. F. C. Sturrock took over finance. The reshuffle of portfolios also involved the departments of economic development, the interior, posts and telegraphs, public works, social welfare and transport.

[2] Deborah, mother of J. H. Hofmeyr.

[3] For the centenary celebrations.

[4] Smuts had, on one of his cross country walks from Irene to Pretoria, injured a toe so badly that he was for some time unable to walk normally and suffered a good deal of pain.

773 To C. E. Raven Vol. 88, no. 9

Telegram

To: The Master, Christ's College, Cambridge

From: J. C. Smuts

Dated 18 January 1948

I shall deeply appreciate the high honour of representing my old university and accept it with gratitude and pleasure.[1] Your letter just received makes clear that no undue demands will be made on my time in view of my other heavy duties.

774 To M. C. Gillett Vol. 88, no. 232

Groote Schuur
[Cape Town]
24 January 1948

This week brought me a letter from you and another from the little Greek Queen.[2] She wrote after her return from visiting the Greek troops at Konitza where they had been besieged by brigands for more than a week and had suffered heavy casualties. Her story is a most amazing one—her arrival at posts unannounced, surprise and joy and tears in all directions and what she calls a 'Marathon of emotions'. At Konitza she visited a school or clinic for three hundred children which she had established and where the poor things had been hiding for seven days and nights with bullets whistling over their heads. She entered unannounced and unknown, until one child shouted out: 'Basilissa!' (Queen) and then a pandemonium of emotion burst loose! Imagine the scene. She says she shed more tears on this Konitza visit than in her life. What an experience! You will be interested in all this as we have to do with a real and unusual human. And all the time her husband in danger with a fresh attack of enteric at Athens.

Your letter was most welcome as usual. I was much amused by your account of the bout between Richard and Simon—a very unequal affair.[3] But what a dear, brave little thing Simon must be. My heart warms to him the more I hear of him. Your other news quite good and interesting—your life at home alone, your going

[1] Smuts had been nominated as chancellor of the University of Cambridge.

[2] Queen Frederica's letters to Smuts were returned to her, at her request, by his family and there are no copies in the Smuts Collection.

[3] Richard Clark, grandson of Smuts, and Simon Gillett, grandson of A. B. and M. C. Gillett who was fifteen months younger than his attacker.

to Meeting in strange ways and places, your musings over things political. This Cambridge plan is an amazing thing to me. I suppose I have to accept under all the circumstances if I am elected, but what with distance and the heavy burden of politics here you can imagine my embarrassment and difficulties. The honour is great, the good will behind it deeply appreciated, but my dilemma is a very real one. We shall see what happens and how the resulting difficulties will be overcome.

The trouble here is that I shall have to go through with this general election, shall probably win again, and shall then have to carry on for some years more at any rate: and all that when I have been already fifty years at the job and am in my seventy-eighth year! But if I don't continue we shall lose the election and upset the apple-cart for causes dear to me. The Native policies of the opposition will create chaos here and must be frustrated, and the good work of racial peace and economic progress must be continued. But all this means that my slavery will continue, and the things I have meditated for a lifetime must remain in their incubation.

It is all rather saddening and personally disappointing. But I find the pulling out process too much for me. It looks too much like desertion of friends and causes which I have spent much of my life for. So I see no other course but to carry on and await developments and trust to the chapter of the unknown. The Native question especially weighs very heavily on me, although even there I think disappointment and frustration may be in store for me. But rather defeat than running away, when there is still fight in me.

I am much heartened by Bevin's coming over to the Western idea openly and unequivocally, and Winston's warm support.[1] At least we have a great cause in which the British people are once more wholeheartedly united. And what a cause it is! It may mean that Europe is not languishing on a death-bed but is in child-labour. A new birth of time is happening and the sorrows and agonies of the wars are leading to a new life for this old European continent. There is heart and hope and confidence and faith once more. What a wonderful thing it will be if this night is miraculously transformed into day, into a new dawn which will lead to a restoration of the glory which is Europe! This would make the loss and suffering worth while, and not a sheer waste and defeat. If the Western Union

[1] The idea of Western European union, mooted in various forms during and after the Second World War, was adopted by the British cabinet at this time and launched by the foreign secretary, Ernest Bevin, in a debate on foreign affairs in the house of commons on 22 January.

succeeds, the East must also in time fall into line. For the economic and even war potential of the combination of America and Western Europe and the British Commonwealth would be such that no other power on earth could stand up to it or lead to a great set-back again. So at last a great hope dawns. May it not be another disappearing mirage!

So much for great things. Now for the little. My leg is now rapidly recovering from the old sprain. I cannot yet walk a long distance but the pain is gone and in a week or two I can resume my pedestrian routine. Isie writes cheerfully from home. Daphne [Smuts] will, I hope, soon be able to join me here where I am now living alone. I cannot ask Bibas [Smuts] to come here unless there are other females, as I fear another breakdown for her if not looked after.[1] The Athlones are enjoying themselves here and will spend next week-end with me. I think this is a happy visit and change and rest for them. I shall take them out to du Toit's kloof[2] which is now in order and one of our new glories. There are many other important visitors to South Africa from abroad and I give them such entertainment as my time allows. But you know how occupied I myself am all the time with my own and the country's affairs. Still, it is good publicity for South Africa.

To return to Europe. I like the new development also because it creates a platform on which parties in Britain can work together once more. I hate this rather embittered temper at a time when national unity is so imperative in the national interest. A coalition may not be desirable or feasible, but at least a line of policy could be embarked upon which will entail national co-operation rather than the party dog-fight. And what better than that a united Britain should sponsor the cause of a united, restored, progressive Europe? I think the leadership in this vast issue should be with Britain, and that means a united front and effort. So good may come out of evil, and life out of what promised to be a process of decay and death.

This sounds rather high flying; but you can understand how I look to and welcome any sign of the new, better world we have striven for. My dear love ever,

Jan

[1] She had had a diabetic collapse on an earlier visit to Groote Schuur where, said Smuts, she was unable to resist sweet dishes.

[2] A mountain pass between Paarl and Worcester in the western Cape Province.

775 To F. Lamont Vol. 88, no. 18

Telegram

To: Florence Lamont

From: J. C. Smuts

Dated [3] February 1948

Dear Florence, in this hour of common loss[1] we hold your hand in deepest sympathy with you and your children.

776 To C. E. Raven Vol. 88, no. 22

Telegram

To: The Vice-Chancellor, Christ's College, Cambridge

From: J. C. Smuts

Dated 3 February 1948

The press reports my unanimous nomination as chancellor. My warmest thanks for this great honour and the good will behind its unanimity. It also emphasizes the Commonwealth character of the university which has played so great a part in the highest academic training of Dominion men.

777 M. C. Gillett Vol. 88, no. 233

Groote Schuur
[Cape Town]
9 February 1948

Sunday afternoon. My leg is quite recovered. Yesterday I walked up to the gate on the upper contour path which opens into Groote Schuur estate, and back. I felt no discomfort. This morning I motored pleasantly in Mercury to Cape Point, and then walked up the last lap to the lighthouse. Again no discomfort. So I am healed and whole again and can indulge my old appetite for peripatetics—that is the Aristotelian term. Far more lucky I am than you, poor dear, who cannot walk at home and have to enjoy that luxury—moderately—in South Africa. Of course I must be careful about the old heart; its love for mountains must be carefully moderated. 'Six presidents of the Alpine Club have died of heart' as the wise president said to me. Isie will be specially pleased to

[1] The death of her husband, Thomas W. Lamont, on 2 February.

hear of my healing for the accident disturbed her. But what a joy it is to walk again, and to climb, even up to the contour path!

So Cambridge has gone mad and done it, and I am now chancellor. However shall I fit this into my already crowded programme? Next June, Cambridge; and at the same time I shall be in, or preparing for, my final general election in South Africa. With me the problem of the time-table is generally the most difficult of all. I see no solution yet, and let time solve the problem of the time-table! I think there has been a conspiracy among my friends, yourself and Cato [Clark] and Raven and the rest included.[1] Is there no pity in the universe? Is there no mercy in our ethics?

Thank you for another good letter. I have already thanked you for the books, especially the Brontë poems. This new edition, based on real research, is indeed valuable. Those Gondal pieces[2] throw a flood of light on her as person and as poetess. She had an intensity and a poetic capacity which I think do place her first among English poetesses. She faces out ultimate issues in a way which is really breath-taking for one so young and so little cultured. In moments of the deepest feeling she reaches the fundamental insight that 'I am God'. That underlies several of her most wonderful little poems. Our inner light is the Light itself! It is breath-taking in its daring.

I am also reading G. Murray's *Greek Studies*[3] which I find full of very good stuff. His first paper on 'Hellenism' is one of his best surveys. That the essence of the Greek way of life is also ours is a very valuable contribution, and he argues it out with great force and persuasiveness. Surely the Altar of Pity which stood in the market-place should be our war memorial in this age of horrors! 'Euripides' Tragedies of 415 BC' is also a very remarkable paper. Reading that paper and especially his conclusions on *Troades* (*Trojan Women*), I find something which carries me into the insights of Emily Brontë. 'Death the most holy' is a wonderful thought.[4]

[1] Professor E. A. Walker to Smuts (6 February 1948): 'To the best of my knowledge the first mention of your name as our future chancellor was made...at the St John's dinner on 27 December last. The Master of St John's (Mr E. A. Benians) was delighted with the suggestion, for which plenty of support was found at once in the university. At an informal senate meeting a week or two later, the Master of St John's proposed your name, the Masters of Queens' and Magdalene Colleges supported him, and I confess that I, as a humble professor, suggested that your seventy-seven years sit lightly on you...' (Smuts Collection, vol. 88, no. 233).

[2] *See supra*, p. 64, note 1.

[3] Published in 1946.

[4] '...Hecuba kneels and beats upon the ground, crying to those who must have pity...above all to Priam. But Priam cannot hear her...He has gone away from the foulness of war, he is with Death the Holy' (p. 147).

Both poets reach it in their most tragic moment—Euripides with Troy before him, Emily with T.B. ending her life. Suffering at its extreme limit creates an inspiration and insight such as life itself cannot reach.

I had to write a letter of consolation this morning to Florence Lamont who had just lost her Tom. I find these things most difficult and could only lapse into the line of thought which these poets, and indeed my own reflections, had opened up to me. The 'Anatomy of Suffering' is a book which should be written in our age of suffering, unequalled in our human record. The danger is that our sense is so dulled by this piled-up horror that we lose its real significance and fail to realize that it is a way of experience which leads us into a deeper appreciation of the fundamental meaning of life and human destiny. The Cross is not an accident, and the Christian reading of it is a very true and profound one. Suffering is one of the sure trails to understanding of what is deepest in us. But our senses are dulled instead of sharpened by it.

This reads like Sunday talk! But I have my light moments, and last Sunday I could enjoy du Toit's Kloof and this Sunday Cape Point. So you must not think I am plunged in woe! I wonder whether Jan [Gillett] will be affected by these silly developments in Iraq.[1] The Palestine situation is lapsing into sad chaos, and I fear the British will be largely blamed for the chaotic ending of what in itself is a great tragedy. Their manner of going must surely mean a complete chaos, with no authority to control the situation.[2] Ever lovingly,

J.C.S.

[1] In January 1948 a new treaty was signed between Great Britain and Iraq which revised long-standing British military commitments there. Iraqi nationalists rioted in protest against the treaty which in consequence was not ratified. Jan Gillett was a government botanist in Iraq.

[2] On 26 September, in the absence of any agreed solution of the Arab–Jewish conflict, the British government announced the early withdrawal of the British forces and administration from Palestine. On 29 November 1947 the United Nations general assembly approved the partition plan (*see supra*, p. 168, note 1). The Arabs would not accept it and guerilla war broke out almost at once. On 11 December the British government announced the termination of the mandate on 15 May 1948.

778 To L. S. Amery Vol. 88, no. 30

House of Assembly
Cape Town
12 February 1948

My dear Leo, Thank you for your note enclosing your article on Gandhi.[1] I read this article with much interest. Gandhi has played a very large part in the world and produced an effect on opinion which has in some respects surpassed that of any other contemporary of ours. And he *succeeded*. And his success was due not only to his personality but to strange methods, never resorted to by other leaders. Altogether he was a strange human phenomenon.

I was looking through your recent books with much interest. Thank you for sending them to me. It looks as if a crisis may come in 1948. There are so many indications and symptoms. Not war, but something that will shake the existing political and financial structure. As I have to be in London in June in connection with my duties as chancellor of Cambridge University I may have an opportunity to talk things over with you. Here things are normal, but a general election is approaching, and I don't know how it will be possible to fit a visit to London in June into this picture. I am naturally very anxious to win this final battle.

My love to dear Mrs Amery, and kind regards to you. Ever yours,

s. J. C. Smuts

779 To J. Talman Vol. 88, no. 38

Cape Town
16 February 1948

Dear Dr Talman, I enclose the little contribution on Campbell-Bannerman which I promised to write for your school magazine. I trust it will arrive in time and be found suitable for your purpose. I have written it with real pleasure and as a debt of honour to the memory of a great statesman.

It is of course possible that the little article may attract wider attention, and other papers may desire to quote from it or to reproduce it. It is my wish that no objection should be raised to this. Let it all be to the honour of Campbell-Bannerman and his remembrance in these confused days. Yours sincerely,

s. J. C. Smuts

[1] Gandhi was assassinated on 30 January 1948 by a Hindu who held him responsible for partition.

780 Article (1948) Box E, no. 12

This article appeared in the June 1948 issue of the Glasgow High School Magazine.

SIR HENRY CAMPBELL-BANNERMAN AND SOUTH AFRICA

I am glad to place on record some of my recollections in connection with Sir Henry Campbell-Bannerman's share in the grant of self-government to the Transvaal and Orange Free State in 1906. His action will ever remain one of the highlights of British statesmanship, with far-reaching effects on the future course of events. In these days of swiftly moving events and fading memories it is right that his great action should be remembered. And the pages of a magazine conducted by his old Scots school is a proper place in which to record his action once more.

After the conclusion of the South African War in 1902 crown colony rule of the standard type was imposed on the conquered republics. It was to be feared, in view of the length and obstinacy of the Boer resistance, that there might be a renewal of the trouble. But nothing happened. The behaviour of the Boer people, intent only on rebuilding their homes and restoring their destroyed country, was in every way exemplary. Nothing happened to disturb the peace or internal security. It soon became evident to the British authorities that in a country like the Transvaal, with a Boer population traditionally wedded to law and order, and a British population always restive under the restraint of crown colony rule, the position was becoming untenable. And so in 1905 a plan was evolved by the then Conservative government to grant what is called representative government to the Transvaal; that is to say there would be popular representation in a legislative assembly, but the government would remain under the crown. Both among the Boer and the British inhabitants there was considerable feeling against such a half-way solution, and it was clear to the Boer leaders that the scheme was likely to lead to differences between the British governing authority and the people, and so likely to disturb the good relationship which had existed since the peace.

Towards the end of 1906 a general election was pending in Britain, and it appeared likely that the Conservative party might be beaten by the Liberal party led by Sir Henry Campbell-Bannerman. Personal exchanges between Lord Kitchener and myself at the peace conference in 1902 had raised hopes that the Boer people might look forward to a change of the crown colony régime when such a change of government should take place. My colleagues therefore asked me to go to London and explore the position with the new Liberal government. So I arrived in December 1905 on my errand in London, where I had last been as a student ten years before. My presence was noted, and I remember an evening paper making a remark that the most dangerous man then walking the streets was a Boer emissary bent on upsetting the Boer War settlement. This looks a bad prophecy in the light of after events; but it still remains a question whether it might not have been a good shot if my mission had turned out a failure. Little more than ten years later I was once more walking the streets of London, but this time as a member of the British war cabinet, helping in the conduct of the Great War. What an extraordinary turn of events which completely upset the newspaper prophecy and amazed the world!

The man who wrought the miracle was Sir Henry Campbell-Bannerman, to all appearances an ordinary man, almost commonplace to the superficial view, but a real man, shrewd and worldly wise, but rooted in a great faith which inspired a great action. I discussed my mission with many members of the cabinet—perhaps the most brilliant government Britain had had for a long time, and with men among them like Asquith, Edward Grey, Lloyd George, John Morley, and last but not least Winston Churchill. Campbell-Bannerman looked the least distinguished in that galaxy of talent. But what a wise man, what statesmanship in insight and faith, and what sure grip on the future! My mission failed with the rest, as it was humanly speaking bound to fail. What an audacious, what an unprecedented request mine was—practically for the restoration of the country to the Boers five years after they had been beaten to the ground in one of the hardest and most lengthy struggles in British warfare. But with Campbell-Bannerman my mission did not fail. I put a simple case before him that night in 10 Downing Street. It was in substance: 'Do you want friends or enemies? You can have the Boers for friends, and they have proved what quality their friendship may mean. I pledge the friendship of my colleagues and myself if you wish it. You can choose to make them enemies, and possibly have another Ireland on your hands. If you do believe in liberty, it is also their faith and their religion.' I used no set arguments, but simply spoke to him as man to man, and appealed only to the human aspect which I felt would weigh deeply with him. He was a cautious Scot, and said nothing to me, but yet I left that room that night a happy man. My intuition told me that the thing had been done.

The rest of the story has been told by Mr Lloyd George: how at a cabinet meeting next day the prime minister simply put the case for self-government to the Transvaal to his colleagues, and in ten minutes had created such an impression that not a word was said in opposition, and one of the ministers had tears in his eyes.

A mission to work out details was sent to the Transvaal,[1] and next year the country had its free constitution, and a government in which Boer and Englishman sat together, under a prime minister who had been the commander-in-chief of the Boer armies in the field. But Botha was a man of like stature to Campbell-Bannerman. Greatness of soul met equal greatness of soul, and a page was added to the story of human statesmanship of unfading glory and inspiration to after ages. Seven years later Campbell-Bannerman had passed away, but Botha was once more a commander-in-chief in the field, but this time in common cause with Britain, and over forces in which both Dutch and British were comrades. The contagion of magnanimity had spread from the leaders to their peoples. Nor does the story end there. It was continued in the Second World War, after Botha had also passed away. It has even been suggested that the action of South Africa saved our cause in the years that followed the Battle of Britain and when America had not entered the war. The story may never end. To great deeds wrought by the human soul there is no end.

Today we are living in distraught times, where in the confusion it is not easy to recognize the way. But in this simple story I have told there is a light of statesmanship which shines like an indistinguishable beacon above the raging storm. We shall remember Campbell-Bannerman.

Last year, when the royal family visited South Africa, the King did my simple house (a relic from a British military camp of the Boer War)[2] the honour of a visit. There in my study he saw a large portrait of Campbell-Bannerman hanging above my chair. And later he said to me: 'I was so glad to see that portrait in your study. One seldom sees it in Britain today.' Alas!

And so I say to my young Scots friends, and my friends in all our Commonwealth, and to mankind everywhere where greatness of soul is honoured: Don't forget Campbell-Bannerman.

[1] *See* vol. II, p. 243, note 1. [2] *See* vol. II, p. 537, note 2.

781 To C. E. Raven Vol. 88, no. 36

Prime Minister's Office
Cape Town
16 February 1948

My dear Master, You cannot know what pleasure your telegrams and your final letter of 2 February about my election to the chancellorship have given me. It was all so surprising and unexpected and I feel myself so unworthy of this honour 'thrust upon me' in Bacon's phrase.[1] It is indeed a great personal honour, but it also has its wider significance which was no doubt in the minds of the electors. For your own interest and trouble in the matter I thank you most warmly. For Christ's to have the vice-chancellor for the time being and the chancellor must be an unusual circumstance, and I feel very proud of my old college.

I shall manage to attend the central ceremony[2] on 10 June, but as regards other engagements and a longer stay at Cambridge I am most awkwardly situated. We have a general election in South Africa which will probably be held in June more or less about the same time, and you can imagine my embarrassment in being absent from the country at such a time. I shall therefore have to curtail my visit to a few days and hurry back as soon as possible. The election will be one of very special importance, both from a local and a Commonwealth point of view, and I am therefore specially anxious to win it. My presence here will be of critical importance from this point of view, as you can well understand. Later on I may have more definite information to give you on this point, and I shall do so as soon as the time-table is clearer.

At the moment I have no particular nominees in my mind for honorary degrees and shall be glad to have your assistance in the matter. My feeling is all in favour of the 'common man'—the men who contribute by distinguished service in science and the arts but who are usually passed by on these occasions when the big guns are singled out for honour.

I shall personally contact Winston Churchill and find out whether it will be possible for him to attend personally.

Invitations to attend functions are already coming to me from individual colleges, but I am for the present putting them off on the plea of uncertainty about my dates.

Once more expressing my gratitude to you and my gratification at the signal honour done me, Ever yours sincerely,

J. C. Smuts

[1] Smuts must have had in mind Shakespeare's phrase 'some have greatness thrust upon them' (*Twelfth Night*, II.v.158).

[2] His installation.

782 To G. N. J. van Loggerenberg Vol. 88, no. 39

Kaapstad
17 Februarie 1948

Waarde van Loggerenberg, U vra my omtrent Kapt. Danie Theron, en besonderhede omtrent hom wat in herinnering behoort gehou te word deur die jong geslag wat hom nie persoonlik geken het nie. Ek stuur u 'n paar items wat miskien van balang kan wees, en dit spyt my dat ek nie die tyd kan vind vir 'n breedvoeriger verhaal, wat hom meer waardig sal wees nie.

Danie Theron het ek leer ken in die jare voor die Boereoorlog, toe hy 'n prokureur te Krugersdorp was en ek Staatsprokureur te Pretoria. Hy het my dikwels oor regsbesigheid kom raadpleeg en sy moeilikhede voor my gelê. In daardie verre dae had ek 'n gedurige stryd in verband met speur en polisie dienste en viral met moeilikhede in die administrasie van die drankwet en goud diefstalle. Sy professionele werk het hom in noue aanraking met hierdie sake gebring en in sy verleendheid is hy dikwels na my gekom. Ek het toe gevind dat hy 'n man van hoogstaande karakter was, met 'n vurige haat teen alle onreg, en onberispelik in sy professionele gedrag.

In daardie dae voor die oorlog was die politieke atmosfeer ook dik bewolk, en dikwels het hy die sake wat op oorlog sou uitloop met my aangeroer. Hy was 'n vurige patriot en het vir niks gestuit in sy ywer om ons goeie saak te bevorder. Met die vyandiggesinde Engelse pers te Johannesburg had hy 'n gedurige stryd, wat uiteindelik daarop uitgeloop het dat hy die redakteur van die *Star*, die destyds bekende heer Monneypenny, met geweld in sy kantoor aangerand het, en homself in 'n baie moeilike posisie as regspraktisyn gebring het.

Toe eindelik die oorlog uitbreek is hy dadelik na die vegterryn in Natal, en het daar dieselfde voortvarendheid van gees aan die dag gelê. Hy was 'n man van ontembare moed, wat op die roekeloosheid gegrens het. Hy was 'n gebore verkenner vir wie geen posisie gevaarlik genoeg was om dit van naby en nou te inspekteer nie.

Dit het ook nie lang geduur voor hy die gewone kommando organisasie veels te stadig en lamlendig gevind het, en verlof gevra en gekry het om sy eie spioenkorps op te rig. So is die Theron Spioenkorps ontstaan waarvan hy die siel en lewe was. Baie van ons uitstekenste offisiere in die later jare van die oorlog het begin as lede van die Korps en daar hul vuurproef deurgegaan. Ek dink aan Generaal Barnie Enslin en Generaal Malan en vele andere van ons jonger helde in die oorlog. Met die terugval van ons magte onder Generaal Cronjé van Magersfontein na Bloemfontein en die vaskeer van ons magte te Paardeberg was alle verband met die regering te Pretoria afgesny en wis ons vir dae nie wat gaande was nie. Die keuse is toe op Danie Theron geval om tussen die Britse linies deur te gaan en verbinding tussen die Generaal en die regering te herstel. Dit was 'n waagstuk van die gevaarlikse aard, maar in één nag is hy daardeur met sy depêches vir die Generaal, en die volgende nag op nog gevaarliker wyse is hy weer terug met sy treurige tyding dat die posisie onherstelbaar was en die ramp van die verskriklike oorgawe onvermydelik was. Geen groter waagstuk is in die hele oorlog gedoen nie.

Na die val van Pretoria was dit sy keuse om by Generaal de Wet aan te sluit, daar die groter beweeglikheid van die oorlog in die Vrystaat 'n meer bepaalde aantrekking vir hom had. En so is hy tot sy einde op en af die twee republieke deurgeveg, altyd op die gevaarlikste punte, waar die vegtery die ergste was.

Die einde is geheel onverwag gekom in die rande langs die Johannesburg-Potchefstroom pad. Daar was hy op 'n koppie met verkyker besig om die beweging van 'n vyandelike kolom te volg. Die vyand was besig los kanonskote op die rand te vuur, maar op 'n afstand wat dit twyfelagtig maak of hy gesien was en of op hom bepaald gemik was. Een bom het hom getref, en dit was sy laaste deelname aan die oorlog. Sy verlies is diep gevoel en betreur en onherstelbaar, en algemeen was dit erken dat in Danie Theron ons een van ons dapperste helde verloor had. Twee jaar lang het die oorlog nog voortgeduur, maar onder al die helde gemis van die oorlog was daar niemand wat die naam en roem van Danie Theron bereik of oortref het nie.

Na die oorlog is hy te Eikenhof herbegrawe. Ek had die eer die lykrede daar te voer, en die opskrif op die grafsteen is deur my opgestel. Dit was een van die hartroerenste funksies wat ek ooit bygewoon het. Maar daar was nie net 'n gevoel van weemoed nie. Daar was 'n gevoel van opgewektheid en van trots op die held, wie se dade en naam onsterflik sou bly in ons geskiedenis. Vir helde soos hy is die graf te klein. Die dankbare hart van 'n volk is alleen groot genoeg om 'n rusplaas vir hom te vorm. En daarom begin die opskrif met die woorde: 'Nie Hier'. Hy word bewaar in die hart van sy volk en nie alleen van die geslag wat hom geken het, maar ook van die ontelbare ongebore geslagte wat die toekoms vorm en wat sy gedagtenis beroemd en warm sal hou. Die uwe,

get. J. C. Smuts

TRANSLATION

Cape Town
17 February 1948

Dear van Loggerenberg,[1] You ask me about Captain Danie Theron and particulars about him which should be remembered by the younger generation who did not know him personally. I send you a few items which may be of interest and regret that I cannot find time for a more detailed story which would be more worthy of him.

I got to know Danie Theron in the years before the Anglo-Boer War when he was an attorney at Krugersdorp and I state attorney in Pretoria. He often came to consult me about legal business and to put his troubles before me. In those distant days I had a constant struggle with the detective and police services and especially with difficulties in the administration of the liquor law and gold thefts. His professional work brought him into close contact with these matters and in his embarrassment he often came to me. I then found that he was man of high character, with a fiery hatred of all injustice, and irreproachable in his professional conduct.

In those days before the war the political sky was darkly clouded and he often broached to me those questions which might lead to war. He was an ardent patriot and stopped at nothing to advance our good cause. He was always in conflict with the hostile English press in Johannesburg and this ended in his violently assaulting the editor of the *Star*, the well-known Mr [W.F.] Monypenny, in his office and so putting himself into a very awkward position as a practitioner of the law.

When finally war broke out he went at once to the front in Natal where he displayed the same impetuous spirit. He was a man of untamable courage which verged on recklessness. He was a born scout for whom no position was too dangerous to inspect at close quarters and in detail.

It was not long before he found the ordinary commando organization much too slow and poor and had asked, and obtained, permission to establish his own reconnoitring corps. And so Theron's Scouts came into existence, of which he was the heart and soul. Many of our most outstanding officers in the later years of the war began as members of this corps and had their baptism of fire there. I am thinking of General Barnie Enslin and General [W.C.] Malan and many others of our younger heroes in the war. When our forces under General [P.A.] Cronjé retreated from

[1] Principal of the Danie Theron School at Eikenhof in the district of Johannesburg.

Magersfontein to Bloemfontein and were surrounded at Paardekraal, all contact with the government at Pretoria was cut off and we did not know for days what was going on. Danie Theron was then chosen to go through the British lines and restore communication between the General and the government. It was a risk of the most dangerous sort but he got through in one night with despatches for the General; and the next night, in even more dangerous fashion, he was back again with the sad tidings that the position was irrecoverable and the disaster of the terrible surrender unavoidable. No more daring feat was ever performed in the whole course of the war.

After the fall of Pretoria he chose to join General [C. R.] de Wet, as the greater mobility of the war in the Free State was definitely more attractive to him. And so, until his end, he ranged fighting through both the republics—always at the most dangerous places where the fighting was hardest.

The end came quite unexpectedly in the hills along the Johannesburg–Potchefstroom road. He was on a koppie there following through field-glasses the movements of an enemy column. The enemy were firing occasional artillery shots at the hill, but at a range which makes it doubtful whether he was seen or whether he was deliberately aimed at. One shell hit him—and that was his last role in the war. His loss was deeply felt and mourned and it was irreparable, and it was generally recognized that in Danie Theron we had lost one of our bravest heroes. The war lasted two more years but among all the war's heroic dead there was no one who equalled or excelled the fame of Danie Theron.

After the war he was reinterred at Eikenhof. I had the honour of delivering the funeral oration there and the inscription on the grave-stone was composed by me. It was one of the most heart-rending ceremonies that I have ever attended. But there was not only a feeling of sorrow. There was also a feeling of uplifted spirits and of pride in the hero whose deeds and name would remain immortal in our history. For heroes such as he the grave is too small. Only the grateful heart of a nation is big enough to be a resting-place for him. And that is why the inscription begins with the words: 'Not here'.[1] He is laid up in the heart of his

[1] The inscription reads: *Daniel Johannes Theron. Kommandant Theron's Verkenning Corps. Geboren 9 den Mei 1872. Gesneuweld 5 den September 1900, te Elandsfontein, distr. Potchefstroom.*

Niet hier. Nog steeds voert hij hen aan,
De jonge strijders van zoon' meen'gen slag
En aan de spits der helden zal hij staan
Wanneer verrijzen zal de lang verbeide dag.

[*See opposite*]

people, and not only of the generation that knew him, but also of the innumerable generations unborn who will make the future and keep his memory famous and warm. Yours sincerely,

s. J. C. Smuts

783 To M. C. Gillett — Vol. 88, no. 239

Groote Schuur
[Cape Town]
21 March 1948

My letters to you are becoming very scrappy and unsatisfactory. But we are in the last days of the session. Last week I had to be at Cradock for a [agricultural] show and at Oudtshoorn for a centenary. Calls on my time are more than I can cope with, and correspondence has to take its chance, and a poor chance at best. Now Sunday night before bedtime I send this in order not to break an honourable cycle!

Much of my time is taken up with election matters. I have had a long and tiresome negotiation with our little Labour party with whom an accord has finally been reached. The prospects appear fair, but in these matters it is dangerous to be certain of what will happen. It will be a dirty election which it will be difficult to maintain on a decent level. Still, I hope to do so and risk the consequences. My main underlying note will be that in times of grave crisis such as the world is now passing through it is on the whole best to stick to the tried leadership which has proved successful in the past, rather than to embark on risky changes. This sounds egotistical, but in essence it is not an unreasonable point to make.

There is a crisis on, or one not far off. Never has the prospect been so obscure and even black as today. Yet I think Russia has over-reached herself and raised a reaction against her policies which will lead to their failure or frustration. America is already thoroughly awakened and alarmed, and isolation is ending. The way the Greeks have held out[1] has opened people's eyes to what is afoot. Czechoslovakia has been a terrible eye-opener, in spite of

[1] The Greek government, in spite of severe economic difficulties, was engaged in a constant struggle against the Communist guerillas who were aided by Yugoslavia, Albania and Bulgaria.

Not here. Still he leads them—
The young fighters of so many battles
And he will be in the forefront of the heroes
When the long awaited day shall dawn.

Russia's apparent success.[1] The Finnish negotiation has thoroughly alarmed Scandinavia.[2] The Western Union is making good progress, and the Marshall plan is being hurried on to fulfilment. These developments are the silver lining to the ominous cloud. Now you see the report Crossman [R.H.S.] has brought back from Prague,[3] and the resignation of the *Worker's* editor.[4]

I have spoken repeatedly with the object of awakening attention to this sinister cold war. To the American correspondents[5] I pointed out that next time Britain will not be America's front line. America will herself be in the front line and will have to wage war from the first moment if it should come. Two world wars have exhausted Britain and so weakened Europe that the war may begin on the Atlantic coast of Europe. One of these American editors told a friend that my frank statement on the whole position was the clearest and most convincing he and his colleagues had ever listened to. I am not a warmonger, but Stalin is following the Hitler technique—and the results may be the same. But enough of all this.

In two days I fly home with Daphne [Smuts] and her babes and send Bibas [Smuts] back to Hermanus. Then the final struggle will begin for me, which will end in the general election on 26 May. I shall thus be free to go to Cambridge either as prime minister or as a free man. Then, after a short interval, to parliament again with a heavy programme. Pretty tough going as you will admit. Now good-night—and blessings on you.

Jan

784 To C. Weizmann Vol. 88, no. 60

The document in the Smuts Collection is a draft in Smuts's handwriting. On page 3 of the draft is the following annotation: 'This correspondence to be published immediately'.

[1] The Czech Communist party, under Klement Gottwald, had, with the support of the 'purged' Social Democrats, brought about a *coup* which excluded the democratic parties from the government. It was a victory for alliance with Russia as against acceptance of American support under Marshall Aid.

[2] Negotiations were to open in Moscow on 22 March for the conclusion of a mutual assistance treaty between Finland and the Soviet Union. Such a treaty came into force on 31 May 1948.

[3] 'Prague's February Revolution', published in the *Nation*, 27 March 1948.

[4] Douglas A. Hyde had resigned from the position of news editor of the *Daily Worker* and from his membership of the Communist party.

[5] Smuts Collection, Box G, no. 14.

Telegram

To: Dr Chaim Weizmann

From: Field Marshal Smuts

Dated 29 March 1948

Your message of 24 March.[1] I do not assume that partition is in immediate danger. American proposal for U.N.O. trusteeship[2] appears intended as interim measure to prevent terrible situation such as may arise immediately on termination of British mandate and has already begun. I myself feel deeply concerned over possibilities of this situation. Something may happen in that vacuum of public authority after British withdrawal and before new régime is in working order which may shock world conscience and even precipitate an international crisis. Britain unfortunately has grave difficulties of her own and suffers from bitter disappointment over Palestine, and under these circumstances an appeal to U.N.O. who sponsored partition is not unreasonable. I see no alternative to partition, but nobody wishes it to be achieved through massacres and international complications, and some interim measures may yet prevent irremediable mischief.

My deep sympathy and warm good wishes go to you, my old friend, who have laboured so hard for the cause and been wounded in the struggle for it. May your work yet be crowned with success before the end.

785 To M. C. Gillett — Vol. 88, no. 241

Doornkloof
[Transvaal]
2 April 1948

I returned home last night after a three days' absence to Cape Town and Kimberley on official business, and found two letters from you and Arthur awaiting me. Thank you. Your news was good, especially about yourself and your health. Arthur writes about the puzzle which is Russia. Of course Russia is not very easy to understand and calls for caution and reserve on our part. She uses different language from us and where she uses our language it

[1] Weizmann wished Smuts to support partition publicly in view of Dr Evatt's statement of 23 March regarding the attempt to revise the decision of the general assembly of U.N.O. (Smuts Collection, vol. 88, no. 326).

[2] On 19 March 1948 the United States delegation at U.N.O. had proposed that partition be suspended and a temporary U.N.O. trusteeship over Palestine effected.

must be with a different meaning. 'Democracy' for instance means to her exactly what Tsarism and dictatorship mean to us. But of course it is difficult to avoid the impression that she wants to steal a march on the rest of the world in its present deplorable plight. She is remorselessly moving forward in her march to world Communism. And it would almost look as if things may come to a head over Germany, and more especially in Berlin, which is situated in the Russian zone, although occupied by all three powers. Perhaps the hated atomic bomb is the only deterrent from a fresh outbreak of vast trouble. If this is so one can but be thankful for this unmercy!

The political game meanwhile is on here, and we are all hard at it. Dr Malan has just issued a manifesto[1] which threatens to take away from Natives and Coloureds the little political rights which they still have after the retrograde movements of Hertzog's day. But it looks as if we shall beat them in spite of their cry of a black peril over the head of South Africa. My time-table is formidable, but I hope I shall stand and survive this last fight of mine. My heart is not in it, but compulsion is laid on me.[2] My real concern is more over what is happening in Europe, where so much is at stake for the future of this world. We have already little hope of a better order for the future and, unlike the Christians in the decline and fall of the Roman Empire, we have now no vision of the City of God in the advance of the church. We can but hope to hold on grimly to what we have of human rights, which have been saved from the wreckage of two world wars. There is an air of despondency and a sense of failure over our world and its prospects. And yet we know that the light will rise again, and gladness will once more return to the earth. But when, O Lord?

I can but send love and good wishes to you and all the dear ones at Street.

Jan

[1] *See Die Burger*, 29 March 1948, p. 3; 30 March 1948, p. 3. Also D. W. Krüger, *South African Parties and Policies 1910–1960*, pp. 402–7.

[2] 'for necessity is laid upon me'. *1 Corinthians* ix.16.

786 To D. Moore Vol. 88, no. 72

Doornkloof
Transvaal
8 April 1948

My dear Daphne, I had quite a nice letter from Senanayake a little while back and today I wrote him an even nicer letter in return. This was done partly because of the good opinion you have of him, and partly I think it is good policy to cultivate decent relations with that Oriental world now turning away from the West. Hard and bitter experience which surely awaits them may turn them once more towards us.

Since I last wrote to you I have been much on the move. So, last week I spent in the Cape Province on political and other official business. Two days at Cape Town enabled me to cap the governor-general[1] who was made an LL.D. of the University. Another day was spent at Kimberley in connection with a show and other functions. A longish absence always means heavy arrears at Pretoria which have then to be worked off. With the political campaign on, many of my colleagues are away and their work naturally comes to me. Much work also falls on me as leader of the United party in the direction of the campaign all over the country. You will therefore sympathize with me when I say my time is very fully taken up. Still, for a change, I indulge in a long veld walk occasionally, and tomorrow (Saturday) I am going with Jannie [Smuts] to Rooikop to see how his farming operations are progressing.

I think I wrote you about the visit of American newspaper men to South Africa and my contacts with them. I now find a big crop of articles and speculations about this country and its future and myself in the American press. Much of it is really amusing—some of it makes out that I am a sort of superman—some ancient Odysseus returned from many wars and now directing the affairs of his little Ithaca with much experience and enthusiasm. All very amusing.

My great friend Tom Lamont, the leading figure in the Morgan Bank, has passed away and I have condoled with his wife Florence who is one of my special friends. Tom was slightly older than I, and Florence is a few years younger. A really lovely woman and one of my special friends. I have a weakness for women, not in the sexual sense, but from some inner affinity and appeal, and if I have to go through the list of my very special friends in life I find

[1] G. Brand van Zyl.

they are largely women—some of my young life to whom I have remained attached and with whom correspondence still goes on across the years. To me women are more interesting. I suppose it must be because I am more fully a male type, and the opposites attract as in electro-magnetism.

By the way I did not see Deirdre [O'Neill] in Cape Town and Cooper and myself were like hermits in Groote Schuur. Deirdre must be very busy—I don't really know. I shall be again there in the beginning of May and then shall make a point of seeing her. Otherwise I may never see her again. She thinks of England and you think of taking her to Australia. I am a bad parter from those I love, and it troubles me that this dear child may disappear from my horizon. She looked very well when I saw her last.

In my busy life I have the opportunity to meet many interesting people. Thus yesterday afternoon I had here two very interesting Americans—Professor Camp and his wife of Berkeley University, California. He is here as the leader of an American scientific expedition to inquire into our prehistoric life and palaeontology. They were very anxious to see Isie who has a curious reputation far and wide over the world—much as she resents publicity. We discussed the rise of man through the hundreds of thousands of years, of which there is such abundant evidence in South Africa. We discussed holism and its part in evolution. Why is it that there is an upward trend in evolution, and higher and more advanced forms arise from lower, more primitive forms? Why is there a curiously pronounced progress towards the higher. Is there direction, is there a trend, a bias in a certain direction? Is there design and Providence? This of course is the central problem in the great mystery of life. Matter runs down like water, life and mind rise up to ever higher levels. How and why is this? I tried to explain how my theory of holism tries to account for this tendency which is so apparent and yet so mysterious on purely scientific lines of thought. I hope I did not confuse them. I told them I intended still to continue my work on holism and deal with some of the deeper problems which I deliberately left alone in my earlier work. The question is just whether I can live and remain sane long enough to do this! The indications are that we shall win the elections once more, and that I shall be compelled to carry on as prime minister. But how long, O Lord?[1] Will there be no quiet afternoon for release and reflection? The burden and the strain continues. I fear when I am in London in June the world situation will have to be reviewed on the highest levels, and

[1] 'And they cried with a loud voice, saying, How long, O Lord...' *Revelation* vi.10.

I shall return from Cambridge and London more exhausted than ever for a new session of parliament. Such is life: it is difficult to get into the job, and it may be still more difficult to get out of it. Not even a general election will release me, as it should under normal circumstances.

Now good-night. I think of you and Henry, and I sometimes doubt whether you will stay on in Ceylon till the end of 1949. You may have better luck than I! Ever yours,

J.C.S.

787 To L. S. Amery — Vol. 88, no. 78

[Doornkloof
Transvaal]
13 April 1948

My dear Amery, You have never *belaboured* me, as you say, but all you send me is carefully read and considered most informative and helpful. Thank you for this latest from [Lord] Layton.[1] I shall read it with interest.

I do hope to see you when I am in London for a short while in June. We must talk the situation over. I never saw the like of it in my time.

I am very sad over Palestine. We shall be leaving behind a trail of ruin, and I believe very heavy criticism. I did my best to represent to the British authorities the necessity of providing for local security both in Jerusalem and at other points. But the police were adamant in favour of scuttle. We can't scuttle from responsibility before history. All kind regards, Ever yours,

s. J. C. Smuts

788 To C. E. Raven — Vol. 88, no. 88

Prime Minister's Office
Pretoria
4 May 1948

My dear Master, Egeland, who has seen you, has informed me of the provisional programme for the installation and other functions, and I have wired him my approval which he has no doubt conveyed to you.

[1] A pamphlet on European union which argues 'that a European customs union is not practical politics' and advocates 'an advance towards economic unity by way of mutual preference' (Smuts Collection, vol. 85, no. 12).

My dear Oxford friends the Gilletts who now live at Street in Somersetshire are anxious to attend the Christ's garden party, and I shall much appreciate your inviting them if convenient to you. I give their address below.

In regard to the recipients for honorary degrees another name has occurred to me, which you might consider if it is not already too late. It is that of Gregg the Anglican Archbishop of Armagh and Primate of Ireland who was a Christ man of my time and a close friend of those years.[1] I have lost touch with him in later life, but as a distinguished Christ man I would like to sponsor him, if not too late and if the university has not already honoured him.[2]

I am in a frightful time-table tangle, as I face a general election on 26 May and the formation of a cabinet thereafter before I leave early in June—with all the negotiations and preparations which accompany such matters. However, I hope I shall get through it all in time before leaving.

My address at the installation, which I am thinking over, will probably occupy some twenty-five minutes if that is not too long. My idea is to make extended reference to the two ideological trends now dividing the world and their bearing on our Western outlook. Its bearing on the university is obvious.

I am bringing only my private secretary, Cooper, with me, but you need not provide for him at Christ's if you happen to be cramped for space. With kind regards, Yours sincerely,

J. C. Smuts

789 To D. Moore Vol. 88, no. 93

Doornkloof
Transvaal
6 May 1948

My dear Daphne, This Easter day gives me a chance to write to you. It is a holiday and also a pause in the political battle which has now come to its climax. In another twenty days we shall reach the elections. I have naturally been very busy with this and other pressing questions. Most of my colleagues are away stumping the country, and I have to limit my absences in order to attend to the matters which continue to arise in spite of the elections, and brook no delay...

[1] *See* **755** (vol. III).

[2] C. E. Raven wrote to Smuts that Archbishop Gregg had already received a doctorate from the university.

I am so sorry that I shall have come back from London when you reach it. It would have been such a comfort and joy to have seen you again after this long time, and with the prospect of perhaps not seeing you for another lengthy period. Life, in cutting itself up into individuals, made a sad mistake, and has thus created that pain at the heart of the world which nothing can cure. We are separate, and separated in space and time, even though every yearning in us is towards unity, towards togetherness and the easing of that pain. (I am again falling into my reflective mood, which must be a bore to you.)

There is little consoling to look at in the great world. The Curtain[1] now hung up in the world hides but sorrow and fear and worse in the world. I think of speaking on this ideological splitting up of mankind at my installation next month. And I have just prepared a broadcast on the invitation of the B.B.C. on the changing concept of our Commonwealth under the stresses and strains of the new world and power situation.[2] Never has the world situation been more sombre and perplexing than today. America for the moment is the Atlas[3] which carries most of the burden on her shoulders—and for how long? Unless Europe comes together in a new revival the situation may get worse and worse. I have just sent a message of hope and encouragement to the European Unity Conference at the Hague over which Winston is presiding. That, and Benelux[4] and E.R.P.[5] may turn the tide, which is now flowing very dangerously against us. Communism is on the move and there is nothing to stop it, unless a united halt of the West is called to this advance. Luckily Italy has won in her general election.[6] But in Greece, where the attack is hottest, the confusion is growing and the future very dark. The coalition

[1] The Iron Curtain—a term used to indicate the almost impenetrable barriers dividing the Communist countries and peoples in eastern Europe from the West. The phrase became popular after Churchill used it in an address at Fulton, United States on 5 March 1946. But it was used in a comparable sense by H. G. Wells in 1904 and in 1945 in its present sense by other publicists.

[2] 792.

[3] In Greek mythology one of the Titans condemned to support the heavens on his shoulders.

[4] A customs union between Belgium, the Netherlands and Luxemburg agreed upon in 1944 and brought into existence on 29 October 1947. The common tariff came into force on 1 January 1948.

[5] European Recovery Programme—proposals for economic co-operation made to the United States by the sixteen European states which had formed the Organization for European Economic Co-operation.

[6] The election of April 1948, in which 90 per cent of the electorate voted, was an unexpectedly decisive victory for the Christian Democrat party (De Gasperi) which won more than half the seats while the Communists won somewhat less than one-third.

government[1] seems to be breaking up, and King Paul will find it difficult to get a new team together which will command the confidence of the United Kingdom and the United States. Freddy writes that she and her organization are looking after 20,000 Greek children rescued from the guerillas and from deportation to Yugoslavia. Some 3,000 have arrived in Czechoslovakia in unspeakable condition. And so it goes on. The Greek minister of justice[2] has just been assassinated in Athens, and Communism is making a great all-out effort to create confusion and chaos. I am terribly sorry for our dear Greek friends who are in dire physical peril. She does not know what to do, and I am sure the Americans are doing all they can. But Greece is a minor side-show to them and they have bigger problems to worry over in Europe—not to speak of their troubles at home, and the problems of a coming presidential election.

I had a letter from your prime minister[3] and wrote him a nice note in reply. He seems a decent fellow—but after him what?

Don't think I am despondent. I am perplexed and looking round for the way out, knowing that this is only a phase—a very bad phase—and that there will be a turn of Fortune's wheel.

My love and all the rest to you. And kind remembrances and best wishes to Henry. All well here. Ever yours,

J.C.S.

790 To C. Weizmann Vol. 88, no. 100

Telegram

From: secretary for external affairs, Pretoria

To: South African delegation, New York

Dated 17 May 1948

For Andrews [H.T.] from prime minister:

Please give following message from me to Dr Chaim Weizmann, who wires from New York. Begins: I have your message and thank you warmly for it. My hope and wish is for the success of state of Israel.[4]

[1] The Liberal-Populist government, with T. Sophoulis as prime minister and C. Tsaldaris as deputy prime minister and foreign minister, which had been in power since 5 September 1947.

[2] Christos Ladas, killed in Athens on 1 May by a hand grenade thrown at him by Erstratios Moutsoyannis, presumably a Communist.

[3] Dudley Senanayake (q.v.).

[4] The Jewish state of Israel was proclaimed on 14 May. The termination of the mandate at midnight was anticipated by some hours in order not to break the Sabbath beginning at sunset.

I have already publicly welcomed and expressed good wishes for new state. Official action is still held up by consideration of new situation and necessary consultations. All kind regards. Ends.

791 To M. C. Gillett Vol. 88, no. 246

Doornkloof
[Transvaal]
20 May 1948

Another dear letter from you, full of the colour of sky and earth, and of the dear things of home. I have little to say in these last days of a general election which absorbs most of my attention and leaves little for private intercourse. You have told me that you like MSS. I enclose one I wrote last night as an introduction to a book on Olive Schreiner—*Not Without Honour* by a Mrs Postma,[1] a lecturer at Cape Town University. I was much struck by it as you will be when it appears, and I thought I should give it a good send-off—more personal than usual.

I am much troubled in spirit over this war in Palestine—my sympathy being very much with the Jews who are now beset by the Arabs of six other states.[2] It reads like the Old Testament, and I am sorry to see the British, while appearing neutral, really sympathizing with the Arabs. [Sir John] Glubb and his officers of the Transjordan Legion are seconded from the British army. I feel greatly tempted to recognize the new state of Israel. What a terrible age we live in! And what will be the end of it all? One turns with relief to something else, but you would not call a general election with all its shady excitements and contradictions a relief!

This will be my last note to you before my personal appearance in London on 7 June. So good-bye and *tot siens* to you all. Ever yours,

Jan

792 Speech (1948) Box M, no. 252

By kind invitation of the B.B.C. I am giving this message on the changing conception of the British Commonwealth and Empire. The eve of 24 May is an appropriate occasion for such a review

[1] Vera Buchanan Gould, *Not Without Honour; the Life and Writings of Olive Schreiner* (1949).

[2] Immediately after the termination of the mandate the Arab armies entered Palestine. The six Arab states taking part in the war were: Egypt, Syria, Lebanon, Transjordan, Iraq and Saudi Arabia.

of the change that has come over the face of our great group in recent years. 24 May—Queen's birthday, recognized by law as Empire Day in South Africa—is a link with the great Victorian age, when the British Empire was still the greatest power in the world, and the British navy held sway as the instrument of world security and peace for a century. Gone are those halcyon days—gone that supreme status of the Empire. We have moved into a sombre climate of history, and a great shift has taken place in world power and world security. So far as the British Commonwealth and Empire is concerned two world wars have left their mark, and their wounds from which it is still bleeding. The cause we fought for was worth that sacrifice, but the sacrifice has been greater than the most far-seeing dreamt of, greater than even Britain could bear without almost irreparable damage. This centre of our world group, this heart of the Allied defence, has indeed suffered beyond measure. She has come through the ordeal with victory, and laden with honours which history will forever acclaim. But losses in man-power, and especially in material resources, have profoundly affected both her internal conditions and her position as a world power, and our whole group has suffered, though not to the same extent.

In an address I gave to members of both houses of parliament in 1917,[1] in which I used the name of the British Commonwealth of nations as better descriptive of our group than the British Empire, I called it the most successful experiment in world government ever made, and indeed a real league of nations in working order. That description still holds good after the bloody tests of two world wars which shattered many other empires. Since then two other great experiments in world government have been tried, alas, so far with disappointing results. But our Commonwealth of nations still stands, still faces the world as a proof that human government on a world scale is possible, and that free nations can hold and live together in common association. But the unique world position of our group has suffered in these destructive wars of our generation. At the same time other world powers have come to the fore, and now like colossi bestride the scene. In comparison our stature has suffered. In another address I gave to members of parliament in 1943[2] I foreshadowed this change in what was called an explosive speech which caused widespread comment at the time. Unfortunately my forecast has come only too true. The U.S.A. and the U.S.S.R. now occupy top rank among the world powers.

[1] Vol. III, 750. [2] 624.

In these wars and in the post-war years we have suffered other losses of a very serious character. Our financial and general economic position has gravely deteriorated, with serious effects for both our internal conditions and our external relations and influence. Other European powers suffered similarly, but they had no such exalted position to lose. This lost ground may be recovered, on Mr Churchill's formula, by toil and sweat, blood and tears. But there are other losses which may never be recovered again. I refer to our world communications, which are the links and, as it were, the vital arteries of our group scattered over this great globe. Our territory is not a compact mass like the U.S.A. or the U.S.S.R. and our life as a group depends largely on our sea communications and the ability of our sea power to hold them. Our sea power has suffered heavy losses which can, however, be repaired and even improved by the new scientific discoveries. But our lost communications will never be recovered. I refer to our life line through the Mediterranean and on to the Middle East and to the Far East—from the Commonwealth point of view perhaps the greatest loss we have suffered. We still hold certain points in the Mediterranean, but Egypt has gone, and with it our position as of right to use it as a base. What that base meant was proved in the last war. But for it nothing might have prevented Germany from overrunning the Middle East and linking up with Japan in India. From that base we broke the Italian Empire and Italy itself, so that the final attack on Germany could be made from the West. That line has gone, and other dispositions will have to be made for the Commonwealth to make good that grievous loss.

From this point of view the whole post-war position that has come about among the great powers has to be reviewed in order that the Commonwealth can be fitted into the new pattern of world power. The Commonwealth position has to be reviewed in relation to the whole new world position. What is that position as it is shaping today? We have dreamt of the one world that was to be the outcome of this second world war. Science and technology seemed at last to be destroying all the dividing lines among mankind, and economics to be forcing the nations together into a world community. Greatly daring we were, even before the end of the war, planning a vast world organization in U.N.O. to represent this world unity. But we appear now to have moved faster than human nature. Our time-table has been wrong. Mankind has refused to conform to our vision, and is now visibly splitting into two worlds. It may not be a permanent fission, but for the moment at least it is a real fact, and in a spirit of realism we can but recast our plans accordingly. Perhaps we shall progress in due course from two worlds to one: at present it is two. The Curtain divides them. The Curtain stands for fear, the fear which divides the Communist or totalitarian world from the free peoples of the West. It is not a mere passive inert fear: it is active, aggressive. It has already overwhelmed many small peoples in eastern Europe. It is the sort of fear which may mean great mischief, unless it is kept in check by wise precautions and active vigilance. I need not dilate further on what everybody knows and sees, who has eyes to see. Two great poles of power face each other across the Curtain: the U.S.A. in the West, the U.S.S.R. in the East, while the Far East is still shrouded in the shadows of the future. In this power set-up we have to choose and take our place as a Commonwealth of nations. The world is thus faced with an entirely new alignment of world power, with the two opposed camps in command of colossal, unprecedented war potential. It is against this power background that we must review our concepts of Commonwealth and Empire, and of its position and status. It is no longer a question of our standing alone for our security—or of counting our losses and gains in the world wars. Organization of the West becomes the one paramount issue, for us of the Commonwealth also.

In this connection it is in the first place clear that the United States, by virtue of its secure geographical position, its unequalled industrial resources, and its immense war potential, has a special position in the West. The Commonwealth accepts and welcomes that, all the more because of the United States' affinity in race, language, ideas, outlook and policies with members of the Commonwealth. Association between the two would not only be the most obvious and natural one, but would also mean a concentration of resources and a command of world communications which would give pause to any potential aggressor. No change in the structure of the Commonwealth would be involved. Canada has for long found loyal membership of the Commonwealth compatible with close co-operation with the States, and has thus set a precedent for the Commonwealth as a whole. States and Commonwealth could well work together without any change in their present constitutional arrangements, and certainly without any loss of face.

In the second place, Europe, or at least Europe west of the Curtain, is in a position of special danger, and both for its recovery and its future security its construction on a regional plan has become both necessary and urgent. The doom which has befallen the old motherlands of the West can only be retrieved by the

European peoples coming together. Through Benelux,[1] the Five-Power Brussels Pact,[2] and the European Recovery Plan[3] this great move has begun. With strong American backing and British sponsorship it may yet turn the present defeat and disaster of Europe into one of the finest achievements of statesmanship—a European Union, a new birth of time, which will save our Western civilization. Some Atlantic Plan may bring about a measure of American participation. British participation is necessary and inevitable, both because European Union could not work without her, and also because Britain is part of Europe and no longer an island apart. Besides, her own recovery is directly and intimately bound up with the recovery of Europe. They need each other desperately. If Western Union, with British membership, is thus consummated, a third or middle power group will arise, at least equal to either of the other two, the security set-up of the world will rest on a triangle of power, and will not continue to be precariously poised between two great powers facing each other across a broken Europe. That is how I see the future basis of security and world peace. That, I think, is the course of the next great advance.

It is in this connection that an interesting and most important issue may soon arise for the Commonwealth of which Britain is the leading member. Can she be a leading or important member of both Commonwealth and Western Union? Will the Commonwealth suffer from such a dual relationship of Britain? I have given the matter much consideration and see no insuperable difficulty, but it would be premature to discuss the matter here or at this early stage. One thing is quite certain: Britain will be necessary for both Commonwealth and Western Union. She is the mother of states and she has been the originator and the leader of the most successful existing group of free states. She has unrivalled experience of human affairs in all parts of the world, and has acquired a traditional technique for handling them. Her sense of justice and fairplay and her balanced judgment must now more than ever be invaluable world assets in this time of unsettlement and ruffled tempers. A great human mission lies before her, perhaps greater than any in her glorious past.

[1] *See supra*, p. 197, note 4.

[2] The Brussels Treaty Organization, created in March 1948 between Belgium, France, Luxemburg, the Netherlands and Great Britain, bound the members to mutual assistance in the case of an armed attack on any one of them.

[3] *See supra*, p. 197, note 5.

793 From R. E. Bell Vol. 85, no. 49

National Bank Buildings
Johannesburg
28 May 1948

My dear General, Eve[1] and I are more sorry than words can express over the Standerton result[2] which is not only a heavy blow to you personally and our dear Ouma, but equally to our great party (still great).

After the news came through I conveyed to Mr [J. W.] Higgerty by 'phone, and now want to confirm to you, my offer to resign Houghton,[3] which I know will be very honoured to elect you. I just want to add that I shall do so very readily indeed in a sense of privilege and pleasure.

I am, needless to say, shocked at the general result,[4] and at this early stage am of opinion that the *platteland* vote[5] was anti-Hofmeyr and the miners' vote anti-government. I feel that I must express to you my view that Mr Hofmeyr, despite his ceaseless diligence and in some sense his brilliance, has in the main been a serious embarrassment because of his rather too freely expressed views on the Native and Coloured issues (I think particularly of his speech on the Pegging Act in 1943) and his war taxation measures. His stubbornness to heed responsible representations and afford redress concerning discriminatory taxation measures and violations of principles stamped him as no minister of finance, and this, despite his apparent strength, was the weak link in your wartime cabinet. In any other portfolio than finance he could have been a source of strength. I think I can claim to be well in touch with responsible opinion in financial and business circles in which the opinion I have expressed is widely shared.

There is a rumour current that you are considering retiring. I can understand your considering this as a course of action, but I implore you not to do so. South Africa is in a critical phase which calls for the most careful handling and wisest of leadership. Equally so it demands facing facts, outstanding among whom (from the party point of view) is that Mr Hofmeyr cannot expect to lead the party and is in the circumstances prevailing a serious embarrass-

[1] Born Annie Eva Reine, married R. E. Bell in 1926.

[2] Smuts lost Standerton to W. C. du Plessis by 224 votes.

[3] Smuts accepted the offer of Charles Clark's seat, Pretoria East. Houghton is a Johannesburg constituency.

[4] This was as follows: National party 70, Afrikaner party 9, United party 65, Labour party 6. For an analysis of the result *see* W. K. Hancock, *Smuts—The fields of Force*, pp. 505–6.

[5] Rural vote (Afrikaans).

ment in the way of our retrieving the ground lost. That this should be so is a matter of keen regret to me for I realize his good points. In the present dark mists a beacon light shines out clearly and it is your continued active leadership, which destiny is demanding. From this source the rest must flow. May I in my humble way ask you to review the position from this angle and suggest that you give as early a decision as possible upon this all-important issue.

I have felt it a duty to convey these views to you at the same time as the confirmation of my offer to make Houghton available to you, which, I repeat, I shall do with the utmost willingness.

With deepest regards to you and Ouma and best wishes for a happy trip to Britain and your safe return from Eve and myself,
Yours very sincerely and loyally,

R. Eric Bell

794 From J. F. J. van Rensburg Vol. 88, no. 304

28 Mei 1948

Seer geagte Generaal, Op 'n tydstip waar baie van u vyande uitbundig juig oor die *débâcle* wat u in die stryd oorval het, wil ek, met u verlof, my tot u rig omdat ek die drang daartoe voel.

As teenstander het ek op die oorlogskwessie (en ook in ander sake) skerp van u verskil, en tot die nederlaag wat u so pas gely het, het ook ek wel in sekere mate bygedra.

Maar juis as teenstander, en wel teenstander in die brandpunt van 'n aktivistiese terrein waar die gevaar steeds aanwesig en die katastrofe nooit uitgesluit was nie, was ek dalk beter as meeste mense in staat om te beoordeel hoe seer u, soos weinig andere, bemoeid was om te verhoed dat sake nie hande uitruk nie en daardeur die hele volk in 'n ramp dompel. Die kruitvat het wydoop gestaan en enige vonk kon die ontploffing veroorsaak. Ek het met waardering geleer hoeveel die Afrikaner, bewus of nie, aan u meesterlike geduld verskuldig is.

Insover as individuele toedoen betrokke was, het ek u beskou as meer dan iemand anders verantwoordelik daarvoor dat ons volk in die oorlog beland het en ek het dit bitterlik gewraak en met alle krag my daarteen verset. Maar die onheil wat u ná daardie voldonge feit telkens en nogmaals die volk bespaar het, het my beweeg om nou—waar niemand my motiewe kan misverstaan nie—my respekvolle erkentlikheid aan u toe te bring.

Ek weet nie wat u politieke voornemens is nie, Generaal, maar aan u persoon wil ek in alle eerbied nog baie gesonde en geseënde jare toewens en ek ag dit 'n voorreg dat ek, hoewel 'n aktiewe teenstander, my onder u vereerders kan tel.

Ek hoop dat u my brief nie kwalik sal neem nie, Generaal; dit kom uit die hart! Met respekvolle komplimente,

Hans van Rensburg

TRANSLATION

28 May 1948

Dear General, At a time when many of your enemies are rejoicing exceedingly at the *débâcle* which has overcome you in the fight, I should like, with your permission, to address myself to you because I feel a need to do so.

As an opponent I differed sharply from you on the war question (and also on other matters), and I, too, have, to some extent, contributed to the defeat which you have suffered.

But it was precisely as an opponent, and indeed as an opponent at the focal point in activist territory where danger was always present and catastrophe never excluded, that I was able to judge, perhaps better than most, how concerned you were, as few others, to prevent matters from getting out of hand and so plunging the whole nation into disaster. The powder-barrel was wide open and any spark could have caused an explosion. I learned, with appreciation, how much the Afrikanders, whether or not they were aware of it, owed to your masterly patience.

In so far as individual action was concerned, I regarded you, more than anyone else, as being responsible for landing our people in the war; this I bitterly revenged and resisted with all my strength. But the calamity which, after that *fait accompli*, you repeatedly spared the nation has moved me now, when no one can misunderstand my motives, to offer you my respectful gratitude.

I do not know, General, what your political intentions are but to you personally I should like, with all respect, to wish many healthy and blessed years and I regard it as a privilege that I may count myself, even though an active opponent, among those who honour you.

I hope, General, that you will not take my letter amiss; it comes from the heart. With respectful compliments,

Hans van Rensburg

795 From L. S. Amery Vol. 85, no. 14

112 Eaton Square
S.W.1
29 May 1948

My dear Ou Baas, So the proverbial ingratitude of democracy has been confirmed once more! Never mind. You have behind you a wonderful achievement in world saving and world shaping during these last nine years, and you may well have more opportunities before long to return to your creative work in South Africa, in the Commonwealth and in the world. Meanwhile I am sure it will do you good to shake off the red dust of South Africa from your feet for a few days and see the Cambridge Backs in the full glory of early summer. We may also then, I hope, find an hour for a good talk.

I listened with the greatest interest to your broadcast[1] the other evening. But confess I thought you were unduly pessimistic about our abandonment of the Middle East. The facts of geography and the essential feebleness of those Arab powers will compel us, whether with the Americans or by ourselves, to reassert our position there, even if only to keep the Russians out. We scuttled ignominiously out of the Sudan in the eighties, but were back before the end of the century,[2] and you and I may still see something of the same sort happening in the Middle East in our time.

Meanwhile Winston has at last spoken up and begun to turn the corner from the unfortunate position he took up when he talked about handing back the mandate eighteen months ago. I enclose, for your private eye, a copy of a letter which I have just sent him.[3] As things have turned out I am very glad that you took the decisive step of recognizing the Jewish state. Naturally I agreed with you on the merits of your decision, but I confess I was a little anxious about it from the point of view of Empire co-operation, and would have been happier if other Dominions had joined in with you. Anyhow, now you are entirely free to say what you like about that situation either in South Africa or when you come over here.

Florence joins me in sending you every affectionate greeting and every wish for many years of good health and happiness. Yours ever,

Leo Amery

[1] **792**.

[2] After the revolt of the Mahdi, the death of General Gordon and the fall of Khartoum in 1885, British control over the Sudan lapsed until 1898 when an army under Kitchener reasserted it. In 1899 an Anglo-Egyptian condominium was established.

[3] Not enclosed in the document in the Smuts Collection.

796 To J. N. F. van Rensburg Vol. 91, no. 190

Volksraad
Kaapstad
[Junie 1948]

Waarde Hans, My hartelike dank vir jou welkomme brief van geluk en seënwense. Ek waardeer dit en verstaan die gevoel daaragter, wat spruit uit jare van persoonlike kennis, en jare van verwydering wat ons [mekaar] tog miskien beter leer ken het. Ek wens jou alles wat goed is toe. *Es irrt der Mensch so lang er strebt.* Steeds u toegeneë,

J. C. Smuts

TRANSLATION

House of Assembly
Cape Town
[June 1948]

Dear Hans, My sincere thanks for your welcome letter of good luck and good wishes.[1] I value it and understand the feeling behind it, which springs from years of personal acquaintance and years of separation which nevertheless taught us perhaps to know each other better. I wish you all that is good. *Es irrt der Mensch so lang er strebt.*[2] Yours ever,

J. C. Smuts

797 To J. Hutchinson Vol. 88, no. 107

House of Assembly
Cape Town
[June 1948]

My dear Hutch, My very warm thanks for the *Story of Plants*[3] which has just arrived. It is a most welcome gift, both as coming from you, and for its own sake. I hope to spend many a happy bedtime moment in browsing through these beautiful pages and this interesting information. You may be sure that the book will be a great favourite in the Doornkloof circle, and all the family will remember with glowing affection the writer who spent such happy days with us.

[1] **794**.
[2] Man errs as long as he strives. Goethe, *Faust*, part I, Prologue in Heaven.
[3] J. Hutchinson, *British Flowering Plants* (1948).

The whirligig of politics has once more sent me into the cold shades of opposition, with all its trials and disappointments. But on the whole I remain firm in the faith that this is a good world, worth living in, and even if humans are indifferent or unkind the plants remain ever good friends, with whom to live is a great consolation and inspiration.

I hope you are continuing well and happy in your labours, and that the new Bentham and Hooker[1] is making good progress. With good wishes to you both, Yours ever affectionately,

s. J. C. Smuts

798 To D. Moore Vol. 88, no. 108

Hyde Park Hotel
London S.W.1
8 June 1948

My dear Daphne, Here I sit in the same old room where we foregathered in the past. I arrived here yesterday and have been moving since in a tangle of making and evading appointments. But best of all was your letter of 28 May which awaited me on my arrival. A letter of consolation and sympathy and comfort. Yes, I have lost, but more than what you bewail. I have also lost the prospect of release, of some freedom at the end, and of quietly collecting my thoughts and gaining clarity in my own soul. One must view oneself at a distance and in a perspective, so to say, to understand what has underlain one's life work and dark strivings. But my defeat in South Africa leaves me now no choice. If I go out of public life so much of what has been laboriously built up may be broken down again. I must defend my works—which means I must remain in the fighting line and continue to lead the party. Hofmeyr has been too much under attack, and has been too seriously wounded to do this job, and I must continue in the leadership and keep the team together—a good and useful team, but naturally still relying on the old leadership which they prefer to a change. How I would have welcomed that safari, the lure of Serengeti,[2] and the other prospects which must now be severely denied.

I came here in the old York with Henry Cooper. I stayed two days in Athens with those dear friends[3] who were far more dis-

[1] Hutchinson was working on a new edition of *Genera Plantarum* by George Bentham (1800–84) and Sir Joseph Hooker (1817–1911).

[2] The great game resort of the Serengeti plain in northern Tanzania.

[3] King Paul and Queen Frederica of Greece.

appointed than myself over what had befallen me. They are doing very well indeed. He is trusted, she is adored, as we had expected. She is now looking after refugee Greek children, 10,000 of them, and has collected more than a million pounds from the Greeks for the purpose. You would be proud of her if you saw how she had become a real force for good in this difficult little community. When I arrived they were expecting ex-King Michael and his fiancée[1] who were to be married there. But her illness in Switzerland prevented her arrival and I gladly missed the wedding. But during my stay we could visit some of the more interesting spots I knew from history, and Palo drove us along bad roads like another Jehu.[2] Two days of rest and release, to be followed by the agitated crowded doings of a brief London visit. I am seeing as many of the great ones as possible, from the royal family to the political highbrows.

Tomorrow I move to Cambridge to spend the three days as chancellor among the real highbrows. I feel slightly nervous about it all, but hope it will be all right and that I shall succeed in *not* making a fool of myself. The feeling of sympathy for me in my South African blow may make things better; anyhow I shall tell you later of what has happened. Meanwhile, good night!

12 June. Six days later. The Cambridge campaign is over and won. Everything passed better than I had expected. The good will and sympathy all around me was not only touching but overwhelming. You may have seen some reference to my main speech on Russian policy—'aggression without war'—which has attracted much attention.[3] But I made two others which were off the record and therefore easier and perhaps more effective. Churchill was very good and attracted more attention than the chancellor himself as you may well imagine. He is in happy mood and full of fight—sad over the recession of the Empire, but determined to call a halt to this process of defeatism. I have since my return to Hyde Park Hotel met many of the leading figures and I hope our talks may prove helpful. Leading men in the services are sad and discouraged, but I don't think things are as bad from their point of view as they fear. What I do think probable is a crisis on the financial and economic side which may shake the government and the nation itself. American aid is a temporary palliative, but the crisis is surely rising. The government may anticipate it by an election,

[1] Michael of Rumania (q.v.) and Princess Anne of Bourbon-Parma.

[2] Tenth king of Israel (*c.* 842–814 B.C.). 'And the driving is like the driving of Jehu the son of Nimshi; for he driveth furiously.' 2 *Kings* ix.20.

[3] Entitled 'The World Situation: Communism and Freedom' (Smuts Collection, Box M, no. 256).

but the view here is that they will continue with their nationalization policy to which they are so deeply pledged. We can but await events, which may, however, be more serious on the foreign than the internal front. This all sounds vague, but the situation here is particularly obscure at present...

I had a beautiful letter of sympathy and understanding from Henry [Moore], and add a line for him to this letter. I was very glad to have his note.

Yesterday I had lunch with the royal family and we could talk over many things...Philip was also there and in very good form. He makes a good impression and is evidently an able fellow. His mother[1] and other close relations I met at Athens and could bring him the latest news.

I am deeply sorry that your visit to London could not be earlier so that I could meet you and the daughters here. I trust you will enjoy the change and not find London unduly depressing. Cooper went to see the Academy, with pictures by Simon [Elwes] and Winston—both good in his opinion. Your turn next! Ever affectionately yours,

J. C. Smuts

799 To G. G. A. Murray — Vol. 88, no. 109

Hyde Park Hotel
London
13 June 1948

My dear Murray, Thank you for your more than kind note. I wish you and Lady Mary a good holiday and real change, with renewal of strength and faith.

We missed you at Cambridge. It was a greater success than I had anticipated, and I was enfolded by human kindness on all hands.

We are passing through a tragic period. The immense forces on the move create the impression which Fate created for Greek tragedy. And yet our view goes deeper than that. It is not some alien malign force acting *against* us. This world is whole and of a piece, and part of us. There is a family of the universe, and we are members of that family. There is something of that goodness which the psalmist has expressed with such poignancy, though in language not our own. The Altar of Pity stands not only in the market-place but in all the high places. (By the way I got the information about this Altar from your book.)[2]

[1] Princess Alice of Greece (q.v.).

[2] *See supra*, p. 178.

So good-bye, and enjoy your holiday. Somehow the eternal wings are over us[1] and temper the storm to the shorn lambs.[2] All best wishes to you both. Ever yours,

J. C. Smuts

800 To M. C. Gillett Vol. 88, no. 247

Doornkloof
[Transvaal]
28 June 1948

I borrow this form from Cato [Clark] to tell you of our safe arrival some days ago, after a twenty-seven hours' flight from Athens...

Here the political talks with my associates have started and I can see what a task awaits me. The United party is determined to resume the political fight, and of course the main burden will fall on me. Hofmeyr is wounded by the enemy in their foul attacks against him, and cannot be of much effective use—is rather a liability at the moment. But I shall have to see this matter through and heal the fissures which may arise in the party. This has been much of my task in the past, and must be even more so in the future. What is called Liberalism is at a discount here even more than in Britain, and Hof's liberal views have been exploited against the party in a most unfair way. My successor must be killed in advance of his advent. A heavy programme of meetings and conferences has been arranged which will prevent any holiday before parliament meets on 6 August. So far no housing arrangements at Cape Town have been made and I may have to go to the club[3] or a hotel for the short session in August–October, and make arrangements there for the future. It is bad luck being saddled with such a position at this stage. But there is no help and no way out. In these days I realize the tragic element in the world as much as at any other period of my life. But I suppose all real life is tragedy, and who am I that I should claim exemption from the rule. So onward, Christian soldier!

Cato is very happy, Richard perhaps more so. The life here comes to him as a high romance in a strange world. And he is such a fine little chap. They must crowd as much as possible into a very short stay of a few weeks. So far it has been sheer enjoyment.

[1] 'How excellent is thy loving kindness, O God! therefore the children of men put their trust under the shadow of thy wings.' *Psalm* 36.7.

[2] '"God tempers the wind", said Maria, "to the shorn lamb".' Laurence Sterne (1713–68), *A Sentimental Journey*.

[3] The Civil Service Club.

I look back with great pleasure on my days abroad. Cambridge was very good, Leiden the same—almost better.[1] The dear Hollanders went all out to make me feel one of themselves and to make me realize how much they valued what I had done for them in a fateful moment at the end of the war. But what a world we have moved into since then! Berlin has now become the new storm centre, and though I do not fear war, I do fear vast mischief and suffering for these millions, and especially for those who do not know their right from their left hand. May a purified humanity emerge from this vast human tragedy which has befallen the world. But love remains, and faith, and hope—these three.[2] For us too. So good-bye. Ever yours,

Jan

801 To L. S. Amery — Vol. 88, no. 113

Doornkloof
Irene
Transvaal
2 July 1948

My dear Amery, Your letter of 29 May about Palestine[3] reached me only today, and I am sorry we did not discuss the matter in London. In fact I much regretted seeing almost nothing of you there, although the fault was with my time-table and not with us, dear Brutus.[4]

I consulted the other Dominions and told them of my views about Palestine, but they naturally hesitated to act without the United Kingdom. I finally acted because I wanted to avoid the impression of the Commonwealth ganging up against Jewry, in spite of the actions of the United States and the U.S.S.R.[5] This would have been a very bad impression for the future, and of course quite against the line I have always taken about the national home.

Both Cambridge and Leiden did me good and made me feel

[1] Smuts had received the honorary degree of Doctor of Laws of the University.

[2] 'And now abideth faith, hope, charity, these three...' 1 *Corinthians* xiii.13.

[3] Smuts Collection, vol. 85, no. 14.

[4] The fault, dear Brutus, is not in our stars,
But in ourselves...
Shakespeare, *Julius Caesar*, I.ii.133.

[5] Recognition of the new state of Israel by the government of the Union of South Africa was made independently of the other members of the British Commonwealth. Recognition by the United States had been immediate, followed closely by that of the Soviet Union.

a man and not a worm, in spite of the rebuff from my own people. Thank you for what you so kindly say. The pity is that for some years to come all my time and energy will be taken up with this miserable party strife. But how could I act otherwise under the circumstances? My life-work is at stake and I must defend my own while I have the power to do so.

My warm good wishes to you and dear Mrs Amery. I was very glad to see Julian [Amery] again. Ever yours,

s. J. C. Smuts

802 To D. Moore — Vol. 88, no. 115

Doornkloof
Transvaal
12 July 1948

My dear Daphne, I last wrote to you a brief note from Hyde Park Hotel just before my departure—first for Leiden, and then for Rome and Athens. It was really no letter, but kept up the continuity of correspondence. In Leiden I had a great time as the Dutch think much of what I did for them in the war—more than most of them realize. Leiden went mad, that is to say the young folks. Princess Juliana and the Prince [Bernhard] joined in the fun. How good it was. I felt my lines cast in pleasant places,[1] just as at Cambridge. I would have lost my head in both places, if it had not been so old and so aware of the tragedy that is called life. Sometimes I have a sense or feeling that I am not in reality, but in some strange *ersatz* world, where beauty and joy cover and hide the real nakedness of things. At Cambridge and Leiden it was the beauty and joy. Among my own, my beloved South Africa, it is the nakedness, the pain of frustration, which sometimes threatens to overcome me. But not for long. It is good to know that life is essentially a tragedy. It can never measure up to what it aims at, and so there is the sense of failure, of defeat, and the realization that tragedy, more than slavery, is the badge of all our tribe.[2]

I had a couple of very happy days of peace and release at Athens, where the palace sheltered me from the public, and we could go bathing and sightseeing and visiting the great historic places which I know only from the books. Palo was quite well and happy in his work. Frederica was naturally kindness itself, and as vivacious and dear as ever. But really she was very overworked and tired—more than I had seen her ever before. She is looking after some

[1] *See supra*, p. 128, note 2.

[2] *See supra*, p. 47, note 2.

10,000 refugee children from the north, and tied up in a vast array of social undertakings. Then the palace was full of royalties from different parts. Her brother George, married to the Duchess of Hesse; the Olga family;[1] Queen of Rumania;[2] Duchess of Aosta,[3] and many others. I felt sorry for poor Freddy who is really exhausting herself in her kindness of heart, and looked by no means well. Both king and queen are doing wonders for their country, and even if their statesmen fail, they will pull the country through, as the American General [J.A.] Van Fleet said to me. Freddy asked about you and your plans, and I told her what I knew—which is not much...

I flew away from Athens in the evening and doing it non-stop, except for taking in fuel, arrived in Pretoria the next evening (24 June). Since then I have been in a whirl of functions and meetings and ceaseless activity to get the party on its feet again. Our election defeat has stunned both the party and the country, as such a development had not been foreseen, and never considered even within the range of possibility. So I have been busy to restore order and infuse spirit into my defeated army. I have had terrific receptions at Pretoria and Cape Town, and have just come back from the latter, where I had a reception which people compare to that of the King last year. In a couple of days I am off to Durban, and then back to Johannesburg, where no doubt the same scenes will be repeated. It looks as if people want to make amends to me. They do not realize what a hardened old veteran I am, schooled in all the vicissitudes of defeat as well as victory. But Cape Town was really overwhelming...

I hope this will reach you at the Hyde Park Hotel before you leave for Switzerland. And Australia thereafter! I somehow do not feel attracted to Australia, and may never see it, though I have many pressing invitations. What is left of life will have to be spent on this continent, to which I am so deeply wedded in love and duty. My hope is here, south and north. My work is here, my dream in the north. And beyond that stretches eternity! Good-bye, dear. Ever yours lovingly,

J.C.S.

[1] Olga, born 11 June 1903, eldest daughter of Prince Nicholas of Greece (1872–1935) and Helen of Russia (1882–1957); married, in 1923, Prince Paul of Yugoslavia.

[2] Helen, born 1896, daughter of Constantine I of Greece; married Carol II of Rumania in 1921.

[3] Irene, born 1901, daughter of Constantine I of Greece; married, in 1939, Aymon, fourth Duke of Aosta (1900–48).

803 To A. A. Louw Vol. 88, no. 115A

Doornkloof
Transvaal
12 Juli 1948

Geliefde Vriend, My innige dank vir u liewe brief van 5 Juli, wat ek met aandoening gelees het. Die onverwagte slag was swaar, en die ergste was nog dat my eie kiesafdeling, vir wie ek 24 jare geswoeg het, ook beswyk het. 'n Opponent van my sê op ontvangs van die berig: 'maar die politiek is 'n ondankbare ding!' Die lewe is in sy aard 'n tragedie, en mens moenie anders verwag nie. Maar u brief het my goed gedoen—hartelik dank daarvoor.

Ek beny Danie nie sy goeie geluk nie as dit goeie geluk is! Selfs liewe Cinie sou dit verwelkom het. Maar ook sy sou saamgestem het met wat u skrywe.

Ek weet dat, met al my foute en gebreke, ek eerlik bedoel het my bes vir land en volk te doen. Daar laat ek die saak. Ons is nie regters in eie saak; daar is die Regter, en Hy handel in liefde, wat ons dikwels nie begryp nie.

My hartelike groete aan my ou vriend, 11 jaar ouer as ek self, en nog doende. Steeds u liefhebbende

J. C. Smuts

TRANSLATION

Doornkloof
Transvaal
12 July 1948

Beloved Friend, My deepest thanks for your dear letter of 5 July[1] which I read with emotion. The unexpected blow was heavy, and the worst was that my own constituency, for which I laboured for twenty-four years, also succumbed. One of my opponents said on hearing the report: 'Politics is a thankless affair!' Life is, in essence, a tragedy and one should not expect anything else. But your letter did me good—I thank you sincerely for it.

I do not envy Danie[2] his good fortune—if it is good fortune! Even dear Cinie [Louw] would have welcomed it. But she also would agree with what you have written.

I know that, with all my faults and shortcomings, I have sincerely intended to do my best for my country and people. There I leave the matter. We cannot be judges in our own cause—but there is the Judge, and He acts in love—which we often do not understand.

[1] Smuts Collection, vol. 86, no. 123.

[2] Dr D. F. Malan, who had become prime minister.

My heartiest greetings to my old friend—eleven years older than I, and still up and doing! Always yours affectionately,

J. C. Smuts

804 To M. C. Gillett Vol. 88, no. 249

Doornkloof
[Transvaal]
20 July 1948

What a letter you wrote me about your stay at Windermere, and your return home and your visit to Eastbourne! It was all a sheer joy to read as it must have been to you to write. Your picture of little Matthew and of the growing up Simon[1] was most enchanting. Arthur, Edna,[2] the Bourdillons,[3] Portway—and all the rest. It was worth while writing that lyric[4] on the last sheet of dear Alice's gift of paper to you. Thank you for such a letter—so full of understanding of my own and South Africa's difficulties. It is only the large heart that can make you evaluate our troubles as you do. The deeper human feeling is the only clue to knowledge. *Alle menschliche Gebrechen sühnet reine Menschlichkeit* as Goethe says somewhere.[5] Pure humanness is the only cure for our ills. And many as are the ills, as much is the humanness, if we only knew it.

I have had a hard week, ending up at last in a perfect rest and relaxation at Rooikop. I carried out my heavy programme at Durban and Johannesburg, as I had done the week before at Cape Town, and was glad to wind up in my beloved Bushveld at the end. The receptions given me in all these places rivalled those given the royal family last year. People evidently were deeply moved by the treatment my own people had given me with elections, where the countryside simply ran away from me, even beloved Standerton giving me a 'kick in the pants', as the vulgar saying goes. And all this in the hour of victory and achievement for South Africa that simply outran the wildest imagination. However, you know I am not inclined to be much cast down over

[1] The sons of Jan and Gertrude Gillett.

[2] Born Edna Brown, married Sir Hyde Clarendon Gowan in 1905.

[3] Sir Bernard Bourdillon (q.v.) and his wife, born Violet Grace Billinghurst, whom he married in 1909.

[4] Verses by M. C. Gillett entitled 'The Return: a Fantasy'. *See* Smuts Collection, vol. 85, no. 212.

[5] Pure humanness atones for all human defects. From a verse addressed to G. W. Krüger, an actor who had played in Goethe's *Iphigenie*.

such reverses. I live too much of my real life in another world—'in this world but not of it'. But my heart did go out to South Africa, who is preparing a heavy future for herself by these childish, thoughtless pranks and indulgements of comfortable prejudices. She simply cannot afford them. But she has not cared, and gone her way rejoicing, not thinking of the tears which will follow, but cannot wash out, this shame. It remains a country of a divided soul. Faust's two souls[1] inhabit this good fine beloved people. But in a sense I am, we all are, possessed of these two souls—so why blame poor, honest, sinning South Africa over much? What you write is soothing and healing; thank you!

How good it was to turn away from all the wild tumult of last week to the quiet and peacefulness of the Bushveld...I spent the Saturday and Sunday tramping over Rooikop, seeing game and birds and green wheatfields, and the beloved thorn bush. I read much of Churchill's second volume,[2] given me as an advance copy. I lived again through that awful period when France fell, and England had to face a similar fate. I saw some very good people, who reminded me of the goodness which is round us like the clear air. And I have come back refreshed for what the new week will bring.

But what a world to look out upon as the great picture of events unrolls itself before our eyes! For the moment the trouble has shifted from Greece. Even Palestine may have a few more weeks of truce. But what about Berlin, where the great disease has burst forth in a new boil![3] I still cling to the idea or rather the hope that we may avoid war and that somehow a way out will be found. But things are moving to a crisis so great that neither the West nor Russia can give way without a catastrophe for the one or a revolution for the other. We are moving into Munich times, and we know how they ended. A diversion has arisen in this Tito quarrel,[4] which may have its bearing on Russian recalcitrance. It may be

[1] *Zwei Seelen wohnen, ach! in meiner Brust...*
Two souls live in my breast. *Faust,* part I, l. 112.

[2] *The Second World War.*

[3] Under the Berlin declaration of 5 June 1945 Berlin, although in the Russian zone, was to be governed jointly by France, Great Britain, the United States and Soviet Russia. In practice the city was divided into four administrative sectors. Berlin depended for its food supplies on the main road through Eastern Germany—in the Russian zone. In March 1948 the Russians enforced new traffic regulations designed to force the Western powers out by closing the lifeline to their sectors. They countered by organizing a gigantic airlift into the city.

[4] The Soviet–Yugoslav quarrel was caused by the determination of the Yugoslav Communists under Tito to resist control from Moscow. Attempts to maintain friendly relations broke down in March 1948 when the Soviet Union withdrew its military mission from Belgrade.

a godsend—this breach in the solid Communist front—and may call a pause to Russia. But it may also have just the opposite effect. So we hold our breath and pray for wisdom and patience, and for respite from the new horror approaching us. The Berliners *must* be fed, and the West has made it impossible for itself to go and leave them to their fate.

We are passing through times such as demand more patience and wisdom than we seem to be capable of, after all we have suffered the last ten years and more. Once more it is a case for the Griqua prayer![1]

My dear love to you all of the Portway circle, not excluding Street. Ever yours,

Jan

805 To A. Meyer-Abich Vol. 88, no. 122

27 July 1948

Dear Professor Meyer-Abich, I have your letter of 19 March[2] and thank you for all the interesting information contained in it. I am naturally deeply interested in all you write, and congratulate you on the good work you are doing, and the opportunities for further good work that are coming to you.

At the moment I can do nothing about *Holism*. My political responsibilities at my age (78) are so heavy that I cannot find time for the revision of the old book, nor the writing of the new book which has been simmering in my mind for some years. When I look at the world unrest today and the confusion which prevails in science, in philosophy, in religion, and in our whole human outlook and set-up, I feel more and more that in the concept of holism we have the key to many a door, and the way to ultimate solutions. Something holistic is at the heart of things and in the nature of this universe, which is not a mere chance or random assemblement of items. The detailed things derive most of their meaning, significance and functioning from the whole of which they are but the parts. They are not mere parts but really members of the wholes. Both as a metaphysical and as a scientific concept the whole is basic to our understanding of the world. And in sociology and religion this is more clearly the case. Relativity is only a half-way house to this more fundamental concept.

This being my conviction, you will realize how much importance I attribute to holism, and how anxious I am to give the concept

[1] *See* vol. IV, p. 153.

[2] Smuts Collection, vol. 86, no. 160.

a further push forward. But at present I can do nothing about it, and must leave the spade work to you and other workers who are more happily situated. My political position in South Africa, and to a less extent in the world, is such that I cannot say good-bye to that aspect of my work. But I still hope against hope to return to holism at the end. For me there can be no revision of the old nor the beginning of the new work at the moment.

Please give no further thought to a degree for me from the Hamburg University. I thank you for your kind thought, but I have already so many honours and do not wish for more at my time of life.

I feel deeply concerned about the world position, and not least about Germany, which is at the heart of the European, and indeed the human, problems facing us today. No more critical situation has faced the world in all history. With kind regards and all good wishes for you. Yours sincerely,

s. J. C. Smuts

806 To M. C. Gillett — Vol. 88, no. 251

Mount Nelson Hotel
[Cape Town]
8 August 1948

I write in my rooms, just as good as in the Hyde Park Hotel. Up on the third floor my suite overlooks Cape Town, the sea, and the mountains right and left. Though in the hotel I am not of it, and can have seclusion and quiet as much as I like. So there is nothing to be further wished for by so simple a person as myself. Inquiries about houses have so far had no satisfactory result—few available and prices much too high. But the inquiries will be continued.[1]

Parliament opened yesterday with the usual ceremonial. I sit again in my old opposition seat after fifteen years. It felt like coming home, as I had sat there for nine years before. Here we have no abiding city,[2] and we continue on the march as long as the call is there. But frankly, I don't like it. I would rather be at my real home and relax after all the years and collect my thoughts and put them on record. It may be that at the end I shall have no time left for these things, and my strange experiences will not

[1] A. B. and M. C. Gillett had urged Smuts to buy another house in the Cape Peninsula from a fund made available by them after the sale of 'Tsalta' in 1940.

[2] 'For here we have no continuing city, but we seek one to come.' *Hebrews* xiii.14.

be recorded. Perhaps that will be no loss to the world. What perhaps really matters is to make your humble contribution to the real movement, and thus incorporate yourself with the substance of things. The footprint is not in the writing (unless you are a great literary or philosophical genius) but in the path itself, in the march of events and their direction. Perhaps I may in this practical way continue to make some small contribution to the little world to which I belong and which I dearly love. But of course I know that thinking is also doing, and that great thoughts are as potent as great deeds. But this level of thinking and doing belongs to the select few, and I have no illusions about myself. Thankful indeed am I that I have been accorded some small place in which I could play my part for weal or woe, such as it has been and may still be. There is an inherent justice in the nature of things. You are what you are, neither more or less, and the universe does not expect more or less from you. That is the justice of the universe. People think of justice as either reward or punishment, as the case may be. In fact justice is just *it*, no less and no more—the just measure given to you or expected of you. Neither the joys of heaven nor the punishments of hell belong to the realm of justice. Don't expect success; don't be disheartened by failure. You have your allotted part, and the doing of it is your reward, and the failure to do it is your punishment. There is nothing else in the nature of the universe—the rest is men's fancies and embroideries and frills, whether they be theory, or philosophy or religion. The *real* is the only thing, and the real is the fact, the reality, the justice, and the true and the beautiful. Perhaps this is all too much simplified. But I love to reduce the world—so tangled and confused—to its simplest terms. And to me it appears that in the end the things we are after are just the things that are—that are in the nature of this universe, its law, its reality and its *factual* character. The rest is not operative and not real.

This sounds queer stuff in answer to your welcome letter of 29 July in which you console me for the sad vicissitudes of my hard lot, and go on to tell the dear intimate things of domestic life at Portway House. There may be a little trying and superficial Communism,[1] but it really does not matter. The children in the sand pit are the real thing. That is reality, and the Communism is just the dash of nonsense which acts as a foil to the real. So if the children jar, look at the grandchildren and be at rest in your inner joy. It is a charming picture you paint of the young people

[1] Referring to the political opinions of some of the children of A. B. and M. C. Gillett.

about the countryside, on their cycles or otherwise, smiling, sweating, and enjoying themselves. Of such things is the Kingdom of the Real!

But I have to work in parliament and carry on with the follies and eccentricities of nationalism and all the other items of the unreal. It takes so much to make up this queer world of ours. And perhaps we humans are the queerest of all—at least the grown-ups among us. All love and best wishes. Ever yours,

Jan

807 To S. M. Smuts Vol. 88, no. 131

Mount Nelson Hotel
14 August 1948

Liefste Mamma, Saterdag. Ek gaan by die Barings lunch en vanaand na die Griekse Ballet. Maar dit bly maar koud en winderig, met reën af en toe, ek dus is en vanoggend maar in my suite gebly en kantoor werk hier afgedoen. Ek het weer 'n erge verkoue opgetel, en neem snags 'n hot toddy en gebruik die serocalcin pille, maar sonder gevolg. Maandag begin die debat op die begroting en sal ek my aanval op die Regeering maak.

Bennington het nou kennis gekry om te trek en is al aan klaar maak om alles aan Barky te oorhandig. My boeke en ander goed sal hy na sy huis oorneem. Hierheen het hy my hoede en voetstoeltjie gebreng, daar hy van my verkoue gehoor had. Hy se hy het genoeg vir die opvoeding van die seuns maar niks meer nie. Grootskaalse veranderings word te G. S. gemaak wat hy maar liewers niks oor wil sê nie, maar wat hom treurig maak. Hy weet nie hoeveel nog verander sal word nie en wil dit maar liewer nie sien nie. Ek ook nie! *Sic transit gloria mundi*! Ek kry 'n brief van Meyersville Standerton om my te vermaan om my tog nou tot die Heer te bekeer anders sal dit nog erger met my gaan!

Ek was bly dat al die 5 kleindogters (of is dit 4) na Durban kon gaan en deel in die vroolikhede neem. Sir Vernon het my darem mooi behandel. Ek wonder wat ons vir hom kan doen om ons dankbaarheid te toon. Hy wil geen betaling neem vir my verblyf alhier, en dit sal baie geld beteeken. Ek voel werklik aangedaan daaroor.

Van Cooper het ek ingeslote liewe snap van die familie gekry—van Beresford geteeken. Wat 'n moei groep! Jammer so klein.

Nou maar afsluit daar ek na lunch moet gaan. Denk tog, op 1 Oct. moet ek die Ford Fabriek by Port Elizabeth open, en gee hul my present die eerste Ford in S.A. gemaak! 'Our lines are cast in lovely places' wat motors betref.

Nou liefde, soentjies, en alles van die beste aan al die geliefdes.

Pappa

TRANSLATION

Mount Nelson Hotel
[Cape Town]
14 August 1948

Dearest Mamma, Saturday. I am going to lunch at the Barings[1] and to the Greek Ballet tonight. It is still cold and windy, with rain from time to time, and so I have stayed in my suite this morning and finished off office work here. I have again picked up a bad cold and take a hot toddy at night and use the serocalcin pills—but without effect. On Monday the budget debate begins and I shall make my attack on the government.

Bennington[2] has now been given notice to go and is getting ready to hand everything over to Barky.[3] He will take my books and other things to his house. He brought my hats and footstool here as he had heard about my cold. He says he has enough for the education of the boys but no more. Large-scale alterations are being made at Groote Schuur about which he would rather say nothing, but which make him sad. He does not know how much more will be changed and would rather not see it. Nor would I! *Sic transit gloria mundi*![4] I had a letter from Meyersville, Standerton, exhorting me to be converted to the Lord or it would go still worse with me!

I was glad that all five granddaughters (or is it four?) could go to Durban and share in the fun.

Sir Vernon [Thomson] has treated me very well. I wonder what we can do for him to show our gratitude. He will not accept payment for my staying here[5] and it will mean a lot of money. I feel really moved by this.

I got the enclosed charming snap of the family from Cooper—signed by Beresford. What a nice group! A pity it is so small.

[1] Sir Evelyn Baring (q.v.) and his wife, born Lady Mary Cecil Grey, whom he married in 1935.

[2] Edward Bennington, born 7 April 1882 near Sandringham, England; came to South Africa in 1904; house steward at Groote Schuur 1911–48.

[3] W. J. Barkhuizen, who succeeded E. Bennington.

[4] So passes away the glory of the world.

[5] The Mount Nelson Hotel belonged to the Union Castle Steamship Company of which Sir Vernon Thomson was then the chairman.

Will now close as I must go to lunch. Just think: on 1 October I am to open the Ford factory at Port Elizabeth and they will make me a gift of the first Ford made in South Africa! 'Our lines are cast in lovely places'[1] as far as motor-cars go.

And now love, kisses and everything of the best to all the loved ones.

Pappa

808 From P. O. Sauer Vol. 87, no. 112

Die Volksraad
Kaapstad
18 Augustus 1948

Geagte Generaal, Dit is voorgestel om die hoogste piek op Marion Eiland te laat heet 'Jan Smuts Piek'. Dit dra my volle goedkeuring weg. As die persoon wat aandadig was om Marion die besitting van Suid-Afrika te maak en as 'n ou beroemde klimmer van die bergtoppe, kon 'n meer geskikte naam nie gevind word nie.

Ek hoop dus dat u met my voorneme akkoord gaan. Dienswillig die uwe,

P. O. Sauer

TRANSLATION

House of Assembly
Cape Town
18 August 1948

Dear General, It has been suggested that the highest peak on Marion Island[2] should be called 'Jan Smuts Peak'. This I fully approve.[3] As the person who was concerned in making Marion island a possession of South Africa and as an old and famous climber of the mountain-tops, no more suitable name could be found.

I hope therefore that you approve my intention. Yours sincerely,

P. O. Sauer

[1] *See supra*, p. 128, note 2.

[2] A small island in the Antarctic ocean about 1,200 miles south-east of Cape Town. It was annexed to the Union of South Africa on 4 January 1948 in order to set up a meteorological station which is still maintained there.

[3] P. O. Sauer was at this time minister of transport.

809 To M. C. Gillett Vol. 88, no. 255

Mount Nelson Hotel
[Cape Town]
26 August 1948

I have just been reading your last letter, dated 20 August 1948—pretty good going, you will admit. It was full of interest, though I was very sorry to see that you had received a great shock from your defective lamp. For the rest your letter is full of the grandchildren who are evidently growing on you and getting the better of grandmamma. That is as it should be. You condole with me over my house troubles. But I am still pursuing my inquiries, and who knows whether I may not have some luck yet. You also enclose a copy of Jan's [Gillett] latest, which I found most interesting. It is probably as good and searching an analysis of the Iraq position and of British policy there and in neighbouring centres as I have seen for a long time. The English have developed a curious new habit of backing the wrong horse—so different from the horse sense which is native to them. Their attitude to the Jews and the new state of Israel is a disaster, and in the end I fear the Arabs will hate them as much as the Jews now hate them.

This is Thursday night and I have not gone to the house tonight as I had important visitors who have just left me. Day after tomorrow I fly to Johannesburg for an Air function in the afternoon, and from there I shall pass on to Doornkloof to spend the night and the Sunday with the family, returning here by air on Monday. All very tiring but perhaps a good change, and a pleasant prospect to look forward to. What a joy it will be to spend the two nights and a day there with old and young and to forget the political world in which I now move about without feeling at home in it. One almost develops a distaste, if not a disgust, with this alien political world, so full of the petty and so remote from the worthwhile and the greatness of the world.

Hard as it was I liked the creative and constructive side of public life, with its opportunities to *do* things instead of merely talking and criticizing and bickering generally. I get so tired of mere opposition, which is now my role as leader of the opposition. I almost look upon it as a degradation and cannot understand how the English came to look upon it as an honourable role. If you can't be God, then be at least the Devil! That I suppose derives from the sporting spirit of the English, but sport has never appealed to me, and if I can't *do* things I like to be out of them altogether. But here this purgatory is now my role, and I dislike it thoroughly. A Sunday at home far away will be a refreshment of the soul.

Last Saturday I motored to the cement works at De Hoek near Piketberg, and from there returned via Boplaas (my birthplace) and Riebeeck [West].[1] Boplaas now belongs to the [Portland] Cement Company as a reserve but will not be worked for at least forty years. In honour of me the Company is now restoring the farm and the houses[2] and [will] make a good show of it once more. You remember being with me there many years ago.[3] But oh what a glory the whole country was all that day! A wonderful young wheat harvest, and flowers as of old, creating a magic world with a bewitching effect on my senses and my soul. I don't think there is anything in the world so beautiful as the Swartland[4] in spring. You remember our visit to the Cedarberg[5] in the hallowed past. Such it was again last Saturday. Beyond description, and your memory must tell you more than I can write. It was a loveliness beyond all power of language to express. But I must end on this happy note. I hope you will soon be all well again, and meanwhile think of all things lovely.[6] Ever yours,

Jan

810 To S. M. Smuts — Vol. 88, no. 142

Volksraad
Kaapstad
1 September 1948

Liefste Mamma, Hier veilig eergister aangekom na 'n aangename vlug van begin tot end. Hier is ons in reën weer beland en gister was dit ook weer koud, met sterke wind vannag. Maar vandag stil en aangenaam. Ons is al dadelik in hewige diskussies in die Volksraad geraak en gister was ons besig met die Eerste Minister se begrooting, waar ek kon wys op die gevaar buitenslands van al die veranderinge wat voorgestel word in die wetgewing op naturelle, gekleurdes, en Indiërs. Eric Louw sal maar swaar kry by die V.V. en die regeering maak sy taak al swaarder. Dit lyk

[1] The farm Boplaas is three miles from the village of Riebeeck West which is about fifty miles north of Cape Town.

[2] There were two houses on Boplaas. The smaller of these, in which Smuts was born, has been declared an historical monument.

[3] In August 1920.

[4] The grain-growing district of the south-western Cape Province.

[5] Mountain range in the south-western Cape Province, about 140 miles north of Cape Town.

[6] *See supra*, p. 151.

ook nou of die plan is dat die $\frac{2}{3}$ meerderheid vir wegname van naturelle regte onder die S.A. Wet eenvoudig geminag sal word, met verder ernstige moeilikhede in die land. Dit sou 'n growe verbreking van die S.A. Acte wees. Maar waarom jou oor hierdie dinge pla?

Ek is nog vol van die aangename besoekie aan liewe Doornkloof. Ek het heelmal verfris gevoel in die liewe geselskap van grootes en kleines. Ek was ook bly dat plaaslike [*sic*] kwesties so mooi opgelos kon word. Ek hoop alles sal nou mooi loop en goed uitwerk...Ons sal sien hoe dinge loop.

Niks verder nuus nie. Alles van die beste.

Pappa

TRANSLATION

House of Assembly
Cape Town
1 September 1948

Dearest Mamma, Arrived here safely yesterday after a pleasant flight from start to finish. We found ourselves in rainy weather here and yesterday it was again cold with a strong wind last night. But today it is calm and pleasant.

We were at once involved in violent debates in the house. Yesterday we were busy with the prime minister's vote when I could draw attention to the danger abroad of all the changes that are proposed in Native, Coloured and Indian legislation. Eric Louw will have a hard time at U.N.O. and the government makes his task the heavier. It also looks now as if it is the intention simply to ignore the two-thirds majority for the repeal of Native rights under the South Africa Act—which will mean further serious trouble in the country.[1] It would be a gross breach of the South Africa Act. But why bother you with these things?

I am still full of the pleasant little visit to Doornkloof. I felt quite refreshed in the dear company of grown-ups and children. And I was glad that farm questions could be so well solved. I hope all will now run smoothly and work out well...We shall see how things go.

No further news. Everything of the best.

Pappa

[1] *See* vol. v, p. 371, note 3.

811 To M. C. Gillett Vol. 88, no. 258

Cape Town
8 September 1948

...For the rest your last letter paints a happy picture of your life at Portway House, surrounded by relays of grandchildren to keep you going. And there are the grapes, and the scents and colours of flowers. And the birds sing. And so the frictions in us are absorbed in our unity with nature. In that unity lies largely our peace and happiness. There too lie some of the deepest sources of religion.

I was discussing with two young Calvinist parsons the other day the concept of holism, which they took as purely humanistic and a denial of the theistic concept. I explained to them that I did not agree with Calvin's legalistic conception of human alienation and depravity. With John's Gospel I believed in incarnation—the Word become flesh—the divine immanent in the human, and in matter and its patterns as a revelation of the divine. Holism is therefore the approach towards the theistic concept from the side of nature, and builds as it were a bridge between humanism and divinity. They looked impressed, but perhaps did not take it all in. I told them to consider the concept of incarnation in its wider aspect, and not merely in its biblical context. Under that curious, almost mythological, imagery a bridge was built across the chasm between the human and the divine. In real fact there *is* unity, and only our thinking has created the gap, which our deeper thinking should bridge again.

Of course the bridging is done more in feeling than in thought. Faith, hope and love—these three[1] are the arches of that bridge. I often revert to the Spinoza terminology of *deus sive natura*[2]—and his attempt thus to convey the sense of underlying unity in difference. Perhaps the way back to the truth is once more to be found by our approach through emotion to nature, and so to the deeper feeling which makes us sense the divine in the world. If the total separation between the natural and the divine is made on Calvinistic lines, the natural is of course damned. But the damning is not in the nature of the situation, but in our own creation of a gulf which does not in fact exist. Separate the Word and the flesh, and the one becomes a distant abstraction, and the other the work of the devil. Back to nature means back to God, or the nearest we can approach to that greatest vision of the human race.

Of course there is more. The truly *human* is a deeper inter-

[1] *See* vol. VI, p. 110, note 2. [2] God or nature.

pretation of nature. And so the Lover Divine and perfect Comrade of Walt Whitman's line[1] becomes our God. How far we have wandered away in thought from this truth! And yet how near it is to us in our humblest and simplest human relations all the time. And suffering enters as another essential idea. The Cross becomes another link between life and the divine.

So much for my two young Calvinists!

Now good-bye. Listen to the music in Miss Wuschack's radio,[2] and think loving thoughts of all, dead or alive!

Jan

812 From E. G. Malherbe — Vol. 86, no. 143

Persoonlik en vertroulik

Natal Universiteitskollege
Pietermaritzburg
8 September 1948

Geagte Oom Jannie, Ek voel vreeslik besorgd oor die loop van sake op politieke gebied. As hierdie klomp wat tans die botoon voer aan bewind van sake bly, gaan dit ons land ruineer—ten spyte van al die superambassadeurs wat hulle mag uitstuur om hierdie noodlottige *volte face* in ons land goed te praat. Dit is hierdie besorgdheid wat my noop om aan u te skrywe. Veel liewer sou ek die hele besigheid met u persoonlik wou bespreek het toe ek onlangs in die Kaap was, maar ongelukkig was daar toe nie kans voor nie.

Ek weet dat daar baie mense is wat—gevraagd en ongevraagd—vir u raad gee. Ek het egter rede om te glo dat baie van die raadgewers wat u omring nie behoorlik ingelig is nie en dat diegene wat wel weet wat skort nie altoos die moed het om reguit vir u die ware toedrag van sake in alle opsigte mee te deel nie. Hierdie versuim is soms te wyte aan eiebelang en soms aan vrees vir u. U het in hierdie opsig 'n onherstelbare verlies gely toe Louis Esselen weggeval het. Hy het 'geweet' en hy het u op hoogte gehou.

Ofskoon wat ek hier skrywe die indruk mag wek dat ek met 'n 'holier than thou' houding hier wil poseer, wil ek u die versekering gee dat ek gedwing word deur 'n belangelose vriendskap

[1] Lover divine and perfect Comrade,
Waiting content, invisible yet, but certain,
Be thou my God.

By the Roadside, 'Gods'.

[2] On the death of Miss Wuschack, a teacher of German in Oxford, a radio set given to her by M. C. Gillett was returned. (Note by M. C. Gillett.)

en hoë agting vir u, gepaard met 'n onrusbarende besef van die kritiese tyd wat ons land op hierdie moment deurgaan. Maar genoeg oor motiewe agter hierdie ongevraagde inligting en advies!

U sal onthou dat, op 19 Aug., gedurende die paar minute toe ek u gesien het in die portaal van die Parlementshuis, ek u vertel het dat die Nat.-regering sekere konsessies aan Minister Havenga sou maak en dat hy hulle nie sou aanneem nie, omdat hy persoonlik, en ook sommige van sy volgelinge, diep ongelukkig is in daardie kraal; verder sou hy ook veel liewer met u wou saamwerk.

U het hierdie wenk (wat ek eerstehands gekry het) van die hand gewys op grond van die feit dat u 'nie met 'n klomp Fasciste wil onderhandel nie'.

Ek vrees dat u waardering van die situasie oppervlakkig is. Ek kan dit toeskrywe alleen aan die feit dat u inligtingsdiens swak en oppervlakkig is.

Die feite is as volg:

(1) Havenga gebruik die O.B. grotendeels om daarmee die Nattes te intimideer en om sy 'bargaining power' te versterk en nie omdat hy enige voorliefde vir die O.B.'s of hulle ideologie het nie. Buitendien, met uitsondering van 'n klompie ideologiese leiers, dring die fascisme nie baie diep deur die 'rank and file' van die O.B.'s nie. Dit is nie in die aard van ons mense en rym nie met ons inheemse instellings nie. In afwesigheid van die prikkeling en geleenthede wat die oorlog verskaf het, is hulle mag en getalsterkte vinnig aan die afneem. Selfs van Rensburg besef dit en probeer nou witvoetjie by die meer demokratiese en gematigde elemente soek. Ek sou dus nie te veel gewig heg aan Havenga se opportunistiese affiliasie met die 'Fasciste' nie.

(2) Havenga haat die Broederbond. Dit was hulle wat sy ou vriend Gen. Hertzog in die rug gesteek het. Dit sal hy hulle nooit vergewe nie.

(3) Myns insiens is die belangrikste resultaat van Erasmus se snuffelry in die Argiewe van die Militêre Inligtingsdiens die hoë mate van agterdog en weersydse wantroue tussen die drie seksies wat voor die jongste verkiesings saamgewerk het en die Verenigde Party uitgestof het: (a) Die Broeders, (b) die nie-broeder Nattes, en (c) die O.B.'s. Hulle ontdek nou hoedat indiwidue in hierdie drie seksies—om nie eens die Gryshemde en ander minderbelangrike faksies te noem nie—mekaar ondermyn en probeer uitoorlê het in hulle 'jockeying for power'. Hierdie aspek is nogal amusant, veral vir diegene van ons wat destyds al hierdie streke en kaskenades kon gadegeslaan het. Havenga se kontak met hierdie vete was destyds maar tangen-

sinaal. Hy het hom nooit heelhartig met enigeen van hulle gekompromitteer nie. Weliswaar het hulle beurtelings na hom kom vry.

Ek voel dat u hierdie situasie moet eksploiteer deur, terwyl hierdie leiers en pseudo-leiers nog besig is om hulle gemoedere van hierdie agterdog te bevry, onmiddellik en kragtig op te tree. U en Havenga moet saamkom en onder u gesamentlike leierskap weer ons ou volkie laat koers vat.

In sommige opsigte is die toestand soos in 1932–33, net veel kritieker en gevaarliker. Die groot meerderheid van die Suid-Afrikaanse volk is moeg van hierdie onnatuurlike toestand van verdeeldheid en verlang, net soos in 1932–33, na 'n leierskap wat al die gematigde elemente tot een kragtige party kan saambind.

Ek is seker dat 'n groot seksie van die Nasionaliste nie juis in hulle harte trots voel oor die uitspattings waaraan sommige van die huidige ministers hulle oorgee nie. Die stert swaai die hond in Malan se regering.

Hierdie nuwe oriëntering onder 'n Smuts–Havenga leierskap sal egter nie kan geskied onder die Verenigde Party soos hy vandag saamgestel is nie. Verstaan dit goed: *Die Verenigde Party as sulks is klaar*. Daardie ou Verenigde Party Kabinet sal nooit weer die land regeer nie. Vir hulle om u weer aktief in die party in te gebring het, nadat hulle so'n hopelose gemors van die eleksie gemaak het, om te verwag dat u as 'n ou veteraan op die sinkende skip moes klim en onder 'n wapperende Verenigde Party vaandel saam met hulle naar benede te sink, is niks minder as krimineel nie. Aan die einde van u strydvolle en heldhaftige loopbaan verdien u as Suid-Afrikaanse en wêreldstaatsman iets veel beter as so'n futiele gebaar.

U besef dit selfs beter as ek dat geen party, net soos 'n ou stuk masjinerie, ooit die geestelike en materiële ontwrigtings wat onvermydelik na 'n oorlog kom, kan oorleef nie. Die Verenigde Party het maar net die weg van alle partye onder soortgelyke omstandighede gegaan. Maar dit hoef tog immers nie noodwendig te beteken dat ons ou volkie nou vir goed onder die dwingelandy van die Broederbond moet vergaan nie.

Die débâcle van die Verenigde Party was des te groter om verskeie redes, onder andere—

(a) omdat hy geen positiewe, aggressiewe beleid gehad het nie. Hy was altyd op die verdediging en negatief. Sy sterkste punt was die swart oorlogsrekord van die Nattes en hy het vertrou op goedkoop platform dialektiek. In hierdie opsig was die partypropaganda hopeloos. Ook het hy heeltemal uit die oog verloor dat die helfte van die stemgeregtigdes vrouens is vir wie witbrood veel belangriker was as 'n wêreldoorlog oor ideologiese beginsels. Die onvermydelikheid van kontroles is nooit behoorlik aan huisvrouens verduidelik nie.

(b) omdat hy nie genoeg die gematigde elemente in sy eie kringe beskerm en aangekweek het nie. Hy het hulle toegewyde ondersteuning te veel as vanselfsprekend veronderstel. (Kyk net o.a. na die lamlendige manier waarop die tweetalige skoolbeleid getorpedeer is: enersyds deur die Engelse jingo's en andersyds deur die Broderderbond. Okkie Oosthuizen sal u kan vertel hoedat my ergste voorspellings oor die mislukking van die Transvaalse wetgewing op hierdie punt uitgekom het. Maar hulle wou nie na my waarskuwings luister nie.)

(c) omdat hy *geen tekens van selfverjonging openbaar het nie.* Dit is goed en wel om trou te bly aan die ou karperde wat jarelange diens gedoen het, maar daar kom 'n tyd wanneer hulle uitgespan moet word. Op hierdie reël is u weens u geestelike kragte en liggaamlike jeug 'n skitterende uitsondering. Die Verenigde Party het nie die minste hoop om weer die vertroue van die land te herwin as hy weer met die selfde ou kabinetspan gaan optree nie. Verdiend of onverdiend was die volk moeg en sat van hulle en het na 'n verandering van personeel meer as na 'n verandering van fundamentele beleidsbeginsels verlang. Selfs nou nog skyn die partyleiers dit nie te besef nie. Waar die Verenigde Party die kans gehad het om jong en nuwe bloed in te bring, soos b.v. by Groenpunt, gaan hulle nou wragtiewaar vir Piet van der Byl stel as kandidaat. Hoewel ek goed bevriend is met Piet en hom nie persoonlik wil benadeel nie, kan ek nie dink aan 'n groter stommiteit wat die party kon begaan het op hierdie tydstip nie. Ek is in noue aanraking met die jong, denkende dele van ons bevolking en niks kon bereken gewees het om hulle indruk omtrent die afgeleefheid van die Verenigde Party te sterk as hierdie simptomatiese argaïsme nie. Jong mense word onwillekeurig aangetrek deur enige beweging wat lewenskragtigheid vertoon. Die Verenigde Party wys daar gewis maar min tekens van.

Dit is om hierdie redes dat die Verenigde Party sy houvas op die jong mense verloor en derhalwe *as sulks* geen toekoms het nie. Ek voel dat u hierdie feit onder die oë moet sien en daadwerklik en sonder verdere aarseling behoort op te tree. Hierdie optrede mag in sy gevolge teenoor seker persone as meedoënloos bestempel word. Ook wat u self betref, is dit moontlik dat die oplossing 'n byna te veel gevergde opoffering mag meebring. *Maar die saak van die redding van ons volk is groter as persone.* U eie handelwyse in die verlede het dit reeds bewys.

Dit bring my tot die groot probleem van wat om te doen met mnr. Hofmeyr. Ek het die grootste agting vir sy hoë ideale en administratiewe bekwaamheid. Hy was verreweg die bekwaamste lid van u Kabinet. Maar as gevolg van sy beklemtoning van abstrakte ideale betreffende die nie-blankes (ideale wat die geskiedenis eendag wanneer ons almal dood is, sal bewys as absoluut korrek) juis op hierdie tydstip, het die Nasionaliste 'n karikatuur van hom en sy idees gemaak en so'n 'mental stereotype' in die volksgees teen hom en sy idees opgebou dat dit jare sal neem om daar verby te kom. Daarby is hy aangewys as u opvolger en eerste minister. Hierdie was waarskynlik die vernaamste faktor wat bygedra het tot die neerlaag van die Verenigde Party op die platteland. Die Nasionaliste altans skrywe hulle onverwagte oorwinning hoofsaaklik daaraan toe. (Hierdie punt is seker al 'n gemeenplaas vir u!) Die feit bly egter staan dat Hofmeyr 'n 'embarrassment' sal wees in enige pogings om die groot gros van Verenigde Party aanhangers met die gematigde elemente wat mnr. Havenga van die Nasionaliste met hom sal meebring, tot een soliede, sentrale groep saam te smelt. Hoe ons dit ook al mag betreur, kan ons nie verbykom by die feit dat Hofmeyr as 'n onverteerbare knop in die maag van so'n groep sal bly sit nie. Dit sal onvermydelik vroeër of later ernstige krisisse meebring en sal die hele besigheid uitmekaar laat spat. U sal dus genoodsaak wees om, terwille van die behoud van die eenheid van ons volk, en terwille van die uiteindelike verwesenliking van die ideale waarna Hofmeyr streef, hom uit te laat, tensy hy kopgee oor daardie beginsels van hom. Ek twyfel ten seerste of hy dit sal doen. Hy sal waarskynlik 'n paar liberale elemente met hom meeneem, maar mens sal altoos op hulle kan reken om met die sentrale party saam te staan as dit tot 'n ernstige stryd kom teen die ekstremistiese elemente wat tans die huidige regering so domineer, en wat m.i. skaars een-derde van die land se kiesers agter hulle sal kry as daar 'n nuwe Sentrale Party onder u en Havenga gestig kan word. Met verloop van tyd sal die 'anti-Hofmeyr stereotype' vervaag raak en bes moontlik kan hy weer terugkom. Die verwesenliking van sy ideale is 'n saak van geleidelike opvoeding van die volk en sal selfs onder gunstige leiding nog jare neem. Onder die beleid van die huidige regering word die klok nie alleen agteruit gesit nie, maar kan daar maklik revolusie en bloedvergieting kom. Vir u om op hierdie tydstip van dreigende gevaar nie bereid te wees om groot opofferings, wat persone betref, te maak nie, sal noodlottig wees vir ons volk en ons demokratiese instellings—om nie eens van mnr. Hofmeyr se eie liberale idees te praat nie. Hy behoort dit in te sien.

Om redes hierbo genoem toon die Verenigde Party, soos hy tans georiënteer is, geen groeikrag nie. Hierdie gebrek aan vitaliteit is aansteeklik. Hy is nie bestand teen die doeltreffende organisasie wat die Broederbond met al sy vertakkinge tot stand gebring het nie. As die Verenigde Party met Hofmeyr daarin na die volk gaan, sal hulle definitief weer verloor. Veral as die Nasionaliste die skyn gaan wek dat *hulle* nou die gematigde party gaan wees en die ekstremiste, wat tans so voor op die wa is, in die agtergrond gaan hou, gaan hulle 'n groot deel van die Engelssprekendes se stemme ook vang.

My ervaring van die Engelse (veral in Natal) is dat hulle geheues baie kort is, en dat hulle net so bereid sal wees om die Nattes aan die bewind te sien as wat hulle destyds bereid was om vir Generaal Hertzog te stem. 'After all they cannot be too bad; and, what is more, we trust Klasie Havenga as a sound Finance Minister.' Hulle het 'n grenslose bewondering vir Havenga en sal geredelik vir sy kant stem. Tot vandag toe nog vertel die suikerboere hoe die voormalige Nat.-regering hulle begunstig het.

Vra u my nou wat ek aan die hand kan doen behalwe om negatiewe kritiek uit te oefen, dan besef ek die moeilikheid van die probleem. Ten spyte, egter, daarvan dat dit mag skyn 'n geval te wees van 'fools rushing in where angels fear to tread', wil ek dit tog waag om kortliks aan te stip wat ek reeds hier by implikasie laat deurskemer het: U en Klasie Havenga kom bymekaar en vergeet vir die moment die name 'Verenigde Party' en 'Afrikaner Party' met al hulle konneksies. U stel 'n program van beginsels op waarvolgens u as twee ou-leiers bereid is om saam na die volk te gaan. Die hoofpunt in hierdie program moet wees ***die opbou en voortplanting van Westerse beskawing in Suidelike Afrika***. Hierdie ideaal sluit in:

(a) samewerking tussen die Engels- en Afrikaanssprekende seksies;

(b) die ekonomiese ontwikkeling van Suid-Afrika op landboukundige en industriële gebied;

(c) 'n progressiewe immigrasiebeleid—nie alleen om die getalsterkte van die blanke ras op te bou nie, maar ook omdat ons geskoolde mense broodnodig het om (b) te verwesenlik; (d) die opheffing—ekonomies en opvoedkundig—van die nie-blanke bevolking, waarsonder (b) onmoontlik is. Trouens, die geskiedenis het geleer dat die enigste waarborg vir die voortbestaan van enige beskawing, die voortplanting en verspreiding daarvan is onder diegene met wie so'n beskawing in dieselfde gebiede saamwoon, en onder aangrensende meerderheidsgroepe. Hierdie sal noodwendig 'n geleidelike proses wees;

(e) die handhawing van ons demokratiese lewensbeskouing en die bestryding van fascisme, hetsy in die vorm van 'n broederbond-gestapo-regering of in die vorm van totalitaristiese kommunisme.

Ek is daarvan oortuig dat die saamkom van twee populêre figure soos u en mnr. Havenga die verbeelding van die volk so gaande sal maak dat hulle hierdie algemene doelstelling sonder veel teenkanting (in beginsel altans) sal aanvaar.

Die grootste moeilikheid, myns insiens, in verband met die verwesenliking van die vorming van so'n nuwe Sentrale of Volks-Party is die bestaan van die huidige partyorganisasies wat meebring die nadruk op setels en baantjies vir seker persone. Gevolglik vind ek dat die Verenigde Party organisasie b.v. nie die bos om rede die bome kan sien nie. Hier lê die wortel van die kwaad. Die partymasjien word gehandhaaf, en selfvernuwende, organiese groei en aanpassing word uitgeskakel. Myns insiens moet 'n mens eers die verbeelding en gees van die volk vang—òf deur 'n grootse ideaal òf deur sentimentele gehegtheid aan 'n groot leier, of leiers, en dan sal die kleiner kwessies van setels hulself oplos. Dit is 'n geval van 'Soek eers die Koninkryk der hemele'.

Nou is die kritieke tydstip om so iets te bewerkstellig—voordat mense te ver gaan om standpunt in te neem betreffende ondergeskikte dog moeilike vraagstukke, soos b.v. die Indiërvraagstuk—standpunte wat hulle dan terwille van party- of persoonlike prestige sal moet handhaaf en wat moontlik die saamstaan op die groot sake hierbo genoem gaan bemoeilik of heeltemal onmoontlik maak.

Dit moes u seker ook getref het hoe mnr. Havenga uit sy pad gegaan het om, net waar hy kom, u persoonlik te komplimenteer, hoewel hy die Verenigde Party as sulks gekritiseer het. Hy weet dat baie van sy volgelinge liewer by u wil aansluit as om by Malan te bly.

Maar dit is nie om die klein klompie wat die *Afrikaner Party* uitmaak by die Verenigde Party te voeg en sodoende 'n klein meerderheid in die Volksraad te bekom, dat ek hierdie vertoog aan u rig nie. Nee, dit is omdat ek oortuig is dat u ook die ondersteuning van 'n aansienlike aantal gematigde Nasionaliste sal verkry as u en mnr. Havenga saam na die volk gaan.

U weet net so goed soos ek wat die faksies in die huidige Malan-regering is. By die persoonlike jaloesieë is daar nog steeds die gevoel van die Noorde vs. die Suide. Hulle is dus nie in staat om met so'n soliede front na die volk te gaan as 'n Smuts–Havenga kombinasie nie. Die Malan-regering is tans net 'n bietjie minder kwesbaar as die Smuts–Hofmeyr kombinasie.

Met 'n aansienlike meerderheid van die volk agter u, sal die gesamentlike leierskap van u en mnr. Havenga genoegsame vertroue inboesem dat die nuwe koalisie met vrymoedigheid sal kan eksperimenteer met jonger manne in die Kabinet en om sodoende volksleiers vir die toekoms op te lei en op te bou terwyl u en mnr. Havenga later geleidelik op die agtergrond tree. Die groot saak is dat daar 'n stabiele fondament sal wees om op voort te bou.

Wie die onderhoof van die twee moet wees, wil ek nie sê nie. Net dit: As dit moet blyk dat dit die enigste manier sou wees om die gematigde gedeelte van die Nasionaliste in hierdie sentrale groep in te bring as mnr. Havenga as die hoof en u as die onderhoof optree, dan sal hierdie opoffering myns insiens deur u persoonlike prestige geregverdig wees. U dergelike selflose groot gebaar in 1933 het vir u van allerweë hoë agting verwerf. Dit was 'n daad van selfimmolering wat alleen 'n ware groot man kon verrig het. As gevolg daarvan het u des te groter van aansien geword. Al sou dit ook die laaste politieke daad wees wat u in u eie land kan verrig, sal niks so baie kan bydra tot die rehabilitasie van u eie posisie in Suid-Afrika as so'n staatsmansdaad van selfopoffering nie. Deur die regte elemente weer bymekaar te bring en 'n leidende aandeel te neem in die opbou van 'n nuwe sterk regering wat die vertroue van die grootste deel van ons volk—Engels- en Afrikaanssprekend—sal wegdra, sal u u skitterende loopbaan tot 'n passende klimaks bring.

In sy wordingsjare het u as jong man ons Suid-Afrikaanse volk dikwels deur donkere nagte gelei. In die fleur van u lewe het u hom op die pad van selfstandigheid gevoer. Nou het u die lewensaand bereik. Weer staan Suid-Afrika voor 'n krisis. Dit sal op die verkragting van die Westerse beskawing stuur in die hande van die Fascistiese Broederbond-elemente met hul deur vrees aangejaagde, kortsigtige nie-blanke beleid. Ek besef ten volle hoe ingewikkeld die hele situasie is, maar in u hande, en u hande alleen, seer geagte Oom Jannie, lê die oplossing. U sal die beste kan beslis oor die 'timing' en oor die metodes van aanvoor teneinde hierdie nuwe oriëntering te bewerkstellig. Hoe gouer hoe beter. Anders wat is die alternatief? Die verbrokkeling van die Verenigde Party en 'n toenemende bitterheid en onenigheid wat die prestige van ons volk oorsee sal ondermyn en die ontwikkeling van ons land vir jare sal strem.

Laat die aandster van u loopbaan net so helder Suid-Afrika se beskawingspad deur die woestyn verlig soos die môrester van u vérsiende leiding die donker newels in die verlede deurgedring het. In September 1939 toe die situasie byna onmoontlik en taamlik hopeloos gelyk het, was dit u nugtere leierskap en besliste optrede wat die regdenkendes van alle partye om u laat skaar het en u 'n meerderheid besorg het. Sodoende het u Suid-Afrika van 'n groot ramp gered.

Vandag weer staan ons volk by 'n tweesprong. By u weer lê die verantwoordelikheid om die beslissing te maak. Die oë van die gematigde elemente in ons volk is op u en mnr. Havenga gevestig. Ek bid u, moet ons nie teleurstel nie. Met vriendelike groete, hoogagtend die uwe,

E. G. Malherbe

N.S. Ingeval ek deur bostaande by u miskien die indruk mag gewek het dat ek 'n tweede professor A. C. Cilliers is wat homself soms in die rol van 'n versoener en 'n toenaderingsingenieur gesien het, kan ek u meedeel dat ek geen persoonlike politieke aspirasies het nie. Ek is heeltemal tevrede om my land in my huidige werkkring te dien. Nietemin voel ek dit is my plig as landsburger om, waar ek besondere geleenthede gehad het, en dikwels nog het, om die pols van ons maatskaplike lewe te voel, hierdie voorstelle in alle beskeidenheid voor u te lê. Ek wil vertrou dat u in die lig daarvan die nodige stappe sal doen teneinde 'n nuwe oriëntering in ons land se politieke samestelling teweeg te bring—voordat dit te laat is.

TRANSLATION

Personal and confidential

Natal University College
Pietermaritzburg
8 September 1948

Dear Oom Jannie, I feel terribly worried about the way things are going politically. If this lot who are now on top remain in power, it is going to ruin our country—in spite of all the superambassadors they may send out to try to defend this disastrous *volte face* in our country.[1] It is this concern that induces me to write to you. I would much rather have liked to discuss the whole business personally with you when I was recently in the Cape, but unfortunately there was no chance of this.

I know that there are many people who—asked or unasked—give you advice. I have, however, reason to think that many of

[1] C. te Water (q.v.) had been appointed ambassador-at-large for the Union in 1948 and held this position until 1950.

the advisers around you are not properly informed and that those who do know what is wrong do not always have the courage to tell you frankly and in all respects what the true state of affairs is. This negligence is sometimes due to self-interest and sometimes to fear of you. In this respect you suffered an irreparable loss when Louis Esselen died. He did 'know' and kept you well informed.

In case what I write here may give the impression that I am taking up a holier than thou attitude, I want to assure you that I am constrained by disinterested friendship and a high regard for you, coupled with a disquieting realization of the critical time through which our country is at this moment passing. But enough about the motives behind this unasked information and advice!

You will remember that, on 19 August, in the few minutes that I saw you in the lobby of the house of assembly, I told you that the Nat government would make certain concessions to minister Havenga and that he would not accept them because he personally, and also some of his followers, were deeply unhappy in that *kraal*; also, he would much rather co-operate with you.

You rejected this suggestion (which I had at first hand) on the grounds that you 'did not want to negotiate with a lot of Fascists'.

I fear that your evaluation of the situation is superficial. I can only ascribe to this the fact that your information service is weak and superficial.

The facts are as follows:

(1) Havenga uses the O.B. chiefly to intimidate the Nats and to strengthen his bargaining power and not because he has any liking for the O.B.s or their ideology. Besides, with the exception of a small group of ideological leaders, Fascism does not penetrate very deeply into the rank and file of the O.B.s. It is not in the nature of our people and does not fit in with our indigenous institutions. In the absence of the stimulus and opportunities provided by the war their power and numbers are fast decreasing. Even van Rensburg realizes this and is now seeking to curry favour with the more democratic and moderate elements. I would, therefore, not attach too much weight to Havenga's opportunistic affiliation with the 'Fascists'.

(2) Havenga hates the *Broederbond*. It was they who stabbed his old friend, General Hertzog, in the back. That he will never forgive them.

(3) In my opinion the most important result of Erasmus's ferreting in the military intelligence archives is the high degree of suspicion and mutual distrust between the three sections who co-operated before the last elections and beat the United party:

(a) the *Broeders*, (b) the non-*Broeder* Nats and (c) the O.B.s. They are now discovering how individuals in these three sections —not even mentioning the Greyshirts[1] and other less important factions—undermined and tried to outwit one another in their jockeying for power. This aspect is amusing, especially for those of us who could watch all these tricks and doings at the time. Havenga's contact with this feud was tangential. He never compromised himself wholeheartedly with any of them. To be sure, they courted him in turn.

I feel that you should exploit this situation by acting immediately and strongly while these leaders and pseudo-leaders are still busy freeing their minds of these suspicions. You and Havenga must come together and set our little people on course again under your joint leadership.

In some respects the situation is as in 1932–3, only much more critical and dangerous. The great majority of the South African people are tired of this unnatural condition of division and long, just as in 1932–3, for a leadership which can bind all the moderate elements together into one powerful party.

I am certain that a large section of the Nationalists do not in their hearts feel exactly proud of the extravagances that some of the present ministers indulge in. The tail wags the dog in Malan's government.

This new orientation under a Smuts–Havenga leadership can, however, not come about under the United party as it is constituted at present. Understand this well: *the United party as such is finished.* That old United party cabinet will never again govern the country. That they brought you actively into the party again after they had made such a hopeless mess of the election, that they expect you as an old veteran to board the sinking ship and go down with them under a fluttering United party flag, is nothing less than criminal. At the end of your fighting and heroic career you, as a South African and world statesman, deserve something much better than such a futile gesture.

You realize even better than I do that a party, just like an old piece of machinery, can never survive the spiritual and material dislocations that inevitably follow a war. The United party has simply gone the way of all parties under similar circumstances. But surely this need not necessarily mean that our little nation must now perish for ever under the tyranny of the *Broederbond*.

The *débâcle* of the United party was the greater for various reasons, among others:

[1] This movement for the propagation of the Nazi ideology in South Africa was founded by Louis Weichardt in 1935.

(a) because it had no positive, aggressive policy. It was always on the defensive and negative. Its strongest point was the black war record of the Nats and it relied on cheap platform dialectic. In this respect the party propaganda was hopeless. It also completely overlooked the fact that half the voters are women for whom white bread was much more important than a world war for ideological principles. The unavoidability of controls was never properly explained to housewives.

(b) because it did not protect and foster the moderate elements in its own circles. It took their devoted support too much for granted. (Consider, for instance, the feeble way in which the bilingual school policy was torpedoed: on the one hand by the English jingos, on the other by the *Broederbond*. Okkie Oosthuizen will be able to tell you how my worst prophecies about the failure of the Transvaal legislation on this point were fulfilled.[1] But they would not listen to my warnings.)

(c) because it *has shown no sign of rejuvenation*. It is all very well to remain faithful to the old cart-horses who have given years of service, but there comes a time when they must be outspanned. You, because of your spiritual powers and physical youth, are a brilliant exception to this rule. The United party has not the slightest hope of regaining the confidence of the country if it again appears with the old cabinet team. Deserved or undeserved, the people were tired of and satiated with them and longed for a change of personnel more than for a change in fundamental points of policy. Even now the party leaders do not seem to realize this. Where the United party had the chance to bring in young new blood, as for instance in Green Point, they actually again nominated Piet van der Byl as candidate. Although Piet is a good friend of mine and I do not wish to injure him personally I cannot think of a greater stupidity that the party could have committed at this juncture. I am in close touch with the young, thinking sections of our population and nothing could have been calculated to strengthen them more in their impression of the decrepitude of the United party than this symptomatic archaism. Young people are involuntarily attracted by any movement that displays vitality. The United party certainly shows few signs of that.

It is for these reasons that the United party is losing its hold

[1] After their victory in the 1943 provincial election in the Transvaal the United party introduced dual medium education in secondary schools there. In 1948, when the Nationalist party won the election, this policy was reversed. In South Africa education 'other than higher' is a function of the provincial governments.

on the young people and therefore has, *as such*, no future. I feel that you must face this fact and that you should act forcefully and without further hesitation. Such action may, in its effects, be called heartless. Also, as regards yourself, it is possible that the solution may require almost too great a sacrifice. *But the task of saving our nation is greater than persons.* Your own behaviour in the past has already proved this.

This brings me to the great problem of what to do with Mr Hofmeyr. I have the highest regard for his high ideals and administrative ability. He was by far the ablest member of your cabinet. But, as a result of his emphasis at this particular time on abstract ideals regarding the non-whites (ideals which history will one day, when we are all dead, prove to be absolutely right), the Nationalists made a caricature of him and his ideas and built up such a mental stereotype in the public mind against him and his ideas that it will take years to get past it. Moreover, he is designated as your successor and prime minister. This was probably the chief factor that contributed to the defeat of the United party in the rural areas. At any rate the Nationalists ascribe their unexpected victory mainly to this. (This point is probably already a commonplace to you!) The fact remains, however, that Hofmeyr will be an embarrassment in any attempt to forge into one solid, central group the greater number of the United party supporters and the moderate elements that Mr Havenga will bring with him. However much we may deplore it, we cannot get past the fact that Hofmeyr will remain sticking, like an indigestible lump, in the stomach of such a group. It will inevitably cause serious crises sooner or later and shatter the whole thing. You will therefore be obliged, for the sake of maintaining the unity of our people and for the sake of the eventual realization of the ideals for which Hofmeyr strives, to leave him out, unless he gives in about those principles of his. I strongly doubt whether he will do so. He will probably take a few liberal elements with him but one could always rely upon them to support the central party if it were to come to a serious contest with the extremist elements who now dominate the present government and who, in my opinion, would have hardly one-third of the country's voters behind them if a new central party under you and Havenga can be formed. In the course of time the Hofmeyr stereotype will fade and he can, in all likelihood, return. The realization of his ideals is a matter of the gradual education of the people and will, even under favourable leadership, take years. Under the policy of the present government the clock is not only being put back, but there could easily be revolution and bloodshed.

That you, at this time of threatening danger, should not be ready to make great sacrifices as regards persons will be disastrous for our people and our democratic institutions—not to mention Mr Hofmeyr's own liberal ideas. He should see this.

For the reasons given above the United party, as now orientated, shows no power of growth. This lack of vitality is infectious. It is not proof against the effective organization which the *Broederbond*, with all its ramifications, has built up. If the United party, with Hofmeyr in it, goes to the country, it will definitely lose again. Particularly if the Nationalists now create the appearance that they are going to be the moderate party and keep the extremists, who are at present so forward, in the background, they are going to catch a large part of the English-speakers' vote as well.

My experience of the English (especially in Natal) is that their memories are very short, and that they will be quite prepared to see the Nats in power as they were formerly prepared to vote for General Hertzog. 'After all they cannot be too bad; and, what is more, we trust Klasie Havenga as sound finance minister.' They have a limitless admiration for Havenga and will readily vote on his side. To this day the sugar farmers still tell how the former Nat government favoured them.

If now you ask me what I can suggest apart from making negative criticisms, then I realize the difficulty of the problem. However, in spite of this appearing to be a case of 'fools rush in where angels fear to tread', I venture to indicate briefly what I have already allowed to appear by implication: You and Klasie Havenga come together and forget for the moment the names 'United party' and 'Afrikaner party' with all their connections. You draw up a programme of principles according to which you, as two veteran leaders, are prepared to go together to the country. The chief point of this programme must be *the building up and expansion of Western civilization in southern Africa*. This ideal includes:

(a) co-operation between the English- and Afrikaans-speaking sections;

(b) the economic development of South Africa in agriculture and industry;

(c) a progressive immigration policy, not only to build up the numbers of the white race, but also because we desperately need trained people to realize (b);

(d) the uplifting—economically and educationally—of the non-white population without which (b) is impossible; (Indeed, history has shown that the only guarantee for the survival of any civilization is its expansion and propagation among those who live together in its territory and among majority groups on its borders. This will necessarily be a gradual process.)

(e) the maintenance of our democratic way of life and the combating of fascism, whether in the form of a *Broederbond*–Gestapo government, or in the form of totalitarian communism.

I am convinced that the coming together of two popular figures like you and Mr Havenga will so excite the imagination of the people that they may well accept this general goal (at any rate in principle) without much opposition.

The greatest difficulty, in my view, in connection with realizing the formation of such a Central or People's party is the existence of the present party organizations—which involves emphasis on seats and jobs for certain persons. Consequently I find that the United party organization, for instance, cannot see the wood for the trees. Here lies the root of the trouble. The party machine is maintained and self-renewing; organic growth is eliminated. In my opinion one should first capture the imagination and soul of the people—either by a great ideal or by sentimental attachment to a great leader or leaders, and then the smaller matters of seats will solve themselves. It is a case of 'seek ye first the kingdom of heaven'.[1]

Now is the critical time to bring something like this about—before people go too far in taking up a standpoint about subordinate but difficult questions such as the Indian question—standpoints which, because of party or personal prestige, they will have to maintain and which may perhaps make co-operation on the large matters named above difficult or quite impossible.

It must have struck you that Mr Havenga has gone out of his way to pay you personal compliments wherever he goes although he has criticized the United party as such. He knows that many of his followers would rather join you than stay with Malan.

But I do not make these representations to you in order to add the small group comprising the Afrikaner party to the United party and so to acquire a small majority in the house of assembly. No, it is because I am convinced that you will also get the support of a considerable number of moderate Nationalists if you and Mr Havenga go to the country together.

You know as well as I do what the factions in the present Malan government are. Along with personal jealousies there is still this feeling of the north versus the south. They are therefore not in a position to go the country with such a solid front as a Smuts–

[1] 'But seek ye first the kingdom of God and his righteousness; and all these things shall be added unto you.' *St Matthew* vi.33.

Havenga combination. The Malan government is at present only a little less vulnerable than the Smuts–Havenga combination.

With a considerable majority of the people behind you the combined leadership of yourself and Mr Havenga will inspire enough confidence to allow the new coalition to experiment freely with younger men in the cabinet and so to train and foster national leaders for the future while you and Mr Havenga gradually move into the background. The great thing is that there will then be a stable foundation on which to build further.

Who of the two is to be the deputy leader I do not wish to say. Only this: if it should appear that Mr Havenga as leader and you as deputy leader would be the only way to bring the moderate section of the Nationalists into this central group, then this sacrifice would, in my opinion, be justified by your personal prestige. Your similar selfless great gesture in 1933 brought you high and universal esteem. It was a deed of self-immolation that only a truly great man could have performed. As a result of it your stature became the greater. Even if it should be your last political act in your own country, nothing could contribute more to your own position in South Africa than such a statesmanlike act of sacrifice. By bringing the right elements together once more and taking a leading part in building up a new strong government which will have the confidence of the greater part of our people—English- and Afrikaans-speaking, you would bring your brilliant career to a fitting climax.

In its formative years, you, as a young man, often led our South African nation through dark days. In the prime of your life you put it on the road of independence. Now you have reached the evening of life. Again South Africa faces a crisis. It will head for a violation of Western civilization in the hands of the fascistic *Broederbond* elements with their short-sighted non-white policy which is induced by fear. I fully realize how complicated the whole situation is, but in your hands, and your hands alone, most respected Oom Jannie, lies the solution. You would best decide about timing and the method of procedure in order to bring about this new orientation. The sooner the better. Otherwise, what is the alternative? The disintegration of the United party and an increasing bitterness and disunity which will undermine the prestige of our people overseas and retard the development of our country for years.

May the evening star of your career light up South Africa's path of civilization through the desert as brightly as the morning star of your far-sighted leadership penetrated the dark mists in the past. In September 1939 when the situation seemed almost impossible and fairly hopeless, it was your sober leadership and decisive action that caused right-thinking people of all parties to range themselves around you and give you a majority. So you saved South Africa from a great disaster.

Today our people stand again at a cross-roads. The responsibility of making the decision lies with you. The eyes of the moderate elements of our people are fixed on you and Mr Havenga. I implore you, do not disappoint us. With friendly greetings, Yours sincerely,

E. G. Malherbe

P.S. In case I may by the above have given you the impression that I am a second Professor A. C. Cilliers, who has at times seen himself in the role of a conciliator and engineer of *rapprochement*,[1] I may say that I have no political aspirations. I am quite satisfied to serve my country in my present sphere of work. Nevertheless I feel it is my duty as a citizen who has had, and often still has, special opportunities to feel the pulse of our social life, to lay these suggestions in all modesty before you. I trust that you will, in the light of this, take the necessary steps to bring about a new orientation in the political constitution of our country—before it is too late.

813 To E. G. Malherbe — Vol. 88, no. 154

There is another draft in the Smuts Collection of a reply to **812** (vol. 88, no. 154A). It is in Smuts's handwriting and is more reasoned and serious in tone than the letter printed below which was actually sent to Professor Malherbe.

Kaapstad
13 September 1948

Waarde Malherbe, Ek het jou belangrike brief van 8 deser ontvang. Jy sal natuurlik nie verwag dat ek daarop kommenteer nie. Dieselfde oorwegings het ek ook van andere ontvang. 'n Kombinasie tussen die Verenigde Party en die O.B. kom my darem raar voor en herinner my aan die voorstel jare gelede dat die Sappe met die Roosiete moes verenig, en Tielman desnoods as leier aanneem! Dit alles was baie uit die lug gegrepe, en dit sal maar goed wees stadig oor die klippe met die nuwe idee te gaan. Met groete en beste wense, Steeds die uwe,

J. C. Smuts

[1] In January 1939 Professor A. C. Cilliers (q.v.) published a pamphlet entitled *Quo Vadis* in which he advocated the formation of a new Afrikaner party to bring together the followers of General Hertzog and Dr D. F. Malan. *See also* vol. VI, p. 200, note 2.

TRANSLATION

Cape Town
13 September 1948

Dear Malherbe, I have received your important letter of the 8th. You will, of course, not expect me to comment on it. I have received the same considerations from others also. A combination between the United party and the O.B. appears rather odd to me and reminds me of the suggestion years ago that the Saps should unite with the Roosites and, if necessary, accept Tielman as leader![1] All that was very far-fetched and it would be as well to go slowly with the new idea. With greetings and best wishes, Yours ever,

J. C. Smuts

814 From E. G. Malherbe — Vol. 86, no. 144

This letter is annotated, in Smuts's handwriting, as follows: 'No answer as yet'.

Persoonlik en vertroulik

Natal Universiteitskollege
Pietermaritzburg
18 September 1948

Geagte Oom Jannie, Baie dankie vir u vriendelike briefie.

My voorstelle is miskien nie so naïef as wat u blykbaar dink nie. Mnr. Havenga is nie die O.B. nie. Sy werklike aanhang is veel wyer as die Afrikaner Party en die O.B.'s. Die O.B.'s is maar die vlooie op die hond se stert! Hoewel lastig op die oomblik, sal hulle afspring en mettertyd verdwyn sodra die algemene atmosfeer gesonder word.

Hierdie gesonder atmosfeer kan alleen kom as u en mnr. Havenga kan wegbreek van die huidige party-konnotasies en -benamings en 'n nuwe oriëntering skep wat die verbeelding van Suid-Afrika sal vang. Uit die aard van die saak sal die Broederbond plus hulle geestesverwante wat teer op sensasionalisme en vreesaanjaging dan die opposisie uitmaak, en hoewel ek hulle geensins onderskat nie, voel ek dat hulle op die lange duur nie bestand sal wees teen 'n kragtige sentrale party of groep nie. Met vriendelike groete en hoogagting, die uwe,

E. G. Malherbe

[1] *See* vol. v, nos. **302, 324–5**.

TRANSLATION

Personal and confidential

Natal University College
Pietermaritzburg
18 September 1948

Dear Oom Jannie, Thank you very much for your friendly note.

My suggestions are perhaps not so naïve as you apparently think. Mr Havenga is not the O.B. His real following is much wider than the Afrikaner party and the O.B.s. The O.B.s are only the fleas on the dog's tail! Although a nuisance at the moment, they will jump off and, in due course, disappear as soon as the general atmosphere gets healthier.

That healthier atmosphere can only appear if you and Mr Havenga can break away from the present party connotations and names and create a new orientation which will capture the imagination of South Africa. In the nature of things the *Broederbond* plus their kindred spirits who thrive on sensationalism and agitation will then make up the opposition, and, although I do not in the least underestimate them, I feel that they will not in the long run be proof against a powerful central party or group. With kind regards and esteem, Yours sincerely,

E. G. Malherbe

815 To M. R. Drennan — Vol. 88, no. 159

16 September 1948

My dear Drennan, What an exciting find, if it is correctly understood![1] I can scarcely believe it. Jolly [K.] seems to have got as far down as upper Stellenbosch or Fauresmith. But the Dartians[2] must belong to a far more remote past. To think of our little men feasting on the head of an Australopithecine man-ape is almost more than I can believe.

Anyhow, Peers cave is holding great secrets, and the continued search there has proved very worth while. Ever yours sincerely,

s. J. C. Smuts

[1] K. Jolly had, while excavating Peers cave near Fish Hoek on the False bay coast, found 'a primate tooth' which Drennan thought came from 'a huge Australopithecine type' (*see* Smuts Collection, vol. 85, no. 161).

[2] A reference to Professor Raymond Dart of the University of the Witwatersrand who in 1924 discovered, at Taungs in Bechuanaland, a skull of a creature which he named *Australopithecus* and which had man-like and ape-like characteristics. In the letter cited above Drennan had written: 'Who will believe that the Dartians roamed the False bay coast?'

816 To W. S. Churchill Vol. 88, no. 166

27 September 1948

My dear Winston, I have not troubled you with correspondence knowing how fully your time is occupied, and how deeply you must be concerned with present world developments. But, as in old times, I wish briefly to unburden myself to you.

War preparations are going on all round and alarming speeches are being made by those in authority. Both Marshall and Bevin speak like men standing in the last ditch for peace. I, myself, have not up to now taken the war situation very seriously. As you will remember, in my address at Cambridge I described the real danger before us as the peaceful infiltration which Russia is pursuing through her fifth column in all parts of the world. But in view of what is now happening, and openly said in responsible quarters, I do not feel so certain of that view now. Of course I am cut off from all informed official contacts and can only judge by what appears in the press, and from what is actually happening.

France is so broken by Communist infiltration and lack of leadership and some deeper decay that little can be expected from her, either in a great peace or a war crisis. Britain, our mainstay in the war, remains stricken by war exhaustion and financial dangers, which may come to a head, should America cease to supply her dollar dope. The rest of Europe is ripe for the sickle.

What is to happen if Russia does make up her mind that this is her moment? I have never trusted Russian judgment, which has been clever in small ways but often stupid in big issues. The position now developing in Europe and Asia may appear to her to be her opportunity, and in the near future we may be precipitated, either deliberately or by blunder, in a war for which we are not ready.

I almost hesitate to have to confess it, but I am beginning to think more and more that the wise course for us is boldly and openly to integrate Western Germany with the West, and, instead of continuing to dismantle and cripple her, to put her on her feet again and make her part of our eastern defence wall, as she has been for centuries. The Slav menace has been so successful and is now becoming so great that a drastic change in European strategy and alignment is called for. With the present weakness of the European situation, I see no way out of the Communist menace short of calling on Germany to play her part. At least that is how I begin to view what is now happening in Europe.

It will mean a rather sharp reversal of the politics we have been pursuing so far. It will come as a shock to public opinion. But the shock will be worse if war breaks out suddenly and soon, and Russia marches practically unopposed to the Atlantic and the Mediterranean. The vacuum created by German elimination from our European system will then appear to have been the greatest blunder of all.

Russia has abused our joint victory to fasten her ideology on much of Europe and to open the way to the complete conquest of the West. And our present policy of continuing the German vacuum is helping her in that sinister game. A reversal of that policy has to be considered very seriously.

Instead of making peace with Germany and saving and securing her as an ally for the future equilibrium of peace, we have continued to break her down and expose her and ourselves and the world to this Communist menace. She should rather be saved, if Europe is to be saved and a halt called to the Communist advance from the East. In this new and quite unforeseen situation now developing why not call her in to play her part? Why not call her in to play once more the part she played in the Protestant revolution in the sixteenth century? It is generally recognized that Germany is necessary for the salvaging of Europe.

This may sound explosive stuff. But we live in explosive times, and the question is whether it is not we and our civilization which will be exploded if our present post-war policy in central Europe is continued any longer.

Your proposal for European unity is good and sound and making quite fair progress. But present events are outpacing that progress. Some decisive drastic steps may have to be taken to meet the new situation which Russia has herself created by her ruthless exploitation of our joint victory for her own Communist ends.

My suggestion to you is this: now that Marshall is in Paris, will you not raise this matter with him? You may, if you prefer, put it before him, not as your but my suggestion, and put the onus on me if you like. If I were in Europe now I would certainly approach him direct, but I am tied down to my duties here, and am isolated from all inside information about what is really happening. And the position may not be as menacing as it appears to me at this distance. Both of you may consider my alarm exaggerated and unjustified. If so, I shall leave it at that. But if Stalin is going to play the game of Hitler, something far more drastic will have to be done than has hitherto been considered called for, and in that case we should not for a moment hesitate to call in Germany to take her part in the struggle—and prepare for it in time. The hatred for Russia will strengthen the German response, and be the greatest reinforcement we could have in an otherwise very fateful struggle for the West in its present condition. Yours with every good wish and all my affection,

s. J. C. Smuts

817 To M. C. Gillett Vol. 88, no. 260

Cape Town
29 September 1948

This is a vacant moment in the last days of this session of parliament, and an opening for a few words with you. On my return to Doornkloof I may not soon have another free time. I returned yesterday from another of my tumultuous country visits—this time to Swellendam. The Monday before I had been to a similar function at Worcester. These are great occasions, attended by thousands—partly out of curiosity—and partly from genuine political interest. All very tiring to me, as the meetings are preceded and followed by other engagements which make the visit even more exhausting. But I am back and attending to the concluding business in parliament. In two days I shall be off to Port Elizabeth where I shall crowd four functions into one day. And then off by air to home, sweet home. Although it has been raining here, both Worcester and Swellendam passed off in splendid weather, and I felt as if treading on air, with an elation of the spirit. I am sure these visits do good—if only by establishing human contact. Country people have seen me so seldom in the war years and since that I am a sort of mythical character.

This afternoon I am to receive the Cook Medal of the Royal Society in Australia for distinguished services in science and public life. This is the first award of this medal and therefore a great honour. But I am somewhat nonplussed to make out what my scientific services were. My public services are anybody's guess! But at any rate this is good fun, and I like this sort of thing.

You must have noticed that, what with all these week-end engagements, I have no or very little time for either the country or the mountains. And these are the parts of my week that I love most to be free. But the world is merciless, and I must bow to the will of my masters.

It has been a bad session. Natives, Coloureds and Indians have been under constant attack, and we in the opposition have not been able to ward off the blows struck against those who cannot defend themselves. There is no doubt a wave of reaction rolling over the country, and the sort of policies I have stood for are once more under the hammer. The Black Peril has been exploited to the limit and the prejudices of our good unthinking people have been played upon until they will not listen to any counsel of wisdom or prudence. We shall have much more of all this next year, and politics will become most unpleasant. I do not think people mean evil, but thoughtlessly do evil. In public life they do things of which they would be incapable in private life. So I heard yesterday from a friend how he had been in a hot argument with a Nat over taking away the Native and Coloured franchise. They were in the car of the Nat and when along the road they met an old Coloured person wearily marching along, the Nat stopped his car and picked up the old fellow and drove him on for the next ten or twelve miles. When he had been put down at the end of his journey, my friend said to the kind Nat: 'How does this square with your policy of apartheid?' To which he replied, 'But how could you pass the old fellow by without giving him a lift?' You can note how much better the behaviour was than the politics. It is all a sore trial and I fear we shall pay dearly for all this dangerous colour propaganda now set going. Anyhow I shall soon be away from these apartheid debates for at least a week, perhaps for two. And I shall enjoy the freedom and release of Doornkloof and Rooikop. I shall think of you and Arthur when I enjoy the quiet which we have shared together in old times. To me the goodness of the world and the spirit comes in these quiet times of seclusion and release from the human pressure. My dear love and best wishes. Ever yours,

Jan

818 To M. C. Gillett — Vol. 88, no. 262

Doornkloof
[Transvaal]
11 October 1948

This date is a mark of calamity in my history. On it fifty years ago the Boer War was declared. On it at 12.30 this morning Japie [Smuts] passed away, after an illness of less than twenty-four hours. It was a case of acute cerebral meningitis. Last Saturday afternoon he or Kitty phoned that he was coming over on Sunday morning (yesterday) to fetch two of the small daughters who were staying with us. Sunday morning Kitty phoned that he was not feeling quite well and might not come. That Sunday night he passed away. The doctor had thought it merely an attack of influenza, otherwise an application of penicillin might have done some good—perhaps. But it must have been a very virulent case to have developed with such speed. We heard of the matter only on Sunday night when he had already passed away. Jannie [Smuts] and Sylma [Coaton] hurried by car to their house at Welgedacht mine, but of course it was all over. Tomorrow will be the cremation, to which of course Isie will not be allowed to go, but the rest of us will go, and probably a big crowd of the public, as Japie was one of the most popular mine managers on the Reef. Kitty[1] remains with five small ones, and we propose to bring them all over to Doornkloof which is actually their property. Isie was only told this morning, although she was awake during the night, and noted the going, and must have guessed that something unusual was going on. I broke the news to her at 7 a.m. today and she took it all quietly, I think rather dazed and speechless with inward suffering. 'Death the most holy' had once more come into this family after a long, long absence and taken away perhaps the pick of the bunch, rather snatched him away almost without notice. Better so perhaps. But what suffering is left behind in this very sensitive family! I feel for Isie. I feel for Kitty sitting with that small group of five. But we shall try to stand by her and make what is intolerable tolerable for her. What more can one say? It is curious that last week I had been reading two philosophical discussions on immortality—one by Professor A. D. Ritchie[2] and another by A. N. Whitehead in his last volume of essays.[3] Both very high class and highbrow, but missing the human poignancy of it all. To me the last word in all the great matters is 'mystery'. And death, the most natural of all events, is also the most mysterious—beyond all philosophy, and perhaps beyond all religion. 'O death, where is thy sting?[4] But the sting is in those who remain behind, and no consolation of philosophy or comfort of religion has drawn that sting, in spite of the wonderful words of St Paul on the matter. There is great pain in all partings and the greatest pain in the last parting. Even the Holy Spirit of remembrance cannot fill that void for flesh and blood. And so the veil goes down,[5] and there is silence for ever more. Japie was so much to us. Such a son, such a human, such a comrade—such a joy and pride of life! And some

[1] Born Katharina Bosman; married J. D. Smuts in 1933.

[2] *Essays in Philosophy and other pieces* (1948).

[3] *Essays in Science and Philosophy* (1948).

[4] 1 *Corinthians* xv.55.

[5] 'Death is the veil which those who live call life.' Shelley, *Prometheus Unbound*, III.iii.113.

miserable invisible microbe has robbed us of him! There is here such a problem in the order of the universe that all attempts at explanation seem just silly and make no sense. The last word *is* mystery, before which we bow our heads in silence, and carry on with the tasks of the living before us. Good-bye, beloved son, beloved mate, beloved brother, beloved father. We are all in the Eternal Order, and in *that* togetherness there can be no parting...

What more is there to write, except to thank you for your last long letter...And then there are the happenings in the world—the Security Council gingerly touching Berlin,[1] U.N.O. with endless discussions, the French strike[2] passing over into something like insurrection, the Commonwealth conference.[3] The human scene looking very inhuman! And yet, and yet, that is only part of the story. In infinite homes and hearts the goodness of God is manifesting itself in numberless ways, and the sacred flame is kept burning. You refer to my visit to the Karoo garden[4] and all its wealth of beauty. But is there not the same in the human garden of the soul—flowers of the most exquisite type, perhaps blooming unseen, except to the Eternal Eye. In days like these and on an occasion in my life like this, I sense the Eternal *within* all this transitory scene. It is not all ugliness and misery and pain. The tragedy is highlighted with gleams of the ultimate Good and Beautiful and True—with Faith Hope and Charity too. Ever yours,

J.C.S.

819 To D. Moore — Vol. 88, no. 172

Doornkloof
[Transvaal]
17 October 1948

My dear Daphne, I had your letter from Hyde Park Hotel a few days ago. It was a sad letter, just before parting with your daughters

[1] On 4 October the Security Council met in Paris to consider the complaint by the United States, Great Britain and France against the transport restrictions imposed by the U.S.S.R. (*see supra*, p. 218, note 3). The dispute was put on its agenda but on 6 October it adjourned. Meanwhile some of its members tried to mediate between the Western powers and Russia, which held that the matter did not fall within the competence of the council.

[2] The coal-miners' strike in October for increased wages was also a political move by the strongly Communist trade unions to counteract the economic co-operation proposed in the European Recovery Programme and Marshall Aid. The miners barricaded themselves in the mines and army units were used against them.

[3] This met in London from 11 to 22 October.

[4] At Worcester, south-western Cape Province.

and leaving London for a long change. The daughters will get on quite well. They are both well-equipped in character and training for whatever may lie ahead. I am not so sure about the mother! Once more you have become a seeker. May you find fulfilment and satisfaction. But at bottom life is such a search, and mostly a tragic search. I do not think this life was meant for happiness. Perhaps the search is the thing—the struggle and endless endeavour, and the little snatches of happiness are just flowers to cheer us on the way. Dear Daphne, I do wish Australia will be kind to you. At least it will be a new experience and as such expand the horizons which so far have been too narrow for you, for your questing soul.

We have just passed through a harrowing experience. Sunday a week ago our Japie passed away quite suddenly and unexpectedly, at the beginning of a great life that was opening up before him. Apparently quite fit and well he had gone for a walk that morning and on returning told his wife that he had a headache. It rapidly got worse, in the afternoon he became unconscious and at night he passed away. A virulent attack of cerebral meningitis, the doctor diagnosed. He returned from the U.S.A. a couple of months ago where he had been sent on a mining mission, as he had been marked out for very high position in the mining industry. He leaves a widow and five small children, the youngest another Jan Smuts, and the image of his father. We are taking the family into our household, and indeed this home part of Doornkloof belonged to him. Isie has taken it calmly, but I think she is really dazed by the blow, as he was her favourite child. An exceptionally brilliant career at the university, both here and at Cambridge, ended by a miserable invisible microbe. Such is life. That is our dramatic story. And the public story is not much better. South Africa is passing through a difficult period. Our last general election was fought under an anti-colour complex, in which the forces of reaction won a partial victory, and I had to retire. Spiritually I live in retirement, though still publicly carrying on the fight. Perhaps I had demanded too much of my poor people, moved too fast and too far ahead of their ordinary outlook. So there has been a reversal, and the consequences will be what they will be. I am not sorry for myself but for the causes I stood for and the prospect which had opened before this country in the new African phrase. Things will change again, but whether in time for me once more to take the lead, who can say? The record remains—and perhaps so far as I am personally concerned that is enough. The march will continue—to success I hope, under other leadership perhaps.

I had looked forward to some quiet meditation and gathering

of results at the end, after fifty years of the struggle. But this may not be, as no one has yet appeared to take over the leadership of the party. With you I could have wished for quiet meditation at the close. I could, as an alternative, have wished to be in London and Paris and Washington at this moment, when such vast issues in which I am interested are at stake. But it does not appear that the time for decision there has yet arrived. What a confusion and milling round there is today in world affairs! Has there ever been the like—certainly never before at such a fateful moment. Evil in high places is coming to a head and making its supreme effort for world victory. Did you quote to me: 'Look your last on all things lovely'?[1] Is this a description of our day? I cannot believe it. I do believe that there is a Divinity which shapes our ends, rough hew them as we may.[2] Lovely things will remain, and become more lovely. But that may be only after further sweat and blood and tears.[3] Ours is the tragic march and there is the high note of tragedy right through it and perhaps deepening as we move on.

You can see that I have been dipping into Shakespeare in recent months. I find him full of light and wisdom and consolation. No truer insight into the nature of man and his destiny has been vouchsafed to us. Except perhaps by the Jew of Nazareth, who saw even deeper into the heart of things, and got his due reward for his insight. Love remains the last word. This universe is not built on hatred or evil, but on good and beautiful things, and on love which is the best and most beautiful and truest of all things. But moving in a cloud of prejudices and false views and desires it is very difficult for us to realize the truth of this vision. Shakespeare saw life more holistically, less at its highest peak of achievement, and more as a whole—from the clay to the rainbow in the sky.

I hope this letter will find you in Australia where I am sending it to the address you gave me. Let me sometimes hear from you. I wish I could be helpful to you. But you are going alone on a lone journey in which you must perforce rely on your inner resources more than on the experience of others. But be assured my company though unseen goes with you. Think kindly of me and my idiosyncrasies, which are as much a trial to me as they must be to you! But I am also a wanderer, seeking if haply I may find what perhaps it is for no man to find. Ever yours affectionately,

J.C.S.

[1] *See supra*, p. 151. [2] *See* vol. I, p. 388, note 2.

[3] 'I have nothing to offer but blood, toil, tears and sweat.' Winston Churchill in his first speech as prime minister in the house of commons, 13 May 1940.

820 To M. C. Gillett Vol. 88, no. 264

Doornkloof
[Transvaal]
23 October 1948

How dull the world looks, after a blow such as we have suffered. It is not only the blow itself, but what more it takes out of our lives. I feel as if much of my interest in things has gone. There has been an inward as well as an outward loss and subtraction from us. Yesterday I revisited Japie's residence at Welgedacht mine to see Kitty. I walked the ways which must have been familiar to him. I was more overcome than at the funeral, and had a deeper sense of what has really happened. O what a wrench, what a sense of the void and the hollowness which has come to us! It is a feeling to be resisted, otherwise it will leave us numb and powerless and unwilling to face the world before us. Death is a dulling sensation which must be fought. I know what has been said in praise of death by the poets and the philosophers and the religious mystics. But its stark reality, when it strikes in the inner circle, is more than one can bear. That revisit to Welgedacht has been an eye-opener to me, and I must shake off the shock of such an experience. I have too much else to do. The demands of life on the living are too great and too insistent to allow one a pause at the paralysing thought of death. I am glad Isie did not go with me. She is very quiet and calm—almost too much so. The danger in her case is that she may lose interest in life, and sit down to a blow which is as terrible as it was unexpected.

I have just sent off a message to the Alamein dinner tonight in London. There is this memory of victory won at a fateful moment, snatched so to say from the jaws of defeat. It is a symbol of life itself, of not succumbing and accepting the inevitable, but of fighting back and in the end winning through.

Thank you and Arthur very warmly for your beautiful letters of condolence. We understand, we know what you too must feel. We can understand the aged going, who have had their chance for good or evil. But this senseless thing is almost unpardonable, and looks like blasphemy on the universe. How much fairer and fitter if we had gone, instead of this comparatively young life, with all before it! It is the mystery which is life itself. It is not all a beautiful pattern. Through it all runs this strand of the accidental, the unaccountable, the outrageous, the unforgiveable. It is almost as if the power of chaos is at the heart of things and what is highest in us is *not* responded to, but outraged by a senseless accidentalism in what actually happens. The only excuse I can offer for the universe is that we do not understand, that the mystery is greater than our limited outlook can explain, and that humility rather than violent remonstrance becomes us. Words, words, words. How hollow it all sounds in the void of the human heart!

And so we just return to our ordinary routine, and carry on as best we may, and let time do the rest. It is the healer, perhaps the stupifier, but also the teacher. They say it is the best judge. But what a judge! And what judgments we have to accept!

I follow with grave concern what is happening abroad. What a sad, disillusioned world we have moved into! I am reminded of what Froude said in the seventies of last century when he visited South Africa on a mission from Lord Carnarvon.[1] The Orange Free State volksraad appealed to justice in the dispute with the Transvaal,[2] and Froude said, 'These simple farmers still pathetically believe in justice!' Or the like words. Ever in deepest affection,

J.C.S.

821 From L. S. Amery — Vol. 85, no. 16

112 Eaton Square
S.W.1
26 October 1948

My dear Ou Baas, The Commonwealth conference has been and gone, and has on the whole been useful. I enclose an article in the *Sunday Express* which gives as much about it as could conveniently be said in public.

I am afraid the stickiest representative there was our friend Louw [E. H.], much more concerned with the emphasis on separatism than with the realities of the world today. On the other hand the Indians, in spite of Nehru's being tied down by the republican preamble in their draft constitution,[3] seem anxious to find some

[1] James Anthony Froude (q.v.) had arrived in South Africa in September 1874 ostensibly on a private visit but in fact at the instance of Lord Carnarvon (q.v.) to report on the possibilities of federating the South African colonies and republics.

[2] The dispute concerned the ownership of the territory containing alluvial and dry diamond fields to which the Orange Free State, the South African Republic and two Griqua chiefs asserted varying claims. Following an award which cut off the whole diamond region from the republics, Griqualand West was annexed by the governor of the Cape Colony in 1871. The 'appeal to justice' by the Orange Free State was directed, not to the Transvaal, but to the British government. Froude reported that the Orange Free State had suffered an injustice.

[3] The draft constitution was approved by a constituent assembly in November 1948 and became law on 16 January 1950.

formula which will emphasize the fact that the Commonwealth is an organic living association, not only concerned with mutual support in defence and trade, but embodying a spiritual outlook and having a mission for the world. They may try to find expression for that in the shape of some sort of solemn declaration, the obverse as it were of the king's coronation oath,[1] and I still hope it may not be altogether impossible for them to bring into such a declaration their association with the crown as the symbol of Commonwealth unity. I gather that what sticks in their gizzards is the idea that if they have their own head of the state e.g. a president, that head should owe allegiance to the king, and some such version as association with the crown, not involving the suggestion of personal subordination, might possibly meet the case.[2]

I am rather sorry that the word British has dropped out of the Commonwealth but do not feel as strongly about it as some do. It seems to me to be rather like the dropping of English officially when we absorbed Scotland[3] and invented a new name fished up out of remote history in order to appease Scottish sensibilities. I only wish it were possible to find a good new name, politically neutral and yet inspiring, for the whole Commonwealth. Froude, going back to Sir John [*sic*] Harrington's Cromwellian fantasy, used the title 'Oceana',[4] and that would indeed correspond to the fact that it is essentially a Commonwealth bound together by the oceans.

So far as practical business went, both as regards defence questions and economic questions in relation to Europe, I believe the general attitude was realistic and practical and I am not without hopes that successive conferences may now be got down to real business. Yours ever,

Leo Amery

[1] Part of the coronation oath administered to George VI in 1937 reads: 'Do you solemnly promise and swear to govern the peoples of Great Britain, Ireland, Canada, Australia, New Zealand and the Union of South Africa and of your empire of India according to their respective laws and customs?'

[2] For the declaration agreed upon at the Commonwealth conference in London in April 1949 *see infra*, p. 290, note 1.

[3] The union of England and Scotland was effected by an act of parliament in 1707 which created the United Kingdom of Great Britain.

[4] Sir James Harrington (1611–77) published *The Commonwealth of Oceana* in 1656. J. A. Froude (q.v.), after a visit to Australia, published *Oceana or England and her Colonies* in 1886.

822 To Lord Brand Vol. 88, no. 180

27 October 1948

My dear Brand, My warm thanks for your *Western Union and British Commonwealth* article. As a matter of fact I had seen it in *The Times* before receiving the cutting from you, and had read it with much pleasure and complete approval. The case is put so convincingly by you that it is difficult to be patient with the views of European federation advocated in certain quarters. As it could never work, even in the British Commonwealth, how could it possibly work in the medley of West European states, with all their infinite variety? I remember a member of the war cabinet saying to me in 1917—after my speech to members of parliament, in which I used the term British Commonwealth of nations[1]—that I had torpedoed federation. But the poor thing, though sunk, has floated on, or been dragged along, until today it is suggested as a remedy for European, or even world troubles! The debate continues even in the *Round Table*, to my surprise. You are quite right in pointing out that the powers of government are so pervasive and penetrating in the modern state that a federal government must inevitably clash with any national governments in the federation. European union, to be feasible at all, would have to be of the loosest type possible—perhaps to begin with, more a treaty affair than an organic entity. It would, however, have to be more of a reality than Pan-American Union,[2] with stricter definition of functions and obligations for defence purposes. On that basis a process of periodic revision and improvement could in time achieve something more of substantial unity. But the beginnings will have to be quite modest.

My trouble about Western European union is one of leadership. France's stock has sunk too low to be trusted by the others. Britain has the trust but does not appear anxious to carry the burden of responsibility especially in view of her Commonwealth relations and obligations. America is far off and still not yet quite weaned of isolationism. There must be leadership, or the resultant union will be just a flop. Perhaps time alone can solve this problem.

The whole world outlook is pretty sombre. I hope that Britain

[1] Vol. III, pp. 506–17.

[2] Formed after the first international conference of American states in April 1890 in Washington with the object of fostering political and economic co-operation between the American states. Now the permanent organ and secretariat of the Organization of American States set up in April–May 1948 to co-ordinate the work of all the inter-American organizations and to settle disputes between members peacefully.

will recover from the dollar dole malaise and really assert herself. The fall of Germany has created a fatal vacuum in Europe, and the weakness of Britain has widened this vacuum far beyond Europe. What can be done about it? Ever yours affectionately,

s. J. C. Smuts

823 To G. C. Marshall — Vol. 88, no. 187

Private and personal — 5 November 1948

My dear General Marshall, I have a great desire to write to you personally and quite unofficially in regard to your recent visit to Athens. But before doing so, allow me to send you my warm congratulations on the magnificent victory of President Truman in the presidential and congressional elections. Though the elections will have gone largely on internal policies of the U.S.A., their effect on the world policy of the U.S.A. must necessarily be far-reaching. They give notice to the world that U.S.A. foreign policy is stable and continuous, and in particular that the Truman–Marshall policy of security and recovery in Europe will remain of full force and effect. At this fateful juncture of history nothing could be more helpful than this proof of America's firm and consistent lead in world affairs. It is the best hope for a world in sore need and trouble.

I was glad to read your contradiction of the rumour that you had intimated your intention to retire from office next January. I can understand your feeling after your Herculean labours of these war and post-war years, but I do not see how your services can at this moment be spared. 'To the spirit elect there is no choice!'[1] I remember President Roosevelt's insisting how vital it was to him to have you at Washington in spite of our strong wish that you should have the high command in the West. The position remains unaltered. I do not think President Truman can spare you—at least not yet, now that the last round for victory and peace in the West is being fought out. I am sure you will not mind my saying this to you.

As regards your visit to Athens, it was, if I may say so, at least a fine and wise gesture just at the right moment, when Greece so badly needs some token of personal encouragement from her friends. What that little country has gone through in this Second World War up to now is a great story, the significance of which is not fully realized. She stood up victoriously to Italy; she proved

[1] *See* vol. IV, p. 103, note 1.

staunch against all German overtures and threats, and fought on magnificently until finally overpowered. Very much divided, she yet remained staunch, and is today still continuing the fight against Russia and her satellites, just as bravely as she had fought against Italy and Germany. Compared to the rest of south-east Europe she remains the only exception and a shining light, in spite of exhaustion and political weakness.

And now she is in the front line of the resistance against the Communist onslaught in Europe. If she breaks, Turkey may go too, and the Middle East with its oil resources thereafter, with grave danger to the whole European situation. The strategic position of Greece in the present world situation is therefore all-important, and not only our sympathy, but our vital interest, is deeply involved in saving so gallant and necessary an ally.

My deep interest in Greece derives not only from these high considerations, but is also partly personal. When Greece fell, and Egypt declined to give asylum to the Greek royal family, I offered them asylum in South Africa, and most of the members of the royal family remained our guests for the rest of the war. Among them I found the crown princess, now the queen, a remarkable personality, full of character and ability, and of high human quality. We have remained in personal contact and exchange letters occasionally. She has written me of your visit and of its inspiring effect on the Greek people, just at this critical moment, and has expressed her gratitude for this valuable and opportune service. I have kept in touch with other Greek personalities, many of whom I know, and on my visits to Athens I have also discussed matters with British and American representatives. Among them I have found your General Van Fleet specially capable and helpful.

From all these contacts I have formed the following impression of the Greek situation as a whole. The political situation is bad and discouraging. But Greeks are accustomed to this sort of instability and muddle, and it is therefore not very important. Far more important is the military situation, faced as it now is by the determined Russian and satellite menace. The long continued military strain all these years on the people and the brave troops must be very great, and the danger is that it may reach breaking-point from sheer physical and moral exhaustion. There seems no end to guerilla warfare in such a mountainous country, and with the continual violation of its thousand miles of difficult frontier to the north. Beaten in the north, the guerilla attack has now shifted to the south in the Peloponnese, and it is all the time continuing in the Salonika–Thrace section in the east. It has become a struggle of physical endurance against Russian persistence, very much like the air-lift at Berlin. Indeed, to me it seems very much the same situation, with the same significance in Greece as in Berlin, and a break at either front may be fraught with almost equally fatal consequences for the democratic West. For Berlin the Allies have their plan and have publicly announced their determination to hold on at whatever cost. May I suggest for your consideration that the same be done for Greece. Let there be one Western plan for holding on resolutely against the Communist menace. The Turkish position is equally important, but for the moment quiescent, and not therefore calling for a publicly announced policy. Western Berlin is holding out in reliance on Allied staunchness. Similarly, Greece will hold on in similar confidence and reliance.

Besides this I would also suggest that the air arm be materially strengthened in Greece. It is a powerful weapon in guerilla warfare from many points of view.

I know also from my Greek contacts that there is a persistent appeal for additional troops, and for a high command divorced from undue political influence. Both these points I consider worthy of careful attention, especially from the point of view of Greek morale. Anything which might strengthen Greek resolution should be attended to, for the real danger is a break in the Greek will to resist, ending in a collapse which might open the flood-gates. Of course a first-class military success, leading to complete guerilla defeat, would be best of all.

I bracket Berlin and Athens together as—both of them—vital points in the present defence of the West. The larger long-range policy for the future of the West involves other considerations which I am not going into now.

I cannot conceal my very deep concern for the immediate future in Greece, so vital to the whole West, and which, I fear, is not taken as seriously as it should be. The victory of the Communist policy there will be disastrous, and I fear it is a real possibility, to be faced before a crisis arrives.

Please forgive this expression of my deep concern for Greece. It calls for no answer, but I thought I should put it to you, in view of your own evident interest in the whole matter. Yours very sincerely,

s. J. C. Smuts

824 To W. S. Churchill Vol. 88, no. 190

6 November 1948

My dear Winston, I was very glad to receive your cable approving of my suggestion about incorporating Western Germany into Western union and, in fact, putting it into a position to play its part in the defence of the West against eventual Communist aggression. You have since met Marshall, and I hope you have been able to impress on him the necessity of such a step in view of the increasing threat which Russian policy constitutes for the West.

Meanwhile Marshall has been to Athens, from where I have had reports of his talks with leading personages. As a result I have thought it advisable to send him a letter, putting to him the views I have formed of the Greek position as part of the overall European situation now in process of taking shape. Berlin and Greece are the two focal points on which Russian policy is concentrating for the move against the West, and a break at either of these two points may have very far-reaching consequences.

I do not know whether he has put his views to you in your contacts with him, and at Athens he preserved a more or less non-committal attitude. I thought, however, that what I had written to him should also be communicated to you, for what it is worth.

Russia has not yet finally made up her mind, in view of the atomic bomb and other possibilities, and it would be wise to leave her leader in no doubt of what the consequences will be of continued aggression at either of these two points of attack.

I have much enjoyed your recent grand speeches. Your Fulton policy[1] has been completely justified and has in fact become the policy of the West.

Good luck to you in your leadership of the West. My affectionate regards. Ever yours,

s. J. C. Smuts

[1] Churchill's speech at Westminster College, Fulton, Missouri, on 5 March 1946, with President Truman present, was the first open recognition by a major statesman of the post-war conflict between Russia and its satellite states and the Western powers and a call upon the United States to help the free European states to maintain themselves.

825 From D. F. Malan Vol. 86, no. 142

Kantoor van die Eerste Minister
Pretoria
11 November 1948

Geagte generaal Smuts, Aangehegte telegram van Eric Louw, wat my vanoggend bereik het, sal ongetwyfeld vir u van belang wees.

Louw se opmerkings verg geen kommentaar deur my nie, behalwe miskien dat ek my dit mag veroorloof om te sê dat dit ongelukkig is dat die voorlegging aan die Verenigde Volke van die Unie se standpunt insake 'n aangeleentheid waaromtrent ons onderskeie sienswyse so weinig verskil, bemoeilik word deur moontlik onbesonne uitlatings hier in Suid-Afrika. Met agting, Die uwe,

D. F. Malan

TRANSLATION

Prime Minister's Office
Pretoria
11 November 1948

Dear General Smuts, The attached telegram from Eric Louw which reached me this morning will doubtless be of interest to you.

Louw's remarks need no comment from me except perhaps that I may permit myself to say that it is unfortunate that the submission to the United Nations of the standpoint of the Union, in a matter on which our respective views differ so little, should be impeded by possibly thoughtless utterances here in South Africa. With respect, Yours sincerely,

D. F. Malan

ENCLOSURE

Telegram

From: South African delegation, Paris

To: secretary for external affairs, Pretoria

Dated 10 November 1948

Following for personal attention of the prime minister from minister Louw:

At very moment that I was engaged in fighting South Africa's battle on South West African issue yesterday, Smuts made speech at Durban which is headlined in this morning's Paris edition of the *Daily Mail*—'World has lost confidence in South Africa, says Smuts'. The despatch opens with the following paragraph: 'General Smuts declared today that the people of the world had lost confidence in South Africa.'

My statement yesterday made a good impression, and debate immediately adjourned to give delegates the opportunity for studying of it. There has been a large demand for a copy of the statement. From information received last night, I gained the impression that there is a good prospect of securing milder resolution.[1] In the circumstances, Smuts's speech most lamentable, and has sabotaging effect.

At this morning's session, Mrs Pandit made a vicious attack on South Africa and twice quoted Smuts's speech in support of her attacks. I regard Smuts's action as so serious that I would suggest you deal with it specially.

I will probably reply to Mrs Pandit tomorrow evening or Friday morning. No session during the day.

826 To D. F. Malan — Vol. 88, no. 194

12 November 1948

Hooggeagte Eerste Minister, U skrywe van gister, met insluiting van 'n telegram van Eric Louw, is my ter hand.

Dit spyt my dat u na my aanmerkings op die beleid van die regering refereer as 'moontlik onbesonne uitlatings', en my daarvan beskuldig dat ek die saak van die regering in verband met die S.W.A. Mandaat by die Verenigde Volke bemoeilik.

Nêrens het ek enige referte na daardie saak gemaak of bedoel nie, en my houding daaromtrent is welbekend; en, soos u tereg sê, verskil dit in elk geval weinig van die standput van die regering. My houding in verband met die pas getroffe Windhoek ooreenkoms het niks daarmee to doen nie, en kan dus in geen geval die saak voor die Verenigde Volke bemoeilik nie.

My kritiek gaan oor die beleid van die regering, by die algemene eleksie voorgelê en daarna uitgevoer, wat volgens my beskeie sienswyse Suid-Afrika die vertroue van die buiteland gekos het, en nog kos.

Kan oor daardie verlies van buitelandse vertroue enige twyfel

[1] In 1947 the general assembly of U.N.O. had passed a resolution affirming the recommendation that South West Africa should be placed under international trusteeship. After a debate in the trusteeship committee beginning on 8 November 1948 the general assembly, on 26 November, again adopted the 1947 recommendation.

bestaan? Die plotselinge en byna ongelooflik snelle verandering in die finansieele toestande alhier binne weinige maande is daar die sprekende bewys van, en die feite deur my aangestip skiet nog ver te kort by die werklikheid. Neem as voorbeeld die artikel in die *Rand Daily Mail* van eergister onder die opskrif: 'Overseas Plans for Factories in South Africa Abandoned—Millions of Pounds lost to the Union'. Daardie kritiek is algemeen, en dui aan hoeveel erger die werklikheid en die publieke besorgheid is as my opmerkings te Pietermaritzburg en elders. Ek kan seker nie van onbesonne uitlatings beskuldig word nie, maar eerder van te grote matigheid.

Die feit is dat die werklike waarheid vir sigself spreek, en luider as ek, en die verlies van die wêreld se vertroue is die bewys daarvan. Wat ek gesê het is bedoel, nie om die land skade aan te doen nie, maar alleen om my plig teenoor die land te vervul en die publieke opinie voor te lig omtrent die oorsake van wat gebeur het.

Oor die kwetsende uitdrukkings van Louw in sy telegram en ook in die publieke pers te Parys, ag ek my nie geroepe hier kommentaar te lewer nie.

Soos die ou gesegde lui: 'Things are what they are, and their consequences will be what they will be.' Met die meeste hoogagting bly ek Steeds die uwe,

get. J. C. Smuts

P.S. Ek het hierdie antwoord op u brief geskrywe voor ek so juis u uitbarsting in *Die Transvaler* gesien het. Ek maak hier geen kommentaar daarop.

TRANSLATION

12 November 1948

Dear Prime Minister, I have received your letter of yesterday[1] enclosing a telegram from Eric Louw.

I am sorry that you refer to my remarks on the policy of the government as 'possibly thoughtless utterances' and accuse me of impeding the government's case before the United Nations in connection with the South West Africa mandate.

Nowhere did I make or intend any reference to that matter and my attitude to it is well known; and, as you rightly say, it differs little in any case from the view of the government. My attitude in connection with the lately concluded Windhoek agreement[2] has

[1] 825.

[2] Concluded on 21 October between D. F. Malan and representatives of the inhabitants of South West Africa, the agreement made provision for the representation of South West Africa in the Union parliament and for provincial government in the territory. For details *see* the *Cape Times*, 22 October 1948.

nothing to do with it and therefore cannot in any way impede the matter before the United Nations.

My criticism concerned the policy of the government submitted at the general election and thereafter implemented, which, according to my humble opinion, has cost, and still costs, South Africa the confidence of the outside world.

Can there be any doubt about that loss of foreign confidence? The sudden and almost unbelievably rapid change in financial conditions here within only a few months is striking proof of it, and the facts which I pointed out fall far short of the real state of affairs. Take, for instance, the article in the *Rand Daily Mail* of the day before yesterday under the headlines: 'Overseas Plans for Factories in South Africa Abandoned—Millions of Pounds lost to the Union'. That criticism is general and indicates how much worse the reality and the public anxiety are than my remarks at Pietermaritzburg and elsewhere. I can surely not be accused of thoughtless utterances but rather of too much moderation.

The fact is that the real truth speaks for itself—and louder than I; and the loss of world confidence is the proof of it. What I said was intended, not to damage the country, but merely to do my duty to the country and to enlighten public opinion as to the causes of what has happened.

I do not consider myself called upon to make any comment here on the wounding expressions used by Louw in his telegram and also in the public press in Paris.

As the old saying goes: 'Things are what they are, and their consequences will be what they will be.'[1] With much respect I remain Yours ever,

s. J. C. Smuts

P.S. I wrote this answer to your letter before seeing just now your outburst in *Die Transvaler*.[2] I shall make no comment upon it here.

[1] 'Things and actions are what they are, and the consequences of them will be what they will be: why then should we desire to be deceived?' Joseph Butler (1692–1752), *Fifteen Sermons*, no. 7, para. 16.

[2] In the issue of 12 November Malan was reported as commenting on Smuts's speech at Pietermaritzburg *inter alia* as follows: *Daar is duidelik merkbaar 'n doelbewuste poging om die Suid-Afrikaanse regering, en daarmee ook Suid-Afrika self, in verskillende lande van die wêreld te beswadder, met geen ander doel nie as om vir die wankelende Opposisie-party hulp van buite in te roep...en uit pure haat vir die party wat hom sy nederlaag besorg het.* There is clearly to be seen a deliberate attempt to besmirch the South African government, and with it South Africa, in various countries of the world, with no other purpose than to call in outside help for the tottering opposition party—and out of sheer hatred of the party which brought about its defeat. *Die Transvaler* was established in Johannesburg in October 1937.

827 To M. C. Gillett Vol. 88, no. 268

Doornkloof
[Transvaal]
20 November 1948

I have just returned from my Durban visit where a number of party functions had to be attended to. All passed off with striking success. The journey was, as usual, by air which saves much time. A week ago I was on similar errands to Pietermaritzburg by train, which took me two full nights and parts of the day. I wonder how we ever managed to do our work in the old days. Today you do three or four times as much by air in the same time. I found the party spirit good and heard very little about 'Indians' which generally formed my main political trouble in Natal. Meanwhile we have just had a bye-election at Stellenbosch, where we had hoped at least to reduce the big Nat majority of the general election. However the Nats held their own, and even very slightly improved their position.[1] It is therefore an indication, for what it is worth, that the Nat position is not yet seriously weakened by our assaults or the deterioration in the country's economic and financial position. I have therefore nothing good to report from the political front, in spite of my heavy labours, alas! At home all goes well; abundant rains, and no set-back to report...

Next week I shall be for a couple of days at Bloemfontein at the central congress of our party. Politics, politics, politics! And there is a world heavy in grave trouble, while we continue our bawling on the political platform! And yet, that too has to be done, however futile or unpleasant it may be.

Last night, when I went to bed, I took Spinoza as an opiate. And he begins his *Ethics* with a definition of God or the Ultimate Reality and then, on that assumption or axiom, proceeds to find the pattern of this universe and man and all his riddles. *We* begin at the other end—in the little details and events which make up our world and the world beyond. Which is the correct starting point? How calm and sublime it is to begin with God as the foundation, instead of trying to rise up to Him as the supreme goal. And yet, we have to toil through all this tiring and tiresome experience in our endless quest. You can see how much more pacifying and comforting it is to begin with the Divine. But actually we have to walk over this quaking bog in our quest of today. Wherever we look we see the pain and the vanity or futility

[1] The result of the election was: J. A. Loubser (National party) 6,254; L. Hofmeyr (United party) 4,104—a majority of 2,150. The National party majority in the general election was 2,014.

of it all. But Spinoza satisfies me, especially when I want to go to rest, after the day's toil and trouble. 'In Him is our peace.'[1] Loving wishes and thoughts. Ever yours,

J.C.S.

828 To W. S. Churchill Vol. 88, no. 202

Telegram

To: Winston Churchill, 28 Hyde Park Gate, England

From: J. C. Smuts

Dated 25 November 1948

On balance consider continuance your wartime policy of not repeat not specially punishing Eire for her folly the wiser course.[2]

829 Speech (1948) Box M, no. 260

This speech was broadcast by Smuts on 4 December 1948.

We are passing through days of heavy losses, such as no tongue, no pen can describe. But yesterday I paid my tribute to the memory of Hennie van der Byl, who had passed away the day before. Today, when we are burying him, comes the devastating blow of the passing of Jannie Hofmeyr, that wonder child of South Africa. Within two days of each other these two most highly gifted sons of South Africa have left us. Truly our house as a nation is left desolate unto us.[3] At the height of their powers, at a moment when we could so ill afford to spare them, this noble pair of brothers, *par nobile fratrum*,[4] have been taken away from us. Happy the young country which could, within a few years of each other, produce two such brilliant sons.[5] Unhappy the country which could, within a couple of days of each other,

[1] 'And His will is our peace.' Dante, *Il Paradiso*, III, l. 85.

[2] The government of Eire had introduced a bill to repeal the act which recognized the king in certain external relations and to establish the Republic of Ireland. On 25 November Attlee said in the house of commons that the government of Great Britain would not, were the bill enacted, regard citizens of Eire in Great Britain as foreigners. Churchill said that Southern Ireland should not enjoy Commonwealth advantages without reciprocal obligations and dissociated the opposition from the attitude of the government. During the Second World War no action had been taken against Eire when she declared her neutrality and denied Great Britain the use of her ports.

[3] 'Behold, your house is left unto you desolate.' *St Matthew* xxiii.38.

[4] Horace, *Satires*, II.iii.243.

[5] Van der Bijl was born in 1887, Hofmeyr in 1894. The former died on 2 December 1948, the latter on the evening of the 3rd.

lose both of them. In this moment of grievous loss, of bitter sorrow, we can but brace our hearts and pull ourselves together and move forward to carry on the tasks which, even with them by our side, it would have been difficult for us to fulfil; tasks which without them it will be almost impossible for us to carry on. Our sense of grievous loss is indeed overwhelming.

But first and foremost our thoughts, our deep and affectionate sympathy, go out to the two women whose loss and grief are even greater than our own: to the young widow[1] left with her small children in the one case, to the aged mother[2] in the other, who has lost the apple of her eye, her treasure, who was also a treasure of South Africa. If ever there was a proud mother, a justifiably proud mother, it was Mrs Hofmeyr. Hers was the wonder child of South Africa, with a record to which South Africa shows no parallel, who from his youngest years beat all records, whose achievement in a comparatively brief life shows no parallel in this land, and whose star at the end was still rising. It has been her bitter fate to survive him. Surely in a land of tragedy such as ours, a personal tragedy like this has no parallel. We can but for a moment forget our own sorrow, and stand with bare heads before her noble and tragic figure. She typifies in her person the tragedy of a nation. In such a situation, am I one to complain of what I, too, personally have lost? I who buried my great friend Louis Botha at a moment of South Africa's greatest need, and had with my poor strength to continue his work, I who now lose my right hand and the man who, I had fondly hoped, would have continued my work if he had been spared. We can but console ourselves with the thought that South Africa has survived these national losses, and has through tragedy moved to new and unforeseen achievement. In that knowledge, and strengthened by that faith, we can but nerve ourselves and pass on to the work which lies before us.

But still the wound remains, and the sense of what South Africa has lost in Jan Hofmeyr remains almost more than one can bear. His youthful achievements were the marvel of this land, and still continue an unbeaten record. His brilliant career as a scholar, his professorship in classics at the old School of Mines, Johannesburg, when he had barely passed his student years, his principalship of the new University of the Witwatersrand shortly after, his distinguished administratorship of the Transvaal a few years later, his subsequent distinction in parliament and in the Union cabinet, his brilliant role in our war cabinet, which guided South Africa during the Second World War: who has forgotten that unique record?

[1] Born Ethel Buxton; married H. J. van der Byl in 1942. [2] *See* vol. IV, p. 337.

Once more my thought reverts to what I personally owe to him throughout those years of the great struggle, from which South Africa emerged with such glory, and such added strength and self-confidence. During those years he not only carried the heavy burden of looking after our finances and after several other cabinet portfolios, but during my frequent absences from the country as commander-in-chief and prime minister, he added my heavy burdens in the cabinet to his own, and carried them all with an ability and distinction, and even with a gay and buoyant spirit, which made the world wonder, and made us forget how much he was spending himself. In the end South Africa emerged from the war financially much more solid and secure than she had entered it. What a debt we owe to him in these days for that outstanding war service to South Africa! But looking back now to those years of almost superhuman labours, I cannot avoid the feeling that he carried burdens which even for him were too heavy, and for which the price has now been paid in the tragedy of his loss to the country, which he served with such selfless devotion and such brilliance, and which will now sadly miss him in what may well be another hour of need for her. He too is a war casualty, and perhaps the most grievous of our personal losses. The price was perhaps inevitable and had to be paid, but he devoted himself to his many tasks without thought of self, and [with] a success which will remain part and parcel of the proud record of South Africa. But his loss is and will remain irreparable, and my sense of that loss, both personal and national, is one which I find it impossible to express and almost impossible to bear. One can but console oneself with the thought that tragedy often goes with high service, and that this is particularly true of South Africa, and that in his person and his career and its premature ending he illustrates this truth for the land he served so well.

But the sense of what we have lost in his passing remains and will never leave me. How can I forget that brilliant intellect, those incomparable gifts of the mind, that golden heart, that high integrity of character which regarded anything small or mean or unjust as a stain, that noble spirit which never thought of self, but always in terms of high principle, always of others and especially of those less able to look after themselves. He looked upon life as a sacred trust, and one to be discharged in the true Christian spirit. The formula of Christian trusteeship, which he found to express his conception of Native policy, was descriptive also of his whole outlook on life and on man's role in this world. He has passed on, but his service, and the high spirit in which he sought to serve his country and his fellow men of all races remains our abiding possession. This is a better and richer country for his service, and his message will not be forgotten. We humbly thank God for the gift of Jan Hofmeyr the second, just as we thank Him for the gift of his uncle, the famous Onze Jan.[1] Good-bye, my noble friend and comrade. Au revoir. *Tot siens.*

830 To M. C. Gillett Vol. 88, no. 270

Doornkloof
[Transvaal]
6 December 1948

Last week was one of shocks to us and to South Africa. Both Dr [H. J.] van der Bijl and Hofmeyr [J. H.] passed away within two days of each other. Van der Bijl was our greatest industrialist, and Hofmeyr our most distinguished parliamentarian. You can imagine the surprise and shock and loss. Van der Bijl had suffered for months from internal cancer, and those in the know expected the end, but the public was in complete ignorance. Hofmeyr had two fainting fits at a cricket match eight days before and had to go to bed; but the doctor saw no danger and spoke of fatigue from overwork. In bed his condition did not improve and eventually a specialist found thrombosis with other complications which made the case a serious one.[2] Last Saturday he passed away very suddenly. We buried him yesterday, on the 86th anniversary of his mother. I gave broadcasts for both[3] and spoke at Hofmeyr's burial yesterday. He was our ablest and most high-minded public man, and was in a sense the conscience of South Africa. To me he was my right hand, and his going will add immensely to my labours—already as much as I can bear. He was only fifty-four and was my destined successor. The pity of it that I should have had to bury him.

Simultaneous with these sad events, a fissure of a grave character has arisen between Havenga and the Nats. He has declared his inability to vote for the repeal of the entrenchment clauses in the constitution which protect Coloured and Native rights. A crisis has arisen which, if Havenga is really sincere, may recast the whole political situation.[4] Things are in a flux and at present it is impossible

[1] *See* vol. IV, pp. 337–8.

[2] The account of Hofmeyr's last illness by his biographer differs in some respects from what Smuts relates. *See* A. Paton, *Hofmeyr*, pp. 522–5.

[3] For the broadcast tribute to Hofmeyr *see* **829**.

[4] At the opening of the Afrikaner party congress at Brakpan, Transvaal, on 2 December Havenga said that he supported the apartheid policy but considered

to foresee what will come out of it. Something may be known when you get this letter or shortly after. It is naturally a delicate and, for me, an extremely anxious situation. I am awaiting developments and hope they will be for the good of South Africa...

I am reading your Brontë book[1] with much interest; also another book *In the Steps of the Brontës*,[2] of a more biographical character which is also full of interesting information about that remarkable family in their Yorkshire setting. Some changes in the house have also been made, and part of my eastern block has been converted into a botany room and library to save space for my growing bookshelves. A great improvement. I still dabble off and on in my plants, here and in the veld. And politics all the time—last week at Pietersburg, this week to Zeerust, Swartruggens, and Ermelo.[3] It is not only the meetings but the immense motoring distances. I wonder how I stand it all! But I feel I must repeat my efforts of the 'twenties if I have to save the country from the plans of the Nats. But these things are harder a generation after. However, all may be well, and meantime we shall try to make it so! Ever yours,

J.C.S.

831 To D. Moore — Vol. 88, no. 221

Doornkloof
Transvaal
14 December 1948

My dear Daphne, Your letter of 25 November arrived yesterday and was most welcome. I had waited so long to hear from you and could well understand that delay was unavoidable under the circumstances. Now I rejoice to know you are on the whole happy and also recovering from your ailment. You write of the idyllic surroundings in which you can rest and relax and paint. It is

that the entrenched clauses must be respected because in so fundamental a matter the will of the people (*volkswil*) must be ascertained. Commenting on this, D. F. Malan declared that legal advice had confirmed the competence of parliament to alter the entrenched clauses by means of an ordinary majority but that Havenga's requirements with regard to the will of the people would clearly be met by the result of the provincial election at which the government's colour policy would again be laid before the electorate. (*See Die Burger*, 2 and 4 December 1948.) *See also* vol. v, p. 371, note 3.

[1] L. L. Hinkley, *The Brontës—Charlotte and Emily* (1947).

[2] By E. Raymond, published in 1948.

[3] On campaign for the provincial council elections in which the government sought further support for their apartheid policy.

a pleasing picture, and one is glad to know that there are such places in Australia, from which the news of continual labour and political troubles conveys a very different picture. You deserve a good long holiday and complete change after your labour and long sojourn in an atmosphere of war and tropics. I was also glad to hear that Henry [Moore] is cheerful in the new political set-up.

1948 has been a year of losses and anxieties and frustrations, not only in our domestic circles, but for the whole world. I repeated my failure after the First World War, which sent me into the wilderness for nine years. I hope it will not be so long this time—in fact I do not have such a long time to waste now in the desert! Luckily for me the new government are far from happy. There are internal fissures and there is depression in the offing, while their majority is a small one in parliament.[1] We shall have a provincial election in the Union in March, and even a general election may come in 1949, which may unseat them again. So in my misfortunes I have once more put on my armour and am hard at the political fight. I have never been more busy politically. Perhaps this is as well, not only for the country, which is being sadly misgoverned, but for myself who am thus kept from indulging private sorrows and grievances. The pity is that I have no time left for other things in which I am also deeply interested. I read comparatively little, and much of my time is taken up with following world affairs and local political developments. Parliament will resume in January and will keep me busy till June, when I hope to be free to go to Cambridge to attend for a couple of weeks to my chancellor's duties. I may then have some weeks in London to keep contact with political and world affairs. Apart from the press and occasional private letters I feel very much cut off from happenings abroad and from those personal contacts which are so necessary for an understanding of what is *really* going on.

And what a world it is! With China collapsing the Communist wave seems to be submerging all Asia. In Europe the battle is now being fought out in Berlin, and the future is not bright there. The sickle seems to be getting ready for the ripening harvest.[2] Britain has a feeble government, and many other countries practically none at all. But for the strength of America we might today see a landslide in world affairs. And the twentieth century might inaugurate another Dark Age. This will now not be. But the position remains precarious and unhappy. France is constantly on the edge of collapse. Italy is at work, but government remains

[1] *See infra*, p. 282, note 3.

[2] 'Put ye in the sickle, for the harvest is ripe.' *Joel* iii.13.

weak. Where is the rest of Europe, now kept going by the American dole? Greece has *not* got on top of the guerilla warfare, and Communism there is holding its own. I feel doubly sorry for this excellent little people whose politicians are such poor stuff. The king and queen have done very well and are universally popular but must mind their step to avoid the taint of dictatorship. It is all a very distressing situation. Freddie writes to me occasionally about her work and aims and I give her my blessing; more I have not to give under my present eclipse. I may look them up next June if my programme will allow. The only people winning through today are the Jews who richly deserve success, which indeed they have snatched from the very jaws of disaster. I have supported them at every stage, even when they were a little mad!

Now, dear child, I must not continue this ramble. But I write to you as I talked to you in happier days. What else can one do if one is really interested in this world of ours, with dark clouds shrouding its future?

And so good-bye. Pray for the world in the new year. It may mark a turning-point. And re-establish yourself and return with new zest to the fray, in which you will always play your part. Ever affectionately yours,

J.C.S.

832 From G. C. Marshall — Vol. 86, no. 151

Washington
17 December 1948

Dear Marshal Smuts, Thank you for your letter of 5 November[1] which arrived in Washington while I was undergoing tests just prior to a kidney operation. I am now in the midst of what the doctors call 'recovery and recuperation' but which I find a rather painful and uncomfortable procedure...

I saw Churchill in London in late October and he was good enough to let me read your letter of 27 September[2] to him. So far as concerns the firm induction of Germany into Western Europe, I think that much has been done along this line since your letter was written. Corrective action moves slowly in a democracy and it is often this very slowness which ensures a correct and supported approach to our decisions. I am convinced that we are headed in the right direction and I also believe that time is on our side if we continue to progress and don't stand still.

[1] **823.** [2] **816.**

As to Greece, I hold an equally high opinion of the queen and her husband and I assure you of our firm intention to do our proper best for that country. We have already planned for an increase of 15,000 in the Greek army to provide replacements for the war-weary soldiers, many of whom have not been home for years and are deeply concerned about their families. My views as to Greece coincide with yours, particularly as to its being part and parcel of the entire Soviet problem.

I am sorry that I cannot at this time go into more detail on these problems. The doctors have just come in to feel my pulse, take my blood pressure, remove some stitches, and otherwise involve themselves in matters which up to now I had held rather personally to myself. With warm personal regards and great respect, Faithfully yours,

G. C. Marshall

833 To S. M. Smuts Vol. 91, no. 93

Mount Nelson Hotel
Kaapstad
26 Januarie 1949

Liefste Mamma, Ek het gister my aanval op die Regeering in my mosie van wantrou gemaak. Alles goed afgeloop en die party baie tevrede. Ek het hul die heel geskiedenis vertel van af die Nasionale Konvensie, met spesiale nadruk op al die verklarings op 22 April 1931 toe almal beloof het ewige trou aan die verskanste artikels van die Konstitusie, met wat daarop gevolg het in die deursetting van die Hertzog Wette in 1936 in ooreenkoms daarmee. Baie van dit alles is al vergeet en moes weer gesê word. Dan op die gevare gewys, waarvan Durban maar die begin is. Vandag praat Malan en sal ons sy lamlendige antwoord hoor.

Bibas het my gevra die aand van 19 Febr. wanneer ek te Hermanus praat by haar te bly—ek en Cooper sal dit doen. Ek sluit in briefie aan jou van Vernon Thomson. Die weer bly aan wissel. Ons had baie warm, toe weer betreklik koue met reën. Vandag weer baie warm en ek is in my ligte klere. Gesondheid goed. So is daar niks verkeerd te rapporteer nie. Ek sien baie gaste van die buite wereld hier op die hotel, en vandag kom weer die vrou van die diamant. Ek is bly dat ek haar nie behoef te sê dat dit verlore is nie. Dis duidelik dat sy 'n groot geheime vriendin is wat nie agter publisiteit is soos so baie ander.

Joy het weer pakkie botter gestuur. Maar ek is baie goed van alles voorsien. Vrugte volop, hoewel ek spaarsaam met ete daarvan moet wees. Saterdag aand is ek op Muizenberg vir 'n funksie en toespraak. En so sal dit maar eindeloos voortgaan. Ek hoop spoedig die ou Bossies te gaan besoek en nuus oor te breng. Ek hoop dit gaan jul almal baie goed. Liefde van

Pappa

TRANSLATION

Mount Nelson Hotel
Cape Town
26 January 1949

Dearest Mamma, Yesterday I made my attack on the government in my motion of no confidence.[1] All went off well and the party is most satisfied. I told them the whole story since the National Convention, with special emphasis on all the declarations of 22 April 1931[2] when everyone promised eternal loyalty to the entrenched clauses of the constitution, and all that followed in putting through the Hertzog bills in 1936 in accordance with it. Much of all this has already been forgotten and had to be said again. I then pointed out the dangers, of which Durban[3] is only the beginning.

[1] The motion was as follows: 'I move that this house, deeply conscious of the sacred and binding character of the obligations towards the Native and Coloured peoples, on which the constitution of the Union was founded by the National Convention and agreed to by the parliaments of the constituent colonies, and confirmed by the practice of parliament and by solemn assurances of this house—

disapproves of the policy of the government to abrogate and alter the existing parliamentary rights of these peoples, without a direct and unmistakable mandate from the people of the Union, and by a two-thirds parliamentary majority, as provided by the entrenched clauses of the constitution;

disapproves of the verdict of the people in the forthcoming provincial election being taken as an approval of this policy, as such a misuse of the provincial system would itself be a violation of the spirit and purpose of the constitution;

disapproves of any government which, like the present government, is not truly representative of the broad national will, adopting a policy of tampering with fundamental political rights and obligations, in conflict with the spirit and intention of the constitution, and damaging to our vital interests,

and expresses its want of confidence in the government.' *House of Assembly Debates*, vol. 66, cols. 60 *et seq*.

[2] On this day, during the debate in the Union house of assembly on the proposals of the imperial conference, the following resolution was agreed to: 'That on the understanding that the proposed legislation will in no way derogate from the entrenched provisions of the South Africa Act, this house, having taken cognisance of the draft clauses and recitals which it was proposed by the imperial conference of 1930 should be embodied in legislation to be introduced in the parliament at Westminster, approves thereof and authorizes the government to take such steps as may be necessary with a view to the enactment by the parliament of the United Kingdom of legislation on the lines set out in the schedule annexed.' *House of Assembly Debates*, vol. 17, cols. 2736–64.

[3] In January 1949 extensive riots occurred in Durban when the antagonism between Indians and Zulus flared up after a minor assault. A judicial committee of

Today Malan [D.F.] will speak and we shall hear his feeble reply.

Bibas [Smuts] has asked me to stay with her on the night of 19 February when I speak at Hermanus; Cooper and I will do this. I enclose a letter for you from Vernon Thompson. The weather keeps changing. It was very hot then again relatively cold with rain. Today once more very hot—I am wearing my light clothes. Health good. So there is nothing to report. I see many visitors from abroad here in the hotel and today the diamond woman[1] is coming again. I am glad I need not tell her that it has been lost. It is clear that she is a great secret friend who is not after publicity like so many others.

Joy [van der Byl] has again sent a parcel of butter. But I am very well provided with everything. Lots of fruit—although I must not eat too much of it. On Saturday evening I shall be at Muizenberg for a function and speech. And so it will go endlessly on. I hope to go and see the old Bossies[2] soon and take them the news. I hope you are all very well. Love from

Pappa

834 To S. M. Smuts — Vol. 91, no. 104

Die Volksraad
Kaapstad
29 Januarie 1949

Liefste Mamma,...Die wantroue debat gaan goed, en sal Maandag beslis word. Havenga en sy vrinde gaan vir Malan sy amendement stem. Dit is natuurlik so opgetrek om Havenga 'n opening te gee om by die regeering te bly. Ons gaan weer 'n amendement op Malan se amendement voorstel wat die saak weer baie lastig vir Havenga sal maak. Hy speel 'n dubbelsinnige rol en die Engelse denk hy is die man om te volg, daar hy nie so straf as Jan Tax met hul gehandel het nie. Maar vroeër of later sal hy sy rieme styf loop en sal sy moeilikheid kom net soos in die dae van die goud standaard. Intussen gaan ons voort ons plig teenoor die land te doen. Daar is maar weer die ou twyfel en wankelmoedigheid van die ou Sap dae. Maar ek trap vas, wetende wat die arme land te wagte is.

inquiry found that the outbreak was exceptional and unexpected and that the public authorities were in no way to blame. Some 2,000 buildings were destroyed or damaged, 147 persons killed and 1,087 injured. (*See* U.G. 36 of 1949.)

[1] She had given Smuts a diamond ring.

[2] J. J. H. Bosman and his wife, born Gertruida de Villiers—the parents of Kitty Smuts.

Dit lyk na 'n pragtige naweek en ek hoop 'n bietjie vars lug te geniet. Liefde en beste wense aan jul almal van

Pappa

TRANSLATION

House of Assembly
Cape Town
29 January 1949

Dearest Mamma,...The no-confidence debate is going well and will be decided on Monday. Havenga and his friends are going to vote for Malan's amendment. Of course it has been framed in such a way as to give Havenga an opening to stay in the government.[1] We shall again move an amendment to Malan's amendment,[2] which will once more make the matter very awkward for Havenga. He is playing an ambiguous role and the English think he is the man to follow because he has not pressed them as hard as Jan Tax.[3] But sooner or later he will find himself up against it and will have trouble—as in the days of the gold standard. Meanwhile we shall go on doing our duty to the country. Once more there is the old doubt and irresolution of the early Sap days. But I shall stand fast knowing what is in store for the poor country.

It looks like a beautiful week-end and I hope to enjoy a bit of fresh air. Love and best wishes to you all from

Pappa

835 From L. S. Amery Vol. 89, no. 8

31 January 1949

My dear Ou Baas, I do not know whether your papers gave any full account of the Palestine debate or whether you had time to read the report in *The Times*. What happened is that the unhappy shooting down of our airmen and the wild rush of military pre-

[1] Malan's amendment, moved on 26 January, included a recommendation that the government consider the appointment of a commission of both houses to examine the application of the principle of apartheid 'as approved by the electorate' and that the commission be instructed to 'take special notice of the officially declared Native policy, if any, of the various parliamentary parties, as well as of the findings of the Fagan Native Laws commission' (*House of Assembly Debates*, vol. 66, cols. 113–14).

[2] The counter-amendment was moved on 31 January by J. G. N. Strauss. It accepted a commission of both houses but included an instruction to the commission 'that any recommendation or proposal to abrogate or alter the existing parliamentary rights of the Natives shall be subject to a two-thirds majority as provided by the entrenched clauses of the constitution' (*House of Assembly Debates*, vol. 66, cols. 289–90).

[3] A nickname for J. H. Hofmeyr as minister of finance.

parations led to a violent reaction here against Bevin's folly,[1] with the result that the cabinet insisted on a change and the recognition of Israel. But it seems to have taken a whole week to get Bevin into a mood of rather sulky acquiescence, and even in Wednesday's debate he left the situation so vague that it greatly upset his own party. With an election on the horizon, they were only too willing to let bygones be bygones if Bevin had cheerfully declared that he was going to recognize Israel and possibly even added a sympathetic word directed to that quarter. It was the sulkiness of the speech and the obvious anti-Zionist partiality, of which he himself is largely unconscious, which upset them and led to something like a hundred abstaining from voting, something like half of them doing so ostentatiously in the house itself. I hear also that a good many of those who voted with the government have written privately to Attlee to voice their discontent.

Winston, on the other hand, was at the very top of his form and only the full speech in Hansard gives any idea, not only of its trenchant criticism, but of its broad sweep and of its personal generosity towards Weizmann. He had a difficult task, for there was a moment, two years ago, when he did himself suggest scuttle, but he skated round that corner gracefully. Also he had to keep in mind the necessity of getting the pro-Arab element in the party to vote with him, and so had to lay much of his emphasis on the purely critical side. In this he was well supported by an adroit negative speech by Oliver Stanley. As for Attlee, his defence really amounted only to this, that Churchill should have carried out partition himself in the short interval between V.E. Day and the election. I think he might have done so, or even done so just before the German collapse but, after all, at that moment there was a good deal to do in Europe, not to speak of the imminent prospect of the election.

However, recognition has now been agreed[2] but I am afraid that Bevin will still continue in his rather sulky attitude and be inclined to pick quarrels with Israel if he can. The negotiations at Rhodes[3] seem to be sticky, and this may easily lead to further difficulties.

Meanwhile, the European thing seems to be moving and Bevin's

[1] During the Arab–Israeli War the Israeli forces, in an offensive against Egypt, shot down five royal air force reconnaissance aircraft on 7 January. They claimed that the aircraft had been shot down while over the Negev and refused to accept a British memorandum saying that they had been shot down on the Egyptian side of the frontier because the British government had not recognized the Israeli government. On 11 January the foreign office declared 'the present crisis is the outcome of Jewish aggression'.

[2] Great Britain gave *de jure* recognition in April 1950.

[3] Armistice negotiations between Israel and Egypt began in Rhodes on 13 January under the chairmanship of Dr Ralph J. Bunche.

original stickiness in respect of the British delegation at the European assembly[1] has been overcome to the extent that I do not think our government will press for the British delegates being, not only government nominated, but ordered to vote in a block according to instructions. Yours ever,

L. S. Amery

836 To S. M. Smuts Vol. 91, no. 116

Mount Nelson Hotel
8 Februarie 1949

Liefste Mamma, Ek meen ek het jou al geskrywe van my klim op Leeukop laaste Saterdag en my verlies van my spoorweg badge by 'n val wat ek met die afkom gehad het. Wel, gister is die seuns wat dit kort daarna gekry het op my kantoor gewees en daar oorhandig my klein beursie met beetjie silwer en die goud badge daarin, tesame met my klein knipmes en iodine kannetjie. Was dit nie fluks? Daar was twee van hul, 9 en 10 jaar oud, en hul twee is alleen die kop uitgeklim en so my verlore goed gevind en terug besorg. Ek het albei 'n geteekende portret van dank gegee. Wat meer kon ek doen. Twee seuns op laer skool. Hul sal seker die portrette rond wys onder hul maters.

Die S.W.A. Wet is gister ingedien en ek het dit vannag bestudeer. 'n Vreeslike mengelmoes net bedoel om die Regeering deur S.W.A. ook in te grawe. Vier lede in die Senaat, waarvan twee deur die Regeering aangestel! Die wet maak ons saak met S.W.A. baie moeilik, en ons hou caucus vandag daaroor. Die Regeering is besig hul in te grawe, maar ons moet vermy aanstoot aan S.W.A. te gee. Gister het Havenga ook 'n lang finansieele verklaring gemaak wat net daarop neer kom dat hul nie geld hier of buitelands kan kry nie. En tog is hul die spandawelste Regeering wat ons ooit gehad het. Waarheen gaat dit alles? Ek vrees vir die ergste maar as dit moet kom, hoe gouer hoe beter vir die land. Maar dit is genoeg om die grootste optimis mismoedig vir ons land te maak.

Die dae is nou heerlik. Die ergste wind en hitte albei verby. Jammer maar dat ek elke naweek vas is met funksies totdat ek na die noorde kom.

[1] Negotiations for establishing the Council of Europe (set up on 5 May 1949) were going on. The original members were Belgium, Denmark, France, Ireland, Italy, Luxemburg, the Netherlands, Norway, Sweden and the United Kingdom. Its organs were (a) a committee of foreign ministers and (b) a consultative assembly. Later members were Austria, Cyprus, the German Federal Republic, Greece, Iceland, Switzerland and Turkey.

Nou alles ten beste vir jul almal. Wees nie oor my bekommer nie. Alles sal reg kom: maar wanneer?

Pappa

TRANSLATION

Mount Nelson Hotel
[Cape Town]
8 February 1949

Dearest Mamma, I think I wrote to you about my climb up Lion's Head last Saturday and the loss of my railway badge[1] in a fall I had coming down. Well, the boys who found it shortly afterwards were at my office yesterday and handed over my small purse with a little silver and the gold badge in it together with my pocket-knife and phial of iodine. Wasn't that smart? There were two of them, nine and ten years old. They climbed the peak alone and found my stuff and returned it. I gave both a signed photograph with my thanks. What else could I do? Two boys at primary school. They will probably pass the photographs round among their pals.

The South West Africa Bill[2] was introduced yesterday and I studied it last night—a terrible hotch-potch simply intended to dig the government in[3] by means of South West Africa as well. Four members in the senate, of whom two are to be appointed by the government! The bill makes our case in South West Africa very difficult and we shall have a caucus meeting about it today. The government is busy digging itself in, but we must avoid giving offence to South West Africa. Yesterday Havenga also made a long financial declaration which simply amounted to this: that they cannot raise money here or abroad. Nevertheless they are the most extravagant government we have ever had. Where will all this end? I fear the worst but if it must come, the sooner the better for the country; but it is enough to make the greatest optimist pessimistic for our country.

The days now are delightful. The worst wind and heat are over. The only pity is that I am tied with functions every week-end until I come north.

Now, everything that is best to you all. Don't be worried about me. All will come right: but when?

Pappa

[1] Carried by members of parliament as a free pass on the South African railways.

[2] Act No. 23 of 1949. It gave South West Africa six representatives in the Union house of assembly and four senators.

[3] The National party, supported by nine Afrikaner party members had a majority of five over the other parties and groups in the house of assembly. In the senate the United party members were in the majority.

837 To M. C. Gillett Vol. 92, no. 7

Mount Nelson Hotel
[Cape Town]
12 February 1949

I have just read yours of 3 February and was glad to get it and the news to which I had looked forward. The doctor's report on Arthur makes the position no worse than I had feared. He will in future have to work less and walk less, and that sounds not too bad. Then he should avoid wintering in England, which also seems sensible. So you must arrange your plans in future accordingly. Tell him that as a layman I had independently come to the same conclusion. About yourself you say nothing, so that I assume no change—at least for the worse! I always look forward to improvement with the new treatment. Of course sunshine is what you both want and we must plan for that.

I am interested in your letter quotation from Tona [Gillett].[1] I hope it is not as bad as that, but I do feel deeply concerned about South Africa. My repudiation last May came as a great shock—not so much for me personally as for this country and its future. You know how I love it and have never lost faith in it. One should not rush to conclusions but neither should one shut one's eyes. We must await developments and that is why I have stayed on at this task. My work is a labour of love for South Africa, and partly of faith too, but that faith is now clouded with a doubt. I can say no more. This afternoon I go to Paarl for a big party function in connection with the provincial elections on 9 March. The following Saturday I shall be at Hermanus for a similar purpose. Then on to the Transvaal for meetings there. All tough work, but I must not fail the country, even if it fails me!...

I shall not trouble you with referring to our affairs. Parliament is very hard work; to this has now been added this bitter election, once more on apartheid. I have spent this morning on another abortion of the government in regard to a South West Africa constitution,[2] once more devised to help their party, at whatever cost to this country. And so on.

But I am no less troubled about world developments. Things look like slowly working up to a world climax, in spite of all that

[1] Commenting on Smuts's defeat in May 1948 A. W. Gillett had written in a letter to his mother: 'From an historical point of view this lets Oom Jannie out. What he stood for and what he achieved will be, no doubt, regarded as a Golden Age in South Africa's history. What will be done now will corrupt and disgrace the name of South Africa and it will be the past that will be all that is left.' (Smuts Collection, vol. 89, no. 174.)

[2] *See supra*, p. 282, note 2.

mankind has already endured and lost. The only bright spot, and a very bright one, is American reaction to the world situation. How different from 1920 and following years! But overall what an unhappy world! All, or most, we have worked for and had hoped to have achieved is once more in dire danger. History now reads like a chapter of the Apocalypse. Fear, hunger, disorder, war in the East, loss of faith in the West, and storm clouds gathering all the time. Man as an individual has not altered, but man in the mass seems to be adrift as never before. It is this sombre world situation that fills one with deep anxiety. One does not know how to deal with phenomena on such a scale, and so the drift continues. It is a case neither for pessimism nor for optimism, but just baffling and as it were beyond control. It is a drift, a world-wide drift, and one does not know how to view or deal with it. Nothing like it in all history. South Africa and this obsession with apartheid is just one very small facet of this immense phenomenon. So one but holds on, does the daily task, prays to high heaven, and keeps one's eyes open. The dimensions seem so beyond us! Ever lovingly yours,

J.C.S.

838 To S. M. Smuts — Vol. 91, no. 146

Mount Nelson Hotel
11 Maart 1949

Liefste Mamma, So is die verkiesings virby, en die posisie bly maar baie soos dit was. Ek is teleurgestel met die uitslae by baie kiesafdelings, soos Pretoria distrik, Witbank, Middleburg, Standerton en etlike andere. Ons het gelukkig Paarl en Bredasdorp gewen en Caledon en Hottentots Holland behou. Maar setels wat ek byna seker was ons sou wen het ons tog verloor, ten spyte van die uiterste kragte wat ons ingespan het. Sake sou baie slegter gestaan het had ons nie so hard gewerk nie. Ek wonder wat van die land sal word as hierdie rasse beleid so voortgaan. Dit lyk of maar weer 'n groot ramp soos in 1939 die volk moet tref vor hul oë oop gaan. Arme Suid Afrika! Ek vrees 'n ekonomiese ramp gaan ons nou tref, wat ons nog swaar sal voel, en dit sal grootendeels te wyte wees aan die verlore vertroue van die buitewêreld waarvan ons nou meer afhanklik is as ooit te vore. Die Nattes is natuurlik in die wolke en juig met luidkeels.

Nou ja, agtermiddag is Dr Malan's tuinparty te Groote Schuur, en ek sal maar ook daar wees om al hul jubel te hoor. Maar dit is 'n wonderlike land!

Woensdag is ons veilig aangekom en my ou kamers het vir my verwelkom en voel nou meer gelukkig om nie langer leeg te staan nie...Ons had 'n aangename vlug en ek had goeie geselskap, o.a. Albert Hertzog en Prof Malan! Sondag n.m. sal ek te Somerset West wees vir 'n funksie, by die Moths, en die volgende Saterdag is ek op Durban om die nuwe universiteit te open en die namiddag (19 Maart) vlie ek na Palmietfontein vir die naweek by jul, hoerê. Nou groete en soentjies.

Pappa

TRANSLATION

Mount Nelson Hotel
[Cape Town]
11 March 1949

Dearest Mamma, So the elections are over and the position remains much what it was. I am disappointed at the results in many constituencies such as Pretoria District, Witbank, Middelburg, Standerton[1] and various others. Fortunately we won Paarl and Bredasdorp and retained Caledon and Hottentots Holland.[2] But in spite of exerting our utmost strength we lost seats which I was almost certain we would win. Things would have been much worse if we had not worked so hard. I wonder what will happen to the country if this race policy goes on. It looks as if a great disaster must strike the people, as in 1939, before their eyes are opened. Poor South Africa! I fear an economic disaster will now hit us which we shall yet feel badly, and it will be largely due to the lost confidence of the outside world on which we are now more dependent than ever before. Of course the Nats are in the clouds and rejoice loudly.

Well, Dr Malan's garden-party at Groote Schuur takes place this afternoon and I shall also be there to hear their jubilation. But it is a wonderful country!

We arrived safely on Wednesday and my old rooms welcomed me and now feel happier to be empty no longer...We had a pleasant flight and good company—among others Albert Hertzog and Professor [A. I.] Malan! On Sunday afternoon I shall be at Somerset West for a M.O.T.H.[3] function and the following Saturday I shall be in Durban to open the new university[4] and in the afternoon

[1] All in the Transvaal. [2] All in the south-western Cape Province.

[3] An ex-servicemen's association founded after the First World War.

[4] The University of Natal, situated at Pietermaritzburg and Durban came into existence on 15 March 1949 under Private Act No. 4 of 1948. It grew out of the Natal University College established at Pietermaritzburg in 1909.

(19 March) I fly to Palmietfontein for a week-end with you—hurrah! And now greetings and kisses.

Pappa

839 To V. Norton Vol. 91, no. 135

[Cape Town]
[March 1949]

My dear Norton, Now that the battle is over I wish to tell you how much I have admired and appreciated the support the United party has received from the *Cape Times*. Your publicity and advocacy have been splendid and contributed much to the success we have had.

On the whole I am moderately satisfied with what has been achieved. The party is firmly established and consolidated and the Herenigde Nasionale party remain in the stalemate where it is best for us that they should be for the present.

The fight has now to be kept up relentlessly, and will be. Many thanks.

s. J. C. Smuts

840 To M. C. Gillett Vol. 92, no. 13

Mount Nelson Hotel
[Cape Town]
22 March 1949

I have yours of 17 March, telling of Nathan's[1] return and Mrs Hodgkin,[2] and your own excessive travellings and labours. I wonder how you manage to do all this, in view of your physical disablement.[3] Still it is good to read, and to think that you continue to strive, and *not* to yield, as Tennyson's *Ulysses* poem puts it.[4]

Do not be unduly concerned about me, or my election and other troubles. I can take things philosophically and 'can take it' as they say. I have a curious inner faith, which I suppose is a sort of laziness or indifference, but yet is restful and prevents one from being worn down by the vain endeavour. It is a spirit of acceptance, when I have nothing particular to blame myself for. There is a contrariety in things, a general refractory character in the universe and in life which we must accept, or otherwise go under in the

[1] Son of Roger and Sarah Clark.
[2] Mary Hodgkin, a friend of M. C. Gillett.
[3] As a result of arthritis.
[4] 'To strive, to seek, to find, and not to yield.'

friction and frustration. I believe faith has something to do with it—a vague sense of holding on in spite of it all. It certainly keeps me going...

Here we continue to talk in parliament and cope with our political troubles. The Nats seem determined to take away the Native vote and to put the Coloured vote on a communal roll. They lost several Cape seats and the Coloureds have to be punished. What troubles me deeply is the feeling that, on the whole, white opinion favours this policy because of the fear they have for the future. The Nats behave inexcusably by exploiting this fear, but the man in the street *has* this fear and one feels for him in his ignorance and short-sightedness. Meanwhile the racial situation must surely get worse, and become a dark problem for our future. Perhaps a change may come later and the situation may improve. Meanwhile we must continue the fight against what is a perilous mistake. South Africa is isolating itself from world opinion in a world situation which is full of danger. And it is such a good people, sinning not from evil but more from ignorance as the Greeks would have held. The elections were indecisive, and not so bad as might appear to outsiders. But it is not pleasant for me personally to spend my latter days in these parliamentary quarrels, when I would so much rather have done some quiet, perhaps lazy, thinking! But how does one pull out of such things?

I had a letter from Arthur, asking or rather suggesting that accommodation for you two could be found in Irene village. Of course your place is with us at Doornkloof. There is no question about that, and everything will be in order when you come out. My own movements still remain uncertain. I may or may not be able to come to Cambridge in June, or later in October, when I have the Alamein appointment[1] in London. If I come I could discuss all these matters very pleasantly with you. Meanwhile my love to you and you all. Ever,

J.C.S.

841 To R. F. Harrod — Vol. 91, no. 158

24 March 1949

My dear Harrod, I have received the typescript of your chapters[2] dealing with the making of the peace treaty, and return it herewith.

[1] A dinner to commemorate the battle of Alamein. Smuts did not, in the end, attend.

[2] *The Life of John Maynard Keynes* (1951).

I am glad you gave me the opportunity to read and comment on these chapters.

As far as I am personally concerned, I have no comment to make, as your statement is objective and fair. My attitude on the question of the reparation amount and the inclusion of pensions in it was well understood at the time, and is clearly reflected in the statement of Norman Davis you refer to.[1] I was totally opposed to an inordinate sum being fixed for reparation, and never meant the inclusion of civil pensions to increase the amount contemplated. My sole object was to see that justice was done to Britain in the distribution of the amount settled, and the inclusion of pensions would have helped in that direction. I think Keynes overstressed the pensions aspect in his book.[2] The way the total amount was fixed shocked him, and he would naturally use any fair argument to strengthen his case. I understood all this and never resented his attitude, though I did think he made too much of the pensions case.

Then too, as I told you in London, I thought he had not been judicious in the way he handled Woodrow Wilson in his book. While he was substantially correct in the picture he drew of the leaders, the effect on the public mind was unduly damaging to Wilson, who after all was the leader of the cause for a fair peace. The damage done to Wilson affected the whole cause, and gave unnecessary opportunity to those inclined to blaspheme. The scoffers and cynics rejoiced, and the whole atmosphere worsened in the years of crisis to follow. We still continue in that malaise of public opinion, in which all higher values appear to be at a discount.

You are quite right in your presentation of Keynes, as I knew him. Brilliant in intellect, high-minded and of the highest personal integrity, he was an ornament to the society that produced and nurtured him. But that society was then already getting out of tune with the new tendencies getting to the surface. Idealism was beginning to yield to what was called realism, and in a harder and hardening world the outlines of the new order of things were being shaped. We were then moving into a new atmosphere, and have moved much farther since. It was this temper, more than the peace itself, which did the damage. In this temper the Ruhr invasion took place in 1923, the wild inflation of the mark was started, and the German middle class was ruined and ultimately joined the forces which combined to produce Hitler. After all it is the middle class, not only in Britain, but in Europe, which had

[1] R. F. Harrod, *ibid.* pp. 244–5. *See also* **32, 41, 94**.

[2] *The Economic Consequences of the Peace* (1919).

been the moving force in civilized society and stable progress in the West.

It is not merely ideas but the structure of society which has to be considered in these complicated matters. If I may say so, it is a case of ideas versus public opinion, which expresses largely the social structure and outlook. Keynes stood for the ideas—ethical, economic, intellectual, while the political leaders and the lesser fry stood for public opinion and the social outlook. We now can understand and sympathize with both, we who have now been through a greater war and a greater social and economic upheaval. The plannings of the leaders at Teheran, Yalta and Potsdam,[1] are now taking curious shape in this new atmosphere of public opinion. We have moved farther away from the world of Keynes, alas!

When, as you do in your comparison of the Keynes view with what is happening today, [*sic*] you have to bear in mind this far-reaching shift which has taken place, and which is difficult to describe in detail. The social and political and economic forces, now on the move, are producing a world which looks very unlike the world and the vision of Keynes. Such is life, such is the organic growth which incorporates both good and evil, both right and wrong, in the new social and political structure. Keynes saw the world in the light of high principles, clear ideas, noble ethics. The reality that has resulted in one generation presents a very different and amazing and, in some respects, repellent picture.

The world is at best a strange mixture. And the revolution through which we are still passing presents a strange mixed picture. Any comparisons between 1919 and 1949 are very difficult and may be misleading. Judgment must be suspended while the ferment is proceeding and the process of change still in full flood.

I say this in reference to the reflections you make on then and now, which are interesting to me, but still leave me doubting and perplexed. One can but hope that in the end the light which Keynes saw will prevail, in spite of all present apparent tendencies the other way.

This is not in criticism of what you say, but just to show the hesitation in my mind at present. Perhaps you noticed as much in our London talk.

With kind regards and all good wishes for the success of your book and your work. Yours sincerely,

s. J. C. Smuts

[1] Conferences of the Allied powers (the United States, Great Britain, the U.S.S.R.) in 1943 and 1945.

842 From L. S. Amery Vol. 89, no. 10

112 Eaton Square
S.W.1
2 May 1949

My dear Ou Baas, I need not say that I appreciate the force of your misgivings about this last declaration.[1] But I still remain convinced that it would have been a mistake to have pushed India out unless she accepted the actual position of allegiance to the king. I realize all the difficulties which may arise in a partly coloured Commonwealth. On the other hand, if that Commonwealth can hold together it may avert an ultimate war of races and form the nucleus of a future world union. The new position certainly makes it easier for others to join e.g. Norway or Iceland and even perhaps some day the United States, though I should not welcome that unless and until the Commonwealth has grown to be in resources and world position once more at least a match for America.

Naturally I also realize your own South African dangers, namely that Malan [D. F.] will presently go for a republic and plead that there is no real objection to it. So far, however, he has taken the line of saying that so long as he can be a republic if he wants it, he does not want it, and possibly also he may have some hesitation in advocating South Africa's following India's lead instead of remaining in the white group of the Commonwealth. Is it inconceivable that one of these days republicanism may become the black man's slogan and all whites stand together as monarchists?

What I think is not unlikely is that Pakistan may be forced by some of its elements to align itself with India on the republican issue.[2] Ireland, I feel pretty certain, will take the line of saying that there is nothing doing until 'partition' is got rid of. The fundamental difference anyhow between India and Ireland is that India wants to stay in and has asked to remain a full partner subject to her republican constitution, while Ireland has used the setting up of a republic in order to emphasize the final breaking of the last ties with the Commonwealth.[3] It is all very difficult

[1] Made at the meeting of Commonwealth prime ministers in London in April 1949 to reconcile the republican constitution of India and her unwillingness to continue allegiance to the king with her desire to remain within the Commonwealth. The formula adopted declared India's 'acceptance of the king as the symbol of the free association of its independent member nations and as such the head of the Commonwealth'.

[2] Pakistan became a republic within the Commonwealth on 23 March 1956.

[3] In April 1949 by an act of the parliament of Eire that country became the Republic of Ireland and ceased to be a member state of the Commonwealth.

but I still feel that we have avoided either pushing out an India that asked to stay in or doing something that would have immediately and definitely weakened the position of the crown for the Commonwealth as a whole. Only the event can show. Yours ever,

Leo Amery

843 To S. M. Smuts Vol. 91, no. 196

Volksraad
Kaapstad
3 Mei 1949

Liefste Mamma, Gisteraand het ek afskeid geneem van Kitty en J. C. en hul is seker al weer tuis, met al die nuus van hier. Saterdag wou ek Kitty vir 'n bergklim neem, maar sy wou liewers Cornie in die hospitaal gaan sien. Dus is ek en Cooper toe maar die berg op van Constantia Nek na bo en langs Skeleton weer af—3 uur harde werk. Gister (Sondag) oggend was Kitty weer besig en het ek toe maar met my werk voortgegaan. Die namiddag is ek toe na Moorreesburg en van daar na die familie te Louwsbaken en so terug Kaap toe waar ek 7.15 n.m. aangekom het, en Kitty daar ontmoet en afgesien het. Ma het daar taamlik goed uitgesien en was aan rond loop op twee krukke. Almal te Moorreesburg en Louwsbaken wel. Dit was maar 'n woelige naweek maar dit het my goed gedoen en die besoeke na die familie was baie wenslik. Van Stellenbosch het ek nog niks verneem nie, en hoop dit gaat hul wel.

Ek sien die Malans is nou in Rome en sal seker Vrydag te Pretoria aankom en Saterdag hier. Ek vrees die konferensie besluit gaat Malan help met sy republiek in Suid-Afrika en hy sal nou met Britse steun stoom op vorentoe woel. Dit is treurig maar is nou so. Indië is in die Gemeenebes behou, maar wat gaat van Suid-Afrika word? Nou is daar 'n gerug dat die Nattes gaan hierdie sitting voort om die Kleurstem af te sonder van die blankes, en so 'n aantal setels vir hulself hier in die Weste verseker. Dit mag die sessie vertraag. Intussen kry ek 'n dringende geroep van Cambridge om tog vir 9 Junie daar te wees op Grade Dag. Jy kan dus sien hoe dinge moeilik word vir my. Ek kan nog nie besluit nie.

Ek sluit 'n paar rekenings in wat te Doornkloof behandel moet word.

Verder heerlike weer hier na die reën en koue. Ek hoop die beste vir julle ook. Baie liefde.

Pappa

TRANSLATION

House of Assembly
Cape Town
3 May 1949

Dearest Mamma, Yesterday evening I took leave of Kitty [Smuts] and J.C.[1] and they are probably home again with all the news from here. I wanted to take Kitty for a climb up the mountain on Saturday but she preferred to go and see Cornie[2] in hospital. So Cooper and I went up the mountain from Constantia Nek to the top and down by Skeleton [Gorge]—three hours' hard work. Yesterday (Sunday) morning Kitty was busy again and so I went on with my work. In the afternoon I went to Moorreesburg[3] and from there to the family at Louwsbaken[4] and so back to Cape Town where I arrived at 7.15 p.m. to meet Kitty and see her off. Mother looked fairly well and was walking about on two crutches. All at Moorreesburg and Louwsbaken were well. It was rather an active week-end but it did me good and the visits to the family were most desirable. I have heard nothing from Stellenbosch and I hope all is well with them.

I see the Malans[5] are now in Rome and will probably arrive in Pretoria on Friday and be here on Saturday. I fear the conference resolution[6] is going to help Malan with his republic in South Africa; he will now go full steam ahead with British support. It is sad but it is so. India has been kept in the Commonwealth, but what will happen to South Africa? Now there is a rumour that the Nats will proceed this session to separate the Coloured vote from the white[7] and so assure themselves of a number of seats here in the West.[8] It may prolong the session. In the meantime I have had an urgent call from Cambridge to be there on 9 June for Degree Day. So you can see how things are getting difficult for me. I cannot yet decide.

I enclose a few accounts to be dealt with at Doornkloof.

For the rest it is lovely weather here after the rain and cold. I hope it is good for you also. Much love.

Pappa

[1] Jan Christian, son of Japie and Kitty Smuts.

[2] Cornelia Duckitt, born Bosman, sister of Kitty Smuts.

[3] To see his brother, Boudewyn (Bool).

[4] Smuts's step-mother was then living on this farm near Moorreesburg with her daughter, Hetta Louw.

[5] Dr D. F. Malan and his second wife, born Maria Louw.

[6] *See supra*, p. 290, note 1.

[7] The Separate Representation of Voters Bill was introduced in 1951.

[8] In the western region of the Cape Province, the home of the greater part of the Coloured population.

844 From W. S. Churchill Vol. 89, no. 81

Telegram

From: Winston Churchill, London
To: Field Marshal Rt. Hon. Smuts, Cape Town
Dated 12 May 1949

Let me know how I can cable you privately. Will sign Colonel Warden. Every good wish.

Winston

845 To W. S. Churchill Vol. 89, no. 81

Telegram

From: J. C. Smuts, Cape Town
To: Winston Churchill, London
Dated [12 May 1949]

Cable Henry Cooper Mount Nelson Hotel, Cape Town. Shall appreciate hearing from you.

Smuts

846 To S. M. Smuts Vol. 91, no. 200

Volksraad
Kaapstad
13 Mei 1949

Liefste Mamma, Van hier is waarlik niks te rapporteer nie. Ons werk gaan maar op ou trant voort in die Volskraad. Malan is hierdie week besig gewees met sy rapport oor sy werk in Londen en daaruit is niks van belang gekom nie. Hul mik nou na die republiek maar sal vir hierdie parlement niks in verband daarmee voorbreng nie. Malan sal tevrede wees met 'n republiek binne die Statebond, maar Strydom en andere gaan verder en wil eventueel daaruit. Dit sou dan kwansuis meer vrede en samewerking in Suid Afrika te weeg breng! My argument is dat dit net die teenoorgestelde effek sal hê, soos dit tot hiertoe al gehad het. Intussen word die finansiële toestand in die land vinnig aan slegter en verwag ek 'n haglike toestand a.s. jaar. Maar 26 Mei het gesaai en nou sal ons maar moet maai.

Die reën is virby en die son skyn vandag mooi, dus kan ons 'n goeie naweek verwag. Ek het nog geen planne behalwe die gewone stap langs die berg. Vanaand woon ek die vergadering van ons algemeene raad in die Skiereiland by maar sal niks biesonders sê nie. Daar is 'n stilte in die politieke stryd en ek wonder wat a.s. te Vereeniging sal gebeur. In Port Elizabeth sal ons wen, maar Ver. is minder seker na al die kwaad wat Kalie Rood gedoen het. Daar bly maar 'n slapheid in die party terwyl die teenparty woel dat dit so kraak. Nou is dit apartheid in die skole, en ek sien die Nattes het al hul mosie in die Transvaal voorgebreng om dubbel medium af te skaf, en aparte skole vir Engels en Afrikaans sprekend kinders te hê, met *dwang* om kinders op die huistaal basis te skei. Wat 'n sonde teenoor die opkomende geslag! Die Engelse sal nou nie Afrikaans ken nie, en die Afrikaanse kinders omgekeerd. Die mense is met blindheid geslaan, en apartheid wat met naturelle begin is, gaan nou na die blankes oor, met noodlottige gevolge vir ons toekoms as 'n nasie.

Ek hoop dit gaan goed met jul op die plase. Ek sal maar hier besig wees op 24 Mei en ook 25 Mei, maar dit is moontlik dat ek die namiddag van 26 Mei na jul terugvlie vir daardie naweek. Nog nie seker nie.

Dit begin nou lyk as of ek vir 9 Juni te Cambridge sal moet wees, en dus 3 of 4 dae vroër van hier sal moet vertrek. Maar dit is nog nie seker nie. Ek sal a.s. week bepaald moet beslis. Nou alles van die beste vir jul almal. Baie liefde van

Pappa

TRANSLATION

House of Assembly
Cape Town
13 May 1949

Dearest Mamma, There is really nothing to report from here. Our work goes on in the usual way in the house. Malan [D.F.] was busy this week with his report on his work in London and nothing of importance has come out of it. They are now aiming at a republic but will not put forward anything in connection with it in this parliament. Malan will be satisfied with a republic within the Commonwealth but Strijdom [J.G.] and others go further and wish to leave it eventually. This is supposed to bring about more peace and co-operation in South Africa! My argument is that it will have exactly the opposite effect, as it has already had so far. In the meantime the financial position in the country is fast getting worse and I expect a desperate situation next year. But what we sowed on 26 May[1] we shall now have to reap.

The rain is over and there is nice sunshine today so we can expect a good week-end. I have no plans as yet except the usual walk along the mountain. Tonight I shall attend the meeting of our general council in the Cape Peninsula but shall not say anything in particular. There is a calm in the political fight and I wonder what will happen at Vereeniging. We shall win in Port Elizabeth[2] but Vereeniging is less certain after all the mischief Kalie Rood has done.[3] There is still apathy in the party while the opposing party are going at it hammer and tongs. Now it is apartheid in the schools and I see that the Nats have already introduced their motion in the Transvaal[4] to abolish dual medium and have separate schools for English- and Afrikaans-speaking children with *compulsory* separation of the children on the basis of home language. What a sin against the coming generation! The English will now not know Afrikaans and the Afrikaans children the other way about.[5] These people have been struck with blindness, and apartheid, which began with the Natives, is now being applied to the whites—with fatal consequences for our future as a nation.

I hope all is well on the farms. I shall be busy here on 24 May and also the 25th; but I may possibly fly back to you on the afternoon of 26 May for that week-end. Still uncertain.

It begins to look as if I shall have to be in Cambridge for 9 June and so shall have to leave here three or four days earlier. But this is not yet certain. I shall have to decide finally next week. And now all that is best to you all. Much love from

Pappa

[1] Refers to the general election of 1948.

[2] The result of the bye-election at Port Elizabeth North on 18 May was as follows: J. A. Cull (United party) 5,559; Lt. Col. George Wynne (National party) 4,147. The United party majority was 420 less than at the general election although they polled 235 votes more.

[3] Karel Rood (q.v.), United party member for Vereeniging, resigned his seat because he differed from the party on Native policy. At the bye-election J. H. Loock (National party) won the seat from Dr R. H. Amm (United party) by sixteen votes.

[4] That is, in the Transvaal provincial council. Under the South Africa Act education 'other than higher education' is provided and controlled by the provincial councils.

[5] The question of the language medium in South African schools is complex. For a summary of the position at this time *see* E. G. Malherbe, *The Bilingual School* (1943), pp. 118–19.

847 To W. S. Churchill Vol. 91, no. 207

House of Assembly
Cape Town
21 May 1949

My dear Winston, A week or two ago I had a cable from you, asking me in what name you could cable me, and giving your own cable name as 'Colonel Warden'. I cabled 'Henry Cooper' as my cable name. Since then I have heard nothing further from you, and I do not know whether something may have gone wrong, or your plan has been changed. However, I hope to see you soon now, and no cable is asked for.

I have to be at Cambridge on 8 June in my capacity as chancellor, and shall be there on official business till 11 June (Saturday), and hope to be in London on the following Monday, 12 June, staying at my hotel (Hyde Park Hotel) till Saturday, 18 June, when I fly home via Rome, Athens and Cairo. During that week (12–18 June) I hope to see you and make other contacts as widely as possible in order to learn what is going on behind the scenes. The press is not very helpful when it comes to matters which really matter, and so much is going on at present which one really wants to understand.

As you can appreciate, the London conference on India is going to have its repercussions in South Africa. One could appreciate the deep concern of the British government to keep India, in however loose a form, within the Commonwealth. But the arrangements made for India have given the Nationalists here the very opportunity they have been praying for—that is, some half-way house towards complete secession (which is their policy), which might not prove too difficult for South Africans of both races to accept. Now the problem has been solved for them by the republic which still adheres to the Commonwealth. Since Malan's [D.F.] return the Nationalists are jubilant, and their next move may now well be a republic within the Commonwealth as a stepping-stone to full secession in due course. You will appreciate how much more difficult it has become to fight this sort of republic after the London decision. I have done my best to make it appear an exceptional accommodation for India, but they maintain stoutly that it is a complete change of general future application. It has been made easy for South Africa to travel the same way as Ireland. It is a most unfortunate development, but the British government acquiesced in it with full knowledge, and Malan has welcomed it. As I have expressed it, the Commonwealth may go the way of the

Holy Roman Empire[1] and become nothing but a name, and lose all meaning and reality. I know you must deplore this as much as I do, but we have both been put in the most embarrassing position possible. Already many good, loyal English people here ask what is the harm of a republic, not knowing that there is so much more behind it than the republic. What has happened in Ireland may now be repeated in South Africa. But these matters we can discuss when we meet again.

And there are others too. Your lead when out of office has been most fruitful, and from this point of view it may yet appear that your defeat in 1945 has been a blessing in disguise. You could scarcely have made either your Fulton or your Lucerne speech[2] when in office; and yet the one has become the basis of our Russian policy, and the other the basis of our European policy. You have been the elder statesman of the world and in that way achieved success which would not have been possible to a prime minister in office. Western Union[3] and Atlantic Pact[4] are the foundation stones of the future world structure. Of course they are only a beginning, but in great things it is the beginnings that count.

The pendulum appears at last to be swinging in Britain—how much, you would know better. I am not so much concerned with the internal conditions in Britain as with its world position, where there has been an unbelievable decline since 1945. We have lost much of our world position and influence and face. And this is indeed a world calamity, and not to us only. We might not have the physical force, but we have the moral force which counts even more for eventual victory in the world struggle now going on. I fear the Socialist government has been more concerned over their social programme than over the great issues on which in the end their social aims also depend. In the world revolution now in progress it is essential that the Commonwealth should pull its

[1] Established in 962 under the Emperor Otto I, it included Germany, Bohemia, Austria, Lotharingia, Burgundy, north and central Italy. The appellation Holy Roman Empire was used after 1254. By *c.* 1270 it had been irretrievably broken up but the imperial position survived and became hereditary in the Hapsburg dynasty until 1806 when Napoleon I dissolved the Empire.

[2] Smuts probably refers to the speech made by Churchill at Zürich University on 19 September 1946 when he called for the creation of a European union. For the Fulton speech *see supra*, p. 263, note 1.

[3] *See supra*, p. 281, note 1.

[4] The North Atlantic Treaty Organization was established on 4 April 1949 by a group of ten Western European states and the two North American powers—the United States and Canada. Under the treaty each member will assist any other against armed attack by 'such action as it deems necessary'. Since 1949 the German Federal Republic, Greece and Turkey have joined N.A.T.O.

full weight, instead of creating the impression (perhaps quite mistakenly) of being in retreat and abandoning its world role. I do not know how to put it, but you will understand better what is in my mind. Surely we have not won the war only to appear to lose our proud position and our face before the world? Even America will think less of us as an ally if this were the case.

I long to hear you on these searching matters, which go to the roots of the present mischiefs.

I shall contact you as soon as I am in London. Ever yours affectionately,

s. J. C. Smuts

848 From W. S. Churchill Vol. 89, no. 82

Telegram

From: Churchill (Colonel Warden)

To: Smuts (Henry Cooper)

Dated 22 May 1949

I was distressed to find myself taking a different line from you about the Republic of India and the crown. You know well my views and record on this subject. As Conservative leader I found it my duty to look forward and to have a policy which would not place the Conservative party in a position of permanent antagonism to the new Indian government. When I asked myself the question: 'Would I rather have them in even on these terms or let them go all together', my heart gave the answer, 'I want them in.' Nehru has certainly shown magnanimity after sixteen years imprisonment. The opposition to Communism affords a growing bond of unity.

No one can say what will happen in future years. I cannot think that any Soviet invasion of India would occur without involving U.N.O. against the aggressor. Therefore the burden of Indian defence no longer falls on us alone. Finally I felt it would place the crown in an invidious light if it appear an exclusive rather than an inclusive symbol. For these reasons among others I took my decision, which was accepted without protest by the party.

I am none the less glad you said what you did and you may be sure I should strongly oppose any attempt by the South African Union to repudiate the crown. I have not thought, however, that this was likely because of the risk it would make with Natal and other provinces and the danger of a mortal quarrel among the white minority. Malan now seems not to intend any violence at the present time. I am earnestly looking forward to your return to power. We are not doing so badly here though parties are evenly matched.

Every good wish to you and yours, my lifelong friend and comrade. I should welcome a letter.

849 To W. S. Churchill — Vol. 91, no. 211

House of Assembly
Cape Town
23 May 1949

My dear Winston, I had written to you before your welcome cable arrived, but had not yet posted the letter.[1] I send it forward now, with this additional note.

Be assured that I have no fault to find with your action, and indeed I anticipated you would actually take the line you did. For that reason I had not written you privately, for fear that such a letter would seriously embarrass you in coming to a decision.

The whole issue is indeed a tangled one, presenting different aspects from the Indian and the South African point of view. I was, of course, bound to take the latter, but in your position I might have been sorely tempted to take the line you did. The total secession of India at this stage would have been a very serious loss of face, for Britain primarily, but also for the Commonwealth as a whole. Our stock has been falling badly, as I point out in my other letter, and the total loss of India would have deepened the impression of decline to the outside world.

But from the South African point of view I was bound to take the anti-republican view. The campaign for the republic is coming, and may be in full spate when I am no longer there to combat it. It will tear up South Africa as you indicate in your cable, and it may succeed on the Indian model of a republic within the Commonwealth. But it will not stop there, as the fight since the First World War has been for complete secession, and Malan [D. F.] (who is at heart a moderate) will not be able to control his republican extremists, who are very powerful. The danger is therefore very real, and my public statements were meant more as a warning to South Africa about the danger ahead, than a reflection on the conference declaration. Of course, as you say, the future overall menace may be Communism, and on that issue even the republicans will stand by the Commonwealth, as I imagine even India is likely to do. But in any case the republican propaganda will influence

[1] 847, 848.

racial feeling here as no other issue can. We shall be back in the Boer War atmosphere. However, in this rapidly changing world we should not peer too deeply into the future. I think the world is moving into one of the secular crises of history, and no one can forecast the world picture which will ultimately emerge from it. For the sake of the future I am jealous for the coherence and stability of the Commonwealth which, together with American war potential, will save mankind from the rocks as nothing else will. The present tendency to concentrate on social security, without earning it by work, may lead to a fresh outburst of dictatorship, which follows chaotic economic conditions. If democracy cannot provide efficient leadership, the road is open for dictatorship, as recent history has shown. And dictatorship at once leads to a struggle for world power. The prospect before us is therefore far from bright. You and I shall not see it, but I believe the transition through which we are moving may bring strange developments, from which, one hopes, our free Western culture should once more emerge, purified and strengthened.

It will be a great joy to discuss these and other issues once more with you, and I hope that during the week I shall be in London (June 13–17) this will be possible.

I read your indictment in Scotland[1] of the present indifference to our world position with warm approval. I think that way the long range danger lies. What is lost now can never be retrieved. History does not move backward. With warm affectionate regards to you and Clemmy, Ever yours,

s. J. C. Smuts

850 To S. M. Smuts — Vol. 91, no. 209

Mount Nelson Hotel
22 Mei 1949

Liefste Mamma, Sondag oggend. Bewolk buite en ek spandeer die tyd om briewe te skrywe. So het ek vanoggend al geskrywe na Weizmann, Churchill, Vernon Thomson, Gilletts, Frederica, en Florence Lamont. En ek eindig met 'n lyntjie aan jou voor lunch.

Vereeniging is 'n bitter pil daar ons seker was dit te behou, en ons kon dit gedoen het, as van Vuuren die 350 stemme geregistreer het wat hy versuim het te doen voor dit te laat was. Ons mense is kwaad en mismoedig en onder die Nattes is daar gejubel dat dit kraak. Dit sal nou weer 'n bitter kritiek op die Party en Ockie en

[1] At a Conservative party demonstration in Glasgow on 20 May.

my wees. Ek weet nie waarom ons so ongelukkig is en so wreed gestraf word nie. Dinsdag sal ons 'n kaukus en 'n *post mortem* daaroor hou, en Vrydag weer ons Aksie Committee. Dan Vrydag laat sal ek die plane hier vang, en laat die aand te Doornkloof wees. Ek sê niks, maar die liewe Heer hoor my brom!

Gister was dit heerlike weer, en het ek die namiddag te Kirstenbosch deurgebreng met Cooper en twee liewe ou susters (Holt) wat baie groot vrinde van die I. W. Schlesingers is....

Ek het gister en vanoggend klaar gepak so dat my surplus bagasie môre kan vertrek na Doornkloof. Ek hou hier net die noodsaaklike wat sal dien tot einde van a.s. week (Vrydag 3 Juni) wanneer ek huistoe kom om op 5 Junie na Londen te vlie. Baie liefde.

Pappa

TRANSLATION

Mount Nelson Hotel
[Cape Town]
22 May 1949

Dearest Mamma, Sunday morning. It is cloudy outside and I am using the time to write letters. I have already written this morning to Weizmann, Churchill, Vernon Thomson, the Gilletts, [Queen] Frederica and Florence Lamont. And I end with a line to you before lunch.

Vereeniging is a bitter pill as we were certain of keeping it and we could have done so if van Vuuren had registered the 350 votes which he neglected to do before it was too late. Our people are angry and discouraged and among the Nats there is high jubilation. There will again be bitter criticisms of the party and Ockie [Oosthuizen] and me. I do not know why we are so unlucky and so cruelly punished. On Tuesday we shall hold a caucus and a *post mortem* upon it and on Friday our action committee will discuss it. Then, late on Friday, I shall catch the plane here and be at Doornkloof late that night. I say nothing, but the Good Lord hears my groaning!

Yesterday it was lovely weather and I spent the afternoon at Kirstenbosch with Cooper and two dear old sisters (Holt)[1] who are great friends of the I. W. Schlesingers...

I finished packing yesterday and this morning so that my surplus luggage can go to Dornkloof tomorrow. Here I am keeping only what is essential until the end of next week (Friday, 3 June) when I return home to fly to London on 5 June...Much love.

Pappa

[1] Misses H. and M. Holt.

851 To G. G. A. Murray Vol. 91, no. 224

Hyde Park Hotel
London
13 June 1949

My dear Gilbert, Thank you for a welcome and delightful letter. I like to think of you turning away from the affairs of scholarship and politics to write about your father and your own early beginnings in that far off world of Australia of a bygone age.[1] You are returning to the common man, who after all is a very good and human fellow, as long as he does not think he is able to run the world and do things he has never been trained for. I like to think of Jesus with his 'common men', fishermen and the like, who yet could put across to the future his message which they themselves could scarcely understand. Surely that is one of the miracles of history, and the greatest tribute to the common man! On the purely human level there is nothing better and more sincere than the ordinary man. But only on that level.

It is on that level also that the real good work of our age is being done, and I am much interested in what you write of good works at Oxford for those in distress abroad. I sometimes feel as if in our confused age the real goodness of the world has retired to family life, to those intimate circles of the home where the flame, now burning so dimly in the great world, is kept going. The great world is not a pleasant or good scene today. I was also much cheered by what I saw at Cambridge last week. How exhilarating it was among carefree youth, moving almost unconsciously to the battlefront of the future!

Mind you, we old stagers have much to be thankful for—for one thing in having lived through one of the most tremendous epochs of history, whose real significance we surely do not yet appreciate. Perhaps through painful steps we are moving to the larger groupings of mankind, as in the past the nation state rose from the city state. But shall we ever see the glory that was Greece? I like the glory more than the grandeurs,[2] the soul than the size.

It is a pleasure to hear from and about you. Florence [Lamont] could tell me something of you and Lady Mary. I can but send my greetings and deep affection. Ever yours,

J. C. Smuts

[1] G. Murray, *An Unfinished Autobiography*; with contributions by his friends; edited by Jean Smith and Arnold Toynbee (1960).

[2] . . . the glory that was Greece,
And the grandeur that was Rome.

Edgar Allan Poe, *To Helen*.

852 To W. H. E. Poole Vol. 91, no. 238 (enclosure)

House of Assembly
Cape Town
[26 July 1949]

My dear Poole,[1] I attach a letter from Colonel [R.] Meinertzhagen, one of my old staff in German East, and a letter from General von Lettow[2] to him, our brave and honourable opponent in that campaign. His pension had been cancelled in or after this last war and he was living in extreme penury, according to information that came to me. I accordingly instructed [Major-General B. F.] Armstrong to visit him and see what his circumstances were, and Armstrong fully confirmed the reports that had reached me. I then asked him to move the relevant authorities for the restoration of his pension, and Armstrong succeeded in getting this done. Now it appears that this is not quite correct. I do not know whom to approach in Germany on a matter on which I feel strongly, and I therefore write to you to try and find out what can be done. The old General and his wife and daughters were living in abject poverty, and we should do all we can to see that their misery is ended. They were not Nazis; on the contrary; and preservation of the sympathy of such people is worth more to us than the value of any little pension. I shall be happy if you could be helpful in a matter of this kind, which unites old warriors like us in bonds of sympathy and mutual help. Ever yours sincerely,

s. J. C. Smuts

853 To H. Macmillan Vol. 91, no. 240

26 July 1949

My dear Macmillan, I am much moved by your kind letter of 30 June[3] which has just reached me, after long absence from my Pretoria headquarters. To me it was a pleasure and privilege to meet so many of my old friends on the occasion of the [Lord] Kemsley luncheon, and I was deeply grateful to him for the opportunity of reunion, although I had not intended to say anything in particular.

I feel deeply the heavy onus on us. The Battle of Britain is still on, but in a deeper sense than in 1940; it is also the battle of the world, the battle for humanity. It is in that sense of urgency that I said the few things I did say on that occasion.

[1] Major-General W. H. E. Poole (q.v.) was at this time the South African military representative in Berlin.

[2] *See* vol. IV, p. 395.

[3] Smuts Collection, vol. 90, no. 98.

Here in South Africa things have gone wrong far more than I had believed possible. But here, also, the fight is on, and will continue until once more the cycle changes, and the people see the light again. It is this fight which keeps me in the battle line, in spite of the years.

And this also is my answer to your suggestion about writing a volume of memoirs. It is just a question of time and human limitation. I have something to say at the end, but this is not the time to pull out of the struggle, which takes all my strength and time. All good wishes. Ever yours sincerely,

s. J. C. Smuts

854 To M. C. Gillett Vol. 92, no. 25

Doornkloof
[Transvaal]
26 July 1949

I am back again from the wilds of Mozambique where I spent a most enjoyable time with Santa and Andries [Weyers], Jannie [Smuts] and other hunting friends. They hunted big game, from elephants and buffaloes to smaller animals, while I followed the more painless game of collecting plants and the invisible delights—the glory of the sunrise over the bush, the afterglow of the sunset, sipping tea or coffee. What a release and carefree world, where the radio was the only brief contact with a world in trouble. Now I am home again and coping with stacks of arrear papers and correspondence. But I shall get on top of them too, and then next week once more resume the political fight. I feel refreshed and in good form again, and yesterday afternoon once more did the Doornkloof–Pretoria walk[1] in company with Kitty [Smuts], just to prove that I had recovered my old physical form again. Physical, but perhaps not mental! I find this political grind pretty hard going, and my old memory is no longer what it was or should be. I am always afraid of missing a name at the necessary moment, or of forgetting a fact just when it is vital to your case or your argument. In botany the names also get rusty when I have not worked with them for some time. I suppose this is simply one of the penalties of age, and one must not mind it too much, but it can be pretty distressing at times. But the quiet time in the bush and among congenial surroundings was very welcome to me, and one forgot there all the minor troubles which are part of our lot. It was curious and

[1] A distance of about seven miles over the veld.

interesting to hear nothing but talk of game, of misses and hits, of hairbreadth escapes and all the many features of the hunting life. Wars in the Far East, strikes, and vagaries of the weather, of which the papers are full, troubled us not, and we lived in a sort of dream life apart—or was this the real thing and the turmoil of the world the ravings in a dream!

I could make quite a fair collection for the Herbarium[1] although as you know, the winter here is not the best time for botanical collecting. But the interest of the occupation kept me pleasantly going all the time; and of course there were the long rambles in the course of collecting which were also so interesting and useful. And often there was the danger of sudden contact with elephant or buffalo which might at any moment end in disaster. I returned in one day, motoring 415 miles and crossing the Limpopo river on piles of poles and branches, while the traction was supplied by a dozen or two of Natives. My poor new Mercury got sadly out of form in all this rough handling, and she will be for some days in the hands of the garage people. However, my companion and I arrived safely at home at night. We travelled the Louis Trichard–Sibasa way, and from the latter on by Punda Maria to Pafuri and so further into the Mozambique territory. All well at home and pleased to find us returned without mishap. Santa comes back tonight.

Thank you for the welcome books. Of the Tolstoy I read the last amazing chapter 'Escape'.[2] It is an incredible story, and creates the impression of a mad world and society, so unlike what we Westerners are accustomed to. The family is now reading this wild story. The Shakespeare books[3] are also welcome. An American firm has sent me a book on philosophy which purports to be a new synthesis, by-passing religion and the battle between science and religion. It seems all a muddled affair. But a good deal of one's time is wasted with this sort of thing. Many people look upon me as a sort of referee in their puzzles, forgetting that I am a very hard-pressed individual, with little time for all their muddles and puzzles. But one always reads part of it, for fear of missing the wheat in the chaff, the jewel among the swine.

Your letters are very interesting. What a good time you must have had in that lake country! But I suppose at the end you still say: Portway was the best! I agree, excepting Doornkloof! Good-bye,

J.C.S.

[1] The National Herbarium in Pretoria.

[2] E. J. Simmons, *Leo Tolstoy* (Boston 1946, London 1949).

[3] M. C. Gillett had sent seven books of Shakespeare criticism.

855 To M. C. Gillett Vol. 92, no. 29

Doornkloof
[Transvaal]
20 August 1949

My usual Sunday night letter in answer to yours of a few days ago. First let me thank you very warmly for your recent parcel of books. I have been spending today in reading *From Euclid to Eddington*,[1] which is just the book I wanted to bring my physics up to date. Whittaker is a splendid writer and a most competent guide. My general world view is largely based on physics for, after all, our views of matter must largely influence our view on the biological and spiritual superstructure. A good deal of more or less specialist material is of course beyond me, but most I can follow and appreciate. The satisfying world view would be one which would harmonize it all, and produce a world picture which would make sense. So much in the religion which has been delivered to us is really first-rate stuff, but unfortunately mixed up with a science which makes no sense—hence our throwing away the baby with the bathwater. Of course, I also always thirst after knowledge!

Yesterday I again went with Jannie [Smuts] to Rooikop and had another good two and a half hours over the bush, while he occupied himself with farming business. I went over ground which I had so far missed and was glad to find many *Acacia Giraffae* which I had not suspected before. *Acacia Gillettiae* I also studied more carefully; it is much confined to the Witlaagte valley where you found your specimens. We ought to spend some days on that farm when you come out, and give some time to Zoutpansberg again, if the rainy season is not too fierce. I shall not make excessive walking demands on you, and the vicinity of our camps ought to give you as much joy as you can digest. There are so many delectable spots and the roads are now much improved. And the company will be so good.

Friday I spent at Johannesburg among the money bugs in order to hunt for funds for the party. We shall want a good deal if the election is hastened and comes off next year already. I shall not be surprised if it is sprung on us. The Nats just saved Mayfair with a majority of ten (388 at the general election)[2] and they must know that the longer they wait the worse it will be for them. I shall not be surprised if the big fight comes off quite early. I shall

[1] Sir Edmund Taylor Whittaker, *From Euclid to Eddington* (1949).

[2] The result of this bye-election was: Dr. H. J. Luttig (National party) 4,468; B. N. Swemmer (United party) 4,458.

regret it because the longer they delay the more they will be found out, and surely defeated. I should like to round off my tale with a good victory, and then put the younger men in charge while I retire to collect my thoughts in the beloved bush. What a nice end that would be, after eighty and more than half a century of the fight! But let it be as Providence ordains; I have no grievance against the universe, and have had more luck than I deserved. I never had the ambition that I was called upon to reform the world, and see no reform of it in the near future. I think I told you that the B.B.C. had asked me for a review of the world situation to be broadcast on 29 September. I have finished it and hope to send you a copy.[1] It is just a general appraisal of these post-war developments. Nothing particular. I avoid all discussion of the economic position. I am indeed sorry to see that people in the States are beginning to cut up rough over British delays and troubles. I have little fault to find with the British, except with their government policy, which is badly timed and much too complaisant. But who am I to criticize such men of good will! So I avoid all that. I do think harder times lie ahead for all of us, and it may even be a good thing. Grapes do not grow on thistles.[2] And on the whole we have not done so badly in these difficult post-war times. But I am sure people are too much out for comfort and what they call a good life. It is not good for us, and adversity is a good thing to kill the weeds that grow in the garden.

But perhaps I go too much by my individual lot, which has been a good one, full of interest and work of all sorts. It is different for those who toil uninterestedly on a lower level. I would not be a miner or a shop-keeper or any of the other usual occupations. And how happy you are in your garden! Well, good-night,

J.C.S.

856 To M. C. Gillett — Vol. 92, no. 31

Doornkloof
[Transvaal]
4 September 1949

I have yours of 26 August in which you write of many things, the best for me being to hear that the doctor has passed Arthur as O.K....[3]

[1] Not in the Smuts Collection.
[2] 'Do men gather grapes of thorns, or figs of thistles?' *St Matthew* vii.16.
[3] Arthur Gillett had had heart trouble.

Now for a surprise. While you are on the high seas coming to South Africa I shall be flying to London! The explanation may be brief.

Dr Weizmann's English friends wish to arrange a function in London at which a scheme will be launched to collect a large sum of money to start a forest in Palestine as a memorial to him. He and they fear that the appeal may fail unless it is launched by a person like me, and so they have invited me to be the guest of honour for the function (23 and 24 November). This appeal has put me in a most awkward dilemma from many points of view, but in the end I have decided that I should accept and do what I can to be helpful. You know of my relations to Weizmann and to Israel, and I feel I should do him this honour and Israel this service. But what a request, and what an addition to my already heavy burdens! I shall come back immediately as I have to be at a big party congress on 3 December. On 16 December I have to speak at the centenary monument for the Voortrekkers.[1] Thereafter I hope we shall be free to enjoy ourselves. I call this bad luck, but it has to be cheerfully accepted as so much other bad luck that has recently come my way.

I note what you say about Germany. We are repeating all the old mistakes of 1920–1. It is not ill will, but just that lack of imagination and historical perspective which accounts for so much that is wrong in our policy. I can understand French fears and American inexperience. But the British leadership does not do the great record of Britain justice in these matters. They know, or ought to know, we are once more choking the channels of future good will through which salvation may flow for this good world. I believe that imagination is often the highest wisdom, and not the dreamy business which people take it for.

All well here. Ever yours,

J.C.S.

[1] The unveiling of the monument of which the foundations had been laid in 1938, the centenary of the Voortrekker victory at Blood river.

857 From K. Howard-Browne Vol. 90, no. 32

P.O. Box 17
Putfontein
Benoni District
[Transvaal]
14 September 1949

Dear General Smuts, As vice-chairman of the Putfontein branch of the United party and as a delegate to the general council, I had the honour of hearing your most outspoken and outstanding address in the Darragh Hall last night.

I need not mention that I am one of the most ardent supporters of the party. If I were not, you would not be receiving this communication. I refer to your condemnation of apartheid which, after all, is segregation, and I must say that it is, in my opinion, a most desirable and real thing. Born of English-speaking parents, (my great-grandfather, Robert Hart, a personal friend of that great Voortrekker, Piet Retief, stood security for the latter when Retief tendered for the erection of a Cape Town building contract), I feel that apartheid, wherever possible, should be applied in the interests of both European and non-European citizens. I have noted with regret that you, a great leader and international figure of whom we are exceedingly proud, as well as prominent United party officials and members of parliament and the provincial councils, have ridiculed the advisability of apartheid in South Africa.

I, together with thousands of my fellow party supporters, am wholly in favour of that 'mystic policy'. I fail to see that it is either unfair or unwise and I feel that the Bantu themselves welcome it. In the case of the Cape Coloureds, we all know that they love to be associated with their superiors. Even the most feeble-minded are fully aware that total segregation is out of the question but we still have so-called intelligent party leaders bragging from public platforms that the Nats have failed in their apartheid programme as it cannot be applied a hundred per cent. I discuss the subject with every United party supporter I encounter and must state that so far I have not come across a single person who has disagreed that apartheid on Cape Town suburban trains, universities and Johannesburg and Germiston stations is out of order. In fact, in almost each case it has been suggested that South Africa should introduce it on a large scale.

I have noticed that the delegates to meetings of importance (particularly on the mines where individuals could possibly be victimized through expressing their feelings, thereby antagonizing their superiors) are reluctant to support a question raised concerning any policy introduced by the government in spite of its being of advantage to the country. In private conversation, however, I have received the support of one member of the provincial council, one ex-member, scores of chairmen and secretaries and dozens of honest-to-goodness United party men and women. I have spoken to the good old type of Afrikaans-speaking South Africans who have told me that they were compelled to either stay away from the polling-station or vote Nationalist because of our party's attitude to the Native. I feel that we shall be very lucky indeed if we are returned to power if we do not refrain from ridiculing apartheid—a policy I whole-heartedly support in the interests of my country, my family, my party and the non-Europeans.

The Native today, unfortunately, is striving for social equality. The fool—he should fight for economic security. Does he expect to start where we have landed after centuries of progress? His only award will be scorn and sorrow. We South Africans cannot possibly be subjected to Native insolence caused through his too rapid advancement and I can only foresee national disaster unless we can outnumber him by a substantial majority.

Believe me, General Smuts, I love you as an outstanding example of South African manhood, a great leader, lover of freedom and international statesman. I trust you will overlook my impertinence but I pride myself on being a lover of my country—a true South African.

I feel confident that our party will benefit rather than suffer if we associate ourselves with that wholesome idea of segregation. With kindest regards,

K. Howard-Browne

858 To K. Howard-Browne — Vol. 91, no. 291

26 September 1949

Dear Mr Howard-Browne, I was much interested in your letter of 14th September and thank you for writing to me in the frank spirit you have done.

I quite appreciate your point of view, and myself and other party leaders have repeatedly declared that up to a point apartheid is common ground and the traditional policy of South Africa. Socially and residentially it has always been accepted South African policy.

The Nationalist party are however today proceeding far beyond that policy. Even the old segregation policy of General Hertzog is being abandoned, and the constitutional guarantees for the rights of the Natives and Coloured are now being set aside, and our South Africa Act set aside. A wild campaign is going on which must cause resentment by the non-Europeans, and may in the end lead to coloured nationalism and a common front against the white man. All this is new Nationalist doctrine and very explosive stuff. It is against this new development of Nationalist policy that we have protested, and we take our stand on the common platform which Hertzog and I built up in the fruitful years of fusion. With this I am sure you will agree as wise policy for our country. Yours sincerely,

s. J. C. Smuts

859 From F. C. Erasmus Vol. 89, no. 133

When the National party government came into office on 26 May 1948, it overlooked the fact that the leader of the opposition was the commander-in-chief of the Union forces. Sixteen months later it curtly dismissed him.

Ministerie van Verdediging
Pretoria
7 Oktober 1949

Hoogedelagbare Heer, Ek het die eer u mee te deel dat Sy Eksellensie die Goewerneur-generaal-in-rade, kragtens subartikel (1) van artikel een-en-tagtig van die Zuid-Afrika Verdedigings Wet, 1912, goedkeuring verleen het vir die beëindiging van u aanstelling as Opperbevelhebber van die Unie-Verdedigingsmag te velde, wat in Goewermentskennisgewing No. 1055 bekendgemaak en in die Unie-Staatskoerant van 28 Junie 1940 gepubliseer is. U dienswillige,

F. C. Erasmus
Minister van Verdediging

TRANSLATION

Ministry of Defence
Pretoria
7 October 1949

Dear Sir, I have the honour to inform you that his excellency the governor-general-in-council, in terms of article eighty-one of the South Africa Defence Act, 1912, has approved the termination of your appointment as commander-in-chief of the Union Defence Force in the field which was made known in Government Notice

No. 1055 and published in the Union Government Gazette of 28 June 1940. Yours faithfully,

F. C. Erasmus
Minister of Defence

860 To F. C. Erasmus Vol. 91, no. 303

Doornkloof
Irene
Transvaal
14 Oktober 1949

Hooggeagte Minister, In antwoord op die uwe van 7 Oktober neem ek kennis van die beëindiging van my aanstelling as Opperbevelhebber van die Unie-Verdedigingsmag te velde. Dienswillig die uwe,

get. J. C. Smuts

TRANSLATION

Doornkloof
Irene
Transvaal
14 October 1949

Dear Minister, In reply to your letter of 7 October I note the termination of my appointment as commander-in-chief of the Union Defence Force in the field. Yours faithfully,

s. J. C. Smuts

861 To E. G. Jansen Vol. 91, no. 327

18 November 1949

Geagte Dr Jansen, Ek erken ontvangs van u skrywe van 5 November en neem kennis van die reëlings daarin uiteengesit.

Wat my persoonlik betref hoop ek my optrede by die reëlings aan te pas.

Terwyl ek by my oorspronklike voorneming bly om my toespraak in Afrikaans te lewer, wens ek nogmaals my wenk aan u, by ons vorige gesprek gemaak, te herhaal, naamlik, dat ter wille van algemene tevredenheid redelik voorsiening vir gebruik van Engels gemaak dien te word. Hoogagtend die uwe,

get. J. C. Smuts

TRANSLATION

18 November 1949

Dear Dr Jansen, I have received your letter of 5 November and note the arrangements[1] set out therein.

As far as I personally am concerned, I hope to accommodate my part to these arrangements.

Although I shall abide by my original intention of delivering my address in Afrikaans, I wish to repeat my suggestion, made to you at our earlier conversation, that for the sake of general satisfaction reasonable provision ought to be made for the use of English.[2] Yours faithfully,

s. J. C. Smuts

862 Speech (1949) Box M, no. 266

Delivered on 27 November 1949 in London.

You and the committee who have organized this function have done me the honour to ask me to propose the toast of Dr Weizmann, the president of Israel. I appreciate that honour but we are gathered here tonight to do honour only to him. The size and character of this gathering is itself eloquent testimony to the depth of our feeling and admiration for him.

In spite of distance and heavy pressure on my time in South Africa, I have come here specially to join with you in honouring a great friend, a great man, with whom I have had the privilege to be associated for much of a lifetime. At a time like this when he will be celebrating his seventy-fifth anniversary and at the consummation of his life work, we all feel the urge to do honour to a man who in the history of our age will occupy a place all his own.

In this circle of his friends and admirers it is unnecessary to go into his personal record. Besides, he has himself written his story in a book,[3] which I feel sure will be another monument, a literary monument, to him. It is all so simply and modestly and humanly told. It has itself the stamp of greatness on it.

[1] For the ceremony of the unveiling of the Voortrekker monument. The document in the Smuts Collection has a note by Smuts for his private secretary which reads: 'I have not been officially asked to speak in Afrikaans, but was intending to do so, and am still going to do so. The editor may come and see me about it. It is evidently a delicate matter, as trouble seems to be feared.'

[2] At the unveiling Mr Justice Newton Thompson, as spokesman for the English-speaking South Africans, made his speech in Afrikaans.

[3] *Trial and Error*, published in 1949.

I love to think of that boy from the Russian ghetto rising to his destined place among the great men of his time. In spite of all the opposition he encountered in his hard quest, there is not a harsh or bitter word against anybody. What a fine human spirit pervades it all! And what a story it is of the young chemist who, without any means or even working knowledge of English, an unknown stranger to this land, came to Manchester University, set up his primitive laboratory in a bare basement room, and began his research work, which in the end was to carry him to his high place among the biochemists of the world and to the part he played in our scientific activities in connection with the First World War. In the annals of science I know no more inspiring story than that of the early beginnings of Weizmann. And the rest of his life was in keeping with its strange beginnings.

But he was more than a scientist. He owed a dearer allegiance. In his youth [Theodor] Herzl had appeared with his Zionist message, the return of Israel to the ancient homeland. Weizmann's imagination and heart were fired with the Vision to which he remained faithful when many, even Herzl himself, began to quail before the enormous difficulties. He remained faithful right through to the final fulfilment. One can appreciate the doubts and misgivings which began to oppress others and made them waver. Palestine had become a desert under Turkish rule; there were other more tempting territories. The political and international difficulties appeared almost insurmountable. Weizmann refused to renounce his vision, and would not look at South America or central Africa. It was all or nothing for him. The memory of the ghetto and the pogrom had been burnt into his soul, and even his subsequent preoccupations as a scientist could not turn his mind away from the lure of the vision. But how were the enormous political difficulties to be overcome?

Then came the opening, and his great opportunity, with the Great War. In the first place his outstanding war service as a scientist had made him known and famous in high Allied circles, and his voice carried so much the greater weight in pleading for the Jewish national home. Then again, Turkey was involved in the war on the German side and had to be pushed out of Palestine. Here was the very situation the Zionist cause so urgently needed. There were also other powerful arguments in favour of placing the national home in Palestine among the Allied war aims. It would rally Jewry on a world-wide scale to the Allied cause, and the Jews in those days—with their world-wide connections and activities—were like another power. Even among Christians such a policy would rally fresh support to the Allied cause. Was there not the ancient promise of the Book, which made a great appeal to the Christian conscience? Had the Jews not suffered enough in their agelong dispersion, and had the time not come for history to fulfil the promise? The case itself, and Weizmann's way of presenting it, together with his personal prestige as a scientist and war worker, carried the day with some members of the then war cabinet. Mr Balfour was persuaded, and became a convinced supporter. Likewise Mr Lloyd George, who had not only been educated on the Book, but was particularly sensitive, as a member of a small people, to Weizmann's arguments. As for me, a Boer with vivid memories of the recent past, the Jewish case appealed with peculiar force. I believed with all my heart in historic justice, however long delayed. I also had the strong feeling that something was due from the Christians to the Jews, not only as compensation for unspeakable persecutions, but as the people who produced the Divine Leader, to whom we Christians owed the highest allegiance. Moral and religious motives thus reinforced the political considerations. We were persuaded, but remember it was Weizmann who persuaded us.

It took some time to evolve a suitable formula on which all could agree, and which the American and French governments could also support. And so arose the famous declaration with which the name of Arthur Balfour will always be associated.[1] It did not promise a Jewish state, but only a Jewish national home in Palestine. It was thus practically limited to Jewish immigration, but Weizmann, as a practical man and a realist, knew that no more could be achieved at that stage, and probably felt that something might easily be left to the future. The whole story is well known, and I shall not trouble you with further details. The policy of the national home was embodied in the peace treaty and in the Palestine mandate, which was conferred on the British government.[2] The Jewish cause had at last achieved international recognition in one of the great documents of history. The Arabs also came handsomely out of the bargain. They not only received their full liberation from Turkey, but both in territory and status they came off much better than the Jews. When their gains were finally assessed, they had received three new kingdoms and two other independent states out of the peace settlement.[3] I was under the impression at the peace conference, and rightly so, that Prince Feisal, who represented King Husain of the Hejaz, was fully

[1] *See* vol. v, p. 19, note 1. [2] *See* vol. v, p. 20, note 1.

[3] The new states were Iraq, Syria, Lebanon, Transjordan, Palestine.

satisfied with the settlement and that it would not be reopened thereafter. Weizmann had every reason to be proud of his success.

But remember that but for him there might have been no Balfour declaration and no return to the ancient home. Even many leading Jews were lukewarm towards that policy. When we look today at what has been achieved, at what in the light of great history can only be considered a miracle, we bow in homage and honour to this great leader who was the primary personal force in achieving it. Looking back now after thirty years we must admit that most of what we dreamt of, and worked for, in the First World War has, alas, disappeared. Its main redeeming vision, the League of Nations, is no more. The Balfour declaration on the contrary has borne fruit, and led to one of the most amazing developments in all human history.

But much water had to pass under the bridges before these far-off results were secured. In the early years following on the Balfour declaration immigration remained practically at a standstill. I have always felt that a great opportunity was missed then, when there was no very great opposition to Jewish immigration, and a large population could have entered the country without all the fuss and trouble which developed later. If the policy of the Balfour declaration had been pushed vigorously in those early years, the mandatory power would have saved no end of trouble later, after the Arab temper had changed and the opposition to immigration stiffened. The Arab opposition became organized, and was reinforced by Moslem backing throughout North Africa and the Middle East, as far as India. The policy of the national home felt the impact of international politics which affected both British and French policy. The cause, which at first was viewed with indifference, if not with favour, became bogged in international politics. The psychological opportunity had been missed, and the hesitations and doubts that followed could only be dealt with by time-wasting and largely abortive commissions, one after the other. This is a long story, now best forgotten.

These tedious proceedings were interrupted by the storm of the Second World War. And now the Jews entered upon a phase of their story which of all was the most disastrous. Hitler, even before the outbreak of war, had marked out the Jews as his enemy number one, and had begun their liquidation. After the outbreak of war this policy was relentlessly followed up with diabolical ferocity. Millions of Jews in Germany, and in the countries which later fell under the German sword, were wiped out in a record of war crimes to which history knows no parallel. It has been stated that perhaps as many as six millions of the Jewish race perished in those massacres. This true story, which otherwise might never have been believed in history, was unfolded in the Nuremberg and other war trials. Whatever view one may take of these trials from a judicial point of view, they are of supreme historical value as having proved, on indisputable evidence in proper judicial procedure, facts which otherwise would in future have been dismissed as incredible. Now there can be no doubt, and no question even, about their correctness.

For the Jewish race it seemed almost, if not quite, the end. Well might it have been said at that apparent end: 'Thou hast conquered, O Hitler!' But history has in the final appeal reversed this judgment. Hitler, and all he aimed at and stood for, have gone under, and the state of Israel becomes the answer to Hitler. It is an incredible reversal, an almost incredible ending to one of the most terrible crime stories in all history. Much, very much is due to Jewish endurance and resistance throughout this most awful ordeal of the race. But how much is not due to the leadership of Weizmann, not only in the original launching of the national home policy, but also subsequently in the unprecedented ordeal which befell the Jews later on, and in the confusions after the Second World War?

In the final stage of this drama of a people's fate new factors entered. There was President Truman's declaration in favour of a resumption of a large-scale immigration policy.[1] There was the intervention of U.N.O., once more with its process of commissions. There was a growing exasperation among the Jewish remnants, into whose soul the iron of suffering had entered, and who could bear no more. No wonder extremist elements got out of hand, and forced the pace towards solutions, such as no commission or endless palavers could have brought about. We know that sad story. One need not approve the violent policies of Irgun Zvai Leumi, nor need one abate one's abhorrence of the criminal proceedings of the Stern Gang.[2] But history does not always proceed along the way of law and order. Where reason fails force takes charge, and speeds up the change-over from intolerable conditions. Long delays and continual frustrations do sometimes create an abnormal state of mind, and Jewry as a whole should not be held responsible for such aberrations. A tribute should however be paid to the deep

[1] His official statement was made on 22 December 1945.

[2] Jewish terrorist organizations whose action was directed mainly against the mandatory, Great Britain. The Sternists, founded by Abraham Stern in 1940, were the more ruthless of the two and a much smaller group than Irgun Zvai Leumi or Etzel, founded somewhat earlier and led, from 1944, by Menachem Begin.

interest of U.N.O. and the fine work of the late Count Bernadotte and Dr [R.J.] Bunche, whose patient handling of a very difficult situation also helped to contribute to the successful finale.

Difficult questions still remain to be settled. It is even possible that definite clear-cut solutions are not immediately possible. The Old Testament record goes to show that they were not possible even during the thousand and more years of Palestine history. But Arab and Jew continued to occupy that land alongside each other. The new record may be somewhat like the old historic record. But what a wonderful colourful story it was—it may be so again, more or less. I certainly expect no more than some such uneasy conditions for the immediate future, in which, however, the Jewish genius may once more flower out as it did in the millennium before Christ. The pattern of peace in such cases may be a more varied and intricate one than that prescribed by the rules of the United Nations Organization under great power control, and the success of the effort to introduce uniformity into the racial and political relations of these ancient societies should not be over-estimated. Life might become too drab, and too much living, human interest would be taken out of it. Sport, fun, a certain amount of tension and excitement, and even unruliness have their function in human society. Life is interest, and that interest takes many strange forms. Some sparring among the Semitic elements in Palestine may therefore continue and not be an unmitigated evil. It is a human situation and must be viewed and judged in a human spirit.

But how much else is happening in the new Palestine to make one feel easy and happy about the future! Even under the mandate immigration added some half a million to the Jewish population. These have come from all parts of the world, some from the most advanced societies, but most from the lands of oppression and suppression. These derelicts have escaped from the ghettos and the persecutions of eastern and southern Europe. Cooped up in their urban reserves and enclosures they have escaped, by the aid of the Jewish national fund, to the land, and have become land workers and dwellers. Carried forward by an irresistible ardour of the spirit they have turned that land from swamp and desert conditions once more into the glory that was Palestine in ancient times. No finer effort of recovery and restoration has been made anywhere in the world in post-war times than by these town dwellers, now land workers and farmers in the land of their fathers. I know of no more inspiring effort in our time. And this has now been going on for a generation, and the pace of development is kept up and accelerated in spite of war and rumours of war. It is a blessed work, blessed of heaven, whatever hostile critics may say of it. Somebody has said that wherever you dig in human nature you come on pure gold, if only you dig deep enough. Here is pure gold, dug from the slums and horrors of persecution in the old world. And they are making this old homeland of theirs once more a golden land, a land flowing with milk and honey.[1] The ancient prophetic vision is once more being realized, and the voice of Isaiah is once more heard over these barren lands. The glad return has come, come after thousands of years of waiting and suffering in exile. The bloom is returning to the wasted land, and the music to the hearts of the people. From letters reaching me I read what for instance has been done, what is still being done in Ramat Jochanan, a settlement in the waste land of Israel called after me, and I must confess that I am more deeply moved by it than by many of the great world events now filling the newspaper columns. Here we are at the heart of things, and the heart of man. When these things happen under such untoward circumstances as hamper development in Palestine today, what may one not expect when Israel is able once more to go all out in its own way under favourable conditions. One has to go back to ancient prophetic literature to find language in which to express what is happening, what great things may yet happen in this land, not only of promise, but of fulfilment. I have seen those bare hills, when Allenby and I rode over the hilly country of Judea in the First World War. They must have been covered once with the fig and the olive and the vine. They must remain bare no longer. And so the idea has occurred to friends of Dr Weizmann that part of that area should be set aside for a forest in perpetual honour to him. What more fitting honour and memorial to the man who led Israel back to those bare hills after such long absence, and covered them again with the glory which was theirs in ancient times. Let the Weizmann forest be the memorial of the great planter, who replanted his people in their ancient homeland, and as their tutelary divinity will keep watch and ward over them in the long years of fulfilment to come.

This unique little people, which bequeathed to mankind the noblest spiritual heritage of all history, produced also some great historic leaders of men, foremost amongst them Moses, the mysterious founder who first led them out of bondage to this promised land; David, the shepherd king, the warrior, the musician and poet, the singer beloved of God, the conqueror of Jerusalem which he made the capital of the country. To this select historic list we now add our own contemporary, Chaim Weizmann, the

[1] *Exodus* iii.8.

scientist, the great Zionist, the indomitable leader who, after his people had been all but wiped out in the greatest purge of history, assembled the remnants, led them back to the ancient homeland in face of the heaviest opposition, and welded them once more into a sovereign state among the nations. Surely his achievement bears comparison with that of Moses! Among the leaders of our age we accord high place to this leader who wrought for his people a real miracle of history. We are privileged and proud tonight to do honour to a man who, in his person and his record, is an outstanding example of what we honour most in man, and who has added fresh lustre to our human record.

Nor must we forget Israel tonight. Though only one of the smallest of peoples, it has shown qualities of the greatest. In the disasters which have overwhelmed mankind in our age it has miraculously survived, and arrived. From utter abasement and, as it were, from the grave, it has risen to the heights by sheer soul force. In the Middle East world, in which it now once more occupies a position of power and responsibility, it has before it a unique opportunity, such as Israel never had in its palmiest ancient days. May it at last become a healing influence in that ancient human society. It has the message of mercy and justice and human brotherhood which was the burden of its great prophets. That message points the way by which the new Israel may become a greater blessing and power than ever the old Israel was. That is our hope and prayer for Israel and the whole Middle East world. Our deepest sympathy goes out to that human group which has contributed so much to our human advance.

Nor should we tonight forget the great Commonwealth which stood by the national home from the Balfour declaration to the achievement of national sovereignty. It has been a hard way, sometimes marred by misunderstanding due to the conflicting duties laid on Britain under the mandate. But let Israel never forget that it was Britain that first took Weizmann by the hand, and that that grip should never be relaxed. Forget the smaller differences which have developed on the way. The historic comradeship should continue unbroken for the fruitful service of mankind.

And there is another moral of this remarkable story, to which I would draw your attention. The achievement of Israel has a lesson for all peoples, great and small, today. We are passing through critical times, through a tragic period, such as perhaps has no parallel in history. It reads like some tragic Odyssey, not of one man, but of man, of the human race. And to it we may justly apply the words of Homer: 'The sun has set, and all the ways are darkened.'

Mankind has been exhausted by labours almost beyond its powers, and it now stands perplexed and confused before the future, with no clear light upon the way before it. It is at such a time and in such a scene that we may derive comfort and guidance from the case of Israel. It is in such moments that the human spirit takes control and wins through. The soul, spiritual force, is the answer to the machine. What little Israel could achieve, in spite of Hitler, and against almost unimaginable odds, surely this Western world of ours may achieve on its larger scale. The last reserve, the unconquerable reserve of man, is his resolution, his will to victory, his determination to win though at all cost. And once the peoples of the West make up their mind to sacrifice minor comforts and benefits, to say good-bye to all that,[1] the sun will once more shine upon their way, and the wide prospect of fulfilment will stretch out before them. The peoples of the West have reached this stage of decision in the post-war period, when the acquired cargo of entrenchments and securities may have to be jettisoned to save the ship itself. Such an all-out effort was made here in the Battle of Britain, and repeated in the resurrection of Israel in Palestine. I bracket them together as among the human highlights of our epoch. Let us repeat that supreme effort in a spirit of willingness to lose all in order to win all, and our European civilization will enter upon perhaps its most glorious epoch of history. We thank Israel for having once more reminded us of that last, that only way to salvation. And especially do we think of Chaim Weizmann tonight in honour and gratitude for his great leadership and inspiration to a world looking for leadership and inspiration.

Drink to the health of Chaim Weizmann and with his name we join that of his noble wife, Vera Weizmann.[2]

863 To E. L. Spears Vol. 91, no. 347

14 December 1949

My dear General Spears, Thank you for your letter of 6 December.[3] Could I ever forget you after our association in 1917–19, and on later occasions?

I know that you and I differ on this Zionist question, but it is a matter on which earnest men will always differ, and yet understand each other.

[1] Title of a novel by Robert Graves.

[2] Born Vera Chatzman; married Chaim Weizmann in 1906.

[3] Smuts Collection, vol. 91, no. 56.

My attitude to Zionism is motivated by several considerations, chief among which is fidelity to the policy of the national home, as formulated in the Balfour declaration. I shared the responsibility for it, and have since seen no reason to go back on a declared public policy of great significance in which the great Allies of World War I joined. All that has happened since has followed from the Balfour declaration.

Then, secondly, I imagine Israel is going to play a foremost part in Near East policy. It is in the Jew to play a great part, and in an inefficient society, such as exists in the Near East, the Jews must necessarily play a leading part. For our Commonwealth group the eastern Mediterranean is all-important, and remains so, in spite of the great set-backs which we have suffered in the Mediterranean world since the end of this war. I am anxious that Israel should be with us rather than look East. She is now West. Keep her West, in company with America and the Commonwealth. If she goes East, because of our apparent hostility, or even indifference, we shall suffer still further loss in the Mediterranean. Arab unity has remained a poor, nebulous affair. It will be a broken reed for us to lean on in the hard struggles ahead. The Jews are still inclined to go West; keep them moving West.

These considerations of high policy which concern our future and that of civilization, move me much more deeply than sentimental considerations, to which both you and I are subject.

I think with pleasure of those times when we worked together. What a world we have moved into; and how much more incalculable and how much more dangerous! So much is today at stake that I prefer to stand by principles and policies which promise stability for our poor human society against the new sinister forces now on the march in the East and Far East. Ever yours sincerely and with every good wish for the New Year,

s. J. C. Smuts

864 Speech (1949) Box M, no. 268

This address was delivered by Smuts, as leader of the United party, at the inauguration of the Voortrekker monument on Skanskop, near Pretoria on 16 December 1949. The corner-stone had been laid on 16 December 1938, the centenary of the battle of Blood river, at which the Voortrekkers inflicted a heavy defeat on the Zulus. No political leader had on that occasion delivered an address.

Ons staan vandag op 'n hoogtepunt, waarvan ons terug kan kyk op drie eeuwe van ons geskiedenis, en in seker mate ook vooruit in die skaduwee van die toekoms. 'n Volk is nie die skepping van die dag maar van die eeuwe, van die verlede sowel as van die toekoms. En in dié verband alleen, in die samevatting van die lange jare in die volkslewe, sien ons die deurlopende rigting en kan ons 'n juister begrip vorm van die rigting en koers van ons geskiedenis en van ons verre bestemming. Agter ons sien ons met die diepste dankbaarheid die duidelike bewyse van Hoëre leiding deur doodsgevare, van uitkoms langs onvoorsiene paaie. Hoe meer mens die wordings-geskiedenis van Suid-Afrika betrag, hoe meer kom mens onder die besef dat daar meer was as mense planne of mense leiding. En daarby nog wat 'n kleurryke geskiedenis! Watter jong volk kan op 'n meer romantiese geskiedenis roem, een van meer ingrypende menslike belang? Kleur, insident, tragedie en komedie, nederlaag en oorwinning, vreugde en smart—ons voor-geskiedenis is vol van die aangrypendste menslike belang. Had ons maar die pen van die Grieke, wat 'n literariese bydrae sou ons maak tot ons toekomstige skatte! Daar is goud nie alleen in ons aarde nie, maar nog meer in ons geskiedenis. Daar was so min teken van 'n vas deurdagte plan, so veel van die misterie. Die Voortrekkers was as siende die onsienlike. Die dringende nood het na 'n uitweg uit diep-gevoelde griewe en moeilikhede gesoek. Die uitweg het heel iets anders geblyk as wat voorsien of verwag was, en so is 'n mirakel van die geskiedenis gebore.

Selfs by die oorspronklike aanleg van die volksplanting aan die Kaap was daar nie 'n nedersettings plan nie, maar eenvoudig die bedoeling om vars water en voedsel vir die skeepsvaart op weg na die ooste te verseker. Deur die owerheid in Nederland is gedurig pogings aangewend om 'n volksplanting te voorkom, en veral om die verder verspreiding na die binneland to belet. Allerhande perke, een na die ander, is vasgestel—hier 'n rivier, en daar 'n berg. Maar niks kon die ingebore wanderlus stopset nie, selfs nie die gevaar van ernstige botsing met onbekende inboorling stamme. So is die grenslyn steeds verder verskuiwe, oostwaarts en noordwaarts, totdat die Oranjerivier in die noorde, en die Groot Visrivier in die Ooste bereik is. Hoe verder, hoe erger het die botsinge met die naturelle stamme ontvlam, en het die troebels met die Britse owerheid geword. Uiteindelik is maar wanhopig besluit om weg te trek, die ou geliefde plase te verlaat, die Oranjerivier oor en die onbekende wereld in, om 'n nuwe land as tuiste te soek.

So klein was die begin, maar hoe verbasend groot die uitkoms! Nie alleen die Voortrekkers, maar ook die skeppende gees van die geskiedenis was op tog na die onbekende toekoms. Die onsigbare Hand was besig om groot geskiedenis te skrywe. Ons vandag op hierdie spioenkop kan sien wat geen Voortrekker ooit van gedroom het.

Soos ek gesê het, was die Voortrek geen omvattende georganiseerde beweging nie, maar veel meer 'n aantal afsonderlike trekke van klompies mense onder afsonderlike leiers—Trichardt, van Rensburg, Potgieter, Cilliers, Uys, Maritz, Piet Retief, en eindelik Pretorius. Daar was maar min gesamentlike optrede. Daar was eer onenigheid en verwydering onder die leiers. Die verbasende resultate was gedeeltelik te wyte aan die moed, die volharding, die hoë kwaliteit van siel, wat hier 'n uitstaande menslike drama geskep het; en gedeeltelik te wyte aan die loop van omstandighede, die onberekenbare faktor in die geskiedenis, in alle geskiedenis.

In verband met die Voortrek wil ek korteliks op twee aspekte wys, wat veral die Engelse en naturelle bevolking betref.

In die eerste plaas was daar 'n groot mate van hartelike samewerking tussen die ou Afrikaner bevolking en die nuwe pasaangekome Engelse setlaars in die oostelike grensgebied van die Kaap. Daar was 'n goeie gevoel en daar was gesamentlike optrede in die Kaffer-oorloë. Selfs met die trek was daar sterk Engelse simpatie met die Trekkers in hul duister onderneming. Getuie die Bybel wat as aandenking aan Jacobus Uys deur die Setlaar gemeenskap van Grahamstown geskenk was. Piet Retief in sy afskeids memorie maak geen verwyt teen sy Engelse medeburgers, maar alleen teen die regering. In Natal weer was daar alle bewys van goeie gevoel en relasies tussen die Voortrekkers en die weinige setlaars te Port Natal, en in die slae wat later teen Dingaan gelewer is, het hul saam geveg, en is Engelse bloed langs Afrikaner bloed gestort. Van rassegevoel tussen blankes was daar geen teken.

In die twede plek was daar selfs tussen die Voortrekkers en die naturellebevolking geen besonder vyandelike gevoel nie, hoewel die mense bitter swaar gely het van die strooptogte en vee-roof op die oos grens. Getuie die veilige Uys verkenningstog deur die Kaffer gebiede na Natal en terug. Getuie die vele Afrikaners wat, oorhoop met die Britse regering, veilig verblyf by die Kafferstamme gevind het—die Bezuidenhouts, Trichardts, van Rensburgs, en vele andere. Getuie die groot getalle kaffer en kleurling bediendes wat die Voortrekkers vergesel het en soet en suur, en selfs die dood, met hul gedeel het. Getuie ook die goeie ontvangs en steun wat die Voortrekkers van verskeie kafferhoofde ontvang het, soos onder andere, van Moroka. 'n Slegte gevoel en verhouding is eers daarna ontstaan, as gevolg van die wrede aanvalle en moorde deur Moselekatse aan die Vaalrivier, en Dingaan in Natal. En daarby moet ons nog erken dat albei dwingelande geen onderskeid gemaak het tussen Voortrekkers en hul eie swart stamgenote, wie hul ewe meedoënloos by die honderde-duisend uitgeroei het. Die Voortrekker stryd was nie teen die Naturel as sulks, maar teen die barbaarse opperhoofde wat met hul Zulu leërs die binnelande van Natal, Transvaal en Vrystaat 'n woestyn gemaak het, en so doende onwetend dié wêreld vir blanke nedersetting skoongemaak het. Op die wyse is die Voortrekkers grotendeels 'n ope wêreld ingetrek, waar hul die oorblyfsels van uitgeroeide stamme ontmoet het, en in hul beskerming geneem. Die beskuldiging as sou die Voortrekkers die Naturelle van hul grond beroof het is grotendeels ongegrond. Die vreedsame oorblyfsels van verwoeste stamme is onder Voortrekker beskerming geneem en is in besit van hul grond gebly, en is vandag nog in die reserwes en lokasies wat in ongestoorde Naturelle besit bly. Vegkop, Mosega, Bloedrivier, Makapanspoort, en dergelyke insidente was noodsaaklik om aanvalle te straf en die mag van die barbaarse tiranne vir goed te breek, en wet en orde die erfdeel ook van die Naturel te maak. Die Afrikaner het nie die uitroeiingsbeleid gevolg nie, wat in ander lande die inboorling kwessie van die nuwe inkomelinge opgelos het.

Hierdie helde periode is ongelukkig gevolg deur 'n tyd van onderlinge troebels onder die Voortrekkers toe seker swakhede, waarop ek al gewys het, meer prominent op die voorgrond getree het, en 'n skadu op die glans van die Voortrek gewerp het. Verskille en onenighede onder die leiers het tot verwarring in die beweging gelei. Natal, aan haarself oorgelaat, is vroeg 'n Britse Kolonie geword. Die Vrystaat en Transvaal het geskei, tot nadeel en selfs gevaar vir albei. In die Transvaal is daar gedurige twiste ontstaan, wat in een of ander vorm voortgeduur het tot die opkoms van die kolossale figuur en ferme leiding van Paul Kruger. In gesprekke wat ek met hom had in die jare toe ek Staatsprokureur van die Republiek was het hy my veel kon vertel van daardie tyd toe hy self teen wil en dank in die partytwiste gewikkel was—nie sonder geweld, nie sonder bloedvergieting nie. Dié voortdurende getwis het bygedra tot die innerlike swakheid van die Republiek, wat later voorgegee was as die rede vir die ongelukkige inmenging van die Britse regering en die anneksasie van Transvaal, wat op die eerste Vryheidsoorlog uitgeloop het. Hierdie ongelukkige ontwikkelinge is weer gevolg deur die ontdekking van die diamant- en goudvelde, die instroming van 'n nuwe Europese bevolking, die ontginning en ekonomiese ontwikkeling van die binneland en die intree van Suid-Afrika in 'n heel nuwe fase van haar geskiedenis, met steeds toenemende stremming tussen die oue en die nuwe bevolking, wat uiteindelik deur die Twede Vryheidsoorlog gevolg is, 'n oorlog wat terselfdertyd, hoewel ons dit destyds nie besef het nie, maar die eerste skot was in die groot wêreldoorloë van hierdie eeu. Die oormag in die ongelyke stryd was te groot en by die Vrede van Vereeniging het dit geskyn asof dit die einde was, en asof die grenslose opofferings van die worstelstryd tevergeefs was gewees.

Dit was nie die einde nie, maar slegs 'n nuwe begin. Uit die smarte en weë is gebore die nuwe Suid-Afrika. Ag jaar na Vereeniging is die antwoord daarop gevolg in die verwesenliking van 'n verenigde Suid-Afrika. Die Vereeniging van oorgawe was geword die groter Vereeniging van Suid-Afrika. Die grootste droom van die voorgeslag was op wonderbaarlike wyse verwesenlik geword.

Vir die nuwe verenigde Suid-Afrika het 'n wyer gesigseinder verrys, en het ook 'n nuwe gees in ons blanke rasseverhoudings gekom. Dit was ook net in tyd, voor die storme van ons eeu oor die hele wêreld losgebars het. Dit word algemeen erken dat, as gevolg van die Tweede Vryheidsoorlog, 'n radikale verandering in Brittanje's houding teenoor Suid-Afrika plaasgevind het. Die opofferinge in daardie stryd, oneindig groter as dié van die Voortrek, was nie tevergeefs gewees nie, en binne vyf jaar daarna is selfregering aan die ou Republieke toegeken. As gevolg weer van hierdie verandering het Suid-Afrika haar deel geneem aan die twee wêreldoorloë wat daarop gevolg het. Van weerskante is dus die brug gebou oor die klowe wat in die neëntiende eeu in Brits-Afrikaanse relasies ontstaan het. Versoening en medewerking het die ou vervreemding vervang. En so is onder Hoër leiding die goede uit die kwade gebore.

Langs hierdie moeilike weg het die jonge Staat sy koers deur twee wêreldoorloë kon vind, en steeds in aansien en status kon groei, totdat hy sy volkome internasionale erkenning verkry het en sy plaas in die staterei van die volke as gelyke ingeneem het. Daar staan ons vandag, en met trots en dankbaarheid kan ons terugkyk na die heldeverlede.

Wat van die toekoms? Die weg deur die wêreld is nooit sonder gevaar, en minste van al vandag, in die groot wêreldrewolusie wat die lot van die mensheid oorskadu. En in die besonder sal die pad van die Europese gemeenskap op hierdie Afrikaanse vasteland nie een van rose wees nie. Laat ons dus nie dweep met ons verlede nie, en nie deur ons verlede te romantiseer op 'n dwaalspoor geraak nie, maar met ope oë en gesonde verstand nugter die toekoms tegemoet gaan. Die heimwee na die verlede kan in 'n verkeerde rigting lei. Ons is 'n toekoms volk, en ons toekoms lê op die weg en in die geselskap van die Westerse beskawing.

Paul Kruger, in sy laaste boodskap aan die volk, het ons opgeroep om in die verlede te soek wat goed en skoon is, ons ideaal daarna te vorm en vir die toekoms te verwesenlik. Die goede en die skone! Geregtigheid verhoog 'n volk. Alleen op daardie dieper fondament kan die goeie samewerking en die broederskap tussen ons blanke volksdele gekonsolideer word, en die toekoms van ons blanke gemeenskap blywend gewaarborg word. Op dieselfde etiese basis, meer as op politieke grondslag, kan ook 'n oplossing gesoek word van die grootste vraagstuk wat ons van die voorgeslag geërf het—die vraagstuk van ons naturelleverhoudings. Die vraagstuk neem steeds duideliker vorme aan met die voortdrang van die Europese besetting en beskawing op die Afrikaanse vasteland as integrale deel van die Weste. In die gees van menslikheid, van die goede en die skone, waarop Paul Kruger die nadruk gelê het, kan ons die sleutel vind vir die oplossing ook van hierdie moeilikste van al ons vraagstukke en die finale toets van ons Westerse Kristelike beskawing.

Bo-op die Andes gebergte van Suid-Amerika, op die grens tussen Argentinië en Chile, staan daar 'n monumentale kruis, die Kristus van die Andes genoem, opgerig na lange stryd tussen hul as simbool van ewigdurende vrede. Laat hierdie monument van ons wordingsgeskiedenis 'n soortgelyke simbool wees, die Kristus van Afrika, simbool nie alleen van die verlede stryd, van die bloed en trane, maar ook van ons versoening en ewigdurende vrede, en van ons gelofte om ook in ons ras- en kleurverhoudings steeds die regverdige, die goede en die skone na te volg.

TRANSLATION

Today we stand on a vantage point from which we can look back upon three centuries of our history and also, in some measure, forward into the shadows of the future. A nation is not the creation of a day but of centuries—of the past as well as of the future. Only in this context, in summing up the long years of a people's existence, do we discern the continuous direction and can we form a truer conception of the tendency and course of our history and of our distant destiny. Behind us we see, with the deepest thankfulness, the clear evidence of higher guidance through deadly dangers, of escape by unforeseen paths. The more one reflects upon the genesis of South Africa, the more one comes to realize that there was more than human planning and human leadership. And what a colourful history as well! What young nation can boast a more romantic history, one of more far-reaching human interest? Colour, incident, tragedy and comedy, defeat and victory, joy and sorrow—our early history is full of the most gripping human interest. If only we had the pen of the Greeks, what a literary contribution we should make to our future treasures! There is gold, not only in our earth, but still more in our history. There was so little sign of any preconceived plan, so much of mystery. The Voortrekkers were as seeing the invisible.[1] Their urgent need sought a way out of deeply felt grievances and difficulties. That way out appeared as something quite different from what was foreseen or expected, and so a miracle of history was born.

Even when the original colony at the Cape was begun[2] there was no plan of settlement but simply the intention to ensure fresh water and food for shipping en route to the east. The authorities in the Netherlands made constant attempts to prevent the planting of a colony and especially to forbid further expansion to the interior. One after the other all sorts of limits were set—here a river, there a mountain. But nothing could stop the inborn wanderlust, not even the danger of serious clashes with unknown Native tribes. So the frontier was always shifted further, eastwards and northwards, until in the north the Orange river and in the east the Great Fish river were reached. The further it moved, the worse did conflicts with the native tribes and troubles with the British authorities become. At last, in despair, it was decided to trek away, to leave the old beloved farms, to move over the Orange river into unknown country and seek a new homeland.

The beginning was so small, but how astonishingly great was the outcome! Not only the Voortrekkers but also the creative spirit of history was on a journey to an unknown future. The invisible Hand was busy writing great history. We today on this vantage point can see what no Voortrekker ever dreamed of.

As I have said, the Trek was not a comprehensive, organized movement, but far more a number of separate treks of groups of people under different leaders—Trichardt [L.], van Rensburg [J.J.J.], Potgieter [A.H.], Cilliers [S.A.], Uys [J.J.], Maritz [G.M.], Piet Retief, and finally Pretorius [A.W.J.]. There was little combined action. Rather was there discord and estrangement among the leaders. The astonishing results were partly due to the courage, the persistence, the high qualities of soul which here created an outstanding human drama; and partly to the course of circumstances, the incalculable factor in history, in all history.

[1] 'By faith he forsook Egypt, not fearing the wrath of the king: for he endured, as seeing him who is invisible.' *Hebrews* xi.27.

[2] Jan Anthonisz van Riebeeck arrived in Table bay on board the *Drommedaris* on 6 April 1652 to establish a supply station for the ships of the Netherlands East India Company.

In connection with the Trek, I wish to refer briefly to two aspects which concern especially the English and the Native population.

In the first place there was a large measure of hearty co-operation between the old Afrikander population and the new, recently arrived English settlers[1] in the eastern frontier districts of the Cape. There was good feeling and combined action in the Kaffir wars. Even as regards the Trek there was strong English sympathy with the Trekkers in their strange undertaking. Witness the Bible which was presented to Jacobus Uys by the Settler community of Grahamstown. Piet Retief in his farewell manifesto makes no reproach against his English fellow-citizens, but only against the government. Again, in Natal there was every evidence of good feeling and good relations between the Voortrekkers and the few settlers at Port Natal; they took part in the battles later fought against Dingaan and English blood was shed along with Afrikander blood.[2] There was no sign of racial feeling between the whites.

In the second place there was, even between the Voortrekkers and the Native population, no particularly antagonistic feeling although the people suffered bitterly and heavily from raids and cattle-stealing on the eastern frontier. Witness the safe reconnoitring journey of Uys[3] through the Native regions to Natal and back. Witness the many Afrikanders who, at loggerheads with the British government, found safe lodgement with the Native tribes—the Bezuidenhouts,[4] Trichardts, van Rensburgs, and many others. Witness the large numbers of Native and Coloured servants who accompanied the Voortrekkers and shared with them the sweet and the sour and even death. Witness also the good reception which the Voortrekkers received from various Native chiefs, such as, among others, from Moroka. Bad feeling and a bad relationship appeared only afterwards as a result of the cruel attacks and murders by Moselekatse on the Vaal river and Dingaan in Natal. Moreover, we must admit that both tyrants made no distinction between the Voortrekkers and their own black fellow-tribesmen whom they

[1] They had arrived in 1820.

[2] Alexander Harvey Biggar (1781–1838) and his sons Robert (1812–1838) and George (1820–1838) were all killed while fighting with the Voortrekkers in Natal against the Zulus.

[3] In September 1834 P. L. Uys led a reconnoitring expedition from Uitenhage along the coastal route to Port Natal. He returned early in 1835.

[4] Johannes and Frederik Bezuidenhout and other inhabitants of the extreme eastern frontier of Cape Colony repeatedly defied the British authorities and lived for the most part among the Xosa tribes. In 1815 the Bezuidenhouts started the unsuccessful Slachter's Nek rebellion after a vain attempt to enlist the help of the Xosa chief, Gaika.

exterminated just as mercilessly by the hundred thousand. The Voortrekker struggle was not against the Native as such, but against the barbaric chiefs who, with their Zulu armies, made a desert of the interior of Natal, the Transvaal and the Free State and, in doing so, unwittingly cleared that country for white settlement. In this way the Voortrekkers moved into largely open country where they met and took under their protection the remnants of exterminated tribes. The accusation that the Voortrekkers robbed the Natives of their land is for the most part unfounded. The remnants of shattered tribes were taken under Voortrekker protection and remained in possession of their land and today are still in the reserves and locations which remain in undisturbed Native possession. Vechtkop,[1] Mosega,[2] Blood river, Makapanspoort[3] and similar incidents were necessary to punish attacks and break the power of the barbaric tyrants for good, and to make law and order the heritage of the Natives as well. The Afrikanders did not follow the policy of extermination which, in other countries, solved the Native question for the newcomers.

This heroic time was unfortunately followed by a period of troubles among the Voortrekkers when certain weaknesses to which I have already referred came more prominently to the fore and cast a shadow on the lustre of the Trek. Differences and divisions among the leaders led to confusion in the movement. Natal, left to itself, early became a British colony.[4] The Free State and the Transvaal separated, to the disadvantage, and even danger, of both. In the Transvaal constant disputes appeared, which persisted in one form or another until the rise of the colossal figure and firm leadership of Paul Kruger. In conversations which I had with him in the years when I was state attorney of the Republic he could tell me much about that time when, in spite of himself, he became involved in the disputes of the factions—not without violence, nor without bloodshed. This continual quarrelling contributed to that inner weakness of the Republic which was later professed as the reason for the unfortunate intervention of the

[1] On 19 October 1836 forty Voortrekkers under Hendrik Potgieter beat off an attack by some 5,000 Matabele at Vechtkop in the north-eastern Orange Free State.

[2] In January 1837 a punitive expedition led by Hendrik Potgieter attacked the Matabele at Mosega, north of the Magaliesberg, killing some 400 men and recovering 7,000 head of cattle. *See also* vol. I, p. 649.

[3] In June 1868 Paul Kruger led a force of about 750 Boers against the tribesmen of Mapela and Makapan at Makapanspoort in the Waterberg range in the Transvaal.

[4] English traders and hunters first settled at Port Natal in 1824. In 1837 a British official was sent there to act as magistrate. An attempt to establish a Voortrekker republic in Natal was frustrated by British military occupation and formal annexation as a district of the Cape Colony took place in August 1845.

British government and the annexation of the Transvaal that ended in the first war of liberation.[1] These unfortunate developments, again, were followed by the discovery of the diamond and gold fields,[2] the streaming in of a new European population, the exploitation and economic development of the interior and the entrance of South Africa upon an entirely new phase in her history, with ever increasing strain between the old and the new population, which in the end was followed by the second war of liberation[3]—a war which at the same time (although we did not realize it then) was but the first shot in the great world wars of this century. The superior power in the unequal contest was too great and at the peace of Vereeniging[4] it seemed as if it was the end and as if the limitless sacrifices of the struggle had been in vain.

It was not the end, but only a new beginning. Out of pain and grief a new South Africa was born. Eight years after Vereeniging the answer to it was given in the realization of a united South Africa. The 'Union'[5] of surrender had become the greater Union of South Africa. The greatest dream of our ancestors had, in miraculous fashion, been realized.

For the new united South Africa a wider horizon opened and a new spirit informed white race relations. And it was only just in time, before the storms of our century burst upon the whole world. It is generally acknowledged that, as a result of the second war of liberation, a radical change took place in Britain's attitude to South Africa. The sacrifices made in that struggle, infinitely greater than those of the Trek, had not been in vain and within five years self-government was granted to the republics. Again, as a result of that change, South Africa had her share in the two world wars that followed. So, from both ends, the bridge was built over the chasm which existed in British–Afrikander relations in the nineteenth century. Reconciliation and co-operation replaced the old estrangement. And so, under the higher guidance, good was born out of evil.

Along this difficult road the young state was able to find its way through two world wars and constantly to grow in prestige and status until it won full international recognition and took its place in the array of the nations as an equal. There we stand today and we can look back with pride and gratitude to the heroic past.

[1] *See* vol. I, p. 104, note 1.

[2] The alluvial diamond diggings at the junction of the Vaal and the Harts rivers date from 1868; the dry diggings, where Kimberley now stands, from 1871. The main gold-bearing reef of the Witwatersrand was discovered in February 1886.

[3] The Anglo-Boer War (1899–1902).

[4] Signed on 31 May 1902.

[5] *Vereeniging* means union (Afrikaans).

What of the future? The way through the world is never without danger, least of all today in the great world revolution which overshadows the lot of mankind. More particularly, the path of the European community in this African continent will not be one of roses. So let us not be fanatical about our past and, by romanticizing it, get on to the wrong track; but let us face the future soberly with open eyes and commonsense. Nostalgia for the past could lead us in the wrong direction. We are a people of the future and our future lies on the road of Western civilization and in its company.

Paul Kruger, in his last message to the people, called upon us to seek in the past what is good and beautiful—to shape our ideal accordingly and realize it for the future. The good and the beautiful! Justice exalts a people.[1] Only on that deeper foundation can fruitful co-operation and brotherhood between our white peoples be consolidated and the future of our white community be lastingly ensured. On the same ethical rather than political basis a solution might also be sought of the greatest problem which we have inherited from our ancestors—the problem of our Native relations. The problem continues to take clearer shape as the European occupation and civilization of the African continent as an integral part of the West surges forward. In a spirit of humanity, of the good and the beautiful which Paul Kruger stressed, we might find the key to the solution of this problem too—the most difficult of all and the final test of our Western Christian civilization.

On the top of the Andes mountains of South America, on the border between the Argentine and Chile, there rises a monumental cross called the Christ of the Andes, set up after long strife between them as a symbol of eternal peace. May this monument of our historic beginnings be a symbol of the same kind—the Christ of Africa—a symbol not only of past strife, of the blood and tears, but also of our reconciliation and eternal peace—and of our vow always to pursue, in our race and colour relations as well, the just, the good and the beautiful.

865 To S. G. Millin — Vol. 102, no. 174

Doornkloof
Transvaal
20 December 1949

My dear Sarah, Thank you for your note. No, I shall be away this week and early next week, so as to shake off the dust of recent

[1] 'Righteousness exalteth a nation.' *Proverbs* xiv.34.

events and doings. So I shall not see you before I go down to the Cape, where I look forward to bathing in your waters. I hope to be back at the Mount Nelson by 10 January.

The celebration of the monument has come and gone—and all the better so. What its ultimate effect will be is 'anybody's guess'. Let us hope that its evil will be forgotten and some of its good remain. For our European relations it has on the whole been good. But its repercussions on our non-European relations will be bad, and that is what weighs heaviest. But why dilate on that vast theme? The whole world is moving into a 'Colour' phase of history, with results none can foresee and South Africa should dread most. Still, the worst, like the best, never happens.

A happy, fruitful new year to you and Phil, and may the good God give you your heart's desire. Ever yours,

J. C. Smuts

866 To L. S. Amery — Vol. 91, no. 355

Doornkloof
Irene
Transvaal
23 December 1949

My dear Amery, Just a line of warm good wishes to you and dear Mrs Amery for the new year. You may remember Carlyle's translation of one of Goethe's symbolism verses:

> The future hides in it gladness and sorrow,
> Nought that abides in it damping us,
> Forward!

And so we move on to 1950 which may prove a very eventful year in an age of rapid transition. May it hold more gladness than sorrow for all of us, and for mankind now labouring in the trough of the sea.

I have just been reading *Thought and Language*[1] which you kindly sent me while in London. It is full of good stuff and I have enjoyed all of it very much.

Here our centenary Voortrekker celebrations have passed without a hitch, which so many feared. But the Nationalists have reaped a rich harvest of emotionalism from it. May 1950 be a good year for you in England and for us here. We shall see! With kind regards and real affection for both you and Julian, Ever yours,

s. J. C. Smuts

[1] Amery's presidential address to the English Association, published in 1949.

867 To S. M. Smuts Vol. 95, no. 108

Mount Nelson Hotel
Kaapstad
14 Januarie 1950

Liefste Mamma, Gister veilig hier aangekom, maar O so'n reis vir 4 uur op my sterk [*sic*] wat al ondraagliker geword het! Maar ook dit het tot 'n einde gekom. Toe na die hotel waar Frankie Forman met sy instrumente was na lunch en my goed ondersoek het, na al die inligtings wat Louis hom gestuur het. Hy het toe my ruggraat ondersoek totdat hy die verplaatste vertebra gekry het en daarin het hy 'n teëgif ingespuit. Hy glo nie baie in die idee van Louis en Guy Elliot, wat maar in seker gevalle van toepassing is. Maar na 'n nag alhier moet ek sê dat et tot hier toe geen verbetering in die Forman behandeling vind nie. Hy sal natuurlik weer kom sodra ek hom laat roep, en so sal ek maar moet voortsukkel. Vannag goed geslaap, maar die sit en loop bly maar baie pynlik.

Hier was die Gilletts op dieselfde vloer en ek sal baie van hul sien daar hul liefderik is en sonder eenig ander besigheid! Gisteraand was Daphne Moore hier vir ete en kon my vertel dat Henry nou al byna 'n maand in pleister by die Monastery lê...Hier op die hotel was alles vir my mooi gereed en ek het in my ou woonstel ingetrek. Vernon Thomson het my kom sien voor sy vertrek en hy het baie liefde vir Ouma gestuur. Hy is heeltemaal verlief op jou en ek sal hom moet waarsku! Nou groete en baie liefde aan jul almal.

Pappa

Alles hier in order gevind en tot dus ver lyk niks te Doornkloof vergeet nie, behalwe die liefde wat altyd agter bly!

TRANSLATION

Mount Nelson Hotel
Cape Town
14 January 1950

Dearest Mamma, Arrived here safely yesterday but oh, that journey of four hours on my bottom which became more and more unbearable![1] But that also came to an end. Then to the hotel where Frankie Forman appeared after lunch with his instruments and gave me a thorough examination after all the information Louis [McIldowie] had sent him. He then examined my spine

[1] Smuts was suffering from an acute pain in his back and left hip which began suddenly at Doornkloof shortly before he left for the parliamentary session in Cape Town.

until he found the displaced vertebra and into that he injected an antitoxin. He has not much belief in Louis' and Guy Elliott's idea, which applies only in certain cases. But after a day here I must say that I have up to now not felt much improvement from the Forman treatment. He will of course come again as soon as I call him in; so I shall just have to struggle on. Slept well last night but sitting and walking remain very painful.

The Gilletts[1] were here on the same floor and I shall see a good deal of them as they are affectionate and have no other concerns! Yesterday evening Daphne Moore was here for dinner and could tell me that Henry [Moore] has now been lying in plaster at the Monastery[2] for almost a month...Here at the hotel everything was ready for me and I moved into my old suite. Vernon Thomson came to see me before his departure and he sent Ouma much love. He is quite in love with you and I shall have to warn him! Now, greetings and love to you all.

Pappa

Found everything in order here and so far it does not seem that anything has been forgotten at Doornkloof, except the love which always has to be left behind!

868 To L. Curtis — Vol. 95, no. 111

18 January 1950

My dear Curtis, I have your letter and enclosure of 13 January, and have read both with deep interest. I have also read your other recent statements on international developments. It is indeed encouraging to see how deeply you remain interested in the world situation, especially as it affects the peace situation.

We have arrived at such a moment in world history, with dangers so beyond even our imagination, that we sit baffled before the prospect. 'Achilles sits pondering in his tent!'

My hope is that at some early stage we shall see some opening in the darkness, some point where effective action can be directed against the menace, and that then the moment will be grasped.

European union and North Atlantic defence are already advancing far beyond anything dreamt of as possible only a few years ago. So let us not despair. They are not enough, but they are a great advance. It may be that events are outpacing our advances. But it may also be that our own tempo will increase with that of the

[1] M. C. and A. B. Gillett were then staying at Hermanus on the south coast.

[2] A hospital in the Cape Peninsula.

events. So let us not lose heart and cry havoc.[1] You and others like you remain as watchers on the towers, and I hope your counsel will not go unheeded.

Good-bye, my friend and old colleague. All warm good wishes. Ever yours sincerely,

s. J. C. Smuts

869 To S. M. Smuts — Vol. 95, no. 112

Mount Nelson Hotel
Kaapstad
19 Januarie 1950

Liefste Mamma, Baie dankie vir jou brief van 16 deser, met al die nuus daarin. Ek is jammer te hoor dat jy weer die hoofpyn aanval gekry het, en dat pokkies op die plaas is. Laat ons na beterskap uitsien.

Wat my betref gaan dit stadigaan beter. Mrs Malan die elektriese masseuse wat ook Dr Malan behandel het is al 4 keer hier gewees om my te karnuffel en kom nog aldag. Dit was op advies van Forman wat ook aldag kom. Die pyn in die rug is nog daar en sit en lê bly swaar. Maar stadigaan verbeter dit. Agtermiddag sal ek ons kaukus bywoon en môre die opening van die parlement. Ek *moet* gaan omdat daar wilde praatjies oor my toestand aan gang is. En dit is ook die rede waarom ek maar liewers hier sal moet bly vir behandeling. Die ontmoediging in die land sou anders te groot wees. Maar dit gaan stadig beter, en Forman en Mrs Malan is albei tevrede met my vooruitgang. Dus wees nie ongerus nie. Dinsdag sal ek die wantroue mosie in die Volksraad voorstel, en dit sal miskien die slegste wees. Nuus van Bibas en die Gilletts te Hermanus is goed. Ek is ook maar bly bietjie los van gedurige besoek te wees. Maar parlementslede en vreemde besoekers bly maar steeds op my spoor. Die sit bly nog die swaarste, en ek sou beter doen deur na bed vir 'n tyd te gaan, maar kan dit nie doen nie.

Mrs Malan is 'n liewe vrou en ek hou van haar. Sy kyk na Mushet en so het ek op haar spoor gekom. Allerhande raad word my gegee en nuwe raadgewers aanbeveel. Ek bly maar by Forman en Malan. 'n Pragtige box chokola is my deur 'n Engelse besoeker gegee (Weston) maar ek het dit maar aan die Formans oorgemaak. Die Gilletts kom Maandag terug. Joy is al hier. Sarah Millin is ook op my spoor. Dus kan jy sien wat op my pad lê!

[1] 'Cry, "Havoc!" and let slip the dogs of war.' Shakespeare, *Julius Caesar*, III.i.273.

Stuur my tog nog twee pyjamas, daar ek kortloop—een dun, een warm.

Pappa

TRANSLATION

Mount Nelson Hotel
Cape Town
19 January 1950

Dearest Mamma, Many thanks for your letter of the 16th with all its news. I am sorry to hear that you again had migraine and that there is chicken-pox on the farm. Let us hope things will get better.

As far as I am concerned there is a slow improvement. Mrs [L.] Malan, the electrical masseuse who also treated Dr Malan, has already been here four times to pummel me and still comes every day. This is on the advice of Forman who also comes every day. The pain in my back is still there, and sitting and lying down remain difficult. But it is improving slowly. This afternoon I shall attend our caucus and tomorrow the opening of parliament. I *must* go because wild talk is going on about my condition. And that is also the reason why I had better stay here for treatment. The disheartenment in the country would otherwise be too great. But I am getting slowly better and Forman and Mrs Malan are both satisfied with my progress. So don't be uneasy. On Tuesday I shall propose the motion of no confidence in the government and that will probably be the worst. There is good news of Bibas [Smuts] and the Gilletts at Hermanus. I am rather glad to be free of constant visits. But members of parliament and visitors from abroad are continually on my track. Sitting is still the hardest part and I would do better to go to bed for a while but cannot do so.

Mrs Malan is a sweet woman and I like her. She looks after Mushet [J.W.] and that is how I got to know about her. All manner of advice is offered to me and new counsellors recommended. But I shall keep to Forman and Malan. A beautiful box of chocolates was given to me by an English visitor (Weston) but I passed it on to the Formans. The Gilletts return on Monday. Joy [van der Byl] is already here. Sarah Millin is also on my track. So you can see what lies ahead on my road!

Send me two more pairs of pyjamas as I am running short—one thin, one warm.

Pappa

870 To S. M. Smuts Vol. 95, no. 118

Mount Nelson Hotel
25 Januarie 1950

Liefste Mamma, Dankie vir jou brief. Gister het ek my aanval op die Regeering kon maak, hoewel nie sonder pyn nie. Ek het omtrent een uur gepraat ten einde my linker been nie te ooreis nie. Alles goed afgeloop. Die debat sal nou tot Maandag nog voortduur. Die gees in die Party is goed, en ek bespeur 'n groeiende mate van benoudheid aan die ander kant. Maar devaluasie sal hul van jaar nog op die kussens hou.

Bibas was Saterdag hier en siet daar biesonder goed uit. Die Gilletts sal a.s. terug kom en weer na die hotel. Ek glo nie dat hul plek by Mrs Bolus sal kry nie. Ek hoop maar dat hul nie onnoodig my tyd in beslag sal neem nie. Arthur en David hou geselskap in swem en bergklim te Hermanus. Ek hoop hul sal bly rond ry en ander plekke besoek. My toestand laat nie rond flenter toe nie!...

Hier was aangename geselskap op die hotel toe Freddie's twee neefs, seuns van die ou Kroonprins, hier aangekom het. Liewe mense, en met Cooper het ek hul Sondag na Kaappunt gestuur. Die oudste (Hubertus) kom in S.W. Afrika woon. Maar die jonger (Frederick) is met 'n ryk Engelse dame getroud en gaat na Engeland terug. Ek het dit aan Freddie meegedeel. Nou soentjies en groete.

Pappa

Die behandeling gaan voort, maar die pyn in die been bly ook maar voortduur.

TRANSLATION

Mount Nelson Hotel
[Cape Town]
25 January 1950

Dearest Mamma, Thank you for your letter. I was able to make my attack on the government yesterday, though not without pain. I spoke for about an hour in order not to overstrain my left leg. All went off well. The debate will continue until Monday. There is a good spirit in the party and I detect an increasing measure of anxiety on the other side. But devaluation will keep them in office this year.[1]

Bibas [Smuts] was here on Saturday and looks particularly well. The Gilletts will shortly be back and in the hotel. I do not think they will find room at Mrs Bolus's. I only hope they will not take

[1] The pound sterling had been devalued on 18 September 1949 and the Union followed suit.

up my time unnecessarily. Arthur [Gillett] and David[1] swim and climb together at Hermanus. I hope they will go on driving about and visiting other places. My condition does not allow of gadding about!...

There was pleasant company in the hotel when Freddie's[2] two cousins, sons of the old crown prince,[3] arrived here. Nice people; I sent them to Cape Point with Cooper on Sunday. The eldest (Hubertus)[4] is coming to live in South West Africa. But the younger (Frederick)[5] is married to a rich Englishwoman and is returning to England. I have told Freddie this. Now, kisses and good wishes.

Pappa

The treatment goes on, and the pain in the leg also continues.

871 To S. M. Smuts — Vol. 95, no. 146

Die Volksraad
Kaapstad
19 Februarie 1950

Liefste Mamma, Jy sal bly wees te verneem dat ek baie beter is, en gister 'n wandel van 1½ uur te Christian Beach met gemak kon neem. A. en Margaret het meegewandel—sy vir omtrent half die afstand. Albei lyk baie beter na hul verblyf by Hermanus, en dit is seker dat die visite na Suid-Afrika en viral na Doornkloof vir hul baie goed gedoen het. Maar A. val aan slaap selfs by sy ete! Vrydag vertrek hul van Lulu Bolus na Engeland...

Eergister was daar 'n tuin party by Westbrooke en daarna 'n cocktail by die Watersons. Ek het albei met genoë bygewoon...

Strauss is terug na Johannesburg om die saak van Conroy teen Nicol waar te neem en sal miskien 3 weke weg wees, met meer las op my. Parl. werk gaan maar baie stadig aan, maar ons dons hul maar goed op. Beyers, Marshall Clark, die Johburg onluste en die vroue oor C.O.L. maak hul die lewe baie lastig. Ek verheug my in hul welverdiende leed. Verder alles wel. Suster Malan kom nog maar paar maal per week vir knoppe weg masseer. Maar alles gaan goed vooruit. Weer hier lekker. Liefde en soentjies aan almal.

Pappa

1 David Scott, a university student, who was acting as chauffeur to the Gilletts.

2 Queen Frederica of Greece.

3 Crown Prince Wilhelm of Germany (q.v.).

4 Prince Hubertus of Prussia, born in 1909, came to live on family land in South West Africa in 1950. He died in Windhoek on 8 April 1950.

5 Prince Frederich Georg of Prussia married Lady Brigid Guinness, daughter of the Earl of Iveagh; died 1 May 1966.

TRANSLATION

House of Assembly
Cape Town
19 February 1950

Dearest Mamma, You will be glad to hear that I am much better and could take a walk of one-and-a-half hours on Christian Beach[1] yesterday with ease. Arthur and Margaret [Gillett] also walked—she for about half the distance. Both look much better after their stay at Hermanus, and it is certain that the visit to South Africa and especially to Doornkloof has done them a lot of good. But Arthur falls asleep even at meals! On Friday they leave Lulu Bolus's for England...

The day before yesterday there was a garden-party at Westbrooke[2] and after that a cocktail party at the Watersons. I attended both with pleasure...

Strauss has returned to Johannesburg to take charge of [A. H.] Conroy's case against Nicol[3] and may be away for three weeks—which means a greater burden on me.[4] Parliamentary work goes on slowly but we are letting them have it good and hearty. [General L.] Beyers,[5] Marshall Clark,[6] the Johannesburg disturbances[7] and the women about C.O.L.[8] make life very difficult for them. I rejoice in their well deserved sufferings.

For the rest all is well. Sister Malan comes only a few times a week to massage the lumps away. But everything is going on well. The weather here is pleasant. Love and kisses to all,

Pappa

[1] At Muizenberg in the Cape Peninsula.

[2] Residence of the governor-general at Rondebosch in the Cape Peninsula.

[3] An action for defamation brought against the Reverend W. Nicol (q.v.). A. H. Conroy's claim for damages was dismissed in the Transvaal division of the supreme court and subsequently in the court of appeal in Bloemfontein.

[4] J. G. N. Strauss had, since the death of J. H. Hofmeyr, assisted Smuts in his political work.

[5] General L. Beyers, chief of the general staff, was retired prematurely on 15 March following differences on Defence Force matters with the minister of defence which were not fully disclosed.

[6] The appointment in October 1945 of W. Marshall Clark as general manager of the South African railways was found by the commission of inquiry into the grievances of railway servants (25 January 1950) to have constituted an unjust discrimination 'on account of political considerations' against W. Heckroodt, the then deputy general manager. On 8 February Marshall Clark made it known that he had agreed to retire at once as general manager 'at the repeated and earnest request of the prime minister and the minister of transport'. Two days later Heckroodt succeeded him. *See* the *Cape Times*, 26 January, 8 and 10 February 1950.

[7] On 29 January and 13–14 February riots occurred in the Newclare Native township following arrests for illegal possession of liquor and non-possession of passes. The rioters used stones and revolvers and fired and looted shops. The police used tear-gas and exchanged shots with the rioters.

[8] The rise in the cost of living.

872 To S. M. Smuts Vol. 95, no. 151

Mount Nelson Hotel
22 Februarie 1950

Liefste Mamma, Hartelik dank vir jou laaste brief en vir al die nuus omtrent die Scout Kamp en die Rowallan ontmoeting. Dit was alles interessant en ek is bly dat jul en R. alles so geniet het. Ek sal hom natuurlik hier sien en die goeie indruk nog verder versterk. Ek hoop nou dat jul reën sal kry na die langdurige warm dae. Hier is daar niks oor die weer te kla nie. Wind is somtyds erg en dan brand groot gedeeltes van Tafelberg af, soos nou weer vannag gebeur het.

Ons bly maar besig met die werk in die Volksraad en ek voel tevrede oor die deel wat ons party bydra. Die gevegte word al skerper en van a.s. week sal ons met die Registrasie van die bevolking begin wat seker die hardste gevegte van die sessie sal beteeken. Die eenigste bedoeling van die regeering is natuurlik om die gekleurdes apart vir kiesdoeleindes te registreer en sodoende 'n groot aantal setels in Wes Kaapland vir die Nattes te verseker. Maar jy kan begryp hoe onmoontlik dit is om blank en gekleurd hier van mekaar te onderskei, en al die smart en bitterheid wat dit gaan veroorsaak waar dit byna onmoontlik is 'n lyn te trek. Broers en susters, man en vrou sal nou die gevaar loop van aparte registrasie...

Ek sluit in 'n briefie van Queen Mary se sekretaris. Ook kom daar weer 'n Clothmakers geskenk. Liefde vir almal

Pappa

TRANSLATION

Mount Nelson Hotel
[Cape Town]
22 February 1950

Dearest Mamma, Many thanks for your last letter and for all the news about the Scout camp and the meeting with Rowallan. It was all interesting and I am glad that you and Rowallan enjoyed it so much. I shall of course see him here and strengthen the good impression. I hope that you will now have rain after the long hot days. Here there is nothing to complain of in the weather. The wind is strong at times and then large parts of Table mountain burn out, as happened again last night.

We are still hard at work in the house of assembly and I am satisfied with the share our party is taking in it. The encounters are becoming sharper and from next week we shall begin with the registration of the population[1] which will probably mean the hardest fights of the session. Of course the sole intention of the government is to register the Coloureds separately for election purposes and so ensure a large number of seats in the western Cape for the Nats. But you will understand how impossible it is to distinguish white from coloured here, and all the pain and bitterness that will be caused where it is almost impossible to draw a line. Brothers and sisters, husband and wife will now be in danger of separate registration...

I enclose a note from Queen Mary's secretary. And there is another present from the Clothmakers.[2] Love to all

Pappa

873 To S. M. Smuts — Vol. 95, no. 155

Mount Nelson Hotel
24 Februarie 1950

Liefste Mamma, Die Gilletts vertrek vandag en gisteraand het hul by my ge-eet. Arthur het vroeër weer Skeleton Gorge alleen gaan klim en op verkeerde voetpad geraak, en geëindig met kramp in die been, waaruit 'n meid hom by die Nasionale tuin moes help. Arme Margaret is baie besorg en ek denk werklik dat hy hier in Suid-Afrika gevaarlik kan word.

Ek sluit in knipsels uit die *Times* en *Burger* waaruit jy sal sien van die plan om vir my 'n huis langs die hange van Tafelberg te gee wat deur 'n fonds gebou sal word. Die plaas moet nog deur my gekies word—òf bo Kirstenbosch òf bo Kaapstad. Ek het maar aangeneem omdat dit 'n biesonder eerbewys is, en nie omdat ek met die idee self erg opgenome is nie. Ons sal nog sien wat van die saak sal word, maar dis 'n beetjie laat vir my daarbo te gaan woon gedurende parlements sitting; ek sou denk dat die hemel self 'n geskikter plek sou wees! En wat van die vuurbrande wat my daar kan tref? Ons sal maar afwag wat van die idee gaan word.

My been is nou, so te sê, gesond. Maar ek bly nog hinkende, en Forman kom my môre oggend sien. Dit lyk of my een voet (linker) beetjie meer uitstaan na links as die ander voet, en dit kan die rede van my hink wees. Maar verder geen pyn of ongemak. Suster Malan kom nog elke ander oggend om knoppe weg te masseer.

[1] The Population Registration Act (No. 30 of 1950) was enacted on 22 June.

[2] Smuts had been made a member of the Clothworkers' Company in England in 1917.

Dit lyk vanoggend of die Labourites weer die Engelse eleksie gewen het. Dis jammer. Hier in die Volksraad gaan dit maar op ou trant vorentoe.

Ek het nie gehoor of Bancroft weer terug is in Engeland. Liefdegroete,

Pappa

TRANSLATION

Mount Nelson Hotel
[Cape Town]
24 February 1950

Dearest Mamma, The Gilletts leave today and they dined with me last night. Arthur had earlier again climbed Skeleton Gorge alone, got on to the wrong footpath, and ended with cramp in the leg; he had to be helped out by a maid at the National gardens. Poor Margaret is very worried and I really think he may become a danger here in South Africa.

I enclose cuttings from the [*Cape*] *Times* and *Die Burger* from which you will learn of the proposal to give me a house on the slopes of Table mountain to be built out of a fund. The site is to be chosen by me—either above Kirstenbosch or above Cape Town. I have accepted because it is an exceptional honour, and not because I am myself much taken with the idea. We shall see what comes of it, but it is a bit late for me to go and live up there during the parliamentary sessions. I should have thought that Heaven itself would be a more suitable place! And what about the mountain fires that may hit me there? We shall wait and see what will come of the idea.

My leg is now practically cured. But I continue to limp and Forman is coming to see me tomorrow morning. It looks as if one of my feet (the left) is slightly more turned to the left than the other foot, and that may be the cause of my limp. But there is no pain or discomfort. Sister Malan still comes every other day to massage the lumps away.

It looks this morning as if the Labourites have again won the English election. That is a pity. Here in the house of assembly things go forward as usual.

I have not heard whether Bancroft [Clark] has returned to England. Loving wishes,

Pappa

874 To S. M. Smuts Vol. 95, no. 156

Die Volksraad
Kaapstad
25 Februarie 1950

Liefste Mamma, Ek begin weer goed loop. Gister (Vrydag n.m.) het ek van die hotel na Kloofnek geloop en terug. Vandag (Sat.) weer van Christian Beach langs die see vir 'n uur in geselskap van Daphne Moore wat later by my lunch geneem het. Forman was ook vanoggend hier en is tevrede met my toestand, hoewel die voet 'n beetjie skeef loop—hy sê dit sal van self reg kom. Dus sover goed.

Ek sluit in paar knipsels oor die Berg Cottage wat ek môreoggend 'n geskikte plaas voor gaan uitsoek—òf by Kirstenbosch òf op die berg pad van Kloofnek. Ek wonder of ek eenige van die plekke sal lyk, maar skryf later.

Die geboorte viering gaan baie lastig wees—24 Mei op Johburg, 27 Swartkop, 31 Mei Kaapstad, en daar kom nog 29 Mei te Durban by. Mense is gedetermineerd my gou dood te maak. Hierby moet nog die politieke dae gevoeg word, waarvan daar 'n heel aantal al vasgestel is. Ek wonder of ek op 9 Juni te Cambridge vir Degree Dag sal kan wees.

Soo is die Engelse verkiesings virby, met 'n klein meerderheid vir die Arbeiders. Ek wonder hoe lang hul dit sal kan volhou voor 'n ander verkiesing noodsaaklik word. Dit spyt my dat Churchill nie gewen het nie, en ek vrees dit gaan Engeland kwaad doen, viral in Amerika waar opinie teen die Sosialiste gekant is.

Verder niks te rapporter. Ek sal later rapporteer oor die plaas vir die Smuts-Berg-Huis.

Pappa

TRANSLATION

House of Assembly
Cape Town
25 February 1950

Dearest Mamma, I am beginning to walk well again. Yesterday (Friday afternoon) I walked from the hotel to Kloof Nek and back. Today (Saturday) for an hour along the sea from Christian beach in the company of Daphne Moore who later lunched with me. Forman was here this morning and is satisfied with my condition, although the foot is slightly crooked. He says it will cure itself. So far, so good.

I enclose a few cuttings about the mountain cottage for which

I must choose a suitable site tomorrow morning—either at Kirstenbosch or on the mountain road from Kloof Nek. I wonder if I shall like any of the sites—but shall write later.

The birthday celebrations[1] are going to be a great nuisance—24 May in Johannesburg, 27 May at Swartkop, 31 May in Cape Town—to which must be added 29 May in Durban. People are bent upon killing me quickly. Besides this there are the political days, of which quite a number have already been fixed. I wonder whether I shall be able to be in Cambridge for Degree Day.

And so the English elections are over, with a small majority for the Labourites.[2] I wonder how long they will be able to hold out before another election becomes necessary. I am sorry Churchill did not win and I fear it will injure England, especially in America where public opinion is against the Socialists.

Nothing further to tell. I shall report later on the site for the Smuts Mountain House.

Pappa

875 To S. M. Smuts — Vol. 95, no. 157

Die Volksraad
Kaapstad
26 Februarie 1950

Liefste Mamma, Ek was vanoggend uit om 'n plek te kies vir die Kaapstad gift. Ek het gekies 'n pragtige plek naby Kirstenbosch tuin, net anderkant die ou Herbarium. Dit is mooi geleë tussen silver en ander protea bome en inheemse wilde Afrikaanse plante, in vol gesig van die berg en die tuine, en die verre vlaktes na die noorde waar ek gebore is. As die huis net so lieflik is as die ligging, dan sal niks verder te wens wees nie. Nou sal die stadsraad verder beslis. Jy kan begryp hoe hoog ek die eer en die mooi gevoel waardeer wat tot so 'n gift gelei het. Selfs jy sal dit lyk om hier vir 'n tydjie te vertoef, om nie van die kinders en familie te praat nie. Dit is lief om so deur liefde omring te word te midde van alles wat pla en ontmoedig.

Pappa

[1] Smuts's eightieth birthday on 24 May.

[2] The results of the general election on 23 February were: Labour party, 315; Conservative party, 296; Liberal party, 10; Irish Nationalists, 2.

TRANSLATION

House of Assembly
Cape Town
26 February 1950

Dearest Mamma, I was out this morning to choose a site for the Cape Town gift. I chose a beautiful spot near Kirstenbosch gardens, a short distance from the old herbarium. It is pleasantly situated among silvertrees and other proteas and indigenous South African wild plants, in full view of the mountain and the gardens and the distant flats to the north where I was born. If the house is as charming as the situation, nothing more could be wished for. Now the city council will have to decide further. You will understand how much I value the honour and the good feeling which have led to such a gift. Even you would like to stay here for a while —not to speak of the children and the family. It is sweet to be thus surrounded by love in the midst of everything that tries and discourages.

Pappa

876 To W. S. Churchill — Vol. 95, no. 158

House of Assembly
Cape Town
27 February 1950

My dear Winston, I need not tell you how much my thoughts have been with you these last weeks and how sorry I am that you did not achieve a full measure of success. Still, your own stock stands very high and complete victory in the near future now appears a certainty. Both in Britain and abroad the continuance of the present government in power is awkward, but if there had to be a stalemate, it was better for the Labour government to carry on than for you to struggle under such a handicap. Labour will be impotent and the Liberals have been practically eliminated, so that you will be able to look forward to a resounding victory. All your principal colleagues are in, and so are Sandys [D.] and Soames [C.].[1] I much regret Randolph's [Churchill] defeat.

I trust your heavy labours have not imposed too heavy a strain on you. Your speeches have been magnificent and had all the old ring and appeal. The rest will follow in due course.

Here the Nationalist government are continuing to lose ground

[1] Sons-in-law of Churchill.

all round, and I look forward to my victory following yours in Britain in due course.

With warm regards to you and Clemmie and the family, Ever yours affectionately,

s. J. C. Smuts

877 To L. S. Amery Vol. 95, no. 170

7 March 1950

My dear Leo, I am glad that you have been helpful to Oosthuizen, and hope he will return with useful tips for his future task when we face a general election. The government here are steadily losing support and next year may see a general election.

I assume that the Socialist government will avoid extreme measures and hang on as long as possible. The monetary position, plus the extreme left wing, may render this difficult, if not impossible.

It is indeed regrettable that two men like you[1] and John Anderson are not in the new house. I hope a way out (or in) will soon be found.

I read with great pleasure what you wrote about Julian [Amery]. His mother must be specially pleased with his performance.

Yes, Winston's gesture[2] was a good one, from whatever angle it is viewed. However, personally I expect very little real response from Russia. Russia is on the march unopposed to virtual occupation of the Far East, which the other European powers have evacuated. This is a conjunction of circumstances which has given her a unique opportunity of which she will avail herself to the limit. It is a fateful prospect, not only for the Far East, but for Europe and the whole world. I sometimes think we do not realize the significance of this moment in world history. The only cheerful possibility is that she may leave the West alone and give it an opportunity to integrate and consolidate itself on a scale which will be worthy of the opportunity. Ever yours,

s. J. C. Smuts

[1] Amery did not stand for election.

[2] In the course of an electoral campaign speech at Edinburgh on 14 February Churchill had made a plea for 'another talk with Soviet Russia upon the highest level—a supreme effort to bridge the gulf between the two worlds'.

878 To W. S. Churchill Vol. 95, no. 180

16 March 1950

My dear Winston, In reply to your cable for my views on the Seretse affair,[1] I send you the following note.

The matter has various aspects. In the first place, as regards the way in which Seretse [Khama] has been treated, there is much to be said for his view that he has been tricked into the London visit, and that once having been inveigled to London, he has then been forbidden to return. He should at least have been warned in advance of this possibility. I imagine this is appreciated, and it is possible that the government may now allow him to return, and thereafter banish him from the territory.

As regards the non-recognition of Seretse, I do not see how the government can change their announced decision without grave damage from the South African point of view. A form of passive resistance, or boycott, has already been started by the tribe against the government, and any change now by the government will be looked upon as a capitulation, which might seriously damage British authority, and indeed, all government authority in South Africa. Our Native situation is already a troubled one, and it would be an inducement to Natives in the Union to do likewise, with far-reaching consequences. We have repeatedly had cases where we had to refuse to acknowledge claimants for chieftainship, and it has generally been accepted. Natives traditionally believe in authority, and our whole Native system will collapse if weakness is shown in this regard.

This argument would apply in any case of an unsuitable candidate, but it is here aggravated by the undesirable marriage of Seretse. People, both in South Africa and Rhodesia, are as a whole united in their opinion against Seretse's marriage to a white woman. Indeed, in both countries miscegenation of this kind is legally criminal and would certainly be fatal to any claim to the chieftainship.

Should the British government ignore this sentiment in South Africa, public opinion here would harden behind [D. F.] Malan's claim for the annexation of the protectorates to the Union, and in case this claim were refused, the extreme course of declaring South Africa a republic would at once become a live issue. This

[1] Tshekedi Khama (q.v.) was regent of the Bamangwato tribe in the Bechuanaland protectorate. Seretse Khama (q.v.) his nephew, was heir to the throne. Both were at this time in England where Seretse had married an Englishwoman, Ruth Williams. A faction in the tribal assembly refused to accept her as queen; another faction demanded the return of Tshekedi as ruler. The British government detained Tshekedi, withheld recognition of Seretse as chief, and forbad him to visit his country for five years.

is already the declared policy of the Nationalist party, and any surrender of the British government on the Seretse issue would at once give the Nationalists a very strong argument in favour of annexation, and if refused, of adopting the extreme course of attempting to realize their republic propaganda.

I think this, from a South African point of view, the most serious aspect of the Seretse case. Its gravity for the whole Commonwealth must be evident. South African public opinion might be mobilized in favour of a republic because of the Seretse affair and the refusal of annexation of the territory thereafter.

I believe the feud between the Tshekedi [Khama] and the Seretse factions is another plausible excuse which the British government may have for banishing both from the territory. Whether they will make use of this I cannot at present say. But from all this you will see that the Seretse case in its full implications is full of dynamite, and I think it would be a mistake to exploit British feeling in favour of Seretse to an extent which may damage the relations of South Africa to the Commonwealth and the Commonwealth itself.

I would therefore counsel caution in this matter, as it may raise an issue between South Africa and Britain which I am naturally most anxious to avoid.

I assume this is an expression of my opinion which you want to have. With all good wishes, Ever yours sincerely,

s. J. C. Smuts

879 To J. L. Hotson — Vol. 95, no. 205

House of Assembly
Cape Town
12 April 1950

Dear Dr Hotson, Your letter of 27 March,[1] so unduly flattering to me, calls for a response, which I am very glad to send you.

I heard of your book *Shakespeare's Sonnets Dated* under the following circumstances. When my friend, the actress Marie Ney, was in South Africa last year, we had a talk in the course of which I said that Shakespeare's plays, in my opinion, were founded on personal experience and gave sure evidence that he had passed through deep waters of the spirit and was not merely drawing on his creative imagination. I suggested that the sonnets perhaps

[1] Smuts Collection, vol. 94, no. 35. Dr Hotson had seen in a newspaper that Smuts had been given a copy of his book.

contained the key to his personal story, and on that account also, apart from their supreme quality as poetry, they had always intrigued me. Shortly afterwards, and, I guess, as a result of our talk, she sent me your book of that name.

The interest of the book was for me twofold: (a) it supplied what appeared to me very strong evidence of the dating of the sonnets as far back as 1589, and (b) it confirmed my impression that Shakespeare had passed through the deep experiences referred to in the sonnets in his young years, and before he had begun his career as a playwright.

Your book confirms both these impressions of mine. The references to important contemporary events—the defeat of the Armada, the re-erection of the Egyptian obelisks in Rome by Pope Sextus, the assassination of Henry III of France after his murder of the Guises—all dating from 1588, all well attested as remarkable events by the English contemporary literature, leave little, if any, doubt about the meaning of the apparently cryptic references in sonnets 107, 123, and 124. If I may say so, you deserve great credit for having unearthed the historical material which gives the correct explanation of these references in these sonnets. These references, in their contemporary interest, must have been well understood by Shakespeare's friends but not by posterity after some centuries.

From all this there must be at least a high probability that the sonnets were written about 1589, when Shakespeare was a young man of about twenty-five. And this dating stands in spite of the impression created by the subsequent *Venus and Adonis*, and *Rape of Lucrece*.

This is your dating of the sonnets, and it throws this great light on the dark period of Shakespeare's young manhood—that in these years he passed through a terrific experience such as is revealed in the sonnets, and his genius flowered forth in superb poetry, which places him in the same category of early poetic maturity as Goethe, Shelley, Keats, Wordsworth, to mention no others.

His supreme poetic power appears not only in his later dramas, which are the glories of the world's literature, but already in his admittedly early plays. Through them all there is a reading of the riddle of the human heart which is unmistakable, which appears already most clearly in these sonnets of his comparative youth, and which tells the story of his great passion, of his great initiation and awakening. There is a ring of personal sincerity through them all, and of deep contrition and repentance in the final sonnets, which sound the very depths.

What language, what insight one finds in these early productions!

They are a real revelation, not only of poetic genius at its highest, but also of the human spirit at its deepest. Have you noticed his phrase in sonnet 107, 'the prophetic soul of the wide world dreaming on things to come'? The reference is merely to possibilities of change, but the actual language used compasses the whole range of natural evolution in terms which transcend the vision of Darwin, and which rank with St Paul's great expression of the whole creation labouring in anguish for the Sons of God to come.[1] It is more than majestic poetry; it is an insight into the heart of this universe. And this from a young beginner in poetry. And the sonnets are full of these revelations of the spirit and of reality.

My point is that the sonnets are not only great poetry, but great experience, and if (as now appears probable) they were written by Shakespeare in his youth, the wonder that is Shakespeare becomes all the greater as one of the master spirits of the human race—the wonder boy whose early passionate experience set the whole course of his amazing life-work.

If you are right, as I think you are, you have made a real contribution to the unlocking of a great secret of literature. And I want to thank you for your book, and not merely for your kind letter to me. Yours sincerely,

s. J. C. Smuts

880 To C. van Riet Lowe — Vol. 95, no. 201

12 April 1950

My dear van Riet Lowe, I have read the draft of your Salisbury address[2] with much interest. You indicate that no major alteration is invited, and this makes my task all the easier.

I, myself, would not have emphasized the religious aspect so much, as I doubt whether prehistory bears very clear testimony on that grave issue. But on that point I have no further suggestion to make.

When, however, you suggest Africa as the place of human origin, you, as a scientist, should at least indicate your reasons. The oldest human remains date, not from Africa, but from China and Java. It is only when you pass beyond prehistory that you come to Africa. Taungs, Sterkfontein and Makapan indicate the rock from which the human stock may possibly have been hewn.

[1] *Romans* viii.18–25.

[2] Presidential address to the South African Association for the Advancement of Science at their meeting in Salisbury on 3 July 1950 entitled 'Prehistory and the Humanities' (*South African Journal of Science*, vol. 47, no. 1).

But on this you say nothing at all. I suggest that you strengthen your case by at least a reference to this vastly important scientific work in the Transvaal bearing on the question of human origin. This is merely a point for you to consider. All good wishes to you. Yours sincerely,

s. J. C. Smuts

P.S. I have contacted van der Walt [H.S.] about the Abbé and Miss Boyle, and have received a favourable answer.

881 To M. C. Gillett — Vol. 95, no. 286

In Parliament
17 April 1950

I have letters last week from both you and Arthur. Both make a happy impression of your activities and domesticities. How good the world can be and is in its personal domestic doings, away from the more general activities of mankind! Last week-end I was reading a lot of stuff concerning world affairs in order to keep in touch with developments. The impression is that of a situation which is more and more beyond us and almost beyond human control. Take Germany's part in the West, which is now in its most critical phase—to be in or not in Western Europe. I was so shocked and disappointed to see Bevin's cold statement in the commons that Nazism *is* the German character, and not very much due to Hitler![1] I can appreciate [K.] Adenauer's indignation and what decent Germans must feel when a leading British statesman passes such a judgment on them. It is almost to make one despair of our present statesmanship. I was glad to read Churchill's decided 'no' to this[2]—but the harm is done, and it is very great. It shakes my confidence in the competence of these people to deal with the tangled problem which is Germany. I must say I am becoming more and more dissatisfied with British handling of Western Europe and of Germany, and I sometimes feel that the golden moment is already past, and that now again, as in 1919, the great opportunity has been missed. I read with much appreciation [J.J.] McCloy's fine speech at the Pilgrims' dinner,[3] and it almost appears as if Britain is the nigger in the woodpile, and that 1950,

[1] Speaking on the question of the accession of Germany to the Council of Europe Bevin said: 'The Hitler revolution did not change the German character very much. It expressed it.' (*House of Commons Debates*, vol. 473, col. 323.)

[2] Churchill's comment was confined to the word *no*.

[3] Speech by the United States high commissioner for Germany on 4 April at the Savoy Hotel, London.

like 1919, will be written down as the point where we took the wrong turning. Oh for a Campbell-Bannerman to try the experiment of trust and generosity and imagination! It looks all so wooden and stupid and tired today, as if the creative touch has left our statesmanship. Meanwhile Russia is pursuing a much cleverer course, although her policy is one of evil. We mean good, but we don't trust ourselves to do it, and stand shivering on the brink. Poor Europe, poor world! And for relief we revel in the absurdities of Seretse Khama and worse. Really I do not know what to say in public about these things.

I had a great *braaivleis*[1] last Saturday night in the suburbs, and next Friday I shall have another at Stellenbosch. All this is to beat the tomtom of politics and work up the spirit for the fight... But I must have done too much walking on Saturday and Sunday, as my dicky leg has been giving me trouble again since. I thought that more exercise would be helpful, but I was wrong, although at Doornkloof the walking did me no harm. However I hope to be in order again soon as I have very much to do, and all my time-table is fully booked up.

Today I have been at the conference and the lunch of our ex-soldiers' organization—the B.E.S.L.[2] and had to make speeches on both occasions. I wish that public speaking was not such a feature of public life!

There is still quite a spate of travellers from abroad, who pass through my hotel, and pass the time with me—some very interesting and informative people, but many simply bores who want to see me and no doubt tell others about it. I would so much rather give my time and attention to other things, but I daresay we must live in our world, even if we are not of it. I can enjoy a book or the foreign journals, or even my own company, but this continual presence and pressure of others, and often casuals, try me very severely. I have some good friends in the hotel—Daphne Moore, two Holt sisters who are old South Africans now returned to South Africa, full of interesting talk and knowledge of a social world that I don't know. And others also. But ever and always the cry is for time, and for some privacy to attend to the things I have to do or like to do. I wish I could buy time from these people, but that somehow does not work. Now good-bye. Ever yours,

J.C.S.

[1] Barbecue (Afrikaans). [2] The British Empire Service League.

882 To M. C. Gillett Vol. 95, no. 287

Mount Nelson Hotel
[Cape Town]
22 April 1950

Many thanks for your last letter, which touched me deeply, where you write about the Liberal traditions of your background, and the great changes since in the world and the human outlook. I attach the deepest importance to that old Liberal faith, which was the faith of man, the belief in the divine in us, and which nothing should ever touch. But there can be no doubt that that faith was a simplification of the human situation, and stressed only one side of the picture. Since then we have learnt to appreciate more the force of evil in the world, or rather let me say the vast role which force plays in the world. That has come right into the picture of our time, and we have to build both faith and power into our concept of reality. The devil is also in us, and in our day the devil is having a very good run. With this we must reckon, without glossing it over or attempting to conceal it. I call it evil, but perhaps that is not the right word. In the intellectual sphere we distinguish between fact and value—science dealing with the one and the human sciences with the other. Our liberal human ideals correspond to the element of value in our world, while force, power, represent the element of fact, which has equally to be taken into our reckoning. And there is no doubt that in our age the emphasis of events is on this aspect of force and power. Idealism is almost pushed out, and power with a capital P rules our world. We have to reckon with this as the fact, the governing fact of our age. It stands forth now as a power world, with power groupings relying on the power of territory, government, finance, arms and all the resources at the command of force. Force is now the king. Our ideals and our finer human outlook have to reckon with this situation, and must have power and force behind it to pull through this crisis of history.

It is from this point of view that I am so anxious that our human faith should have behind it that power grouping which will prevent it from being overwhelmed in our day. Russia is now the embodiment of power on the one side, and the United States on the other, and we must form a third grouping based on Europe, and for the present on Western Europe, in order to preserve the essence of that civilized human outlook which Europe has evolved and stood for through the ages. If necessary force must be met by force, in order that force shall not extinguish liberty and our other ideals. I have always looked upon Africa as a part of Europe in this connection, and the British Commonwealth as the political core of it. But Africa is drifting sadly, and the Commonwealth is uncertain and confused and weakened beyond belief. A united Western Europe, in which Britain and the Commonwealth play a strong hand as the guardian of our fundamental political ideals, is necessary to the new set-up we wish to establish against the menace of force and anarchy. At bottom it is a great moral and spiritual issue. But morals and spiritual idealism are in danger unless valiantly backed up by adequate force of its own. In this sense force is necessary for our faith, and must not be derided as evil. May we prove strong enough to hold the fort of liberty and our civilized human faith in the great power struggle now raging in the world. The good is still like an infant crying in the night,[1] and it must not cry in vain, and be allowed to perish. The spirit must be wedded to strength. Such seems to be the meaning of the call to us. The weak ideal must be incarnated into the alien force which will see it through the crisis. Forgive this disquisition which is not a letter, but was prompted by your memory of a simpler and easier world from which we have now drifted sadly and far away. Ever lovingly yours,

J.C.S.

883 To S. M. Smuts Vol. 95, no. 240

Die Volksraad
Kaapstad
29 April 1950

Liefste Mamma, Ek staan net op die punt na die Marsh Home te gaan vir die funksie daar en sal maar eers 'n lyntjie aan jou skrywe. Is vandag of môre ons trou dag? Ek meen môre, maar is nie seker nie. In elk geval denk ek met diepe dankbaarheid aan daardie 53 jaar van ons hoogs gelukkige huweliks lewe. Wat al nie deurgegaan! Wat winste en wat verliese! Wie sou ooit kon gedroom het dat dit ons lewensloopbaan sou wees! As ek vandag terugkyk na dit alles dan lyk dit soos 'n droom. En soos 'n droom het dit ongelooflyk snel virby gegaan. Ons het veel om voor dankbaar te wees, en vir die geskiedenis waarop ons met dank en trots terug kan sien.

Ek is baie besig, nie alleen met die parlementaire werk, maar

1
An infant crying in the night:
An infant crying for the light:
And with no language but a cry.
Alfred Tennyson, *In Memoriam*, liv.

ook met al die voorbereidsels vir die geboorte vierings en vir die afreis na Europe. Daar is baie werk aan dit alles verbonde. Mei 31 vlie ek terug na Irene van hier, om dan Vrydag 2 Juni per K.L.M. na Londen te vlie. Weer 2 uur p.m. soos gewoonlik. Dit breng ons Saterdag 8.30 a.m. te Londen aan. Ek kies die K.L.M. omdat dit slaapkans gee, en ook 'n ander koers oor die Congo en Sahara na N. Afrika neem. Ek sal dus 'n beetjie kan tuis bly om vir die reis te pak. 29 Mei is ek op Durban en vlie dan 30 Mei daar weg vir die groot Kaap ontvangs op dieselfde dag. (23 Mei Johburg, 24 Mei Pretoria en 27 Mei Germiston). Op 19 Mei is daar die Universiteits dinner hier vir my en op 20 Mei vlie ek na Irene, en dan volg die Johburg ontvangs op 23 Mei en Pretoria op 24 Mei deur die vroue van Arcadia. Al die dae sal baie vol wees, en ek sal bly wees wanneer dit alles oor is. En wat 'n tyd sal ek nie oorsee hê nie! Dit is genoeg om mens by voorbaat bang te maak.

My verkoue bly maar baie lastig, die voet ook maak my nog mank. Maar verder is my gesondheid goed. Nou alles van die beste,

Pappa

TRANSLATION

House of Assembly
Cape Town
29 April 1950

Dearest Mamma, I am on the point of leaving for the Marsh [Memorial] Home for the function there and shall first write you a line. Is our wedding anniversary today or tomorrow?[1] I believe it is tomorrow but am not sure. However, I think with deep thankfulness of those fifty-three years of our most happy married life. How much we have experienced! What gains and what losses! Who could ever have dreamed that this would have been our life's course? When I look back at it all today it seems like a dream. And like a dream it has gone by—incredibly fast. We have much to be thankful for, and for a history which we may regard with gratitude and pride.

I am very busy, not only with parliamentary work, but also with all the preparations for the birthday celebrations and for the journey to Europe. There is much work connected with all this. On 31 May I fly back to Irene from here so as to fly to London by K.L.M. on Friday 2 June—again at 2 p.m. as usual. This will get us to London on Saturday at 8.30 a.m. I choose the K.L.M.

[1] It was 30 April.

because it gives one a chance to sleep and because it follows a different route via the Congo and the Sahara to North Africa. So I shall be able to have some time at home to pack for the journey. On 29 May I shall be in Durban and fly from there on 30 May for the big Cape Town reception on the same day. (On 23 May, Johannesburg; on 24 May, Pretoria; on 27 May, Germiston.)[1] On 19 May there is the university dinner here in my honour and on 20 May I fly to Irene after which follow the Johannesburg reception on 23 May and Pretoria's on 24 May by the women of Arcadia.[2] All these days will be very full and I shall be glad when it is all over. And what a time I shall have of it overseas! It is enough to frighten one in advance.

My cold is still very troublesome and my foot still makes me limp. But otherwise my health is good. And now I wish you all that is best.

Pappa

884 To H. M. L. Bolus — Vol. 95, no. 251

The Smuts Collection (Box E) contains drafts and typescripts of sixty-nine forewords written by Smuts between 1917 and 1950. Twenty-eight of these were written during his last premiership and twenty between 1948 and 1950.

House of Assembly
Cape Town
9 May 1950

My dear Lulu, I enclose a draft foreword for *Wild Flowers of the Cape of Good Hope*,[3] which I want you to look through before finalizing it. I have no authorities at hand here, and may have made some botanical misstatements which you could at once put right. If you notice any such, please draw my attention to them.

The foreword is longer than usual, or than is perhaps necessary. But what I say may be of interest to others who do not know some of the facts or theories about our Cape flora.

I have written in great hurry, as I am oppressed with other duties in a very exacting time-table. Ever yours,

J. C. Smuts

[1] The programme was interrupted by Smuts's illness. His last public appearance was on 24 May at Pretoria. On the night of 27–8 May he suffered a coronary thrombosis and was put to bed the next day. See 'The last days of General Smuts'—article by G. A. Elliott in *U.C.T.*, June 1953.

[2] A suburb of Pretoria.

[3] By Elsie Garrett Rice and R. H. Compton, published in 1951.

ENCLOSURE

Foreword (1950)

This is the work for which I have been looking for a long time. And I am not alone. Visitors to South Africa, struck by the beauty and unique character of our Cape flora, have continually asked for some illustrated handbook of our flora, such as most other countries have of theirs. And the answer has always been in the negative. Our flora has an extensive literature and has been deeply studied by scientists, but the results are mostly contained in specialist works beyond the scope of the ordinary plant lover. The books of Dr Marloth[1] are almost unprocurable, and in any case too technical for common use. Our orchids and ericas, our aloes and other distinctive groups have an extensive illustrated literature, and European botanists and artists have vied with one another in describing and painting our plants and flowers. We have also the magnificent *Flowering Plants of Africa*, now in its 26th volume, issued by the botanical division of our agricultural department, which deals largely also with our Cape flora. And there is much other illustrated literature, including journals. But no compendious illustrated handbook of this particular area has been prepared. Now we have an approach to it in this volume, and I for one am truly grateful to Mrs Garrett Rice for these exquisite floral paintings, and to the Botanical Society of South Africa for having made them available to the public. The paintings have the double merit of beauty and of scientific correctness. They will therefore be welcomed, not only by the lovers of our beautiful flowers, but also by students interested in their scientific aspects. From both points of view they are a valuable addition to our floral literature.

And it is from both these points of view that exceptional interest attaches to our South African botany—its beauty and its scientific significance. One can imagine the strange attractiveness which our plant forms and flowers must have had for the early botanists from Europe, who visited the Cape in the seventeenth and eighteenth centuries. They found not only a flora of surpassing beauty, but a flora largely new to them, and of puzzling relationships to the plant life of the old world familiar to them. The beautiful new forms, belonging to families well known in Europe, were collected by them and sent to Europe, to pass into the gardens and herbaria of the old world. They were famous collectors, whose names are honourably remembered, both in South Africa and in Europe, and, through their diligent service to botany, many of the most distin-

[1] R. Marloth, *The Flora of South Africa* (1913, 1915, 1924, 1932).

guished bulbous and dicotyledonous forms, now of world-wide cultivation, passed into botanical world currency from South Africa. Europeans are not aware that many of their floral glories which are now domesticated over the world were introductions from South Africa. Here, as so often in wider respects, justice has not been done to South Africa, except in the select circle of those who know!

But a second point of great scientific interest, to which I wish to draw attention, is the marked scientific difference between the Cape flora and that of Europe, or the northern flora generally. A large number of Cape plant families are endemic to the Cape, or are found nowhere else, except in a number of related genera in South Australia, or South America. This difference raises the intriguing problem of plant origins—the question, namely, whether in addition to the northern origin, which is generally accepted, there was also another independent southern origin, still represented in the Cape flora, with affiliations in some other southern lands. This question concerns not only the plants, but other aspects of the past of this globe.

The possibility of such a second source or origin of our plants was first raised by Sir Joseph Hooker, after a study of Australian botany and that of other southern areas, and it found some measure of support from Charles Darwin. Subsequently the Wegener theory of continental drift seemed to lend further support to this theory of dual origin, and pointed to the possibility of a larger Antarctic continent in the Mesozoic past, which split up in earth movements and lost portions of its territories to other lands. The Gondwanaland theory, connecting southern Africa with southern India geologically, appears to have a bearing on this larger issue. It is also known, from the fossil remains, that the Antarctic continent, as at present known, had about that period a temperate and even subtropical climate, and it may therefore have had an independent flora, now surviving most markedly in its remains in that remnant of Antarctica which attached itself to the toe of Africa, while other connecting land links with Antarctica now lie at the bottom of the Indian or southern ocean. There is further curious evidence in the researches of Dr Marloth, who found that the Cape flora is an ancient, decaying one, now yielding before the younger more vigorous invading flora from the north. He actually thought that he had found at the Cape the shifting battle front between these two flora. Bews [J.W.], again, in his book on *Plant Forms*,[1] has traced the changes of the northern or tropical flora as it passed, or is supposed to have passed, south from the tropics to the temperate part of South

[1] J. W. Bews, *Plant Forms and their Evolution in South Africa* (1925).

Africa. From all these and other lines of thought there seems to be corroborative evidence, pointing to some mysterious southern source of plant life, now surviving most markedly in the small area represented by the Cape flora, with some branch forms in other southern lands.

Of course, it may be said that this has little or nothing to do with the subject matter of this book, but at any rate it emphasizes the mystery which surrounds the unique Cape flora, and it helps to show how the mystery of that flora is part of a larger mystery of this globe, and links up intriguing problems, not only of palaeontology, but also of palaeogeography. South Africa has its mysteries, and they form part of still larger mysteries which belong to the distant past, when the world and its plant and animal life looked very different from what they do as distributed now in newer continents. Science is continuing to probe into these mysteries, and in the meantime we can enjoy them as mysteries, stirring up strange interest in the problems of the origins and movements of life on this globe.

Coming to more recent times, we find that much of this unique Cape flora has been destroyed by man in his veld fires, and in his commercialization of our floral beauty during the centuries of European occupation. Much has disappeared from Table mountain and the other coastal ranges, and is today known to us only from specimens collected by the old scientific collectors, and now found in the herbaria, or as cultivated garden plants. But even so, much, very much, remains which is of priceless beauty and interest. This book will supply ample evidence in support of this statement. Of course, in this destructive process some of the surviving families had been reduced to a single living species, such as *Geissoloma*, now found only in one small portion of the coastal range. (I found some samples once in an area which other parties had ransacked for days in vain.) Another single species of a whole family or order is the remarkable *Welwitschia*, a gymnosperm, surviving in the deserts of the west coast of South West Africa and Angola. In other cases we have a few living survivors of whole genera which have been destroyed by veld fires or collectors; such as the *Orothamnus*, or mountain rose, a most beautiful form still found in a small corner of the coastal range. This ancient flora has plenty of families or genera, represented now by only one or a few living species—remnants of plenty in a glorious past. They, too, form a problem in our botany, which is full of scientific interest.

I may here be allowed to point out a difference in this respect between the botany of northern and central Europe, and that of the Cape. Ours is an ancient aging flora, coming from the time before the south was overwhelmed by the Antarctic ice which still prevails on that continent. The northern flora of Europe, on the other hand, is a young and vigorous one, formerly expelled from most of the north, now once more returning from its southern retreat in the great ice age, and once more reoccupying its old home territory. Europe is now the scene of this return from southern Europe, and the march northwards of this flora can be watched with interest. In South Africa there is the opposite movement, a retreat of the Cape flora before the invading northern flora. Both movements appear to be going on and can be watched by the plant geographers.

For those who care less about these plant movements there remain the still more profound interest in, and enjoyment of, the beautiful, towards which this book will be a valuable contribution. There is here no problem of the strife, and of the beginning or the ending, but only the enjoyment of beauty itself, in its maturity. The vision of beauty, and the enjoyment of beauty in the universe in its purest form can perhaps best be realized in plants. And to see the Cape flora in its full glory in spring or at other seasons after rain—with all its exquisite variety and colour—is an experience never to be forgotten. And when this perfect blending of form and colour is added to other features of the natural scene—the song of birds and the hum of insects and the intoxication of scents—the magic of life is seen and felt in a way which it would be difficult to match elsewhere. Nature blends with the human spirit in what we cannot but call a revelation of what is deepest in both. Something of this spirit may be caught from the paintings in this book.

885 To J. D. Rheinallt Jones Vol. 95, no. 255

10 May 1950

My dear Rheinallt Jones, Thank you very warmly for your letter of 5 May[1] and your anniversary good wishes. I need not say how much I appreciate them and your good will.

I have read the copy of your letter to the prime minister with deep interest, as you will realize. The subject gives me deep anxiety from many points of view. So far all overtures for co-operation on the Native question have been made subject to the apartheid policy,[2] which of course begs the whole question and

[1] Vol. 94, no. 52, enclosing a letter to the prime minister (Smuts collection).

[2] This refers to an exchange of letters between the prime minister, Dr D. F. Malan, and Smuts from 5–25 February 1949 (Smuts Collection, vol. 90, nos. 101–4; vol. 91,

makes a nullity of the constitution guarantees for Native rights. We must now await the prime minister's response to the plea which Senator Brookes and Mrs Ballinger have made to him. Yours sincerely,

s. J. C. Smuts

886 To M. C. Gillett Vol. 95, no. 289

Mount Nelson Hotel
[Cape Town]
11 May 1950

I have just read your last letter (6 May 1950) and enjoyed all your news very much. Thank you for sending me your Dorothy Wordsworth[1] which I shall read with all the more pleasure as it is your copy, and now my birthday gift. I have been reading a good deal of stuff about Wordsworth recently in connection with his centenary. These centenaries remind us how remote that great age of literature is which produced the Lake poets, and the Byron–Shelley–Keats constellation, not to speak of Goethe and Schiller. How poor we appear today, with our scientists and atomic bombs! But the great age will return again. The world's great age may be waiting round the corner although we know it not. All the other news is so delightful—Malcolm Darling,[2] Arthur's travels, the Gillett family with its expansion in the world, visits to Kew and its delights, and so on. It is a good story, and it proves that your life continues as full of interest as ever. And I love to think of you in your glass case[3]—full of warmth and sunshine and the light of the spirit shining within.

How different from my lot! In parliament we are grappling with apartheid and Communism and all the ills poor South Africa fancies herself suffering from. And to add to my burdens the birthday is nearing, and I am overwhelmed with the attentions and loves and congratulations and gifts and what not of a host of friends and interested people. Think of all the correspondence and functions and preparations for functions and speeches. And beyond all looms

nos. 117, 126, 131, 132) which followed a resolution of the house of assembly that Native policy should be examined by an all-party commission consisting of members of both houses. The proposal foundered on the point mentioned by Smuts. The correspondence was published in the press. *See also supra*, p. 279, notes 1 and 2.

[1] E. de Selincourt, *Dorothy Wordsworth. A Biography* (1933).

[2] Sir Malcolm Lyall Darling (q.v.) had returned from a tour in the Middle East to study agricultural co-operatives.

[3] A small greenhouse used by M. C. Gillett as a garden room.

the visit to London and Cambridge which also means a lot of planning and preparing of all kinds. How happy I would be to be for once a forgotten man, and to be free of all these tiresome attentions and preparations. But I cannot see a way of escape. Even my London visit means a pressure on my time from all directions which even in prospect appears heart-breaking. And yet I do wish to get into touch with what is happening in the world and with those who are supposed to know at first hand of what is happening. One can but do one's best to make one's way through this jungle of human pressure, and hope to come out alive at the other end. The darker side of all this is that one secretly fears whether one can do any good in this confused situation and whether one's concern about it does not merely add to the trouble. I sometimes feel rather despondent about it all, and almost inclined to leave alone what is not directly my job. But that again is defeatism.

I am sorry to drag you into discussions of this character, and to bore you with my own insoluble problems. But I hope you will not mind and not feel called upon to answer my conundrums. They reveal my state of mind, and throw no particular onus on yours. I wish I saw the way clearly before me, but partly ignorance and partly the inherent human tangle in its complexity proves too much for me. How much easier the way would be if one saw things in their simplicity and one's duty as a clean and straightforward affair. But it is only at certain times and seasons that a clear light shines on one's way, and the way becomes a joy to go. Now good-night. Ever yours,

J.C.S.

887 From W. S. Churchill Vol. 93, no. 112

Chartwell
Westerham
Kent
14 August 1950

My dear Jan, Your faithful and devoted high commissioner[1] has come down here to say 'Good-bye', and I send you by him a line to tell you with what joy Clemmie and I have watched from afar, but every hour, your grand recovery.[2] I look forward so keenly to see you again. God protect you.

[1] L. Egeland (q.v.).

[2] From the middle of July Smuts had begun to recover from his first heart attack and after 6 August he had been allowed to go for drives.

How strange and terrible to be here, five years from the unconditional surrender of all our mighty foes, in a peril the like of which I have never seen or imagined.

The poor, good people will awake from their helpless pillow, but who shall say it will not be *too late*?

Anyhow we have both done our best, and will keep on to the end of the road. Your affectionate friend,

Winston

888 From L. McIldowie to F. Lamont Vol. 94, no. 144A

12 Ashford Road
Parkwood
Johannesburg
17 October 1950

My dear Aunt Florence, Thank you so much for your very sweet letter. It has been a great comfort to my mother and us all to receive the hundreds of loving messages from all over the world and to feel that we do not mourn alone. My mother was writing to you herself and was suggesting you contact Dr Selzer (Mrs Forman) who is staying at International House for a few months. Her husband was one of the Oubaas's specialists during his illness and they are very good friends of ours.

But I felt you would like to hear of the Oubaas's last months from me too, so I am writing.

Just before the Oubaas came up from Cape Town for his birthday celebrations he started complaining of a pain in his chest suggestive of a coronary thrombosis. How he got through all his celebrations I don't know for he was very ill all the time, but would not give in. Two days before he was due to leave for England he had a very bad collapse and all his plans were cancelled. For the next six weeks he was extremely ill and several times I called the family in as I thought the end had come. Then he improved up to a point and we were all hopeful. A mild bout of flu laid him low again and then it was obvious that his heart was so badly affected that he would never be well again. The last weeks were spent taking him for drives to see the country he loved so much and letting the grandchildren play where he could watch them. My little son—born early in August—gave him great joy and he loved to sit with the little chap on his lap. He would never have been able to climb or walk again as he used to and would not have been able to take an active part in politics again. For that reason, Aunt

Florence, we feel it is best that he went. He would never have been able to tolerate ill health. He died very peacefully and looked so happy in death, with just a suggestion of a smile on his face.

Just the day before he died he still sat chatting to us about that glorious trip we did to the Victoria Falls with you and Uncle Tom and he said that he really must dictate a letter to you to one of us. But alas, it was never done.

My mother has been simply wonderful and carries on with her little daily tasks full of courage and cheerfulness. She has lost about thirty pounds in weight and looks a little thin but is just full of energy. I think she too feels that the Oubaas would not have made a happy semi-invalid and, also, she feels the separation won't be so very long...

Denis joins me in sending our fond love to you Aunt Florence.
Yours very sincerely,

Louis McIldowie

BIOGRAPHICAL NOTES, INDEX

BIOGRAPHICAL NOTES

These notes give information chiefly about the public life of the persons concerned and include, as a rule, their full names, the date and place of their birth, the schools and universities they attended, their main occupation and the date of their death.

Biographies or information about persons not included in the notes below will be found either among the entries in volume IV, pp. 293–401, or in footnotes to the text of volumes V–VII. About ten persons remain unidentified.

Adams, Sir John. Educationalist. Born 2 July 1857, Glasgow, Scotland; educated University of Glasgow; first a schoolmaster, then principal of Free Church training colleges at Aberdeen and Glasgow; lecturer in education, University of Glasgow; principal of London Day Training College; professor of education in the University of London 1902–22; knighted 1925; wrote several books on educational subjects. Died 30 September 1934.

Adenauer, Konrad. German statesman. Born 5 January 1876; educated Universities of Freiburg, Munich and Bonn; practised law in Cologne of which he was lord mayor 1917–33 and 1945; member of provincial diet of the Rhine Province 1917–33; member of the executive committee of the Central party until 1933; founded Christian Democratic Union 1945; chancellor of West Germany 1949–63 and foreign minister 1951–5; advocated German reunification and West European solidarity; resigned office 1963; retired 1966. Died 19 April 1967.

Adler, Alfred. Psychiatrist. Born 7 February 1870, Vienna; qualified in medicine at the University of Vienna; rejected the Freudian psychology and founded a school of individual psychology in 1911; founded child guidance clinics in Vienna 1919; settled in the United States of America 1935; author of a number of books on psychology, notably *The Practice and Theory of Individual Psychology* and *Problems of Neurosis*. Died 28 May 1937.

Aga Khan III, Aga Sultan Sir Mahomed Shah. Indian prince. Born 1877; succeeded his father as head of the Ismaili Mohammedans 1885; founded the All-India Moslem League in support of British rule in India 1906; represented India at the League of Nations in the 'thirties; a well-known owner of race-horses; privy councillor 1934. Died 11 July 1957.

Ahmad Khan, Sir Shafa'at. Indian politician and university professor. Born 1895; educated Universities of Cambridge and Dublin; professor of modern history, University of Allahabad 1921; chairman of All-India Muslim conference 1933–4; high commissioner for India in the Union of South Africa 1944; author of *The Indian Federation: an Exposition and Critical Review* and various works on economics and history.

Alanbrooke, Alan Francis Brooke, first Viscount. British soldier. Born 23 July 1883 in France; educated Royal Military Academy, Woolwich; entered British army 1902; served in India until 1914, then in France; general staff officer 1918–27; commandant, School of Artillery 1929–32; army instructor, Imperial Defence

College 1932–4; inspector, royal artillery; director of military training, war office 1935–7; general officer commanding anti-aircraft command 1939, southern command 1940; commander-in-chief, home forces 1940–1; chief of the imperial general staff 1941–6; field marshal 1944; created baron 1945, then viscount; lord lieutenant, county of London 1950–5. Died 17 June 1963.

Albert I. King of the Belgians. Born 8 April 1875, Brussels; younger son of Philip, Count of Flanders and Princess Marie of Hohenzollern; became heir presumptive in 1891; trained at the École Militaire; married Elizabeth (1876–1965), daughter of the Duke of Bavaria in 1900; succeeded to the throne 1909; commanded the Belgian forces which resisted the German invasion in August 1914 and remained with his troops throughout the war; commanded the northern army group in the allied offensive of October 1918; presided at the colonial congresses (Congo) of 1920 and 1926. Killed while rock climbing near Namur on 17 February 1934.

Alexander, Harold Rupert Leofric George, first Earl, of Tunis and of Errigan. British soldier. Born 10 December 1891, third son of the fourth Earl of Caledon; educated Harrow and Sandhurst; served in France 1914–18; commanded a brigade in India, 1932–4; commander of first brigade 1938; in chief command of the final stages of the Dunkirk evacuation 1940; general officer commanding in Burma 1942; from August 1942 commander-in-chief, Middle East; commander-in-chief, allied armies in Italy and the Mediterranean theatre 1943–5; governor-general of Canada 1946–52; minister of defence 1952–4; promoted general 1942, field marshal 1944. Created viscount 1946, earl 1952; author of *The Alexander Memoirs*. Died 16 June 1969.

Alexander, Samuel. Philosopher. Born 6 January 1859, Sydney, Australia; educated Wesley College, Melbourne; Balliol College, Oxford; fellow of Lincoln College; professor of philosophy, University of Manchester 1893–1924 when he retired; author of *Space, Time and Deity*; *Spinoza and Time*; *Beauty and Other Forms of Value*, etc.; awarded the Order of Merit 1930. Died 13 September 1938.

Alice, Princess, Countess of Athlone (Alice Mary Victoria Augusta Pauline). Born 25 February 1883, daughter of Prince Leopold George Duncan Albert, fourth son of Queen Victoria; married, in 1904, the first Earl of Athlone (q.v.); commandant-in-chief, women's transport service in First World War; chairman of governors, Royal Holloway College 1936–58; active in many philanthropic organizations during her husband's term of office in South Africa 1923–31, notably child welfare, nursing, the Girl Guides.

Alice, Princess, of Greece (Victoria Alice Elizabeth Julia Marie). Born 25 February 1885, eldest daughter of Prince Louie Alexander of Battenberg; married, in 1903, Prince Andrew of Greece who died 3 December 1944; their only son was Prince Philip of Greece (q.v.), afterwards Duke of Edinburgh. Died 5 December 1969.

Allen, Sir Carleton Kemp. Lawyer. Born 7 September 1887, Sydney, Australia; educated Newington College, Sydney; New College, Oxford; served in France 1914–19; Stowell civil law fellow, University College, Oxford 1920; Tagore professor, University of Calcutta 1926; professor of jurisprudence, Oxford 1929–31; secretary to the Rhodes Trustees and warden of Rhodes House, Oxford 1931–52. Author of legal works, notably *Law in the Making*; a novel and short stories.

Allen, Reginald Clifford, first Baron, of Hurtwood. Labour publicist. Born 9 May 1889 Newport, England; educated University College, Bristol; Peterhouse, Cambridge; general manager of first Labour daily newspaper, *Daily Citizen* 1911–15; chairman, No Conscription Fellowship 1914–18; chairman, Independent Labour party and of the *New Leader* 1922–6; director of *Daily Herald* 1925–30. Created baron 1932; author of books on Labour politics. Died 3 March 1939.

Altrincham, Edward William Macleay Grigg, first Baron, of Tormarton. Politician and journalist. Born 8 September 1879; educated Winchester; New College, Oxford; on editorial staff of *The Times* 1903–5, 1908–13; assistant editor of the *Outlook* 1905–6; served in Grenadier Guards 1914–18; military secretary to the

Prince of Wales 1919; private secretary to Lloyd George; member of parliament 1922–5, 1933–45; secretary to the Rhodes Trustees 1923–5; governor of Kenya 1925–31; held junior ministerial offices 1939–42; minister resident in Middle East 1944–5; created baron 1945; author of books on imperial and political questions. Died 1 December 1955.

Amery, Julian. Politician. Born 27 March 1919; educated Summerfields; Eton; Balliol College, Oxford; war correspondent in Spain 1938–9; attaché, British legation, Belgrade 1939–40; served in the Second World War in the Middle East and Albania 1941–4; Conservative member of parliament 1950–66, 1969; delegate, consultative assembly, Council of Europe 1950–3, 1956; parliamentary under-secretary, war office 1957–8 and colonial office 1958–60; secretary of state for air 1960–2; minister of aviation 1962–4; author of biographical works on Joseph Chamberlain.

Ames, Sir Herbert Brown. League of Nations official and politician. Born 2 June 1863, Montreal, Canada; educated Amherst College, Massachusetts; member of house of commons, Montreal 1904–21; financial director of League of Nations secretariat 1919–26; lecturer for the Carnegie Endowment for International Peace 1929–38. Died 31 March 1954.

Anderson, Sir John. See **Waverley.**

Anderson, Peter Maltitz. Mining engineer. Born 1879, Heilbron, Orange Free State, South Africa; educated Pietermaritzburg College; South African College; School of Mines, Kimberley; went to the Witwatersrand 1902; joined A. Goerz and Company, later the Union Corporation, 1911 of which he was consulting engineer 1917, manager 1922, director 1928 and deputy chairman 1945; president of the Chamber of Mines 1925, 1930, 1933, 1937, 1940–1 and chairman of various gold mining companies and mining and geological societies; unofficial adviser of the Union delegation at the Ottawa conference 1934; chairman of Council, University of the Witwatersrand 1936; active during the Second World War in building up the national war fund and in the mines engineering brigade. Died 5 November 1954.

Andrews, Reverend Charles Freer. Vice-President, Tagore Institution, Bengal, India. Born 12 February 1871, Carlisle, England; educated King Edward VI School, Birmingham; Pembroke College, Cambridge of which he became a fellow 1900; went to India 1904; joined Tagore Institution at Santiniketan 1913; went to South Africa in connection with Indian affairs 1913–14, 1925–7 and to Fiji in connection with indentured Indian labour 1915 and 1917; correspondent of various newspapers and author of a number of books on religion and Indian affairs. Died 5 April 1940.

Andrews, Ernest Thomas Edward. Company director. Born 25 September 1880, Pinetown, Natal, South Africa; educated Stamford Hill Academy, Durban and in Wales; member, Institute of Mining and Metallurgy; chairman, Harlands Saligna and gold-mining companies; part owner, Kamhlabane Plantations.

Andrews, Harry Thomson. Diplomat. Born 11 December 1897, Cape Town, South Africa; educated Marist Brothers' College, Cape Town; University of Pretoria; entered South African civil service 1913; served in France in the First World War; advocate of the supreme court (Transvaal) 1927; political secretary, South Africa House, London 1930–5; South African representative, League of Nations 1936–40; head of South African government supply mission to the United States 1942–5; South African ambassador to the United States and permanent representative to U.N.O. 1945–9; South African ambassador to France 1949–57.

Armstrong, Major-General Bertram Frank. Soldier. Born 25 January 1893, Cape Town; educated there and in the Transvaal; joined the Natal police 1910; transferred to the Union defence force and served in South West Africa, France and Palestine 1915–18; battery commander, permanent garrison artillery, at Simonstown; lieutenant-colonel commanding coast artillery brigade 1933; officer commanding Cape command 1937; adjutant-general, Union defence force 1939; during the Second World War commanded the 5th South African brigade, was taken prisoner at Sidi Rezegh, escaped from a prison camp in Italy 1944; returned to South Africa as officer commanding Witwatersrand command; Cape Fortress commander 1946; head of the South African military mission in Berlin 1946–8; acting quartermaster-general 1949; retired 1950. Died 24 December 1971.

Armstrong, Captain Harold Courtenay. Writer and soldier. Born 20 October 1892; educated King's School, Worcester; University of Oxford; served in Indian army and in Mesopotamia; assistant to the British high commissioner, Constantinople; on staff of the commander-in-chief, Allied occupation forces in Turkey. Wrote biographies of Mustafa Kemal (*Grey Wolf*), Ibn Saud (*Lord of Arabia*), General J. C. Smuts (*Grey Steel*). Died 25 August 1943.

Arnim, Dietloff Jürgen von. Army officer. Born 1891, Ernsdorf, Germany; became expert in tank warfare; served on the general staff 1939; commanded an armoured division on the Russian front 1941–2; commanded the 4th army in Tunisia and, in March 1943, took over command of the Axis forces there from Rommel (q.v.); surrendered to Allied forces at Cape Bon, May 1943; prisoner of war in England and the United States.

Arthur, Sir George Compton Archibald, third Baronet. Writer and soldier. Born 30 April 1860; educated Eton; Christ Church, Oxford; joined the British army 1880; served in Egypt 1882–5 and South Africa 1900; private secretary to Earl Kitchener 1914–16; with intelligence department in France 1917–18. Author of several biographies, notably *The Life of Lord Kitchener of Khartoum.* Died 14 January 1946.

Astor, Waldorf, second Viscount. Politician and newspaper proprietor. Born 19 May 1879; educated Eton; New College, Oxford; Unionist member of parliament 1910–19; proprietor of the *Observer* from 1911; inspector of ordnance factories 1914; parliamentary private secretary to Lloyd George 1917; parliamentary secretary to the ministry of food 1918 and to the ministry of health 1919–21; succeeded to the viscountcy 1919; married Nancy Witcher Shaw who became the first woman member of the house of commons in 1919; delegate to the League of Nations 1931; joint author of books on agriculture; lord mayor of Plymouth 1939–44. Died 30 September 1952.

Ataturk, Kemal, known before 1934 as Mustafa Kemal or Kemal Pasha. Soldier and founder of modern Turkey. Born Salonika 1880. Joined Turkish army; banished as a revolutionary 1904–7; fought in Tripoli 1911 and the second Balkan War; commander at Gallipoli 1915; commanded an army corps in Palestine 1917–18; organized the Nationalist party and army in Anatolia 1919; set up a rival government at Ankara 1920; expelled the Greeks from Anatolia 1921–2; abolished the sultanate; at Lausanne conference secured favourable boundaries and established the Turkish Republic with himself as president and dictator 1923; carried out comprehensive reforms to westernize Turkish institutions during his four terms of office. Died 10 November 1938.

Athlone, Alexander Augustus Frederick William Alfred George Cambridge, first Earl of; third son of the Duke of Teck. Soldier and administrator. Born 14 April 1874 at Kensington Palace; educated Eton; Sandhurst; served in Matabeleland 1896, South Africa 1899–1900 and in the First World War; governor-general of the Union of South Africa 1923–31; governor-general of Canada 1940–6; chancellor of the University of London 1932–55. Died 16 January 1957.

Attlee, Clement Richard, first Earl. Statesman. Born 3 January 1883, London; educated Haileybury College; University College, Oxford; barrister of the Inner Temple; lecturer, Ruskin College 1911 and London School of Economics 1913–23; mayor of Stepney 1919–20; served in Gallipoli, Mesopotamia, France in the First World War and promoted major 1917; Labour member of parliament 1922–55; under-secretary for war 1924; chancellor of the Duchy of Lancaster 1930; postmaster-general 1931; leader of the opposition 1935–40; lord privy seal 1940–2; secretary for the Dominions 1942–3, lord president of the council 1943–5; prime minister 1945–51; leader of the opposition 1951–5; created earl 1955; author of books on Labour politics and an autobiography. Died 8 October 1967.

Auchinleck, Field Marshal Sir Claude John Eyre. Soldier. Born 21 June 1884, Ulster, Ireland; educated Wellington College; joined 62nd Punjabis 1904; served in Egypt and Mesopotamia 1914–19, then in India; deputy chief of general staff, army headquarters, India 1936–8; commander-in-chief, India 1941 and 1943–7; commander-in-chief, Middle East 1941–2; made a field marshal 1946.

Avon, Robert Anthony Eden, first Earl of. Statesman. Born 12 June 1897 County Durham, England; educated Eton; Christ Church, Oxford; served in the First World War; Conservative member of parliament 1923–57; private secretary to secretary of state for foreign affairs 1926–9; parliamentary under-secretary, foreign office 1931–3; lord privy seal 1934–5; secretary of state for foreign affairs 1935; resigned 1938 after the Munich agreement; secretary for the Dominions 1939–40; secretary for war 1940; secretary for foreign affairs 1940–5, 1951–5; prime minister 1955–7 when he resigned; knighted 1954; created earl 1961; chancellor of the University of Birmingham; author of *The Eden Memoirs*.

Badenhorst, Alida M., born de Wet. Diarist. Born 14 December 1867, Aliwal North, Cape Province, South Africa; married F. J. Badenhorst 1886; wrote a diary published under the pseudonym of 'Tant Alie van Transvaal'. Part of the diary deals with her experiences in the Anglo-Boer War. Died 1 April 1908.

Badoglio, Marshal Pietro. Administrator and soldier. Born 8 September 1871, Piedmont, Italy; educated Military School, Turin; served in Abyssinia 1895–6, Libya 1911–12 and the First World War after which he became chief of the general staff 1918; ambassador to Brazil 1924; governor-general of Libya 1928–33; high commissioner for East Africa 1935; viceroy of Abyssinia 1936. After the resignation of Mussolini (q.v.) he formed a new government which concluded an armistice with the Allies 1943; made a marshal 1926. Died 31 October 1956.

Baillieu, Clive Latham, Baron, of Sefton, Australia and of Parkwood. Government official and company director. Born 24 September 1889, Melbourne, Australia; educated University of Melbourne; Winchester; Magdalen College, Oxford; barrister, Inner Temple 1914; served in the Australian forces in the First World War; represented the British government at imperial wireless and cable conference 1928; Australian representative on imperial economic committee 1930–47; during the Second World War headed various supply organizations; member, advisory council, British Broadcasting Corporation 1947–52; head of British trade mission to Argentine 1948; chairman, Dunlop Rubber Company, Central Mining and Investment Corporation; director, Midland Bank; governor, National Institute of Economic and Special Research 1958; knighted 1938; created baron 1953. Died 18 June 1967.

Baker, Sir Herbert. Architect. Born 9 June 1862, Cobham, Kent, England; educated Tonbridge School; associate of Royal Institute of British Architects 1889; went to South Africa 1892; practised in Cape Town and received commissions from Cecil Rhodes for whom he designed 'Groote Schuur'; moved to the Transvaal in 1902 where his most important work is the Union Buildings, Pretoria, completed 1913; later practised in London and Delhi; knighted 1923; author of *Cecil Rhodes by his Architect*. Died 4 February 1946.

Baldwin of Bewdley, Stanley, first Earl. Statesman. Born 3 August 1867, Bewdley, Worcestershire, England; educated Harrow; Trinity College, Cambridge; entered the family iron-founding business; Conservative member of parliament 1908–37; financial secretary to the treasury 1917–21; president of the board of trade 1921–2; chancellor of the exchequer 1922–3; prime minister 1923–4, 1924–9; lord president of the council 1931–5; prime minister 1935–7; resigned after the coronation of George VI 1937; rector of the Universities of Edinburgh 1923–6 and Glasgow 1928–31; chancellor of St Andrews University 1929 and of the University of Cambridge 1930; created earl 1937; author of *The Classics and the Plain Man*. Died 14 December 1947.

Ballinger, Margaret Livingstone, born Hodgson. Politician and university lecturer. Born 11 January 1894, Glasgow, Scotland; went to South Africa as a child; educated Huguenot College, Wellington; Rhodes University College, Grahamstown; Somerville College, Oxford; lecturer in history, University of the Witwatersrand; married W. G. Ballinger (q.v.) 1934; member of parliament representing Natives of the Cape Province 1937–60; first leader of the Liberal party of South Africa 1953; author of *From Union to Apartheid.*

Ballinger, William George. Politician. Born 21 September 1894, Birmingham; educated Birmingham and Motherwell, Scotland; extramural student, University of Glasgow; town and parish councillor, Motherwell 1922–8; went to South Africa as adviser on African trade union organization 1928; elected senator of the Union parliament representing the Natives of the Transvaal and the Orange Free State 1948–60.

Ballot, Diederik William Ferdinand E. Attorney and farmer. Born 1 July 1887, George, Cape Province; educated St Mark's College, George; Diocesan College, Rondebosch; elected member of the legislative assembly of South West Africa 1926–34; nominated member 1935–45; member of the executive committee 1934–45.

Baring, Sir Evelyn. Administrator. Born 29 September 1903; educated New College, Oxford; entered Indian civil service 1926; retired 1934; governor of Southern Rhodesia 1942–4; British high commissioner in the Union of South Africa 1944–51; governor of Kenya 1952.

Barlow, Arthur Godfrey. Journalist and politician. Born 4 May 1876, Bloemfontein, Orange Free State, South Africa; educated St Andrew's College, Grahamstown; entered journalism as a reporter in the Orange Free State volksraad; edited the *Friend* during the British occupation of Bloemfontein; member of the Orange Free State legislative assembly 1907–10; Labour member of the Union parliament 1921–9; political correspondent of the *Rand Daily Mail* 1930–3; edited the *Sunday Express* 1934 and later founded *Arthur Barlow's Weekly*; United party member of parliament 1943–53 when he was expelled from the party; sat as independent member until 1958. Died 18 May 1962.

Barry, Richard Alan. Mining engineer. Born 20 October 1874, Kimberley, South Africa; educated St Andrew's College, Grahamstown; Sherborne School, Dorset; Camborne School of Mines, Cornwall; employee of gold-mines on the Witwatersrand 1893–8 where he began business as a mining engineer; served with the British forces in the Anglo-Boer War and later as lieutenant in the Imperial Light Horse volunteers; general manager, Transvaal Mining Estates Ltd. Died *c.* 1930.

Barthou, Jean Louis. Politician and lawyer. Born 25 August 1862, Orlon-Sainte-Marie, France; educated Lycée de Pau; practised as a barrister; elected to chamber of deputies 1889; minister of public works 1894–5; minister of the interior 1896–8; resumed legal practice 1898–1906; minister of public works 1906–9; minister of justice 1909–10; premier 1913; minister without portfolio 1914–19; minister of war 1921; elected senator 1922; president, reparations commission 1922–6; minister of justice 1926; in Briand's cabinet 1929; foreign minister 1934; assassinated at Marseilles with King Alexander of Yugoslavia 9 October 1934.

Barton, Robert Childers. Irish nationalist leader. Born 1881; educated Rugby; Christ Church, Oxford; joined Sinn Fein after the Irish rebellion 1916; member of parliament for Wicklow 1918; member of the republican government as minister of agriculture 1919–21 and economic secretary 1921–2; signatory of the treaty with Great Britain 1921; chairman, Agricultural Credit Corporation 1934–59.

Baruch, Bernard Mannes. Financier and philanthropist. Born 19 August 1870, South Carolina, United States of America; educated College of the City of New York; became a stockbroker and made a large fortune; chairman of war industries 1918; active in the economic sections of the American delegation to the peace conference 1919; member of government conferences on labour and agriculture 1919–22; government adviser on ordnance and post-war planning during the

Second World War; United States representative on the atomic energy commission 1946; made large donations to universities, medical schools and the American Red Cross; wrote an autobiography and books on the First World War. Died 20 June 1965.

Bayford, Sir Robert Arthur Sanders, first Baron, of Stroke Trister. Lawyer and politician. Born 20 June 1867, Isle of Wight; educated Harrow; Balliol College, Oxford; barrister of the Inner Temple 1891; Unionist member of parliament 1910–23; served in Gallipoli, Egypt, Palestine 1914–17; treasurer of the household 1918–19; junior lord of the treasury 1919–21; under-secretary for war 1921–2; minister of agriculture and fisheries 1922–4; deputy lieutenant of Somerset; created baronet 1920, baron 1929. Died 24 February 1940.

Beaverbrook, William Maxwell Aitken, first Baron. Newspaper proprietor and statesman. Born 25 May 1879, Maple, Ontario, Canada; educated Newcastle, New Brunswick; became a stockbroker 1907 and made a large fortune; went to London; Conservative member of parliament 1910–16; minister of information 1918; after resigning office acquired the *Daily Express*, founded the *Sunday Express* and secured control of the *Evening Standard*; launched his 'Empire free trade' policy 1929; minister for aircraft production 1940–1; minister of state 1941; minister of supply 1941–2; lord privy seal 1943–5; knighted 1911, created baron 1917; author of *Canada in Flanders*; *Politicians and the War*; *Men and Power*, etc. Died 9 June 1964.

Bell, Robert Eric. Politician and company director. Born 2 May 1899, Transvaal, South Africa; educated Michaelhouse School, Balgowan, Natal; served in the royal air force in the First World War; United party member of parliament 1940–53; chairman, Eric Bell and Co.; director, Mayfair Gold Mining Co. Died 12 March 1966.

Benes, Eduard. Statesman. Born 28 May 1884, Kozlany, Czechoslovakia; educated Universities of Prague, Paris, Dijon; lecturer, then professor of sociology, University of Prague 1912–22; general secretary of the Czech national council 1915; foreign minister of Czechoslovakia 1918–35; delegate at Paris peace conference 1919; member of council of the League of Nations 1923–5; succeeded Masaryk as president 1935; resigned after the Munich agreement 1938; head of Czech government in exile during the Second World War; re-elected president 1945; resigned when Klement Gottwald formed a Communist government under Russian aegis 1948; published memoirs 1947. Died 3 September 1948.

Benn, William Wedgwood. See **Stansgate.**

Bernadotte, Count Folke. Internationalist. Born 2 January 1895, Stockholm; nephew of Gustaf V of Sweden; educated Officers' Military School, Karlberg; vice-chairman of Swedish Red Cross during the Second World War; aided the exchange of German and British prisoners of war; arranged the transfer of Danish and Norwegian political prisoners from Germany to Sweden; appointed mediator between the Arabs and the Jews in Palestine 1948. Assassinated by Jewish terrorists in Jerusalem 17 September 1948.

Bernhard, Prince, of the Netherlands (Bernhard Leopold Friedrich Eberhard Julius Kurt Karl Gottfried Peter). Born 29 June 1911, Jena, Germany; son of Prince Bernhard of Lippe-Biesterfeld; educated Universities of Lausanne, Munich, Berlin; married Princess Juliana of the Netherlands 1937 and became a Dutch subject; appointed chief liaison officer between the Dutch and British forces 1940.

Beveridge, William Henry, first Baron, of Tuggal. British economist. Born 5 March 1879, Bengal, India; educated Charterhouse; Balliol College, Oxford; member of the Central Unemployed Body for London 1906–8; director of labour exchanges at the board of trade 1908–16; in the ministries of food and munitions during the First World War; director of the London School of Economics 1919–37; served as chairman of various social service committees; responsible for a comprehensive and influential social security plan published as *Social Insurance and Allied Services*

(Cmd. 6404 of 1942); knighted 1919; created baron 1946; author of a number of books on social insurance and unemployment, notably *Full Employment in a Free Society*. Died 16 March 1963.

Bevin, Ernest. British statesman and trade union leader. Born 9 March 1881; educated at an elementary school; organizer, Dockers' Union 1910–21; founder and general secretary, Transport and General Workers' Union 1921–40; member, general council of trades union congress 1925–40; Labour member of parliament 1940–51; minister of labour and member of the war cabinet 1940–5; secretary of state for foreign affairs 1945–51. Died 14 April 1951.

Bews, John William. Botanist. Born 16 December 1884, Kirkwall, Orkney, Scotland; educated University of Edinburgh; lecturer in botany, Universities of Manchester 1907–8 and Edinburgh 1908–10; professor of botany, Natal University College, Pietermaritzburg, South Africa 1910–25, 1927–30; principal, Natal University College 1930–8; author of botanical works, mainly on grasses and ecology. Died 10 November 1938.

Beyers, Lieutenant-General Leonard. South African soldier. Born 1894; educated Military College, Camberley, England; entered the Union defence force and became officer commanding the Pretoria military district in 1932 with the rank of lieutenant-colonel; director of prisons 1933–44; adjutant-general 1941–5. After a period of retirement because of illness he was recalled in 1949 to become chief of the general staff but resigned in 1950 over differences with the minister of defence, Mr F. C. Erasmus (q.v.). Died 15 April 1959.

Bezuidenhout, Willem W. J. J. Farmer and politician. Born 1869 in South Africa; member of the Cape provincial council; South African party member of parliament 1912–24; chairman of the Heidelberg (Cape) branch of the party. Died 6 October 1946.

Bicester, Vivian Hugh Smith, first Baron, of Tusmore. Born 9 December 1867; educated Eton; Trinity Hall, Cambridge; director of the Royal Exchange Assurance Corporation 1894–1955 and governor 1914–55; lord lieutenant, county of Oxford 1934–54. Died 17 February 1956.

Bidault, Georges. French statesman. Born 5 October 1899; educated Jesuit school in Italy; University of Paris; served with army of occupation in the Ruhr 1919; after teaching history at lycées joined editorial staff of *L'Aube* 1932–9; during the Second World War was at first imprisoned by the Germans and then joined the resistance; foreign minister in General de Gaulle's provisional government 1944; prime minister 1946, 1949–50; foreign minister 1946–8, 1953; minister of national defence 1951–2; wrote a political autobiography 1967.

Binyon, Robert Laurence. Poet. Born 10 August 1869, Lancaster, England; educated St Paul's School; Trinity College, Oxford; employed in British Museum department of printed books 1893–1909; became assistant keeper, department of prints and drawings 1909–13; deputy keeper 1913–32; lectured in the United States and Japan; professor of poetry, Harvard University 1933–4; Byron professor, University of Athens 1940; published poems, plays and books on oriental art. Died 10 March 1943.

Birkenhead, Frederick Edwin Smith, first Earl of. Statesman and lawyer. Born 12 July 1872, Birkenhead, England; educated Birkenhead; Wadham College, Oxford; lecturer in history, Oxford and Victoria University 1896–1900; barrister of Gray's Inn 1899; Conservative member of parliament 1906–19; solicitor-general 1915; attorney-general 1915–19; lord chancellor 1919–22; secretary of state for India 1924–8; rector of Universities of Glasgow 1922 and Aberdeen 1926; knighted 1915; created viscount 1919, earl 1922; author of several legal and historical books, notably *International Law*. Died 30 September 1930.

Black, Hugo Lafayette. Jurist. Born 27 February 1886, Harlan, Kentucky, United States of America; educated public schools Ashland, Alabama; University of Alabama; began practice in Birmingham, Alabama 1907; police judge 1910–11; prosecuting attorney, Jefferson County, Alabama 1915–17; in general practice,

Birmingham 1919–27; United States senator for Alabama 1927–37; associate justice, United States supreme court 1937.

Blackwell, Leslie. Judge and politician. Born 27 February 1885, Sydney, Australia; went to South Africa 1895; educated Jeppe High School, Johannesburg; South African College, Cape Town; served in German East Africa 1916–17; South African party member of parliament 1915–43; judge of the Transvaal division of the supreme court 1943–55. Author of popular books on South African politics.

Blommaert, Willem. Historian. Born 15 June 1886, Maria-Hoorebeke, East Flanders, Belgium; educated there and at the University of Ghent; professor of history, Victoria College, Stellenbosch 1910–34; chairman of the university senate 1926–34; co-author of *Uit ou Reisbeskrywinge*; *Dagverhale en ander letterkundige bronne oor die Kaap*; *Die Joernaal van D. G. van Reenen*. Died 18 October 1934.

Blum, Léon. Statesman and writer. Born 9 April 1873, Paris; educated École Normale Supérieure; University of Paris; became literary and dramatic critic; with Jaurès formed the new French Socialist party 1902; elected to chamber of deputies 1919, 1929, 1932, 1936; prime minister of the Popular Front government 1936; resigned 1937; prime minister 1938; during the Second World War was brought to trial by the Vichy government and later interned by the Germans; leader of economic missions to the United States and elsewhere 1946; formed a caretaker government December 1946; retired from public life 1947; author of books on politics and literary and dramatic criticism. Died 30 March 1950.

Boetzelaer, Constant. See **Van Boetzelaer.**

Bohr, Niels Henrik David. Physicist. Born 7 October 1885, Copenhagen, Denmark; educated there; worked under Sir J. J. Thomson and Sir Ernest Rutherford (qq.v.); professor of physics at Copenhagen 1916; awarded Nobel prize for physics 1922; fellow of the Royal Society 1926; during the Second World War worked in England and the United States on atomic fission. Author of various publications on atomic physics. Died 18 November 1962.

Bolus, Frank. Botanist. Born 10 March 1870, Graaff Reinet, Cape Province, South Africa; educated Diocesan College, Cape Town and privately; practised for a time as an attorney in Mafeking 1898–1902; thereafter managed the country estate of his father, Harry Bolus, and worked in the herbarium begun by him in 1865; made a special study of grasses; kept a continuous diary from 1897 to 1945. Died 13 May 1945.

Bolus, Harriet Margaret Louisa, born Kensit. Botanist. Born 31 July 1877, Burgersdorp, Cape Province, South Africa; educated Girls' Collegiate School, Port Elizabeth; the South African College, Cape Town; curator of the Harry Bolus Herbarium 1903; married Frank Bolus (q.v.) 1912; awarded honorary D.Sc. of the University of Stellenbosch for eminence in botanical research. Died 5 April 1970.

Bonaparte, Princess Marie. Born 2 July 1882, St Cloud, Paris; daughter of Prince Roland Bonaparte; married, in 1907, Prince George of Greece (q.v.), brother of King Constantine I of the Hellenes; gained repute as a student of psychoanalysis. Died 21 September 1962.

Bonnet, Georges Etienne. Politician. Born 23 July 1889, Bassillac, Dordogne, France; educated Lycée Henri IV; École Libre des Sciences Politiques; chef de cabinet, minister of posts and telegraphs 1919–21; advocate in the court of Paris 1928; member of chamber of deputies, 1924, 1929, 1932, 1936, 1956–8; minister of finance 1925, 1933–4; minister of housing 1926; minister of commerce and posts and telegraphs 1930; minister of public works 1932; minister of commerce 1935–6; ambassador to the United States 1936–7; minister of state 1938, minister of foreign affairs 1938–9; minister of justice 1939–40; wrote his memoirs.

Bosanquet, Bernard. Philosopher. Born 14 June 1848 near Alnwick, Northumberland, England; educated Harrow; Balliol College, Oxford; lecturer, University College, Oxford 1870–80; professor of moral philosophy, University of St Andrews 1903–8; author of *Knolewdge and Reality; Essentials of Logic*, etc. Died 8 February 1923.

Boshoff, Stephanus Petrus Erasmus. South African philologist. Born 1891; educated University of Amsterdam; professor at the Universities of Potchefstroom 1927 and Cape Town 1932–4; became principal of a correspondence college and then director of the technical terminology (Afrikaans) bureau 1950–7; author of an etymological dictionary of Afrikaans.

Bourdillon, Sir Bernard Henry. Administrator. Born 3 December 1883, Emu Bay, Tasmania; educated Tonbridge; St John's College, Oxford; joined Indian civil service 1908; under-secretary to government of United Provinces 1913; registrar, high court, Allahabad 1915; served in Mesopotamia 1918; political secretary to high commissioner, Iraq 1921; secretary 1922; counsellor 1924–9; acting high commissioner 1925–6; colonial secretary, Ceylon 1929–32; acting governor 1930–1; governor of Uganda 1932–5; governor of Nigeria 1935–43; director, Barclay's Bank (D.C. and O.); knighted 1931. Died 6 February 1948.

Bower, Sir Graham John. Government official and naval officer. Born 15 June 1848, Ireland; educated Naval Academy, Gosport; entered royal navy 1861; served until 1880 when he became private secretary to Sir Hercules Robinson (q.v. vol. IV); retired from the navy with rank of commander 1884; imperial secretary to the high commissioners for South Africa 1884–97; colonial secretary of Mauritius 1898–1910; retired 1910; knighted 1892. Died 2 August 1933.

Boycott, Arthur Edwin. Pathologist. Born 6 April 1877, Hereford, England; educated Hereford Cathedral School; Oriel College, Oxford; St Thomas's Hospital; lecturer in pathology, Guy's Hospital 1907; professor of pathology, University of Manchester 1912–15; and University of London 1915–38; author of many papers on pathology. Died 12 May 1938.

Boydell, Thomas. Politician. Born 15 December 1882, Newcastle-upon-Tyne, England; went to South Africa 1902; trade union organizer; Labour party member of parliament 1912; minister of posts and telegraphs 1924–5; minister of labour 1925–9; senator 1929–39; wrote an autobiography. Died 5 July 1966.

Bradley, Sir Kenneth Granville. English government official. Born 5 January 1904; educated Wellington College, Berkshire; University College, Oxford; district officer, Northern Rhodesia 1926–39; information officer, Northern Rhodesia 1939–42; colonial and financial secretary, Falkland Islands 1942–6; under-secretary, Gold Coast 1946–9; retired 1949; edited *Corona*, colonial service journal 1948–53; director, Commonwealth Institute since 1953; knighted 1963; author of several books on Northern Rhodesia and the colonial service.

Braithwaite, William Charles. English banker. Born 1862; educated Oliver's Mount School, Scarborough; University College, London; practised as a barrister until 1896, then became a partner in Gillett and Company, bankers, Banbury and Oxford; on their amalgamation with Barclay's Bank became a local director 1919; author of histories of the Quakers. Died 28 January 1922.

Brand, Thomas Henry. See **Hampden.**

Bremer, Karl. Politician and medical practitioner. Born 27 April 1885, Hopefield, Cape Province, South Africa; educated Huguenot College, Wellington; Victoria College, Stellenbosch; Cornell University, United States; St Bartholomew's Hospital, London; in general practice 1909–15; served in the medical corps in East Africa; first medical inspector of schools in Cape Province; returned to general practice 1919–29; practised as ear, nose and throat specialist 1931–47; member of Cape provincial council 1920–3; National party member of parliament 1924–5, 1929–47, 1952; senator 1948–51; minister of health 1951–3; president, medical council 1943–51. Died 5 September 1953.

Breuil, Abbé Henri Edouard Prosper. Archaeologist. Born 28 February 1877, Mortain, Manche, France; educated Lycée St Vincent, Senlis; Seminary of St Sulpice, Paris; University of Paris; after ordination became an archaeologist; lecturer at the University of Fribourg, Switzerland 1905–10; professor of palaeontology at L'Institute de Paléontologie Humaine, Paris; undertook research in western Europe, China, South Africa; professor of prehistory at the Collège de

France 1929–47; held honorary professorship at the University of the Witwatersrand 1942–5; was a member of many learned societies and received numerous honours; wrote several books and papers, notably *Quatre cents siècles d'art pariétal*, illustrated with his own copies of paintings and engravings. Died 14 August 1961.

Briand, Aristide. Statesman. Born 28 March 1862, Nantes, France; educated Collège de St Nazaire, Lycée de Nantes; became a barrister and later editor of the socialist *La Lanterne*; co-founder of *L'Humanité*; elected to chamber of deputies 1902; minister of public instruction 1906; expelled from the Socialist party; prime minister 1909–11, 1913; minister of justice 1914; prime minister 1915–17, 1921–2, 1925–6; minister of foreign affairs 1926–9; prime minister 1929; unsuccessful candidate for the presidency 1931; received Nobel peace prize 1925, 1926. Died 7 March 1932.

Bridges, Robert Seymour. English poet. Born 23 October 1844; educated Eton; Corpus Christi College, Oxford; St Bartholomew's Hospital, London; held hospital staff appointments until 1882 when he ceased to practise medicine. His published works include poems, notably *The Testament of Beauty* (1929), essays on Milton and Keats, several anthologies and a number of plays. He was made poet laureate in 1913 and awarded the Order of Merit in 1929. Died 21 April 1930.

Brink, Lieutenant-General George Edwin. Soldier. Born 27 September 1889, Orange Free State, South Africa; commissioned in the Union defence force 1914; served during the 1914 rebellion and in South West and East Africa 1915–17; went to England for further military training; appointed commander of the South African Military College; during the Second World War commanded the first South African division; subsequently chairman of the immigrants selection board until 1950. Died 30 April 1971.

Broad, Charles Dunbar. Philosopher. Born 30 December 1887, London; educated Dulwich; Trinity College, Cambridge; lecturer, Trinity College and University of St Andrews; professor of philosophy, University of Bristol; professor of moral philosophy, Cambridge 1933; Donnellan lecturer, Trinity College, Dublin. Author of several philosophical books, notably *Scientific Thought*; *The Mind and its Place in Nature*; *Perception, Physics and Reality*.

Brodetsky, Selig. Zionist leader. Born 10 February 1888, Olviopol, Ukraine; went with his parents to London; educated there and at Trinity College, Cambridge and University of Leipzig; first reader in, then professor of applied mathematics, University of Leeds 1924–8; elected to executive of the world Zionist organization 1928; president of the board of deputies of British Jews 1939; president of the Hebrew University of Jerusalem 1949; retired 1952. Died 18 May 1954.

Brooke, Alan. See **Alanbrooke.**

Brookes, Edgar Harry. Historian and politician. Born 4 February 1897, Smethwick, England; educated Natal University College; the London School of Economics; professor of political science, Transvaal University College 1924; South African delegate to the League of Nations assembly 1927; president, South African Institute of Race Relations 1932, 1946; senator representing Native electors of Natal 1937; member, social and economic planning council 1942–52; member, Native affairs commission 1945–50; professor of history, University of Natal 1959; author of *History of Native Policy in South Africa* and other books on the colour question.

Broom, Robert. Palaeontologist and medical practitioner. Born 30 November 1866, Paisley, Scotland; educated University of Glasgow; practised medicine in Australia 1889–97 and South Africa 1897–1903, 1910–34; professor of zoology and geology, Victoria College, Stellenbosch 1903–9; keeper of the department of vertebrate palaeontology and anthropology, Transvaal Museum 1934. His important researches on the mammal-like reptiles and on early man culminated in the discovery of a skull of Australopithecine type at Sterkfontein, Transvaal in 1936. Author of *Mammal-like Reptiles in South Africa*; *The Coming of Man*; *The South African Fossil Ape-men*; etc. Died 6 April 1951.

Bruce, Stanley Melbourne, first Viscount, of Melbourne. Statesman. Born 15 April 1883 Melbourne, Australia; educated Melbourne Grammar School; Trinity Hall, Cambridge; barrister of the Inner Temple 1907; served in the First World War; member of the Commonwealth parliament 1918–29; 1931–3; Commonwealth treasurer 1921–3; prime minister 1923–9; minister without portfolio and Australian minister in London 1932–3; high commissioner for Australia in London 1933–45; Australian representative at the League of Nations 1921, 1932–8; chairman, world food council 1947–51; created viscount 1947. Died 25 August 1967.

Brüning, Heinrich. Statesman and university professor. Born 26 November 1885, Münster, Westphalia, Germany; educated in philosophy and economics; director of the German trade union council 1920–30; member of the Reichstag (Centre party) 1924–33; chancellor 1930–2 when he was dismissed; leader of the Centre party until its dissolution in July 1933; went to the United States where he became a professor at Harvard University 1937; returned to Germany to take up a professorship in Cologne 1952. Died 30 March 1970.

Buchanan, Douglas Mudie. Lawyer and politician. Born 27 June 1881, Cape Town; educated Diocesan College, Cape Town; St John's College, Cambridge; barrister of the Inner Temple 1903; practised as advocate in Cape Town; member of parliament representing the Native voters of the Transkei 1947–8; agent of the London Missionary Society. Died 1 August 1954.

Bunche, Ralph Johnson. American negro internationalist and university professor. Born 7 August 1904, Detroit, Michigan; educated University of California; Harvard University; London School of Economics; lecturer in political science 1925–38; professor at Harvard University 1938; with the office of strategic services 1941–4; director, United Nations trusteeship division 1946–55; United Nations under-secretary for special political affairs from 1955; professor of government, Harvard University 1950–2; awarded Nobel peace prize 1950; author of books on American and African politics.

Burckhardt, Carl J. Diplomat, international official, historian. Born 10 September 1891, Basle, Switzerland; educated gymnasia at Basle and Glarisegg; Universities of Basle, Zürich, Munich, Göttingen, Paris; attaché, Swiss legation in Vienna 1918; professor of modern history, Zürich University 1928; professor, Institute for International Studies, Geneva 1932; high commissory of the League of Nations in Danzig 1937; member, international committee of the Red Cross 1933 and president 1944; Swiss minister plenipotentiary in France 1945–9; author of historical works and memoirs.

Burgess, Robert Ernest. Bank official. Born 25 March 1893, Wimbledon, England; architectural draughtsman 1907–12; entered Westminster Bank 1912; joined Barclays Bank, Durban 1915; served with the South African contingent in the First World War; superintendent, premises department, Barclays Bank, Cape Town 1929–46 when he retired. Died 8 September 1946.

Butler, Nicholas Murray. American educationalist. Born 2 April 1862. Founder and editor of the *Education Review* 1889–1919; president of Columbia University 1902–45; active in the cause of international peace; author of books on education and international relations. Died 7 December 1947.

Butler, Major-General Stephen Seymour. English soldier. Born 1880; educated Winchester; entered British army 1899; served in South Africa; Egypt 1909–15; in intelligence department, G.H.Q., France 1916–18; head of naval intelligence, Constantinople 1919–20; military attaché, Bucharest 1923–6; inspector-general, royal West African frontier force 1926–30; commander, 48th division, territorial army 1935–9; retired 1939, re-employed; head of military mission, Turkey 1939–40; liaison, Africa 1940–1; head of military mission, Ethiopia. Died 16 July 1964.

Byrnes, James Francis. American politician. Born 1879. Practised law 1909–11, 1925–30; member of house of representatives 1911–25; senator for South Carolina 1930–41; associate justice, supreme court 1941–2; director of economic stabilization

1942–3; director, office of war mobilization 1943–5; secretary of state 1945–6; governor of South Carolina 1951–5; wrote memoirs.

Byron, Brigadier-General John Joseph. Born 1864, County Wexford, Ireland; served in Australia commanding the Queensland regiment of the royal Australian artillery 1895–9; aide-de-camp to Lord Roberts during the Anglo-Boer War; member of the legislative council of the Orange Free State 1907–10; Union senator 1910–20; commanded an infantry brigade in the South West and East African campaigns and served in Flanders in the First World War. Died 17 February 1935.

Cabrol, Right Reverend Fernand. Benedictine abbot. Born 1855, Marseilles, France; ordained 1882; prior of Solesmes 1890–6; first prior of St Michael's Abbey, Farnborough from 1896; vice-president, Lingard Society 1927; committee member, Catholic council for international relations; author of books on the history of religion. Died 4 June 1937.

Caldecote, Thomas Walker Hobart Inskip, first Viscount. Statesman and judge. Born 5 March 1876, Bristol, England; educated Clifton College; King's College, Cambridge; barrister of the Inner Temple 1899; served in naval intelligence division, admiralty 1915–18; Conservative member of parliament 1918–29, 1931–9; solicitor-general 1922–8; attorney-general 1928–9, 1932–6; minister for the co-ordination of defence 1936–9; secretary of state for the Dominions 1939, 1940; lord chancellor 1939–40; lord chief justice 1940–6; knighted 1922; created viscount 1939. Died 11 October 1947.

Camp, Charles Lewis. Palaeontologist. Born 12 March 1893, Jamestown, North Dakota, United States of America; educated Throop Polytechnic Institute; University of California; Columbia University; assistant, Museum of Vertebrate Zoology 1908–15; assistant, American Museum of Natural History 1919–21; research associate, then assistant professor, University of California 1924–39; director, Museum of Palaeontology from 1931; professor of palaeontology, University of California from 1940; author of books and papers on palaeontology and frontier history.

Carr, Herbert Wildon. English philosopher. Born 16 January 1857; educated King's College, University of London where he became professor of philosophy 1918; president of the Aristotelian Society 1916–18; visiting professor, University of Southern California 1925; author of several philosophical works. Died 8 July 1931.

Carter, Right Reverend William Marlborough. Archbishop of Cape Town. Born 11 July 1850, Eton, England; educated Eton; Pembroke College, Oxford; ordained 1874; curate at West Bromwich and Bakewell 1874–80; conducted Eton Mission, Hackney 1880–91; Bishop of Zululand 1891–1902; Bishop of Pretoria 1902–9; Archbishop of Cape Town 1909–30; knighted 1931. Died 14 February 1941.

Casement, Tom. Government official and hotel-keeper. Brother of Sir Roger Casement. Born *c.* 1862 at sea off Boulogne; from the age of thirteen spent some twenty years as a seaman, reaching South Africa *c.* 1895; joined the Imperial Light Horse 1899; commissioner of mines and Native affairs at Barberton 1900–2; claim inspector for the Transvaal 1904–14; served in East Africa in the First World War and then kept an hotel in Basutoland; returned to Ireland *c.* 1922 and started the coast life-saving service. Found drowned March 1938.

Casey, Richard Gardiner, first Baron, of Berwick. Statesman and administrator. Born 29 August 1890, Brisbane, Australia; educated Universities of Melbourne and Cambridge; served in the First World War on the general staff; Australian political liaison officer in London 1924–31; member of the house of representatives 1931–40, 1949–60; assistant federal treasurer 1933–5; federal treasurer 1935–9; minister for scientific and industrial research 1937–9; Australian minister to the United States 1940–2; United Kingdom minister of state for Middle East 1942–3; governor of Bengal 1944–6; minister for national development and works and housing 1949–51; minister for external affairs 1951–60; created life peer 1960; governor-general of Australia since 1965. Author of biographical books.

Caton-Thompson, Gertrude. English archaeologist. Born 1 February 1889; educated Eastbourne; Paris; employed by ministry of shipping 1915–19; student at British School of Archaeology in Egypt 1921–6; organized archaeological and geological survey of the northern Fayum 1924–6; field director of Royal Anthropological Institute 1927–8; conducted excavations at Zimbabwe 1928, the Kharga oasis 1930–3, and in South Arabia 1937–8; author of various archaeological books and papers including *The Zimbabwe Culture* and *Kharga Oasis in Prehistory*.

Chamberlain, Arthur Neville. Statesman. Born 18 March 1869, Edgbaston, Birmingham, England; educated Rugby; Mason College, Birmingham; managed sisal plantation in Bahamas 1890–7; entered business in Birmingham 1897; elected to city council 1911; lord mayor 1915–16; director-general of national service 1916–17; Conservative member of parliament from 1918; postmaster-general 1922–3; minister of health 1923, 1924–9, 1931; chancellor of the exchequer 1923–4, 1931–7; prime minister 1937–40; resigned 10 May 1940 becoming lord president of the council until September; author of *The Struggle for Peace*. Died 9 November 1940.

Chancellor, Lieutenant-Colonel Sir John Robert. Soldier and administrator. Born 20 October 1870, Edinburgh; educated Royal Military Academy, Woolwich; entered British army 1890; served in Egypt and India 1896–8; assistant secretary to committee of imperial defence 1904; secretary to colonial defence committee 1906; governor of Mauritius 1911–16; governor of Trinidad 1916–21; governor of Southern Rhodesia 1923–8; high commissioner, Palestine 1928–31; vice-chairman, British Council 1940–1; vice-president, Royal Empire Society; knighted 1913. Died 31 July 1952.

Chandos, Oliver Lyttelton, first Viscount, of Aldershot. English statesman. Born 15 March 1893; educated Eton; Trinity College, Cambridge; served in the First World War; Conservative member of parliament 1940–50; president of the board of trade 1940–1; minister of state 1941–2; minister of production 1942–5; secretary of state for the colonies 1951–4; chairman, Associated Electrical Industries Ltd. 1945–51, 1954–63; president, Manchester College of Science and Technology 1956–61; trustee of the National Gallery 1958–65; created viscount 1954; wrote his memoirs.

Chappell, Sir Ernest. Financier. Born 1864. London; educated Woodbridge Grammar School; went to South Africa 1890; member of Pretoria city council 1904–7; president, Associated Chambers of Commerce of South Africa; member of various government commissions on finance and taxation; director, South African Reserve Bank; chairman, East African trade commission; adviser to the South African delegation to the economic conference 1923; knighted 1922. Died 3 August 1943.

Charles, Prince, of Belgium (Charles Theodore Henri Antoine Meinrad, Count of Flanders). Born 10 October 1903, second son of Albert I; went to England during the First World War after which his education continued in Belgium; went to the United States in 1931 to work in Thomas Edison's laboratory and later in locomotive and automobile plants; worked with resistance groups during the Second World War; elected Regent of the Realm on 20 September 1944, his brother, Leopold III (q.v.) having been imprisoned by the Germans; held the regency until Leopold abdicated in 1951 in favour of his son, Baudouin.

Chiang Kai-shek. Chinese generalissimo. Born 1887, Ningpo, Che Kiang; educated Paoting; Tokyo Military Academy; took part in the republican revolutions under Sun Yat-sen 1911, 1912, 1917 and was on his staff until 1922; founder and head of the Whampoa Military School 1924; succeeded Sun Yat-sen as leader of the Kuomintang party 1925; set up independent government at Nanking 1927 and exercised virtually dictatorial powers as president of the Executive Yuan (prime minister)—a position he maintained against Communist and other opposition; led Chinese resistance to Japan 1937–45; president of China 1943–9; during the civil war was defeated by the Communists and driven from the mainland but has exercised the presidency of Nationalist China in Taiwan (Formosa) since 1950; author of *China's Destiny*, etc.

Chicherin, Georgi Vasilyevich. Russian politician. Born 1872, Tambor Province; educated University of St Petersburg; employed in the Russian foreign office; became a revolutionary in 1897; resigned his post 1904 to become a Menshevik propagandist in various European countries; imprisoned in England 1917–18; foreign minister of Soviet Russia 1918–29 when he resigned; negotiated treaty of Rapallo and recognition of Russia by the great powers at the Genoa conference 1922. Died 1936.

Childers, Robert Erskine. Writer and Irish Nationalist leader. Born 1870: educated Haileybury: Trinity College, Cambridge; served in the Anglo-Boer War; junior clerk in the house of commons 1895–1910; served in the royal naval air service in the First World War; wrote *The Riddle of the Sands*; volume 5 of *The Times History of the South African War*, etc.; joined the Sinn Fein movement and took part in the armed resistance to the Irish Free State government set up under the treaty of 1921; captured and executed 24 November 1922.

Christie, John. Politician. Born 1883, Scotland; went to South Africa 1901 where he became a pharmaceutical chemist; mayor of Johannesburg 1920; Labour member of parliament 1921–33, 1936–8, 1943–53; leader of the parliamentary Labour party 1948. Died 19 July 1953.

Churchill, Randolph Frederick Edward Spencer. Politician. Born 28 May 1911, London; educated Eton; Christ Church, Oxford; served in the Second World War on general staff (intelligence) in the Middle East; Conservative member of parliament 1940–5, 1950, 1951; author of a number of books on politics and an unfinished biography of his father, Sir Winston Churchill. Died 6 June 1968.

Cilliers, Andries Charl. Physicist. Born 1 January 1898, Wellington, Cape Province, South Africa; educated Paarl Gimnasium; University of Stellenbosch; Frankfurt-am-Main; senior lecturer in mathematics, University of Cape Town 1924–5; senior lecturer in theoretical physics, University of Stellenbosch 1925–40, then professor 1940–63 when he retired; member of the university council 1948–64; chairman, government universities advisory committee 1963–5; author of *Life on the Sigmoid*, several political pamphlets and an autobiography.

Cilliers, Sarel Arnoldus. Voortrekker leader. Born 7 September 1801, Klein Drakenstein, Cape Colony, South Africa; settled in Colesberg district 1829; led a trek north-eastwards 1836 joining Hendrik Potgieter's (q.v.) party; took part in battles of Vegkop, Mosega, Italeni, Blood river 1836–8; settled at Pietermaritzburg 1840 but withdrew when British authority was asserted over Natal 1843 and settled in Kroonstad. Died 4 October 1871.

Clarendon, George Herbert Hyde Villiers, sixth Earl. Administrator and lord chamberlain. Born 7 June 1877; educated Eton; chief government whip, house of lords 1922–5; parliamentary under-secretary of state for Dominions 1925–7; chairman, British Broadcasting Corporation 1927–30; governor-general of the Union of South Africa 1931–7; lord chamberlain 1938–52; permanent lord-in-waiting to the queen 1952–5. Died 13 December 1955.

Clark, General Mark. Soldier. Born 1 May 1896, New York; educated United States Military Academy; Infantry School; General Staff School; Army War College; served in the First World War; deputy chief of staff, civilian conservation corps 1936–7; commander-in-chief, ground forces in Europe 1942; commander, fifth army during invasion of Italy 1943–4; commander, 15th general army group 1944; commanding general, United States forces in Austria 1945–7; commanding general, 6th United States army 1947–9; chief of United States army field forces 1949–52; commander-in-chief, Far East 1952–3; author of books on his war experiences.

Clark, William Bancroft. Manufacturer. Born 1902, Street, Somerset, England; educated Sidcot School, Somerset; Bootham School, York; King's College, Cambridge; employed by the shoemaking firm of C. and J. Clark Ltd. of Street since 1919; director since 1927; chairman since 1942.

Clark, Sir William Henry. Government official. Born 1 January 1876, Cambridge, England; educated Eton; Trinity College, Cambridge; clerk, board of trade 1899;

secretary, special mission to Shanghai 1901; acting second secretary, diplomatic service 1902; private secretary to D. Lloyd George 1906–8; member, council of viceroy, India 1910–16; comptroller-general, department of overseas trade 1917–28; high commissioner in Canada 1928–34; high commissioner in the Union of South Africa 1934–9; retired 1940; knighted 1915. Died 22 November 1952.

Clark, William Marshall. Railway engineer. Born 1 June 1900, Harlesden, England; parents emigrated to South Africa 1902; educated King Edward VII High School, Johannesburg; University of Cape Town; joined South African Railways as pupil engineer 1921; assistant and then district engineer in all provinces of the Union 1921–34; resident engineer in charge of construction work on the Witwatersrand 1935–41; served in the Second World War as lieutenant-colonel, South African engineering corps, in command of railway construction group in Kenya and the Middle East; recalled to civil service as chief works and estate officer 1942; controller of ship repairs for the Union 1943; chief technical officer in charge of post-war railway reconstruction 1944; general manager of the South African Railways and Harbours 1945. This appointment became a political issue which led in 1950 to the appointment of Clark by the next government to a nominal post. He then became an executive director of the Anglo-American Corporation and director of various other companies. Died 26 February 1966.

Clarkson, Charles Francis. Politician. Born 1 November 1881, Durban, South Africa; educated there; practised as attorney from 1905; secretary, Natal Unionist party; member of the provincial council and executive committee of Natal; Union senator 1930–57; minister of posts and telegraphs 1933; minister of the interior 1945–8. Died 1959.

Clay, Sir Henry. Economist. Born 1883; educated Bradford Grammar School; University College, Oxford; lecturer, workers' educational tutorial classes in Leeds, London and Oxford 1909–17; attached to ministry of labour 1917–19; professor of economics, University of Manchester 1922–30; economic adviser to Bank of England 1930–44; warden of Nuffield College, Oxford 1944–9; author of works on economics, industrial relations and unemployment; knighted 1946. Died 30 July 1954.

Clayton, Brigadier-General Sir Gilbert Falkingham. Soldier and administrator. Born 6 July 1875, Sandown, England; educated Isle of Wight College; Royal Military Academy, Woolwich; entered British army 1895; served in Egypt and the Sudan 1898–1910; director of intelligence, Egypt 1914–17; chief political officer, Egyptian expeditionary force 1917–19; adviser to Egyptian minister of the interior 1919–22; chief secretary, government of Palestine 1922–5; high commissioner for Iraq 1929; knighted 1919. Died 11 September 1929.

Clegg, William Henry. Banker. Born 10 March 1867, Bloemfontein, Orange Free State, South Africa; returned with parents to England and educated there; entered the Bank of England 1886; assistant to the auditor 1895; first auditor 1900; principal of the branch banks office 1914; chief accountant 1919; first governor, South African Reserve Bank 1920–31; director, Bank of England 1932–7; lieutenant of the city of London from 1932. Died 16 March 1945.

Coghlan, Sir Charles Patrick John. Statesman. Born 24 June 1863, King William's Town, Cape Province, South Africa; educated St Aidan's College, Grahamstown; South African College, Cape Town; served in Anglo-Boer War as captain in the Kimberley town guard; member of the legislative assembly of Southern Rhodesia; first prime minister of Southern Rhodesia from 1923. Died 18 August 1927.

Coleraine, Richard Kidston Law, first Baron, of Haltemprice. Politician and journalist. Born 27 February 1901, Helensburgh, Scotland, son of Andrew Bonar Law (q.v. vol. IV); educated Shrewsbury School; St John's College, Oxford; member of the editorial staff, *Morning Post*, *New York Herald Tribune*, *Philadelphia Public Ledger* 1927–9; Conservative member of parliament 1931–54; financial secretary war office 1940–1; parliamentary under-secretary for foreign affairs 1941–3; minister of state 1943–5; president of the board of trade May–July 1945;

minister of education 1945; chairman, national youth employment council 1955–62; director of various companies; created baron 1954; author of *Return from Utopia*.

Collins, Michael. Irish nationalist leader. Born 1890, Clonakilty, County Cork, Eire; educated there and at King's College, London; entered the civil service in Dublin; took part in the Easter Rebellion 1916; Sinn Fein member of parliament 1918; organized Irish Volunteers and commanded the Republican army; signed the treaty of 1921 and was minister of finance in the subsequent provisional government. During the ensuing civil war he was killed in an ambush near Brandon, County Cork on 22 August 1922.

Collins, Colonel William Richard. Politician. Born 31 December 1876, Lydenburg, Transvaal, South Africa; educated in Pretoria; practised as an attorney in Ermelo; served in the Boer forces in the Anglo-Boer War; elected Het Volk member of the Transvaal legislative assembly 1907; served in the First World War; South African party member of parliament 1916–44; minister of agriculture and forestry 1939–44; food controller 1942–4. Died 28 February 1944.

Connaught, Arthur Frederick Patrick Albert, Prince of. Administrator and soldier. Born 13 January 1883, Windsor, England—only son of the Duke of Connaught; educated Eton; Sandhurst; entered the British army 1901; served in the First World War on the staff of the commander-in-chief; retired from the army 1919; governor-general of the Union of South Africa 1920–3; personal aide-de-camp to the king from 1936. Died 12 September 1938.

Conradie, David Gideon. Administrator, politician, lawyer. Born 24 August 1879, Ceres, Cape Province, South Africa; educated there and at Victoria College, Stellenbosch and University of Dublin; after admission to the bar entered the public service 1909; in practice as attorney in the Orange Free State 1915; member of the Orange Free State provincial council 1920–6 and of the executive committee 1923–6; National party member of parliament 1927–33; administrator of South West Africa 1933–43; Afrikaner party member of parliament 1948–57 and deputy speaker; retired from politics 1957. Died 30 September 1966.

Constantine II. King of the Hellenes. Born 2 June 1940 in Athens; only son of King Paul (q.v.) and Queen Frederika (q.v.); lived in South Africa with the refugee royal family 1941–6; educated Anavryta; the army, navy and air force academies of Greece; the University of Athens; appointed regent during his father's illness; succeeded to the throne 6 March 1964; after a *coup d'état* by the army the king and the royal family fled to Italy in December 1967.

Coolidge, Calvin. President of the United States of America. Born 4 July 1872, Plymouth, Vermont; educated Amherst College; practised as a lawyer at Northampton, Massachusetts of which he was mayor in 1910; elected senator 1912; lieutenant-governor of Massachusetts 1916–18; governor 1919–20; vice-president of the United States 1921–3; became president on the death of Harding (q.v.); re-elected 1924; retired 1929. Died 5 January 1933.

Cooper, Alfred Duff, first Viscount Norwich. Politician and diplomat. Born 22 February 1890; educated Eton; New College, Oxford; served in the First World War; Conservative member of parliament 1924–9, 1931–45; financial secretary to the war office 1928–9, 1931–4; financial secretary to the treasury 1934–5; secretary of state for war 1935–7; first lord of the admiralty 1937–8; minister of information 1940–1; chancellor of the Duchy of Lancaster 1941–3; representative of the British government with the French committee of national liberation 1943–4; ambassador to France 1944–7; knighted 1948; created viscount 1952; author of *Talleyrand*; *Haig*; *Old Men Forget*, etc. Died 1 January 1954.

Cooper, Henry William Alexander. Government official. Born 19 July 1895, Swaziland; educated Diocesan College, Cape Town; Transvaal University College; joined the South African public service 1910; private secretary to various ministers; served in East Africa in the First World War; private secretary to the prime minister 1942–8; private secretary to Field Marsha Smuts 1948–50; member of the executive committee of the national committee of the United party 1957–61. Died 26 August 1968.

Cope, John Patrick. Journalist and politician. Born 17 March 1906, Mooi River, Natal, South Africa; educated St Andrew's College, Grahamstown; reporter, *Rand Daily Mail* 1924–9; held senior posts on *Natal Mercury* 1930–8; war correspondent in China 1938; editor, *The Forum* 1940–5, 1948–52; member of the house of assembly, United party 1953–9, Progressive party 1959–62.

Coulter, Charles William Albert. Attorney and politician. Born 17 April 1883, Kokstad, Cape Province, South Africa; educated High School, Durban; South African College, Cape Town; practised in Cape Town; South African party member of parliament 1924–39. Died 7 December 1949.

Craig, Sir James. See **Craigavon.**

Craigavon of Stormont, James Craig, first Viscount. Statesman and soldier. Born 8 January 1871, Craigavon, Down, Northern Ireland; educated Merchiston School, Edinburgh; joined the British army and served in the Anglo-Boer War as captain; Ulster Unionist member of parliament 1906; parliamentary secretary to the ministry of pensions 1919–20; parliamentary and financial secretary to the admiralty 1920–1; first prime minister of Northern Ireland 1921–40; created baronet 1918; viscount 1927. Died 24 November 1940.

Craigie, Sir Robert Leslie. Diplomat. Born 6 December 1883, Southsea, Hampshire, England; educated Haileybury; University of Heidelberg; entered foreign office 1907; acting third secretary in diplomatic service 1908–16; second secretary at Berne 1916–18; first secretary 1919; first secretary at Washington 1920; chargé d'affaires 1921; transferred to foreign office 1923; assistant under-secretary of state, foreign office 1934–7; ambassador to Japan 1937–41; British representative, United Nations war crimes commission 1945–8; knighted 1936. Died 16 May 1959.

Cranborne, Robert Arthur James Gascoyne-Cecil, Viscount, subsequently fifth Marquess of Salisbury. Politician. Born 27 August 1893; educated Eton; Christ Church, Oxford; served in France in the First World War; elected Conservative member of parliament 1929; parliamentary private secretary to Anthony Eden (q.v. under Avon); secretary of state for Dominions 1940–2, 1943–5; secretary of state for the colonies 1942–3; lord privy seal 1942–3; secretary of state for Commonwealth relations 1952; lord president of the council 1952–7; chancellor of the University of Liverpool from 1951.

Cripps, Sir Richard Stafford. English politician and lawyer. Born 24 April 1889; educated Winchester; University College, London; barrister of the Middle Temple 1913; bencher 1930; Labour member of parliament 1931–50; solicitor-general 1930–1; British ambassador to Russia 1940–2; lord privy seal 1942; minister of aircraft production 1942–5; president of the board of trade 1945; minister for economic affairs 1947; chancellor of the exchequer 1947–50; rector, University of Aberdeen 1942; knighted 1930; author of books on politics, law and religion. Died 21 April 1952.

Cromer, Evelyn Baring, first Earl of. Administrator. Born 26 February 1841, Cromer Hall, Norfolk, England; educated Ordnance School, Carshalton; Royal Military Academy, Woolwich; entered the British army 1858; aide-de-camp to Sir Henry Storkes in Ionian Islands 1861; private secretary to the viceroy of India 1872–6; British commissioner in Egypt 1877–9; controller-general, Egypt 1879; member of the council of the governor-general of India 1880–3; British agent and consul-general in Egypt 1883–1907 when he resigned; created baron 1892; viscount 1897; earl 1910; author of *Modern Egypt,* etc. Died 29 January 1917.

Crossman, Richard Howard Stafford. English politician and journalist. Born 15 December 1907; educated Winchester; New College, Oxford; fellow and tutor of New College 1930–7; Labour member of Oxford city council 1934–40; assistant editor, *New Statesman and Nation* 1938–55; Labour member of parliament from 1945; member of the Labour party executive from 1952; minister of housing and local government 1964–6; lord president of the council 1966–70. Author of a number of books, mainly on politics.

Cunningham, General Sir Alan Gordon. English soldier. Born 1 May 1887; educated Cheltenham; Royal Military Academy, Woolwich; entered the British army 1906; served in France throughout the First World War; general staff officer, Straits settlements 1919–21; instructor, machine-gun school 1928–31; commander, royal artillery, first division 1935–9; general officer commanding East Africa forces 1940–1; commander-in-chief, Middle East 1941; commandant, Staff College, Camberley 1942–4; commander-in-chief, Eastern command 1944–5; promoted general 1945; high commissioner, Palestine 1945–8; knighted 1941.

Cuno, Wilhelm. Politician and shipping magnate. Born 2 July 1876, Thüringen, Germany; educated in law; entered the civil service 1900; appointed food controller 1916; director, then chairman of the Hamburg-Amerika shipping line 1917; prime minister 1922–3; co-founder of the Anglo-German alliance 1926. Died 3 January 1933.

Damaskinos, Archbishop (Damaskinos Papandreou). Greek prelate. Born 1891, Dobritza, Thessaly; educated University of Athens; served in the Greek army during Balkan War of 1912; took holy orders 1917; Bishop of Corinth 1922; appointed Metropolitan 1930; his election as Archbishop of Athens and all Greece in 1938 was annulled by premier John Metaxas in favour of Bishop Chrysanthos; in exile until the German invasion in 1941 when he was recalled to replace Chrysanthos; became a leader of the resistance movement; was regent of Greece 1944–6 when King George II (q.v.) was recalled to the throne. Died 20 May 1949.

Darlan, Jean Louis Xavier François. Naval officer. Born 7 August 1881, Nérac, Lot-et-Garonne, France; educated Lycée St Louis, Paris; entered the French naval school 1899; reached the rank of captain 1918; commanded a naval battery on the western front in the First World War; was 'Directeur du Cabinet' to several navy ministers 1926–8, 1929–34; rear-admiral 1929; vice-admiral 1931; chief of naval staff 1939; full admiral and naval commander-in-chief June 1939. After the fall of France he supported the Vichy government and was navy minister and minister for national defence in Marshal Pétain's cabinet 1941–2. He was not in Laval's cabinet but remained commander-in-chief of the armed forces. He was in French North Africa when United States forces occupied it and then supported the allied cause assuming office in December 1942 as French chief of state in North Africa. He was assassinated in Algiers 24 December 1942.

Darling, Sir Malcolm Lyall. Government official. Born 10 December 1880; educated Eton; King's College, Cambridge; joined Indian civil service 1904; registrar, co-operative societies 1927; financial commissioner, Punjab 1936–9; vice-chancellor, University of the Punjab 1931; retired 1940; Indian editor, British Broadcasting Corporation 1940–4; on special duty with the government of India (war department) 1945–6; undertook special missions for the British Council, the government of Pakistan, etc. 1951–60; author of books on co-operatives and the Punjab. Died 1 January 1969.

Dart, Raymond Arthur. Anatomist and palaeontologist. Born 4 February 1893, Toowong, Brisbane, Australia; educated Ipswich Grammar School, Queensland; Universities of Queensland and Sydney; senior demonstrator in anatomy, University College, London 1919–21; professor of anatomy, University of the Witwatersrand, Johannesburg 1923–58; member of the international commission on fossil man since 1929; member of the board, South African Institute for Medical Research 1934–48; president, anthropological section, first pan-African congress on prehistory 1947–51; author of books on anthropology and palaeontology including *The Oriental Horizons of Africa*; *Adventures with the Missing Link*, etc.

Davis, Sir Charles, first Baronet. English engineer. Born 1878; member, Port of London Authority 1928–50; chairman, Medway Conservancy 1936–45; sheriff, city of London 1942–3; lord mayor of London 1945–6; knighted 1944; baronet 1946. Died 27 October 1950.

De Gasperi, Alcide. Statesman and journalist. Born 3 April 1881, Trento, Italy; educated University of Vienna; editor, *Il Nuovo Trentino* 1905–26; deputy in Austrian reichstag 1911–18; deputy in Italian chamber 1921–4; secretary of Popular party 1924–6; imprisoned by the Fascists 1926; assistant, Vatican library 1929–39, then secretary 1939–43; minister without portfolio 1944; minister of foreign affairs 1944–5; prime minister 1945–7, 1948–53. Died 19 August 1954.

De Gaulle, Charles. See **Gaulle.**

Dégoutte, General Jean Marie Joseph. Soldier. Born 9 October 1866, Charnay, France; educated École Normale Supérieure; Saint-Cyr Military Academy; served in the colonies; brigadier-general in command of Moroccan division on the Somme and at Verdun 1916; promoted general and commanded the 6th army at the second battle of the Marne 1918; commander-in-chief, Allied occupation armies in Germany 1920–4; carried out occupation of the Ruhr 1923. Died 31 October 1938.

d'Egville, Sir Howard. Organizer and first secretary of the Empire Parliamentary Association. Educated St Catharine's College, Cambridge; barrister of the Middle Temple; member of the war cabinet secretariat 1917; knighted 1920; editor, *Journal of the Parliaments of the Empire*; *Report on Foreign Affairs*; *Journal of the African Society* (joint editor); author of books on imperial questions. Died 9 January 1965.

Delamere, Hugh Cholmondeley, third Baron. Farmer. Born 28 April 1870, London; educated Eton; entered the British army and became captain; emigrated to Kenya 1897 where he was a pioneer farmer on a large scale; member of the first legislative council 1907; elected member 1920; member of the executive council; protagonist of permanent white settlement in Kenya. Died 13 November 1931.

De la Rey, Adolf Johannes. Commandant and politician. Born 17 December 1875, Delareysrust, near Krugersdorp, Transvaal; served in the Anglo-Boer War, under General Botha in the 1914 rebellion, and in South West Africa, and during the 1922 rebellion; member of the Transvaal provincial council 1924–46; United party senator from 1948. Died 10 July 1967.

Delfos, Cornelis Frederick. Industrialist. Born 21 June 1868, Rotterdam, the Netherlands; educated Amsterdam; went to Pretoria 1890 and set up an electrical engineering firm there and a blast furnace for the production of iron and steel 1918; director of the South African Iron and Steel Corporation in the establishment of which he had an important part. Died 23 October 1933.

Deshmukh, Ramrao Madhavrao. Politician. Born 25 November 1892, Pimplod, Berar, India; educated University of Cambridge; called to the bar 1917; member, Nagpur legislative council 1920–30; member, all-India Congress committee 1920–5; minister, Madya Pradesh 1927–30, 1937–8; political minister, Dewas state 1939–41; finance minister, Gwalior 1941–4; high commissioner for India in the Union of South Africa 1945–7; director, Reserve Bank of India 1949–52; elected to Rajya Sabha 1952.

De Valera, Eamon. Irish statesman. Born 14 October 1882, New York; went to Ireland as a child; educated Christian Brothers School, Rathluire; Blackrock College, Dublin; school-teacher and university lecturer; joined Irish Volunteers 1913; commandant in the Easter Rebellion 1916 after which he was imprisoned; released 1917 and elected member of parliament; president of Sinn Fein 1917–26; president of the Irish Republic 1919–22; founder and president of Fianna Fail 1926–59; prime minister of Eire 1933–48, 1951–4, 1957–9; president since 1959.

De Villiers, Cornelius Gerhardus Stephanus (Con). Zoologist and literary translator. Born 16 December 1894, Caledon, Cape Province, South Africa; educated Caledon; Victoria College, Stellenbosch; University of Zurich; lecturer in zoology, Transvaal University College 1916–20; professor of zoology, University of Stellenbosch until his retirement 1957; member of the board of governors, South African Broadcasting Corporation 1948; trustee of the South African Museum 1952–5; translator of novels, plays, etc. from the Italian, German, French and Scandinavian languages into Afrikaans; author of prose sketches and stories, chiefly about the Caledon district.

De Villiers, Major-General Isaac Pierre. Soldier, attorney, company director. Born 20 August 1891, Somerset East, Cape Province, South Africa; educated Gill College; South African College; served in South West Africa, France and Palestine in the First World War; in practice as attorney in Cape Town 1919–27; became commissioner of police 1928–45; appointed general officer commanding the second South African division 1940 and served in the Middle East 1941–2; general officer commanding the coastal area with headquarters at Cape Town; chairman, Union immigration selection board 1946–8; director of De Beers Consolidated Mines and other companies 1945–65. Died 11 October 1967.

Devonshire, Edward William Spencer Cavendish, tenth Duke of. Politician. Born 6 May 1895; educated Eton; Trinity College, Cambridge; served in the First World War in Egypt, Gallipoli, France; assistant private secretary to his father (q.v.) 1923; Conservative member of the house of commons 1923–38 when he succeeded to the dukedom; parliamentary under-secretary of state for the Dominions 1936–40, for India 1940–2, for the colonies 1942–5; chancellor of the University of Leeds from 1938; president, Zoological Society of London 1948. Died 26 November 1950.

Devonshire, Victor Christian William Cavendish, ninth Duke of. Politician and administrator. Born 31 May 1868; educated Eton; Trinity College, Cambridge; Unionist member of the house of commons 1891–1908 when he succeeded to the dukedom; financial secretary to the treasury 1903–5; civil lord of the admiralty 1915–16; governor-general of Canada 1916–21; secretary of state for the colonies 1922–4; chancellor of the University of Leeds from 1909; president of the Royal Agricultural Society 1932. Died 6 May 1938.

De Vos, Reverend Pieter Jacobus Gerhardus. Theologian and minister of religion. Born 29 October 1942 near Worcester, Cape Province, South Africa; educated in Cape Town, Scotland and the Netherlands; minister at Piquetberg 1867, Caledon 1871, Riversdal 1880; professor at the Theological Seminary, Stellenbosch 1883–1919. Died 1 October 1931.

De Waal, Jan Hendrik Hofmeyr. Writer and politician. Born 30 December 1871, Bakkerskloof, Somerset West, Cape Province; educated Normal College and South African College, Cape Town; became a teacher; called to the bar 1897 and practised in Cape Town; editor of *De Goede Hoop* 1903–14; one of the founders of the Afrikaanse Taalvereniging; National party member of parliament from 1915; author of several Afrikaans novels, plays and short stories and of a grammar of Afrikaans. Died 30 October 1937.

Dill, Field Marshal Sir John Greer. Soldier. Born 25 December 1881, Belfast, Northern Ireland; educated Cheltenham and Sandhurst; served in Anglo-Boer War and in the First World War when he was brigadier-major; major-general 1921; commandant of Camberley Staff College 1931; director of operations and intelligence, war office 1934; general, in charge of Aldershot infantry base 1937; corps commander in France 1939; chief of the imperial general staff 1940–1; promoted field marshal 1941; special duties in Washington, India and China and attended various war conferences 1941–4; knighted 1937. Died 4 November 1944.

Dolfuss, Engelbert. Statesman. Born 4 October 1892, Texing, Lower Austria; educated Universities of Vienna and Berlin; served as officer in the Austrian army during the First World War; leader of chamber of agriculture of Lower Austria 1927; president of Austrian federal railways 1931; minister of agriculture and forestry March 1932; chancellor and minister of foreign affairs May 1932; as an opponent of the *anschluss* with Germany he was assassinated by Austrian Nazis on 25 July 1934.

Dommisse, Jan. Actuary and politician. Born 24 September 1902, Piquetberg, Cape Colony; educated there and at the University of Cape Town; private secretary to General Smuts 1925; lecturer in mathematics, Grey University College 1926–8; on staff of S.A.N.L.A.M. 1928–35, then South African Mutual 1936; member of the Cape provincial council since 1959; member, Cape Town city council since 1964; mayor of Cape Town 1969.

Donald, Sir Robert. Journalist and publisher. Born 29 August 1860, Banffshire, Scotland; editor, *Daily Chronicle* 1892–1918; founded the *Municipal Year Book* 1893; proprietor of *The Referee*; part owner of the *Yorkshire Observer*; managing director, Everyman Publishing Company; served in ministry of information during the First World War; chairman of the committee on imperial wireless telegraphy 1924; knighted 1924; author of books on contemporary politics. Died 17 February 1933.

Donnan, Frederick George. Chemist. Born 6 September 1870, Holywood, County Down, Ireland; educated Queen's University, Belfast; Universities of Leipzig, Berlin, London; assistant professor, University College, London 1902; lecturer in chemistry, Royal College of Science, Dublin 1903–4; professor of physical chemistry, University of Liverpool 1904–13, University College, London, 1913–37. Died 16 December 1956.

Drennan, Matthew Robertson. Anatomist and archaeologist. Born 1885, Ayrshire, Scotland; educated Ayr Academy; University of Edinburgh; went to South Africa 1913; medical practitioner at Aliwal North, Cape Province 1914; served as medical officer in the First World War; lecturer in anatomy, South African College 1916; professor of anatomy, University of Cape Town 1918–55. Died 27 July 1965.

Drummond, Sir James Eric. See **Perth.**

Duggan, Eamon John. Irish politician. Born 1874; educated in law and admitted as a solicitor in Ireland 1914; joined Sinn Fein party and was elected member of parliament 1918; commandant of the Irish Republican Army 1920–1; signed the Irish Free State treaty 1922; minister for home affairs and then without portfolio in the provisional government 1922–3; secretary to the president of the council, W. T. Cosgrave, 1927–32; member of the dail 1921–32; senator 1933. Died 6 June 1936.

Dulles, John Foster. Statesman and lawyer. Born 25 February 1888, Washington D.C.; educated Princeton University; the Sorbonne; George Washington University; began law practice 1911; army captain at war trade board 1917; adviser to the United States delegation at Paris peace conference 1919; leading member of the Republican party; adviser to United States delegation at San Francisco conference 1945; United States senator 1949; adviser to secretary of state 1950; secretary of state 1953–9. Died 24 May 1959.

Duncan, Patrick Baker. Government official. Born 29 June 1918, Johannesburg, South Africa; educated Winchester; Balliol College, Oxford; private secretary to the high commissioner for the British territories 1946–7; assistant district officer, Basutoland 1947–9; judicial commissioner, Basutoland 1950–2. From 1952 to 1963 he actively opposed the policies of the South African government on Africans and Indians, served a prison sentence, and was confined to the Cape Peninsula. Defying this ban he went to Basutoland, joined the Pan-African congress, was excluded from Basutoland, Bechuanaland and Swaziland and went to England. Died 4 June 1967.

Du Preez, Daniel Wynand. Farmer. Born 6 June 1911, Standerton, Transvaal, South Africa; educated Agricultural College, Potchefstroom; developed the well-known Langverwyl Friesland cattle stud; served in the Middle East in the Second World War reaching the rank of captain; secretary of the Standerton branch of the United party; executive member, South African Friesland Breeders' Association and Witwatersrand Agricultural Society.

Du Toit, Alexander Logie. Geologist. Born 14 March 1878, Rondebosch, Cape Town, South Africa; educated Diocesan College, Rondebosch; Royal Technical College, Glasgow; lecturer, Glasgow University 1900; secretary, Cape geological commission 1903–19; engaged in research in South Africa and South America 1919–24; advisory geologist, De Beers Consolidated Mines from 1927; led government expedition to the Kalahari 1925; author of *Geology of South Africa*; *Our Wandering Continents*. Died 25 February 1948.

Eddington, Sir Arthur Stanley. Astronomer. Born 28 December 1882, Kendal, England; educated Owens College; Trinity College, Cambridge; senior wrangler 1904; chief assistant, Royal Observatory, Greenwich 1906–13; fellow of Trinity College 1907; professor of astronomy and director of the observatory, Cambridge from 1913; knighted 1930; awarded Order of Merit 1938; author of books on science and astronomy, notably *The Nature of the Physical World*; *Science and the Unseen World*; *The Expanding Universe*; *The Relativity Theory of Protons and Electrons*. Died 22 November 1944.

Eden, Robert Anthony. See **Avon.**

Edward VIII (Edward Albert Christian George Andrew Patrick David). King of Great Britain. Born 23 June 1894, White Lodge, Richmond, Surrey, eldest son of George V and Queen Mary (qq.v.); educated Royal Naval College, Osborne and Dartmouth; Magdalen College, Oxford; gazetted to Grenadier Guards and served in France, Italy and Egypt 1914–17; visited many of the countries of the Commonwealth 1919–27; succeeded to the throne 20 January 1936; abdicated 11 December 1936 following public criticism of his matrimonial intentions; created Duke of Windsor 27 May 1937; married Mrs Wallis Warfield, formerly Simpson, 3 June 1937; was governor of the Bahama Islands 1940–5. Died 28 May 1972.

Egeland, Leif. Politician, lawyer, diplomat, company director. Born 19 January 1903, Durban, South Africa; educated Durban High School; University of Natal; Trinity College, Oxford; barrister of the Middle Temple; advocate of the supreme court of South Africa 1931; United party member of parliament 1933–8, 1940–3; served in the Middle East 1943; South African minister to Sweden 1943–6, and to the Netherlands and Belgium 1946–8; high commissioner in London 1948–50; elected bencher of the Middle Temple 1948; director of a number of South African companies.

Einstein, Albert. Physicist. Born 14 March 1879, Ulm, Germany; educated Swiss Federal Polytechnic School, Zürich; University of Zürich; became a Swiss citizen 1900; technical expert in the patents office at Bern 1902–5; professor at University of Zürich 1909, at University of Prague 1910, at Swiss Federal Polytechnic School 1912, at University of Berlin 1913; published his great paper on the general theory of relativity 1916; received Nobel prize in physics 1922; emigrated to the United States in 1933, joined the Institute for Advanced Study in Princeton and became a United States citizen in 1940; author of *The Meaning of Relativity*; *About Zionism*; *Builders of the Universe*; *Why War?*; *The World as I see it*; *The Evolution of Physics*; *Out of my Later Years*. Died 18 April 1955.

Eisenhower, General Dwight David. Soldier and president of the United States. Born 14 October 1890, Denison, Texas; educated West Point Military Academy; company officer in the United States army 1915–17; commanded a tank corps 1918–22; graduated Command and General Staff School 1926; assistant executive, office of assistant secretary for war 1929–33; assistant military adviser, Philippine Islands 1935–40; in command European theatre of operations 1942; commander-in-chief, Allied forces in north Africa 1942–4; supreme commander, Allied expeditionary force in western Europe 1944–5; supreme commander, North Atlantic treaty forces in Europe 1950–2; resigned from the army 1952; president of the United States 1953–61; author of *Crusade in Europe*. Died 28 March 1969.

Elliot, Walter. Politician. Born 1888, Lanark, Scotland; educated Glasgow Academy; University of Glasgow; served in the First World War 1914–18; Conservative member of parliament 1918–23, 1924–45; member for the Scottish universities 1946–50; parliamentary under-secretary for health 1923–6; parliamentary under-secretary for Scotland 1926–9; financial secretary to the treasury 1931–2; secretary of state for Scotland 1936–8; minister of health 1938–40; director of public relations, war office 1941–2; rector of Aberdeen University 1933–6 and of Glasgow University 1947–50; Companion of Honour 1952; author of *Toryism and the Twentieth Century*; *Long Distance*. Died 8 January 1958.

Elliott, Sir Charles Bletterman. Government official. Born 8 May 1841, Uitenhage, Cape Province, South Africa; educated South African College, Cape Town; entered civil service as clerk in the office of the colonial secretary 1859 where he served until 1863 and 1867–72; secretary to the Board of Public Examiners 1863–73; acting resident magistrate at Wynberg and Cape Town; admitted as advocate of the supreme court 1875; assistant commissioner of crown lands and public works 1876; general manager, Cape Government Railways 1880; special commissioner of railways 1901–2; knighted 1901. Died 10 April 1911.

Elliott, Guy Abercrombie. Physician. Born 5 November 1905, Wynberg, near Cape Town; educated South African College School; University of Cape Town; physician, Groote Schuur Hospital; served in the Second World War as colonel in the South African medical corps; professor of medicine, University of the Witwatersrand; senior physician, Johannesburg General Hospital; retired 1967.

Ellis, George Rayner. Journalist. Born 5 October 1897, London; educated Latimer School; University of Cambridge; served in the First World War; on staff of the League of Nations; editor of the religious paper *Outward Bound*; went to South Africa 1926 and joined the staff of the *Rand Daily Mail* of which he became editor in 1941. Died 6 November 1953.

Ellis, Mervyn. Journalist. Born 1896; educated Cardiff High School; entered journalism 1913 on staff of the *South Wales News* and *Echo*, Cardiff; news editor, then assistant editor of the *Morning Post*, England; editor of the *Natal Mercury* 1938–59. Died 9 February 1968.

Elwes, Simon. Painter. Born 29 June 1902, Theddingworth, Rugby, England; educated the Oratory School, Edgbaston; Slade School; served in the Second World War 1939–45; a portrait painter in oil; associate of the Royal Academy 1956; Royal Academician 1967; vice-president, Royal Society of Portrait Painters from 1953.

Engler, Heinrich Gustav Adolf. Botanist. Born 25 March 1844, Sagan, Lower Silesia, Germany; educated University of Breslau; teacher at Breslau Gymnasium 1866–71; engaged in research at Munich 1871–8; professor of botany at University of Kiel 1878–83, Breslau 1884–9 and Berlin 1889–1914; visited Cape Town 1902 and South West Africa 1913; founder and editor of the *Botanische Jahrbücher*; author of *Pflanzenwelt Afrikas*. Died 10 October 1930.

Erasmus, François Christiaan. Politician and diplomat. Born 1896, Merweville, Cape Province, South Africa; educated Worcester High School; University of Cape Town; practised as advocate 1925–7; assistant attorney-general, South West Africa, then National party organizer in Cape Province; member of parliament 1933–60; minister of defence 1949–59; minister of justice 1960; ambassador to Italy 1961–5 when he retired. Died 7 January 1967.

Evans, Sir Charles Arthur Lovatt. Physiologist. Born 1884 in England; educated University of Birmingham; University College, London; University of Freiburg; assistant, University College 1911–17; served in royal army medical corps 1916; professor of physiology, University of Leeds 1917–19; engaged in research, National Institute of Medical Research, London 1919–22; professor of physiology, University College 1926–49; chairman, military personnel research committee, war office 1948–53; consultant, ministry of supply 1949–59, war office from 1959; knighted 1951; author of *Recent Advances in Physiology*; *Principles of Human Physiology*. Died 29 August 1968.

Evatt, Herbert Vere. Politician and judge. Born 30 April 1894, East Maitland, New South Wales, Australia; educated St Andrews College; University of Sydney; admitted to the New South Wales bar; judge of the high court of Australia 1930–40; member of the Australian war cabinet 1941–6; attorney-general and minister for external affairs 1946–9; Australian representative at U.N.O. 1947; president, United Nations assembly 1948; leader of parliamentary Labour party 1951–60; chief justice of New South Wales 1960–2; author of a number of books on Commonwealth and Australian politics.

Fagan, Henry Allan. Judge, politician, writer. Born 4 April 1889, Tulbagh, Cape Province, South Africa; educated Victoria College, Stellenbosch; University of London; barrister of the Middle Temple; practised as an advocate in Cape Town 1914–16, 1921–38, 1940–3; assistant editor, *Die Burger* 1916–19; professor of law, University of Stellenbosch 1920; National party member of parliament 1933–43; minister of native affairs, education and social welfare 1938–9; judge of the supreme court 1943–50; judge of the court of appeal 1950–9; chief justice of the Union of South Africa 1957–9; United party senator 1962; chairman, Native laws commission 1946–8; author of books on South African colour questions and of stories, poems and plays in Afrikaans; awarded the Hertzog prize for drama 1935; devised a new system of shorthand. Died 6 December 1963.

Fahey, Frank J. Politician. Born in Canada; emigrated to South Africa 1898 as a linotype operator; employed by the *Star*, the *Natal Witness* and the *Natal Mercury*; joined the Labour party and mediated in a dispute between sugar-planters and millers; member of the Natal provincial council 1922–4; member of the board of trade and industry 1924, and chairman from 1932; chairman, cost of living commission 1933; Union delegate on the eastern group supply council in India during the Second World War. Died 25 January 1943.

Farouk I. King of Egypt. Born 11 February 1920; educated privately and at Woolwich Military Academy; succeeded his father, Fouad I, as regent 1936; became king 1937; abdicated 1952 when his government was overthrown by a military coup; thereafter lived in Italy. Died 18 March 1965.

Feisal I (Feisal ibn Husain). King of Iraq. Born 20 May 1885 near Taif in the Hejaz; third son of Husain ibn Ali (q.v.); educated in Constantinople; deputy for Jiddah in the Turkish parliament 1913; took a leading part in the Arab revolt in the Hejaz commanding Arab forces under General Allenby until the capture of Damascus in 1918; proclaimed king of Syria in March 1920 but deposed in July when the French mandate was assumed; elected king of Iraq in August 1921 under British mandate; secured eventual recognition of Iraq as a fully independent state in 1930. Died 8 September 1933.

Fitzalan-Howard, Edmund Bernard, first Viscount of Derwent. Politician. Born 1 June 1855; assumed the name Talbot 1876, reverted to Fitzalan-Howard 1921; educated Oratory School, Edgbaston; Unionist member of parliament 1894–1921; junior lord of the treasury 1905, joint parliamentary secretary 1915–21; chief Unionist whip 1913–21; viceroy of Ireland 1921–2; knighted 1919; created viscount 1921. Died 18 May 1947.

Forman, Frank. Physician. Born 1898, Paarl, Cape Province, South Africa; educated Universities of Cape Town and Aberdeen; appointed to the faculty of medicine, University of Cape Town 1924; professor of clinical medicine, University of Cape Town 1938–54; fellow of the Royal College of Physicians 1942; resigned his chair 1954 but remained a senior lecturer at the medical school until 1963.

Forsyth, Douglas David. Government official. Born 4 March 1896, Pietermaritzburg, Natal, South Africa; educated Boys' Model School, Pietermaritzburg; Transvaal University College; joined civil service 1911; in the department of defence 1912–20; served in South West and East Africa campaigns 1914–18; held magisterial posts 1920–34; public service inspector 1934–7; under-secretary for social welfare 1937–9; secretary for South West Africa 1939–41; secretary to the prime minister 1941; secretary for external affairs 1941–56; director, De Beers Consolidated Mines since 1956.

Fourie, Adrianus Paulus Johannes. Politician. Born 11 August 1882, Phillipstown, Cape Province, South Africa; became a schoolmaster; fought in the Anglo-Boer War with the republican forces; qualified and practised as an attorney; National party member, Cape provincial council; administrator of the Cape Province 1926; minister of mines and industries 1929–33; minister of labour and social welfare 1933–9; nominated senator 1938. Died 6 July 1941.

Fourie, Bernardus Gerhardus. Diplomat. Born 13 October 1916, Wolmaransstad, Transvaal, South Africa; educated there and at the University of Pretoria and New York University; joined the office of the controller and auditor-general 1934; transferred to the department of external affairs and was attached to the South African legation in Berlin 1939; subsequently held several diplomatic posts; stationed in London during the Second World War until 1947; member of the South African delegation at the San Francisco conference 1945 and at the first meeting of the United Nations general assembly in London 1946; member of the permanent South African delegation at the United Nations 1947–52; in the head office of the department of foreign affairs 1952–8; permanent representative of South Africa at U.N.O. 1958–62; under-secretary in charge of the African division, department of foreign affairs 1962; secretary for information 1963–6; secretary for foreign affairs 1966.

Franco Bahamonde, General Don Francisco. Head of the Spanish state and generalissimo. Born 4 December 1892, El Ferrol, Spain; educated Infantry Academy, Toledo; commissioned in 1910; served in Morocco 1912–17; with Oviedo garrison 1917–20; deputy-commander, foreign legion, Morocco 1920–3 and commander 1923–7; director-general, Military Academy, Saragossa 1927–31; captain-general, Balearic Islands 1933–5; commander-in-chief, Moroccan army 1935; chief of the general staff 1935; led the victorious insurgent forces in the civil war of 1936–9; since then ruler of Spain and commander of the national forces governing since 1947 as regent pending the assumption of the throne by the restored monarchy.

Frederica Louise. Consort of Paul I, King of the Hellenes (q.v.). Born 18 April 1917, Blankenburg Castle, Germany; only daughter of the Duke of Brunswick-Lüneberg; educated at schools in Kent, in Obenkirchen and in Florence; married Prince Paul 1938; spent four years in South Africa during the Second World War and returned to Greece in 1946. After the accession of her husband to the throne and the defeat of the Communists she organized an extensive relief fund. Left Greece with the royal family after the *coup d'état* of 1967.

Friend, George Alfred. Farmer and politician. Born 28 September 1890, Vryheid, Natal, South Africa; educated privately; partner in Friend Bros., large merino sheep farmers in Natal; member of the executive, South African party in Natal 1915; member, house of assembly 1929–33, 1938–48; chairman, general council of the South African party of northern Natal 1932, 1951; Natal party whip until 1948; senator 1956–65.

Froude, James Anthony. Historian. Born 23 April 1818, Dartington, Devon, England; educated Westminster; Oriel College, Oxford; fellow of Exeter College, Oxford 1842–8; wrote his great *History of England* 1856–71; editor of *Fraser's Magazine* 1860–74; undertook missions to South Africa to promote federation 1874–5; rector of the University of St Andrews from 1868; regius professor of modern history at Oxford 1892–4. Among his other works are *The English in Ireland in the Eighteenth Century* (1872–4), *The Life and Letters of Erasmus* (1898) and books on the life of Carlyle. Died 20 October 1894.

Gandhi, Manilal Mohandas. Journalist. Born 1892, son of M. K. Gandhi (q.v. vol. IV); editor of *Indian Opinion* founded 1903 in South Africa by his father of whose political views and methods he was a lifelong protagonist; undertook various campaigns in South Africa and abroad to oppose what he regarded as injustices in race relations. Died 5 April 1956.

Gardiner, Alfred George. Journalist and writer. Born 1865, Chelmsford, England; editor of the *Daily News* 1902–19. Under the pen-name Alpha of the Plough he wrote a series of sketches of well-known contemporaries; author of biographies of Sir William Harcourt and George Cadbury. Died 3 March 1946.

Gaulle, General Charles André Joseph Marie de. Statesman and soldier. Born 22 November 1890, Lille, France; educated Saint-Cyr Military Academy; served as captain in the First World War; lecturer in military history, Saint-Cyr 1921;

undertook mission to Iraq, Iran and Egypt; secretary-general to the council for national defence 1932; general of brigade and commander, 4th armoured division 1939–40; leader of the Free French, then president of the French national committee in London 1940–2, and Algiers 1943; president of the provisional government of the French Republic and chief of armies 1944–6; founded *Rassemblement du peuple français* 1947; president 1947–54; in retirement until 1958 when he formed a government and secured a new constitution; elected president January 1959, 1966; author of *La France et son armée*; *Vers l'armée de métier*; memoirs. Died 9 November 1970.

Gayda, Virginio. Journalist. Born 12 August 1885, Rome; educated University of Turin. His early assignments were to Turkey and Austria; during the First World War worked in Rome and was special press envoy to Russia 1915–18 and thereafter to Stockholm, London, Paris and Berlin; editor in Rome of *Messaggero* 1921–6, and *Giornale d'Italia*, the mouthpiece of Mussolini, 1926–43; author of books on European politics. Died 14 March 1944 during an air raid on Rome.

Geldenhuys, Lourens. Goldfields pioneer, farmer, politician. Born 6 December 1864 near Heidelberg, Transvaal; took part in opening up the main Witwatersrand reef at Geldenhuys Estate; joint owner with his brother of Braamfontein farm; member of the second volksraad for the Witwatersrand 1895–9; served with the Krugersdorp commando in Natal during the Anglo-Boer War; South African party member of parliament 1910–29. Died 1929.

George II. King of the Hellenes. Born 20 July 1890, Tatoi, Athens; son of King Constantine and Princess Sophia of Prussia; received military and naval training; married in 1921 Princess Elizabeth of Rumania who divorced him in 1935; succeeded to the throne 27 September 1922 on the deposition of his father but left Greece in December 1923 after the failure of a monarchist revolution and the subsequent deposition of the dynasty by the assembly; returned as king in November 1935 after the restoration of the monarchy by the assembly and a plebiscite; left Greece again after the German invasion in 1941 and lived in Cairo, Cape Town and London until a plebiscite brought him back to the throne on 27 September 1946. Died 1 April 1947.

George V. King of Great Britain. Born 3 June 1865, Marlborough House, London; second son of the then Prince of Wales; joined the training ship *Britannia* as a naval cadet 1877; served in the *Bacchante* 1879–82; abandoned his naval career on the death of his elder brother 1892; married Princess Mary of Teck (q.v.) 1893; created Duke of York 1892, Duke of Cornwall 1901, Prince of Wales 1901; succeeded to the throne 1910. His guidance and personal intervention in the crises over the powers of the house of lords, home rule in Ireland, the general strike and the formation of the national government in 1931 were important. Died 20 January 1936.

George VI (Albert Frederick Arthur George). King of Great Britain. Born 14 December 1895, Sandringham, Norfolk; second son of George V; educated by tutors; at Royal Naval College, Osborne; Dartmouth; Trinity College, Cambridge; served in the royal navy from 1913 and in the First World War; became an air pilot and was commissioned in the royal air force 1919; created Duke of York 1920 and entered the house of lords; began a lifelong interest in improved social and industrial conditions; president of the Industrial Welfare Association; sponsor of boys' camps 1921–39; succeeded to the throne on the abdication of Edward VIII (q.v.) on 11 December 1936; married Lady Elizabeth Bowes-Lyon, daughter of the Earl of Strathmore in 1923. Died 6 February 1952.

George, Prince, of Greece. Born 24 June 1869, second son of King George I of the Hellenes and Olga, Grand-Duchess of Russia; married, in 1907, Princess Marie Bonaparte (q.v.); served in the Balkan Wars; was an admiral in the Greek navy and aide-de-camp to his father. Died 27 November 1957.

George Wilhelm, Prince. Born 25 March 1915, Brunswick, second son of Ernst August, Duke of Brunswick-Lüneberg and Princess Viktoria Luise, only daughter of Wilhelm II, emperor of Germany; brother of Frederica of Greece (q.v.);

married, in 1946, Princess Sophia, widow of Prince Christopher of Hesse and daughter of Prince Andrew of Greece.

Gie, Stephanus François Naudé. Diplomat, educationist, historian. Born 13 July 1884, Worcester, Cape Province, South Africa; educated Boys' High School, Worcester; Victoria College, Stellenbosch; Universities of Amsterdam and Berlin; held teaching posts at Cradock and Worcester 1906–9; inspector of schools 1910–11; principal, Teachers' Training College, Graaff Reinet; professor of history and subsequently rector of the University of Stellenbosch; secretary for education 1926–34; minister in Berlin 1934–9, in Stockholm 1939–44, in Washington 1944–5; author of *Geskiedenis van Suid-Afrika.* Died 10 April 1945.

Gillett, Sir George Masterman. Politician. Born 1870, Islington, London; member, Finsbury borough council 1900–6; member, London county council 1910–12; member of parliament 1923–35; secretary, department of overseas trade 1929–31. Died 10 August 1939.

Giraud, General Henri Honoré. Soldier. Born 18 January 1879, Paris; educated Saint-Cyr Military School; joined 4th Zouave regiment and served in Morocco and as captain in the First World War; succeeded Lyautey as commander of the French forces in Morocco 1925; military governor of Metz 1936; commander of the 7th army 1939; captured and imprisoned in Saxony 1940; escaped to unoccupied France, thence to Algeria and succeeded Darlan as high commissioner and commander-in-chief of French West and North Africa 1942; co-chairman with De Gaulle (q.v.) of the French committee of national liberation May–November 1943; retired on the abolition of the post of commander-in-chief 1944. Died 11 March 1949.

Glubb, Sir John Bagot. English soldier and writer. Born 16 April 1897; educated Cheltenham; Royal Military Academy, Woolwich; served in France in the First World War; political officer in Iraq 1920–6; administrative inspector, government of Iraq 1926–30; transferred to Transjordan as officer commanding, desert area 1932; officer commanding Arab legion, Transjordan 1939–56 when he was dismissed by King Hussein; author of books on the Arab legion, Arab history and Middle East politics.

Gluckman, Henry. South African politician and medical practitioner. Born 12 July 1893; educated King Edward VII School, Johannesburg; University of London; served in medical corps in the First and Second World Wars; United party member of parliament 1938–58; chairman, national health service commission 1942–4; minister of health and housing 1945–8; member of the board of governors, Hebrew University of Jerusalem.

Goddijn, Wouter Adriaan. Botanist. Born 9 April 1884, Leiden, the Netherlands; educated Gouda; University of Leiden; assistant, Rijksherbarium 1910, conservator 1914–34; professor of pharmacography, University of Leiden from 1934; editor of *Genetica* from 1939; retired 1952; author of *Pharmacognosie* and articles on hybridization and evolution.

Godley, Richard Sherman. Police officer. Born 1876, Woolwich, England; educated Imperial Services College, Westward Ho; worked as office-boy in London 1893–5; went to South Africa 1896 and joined the forces dealing with the risings in Matabeleland and Mashonaland; commissioned in Mashonaland police 1897; in charge of Enkeldoorn police district 1898; served in Anglo-Boer War 1900; transferred to South African constabulary, Transvaal 1901–2; district commandant, Wakkerstroom, Potchefstroom, Krugersdorp 1903–13; divisional inspector with rank of major 1913; acting deputy commissioner, Natal, with rank of lieutenant-colonel 1914–20; deputy commissioner, Witwatersrand 1921–31 when he retired; returned to England 1937; wrote memoirs. Died 3 December 1950.

Goebbels, Joseph Paul. Politician. Born 29 October 1897, Rheydt, Rhineland, Germany; educated at various universities, graduating Ph.D. at Heidelberg; worked as a journalist and became National Socialist propagandist 1922; party leader for Berlin 1926; founded *Der Angriff* 1927; elected to reichstag and made chief of party propaganda 1928–30; minister of propaganda and enlightenment controlling press, radio, cinema, theatres, etc. 1933; later *Reichsleiter* in the party and president of the *Reichskulturkammer*; wrote diaries. Died 1 May 1945 by suicide.

Goering, Hermann Wilhelm. Politician. Born 12 January 1893, Rosenheim, Bavaria, Germany; educated Cadet College, Karlsruhe; served in the First World War in the air force and became a combat ace; adviser in Danish airways 1919; transport pilot in Sweden 1920–1; joined the National Socialists 1922 and took part in the Munich *putsch*; lived in Italy and Sweden 1923–7; elected to reichstag 1928; president of reichstag 1932; minister for air and of the interior 1933, in which posts he founded the Gestapo (secret police) and began to build up German air power; took a leading part in the purge of June 1934 and the army crisis of February 1938; became chief of the *Luftwaffe* 1935 and marshal of the reich 1940; directed the German economy with full powers 1937–43. Sentenced to death at the Nürnberg trials. Died 16 October 1946 by suicide.

Goldschmidt, Viktor. Mineralogist. Born 1853, Mayence, Germany; instructor at the University of Heidelberg 1888, subsequently professor 1893 and honorary associate professor 1903; author of *Atlas der Kristallformen der Mineralien* and many other works on mineralogy. Died 1933.

Goodenough, Frederick Cranfurd. English banker. Born 1866, Calcutta; educated Charterhouse, University of Zurich; member of the India council 1917–30; chairman of Barclays Bank; director, Alliance Assurance Company and Westminster Chambers Association; member of the council of foreign bondholders. Died 1 September 1934.

Goodwin, Astley John Hilary. Archaeologist. Born 27 December 1900, Pietermaritzburg, Natal, South Africa; educated St John's College, Johannesburg; Selwyn College, Cambridge; research assistant in ethnology, University of Cape Town 1923; senior lecturer 1926; developed standard terminology of South African archaeology; honorary secretary, Royal Society of South Africa from 1934; honorary secretary and founder, South African Archaeological Society from 1944; member of various expeditions, notably the Dewer expedition in the south Kalahari; went with the Abbé Breuil on his first South African tour (1929); author of *The Stone Age Cultures of South Africa*; *Method in Prehistory*; and many scientific papers. Died 5 December 1959.

Gort, Field Marshal John Standish Surtees Prendergast, first Viscount, of Hamsterley. Soldier. Born 10 July 1886; educated Harrow; Royal Military College, Sandhurst; served in France 1914–18, first as aide-de-camp to Earl Haig, then in command of battalions as brigade-major; awarded the Victoria Cross; director of military training in India 1932; military secretary, war office and then chief of the imperial general staff 1937; commanded British expeditionary force in France September 1939–May 1940; inspector-general of the forces; governor-general, Gibraltar 1941; governor of Malta 1942–3; high commissioner, Palestine and Transjordan 1944; became ill and resigned 1945; promoted field marshal 1943; created viscount 1945. Died 31 March 1946.

Graaff, Sir de Villiers, second Baronet. South African politician. Born 8 December 1913; educated Diocesan College, Rondebosch; Universities of Cape Town and Oxford; barrister of the Inner Temple; advocate of the supreme court of South Africa; served in the Second World War and was taken prisoner 1939–45; United party member of parliament since 1948; leader of the United party and the opposition since 1956.

Gregory, Joseph Tracy. Palaeontologist. Born 28 July 1914, Eureka, California, United States of America; educated University of California (Berkeley); Institute of Meteorology, Chicago; lecturer in zoology, Columbia University 1939–40; instructor in geology, University of Michigan 1941–6; associate professor of geology, Yale University 1946–60; professor of palaeontology and curator of the museum of palaeontology, University of California (Berkeley) from 1960; co-editor, *American Journal of Science* 1955–60; served with the United States army 1942–6.

Griffith, Arthur. Irish journalist and nationalist leader. Born 31 March 1872, Dublin; educated Christian Brothers School, Dublin; became a compositor and joined the Gaelic League and the Irish Republic Brotherhood; founded and edited the *United Irishman* 1899, which became *Sinn Fein* in 1906, then *Eire*, which was suppressed 1914 and reappeared under various names. He did not take part in the Easter Rebellion of 1916 but had supported the Irish Volunteers and was imprisoned with the other rebel leaders and again in 1918 and 1920; elected to the dail Eireann and as vice-president of the proclaimed Irish Republic; took a leading part in negotiating the treaty of 1921 with Great Britain; elected first president of the Irish Free State 1922 and began the suppression of a revolt against the treaty. Died 22 August 1922.

Grigg, Edward. See **Altrincham.**

Gyngell, Albert Edmund. Painter. Born 1866 near Worcester, England; educated Royal Academy schools; went to South Africa for reasons of health 1893; worked as storekeeper in Johannesburg and station-master in Namaqualand; was teaching art and painting in Johannesburg by 1913; first curator of the Johannesburg Art Gallery 1911–28; mainly a portrait painter in charcoal; some of his lectures on art have been published. Died 1949.

Haakon VII. King of Norway. Born 3 August 1872; second son of Frederick VIII; known as Prince Charles of Denmark; married, in 1896, Princess Maud, youngest daughter of Edward VII of Great Britain; accepted the throne of Norway 1905, crowned 1906; escaped to England after the German invasion of Norway 1940; returned to Oslo 1945. Died 21 September 1957.

Haile Selassie. Emperor of Ethiopia. Born 23 July 1892, near Harar, as Lij Tafari, a son of Ras Makonnen, adviser of the Emperor Menelik II; educated by French missionaries at Harar; appointed governor of province of Sidamo 1908; governor of Harar 1910; leader of the party which deposed the Emperor Lij Yasu who had succeeded Menelik in 1913; as Ras Tafari became regent and heir-apparent when Zauditu, daughter of Menelik, was crowned empress in 1916; crowned king of Ethiopia 1928 and emperor in 1930 when Zauditu died; took name of Haile Selassie; went into exile in England in 1936 after the invasion of Abyssinia by Italy; restored as emperor May 1941; promulgated constitutions in 1931 and 1955; among honours bestowed him are those of Knight of the Garter (1954) and an honorary field-marshalship of the British army.

Hailsham, Douglas McGarel Hogg, first Viscount. English politician. Born 28 February 1872; educated Eton; studied sugar-growing in the West Indies; served in the Anglo-Boer War; called to the bar 1902 and became a leading counsel; Conservative member of parliament and attorney-general 1922; lord chancellor 1928; secretary of state for war 1931; lord chancellor 1935–8; British delegate to the Ottawa conference 1932 and the world economic conference 1933; knighted 1922; created viscount 1929; edited a new edition of *Halsbury's Laws of England*. Died 16 August 1950.

Haldane, John Scott. Scientist. Born 1860, Edinburgh; educated Edinburgh Academy; Universities of Edinburgh and Jena; engaged in scientific research and teaching from 1885, chiefly in the Universities of Oxford and Birmingham; held lectureships at Yale, Glasgow, Dublin; served on various royal commissions; Companion of Honour; author of works on physiology, biology and philosophy. Died 15 March 1936.

Halifax, Edward Frederick Lindley Wood, first Earl of, third Viscount. Politician and administrator. Born 16 April 1881, Powderham Castle, Devon, England; educated Eton; Christ Church, Oxford; Conservative member of parliament 1910; served in France in the First World War; under-secretary of state for colonies 1921–2; president of the board of education 1922–4, 1932–5; minister of agriculture 1924–5; as viceroy of India 1925–31 advocated dominion status for India; lord privy seal 1935–7; lord president of the council 1937–8; foreign secretary 1938–9; supported the policy of appeasement; ambassador to the United States 1940–6 when he resigned; author of memoirs. Died 23 December 1959.

Hall, Hessel Duncan. Historian, international official. Born 8 March 1891, Glen Innes, New South Wales, Australia; educated University of Sydney; Balliol College, Oxford; Australian *Manchester Guardian* correspondent 1921–6; professor of international affairs, Syracuse University 1926–7; senior member, League of Nations secretariat 1927–39; member, British raw materials mission, Washington 1942–5; editor of war histories and historical adviser, British embassy, Washington 1945–55; author of books on the British Commonwealth and articles on international affairs.

Hampden, Thomas Henry Brand, Baron Dacre, fourth Viscount. Banker. Born 30 March 1900; succeeded 1958; educated Eton; began his connection with the banking house of Lazard Brothers and Co. Ltd. 1922; managing director 1930–65, chairman 1965; chief executive officer for Great Britain of the combined production and resources board in Washington 1942–4; chairman of the official supplies committee for liberated areas 1944–5. Died 17 October 1965.

Hansen, Otto John. Engineer. Born 1 March 1891, Sandflats, near Port Elizabeth, South Africa; educated Royal Technical College, Glasgow; Glasgow University; chief engineer Iscor 1933–47; director-general of war supplies (technical) and of technical services; general manager, then director and consulting engineer Vecor since 1947.

Harding, Sir Edward John. Government official. Born 1880, England; educated Dulwich College; Hertford College, Oxford; entered board of trade 1903; transferred to colonial office 1904; assistant private secretary to the secretary of state for the colonies 1912; barrister of Lincoln's Inn 1912; secretary, Dominions royal commission 1912–17; served in the First World War 1918; assistant under-secretary, Dominions office 1925–30, permanent under-secretary 1930–40; high commissioner in the Union of South Africa 1940–1; high commissioner's representative in Cape Town 1942–4; member of the council, Royal College of Music. Died 4 October 1954.

Harlech, William George Ormsby-Gore, fourth Baron. Politician and diplomat. Born 11 April 1885; educated Eton; New College, Oxford; Conservative member of parliament 1910–18; assistant secretary, war cabinet 1918; under-secretary of state for the colonies 1922–9; postmaster-general 1931; minister of public works 1932–6; secretary of state for the colonies 1936–8; regional commissioner for Yorkshire 1939–41; high commissioner for the United Kingdom in the Union of South Africa 1941–4; trustee, British Museum and National Gallery; publications include *Florentine Sculptors of the Fifteenth Century*. Died 14 February 1964.

Harris, James Rendel. Biblical scholar and archaeologist. Born 27 January 1852, Plymouth, England; educated Plymouth Grammar School; Clare College, Cambridge where he was lecturer in mathematics 1875–82; professor of greek, Johns Hopkins University 1882–5; professor of biblical languages and literature, Haverford College, Pennsylvania, a Quaker institution, 1885–92; lecturer in palaeography, Cambridge 1893–1903; first director of studies, Woodbrooke settlement for religious and social studies founded by the Society of Friends 1903–18; curator, eastern manuscripts, John Rylands Library, Manchester 1918–25; author of books on oriental manuscripts and religion. Died 1 March 1941.

Harris, Sir John Hobbis. Philanthropist and politician. Born 29 July 1874, Wantage, England; spent some years as a missionary and traveller in tropical Africa; became organizing secretary of the Anti-slavery and Aborigines Protection Society; Liberal member of parliament 1923–4; author of books on Africa and slavery; knighted 1933. Died 30 April 1940.

Harrod, Sir Roy Forbes. British economist. Born 13 February 1900; educated Westminster School; New College, Oxford; lecturer at Christ Church 1922–4; University lecturer in economics 1929–37; 1946–52; served on Sir Winston Churchill's private statistical staff 1940; statistical adviser, admiralty 1943–5; joint editor, the *Economic Journal*; member, United Nations sub-commission on employment; economic adviser, International Monetary Fund 1952–3; member, migration board, Commonwealth relations office 1953–66; author of works on economics and *The Life of John Maynard Keynes*.

Harvey, George Brinton McClellan. Journalist and diplomat. Born 16 February 1864, Peacham, Vermont, United States of America; educated Peacham Academy; Universities of Nevada and Vermont; after four years as reporter (1882–6) became managing editor of the *New York World* 1891; proprietor and editor of the *North American Review* 1899–1926; president of Harper Bros., publishers 1900–15; United States ambassador in London 1921–4. Died 20 August 1928.

Hay, George Alexander. Politician. Born 1855, Grahamstown, South Africa; member of the first legislative assembly of the Transvaal, subsequently member of the Transvaal provincial council; became Labour member of parliament for Pretoria West when he defeated Smuts in 1924. Died 1932.

Heathcote-Smith, Sir Clifford Edward. British diplomat. Born 26 March 1883; educated Pembroke College, Cambridge; vice-consul at Smyrna 1908; consul at Salonica 1915–18; commander R.N.V.R. 1918–19; consul at Casablanca 1922–4; consul-general at Alexandria 1924–39; vice-consul at Tehran 1942, Kweilin 1943; political adviser at Hong Kong 1947; commercial counsellor at Montevideo 1951, at Ankara 1956, at Copenhagen 1960; knighted 1943. Died 3 January 1963.

Helfrich, Conrad Emile Lambert. Dutch naval commander. Born 11 October 1886, Semarang, Java; educated Royal Naval Academy, Den Helder, Netherlands; entered royal Netherlands navy 1907; commanded destroyer flotilla 1931–3; commanded squadron in Netherlands East Indies 1935–6; commander-in-chief of the fleet, Netherlands East Indies 1939; supreme commander of Allied naval forces in south-western Pacific 1942; commander-in-chief of the Netherlands forces in the East 1942–6; commander-in-chief, royal Netherlands navy 1946–9 when he retired; author of memoirs.

Helps, John Stuart Doveton. Politician and military contractor. Born 1878, Rondebosch, Cape Town, South Africa; educated privately; served in Rhodesia during the Matabele rebellion 1896, in Swaziland 1898 and in the Anglo-Boer War; while settled in Natal as a military contractor became politically active, notably in 1929 when he was a founder of the Natal Devolution League, a separatist movement. Died 23 April 1957.

Hemming, Gordon Kingswood. South African politician. Born 1887; served in the First World War; member of the Union parliament representing African voters of the Transkei 1937–47. Died 22 March 1947.

Henderson, Sir Nevile Meyrick. British diplomat. Born 10 June 1882; educated Eton; attaché 1905; between 1905 and 1921 secretary at St Petersburg, Tokyo, Rome, Paris; acting British high commissioner in Constantinople 1922–4; minister plenipotentiary in Cairo 1924–8, Paris 1928–9, Belgrade 1929–35; ambassador to Argentina and Paraguay 1935–7 and in Berlin 1937–9; knighted 1932; author of *Failure of a Mission* and an autobiography. Died 30 December 1942.

Herbst, John Frederick. Government official. Born 1874, Swellendam, Cape Province, South Africa. Joined the Cape civil service in 1891; appointed magistrate at Rietfontein in the Kalahari desert 1905; became secretary for Native affairs; retired 1934. Died 1961.

Hertzog, Albert. Politician. Born 4 July 1899, Bloemfontein, Orange Free State, South Africa, son of General J. B. M. Hertzog (q.v. vol. IV); educated Grey College, Bloemfontein; Universities of Stellenbosch, Oxford, Leiden, Amsterdam; practised as an advocate in Pretoria; in 1936 played a leading part in founding the Nywerheidsbond to draw Afrikander mine workers away from the established Mine Workers' Union and gain their political support; member of the Pretoria city council 1944–51; National party member of parliament 1948–70; minister of posts and telegraphs and of health 1958–68; expelled from the National party and formed the Herstigte Nasionale party 1969; co-founder of Volkskas and Afrikaner Pers.

Herzl, Theodor. Zionist leader and journalist. Born 2 May 1860, Budapest, Hungary; educated University of Vienna; joined the staff of *Neue Freie Presse* 1884, was its foreign correspondent in Paris 1891–6 and thereafter its literary editor. His Zionist views were first propagated in a pamphlet *Der Judenstaat* in 1896. He gave the Zionist movement a world-wide organization and became its recognized leader after 1897. His novel *Altneuland* contains his vision of the future Zionist state. Died 3 July 1904.

Hess, Rudolf. German politician. Born 26 April 1894, Alexandria, Egypt; educated Godesberg; served in the air force in the First World War; joined the Nazi party 1920; took part in the Munich *putsch,* shared imprisonment with Hitler (q.v.) and became his private secretary 1925; chairman of the central commission of the party 1932; deputy-führer and reichs-minister 1933. In May 1941 he made an unauthorized flight to Scotland in order to bring about peace and a joint Anglo-German attack on Russia. He was interned and at the Nuremberg trials in 1946 condemned to life imprisonment which he is serving in Spandau.

Hewart, John Gordon, first Viscount and Baron, of Bury. Judge. Born 7 January 1870, Bury, England; educated Bury and Manchester Grammar Schools; University College, Oxford; after five years in journalism called to the bar, Inner Temple 1902 and built up an extensive practice; Liberal member of parliament 1913; solicitor-general 1916; attorney-general 1919; lord chief justice 1922–40; created viscount 1922; author of *The New Despotism,* etc. Died 5 May 1943.

Heys, George. Transport contractor. Born *c.* 1850 Durban, South Africa and educated there; went to Kimberley *c.* 1870 and established a coaching business; moved to Pretoria in 1879; transport contractor to the South African Republic department of posts; member of the Pretoria town council 1903. Died 23 September 1939.

Higgerty, John Waterson. Chartered accountant, company director, politician. Born 27 June 1903; educated St John's College, Johannesburg; South African College School, Cape Town; practised as accountant; director, Chrome Corporation Pty. Ltd.; member of Transvaal provincial council 1930–3; member of Johannesburg city council 1932–3; United party member of parliament since 1933; United party whip for Transvaal 1938; chief whip since 1939; later treasurer and chairman of the central executive and head committee of the party; retired from politics 1970.

Hill, Sir Arthur William. Botanist. Born 11 October 1875, Watford, England; educated Marlborough College; King's College, Cambridge; university demonstrator in botany 1899 and lecturer 1904; assistant director of Royal Botanical Gardens, Kew 1907 and director 1922; contributed to various *Floras* and edited Hooker's *Icones Plantarum* and other important botanical works; undertook expedition to the Andes of Bolivia and Peru 1903 and visited most of the British Dominions and colonies as botanical adviser to the secretary of state; knighted 1931. Died 3 November 1941.

Himmler, Heinrich. German politician. Born 7 November 1900, Munich; educated Landshut school, Bavaria and trained in agriculture; joined the Nazi party soon after its formation and took part in the Munich *putsch*; became leader of the S.S. (*Schutzstaffel*) 1929; member of the reichstag and of the Prussian state council 1933; head of the entire German police system 1936; deputy head of the reich administration 1939; notorious for his brutal extermination of untold numbers of opponents of the Nazi régime; became minister of the interior 1943 and in November 1944 assumed executive control of Germany; arrested 21 May 1945 and committed suicide by taking poison two days later.

Hirst, Francis W. British economist. Born 1873; educated Clifton College; Wadham College, Oxford; called to the bar 1899; editor of *The Economist* 1907–16; lectured on economics in California 1921 and South Africa 1923; governor of the London School of Economics; author of a number of books on economics and politics and biographies of Adam Smith, Jefferson, John Morley, Gladstone. Died 22 February 1953.

Hitler, Adolf. German dictator. Born 20 April 1889, Braunau, Austria; educated at secondary schools at Linz and Steyr until the age of sixteen; refused admission to the Academy of Fine Art in Vienna where he lived a hand-to-mouth life from 1907 to 1913. On the outbreak of war he volunteered for a Bavarian infantry regiment and in 1918 received the Iron Cross, First Class. After the war he lived in Munich and joined the German Workers' party which he built up into the National Socialist German Workers' (Nazi) party. He attempted, with Ludendorff, the unsuccessful Munich *putsch* to overthrow the Bavarian government and was imprisoned for thirteen months during which he wrote *Mein Kampf* setting forth his ideas. By means of consummate propaganda, a private army, the financial support of certain industrialists and his own demagogic powers he used the political and economic weaknesses of the Weimar Republic to make his party the largest in the reichstag by 1932. Defeated by Hindenburg for the presidency in that year he became chancellor in January 1933 and then dissolved all opposition parties and murdered his chief critics and rivals. In August 1934 he became president as well as chancellor and supreme commander of the armed forces. Between 1935 and September 1938 his control was extended over the Saar, the Rhineland, Austria and Czechoslovakia but his invasion of Poland in September 1939 caused Great Britain and France to declare war on Germany. Early success encouraged Hitler to order the invasion of Russia in 1941 and to take the direction of the war more and more into his own hands. Internally his racist theories issued in the extermination of millions of Jews and his rigid dictatorship required the elimination by imprisonment, torture and execution of all suspected opponents. An attempt mainly by army officers to assassinate him failed in 1944. On 30 April 1945, when the allied armies were closing in on Berlin, he committed suicide.

Hoare, Major-General Francis Richard Gurney. Soldier. Born 1879 in England; educated Harrow; Trinity College, Cambridge; entered the British army 1894; served in the Anglo-Boer War; spent nine years in the Transvaal civil service; joined Transvaal Horse Artillery 1912; seconded to army ordnance department 1914; entered royal flying corps 1917 as temporary lieutenant-colonel and became staff officer, air equipment department; entered Union defence force as inspecting ordnance officer 1919; lieutenant-colonel, South African ordnance corps 1933 and director of technical services; retired from the army 1937; was subsequently chairman of the Union war supplies board, director-general of supplies and South African representative on the Eastern Group supply council in Delhi from March 1941. Died 29 May 1959.

Hoare, Sir Samuel John Gurney. See **Templewood.**

Hoernlé, Reinhold Frederick Alfred. Philosopher. Born 27 November 1880, Bonn, Germany; educated Gymnasium Ernestinum, Gotha; Balliol College, Oxford; senior demy, Magdalen College; lecturer in philosophy, University of St Andrews 1905–7; professor of philosophy, South African College, Cape Town 1908–11; Armstrong College, Newcastle-upon-Tyne 1912–14; Harvard 1914–20; University of Durham 1920–3; University of the Witwatersrand 1923–43; president, South African Institute of Race Relations; author of *Matter, Mind, Life and God*; *South African Native Policy and the Liberal Spirit*, etc. Died 21 July 1943.

Hogg, Douglas McGarel. See **Hailsham.**

Holland, Sir Reginald Sothern, first Baronet. Government official and financier. Born 15 March 1876, Alexandria, Cape Province, South Africa; educated St Andrew's College, Grahamstown; entered Cape civil service 1894, served in the office of the colonial secretary and the Native affairs department 1896–1903; private secretary to the prime minister 1905; head of prime minister's department 1905–8; British trade commissioner in South Africa 1908–13; organized explosives supplies and directed munitions inspection for the war office and the ministry of munitions 1914–18; director and chairman, Central Mining and Investment Corporation 1920–45; Rhodes trustee from 1932; created baronet 1917. Died 14 September 1948.

Holland, Sir Thomas Henry. Geologist. Born 22 November 1868, Cornwall, England; educated Royal College of Science; joined Indian service 1890; director of geological survey, India and reader, Calcutta University 1903–9; professor of geology and mineralogy, University of Manchester 1909–18; member of governor-general's council, India 1920–1; rector, Imperial College of Science and Technology 1922–9; president, British Association 1929; vice-chancellor, University of Edinburgh 1929–44; knighted 1908; author of books on mineralogy and geology. Died 15 May 1947.

Hollander, Felix Charles. Politician and jeweller. Born January 1875, Birmingham, England; emigrated to South Africa 1894 and became a jeweller in Durban; mayor of Durban 1910–13; member of Natal provincial council 1914 and subsequently of its executive committee; Union senator 1939; foundation member, national roads board. Died 1955.

Holloway, John Edward. South African government official and economist. Born 4 July 1890; educated University of Stellenbosch; London School of Economics; lecturer, Grey University College 1917–19; professor, Transvaal University College 1919–25; director of census and statistics 1925–33; economic adviser to the treasury 1934–7; secretary for finance 1937–50; served on various government commissions and represented the Union of South Africa at world economic conferences; ambassador in Washington 1954; high commissioner for the Union of South Africa in London 1956–8; author of *Apartheid: a Challenge* and articles on the monetary system and race relations.

Hoogenhout, Petrus Imker. Government official and educationist. Born 2 February 1884, Wellington, Cape Province, South Africa; educated there and at Victoria College, Stellenbosch and South African College, Cape Town; headmaster, Educational Institute, Jeppe 1908–10 and Hoogenhout High School, Bethal 1910–20; inspector of education 1921–7; chief examiner, Transvaal education department 1927–9; secretary for the interior 1929–37; chairman, national roads board and immigration board 1937–43; administrator of South West Africa 1944–51; ambassador at The Hague 1952–6. Died 18 November 1970.

Hooker, Sir Joseph Dalton. Botanist. Born 30 June 1817, Halesworth, Suffolk, England; educated Glasgow where he took a medical degree; went as assistant surgeon on Sir James Ross's Antarctic expedition 1839; led botanical expedition to North India 1848; appointed assistant director, Kew Gardens 1855 and succeeded his father as director 1865; president, Royal Society 1873–7; knighted 1877; awarded Order of Merit 1907; wrote *Genera Plantarum* (1862–83) and other botanical works. Died 10 December 1911.

Hore-Belisha, Leslie, first Baron, of Devonport. Politician. Born 7 September 1893, Kilburn, London; educated Clifton College, Bristol; St John's College, Oxford; served in the First World War in France, Salonika, Cyprus; began to read law and practise political journalism; Liberal member of parliament 1923–42; financial secretary to the treasury 1932–4; minister of transport 1934–7; secretary for war 1937–40; sat in house of commons as an independent 1942–5; minister of national insurance 1945; created baron 1954. Died 16 February 1957.

Hotson, John Leslie. Professor of English literature. Born 16 August 1897, Ontario, Canada; educated Harvard University; held fellowships at Harvard and Yale 1923–7; associate professor of English, New York University 1927–9; professor of English, Haverford College, Pennsylvania 1931–41; served in United States army 1939–45; research associate, Yale 1953; fellow of King's College, Cambridge 1954–60; author of various books, mainly on Shakespeare.

Howarth, Osbert John Radclyffe. Scientist. Born 18 November 1877. London; educated Westminster; Christ Church, Oxford; geographical assistant to editor, *Encyclopaedia Britannica* 1904–11; secretary, British Association for the Advancement of Science 1909–46; president, Down House 1929–53; served in naval intelligence in the First World War; joint editor, *Oxford Survey of the British Empire*; *The British Association: a Retrospect 1831–1931*. Died 22 June 1954.

Hubbard, Charles Edward. English botanist. Born 23 May 1900; educated King Edward VII Grammar School, King's Lynn; served in royal air force 1918–19; student gardener at Royal Gardens, Sandringham; Royal Gardens, Oslo and Kew Gardens 1916–22; held various positions at Kew becoming botanist 1930–46, senior principal scientific official 1956–9 and deputy director and keeper of the herbarium 1959–65; author of a number of books and articles on grasses.

Huddleston, Major-General Sir Hubert Jervoise. Army officer and administrator. Born 1880, Norton, Suffolk, England; educated Bedford and Felsted; served in the Anglo-Boer War, the Sudan (1910) and the First World War; general officer commanding, Sudan 1924–30; brigade commander 1930–3; held commands in India 1934–8 when he retired from the army; governor-general of the Sudan 1940–7; knighted 1940. Died 2 October 1950.

Huggins, Sir Godfrey. See **Malvern.**

Hughes, Charles Evans. Judge and politician. Born 11 April 1862, Glen Falls, New York; educated Colgate, Brown and Columbia Universities; Harvard; Yale; admitted to New York bar 1884; practised law in New York 1884–1906; governor of New York State 1907–10; judge in the supreme court 1910; Republican presidential candidate opposing Wilson 1916; secretary of state 1921–5; judge in the permanent court of international justice 1928–30; chief justice, supreme court 1930. Died 27 August 1948.

Hull, Cordell. Politician. Born 2 October 1871, Overton County, Tennessee, United States of America; educated Cumberland University; Universities of Notre Dame and Wisconsin; George Washington, Columbia and Michigan Universities; admitted to Tennessee bar 1891; member, Tennessee house of representatives 1893–7; circuit judge 1903–7; member of congress 1907–31; senator for Tennessee 1931–3; secretary of state 1933–44; delegate to San Francisco conference 1945; awarded Nobel peace prize 1945. Died 23 July 1955.

Husain, ibn Ali. King of the Hejaz. Born *c.* 1854, Mecca; brought up as a Bedouin; spent much of his life in Constantinople; became amir of Mecca 1908–16; during First World War co-operated with the British and in October 1916 was recognized as king of the Hejaz; defeated in a war with Ibn Saud in 1924, he abdicated and lived in Cyprus until 1930. Died 1931 at Amman.

Husseini, Haj Amin El. Arab religious and political leader. Born *c.* 1896; educated Jerusalem; Al-Azhar University, Cairo; served as officer in the Turkish army in the First World War; took part in anti-Jewish movements in Jerusalem 1920; fled to Transjordan; returned under amnesty; appointed mufti of Jerusalem and elected president, supreme Moslem council 1922; president, Arab higher committee for Palestine 1936; arrested for taking part in Arab attacks on Jews but escaped 1937; helped to lead an abortive pro-German revolt in Iraq 1941; engaged in Nazi propaganda in Berlin 1941–5; given asylum by King Farouk (q.v.) 1946 and re-elected president of the Arab higher committee; chairman of Palestine Arab delegation to Bandung conference 1955; resident in Beirut, Lebanon.

Hutchinson, George Thomas. Barrister. Born 30 July 1880; educated Marlborough College; Magdalen College, Oxford (history demy); barrister of the Inner Temple 1906; treasurer of Christ Church, Oxford 1910–45; served in France in the First World War; Rhodes trustee. Died 17 January 1948.

Hutchinson, John. English botanist. Born 7 April 1884; educated privately and at Rutherford College, Newcastle; assistant at Royal Botanic Gardens, Kew 1907–19; assistant-in-charge, African section 1919–36; keeper of museums 1936–48; undertook botanical tours of South Africa, Rhodesia, Cameroons; author of a number of books on African flora and British wild flowers.

Huxley, Sir Julian Sorell. English biologist. Born 22 June 1887, grandson of Thomas Henry Huxley (q.v.); educated Eton; Balliol College, Oxford where he was lecturer 1910–12; research associate, then assistant professor, Rice Institute, Houston, Texas 1912–16; staff-lieutenant, G.H.Q., Italy 1918; university demonstrator in zoology at Oxford 1919–25; professor of zoology, King's College, London

1925–7 and honorary lecturer 1927–35; secretary, Zoological Society of London 1935–42; director-general of Unesco 1946–8; has written a number of books of popular exposition of biological and general science.

Huxley, Thomas Henry. Biologist. Born 4 May 1825, Ealing, England; educated London University and graduated in medicine 1845; discovered layer of cells in inner sheath of hair; assistant-surgeon on H.M.S. *Rattlesnake* 1846–50 and began animal studies; elected fellow of the Royal Society 1851; lecturer on natural history, School of Mines 1854; naturalist to geological survey 1855; wrote works mainly on fossil forms 1855–9; defended Darwin's evolutionary theories and wrote *Zoological Evidences as to Man's Place in Nature* 1863 and other works on animal physiology and anatomy during the next ten years; undertook various public duties as secretary (1871–80) and president (1883–5) of the Royal Society and member of the London school board and engaged in controversies on orthodox religious beliefs and agnosticism, which he defended. Died 29 June 1895.

Hyat-Khan, Sir Sikander. Indian statesman. Born 5 June 1892; educated Aligarh; University College, London; recruiting officer during the First World War; served on north-west frontier and in third Afghan War 1919; first class honorary magistrate 1919–30; member of Punjab legislative council from 1921; revenue member, Punjab government 1930–7; acting governor of the Punjab 1932, 1934; prime minister of the Punjab from 1937; deputy-governor, Reserve Bank of India from 1935. Died 26 December 1942.

Hyde, Lord. See **Villiers.**

Ilbert, Sir Courtenay Peregrine. British government official. Born 12 June 1841; educated Marlborough College; Balliol College, Oxford; barrister of Lincoln's Inn; legal member, governor-general's council, India 1882–6 and president 1886; vice-chancellor, University of Calcutta 1885–6; assistant parliamentary counsel to treasury 1886–9; and parliamentary counsel 1899–1901; clerk of the house of commons 1902–21; member board of governors, London School of Economics; author of books on Indian and British constitutional matters. Died 14 May 1924.

Impey, Robert Lance. Medical practitioner. Born 11 July 1888, Queenstown, South Africa; educated Kingswood College; University of Edinburgh; served in the R.A.M.C. in Flanders in the First World War and in the S.A.M.C. in the Second World War when he was assistant director of medical services, Cape fortress command.

Imroth, Gustav. Mining financier. Born 1862. Germany; went to Kimberley, South Africa some twenty years later; founder, with Barney Barnato, of Johannesburg Consolidated Investments (1889) of which he later became managing director until his retirement in 1920. Died 1946.

Irene, Princess, of the Netherlands (Irene Emma Elizabeth). Born 5 August 1939, Amsterdam, second daughter of Queen Juliana and Prince Bernhard (qq.v.); received into the Roman Catholic Church January 1964; married Prince Carlos Hugo of Bourbon-Parma April 1964 and renounced the right of succession to the throne of the Netherlands.

Irvine, Sir James Colquhon. Chemist and university principal. Born 9 May 1877, Glasgow; educated Royal Technical College, Glasgow; Universities of St Andrews and Leipzig; professor of chemistry, St Andrews and principal 1921–51; chairman of various committees on education and science; held lectureships at Princeton, Yale, etc.; author of many papers, mainly on the chemistry of sugars; knighted 1925. Died 12 June 1952.

Irwin, Lord. See **Halifax.**

Isaacs, Godfrey. Business man. Born *c.* 1864, London; younger brother of Rufus Daniel Isaacs, afterwards Lord Reading; educated University College School, London and in Brussels and Hanover; entered his father's firm of fruit merchants; became managing director of the Marconi Wireless Telegraph Company 1910. Died 17 April 1925.

Jabavu, Davidson Don Tengo. Professor of Bantu languages. Born 1885, Kingwilliamstown, Cape Province, South Africa; educated at mission schools; Colwyn Bay (North Wales); University College, London; Tuskegee Institute; University of Birmingham; first lecturer at the South African Native College, later Fort Hare 1916; appointed professor 1942; founder and organizer of the South African Native farmers' association; president, Cape Native teachers' association and the South African federation of Native teachers; chairman of many conferences and conventions concerned with missionary matters and the political advancement of Africans; appeared before various government commissions on African affairs; author of a number of writings in English and Xhosa including *The Black Problem*; *The Segregation Fallacy*; and a biography of his father John Tengo Jabavu. Died 3 August 1959.

Jeans, Sir James Hopwood. Astrophysicist and mathematician. Born 11 September 1877, Southport, Lancashire, England; educated Merchant Taylors' School; Trinity College, Cambridge; university lecturer in mathematics 1904; professor of applied mathematics, Princeton 1905–9; Stokes lecturer, Cambridge 1910–12; secretary to the Royal Society 1919–29; research assistant, Mount Wilson Observatory 1923; knighted 1928; awarded the Order of Merit 1939; author of *Radiation and the Quantum Theory*; *Astronomy and Cosmogony*; and other works on physics and astronomy, including some popular expositions. Died 16 September 1946.

Jenkins, Benjamin. Merchant and politician. Born 5 July 1881, Holyhead, North Wales; educated George Green's School, London; emigrated to South Africa 1904; was a commercial traveller; became an independent mining material merchant in Johannesburg 1920; chairman of the South African Labour party 1926–8; joined the South African party 1932 but withdrew from politics soon after. Died *c.* 1957.

Jeppe, Sir Julius. Financier. Born July 1859, Rostock, Germany; emigrated with his parents to Pretoria, Transvaal 1870; served in the Sekukuni War 1877; the Transvaal War 1880–1; the Anglo-Boer War as head of the Transvaal Red Cross; became a prospector on the Witwatersrand and later founded, with L. P. Ford, the Johannesburg Township Company; subsequently owned interests in the Witwatersrand Townships companies; member of the stadsraad 1888 and of the Johannesburg town council 1903; a founder and executive member of the Chamber of Mines. Died 1 September 1929.

Jinnah, Mohammed Ali. Statesman. Born 25 December 1876, Karachi, India; educated University of Bombay; barrister of Lincoln's Inn, London; practised law in Bombay from 1896 and joined Indian National Congress; member of the provincial legislative council 1909; member of the central legislature 1913–45; joined the Muslim League of which he was president 1916, 1920; became the leader of Muslim separatism, controlling the League as permanent president from 1934 until his death; formulated his scheme for a sovereign state of Pakistan 1940 which was accepted by the British government in 1947; became first governor-general of Pakistan. Died 11 September 1948.

Joachim, Harold Henry. Philosopher. Born 28 May 1868 of Hungarian and English parentage; educated Harrow; Balliol College, Oxford; assistant to the professor of moral philosophy and then lecturer at St Andrews University 1892–4; lecturer in philosophy, Balliol College 1894–7; fellow and tutor in philosophy, Merton College, Oxford 1897–1919; professor of logic, Oxford from 1920; author of *A Study of Spinoza*, etc. and editor of Aristotle. Died 30 July 1938.

Johnson, General Hugh Samuel. Soldier and administrator. Born 5 August 1882, Kansas, United States of America; educated Oklahoma Teachers' College; Military Academy; University of California; entered United States army 1903 and resigned 1919 with rank of brigadier-general after serving in the Philippines and Mexico and organizing the 1917 draft; organized the management of the Moline Implement Company 1919–29; was associated with Bernard Baruch (q.v.) 1927–33; administrator of the national recovery administration June 1933–October 1934. Died 15 April 1942.

Johnson, Louis Arthur. Politician. Born 10 January 1891, Roanoke, Virginia, United States of America; educated University of Virginia; practised as lawyer from 1912; served in the First World War, later as lieutenant-colonel in infantry reserve; member, West Virginia house of representatives 1917; civilian aide to secretary of war, West Virginia 1933; member, federal employment advisory council, department of labour 1936–40; assistant secretary of war 1937–40; personal representative of the president in India 1942; secretary of defence 1949–50; director of companies. Died 24 April 1966.

Jolly, Keith. Archaeologist. Born 4 August 1927, Rondebosch, Cape Town; educated Diocesan College, Rondebosch; Universities of Cape Town and Cambridge; conducted excavations at Peers Cave at Fish Hoek 1946–7; on his return from Cambridge in 1951 held a temporary lectureship in archaeology at the University of Cape Town; in 1953 discovered, at Hopefield in the south-western Cape Province, the major portion of a human skull which he named Saldanha man; later conducted excavations near Willowmore. Died 16 September 1970.

Jones, Sir Clement Wakefield. Government official and company director. Born 26 June 1880, Burnside, England; educated Haileybury; Trinity College, Cambridge; private secretary in New York 1902; served in the First World War 1914–15; assistant secretary, war cabinet 1916; secretary to the British delegation to Paris peace conference 1919; director, Alfred Booth and Co., Sea Insurance Co. Ltd.; served on a number of official boards and committees including the British Overseas Airways Corporation (1946–54), the technical personnel committee (1941–50), the committee for higher appointments (1943); chairman, council of the Royal Institute of International Affairs 1948–53; chairman, Commonwealth shipping committee from 1947; knighted 1946; author of books on shipping and sea trading. Died 29 October 1963.

Jones, John David Rheinallt. University lecturer and politician. Born 1884 in Wales; educated Bangor; Beaumaris; emigrated to South Africa 1905; joined the staff of the South African School of Mines and Technology; lecturer in Native law and administration, University of the Witwatersrand 1927–36; founded the South African Institute of Race Relations 1929 and was its director until 1947; elected to the Union senate as Native representative 1937–42. Died 30 January 1953.

Jones, Reverend Neville. Archaeologist and missionary. Born 8 July 1880, Brixton, London; went to South Africa 1912 and was a missionary at Hope Fountain, near Bulawayo, Rhodesia until 1935; keeper of the department of prehistory and ethnology, National Museum of Southern Rhodesia 1936–48; author of books on the prehistory of Rhodesia and South African archaeology. Died 1952.

Jones, Rufus Matthew. Philosopher. Born 25 January 1863, South China, Maine, United States of America; educated Haverford College; Universities of Heidelberg and Pennsylvania; principal, Oak Grove Seminary, Vassalboro, Maine 1889–92; instructor, Haverford College 1893–1901, associate professor 1901–4; professor of philosophy 1904–34; chairman of the American Friends service committee for foreign relief in and after both World Wars; editor of the *American Friend* 1894–1912; author of devotional works and books on Quaker belief and history. Died 16 June 1948.

Joubert, François Alan. Administrator, politician, farmer. Born 1889, Jansenville, Cape Province; educated Victoria College, Stellenbosch; Trinity College, Dublin; a progressive farmer at Klipheuvel; organizing secretary, South African party in the Cape 1924 and later of the United party; member of parliament 1933–9; administrator of the Cape Province 1939–42. Died 22 September 1942.

Joubert, Jan A. Politician. Born 1873 on the farm Rustfontein, near Wakkerstroom, Transvaal; son of General P. J. Joubert (q.v. vol. IV); took part in the various Native wars, the capture of Jameson and the Anglo-Boer War; wounded on 13 December 1900, he was sent as a prisoner of war to India; a supporter of the National party from its inception; member of parliament 1916–24. Died 5 March 1924.

Juliana (Louisa Emma Maria Wilhelmina). Queen of the Netherlands. Born 30 April 1909, daughter of Queen Wilhelmina (q.v.) and Prince Hendrik of Mechlenburg-Schwerin; studied law and economics at the University of Leiden; married in 1937, Prince Bernhard of Lippe-Biesterfeld; went to Canada after the German occupation of the Netherlands 1940 and to England 1944; returned to the Netherlands 1945; became princess regent 1948 and queen of the Netherlands in September 1948.

Kadalie, Clements. Trade union leader. Born 1896, Nyasaland; settled in Cape Town where he was one of the founders and first secretary of a dockers' trade union which developed into a powerful general union of non-white workers, mainly African, under the name of the Industrial and Commercial Workers' Union of Africa (I.C.U.) of which Kadalie was the national secretary. He was co-editor of its organ, the *Workers' Herald.* Following dissension in the leadership of the I.C.U. Kadalie went to London, Paris and Geneva in 1927 to seek support but the union broke up in 1928. Kadalie resigned in January 1929 and formed the Independent I.C.U. in East London but his influence as an African leader declined. Died 1951.

Kajee, Abdullah Ismail. Indian leader. Born 1896, Surat, India; his parents emigrated to Natal, South Africa when he was an infant; educated Natal; Aligarh College, India; founded, in 1922, his own firm which became one of the largest Indian commercial houses in South Africa; was for many years secretary of the South African Congress and the Indian Workers' Congress; active in the provision of child welfare institutions for South African Indians. Died 5 January 1947.

Katherine, Princess, of Greece (Lady Katherine Brandram). Born 4 May 1913, youngest daughter of King Constantine I of Greece, sister of King George II and King Paul; educated chiefly in England; lived for three years in Cape Town following the German occupation of Greece; married, in 1947, Major R. C. A. Brandram. Princess Katherine renounced her royal perogatives on marriage and was granted by royal warrant the rank of a duke's daughter.

Kayser, Charles Frederick. Politician, merchant, farmer. Born 21 May 1862, King William's Town, Cape Province, South Africa; educated Grey Institute, Port Elizabeth; entered firm of J. and W. Philip as clerk 1879; became a partner in Philip Brothers 1894; South African party member of parliament 1929–35; citrus farmer in Gamtoos valley. Died November 1935.

Keet, Johan Diederik Mohr. Forester. Born 28 December 1882, Ceres, south-western Cape Province; educated there and at South African College; district forest officer, Cape Province 1908; conservator of forests, Transvaal 1923; director of forestry 1934–42; technical assistant, soil conservation 1946; chairman, agricultural policy commission, South West Africa 1953; retired 1956 and became resident director of a private forestry company in the eastern Transvaal.

Kellaway, Frederick George. Politician and journalist. Born 3 December 1870, Bishopston, Bristol, England; became a journalist and edited a group of papers in Lewisham; Liberal member of parliament 1910–22; joint parliamentary secretary, ministry of munitions 1916; postmaster-general 1921–2; managing director, Marconi Company 1924. Died 13 April 1933.

Kelly, Right Reverend Denis. Bishop of Ross. Born 29 February 1852, Kilnaneave, Nenagh, Tipperary, Ireland; educated Ennis College; Collège des Irlandais, Paris; ordained 1877; curate of Roscrea; professor, later president, of Ennis College; Bishop of Ross 1897; member, agricultural board of Ireland from 1900; royal commissioner on poor laws 1906–9. Died 18 April 1924.

Kemal, Mustafa. See **Ataturk.**

Kemsley, James Gomer Berry, first Viscount, of Farnham Royal. Newspaper proprietor. Born 1883, Merthyr Tydfil, Wales; educated privately; associated with his elder brother, Lord Camrose, in newspaper enterprises including control of Amalgamated Press 1926; their interests were separated in 1937 when K. took over Allied Newspapers Ltd., later Kemsley Newspapers Ltd. This, in 1947, included twenty-three newspapers, notably the *Sunday Times* of which K. was editor-in-chief 1937–59. K. was president, University College of South Wales 1945–50 and chairman of various hospitals; created baronet 1928, baron 1936, viscount 1945. Died 6 February 1968.

Kennet, Sir Edward Hilton Young, first Baron, of the Dene. Politician, journalist, lawyer. Born 20 March 1879, Formosa Place, Cookham, England; educated Eton; Trinity College, Cambridge; barrister of the Inner Temple; practised 1904–9; assistant editor, *The Economist* 1909; financial editor, *Morning Post* 1910–14; served in royal navy in First World War 1914–19; Liberal, later Conservative, member of parliament 1915–35; parliamentary private secretary to the president of the board of education 1919–21; financial secretary to the treasury 1921–3; undertook financial missions abroad 1924–30; minister of health 1931–5; chairman, East Africa closer union commission 1928, capital issues committee 1939–59; created baron 1935; author of *The System of National Finance* and books of verse. Died 11 July 1960.

Kenworthy, Joseph Montague. See **Strabolgi.**

Kestell, Reverend John Daniel. Minister of religion, cultural leader, writer. Born 15 February 1854, Pietermaritzburg, Natal, South Africa, son of an 1820 settler; educated Gymnasium and Theological Seminary, Stellenbosch; University of Utrecht; Dutch Reformed Church (N.G. Kerk) minister at Kimberley 1882, Harrismith 1894, Ficksburg 1903, Bloemfontein 1912. On the outbreak of the Anglo-Boer War K. joined the Orange Free State forces as chaplain; secretary, with D. E. van Velden (q.v. vol. IV), at the peace conference at Vereeniging and co-author of the best account of the proceedings; moderator of the N.G. Kerk of the Orange Free State between 1909 and 1918; editor of *Die Kerkbode* 1919–20; rector of Grey University College 1920–7; a founder of the Helpmekaar movement to aid indigent Afrikanders, and of the Zuid-Afrikaansche Akademie. Wrote memoirs of the Anglo-Boer War, biographies of General C. R. de Wet, N. J. Hofmeyr and A. P. Kriel and a number of novels and short stories; was one of the original translators of the Bible into Afrikaans; known as 'Vader Kestell' among Afrikanders. Died 9 February 1941.

Khama, Sir Seretse M. President of Botswana. Born 1 July 1921, Serowe; son of Sekgoma Khama II, paramount chief of the Bamangwato; educated Tiger Kloof; Adams College; Lovedale; Fort Hare College; Balliol College, Oxford. After his father's death in 1925 his uncle, Tshekedi Khama (q.v.), was regent; his marriage, in 1948, to Ruth Williams, an Englishwoman, was opposed by Tshekedi, the Bamangwato chiefs and the South African and British governments. In 1949 the chiefs recognized his succession but the British government exiled him in 1950 and appointed Rasebolai Kgame administrator. Having renounced the throne, Seretse returned with his wife and children to Bechuanaland in 1956. He was elected to the tribal council 1957; became a member of the executive council 1961; formed the Bechuanaland Democratic party 1962 which won the election when self-government was attained 1965; became prime minister and, in 1966, president of the independent nation of Botswana; knighted 1966; chancellor of the University of Botswana, Lesotho and Swaziland.

Khama, Tshekedi. Bechuana ruler. Born 17 September 1905, Serowe; brother of Sekgoma Khama II, uncle of Seretse Khama (q.v.); educated Serowe; Lovedale; Fort Hare College; was regent of Bechuanaland 1926–50; exiled, with Seretse Khama, from Bechuanaland but returned in 1956 after renouncing any claim to the chieftainship; became secretary of the tribal council. Died 10 June 1959.

Khare, Narayan Bhaskar. Politician and medical practitioner. Born 16 March 1882, Panvel, Bombay, India; educated Government College, Jubbulpore, Allahabad; Lahore Medical College, University of the Punjab where he took degrees in medicine; joined Indian National Congress 1918; member of Central Provinces legislature 1924–30; imprisoned for civil disobedience 1930; Congress party member, Indian parliament 1935–7; prime minister, Central Provinces 1937–8; resigned 1938 following differences with Congress leaders; member of the viceroy's executive council in charge of Commonwealth relations department 1943–6; president, all-India Hindu Mahasabha 1949, 1950, 1951; elected to Lok Sabha 1952; author of political and autobiographical books.

King, William Lyon Mackenzie. Statesman. Born 17 December 1874, Berlin, Ontario, Canada; educated Universities of Toronto, Chicago, Harvard; editor, *Labour Gazette* 1900–8; Liberal member of Canadian parliament 1908–11, 1919–49; minister of labour 1908–11; director of industrial research, Rockefeller Foundation 1914–18; leader of Liberal party from 1919 and of the opposition 1919–21; prime minister 1921–30, 1935–48; minister of external affairs 1935–46; retired from public life 1948; awarded the Order of Merit 1947. Died 22 July 1950.

Kingston, Charles Burrard. Engineer. Born 15 May 1867, Montreal, Canada; educated McGill University; emigrated to South Africa 1905; engaged in gold, diamond and coal mining and the development of water supplies and hydro-electric power. Died *c.* 1945.

Kisch, Colonel Frederick Hermann. Soldier and Zionist official. Born 1888, Darjeeling, India; educated Clifton College, England; Royal Military Academy, Woolwich; entered the British army 1909; served in France and Mesopotamia 1914–17; member of the British delegation, Paris peace conference 1919; resigned 1922 to take up work for the Zionist cause; member of the Zionist executive committee in Palestine 1923–7 and chairman 1927–31; re-joined the army in 1939; chairman of the Palestine–British trade association 1942; visited South Africa in 1928 to inaugurate a Palestine foundation fund; author of *Palestine Diary*. Died 7 April 1943.

Kleinenberg, Theunis Johannes. Agent and sworn appraiser. Born 5 July 1865, Calvinia, Cape Province, South Africa; educated in Cape Town; member of head committee of the South African party in the Transvaal; chairman of the district executive of the party; director, Federated Farmers' Co-operative Society. Died *c.* 1928.

Kleinwort, Herman Greverus. British banker. Born 3 July 1856, The Glebe, Denmark Hill, London; educated privately and at the Realgymnasium, Karlsruhe; Institut Supérieur de Commerce, Antwerp; senior partner of the banking house Kleinwort Sons and Co., London and Liverpool; director of various trust and financial companies. Died 18 June 1942.

Klopper, General Hendrik Belsazar. Soldier. Born 25 September 1902, Uitenhage, Cape Province, South Africa; educated Gill College, Somerset East; South African Military College; served in the South African air force; South African staff corps 1933; adjutant, South African Military College 1934; staff officer, Orange Free State command 1934; camp commandant, S.A. air force; deputy director of infantry training 1939, and director 1940; commanded 3rd South African infantry brigade 1941; general officer commanding the Tobruk garrison at its surrender 1942; taken prisoner but escaped 1943; brigadier, Union defence force 1946; inspector-general 1953; commandant-general 1956; retired 1958 to farm; area controller of civil defence, Pretoria 1964–9.

Knollys, Edward George William Tyrwhitt, second Viscount. Chairman of companies and administrator. Born 16 January 1895; educated Harrow; New College, Oxford; served in the First World War; Cape Town director, Barclays Bank D.C. and O. 1929–32; deputy regional commissioner, civil defence 1939–41; governor of Bermuda 1941–3; chairman, British Overseas Airways Corporation 1943–7; minister, British embassy, Washington 1951–2; chairman, Vickers Ltd. 1956–62 and English Steel Corporation 1959–65.

Kotzé, Sir Robert Nelson. Mining engineer and politician. Born 13 April 1870, Darling, Cape Province, South Africa; educated South African College, Cape Town; Royal School of Mines, London; Clausthal Mining Academy, Germany; assistant engineer, Transvaal Gold Fields group, then consulting engineer 1895–1907; government mining engineer of the Transvaal, then of the Union 1908–26; drafted Mines and Works Act 1911; United party member of parliament 1929–38; chancellor, University of the Witwatersrand; knighted 1918. Died 14 March 1953.

Krige, Eileen Claire Berenice, born Jensen. Anthropologist. Born 12 November 1904, Pretoria, South Africa; educated Pretoria High School for Girls; University of the Witwatersrand; married Jacob Daniel Krige (q.v.) 1928; after teaching at schools in Johannesburg 1926–8 did fieldwork among the Lobedu, northern Transvaal 1936–9; lecturer in sociology, Rhodes University 1942–4; lecturer, later professor of social anthropology, University of Natal 1946–70; author of *The Social System of the Zulus*, co-author of *The Realm of a Rain-Queen*.

Krige, Jacob Daniel. Anthropologist and lawyer. Born 15 July 1896, Stellenbosch, Cape Province, South Africa; educated Stellenbosch Boys' High School; Universities of Stellenbosch and Oxford; practised at the Johannesburg bar; lecturer in international law, University of the Witwatersrand 1925–31; director, University Correspondence College, Pretoria 1931–4; fieldwork among Lobedu, northern Transvaal 1936–9; lecturer, later professor of social anthropology, Rhodes University 1940–6, and at the University of Natal 1946–59; author of a number of anthropological papers and co-author of *The Realm of a Rain-Queen*. Died 10 April 1959.

Kylsant, Owen Cosby Philipps, first Baron, of Carmarthen. Ship-owner and politician. Born 25 March 1863; founded the King line on the Clyde 1888; director, then chairman, Royal Mail Steam Packet Company 1902; aquired three other shipping companies, among them the Union-Castle Mail Steamship Company (1912); Liberal member of parliament 1906–10; Conservative member 1916–22; created baron 1923. Died 5 June 1937.

Lamarck, Jean Baptiste Pierre Antoine de Monet, Chevalier de. Naturalist. Born 1 August 1744, Bazantin, Picardy, France; educated Académie des Sciences; custodian of the Jardin du Roi 1788; professor of zoology 1793; noted for the formulation of theories of natural evolution, for the classification of invertebrates and as the founder of invertebrate palaeontology; published *Flore française*; *Histoire naturelle des animaux sans vertèbres*; *Philosophie zoologique*, etc. Died 18 December 1829.

Lamont, Austin. Anaesthesiologist. Born 25 February 1905, Englewood, New Jersey, United States of America; educated Johns Hopkins University of Medicine where he was fellowship surgeon 1934–8; physician anaesthesiology, visiting surgeon, associate in surgery at Johns Hopkins 1942–6; associate professor, clinical anaesthesiology, University of Pennsylvania school of medicine from 1947. Died 21 June 1969.

Lamont, Corliss. Political philosopher. Born 28 March 1902, Englewood, New Jersey, United States of America; educated Phillips Exeter Academy; New College, Oxford; Columbia; instructor in philosophy, Columbia College 1928–32, and New School of Social Research 1940–2; lecturer on Soviet Russia at Cornell and Harvard 1943–4; lecturer in philosophy, Columbia School of General Studies 1947–59; director, American Civil Liberties Union 1932–54; author of a number of books on political philosophy, notably *The Philosophy of Humanism*, and on Soviet Russia.

Lamont, Thomas Stilwell. Banker. Born 30 January 1899, Englewood, New Jersey, United States of America; educated Phillips Exeter Academy; Harvard; Trinity College, Cambridge; with J. P. Morgan and Company from 1922, partner 1929–40, vice-president and director 1940–53, senior vice-president 1953–5, vice-chairman 1955–8, chairman executive committee 1959; vice-chairman, then member, board of directors, Morgan Guaranty Trust Company 1959–64; served on governing bodies of various educational institutions; served as private in First World War and as lieutenant-colonel in army air force 1942–4. Died 10 April 1967.

Lamont, Thomas William. American banker. Born 30 September 1870; educated Phillips Exeter Academy, New Hampshire; Harvard; financial reporter, *New York Tribune* 1893–4; secretary-treasurer, Bankers' Trust Company 1903–5; vice-president, then president, First National Bank 1905–9, 1909–11; became a partner in J. P. Morgan and Company 1911 and chairman of the board 1940; financial adviser of the United States treasury during and after the First World War;

director, U.S. Steel Corporation etc.; trustee, Metropolitan Museum of Art; wrote memoirs of his boyhood. Died 2 February 1948.

Landau, Judah Leo. Jewish rabbi and scholar. Born 1866, Brody, Galicia, Austria; educated University of Vienna; joined the Zionist movement; rabbi in Manchester 1901; chief rabbi in Johannesburg from 1903 and professor of Hebrew, University of the Witwatersrand; writer of an epic and dramas in Hebrew. Died 1942.

Latham, Sir John Greig. Diplomat, judge, politician. Born 25 August 1877, Victoria, Australia; educated Scotch College; University of Melbourne where he became lecturer in philosophy and law; member of the Commonwealth parliament 1925–34; attorney-general 1925–9; minister of industry 1928–9; deputy prime minister, attorney-general, minister for industry and external affairs 1932–4; chief justice of Australia 1935–9; minister to Japan 1940; chancellor, University of Melbourne 1939; knighted 1922; author of books on Australian and international politics. Died 25 July 1964.

Laval, Pierre. Politician. Born 28 June 1883, Châteldon, Puy-de-Dôme, France; educated St. Etienne; Universities of Lyon and Paris; was at first a school teacher at Auvergne; admitted to the bar in Paris 1907; mayor of Aubervilliers 1908; elected as a Socialist to chamber of deputies 1914; served in the First World War; re-elected to the chamber 1924 moving to the political right; minister of public works 1925; foreign minister 1934, 1935, 1936; prime minister 1930, 1931, 1932, 1935, 1936; made, with Sir Samuel Hoare (q.v. under Templewood), the abortive plan to enable Mussolini to acquire Abyssinia 1935. When France fell in June 1940, Laval was foreign minister in Pétain's cabinet until dismissed in December but in April 1942 he became 'chief of government' at Vichy. He fled to Germany when the Allies occupied Paris, then to Spain. Returned to France, he was tried for treason and executed on 15 October 1945.

Law, Richard Kidston. See **Coleraine.**

Lawrence, Harry Gordon. Politician and lawyer. Born 17 October 1901, Rondebosch, Cape Town, South Africa; educated Rondebosch Boys' High School; University of South Africa; practised as advocate in Cape Town; member of parliament 1929–48; minister of labour 1938; minister of the interior and of public health 1940–4; minister of welfare and demobilization 1944–8; head of the Union delegation to U.N.O. 1947; minister of justice and of the interior 1948; national chairman, Progressive party 1959.

Lawrence, William Henry Arthur. Company manager and director. Born 17 May 1894, London; educated William Ellis School, London; Trinity College, Cambridge; served in the First World War; emigrated to South Africa and joined the Central Mining and Investment Corporation 1919 of which he became manager in 1928, general manager in 1942, director in 1947; president, Transvaal Chamber of Mines 1942 and 1944; chairman, Rand Mines Ltd. 1947; chairman, the Argus Company 1949; director of various other mining and industrial companies and of the South African Reserve Bank. Died 15 December 1958.

Layton, Walter Thomas, first Baron, of Danehill. Economist and newspaper proprietor. Born 15 March 1884, London; educated King's College School; Westminster City School; University College, London; Trinity College, Cambridge; lecturer in economics in these universities 1912–28; editor of *The Economist* 1922–38; British delegate, world economic conference 1927; chairman of the *News Chronicle*, the *Star*; director of Reuter's 1930; director-general of programmes, ministry of supply 1941–3; vice-president, consultative assembly, Council of Europe 1949–57; knighted 1930; created baron 1947; author of *Introduction to the Study of Prices*; *Relations of Capital and Labour*. Died 14 February 1966.

Leeper, Sir Reginald Wildig Allen. Diplomat. Born 25 March 1888, Sydney, Australia; educated Melbourne Grammar School; Trinity College, Melbourne; New College, Oxford; appointed to intelligence bureau, British department of information 1917; entered foreign office 1918; first secretary, legation, Warsaw 1923–4, Riga 1924, Contantinople 1925; transferred to foreign office 1929; counsellor 1933; assistant under-secretary 1940; ambassador to Greece 1943–6; ambassador to the Argentine Republic 1946–8; director, De Beers Consolidated Mines etc.; author of *When Greek meets Greek*. Died February 1968.

Leipoldt, Christian Frederick Louis. Poet, medical practitioner, journalist. Born 28 December 1880, Worcester, Cape Province, South Africa; educated privately and at the South African College and Guy's Hospital, London; joined staff of *Het Dagblad* 1897 and the *South African News* 1899; war correspondent of pro-Boer overseas newspapers 1900–2; graduated in medicine in London 1907; medical inspector of schools in Hampstead; first medical inspector of schools in the Transvaal 1914–19, later in the Cape Province 1919–23; assistant editor, *Die Volkstem* 1923–5; practised as pediatrician in Cape Town; editor, the *South African Medical Journal* from 1926; secretary, Medical Association of South Africa 1939–44. His literary works, mostly in Afrikaans and written from 1900 onwards, include stories, novels, plays and, above all, poetry in *Oom Gert Vertel*; *Uit drie Wêrelddele*; *Skoonheidstroos*. Died 12 April 1947.

Leopold III. King of the Belgians. Born 3 November 1901, son of Albert I and Princess Elizabeth of Bavaria; educated privately and at Eton and Ghent University; entered the Belgian army; married, in 1926, Princess Astrid of Sweden who died in 1935; succeeded to the throne 1934; took command of Belgian army when Germany invaded the country early in May 1940 and ordered its capitulation on 28 May; confined to his palace at Laeken; married Mary Lilian Baels 1941; sent to Germany 1944. On the liberation of Brussels his brother, Prince Charles (q.v.), was elected regent by parliament 1944. Differences with his ministers about his conduct and policy during the war prevented his return to Belgium until 1950; abdicated in favour of his eldest son, Prince Baudouin, 1951.

Levick, Sir Hugh Gwynne. English banker. Born 17 March 1870; educated in Port Elizabeth, Cape Province; Malvern College; in Hamburg; went to the United States of America 1886 and entered service of the Bank of Montreal and then of Lee, Higginson and Co., Boston 1902; admitted to partnership 1906; in the London firm from 1917; adviser at the treasury 1917–19; member of British delegation, reparations commission 1919–21; retired 1924 to Wynberg, Cape Town; knighted 1918. Died 19 June 1937.

Lie, Trygve Halvdan. Statesman and lawyer. Born 16 July 1896, Oslo, Norway; educated Oslo University; practised as a barrister; joined the Labour party 1912; legal adviser, trade unions federation 1922–5; minister of justice 1935–9; minister of commerce and of shipping and supply 1939; minister of foreign affairs 1941–6; first secretary-general of the United Nations Organization 1946–53; governor of Oslo and Akershus 1955; ambassador *en mission speciale* 1959; minister of industry 1963–4; author of books on labour legislation and memoirs.

Lindsay, Alexander Dunlop, first Baron, of Birker. Philosopher and university principal. Born 14 May 1879; educated Glasgow University; University College, Oxford; lecturer in philosophy, Victoria University; fellow and classical tutor, Balliol College 1906, then lecturer in philosophy 1911; served in the First World War 1914–18; professor of moral philosophy, Glasgow University 1922–4; master of Balliol College 1924–49; vice-chancellor, University of Oxford 1935–8; principal of University College, North Staffordshire 1949–52; created baron 1945; author of works on Bergson, Karl Marx, Kant, Christian morality, etc. Died 18 March 1952.

Linlithgow, Victor Alexander John Hope, second Marquess of. Administrator. Born 24 September 1889; educated Eton; served in the First World War; civil lord of the admiralty 1922–4; president, Navy League 1924–31; chairman, joint select committee on Indian constitutional reform 1933; viceroy and governor-general of India 1936–43; succeeded his father 1908; knighted 1928; Knight of the Garter 1943. Died 5 January 1952.

Lippmann, Walter. American journalist. Born 23 September 1889, New York City; educated Harvard University; associate editor, *New Republic* 1914–17;

assistant to secretary of war 1917; captain, military intelligence 1918; editor, *New York World* 1919–31; special writer on world affairs, *New York Herald Tribune* 1931–62; Pulitzer prize for international reporting 1962; writer of a number of books on politics and international relations.

Litvinov, Maxim Maximovich. Politician and diplomat. Born Meer Wallach on 17 July 1876, Bialystok, Poland; educated there at the real-school; member of the Kiev committee of the Social Democratic party; imprisoned but escaped abroad; joined the Bolsheviks and contributed to *Iskra*; returned to Russia illegally 1903 and helped to edit *New Life*; lived abroad, mainly in England, after 1905; appointed diplomatic representative of the Soviet government in Great Britain 1917; assistant commissar for foreign affairs 1918; chief Russian delegate at various disarmament conferences during the twenties; commissar for foreign affairs 1930–9; ambassador to the United States 1941–3; deputy minister of foreign affairs 1946 when he retired. Died 31 December 1951.

Livingstone, David. Explorer and missionary. Born 19 March 1813, Blantyre, Lanarkshire, Scotland; worked as a child in the cotton mills; began study at Anderson's College, Glasgow 1836; qualified in medicine in Glasgow 1840 and became a missionary of the London Missionary Society; worked at the mission station of Kuruman in Bechuanaland 1841–9; with two companions discovered Lake Ngami 1849; made journeys to the upper Zambezi 1850–2, from the interior to the west coast 1854, and from the interior to the mouth of the Zambezi in the course of which he discovered the Victoria Falls 1855–6. On further expeditions he discovered Lake Nyasa and attempted to find the sources of the Nile 1859–73. He wrote vivid accounts of his journeys, notably *Missionary Travels and Researches in South Africa* and *The Zambezi and its Tributaries*, and exposed the cruelties of the African slave trade. A search party, led by H. M. Stanley, found him at Ujiji in 1871 after he had been missing for five years. Freshly equipped he continued his exploration but died on 1 May 1873.

Lo, Chung-Shu. Philosopher. Born 3 August 1903, Wu-San, Szechwan, West China; educated West China Union University; Yenching University; Geneva School of International Studies; University of Oxford; dean of studies, West China Union University 1933–4, then professor of philosophy 1934–46; consultant to Chinese delegation, general conference of Unesco 1947; president, East and West Cultural Association since 1941; member, people's political council of Szechwan since 1943; author of books on Greek and Chinese philosophy.

Long, Basil Kellett. Journalist and politician. Born 28 February 1878, Leicestershire, England; educated Norwich School; Brasenose College, Oxford; settled in Cape Town 1902; admitted to the bar 1905; elected to Cape house of assembly 1908; law adviser, South African National convention 1908–9; editor, *The State* 1902–12; member of the Union parliament 1910–13, 1938–43; Dominions editor, *The Times* 1913–21; editor, the *Cape Times* 1921–35; author of *In Smuts's Camp* and a biography of Sir Drummond Chaplin. Died 2 January 1944.

Lotsij, Johannes Paulus. Botanist. Born 11 April 1867, Dordrecht, the Netherlands; educated at Wageningen and Göttingen; lecturer, Johns Hopkins University, Baltimore 1891–5; worked at Bandung and Tjibodas, Netherlands East Indies 1895–1900; lecturer and director, Rijks herbarium at Leiden 1904–9; secretary, Hollandse Mij. voor Wetenschap at Haarlem and later of the experimental gardens at Velp 1909–19; founder of *Genetica* 1919; author of books on botany and theories of evolution. Died 17 November 1931.

Louw, Reverend Andries Adriaan. Missionary. Born 26 February 1862, Murraysburg, Cape Province, South Africa; educated Theological Seminary, Stellenbosch; legitimated as a missionary of the Nederlands Gereformeerde Kerk 1891; founded the mission station Morgenster in Mashonaland; translated New Testament into the Chikaranga language. He was ordained as a minister in 1921 and retired from Morgenster in 1937. Died 12 August 1956.

Louw, Eric Hendrik. Diplomat, politician, lawyer. Born 21 November 1890, Jacobsdal, Orange Free State, South Africa; educated at Beaufort West; Victoria College, Stellenbosch; Rhodes University College; practised as advocate at Grahamstown 1917–18, then managed a family business at Beaufort West; National party member of parliament 1924–5, 1938–63; trade commissioner of South Africa in the United States and Canada 1925–9; high commissioner in London; minister plenipotentiary to the United States 1929–33, to Italy 1933, to France 1933–7; minister of economic affairs 1948–54; minister of finance 1955–6; minister of foreign affairs 1955–63; South African representative at the League of Nations assembly, the United Nations assembly and various international conferences; retired from public life 1963. Died 24 June 1968.

Louw, Francina Susanna (Cinie). Linguist. Born 10 March 1872, Riebeeck West, Cape Province, South Africa; sister of D. F. Malan (q.v. vol. IV); educated at Riebeeck West; Huguenot Seminary, Wellington where she became a school teacher; married, in 1894, the Reverend A. A. Louw (q.v.) with whom she worked at the mission-station at Morgenster; published *A Manual of the Chikaranga Language* 1915 and compiled and translated the hymn book *Nziyo*. Died 25 June 1935.

Lowe, Clarence van Riet. Archaeologist and engineer. Born 4 November 1894, Aliwal North, Cape Province, South Africa; educated South African College; University of Cape Town; served in the First World War in East Africa, Egypt, France; entered the civil service in the public works department; while in charge of bridge construction in the Orange Free State discovered many prehistoric sites and made important collections of implements 1923–8; chief engineer, public works department 1931; director, bureau of archaeology, department of the interior and professor of archaeology, University of the Witwatersrand 1935; co-author of *The Stone Age Cultures of South Africa*; represented South Africa at various international conferences on archaeology. Died 17 June 1956.

Luce, Henry Robinson. Magazine editor and publisher. Born 3 April 1898, of American parentage, in Shantung Province, China; educated Hotchkiss School, Lakeville, Connecticut; Yale University; founded *Time* (1923), *Fortune* (1930), *Life* (1936), *Sports Illustrated* (1954); editor-in-chief of these magazines and of *Architectural Forum* and *House and Home* until 1964, thereafter editorial chairman; trustee, China Institute in America and Metropolitan Museum etc. Died 28 February 1967.

Lugard, Frederick John Dealtry, first Baron, of Abinger. Administrator and soldier. Born 22 January 1858, Madras, India; educated Rossall; Sandhurst; served in Afghan War and in the Sudan and Burma 1879–87; led an expedition against slave-traders on Lake Nyasa 1888; established, while in the service of the East Africa Company, British claims to Uganda 1890–3; secured British control over Northern Nigeria and was appointed high commissioner 1900–6; retired from the army and became governor of Hong Kong 1907–12; governor of Northern and Southern Nigeria 1912–14; first governor-general of united Nigeria 1914–19 when he retired; British member of the permanent mandates commission, League of Nations 1922–36; director, Barclays Bank; knighted 1901; created baron 1928; wrote *The Dual Mandate in British Tropical Africa* and other books on the British East African territories. Died 11 April 1945.

Luther, Hans. Statesman and diplomat. Born 10 March 1879, Berlin; studied law and entered the public service in Magdeburg; secretary to the Association of Prussian and German Towns 1913–18; mayor of Essen 1918–22; minister of agriculture, then minister of finance 1922–4; negotiated the Dawes loan; chancellor and leader of the German delegation at Locarno 1925–6; concerned in management of the state railways 1926–30; president of the Reichsbank 1930–3 when he was forced to retire; ambassador in Washington 1933–7; took part in economic reconstruction after 1945; professor of political science, Münich 1952. Died 11 May 1963.

Lyttelton, Oliver. See **Chandos.**

Lytton, Edward George Earle Lytton Bulwer, first Baron, of Knebworth. Novelist, editor, politician. Born 25 May 1803, London; educated Trinity College, Cambridge; wrote for various periodicals; edited the *New Monthly*, the *Monthly Chronicle*; wrote a number of novels between 1827 and 1873, notably *Pelham*; *The Last Days of Pompeii*; *Rienzi*; *The Last of the Barons*; and three plays; Conservative member of parliament 1852–66; secretary of state for the colonies 1858–9; created baron 1866. Died 18 January 1873.

Macarthur, General Douglas. Soldier. Born 26 January 1880, Little Rock, Arkansas, United States of America; educated West Point Military Academy; served in the Philippines 1905 and Mexico 1914; commanded the 42nd division in the First World War; superintendent, U.S. Military Academy 1919–22; department commander, Philippines 1928–30; U.S. army chief of staff 1930–5; retired 1937 but recalled to active duty to defend the Philippines 1941; commanded the Allied forces in the Pacific 1942–5; supreme commander of the occupation forces in Japan 1945; supreme commander of the United Nations forces during the first nine months of the Korean War, then dismissed by President Truman (q.v.) in a policy dispute 1951; chairman, Remington Rand Incoporated 1952; wrote memoirs. Died 5 April 1964.

McCloy, John Jay. Government official and lawyer. Born 31 March 1895, Philadelphia, Pennsylvania, United States of America; educated Peddie School; Amherst College; Harvard; admitted to New York bar 1921; member of a firm of lawyers 1929–40, 1946, 1961...; assistant secretary of war 1941–5; president, International Bank for Reconstruction and Development 1947–9; United States high commissioner for Germany 1949–52; government adviser and committee member on atomic energy, disarmament, Cuba; director of companies; trustee, Ford Foundation; chairman, Atlantic Institute; author of *The Challenge to American Foreign Policy*.

McConnell, John G. Publisher. Born 6 December 1911, Montreal, Canada; educated Lower Canada College; McGill University; University of Cambridge; formerly a journalist in London and New York; president and director, Montreal Standard Publishing Company since 1938; board member of various Montreal companies; member, international council, Y.M.C.A.

MacDonald, Malcolm John. Administrator and politician. Born 1901, Lossiemouth, Morayshire, Scotland; son of J. Ramsay MacDonald (q.v. vol. IV); educated Bedales School, Petersfield; Queen's College, Oxford; member, London county council 1927–30; Labour member of parliament 1929–45; parliamentary under-secretary, Dominions office 1931–5; secretary of state for Dominion affairs 1935–9; secretary of state for the colonies 1935, 1938–40; minister of health 1940–1; high commissioner in Canada 1941–6; governor-general of Malaya and British Borneo 1946–8; commissioner-general in south-east Asia 1948–55; high commissioner in India 1955–60; leader of British delegation, international conference on Laos 1961–2; Rhodes Trustee 1948–57; chancellor, University of Malaya 1949–61; author of books on birds and south-east Asia.

Machado, Francisco José Vieira. Banker and politician. Born 8 February 1898, Lisbon, Portugal; educated University of Lisbon; member, then vice-president of the council, Banco Nacional Ultramarino 1926–34; under-secretary of state 1934; minister for overseas territories 1936–44; director and president, Banco Ultramarino Brasileiro; member of the administrative council and procurator of the corporative chamber; governor, Banco Nacional Ultramarino; director, Anglo-Portuguese Bank; author of books on Africa.

Mackenzie, Thomas William. Journalist. Born 4 August 1875, Inverness, Scotland; educated High School and Raining's School, Inverness; reporter on his father's paper, the *Scottish Highlander*; went to South Africa 1898 and joined the *Eastern Province Herald*; Reuter's correspondent with the British forces in the Anglo-Boer War; joined the *Rand Daily Mail*; became editor of the *Friend* in Bloemfontein

1908 and managing editor of Friend Newspapers Ltd.; leader of South African press delegations to overseas conferences 1924, 1927, 1930. Died 3 May 1939.

MacKeurtan, Harold Graham. Lawyer. Born 26 February 1884, Durban, Natal, South Africa; educated Durban High School; University of Cambridge; called to the bar 1906; leader of the Natal bar; South African party member of parliament 1921–4; author of *Cradle Days of Natal*. Died 18 December 1942.

Mackie, William Soutar. University professor. Born 31 October 1885, Scotland; educated Universities of Aberdeen and Oxford; head of department of English, Southampton University College until 1921; professor of English language, University of Cape Town 1921–51 when he retired.

Mackinder, Sir Halford John. British geographer and politician. Born 15 February 1861; educated grammar school, Gainsborough; Epsom College; Christ Church, Oxford; extension lecturer in geography 1885–7; reader in geography, Oxford 1887–1905; first director of the school of geography at Oxford 1899; principal of Reading College 1892–1903; held simultaneously a post at the London School of Economics 1895–1925 and was director of the School 1903–8; chairman of the imperial economic committee 1925–31; chairman of the imperial shipping committee 1920–45; Unionist member of parliament 1910–22; put forward the theory of the heartland as the natural seat of power; knighted 1920; author of *Britain and the British Seas*; *Democratic Ideals and Reality*, etc. Died 6 March 1947.

Macmillan, Maurice Harold. Statesman. Born 10 February 1894; educated Eton; Balliol College, Oxford; served in the First World War; aide-de-camp to governor-general of Canada 1919–20; Conservative member of parliament 1924–9, 1931–64; parliamentary secretary, ministry of supply 1940–2; parliamentary under-secretary of state for the colonies 1942; minister resident at Allied headquarters, north Africa 1942–5; secretary for air 1945; minister of housing and local government 1951–4; minister of defence 1954–5; secretary of state for foreign affairs 1955; chancellor of the exchequer 1955–7; prime minister 1957–63; chancellor of the University of Oxford since 1960; chairman, Macmillan and Company since 1963; author of books on British politics and three volumes of memoirs.

Macmurray, John. Philosopher. Born 16 February 1891, Maxwelton, Kirkcudbrightshire, Scotland; educated Grammar School and Robert Gordon College, Aberdeen; University of Glasgow; Balliol College, Oxford; served in the First World War 1914–19; lecturer in philosophy, University of Manchester 1919–20; professor of philosophy, University of the Witwatersrand 1921; fellow, classical tutor, Jowett lecturer in philosophy, Balliol College 1922–8; Grote professor of philosophy, University of London 1928–44; professor of moral philosophy, University of Edinburgh 1944–58; author of a number of philosophical books including *Freedom in the Modern World*; *The Boundaries of Science*; *The Self as Agent*.

Madoc, Henry William. Police officer. Born 1870, Malvern, England; educated at Highgate; went to South Africa 1890; served in Cape regiments 1890–1900; joined the South African Constabulary 1900, rank of major; commanded western Transvaal division 1903–5; subsequently was assistant inspector-general and assistant commissioner, Transvaal police; chief constable, Isle of Man 1911–36; author of *Birds of the Isle of Man*. Died 9 January 1937.

Malan, Avril Ire. Biochemist, politician, company director. Born 31 May 1898; educated Huguenot College, Wellington; University of Stellenbosch; chief research officer, Onderstepoort until 1945; professor of biochemistry, University of Pretoria 1932–45; National party member of parliament 1948–66; deputy speaker 1961–6; chairman, Volkskas Ltd., National Building Society, Transvaal Sugar Ltd., etc.

Malan, Charl Wynand. Attorney and politician. Born 9 August 1883, Paarl, Cape Colony, South Africa; youngest brother of F. S. Malan (q.v. vol. IV); educated Victoria College, Stellenbosch; practised as an attorney at Humansdorp from 1906; an early supporter of General Hertzog; National party member of parliament from 1915; minister of railways 1924–33. Died 6 February 1933.

Malcolm, Sir Dougal Orme. British government official and company director. Born 6 August 1877; educated Eton; New College, Oxford; entered colonial office 1900; private secretary to Lord Selborne (q.v. vol. IV) 1905–10; secretary to Lord Grey in Canada 1910–11; joined the treasury 1912; became a director of the British South Africa Company 1913; chairman of government committee on education and industry 1926–8; member, British economic mission to Australia, 1928; vice-chairman of court of governors, London School of Economics. Died 30 August 1955.

Malcomess, Carl Hermann. Politician and farmer. Born 2 October 1873, Kingwilliamstown, Cape Colony, South Africa; educated there and in Germany; as a young man entered his father's trading company in the eastern Cape Colony; elected to Cape provincial council as independent supporter of the South African party 1931; elected to senate as representative of the Natives of the Cape Province 1937–50. Died 8 September 1950.

Malherbe, Ernst Gideon. Educationalist. Born 8 November 1895, Luckhoff, Orange Free State, South Africa; educated Villiersdorp; University of Stellenbosch; Columbia University, New York; lecturer in education, Cape Town Training College, University of Stellenbosch 1922, University of Cape Town 1924–9; director, National Bureau of Educational and Social Research 1929–39; director of census and statistics 1939–40; director, military intelligence and army education services 1940–5; principal and vice-chancellor, University of Natal 1945–65; member, Social and Economic Planning Council 1946–50 and National Council for Social Research 1945–50; chairman, national war histories committee 1945–9; author of a number of educational works, notably *Education in South Africa*; *The Bilingual School.*

Malvern, Godfrey Martin, first Viscount, of Rhodesia and of Bexley. Statesman and medical practitioner. Born 6 July 1883; educated Malvern College; St Thomas's Hospital, London, where he qualified in medicine; house physician, then medical superintendent, Great Ormond Street Hospital; went to Southern Rhodesia 1911; in general practice until 1921, then as consultative surgeon; served with R.A.M.C. in England, Malta, France 1914–17; member, legislative assembly, Southern Rhodesia 1923–58; minister of Native affairs 1933–49; minister of defence 1948–56; prime minister 1933–53; prime minister, Federation of Rhodesia and Nyasaland 1953–6; created viscount 1955. Died 8 May 1971.

Margriet, Princess, of the Netherlands (Margriet Francisca). Born 19 January 1943, Ottawa, Canada, third daughter of Queen Juliana and Prince Bernhard (qq.v.); educated University of Leiden; married, 10 January 1967, a commoner, Piet van Vollenhoven.

Maritz, Gerhardus Marthinus. Voortrekker leader. Born March, 1797, Graaff Reinet district, Cape Colony, South Africa; learned the trade of carpenter in his father's workshop; became a wagon-maker in Graaff Reniet; also engaged in farming; warden of the town 1827, then acting field-cornet; led a party of trekkers from the district in September 1836 following a northwards and north-eastwards route; elected head of the first Voortrekker government at Thaba Nchu, December 1836 and magistrate, under Pieter Retief (q.v. vol. IV), in the second government formed on 17 April 1837; crossed Drakensbergen to join Retief in Natal towards the end of that year; began to prepare a commando against the Zulus but fell ill. Died 23 September 1838.

Marloth, Hermann Wilhelm Rudolf. Botanist. Born 28 December 1855, Lübben, Germany; educated there and at the University of Berlin; assistant pharmacist in the military reserve 1883; emigrated to South Africa 1883 where he practised as a pharmacist until 1889; lecturer in chemistry, Victoria College, Stellenbosch 1888 and professor 1889–92; part-time lecturer in the natural sciences at Elsenburg agricultural school 1892–1903; honorary director, botanical survey of the western Cape 1919 and director 1927; published a description of the phytogeography of the Cape 1908; undertook wide-ranging studies of the South African flora and wrote three volumes of *The Flora of South Africa*. Died 15 May 1931.

Marshall, General George Catlett. Soldier and statesman. Born 31 December 1880, Uniontown, Pennsylvania, United States of America; educated Virginia Military Institute; during the First World War was chief of operations, first U.S. army in France; later chief of staff, eighth army corps; aide-de-camp to General J. J. Pershing (q.v. vol. IV) 1919–24; stationed in China 1924–7; instructor in various centres reaching rank of brigadier in 1936; promoted general 1939 and was chief of staff of the U.S. army 1939–45; special presidential envoy to China 1945; appointed secretary of state 1946–9; author of the Marshall plan for the economic rehabilitation of Europe; secretary of defence 1950–1; awarded Nobel peace prize 1953. Died 16 October 1959.

Martin, John. Newspaper and mining magnate. Born 19 April 1884, Stirling, Scotland; educated there, then went to Australia as newspaper reporter in Ballarat; moved to South Africa and worked for the *Star* in Johannesburg; manager of the *Bloemfontein Post*; manager of the Argus Company's London office; general manager, Argus Printing and Publishing Company 1915, subsequently managing director and chairman 1926; chairman, Central Mining and Investment Corporation 1926; by 1935 chairman of Rand Mines Ltd. and many other Transvaal companies; director of the Bank of England 1937–46; president, Transvaal chamber of mines 1929, 1932, 1934; adviser to Union delegation, world economic conference 1933; head of Union government supply mission, delegate, imperial conference on post-war aviation 1943; Washington 1942; chairman of the first commission of international civil aviation congress, Chicago 1944. Died 28 March 1949.

Martin, Max Henno. Geologist. Born 15 March 1910, Freiburg, Baden, Germany; educated Realgymnasium, Freiburg; Universities of Bonn, Zürich, Göttingen; private consulting and geological research in South West Africa 1935–45; employed by the administration to supervise water-boring for farms 1945–7; on staff of geological survey of South Africa, South West Africa branch 1947–62; associate professor of geology, University of Cape Town 1963–5; professor of geology, University of Göttingen from 1965; author of *The Pre-Cambrian Geology of South West Africa and Namaqualand* and professional articles.

Marwick, John Sidney. Government official and politician. Born 17 June 1875, Richmond, Natal, South Africa and educated there; served in Native affairs department, Natal 1890–9; served in the Anglo-Boer War 1899–1900; acting Native commissioner, Pretoria, then assistant-secretary for Native affairs 1902–5; Native commissioner, central division 1905–7; retired from the civil service; senior partner in Marwick and Morris, employers of Native mine-workers; manager, municipal Native affairs department 1916–20; elected Unionist member of parliament 1920, later a member of the Dominion party until 1948. Died 18 April 1958.

Mary of Teck. Queen consort of George V of Great Britain. Born 26 May 1867, Kensington Palace, London, eldest child of Francis, Duke of Teck, of the house of Württemburg; studied music under Tosti; lived in Florence 1883–5; became engaged in 1891 to the Duke of Clarence, elder son of the Prince of Wales, who died five weeks later; married, in 1893, the Duke of York, afterwards George V (q.v.); after his death lived in Marlborough House and during the Second World War at Badminton, the home of the Duchess of Beaufort. Died 24 March 1953.

Masefield, John Edward. Poet, playwright, novelist. Born 1 June 1878, Ledbury, Herefordshire, England; educated King's School, Warwick and the training ship *Conway*; went to sea as an apprentice 1893, then lived in New York; returned to London 1897; became literary editor, the *Speaker*; editor, miscellany column of the *Manchester Guardian*; wrote between 1901 and 1911 poems, plays, novels, stories, notably a narrative poem *The Everlasting Mercy* which established his reputation; served during the First World War with the Red Cross and in a hospital ship; his novels include *Sard Harker* and *Odtaa*, his war books, *Gallipoli* and *The Old Front Line*; his *Collected Poems* (1923) sold over 200,000 copies; he became poet laureate in 1930 and was awarded the Order of Merit 1935; his autobiography *So Long to Learn* appeared in 1952. Died 12 May 1967.

Massey, Vincent. Statesman. Born 20 February 1887, Toronto, Canada; educated St Andrew's College, Toronto; University of Toronto; Balliol College, Oxford; lecturer in modern history, University of Toronto 1913–15; on Canadian military staff 1915–18; Dominion minister without portfolio 1925; Canadian minister to United States 1926–30; president, National Liberal Federation of Canada 1932–5; high commissioner for Canada in the United Kingdom 1935–46; governor-general of Canada 1952–9; trustee, National and Tate Galleries, London 1941–6; chancellor, University of Toronto 1947–53; Companion of Honour 1946; author of *On Being Canadian*; *Speaking of Canada*, etc. Died 30 December 1967.

Massey, William Ferguson. Statesman. Born 26 March 1856, Limvady, County Derry, Ireland; educated at schools in Londonderry; emigrated to New Zealand 1870 and farmed near Auckland; active in local government; elected Conservative member of parliament 1894; opposition whip 1895–1903, then leader; prime minister and minister of lands and labour 1912–22; member, imperial war cabinet 1917–18. Died 10 May 1925.

Masterton-Smith, Sir James Edward. Government official. Born 24 August 1878; educated Harrow; Hertford College, Oxford; entered the civil service (admiralty) 1901; private secretary to successive first lords of the admiralty 1910–17; assistant secretary, ministry of munitions 1917–19; war office and air ministry 1919–20; joint permanent secretary, ministry of labour 1920–1; permanent under-secretary of state for the colonies 1921–4 when he retired. Died 4 May 1938.

Matthews, Zachariah Keodirelang. African educationist and political leader. Born 1901, Barkly West, Cape Province, South Africa; educated Lovedale Institution; Fort Hare College; Yale University; principal of Adam's College, Natal; head of the department of African studies, Fort Hare 1936; member of the Native representative council 1941–50; chief organizer of the Pan African convention; Cape chairman of the African National Congress from 1950; visiting professor, Union Theological Seminary, New York 1952–4; acting principal of Fort Hare 1954–6; imprisoned 1960; first ambassador of Botswana in the United States 1966. Died 11 May 1968.

Mears, Walter George Amos. Teacher. Born 29 June 1891, Margate, England, his parents emigrating to South Africa in 1892; lived as a child on a mission station in the Transkei; educated Kingswood College, Grahamstown; Rhodes University College; Emmanuel College, Cambridge; teacher at Kingswood 1914–17, Pretoria Boys' High School 1819–20, Germiston High School 1920–30; headmaster, Rondebosch Boys' High School 1930–52, St Stithians Methodist Church school on the Witwatersrand 1953–9; active in African welfare bodies, notably the Friends of Africa; co-founder, Langa High School, Cape Town 1937.

Meighen, Arthur. Statesman. Born 16 June 1874, Perth County, Ontario, Canada; educated St Mary's Collegiate Institute; Toronto University; called to the bar 1903; practised in Portage la Prairie; Conservative member of the Dominion parliament 1908–32; solicitor-general 1913; secretary of state and minister of the interior 1917; prime minister 1920–1, 1926–32; minister without portfolio 1932–5; government leader in the senate 1932–41; leader of the Conservative party 1941–2. Died 5 August 1960.

Mein, William Wallace. Mining engineer. Born 19 July 1873, Nevada City, United States of America; educated University of California; engaged in gold and nickel mining in South Africa and Canada 1892–1919; president of oil and cement companies; director, banking and insurance companies. Died 5 May 1964.

Meinertzhagen, Colonel Richard. Soldier and ornithologist. Born 1878, of Danish descent; educated Harrow; joined the British army 1899; served in India until 1902, then in the King's African Rifles in Kenya until 1906; staff officer in East Africa, Palestine, France 1914–18; chief political officer in Palestine and Syria 1919–20; military adviser to the colonial office (Middle East department) 1921–4; travelled in Asia, Africa and the United States; on the staff of the war office 1939–40;

served in the home guard 1940–5; author of *Kenya Diary*; *Birds of Egypt*; *Birds of Arabia*; and an autobiography. Died 23 June 1967.

Melchior, Karl. Jurist and financier. Born 1871, Hamburg, Germany; educated at Universities of Berlin, Bonn, Jena; became a judge in Hamburg; entered the banking house of M. M. Warburg 1902 becoming a partner in 1917; served in the Bavarian artillery in the First World War; financial adviser to the German peace delegation 1918–19 and at subsequent conferences but repeatedly declined ministerial office; German commissioner of finance at Geneva 1926; member of the directorate, Bank for International Settlements 1931; member of the central committee to assist Jewish victims of Nazi persecution. Died 1933.

Mendel, Gregor Johann. Austrian scientist. Born 22 July 1822, Heizendorf, Silesia; educated Olmütz; University of Vienna; entered an Augustinian monastery 1843; ordained priest 1847; taught natural science at the Technical High School, Brünn 1854–68; elected abbot of his monastery 1868; discovered the Mendelian laws of heredity which were published in 1868 in *Versuche über Pflanzenhybriden* and are the basis of modern genetics. Died 6 January 1884.

Menzies, Sir Robert Gordon. Statesman. Born 20 December 1894, Jeparit, Australia; educated Gonville College, Ballarat; Wesley College, Melbourne; Melbourne University; practised at the Victoria bar from 1918; entered Victorian parliament 1928; attorney-general, minister of railways of Victoria 1932–4; member of the Commonwealth parliament 1934–66; Commonwealth attorney-general 1934–9; treasurer 1939–40; prime minister 1939–41 and minister for the co-ordination of defence; leader of the Liberal opposition 1943–9; prime minister 1949–66; knighted 1963; Companion of Honour 1951.

Merensky, Hans. Geologist and diamond magnate. Born 1871, Botshabelo, Transvaal, South Africa; educated State Mining Academy and University, Berlin; after a period as government mining official in East Prussia, returned to South Africa in 1904 and became consulting geologist on the Witwatersrand; interned 1914–18; discovered platinum deposits in eastern Transvaal 1923; predicted rich diamond deposits in the Orange river mouth region, which were actually discovered in 1926, and took a leading part in developing these finds; discovered phosphate deposit at Phalabora; sold his diamond interests and retired to undertake agricultural and forestry projects on his farm in northern Transvaal. Died 21 October 1952.

Meyer-Abich, Friedrich Ernst Gustav Adolf. Philosopher. Born 14 November 1893, Emden, Ostfriesland, Germany; educated Universities of Göttingen and Jena; *privatdozent* in philosophy, University of Hamburg 1926–9; professor of philosophy, University of Chile 1929–32; professor of philosophy and history of science, University of Hamburg from 1933; director, Institute for Marine Biology, University of Hamburg from 1946; founder and editor of *Bios* 1934; author of books on philosophy and biology.

Michael. King of Rumania. Born 25 October 1921, Sinaia, son of the heir apparent, Prince Carol, who was excluded from the succession in 1926; succeeded his grandfather, King Ferdinand in 1927 under a regency; became crown prince when his father assumed the throne in 1930 as Carol II; on the abdication of Carol became king again in 1940; opposed the pro-German régime of General Antonescu and supported the *coup d'état* of 23 August 1944 which ended it but abdicated 1947 under pressure from the post-war Communist government.

Michaelis, Sir Max. Mining magnate and art patron. Born 1860, Eisfeld, Saxe-Meiningen, Germany; came to South Africa 1878 and entered the diamond trade; partner in the firm of Sigismund Neumann; later joined the gold-mining house of Wernher, Beit and Co; on retirement became an art patron; founder of the Michaelis School of Art of the University of Cape Town and donator of the Michaelis Collection in Cape Town. Died 26 January 1932.

Millikan, Robert Andrews. Physicist. Born 22 March 1868, Morrison, Illinois, United States of America; educated Oberlin College; Columbia, Berlin and Göttingen Universities; associate professor, 1907–10, then professor of physics,

1910–21, Chicago University; chairman, California Institute of Technology and director, Norman Bridge Laboratory 1921–45; won Nobel prize for work on electrons 1923; author of *The Electron*; *Evolution in Science and Religion*; *Time, Matter and Values*; *Cosmic Rays*; *Autobiography*. Died 19 December 1953.

Millin, Phillip. Judge. Born 1888, Cape Town, South Africa; educated South African College; after some years as journalist admitted to the Transvaal bar 1913; judicial commissioner for Basutoland and president of the special courts of Bechuanaland and Swaziland; appointed to the Transvaal bench 1937; co-author of *The Mercantile Law of South Africa*. Died 15 April 1952.

Millin, Sarah Gertrude, born Liebson. South African writer. Born *c.* 1889–90, Lithuania. Her parents settled on a farm near Kimberley in 1890; educated Kimberley Girls' Seminary; qualified as a teacher of music; married Phillip Millin (q.v.) 1912; author of several novels; biographies of Rhodes and Smuts; histories of South Africa; war diaries; autobiography. Died 6 July 1968.

Minkowski, Hermann. Russian mathematician. Born 22 June 1864 near Kowno; professor in Königsberg, Zürich, Göttingen; formulated mathematical foundations for the theory of relativity; author of *Einführung in die Zahlentheorie*; *Geometrie der Zahlen*. Died 12 January 1909.

Mitchell, Douglas Edgar. Politician, administrator, farmer. Born 8 September 1896, Port Shepstone district, Natal, South Africa; educated Weenen County College, Natal; served in East Africa 1916–17; farmer and general dealer, Port Shepstone; member, Natal provincial council 1933–44, and of the executive committee 1939–44; administrator of Natal 1944–8; United party member of parliament since 1948; chairman of the party in Natal.

Mitchell, George. Politician and business man. Born 1 April 1867, Ayrshire, Scotland; went to South Africa as employee of the Bank of Africa 1889; became general manager, Rhodesia Exploration and Development Company 1901–18 when he retired; member, legislative council, Southern Rhodesia 1911–19; member, legislative assembly 1929–33; minister of mines 1930–3 and of agriculture 1932–3; prime minister, July–September 1933. Died 4 July 1937.

Mitchell, Sir Philip Euen. British administrator. Born 1 May 1890; educated St Paul's School; Trinity College, Oxford; assistant resident, Nyasaland 1912; served in East Africa 1915–18; assistant political officer, Tanganyika 1919; assistant secretary, Native affairs 1926; provincial commissioner 1928; secretary for Native affairs 1928–33; chief secretary 1934–5; governor of Uganda 1935–40; political adviser to General Wavell (q.v.) 1941; British plenipotentiary, Ethiopia 1942; governor of Fiji 1942–4; governor of Kenya 1944–52; knighted 1937; author of *African Afterthoughts*. Died 11 October 1964.

Molotov, Vyacheslav Mikhailovich (pseudonym of V. M. Skryabin). Statesman. Born 9 March 1890, Kukarka, Vyatka province, Russia; joined the Bolshevik party 1906; deported to Vologda 1909; on his release in 1911 studied at the Polytechnic Institute, St Petersburg; party organizer 1912; deported to Irkutsk 1915; escaped 1916 and took part in the revolution of October 1917; secretary of the central committee of the Communist party 1921; member of the politbureau 1926; chairman of the council of people's commissars 1930; commissar of foreign affairs 1939–49; first deputy to Stalin as prime minister 1941; Soviet representative at post-war international conferences and the United Nations; again foreign minister after Stalin's death in 1953 but lost this office and became minister of state control 1956; defeated in the conflict with Krushchev in 1957, he was deprived of all office in the government and party; ambassador to Mongolia 1957–61; permanent delegate to the atomic energy agency 1960–1; expelled from the Communist party 1964. Author of *In the Struggle for Socialism*; *Problems of Foreign Policy*.

Molteno, Donald Barkly. Lawyer and politician. Born 13 February 1908, Wynberg, Cape Peninsula, South Africa; educated Diocesan College, Rondebosch; Pembroke College, Cambridge; barrister of the Inner Temple; practised as advocate in the

Cape division of the supreme court of South Africa from 1932; Native representative in the Union house of assembly for the Cape Western electoral circle 1937–48; senior lecturer in Roman–Dutch law, University of Cape Town 1964–6, professor of public law since 1967; executive member of the South African Institute of Race Relations from 1936 and of the Progressive party since its inception. Died 24 December 1972.

Montgomery, Bernard Law, first Viscount, of Alamein. Soldier. Born 17 November 1887, London; educated St Paul's School; Sandhurst Royal Military Academy; entered the British army 1908; served in the First World War; battalion commander 1931–4 with rank of colonel; general staff officer, Quetta 1934–7; brigade commander, Portsmouth 1937–8; commander, third division in France 1938–9; held south-eastern command in England 1940–2; as lieutenant-general succeeded to command of the eighth army in Egypt; began, with the battle of El Alamein (November 1942), a series of victories in north Africa followed by the invasion of Sicily and Italy; commanded Allied armies in France and Germany, June 1944–May 1945; chief of the imperial general staff 1946–8; chairman, Western Europe commanders-in-chief committee 1948–51; deputy supreme Allied commander in Europe (N.A.T.O.) 1951–8; knighted 1942; field marshal 1944; created viscount 1946; author of books on his campaigns and contemporary politics, a history of warfare, and memoirs.

Monypenny, William Flavelle. Journalist. Born 7 August 1866, Dungannon, County Tyrone, Ireland; educated Trinity College, Dublin; Balliol College, Oxford; entered journalism as contributor to various periodicals; assistant editor, *The Times* 1894–9; editor of the Johannesburg *Star*, March 1899; served in Natal during the early months of the Anglo-Boer War; director of civil supplies in Johannesburg; again edited the *Star* 1902–3; re-joined staff of *The Times*; author of a standard biography of Disraeli of which two volumes were published 1910–12 during his lifetime. Died 23 November 1912.

Moore, Lady. Born Daphne Benson. Painter. Born 21 March 1894, Britstown, Cape Province, South Africa; educated at schools in England, Rome, Johannesburg and at the Slade School of Art and the Royal Academy Schools, London; married Sir Henry Moore (q.v.) 1921.

Moore, Sir Henry Monck-Mason. Government official. Born 18 March 1887, London; educated King's College School; Jesus College, Cambridge; entered Ceylon civil service 1910; served in Salonika and France during the First World War; assistant colonial secretary, Ceylon 1918–21; colonial secretary, Bermuda 1921–3; principal assistant secretary, Nigeria 1924–9; colonial secretary, Kenya 1929–33; governor, Sierra Leone 1934–7; assistant under-secretary of state, colonial office 1937–9; governor, Kenya 1939–44; governor, Ceylon 1944–8; governor-general, Ceylon 1948–9; knighted 1935. Died 25 March 1964.

More, John Rhys. Railway engineer. Born 14 August 1873, Kimberley, South Africa; educated Hereford College, England; joined firm of Pauling and Co. as engineer on railway construction in Cape Colony 1893; joined Cape government railways 1896; district engineer at Mafeking 1899; divisional superintendent of South African Railways 1910; director of railways, South West Africa 1914–17; assistant general manager, Bloemfontein 1918, then Durban 1921; general manager of South African Railways and Harbours 1927–33 when he retired. Died 22 April 1951.

Morel, Edmund Dene. *Nom de plume* of George Edmund Pierre Achille Morel-de-Ville. Journalist, humanitarian, politician. Born 10 July 1873, Paris; educated at Eastbourne and Bedford, England; entered shipping firm in Liverpool as clerk 1890; contributed articles on west Africa to various newspapers; assistant editor, *West African Mail* 1901; started his own paper, *African Mail* 1903–15; founded Congo Reform Association and was honorary secretary 1904–13; with Pierre Mille published *Le Congo Léopoldien*; active as pacifist in the First World War; secretary, Union of Democratic Control; editor, *Foreign Affairs* 1919–24; Labour member of parliament 1922–4; author of books on African and European politics. Died 12 November 1924.

Morgan, Conwy Lloyd. Scientist. Born 6 February 1852, London; educated Royal Grammar School, Guildford; Royal College of Science; lecturer in English and physical science, Diocesan College, Rondebosch, near Cape Town 1878–83; professor of zoology and geology, University College, Bristol 1884–7; principal, Bristol College 1887–1909; vice-chancellor, Bristol University; author of *Animal Behaviour*; *Emergent Evolution*; *Life, Mind and Spirit*, etc. Died 6 March 1936.

Moroka II. Baralong chief. Born *c.* 1795 near Mafeking, then in Bechuanaland; succeeded to the chieftainship in 1830 when the Baralong occupied land on the lower Vaal river. Led by Wesleyan missionaries the clan migrated eastwards to Thaba Nchu 1834. Moroka befriended various parties of Vootrekkers who passed through Thaba Nchu and took part in their expeditions against the Matabele 1837. He also helped the British authorities against the Basuto 1850–1 and the Orange Free State in the Basuto Wars, being recognized by the Republic as independent ally. Died 8 April 1880.

Morrison, Herbert Stanley, first Baron, of Lambeth. Statesman. Born 3 January 1888, Brixton, London; educated there; worked as shop-assistant, telephone operator, newspaper circulation manager; secretary of the Labour party in London 1915–40; opposed Britain's entry into the war; mayor of Hackney 1919; member of the London county council 1922–45; member of parliament 1923–4, 1929–31, 1935–59; minister of transport 1929–31; minister of supply 1940; home secretary 1940–5; member of the war cabinet 1942–5; lord president of the council and leader of the house of commons 1945–51; foreign secretary 1951; created a life peer 1959; president of the British board of film censors 1960; author of *How London is Governed*; *Government and Parliament*; and an autobiography. Died 6 March 1965.

Mountbatten, Louis Francis Albert Victor Nicholas, first Earl. Admiral. Born 25 June 1900, Windsor, England, younger son of the Marquess of Milford Haven; educated Osborne; Dartmouth College; Christ's College, Cambridge; entered the royal navy 1913 and served in the First World War; thereafter as fleet wireless officer, commander, and in the admiralty 1931–9; commanded 5th destroyer flotilla 1939, H.M.S. *Illustrious* 1941; chief of combined operations 1942–3; supreme Allied commander, south-east Asia 1943–5; rear-admiral commanding 1st cruiser squadron, Mediterranean; appointed viceroy of India to carry out transfer of power to the new Dominions of India and Pakistan 1947; governor-general of India 1947–8; commander-in-chief, Mediterranean 1952–4; first sea lord and chief of naval staff 1955–9; chief, defence staff and chairman, chiefs of staff committee 1959; governor of the Isle of Wight 1965; created viscount 1946, baron 1947, earl 1947.

Moyne, Walter Edward Guiness, first Baron, of Bury St Edmunds. Statesman. Born 29 March 1880, Dublin, Eire; educated Eton College; served in the Anglo-Boer War; Unionist member of parliament 1907–31; served in the First World War as brigade major; under-secretary of state for war 1922–3; financial secretary to the treasury 1923–4–5; minister of agriculture 1925–9; secretary of state for the colonies and leader of the house of lords 1941–2; resident minister for the Middle East 1942; created baron 1932; assassinated in Cairo by Jewish terrorists 6 November 1944.

Mudaliar, Sir A. Ramasurami Diwan Bahadur. University principal and government adviser. Born 14 October 1887, India; educated Christian College and Law College, Madras; practised in Madras as advocate; member, legislative council, Madras 1920–6; member, council of state 1930; member Indian legislative assembly 1931–4; member, India council 1936–7; adviser to secretary of state for India 1937–9; member, governor-general's executive council 1939–46; Dewan of Mysore 1946–9; leader, Indian delegation San Francisco conference and first general assembly of the United Nations 1945–6; served on various government committees; vice-chancellor, University of Travancore; knighted 1937.

Munnik, Jan Hendrik. Mining engineer, politician, farmer. Born 30 June 1872, Pietersburg, Transvaal, South Africa; educated Diocesan College, Rondebosch, Cape Town; Royal School of Mines, England; inspector of mines and acting state mining engineer, South African Republic; served in the Anglo-Boer War until April 1901 when he became a prisoner of war in India; practised as a mining engineer on the Rand until 1921 when he became a farmer in the Dordrecht district, Cape Province; National party member of the house of assembly 1920–1, 1924–33. Died 1 November 1942.

Mushet, James Wellwood. Merchant and politician. Born 1882, Kilmarnock, Ayrshire, Scotland; educated there and in Edinburgh; emigrated to South Africa 1899; founded the merchant and manufacturing firm of J. W. Mushet and Co., Ltd.; member of the Union parliament 1920–1, 1938–53; minister of posts and telegraphs 1945–7; minister of economic development 1948; Cape Province chairman, United party 1948–51. Died 31 May 1954.

Mussolini, Benito Amilcare Andrea. Fascist leader. Born 29 July 1883, Varano di Costa, province of Forli, Italy; educated Salesian School, Faenza; Normal School, Forlimpopoli; taught briefly in an elementary school; lived for three years in Switzerland; returned to Italy 1904 and resumed teaching until expelled for socialist propaganda 1909; engaged in journalism in *Il Popolo* and his own paper, *La lotta di classe* 1908–11; editor of the socialist paper, *Avanti*; expelled from the Socialist congress for supporting the Allies in the First World War and founded *Il Popolo d'Italia* 1914; served in the ranks of the Italian army 1915–17; founded a political party, the Fasci Italiani di Combattimento, in 1919 and the movement known as Fascism; elected, with thirty-five followers, to the legislature 1921. In August 1922 the Fascists broke a general strike and in October, on the fall of the government, marched on Rome where the king invited Mussolini to form a cabinet. By 1924 he had established a complete dictatorship. He concluded a concordat with the Pope 1929, intervened in the Spanish civil war, strengthened the Italian navy, carried out the conquest of Abyssinia 1935–6, annexed Albania 1939 and made an alliance with Nazi Germany. In June 1940 Italy entered the war against the Allied powers. Her defeat caused the Fascist grand council to repudiate and arrest Mussolini 1943. He was rescued by the Germans who reinstated him as head of a puppet government. On their withdrawal Mussolini was caught by Italian partisans and executed on 28 April 1945.

Nahas, Pasha, Mustafa Al. Statesman. Born 15 June 1876, Cairo; educated Khedivial School; Khedivial School of Law; in legal practice 1906–14; appointed judge 1914; general secretary, Wafd party 1918; minister of communications 1924; leader of Wafd party 1927–52; president, chamber of deputies 1927; prime minister 1928, 1930, 1936, 1942–4, 1950–2; retired from politics after military *coup* of July 1952 against King Farouk (q.v.) and the Wafd régime. Died 23 August 1965.

Nehru, Jawaharlal. Statesman. Born 14 November 1889, Allahabad, India; educated Harrow; Trinity College, Cambridge; barrister of the Inner Temple; joined nationalist movement under Gandhi 1920; general secretary, all-India Congress committee 1929, president 1929, 1936, 1937, 1939, 1946, 1951; vice-president and minister for external affairs, Indian interim government 1946; prime minister and minister for external affairs 1947–64; minister of defence 1953–64; president, Asian Relations Organization from 1947; author of books on India, on world history and an autobiography. Died 27 May 1964.

Nel, Overbeek Radyn. Attorney and politician. Born 11 September 1883, Rietvlei, Natal, South Africa; educated Fransch Hoek High School, Cape Province; articled in Pietermaritzburg; practised as attorney in Greytown, Natal 1906–24; retired from practice to become South African party member of parliament 1924–41. Died 1941.

Nel, Colonel Piet. Air force pilot and farmer. Born 19 May 1903, Schikspruit, near Kroonstad, Orange Free State, South Africa; educated Kroonstad; Boys' High School, Paarl; entered Military College, Voortrekkerhoogte as a cadet 1924; joined the South African air force 1926 and became a pilot; appointed personal pilot to the prime minister 1940–53 when he retired to farm.

Neser, Johannes Adriaan. Politician and attorney. Born 11 July 1860 near Colesberg, Cape Province, South Africa; educated there and at Victoria College, Stellenbosch; practised as attorney in Klerksdorp from 1888; mayor of Klerksdorp 1904–10; member, Transvaal legislative assembly 1907–10; member, Union house of assembly 1910–20, then senator; active in the organization of the South African party. Died 4 June 1933.

Nevinson, Henry Woodd. Journalist. Born 1856, Leicester, England; educated Shrewsbury School; Christ Church, Oxford; war correspondent of the *Daily Chronicle* in South Africa 1899–1902; investigated the slave trade in central Africa on commission from *Harper's Magazine* and published *A Modern Slavery* 1906; war correspondent of the *Manchester Guardian* in Gallipoli and Egypt during the First World War and special correspondent in the Middle East, Geneva, Washington, 1926–9; on the staff of *The Nation* 1907–23; wrote poems, essays, literary criticism as well as several books on his journalistic experiences such as *Ladysmith*; *Dawn in Russia*; *The Dardanelles Campaign.* Died 9 November 1941.

New, Edmund Hort. Art lecturer and illustrator. Born 1871, Evesham, England; educated Prince Henry's Grammar School, Evesham; Birmingham Municipal School of Art; among his book illustrations are: the Loggan plates of the Oxford Colleges; *Firenze*; *The City and Port of London.* Died 3 February 1931.

Ney, Fred J. Educationist. Born 1884, Westfield, Sussex, England; educated Rye Grammar School; headmaster, English College, Nicosia, Cyprus and St Mary's School, Cairo; emigrated to Canada 1909; headmaster, Russel High School 1909; secretary, department of education, Manitoba; served in the First World War in France; executive secretary, national council of education, Canada; founder and vice-president, Overseas Education League.

Ney, Marie. Actress. Born 18 July 1895, New Zealand; educated St Mary's Convent, Wellington, New Zealand; *début* in Melbourne 1917; leading lady at the Old Vic, London 1924–5; toured in Egypt 1927, the Netherlands 1939, the Middle East, Australia 1940–1, Italy 1945; appeared in a number of English films, on British television and with the South African Broadcasting Corporation 1942–4; married T. H. Menzies 1930; divorced 1949; remarried T. H. Menzies 1959.

Nicholls, George Heaton. Politician, administrator, diplomat. Born 2 February 1876, Hounslow, England; educated Church of England school, Birmingham; joined the British army 1891; served in India, Burma and the Anglo-Boer War; instructor Barotse Native police 1902–7; district commissioner, Northern Rhodesia 1907–8; in Papuan civil service 1908–12; sugar-planter, Zululand from 1912; member of the Union house of assembly 1920–40; appointed to Native affairs commission 1935; administrator of Natal 1941–3; high commissioner in London 1944–7; senator 1948; leader, Union Federal party in Natal 1952–7. Author of *Bayete* and an autobiography. Died 25 September 1959.

Nicholson, Sir William Newzam Prior. Painter and designer. Born 1872, Newark-on-Trent, England; educated there at the Magnus School and trained in Paris; best known as a portrait painter; also produced woodcuts and designed stage costumes and settings; trustee of the Tate Gallery 1934–9; knighted 1936. Died 16 May 1949.

Niemöller, Friedrich Gustav Emil Martin. Minister of religion. Born 14 January 1892, Lippstadt, Westphalia, Germany; educated Elberfelt Gymnasium; midshipman in the Germany navy 1910; submarine commander in First World War; studied theology at Münster, Westphalia and became pastor 1924; pastor of Berlin-Dahlem 1931; imprisoned in concentration camps for resistance to Nazis 1937–45; president of the foreign affairs office of the Evangelical Church in Germany 1945–56; church president, Evangelical Church in Hesse and Nassau 1947–64 when he retired; member, World Council of Churches; several volumes of his sermons have been published and many articles on theology and politics.

Noel-Baker, Philip John. Politician and university professor. Born 1 November 1889, London; educated Bootham School, York; Haverford College, Philadelphia; King's College, Cambridge; vice-principal, Ruskin College, Oxford 1914; served in the First World War in Society of Friends ambulance unit 1914–18; member, League of Nations secretariat 1919–22; professor of international relations, University of London 1924–9; Labour member of parliament 1929–31, 1936 onwards; parliamentary private secretary to secretary for foreign affairs 1929–31; parliamentary secretary, ministry of war transport 1942–5; minister of state 1945–6; secretary of state for air 1946–7; secretary of state for Commonwealth relations 1947–50; minister of fuel and power 1950–1; awarded Nobel peace prize 1959; author of several books on international relations and disarmament, notably *The Private Manufacture of Armaments*.

Noon, Sir Firoz Khan. Statesman and lawyer. Born 7 May 1893, Hamoka, India; educated Aitchison Chiefs' College, Lahore; Wadham College, Oxford; barrister of the Inner Temple; advocate, Lahore high court 1917–26; member, Punjab legislature 1920–36; minister for local government, Punjab 1927–30, minister of education and health, 1931–6; high commissioner for India in London 1936–41; member, viceroy's executive council 1941–5; Indian representative, British war cabinet 1944–5; member, Pakistan legislature 1947–50; governor of East Pakistan 1950–3; chief minister, West Punjab 1953–5; foreign minister of Pakistan 1956–7; prime minister 1957–8.

Norman, Montagu Collet, first Baron. Banker. Born 6 September 1871, London; educated Eton; King's College, Cambridge; served in the Anglo-Boer War; partner in his family's bank; director of the Bank of England 1907; governor of the Bank of England 1920–44; director of the Bank for International Settlements 1930; privy councillor 1923; created baron 1944. Died 4 February 1950.

Norton, Victor. Journalist. Born 12 August 1906, Johannesburg; educated there at Jeppe High School; joined staff of the *Star* 1927; on staff of the *Salisbury Herald*; joined the *Cape Times* 1931; assistant editor 1935; acting editor 1943; editor since 1944.

Norwich. See **Cooper,** Alfred Duff.

Officer, Sir Frank Keith. Diplomat. Born 2 October 1889, Melbourne, Australia; educated Melbourne Grammar School; Ormond College, University of Melbourne; served with the Australian forces in the First World War; political officer, Nigeria 1919–24; in department of external affairs, Canberra 1927–33; external affairs officer, London 1933–7; counsellor, British embassy, Washington 1937–40; counsellor, then chargé d'affaires, Australian legation, Tokyo 1940–3; counsellor, Australian legation, Moscow 1943–4; chargé d'affaires, Chungking 1944–5; minister in South-East Asia 1946; minister to the Netherlands 1946; ambassador to China 1948–9; ambassador to France 1950–5 when he retired; knighted 1950. Died 21 June 1969.

Ogilvie, Reverend Canon George. Headmaster. Born *c.* 1823, Calne, Wiltshire, England; educated Winchester; Wadham College, Oxford; took orders; vice-principal, Bradfield College; head of English school and chaplain to the British community in Buenos Aires; went to South Africa 1858; precentor of St George's Cathedral, Cape Town and headmaster of the attached grammar school; principal of Diocesan College, Rondebosch, Cape Town 1861–84. Died *c.* 1916.

Olga, Princess, of Greece. Born 11 June 1903, castle of Tatoï, Greece; eldest daughter of Prince Nicholas of Greece and Grand Duchess Helen of Russia; married, in 1923, Prince Paul, regent of Yugoslavia 1934–41 during the minority of Peter II of Yugoslavia; cousin of Constantine II of the Hellenes (q.v.).

Olivier, Sydney, first Baron, of Ramsden. Government official and administrator. Born 1859, Winchfield; educated Lausanne; Tonbridge School; Corpus Christi College, Oxford; entered the colonial office 1882; held posts in Honduras and the Leeward Islands 1890–6; secretary, West India royal commission 1897; colonial secretary, Jamaica 1899–1904; principal clerk, colonial office 1904–7;

governor of Jamaica 1907–13; permanent secretary, board of agriculture 1913–17; assistant comptroller and auditor, exchequer 1917–20 when he retired; secretary of state for India 1924; secretary, Fabian Society 1886–90; knighted 1907; created baron 1924; author of books on colonial policy, including *Jamaica, the Blessed Isle*. Died 15 February 1943.

Olsvanger, Immanuel. Author and lecturer. Born 13 April 1888, Grayevo, Poland; educated Universities of Koenigsberg and Berne; active from 1921 as propagandist for the Zionist Organization; later on staff of the propaganda department, Keren Hayesod; author of books on Jewish folklore and translator of *Divina Commedia* and *Decameron* into Hebrew.

Oosthuizen, Ockert Almero. Party secretary and estate agent. Born 14 September 1904, Klerksdorp, Transvaal, South Africa; educated there and at University of Pretoria; employed in Union department of agriculture and by International Harvester Company 1929–31; secretary, United party, Witwatersrand 1933–41; general secretary, United party 1941–51 and editor of its publications; since 1951 partner in an estate agency and active in local public bodies.

Oppenheimer, Sir Ernest. Mining and industrial magnate. Born 22 May 1880, Friedberg, Hesse, Germany; educated at private schools; went to South Africa as representative at Kimberley of a London diamond dealer 1902; member of the Kimberley town council 1908; mayor 1912–15; established the Anglo-American Corporation of South Africa on the Witwatersrand 1917 and the Consolidated Diamond Mines of South-West Africa; chairman, De Beers Consolidated Mines 1929; secured control of and reorganized virtually the whole diamond industry; his other interests included copper mines in Rhodesia and new gold mines in the Orange Free State; director of various finance companies; member of the Union parliament 1924–38; knighted 1921. Died 25 November 1957.

Oppenheimer, Harry Frederick. Mining and industrial magnate. Born 28 October 1908, Kimberley, South Africa; educated Charterhouse; Christ Church, Oxford; served with the South African forces in north Africa 1940–5; United party member of parliament 1948–57 when he retired from politics to take over control of the mining and industrial groups directed by his father, Sir Ernest Oppenheimer (q.v.); left the United party to support the Progressive party 1959; elected chancellor of the University of Cape Town 1967.

Opperman, Madame Kate. Singer. Born 1887, Orange Free State, South Africa; studied music in Johannesburg and in London at the Guildhall School of Music; sang at concerts in the Albert Hall and Queen's Hall and at Sunday League concerts in the London Palladium; returned to South Africa 1914; headed a concert party during the First World War in aid of war funds and to entertain troops; returned to London 1923 as concert singer and teacher of singing; married J. B. Urquhart of Johannesburg. Died 16 February 1955.

Ormsby-Gore. See **Harlech.**

Osborn, Henry Fairfield. Palaeontologist. Born 8 August 1857, Fairfield, Connecticut, United States of America; educated Princeton University where he held professorships in natural science, anatomy, biology and zoology between 1881 and 1910; curator, department of palaeontology, American Museum of Natural History 1891–1910; palaeontologist, U.S. geological survey 1900–24; president of various scientific and cultural societies and of the American Museum of Natural History, 1933. Author of *The Origin and Evolution of Life*; *Fifty-two Years of Research*, etc. Died 6 November 1935.

Pandit, Vijaya Lakshmi, born Swarupkumari Nehru, sister of Jawaharlal Nehru (q.v.). Diplomat. Born 18 August 1900, Allahabad, India; educated privately in India and abroad; married Ranjit S. Pandit 1921; active in the Indian National Congress since early 'twenties; held municipal office in Allahabad; member, legislative assembly of the United Provinces; minister of local government and public health 1937–9; leader, Indian delegation to United Nations 1946–8; ambassador in Moscow 1947–9, in Washington and Mexico 1949–51; president,

U.N. general assembly 1953; Indian high commissioner in London 1954–61; governor of Maharashtra 1962–4; member of the Lok Sabha (House of the People) 1964.

Parnell, Charles Stewart. Irish nationalist leader. Born 26 June 1846, Avondale, Wicklow, Ireland; educated at private schools and Magdalene College, Cambridge; entered house of commons 1875; organized the Land League to unite the Irish people and oppose the British government's agrarian policy; imprisoned 1881 but soon released; arranged support for a Liberal government which then brought in an abortive home rule bill. Following an unsuccessful attempt to connect him with murder, he was discredited by being named co-respondent in a divorce action and retired from politics in 1890. Died 6 October 1891.

Parrack, William James. Building contractor and politician. Born September 1875, Herefordshire, England; educated Moseley Lodge, Birmingham; emigrated to South Africa 1897; member of the Union house of assembly for Denver, Transvaal 1915–20.

Paul I, King of the Hellenes. Born 12 December 1901, Athens. Brother of King George II (q.v.); trained at the Greek Naval Academy; in exile in the United States and in Florence after the deposition of his brother and the dynasty in 1924; returned to Greece 1935; married Frederika Louise of Brunswick-Lüneberg (q.v.) 1938; left Greece after the German invasion 1941; returned 1946; succeeded his brother 1947. Died 6 March 1964.

Pearce, Sir George Foster. Politician. Born 14 January 1870, Mount Barker, South Australia; educated Redhill public school; worked as carpenter; active as trade unionist in Western Australia; president, trade union congress 1899; elected to the federal senate 1906, 1913, 1914–19, 1925, 1931; minister of defence 1908–9, 1910–13, 1914–21, 1931–4; minister for home and territories 1921–6; leader of the opposition, federal senate 1929–31; minister for external affairs 1934–7; knighted 1927; author of memoirs. Died 24 June 1952.

Pechkoff, Zinovi. Diplomat and soldier. Born 16 October 1884, Nizhni-Novgorod, Russia; entered the French army 1914; engaged in missions to the United States, China, Japan, Manchuria 1918–20; officer of the foreign legion, Morocco campaign 1921–6; in the foreign affairs department 1926–30; French high commissioner in the Levant 1930–7; commandant of the legion of Morocco 1937–40; delegate to the Union of South Africa 1941–2; delegate, then ambassador in Chungking, China 1943–5; ambassador to Japan 1946–9 when he retired. Died 28 November 1966.

Perth, James Eric Drummond, sixteenth Earl of. Official and diplomat. Born 17 August 1876, son of the fourteenth earl of Perth; educated Eton; entered foreign office 1900; under-secretary, 1906–10; private secretary to the prime minister 1912–15; and to the foreign secretary 1915–19; first secretary-general of the League of Nations 1919–33; British ambassador to Italy 1933–9; chief adviser on foreign publicity, ministry of information 1939–40; knighted 1916; representative peer of Scotland from 1941; deputy leader of the Liberal party in the house of lords from 1946. Died 15 December 1951.

Pétain, Henri Philippe Benoni Omer Joseph. Soldier and statesman. Born 24 August 1856, Cauchy à la Tour, Pas-de-Calais, France; educated Saint-Cyr; became a lieutenant 1878; instructor at the School of War 1906; army corps commander 1914; in command of the forces defending Verdun 1916; commanded all French forces on the western front and appointed marshal 1918; vice-president, War Council and Council of National Defence 1920–39; minister of war 1934; ambassador to Spain 1939–40; minister of state May–June 1940; arranged an armistice with Germany; head of the government at Vichy until 1945 when he was convicted of high treason and sentenced to life imprisonment. Died 23 July 1951.

Philip, Prince, Duke of Edinburgh. Born 10 June 1921, Corfu; son of Prince Andrew of Greece and Princess Alice of Battenberg (q.v.); educated Cheam School; Gordonstoun School; Royal Naval College, Dartmouth; served in the royal navy in the Second World War; naturalized a British subject adopting the surname of Mountbatten 28 February 1947; created Duke of Edinburgh 20 November 1947; married, on 20 November 1947, Princess Elizabeth, now Elizabeth II; privy councillor 1951; prince of the United Kingdom 1957; awarded Order of Merit 1968.

Phillips, Francis Rudolph. Chairman of companies. Born 11 April 1888, London; younger son of Sir Lionel Phillips (q.v. vol. IV); educated Eton; Balliol College, Oxford; barrister of the Inner Temple; served in France, Bulgaria, Turkey 1914–19; director, Central Mining Corporation 1920; chairman of this and other companies from 1925. Died 24 June 1942.

Phillips, John Frederick Vicars. Ecologist and agriculturalist. Born 1899, South Africa; educated Dale College, King William's Town; University of Edinburgh; ecologist, Tanganyika Territory 1922–7; professor of botany, University of the Witwatersrand 1931; manager and chief adviser, Overseas Food Corporation; consultant in agriculture, Food and Agriculture Organization 1948–51; professor of agriculture, University College, Ghana 1952–60; chairman of committees on the economic resources of Southern Rhodesia (1960–2) and on agro-economic aspects of the Tugela basin (1963–8); author of *Agriculture and Ecology in Africa*; *Kwame Nkrumah and the Future of Africa*, etc.

Phillips, Admiral Sir Tom Spencer Vaughan. Naval officer. Born 19 February 1888, Pendennis Castle, Falmouth, England; entered the royal navy 1903; acting captain in the First World War; captain 1927; chief of staff captain to the commander-in-chief, East Indies 1932–5; director of plans for the admiralty 1935–8; commanded home fleet destroyer flotillas 1938–9; rear-admiral and vice chief of naval staff, admiralty; in command of the Far East battle fleet from 1 December 1941. Drowned 10 December 1941 when his flagship *Prince of Wales* and the battle cruiser *Repulse* were attacked and sunk by Japanese aircraft.

Pickard-Cambridge, Sir Arthur Wallace. Classicist and university principal. Born 20 January 1873, England; educated Weymouth College; Balliol College, Oxford; fellow, Oriel College 1895–7; fellow, Balliol College 1897–1929; joint secretary, Oxford and Cambridge schools examination board 1915–19; chairman of council, St Hilda's College 1920–8; university lecturer, Greek and Latin literature 1926–8; professor of Greek, University of Edinburgh 1928–30; vice-chancellor, University of Sheffield 1930–8; member of the church assembly 1935–45; author of several works on Greek literature; knighted 1950. Died 7 February 1952.

Pienaar, Major-General Daniel Hermanus. Soldier. Born 27 August 1893, Ladybrand, Orange Free State, South Africa; joined the Natal police 1911; served with the South African forces in East Africa, Palestine and Syria in the First World War; joined the permanent force 1919; at the outbreak of the Second World War was in command of the military headquarters at Voortrekkerhoogte, Transvaal with the rank of colonel; commander, first South African brigade in East Africa 1940 and in the western desert 1942 with the rank of major-general. Died 19 December 1942 in an aeroplane crash on the shores of Lake Victoria.

Pirow, Oswald. Lawyer and politician. Born 14 August 1890, Aberdeen, Cape Province, South Africa; educated Potchefstroom, Transvaal; Germany; barrister of the Middle Temple; practised as attorney in Johannesburg, then as advocate in Pretoria; member of Transvaal provincial council 1917–23; National party member of parliament 1924–9, 1933–43; senator 1929–33 and minister of justice; minister of railways and of defence 1933–9; in 1941 founded the New Order—a national-socialist group within the National party which was forced out of the party in 1942; resumed legal practice until 1957; published a weekly news letter; author of African adventure stories and a biography of General Hertzog. Died 11 October 1959.

Pius XII. Pope. Born Eugenio Pacelli on 2 March 1876, Rome; educated Capranica Seminary; Gregorian University; Pontifical Institute of the Apollinare; ordained 1899; member of papal secretariat of state 1901–8; attached to sacred congregation for extraordinary ecclesiastical affairs 1909; became secretary 1914; titular Archbishop of Sardes and nuncio to Bavaria 1917; first papal nuncio to Berlin 1920; created cardinal priest 1929; papal secretary of state 1930; elected Pope March 1939. Died 9 October 1958.

Planck, Max Karl Ernst Ludwig. Physicist. Born 23 April 1858, Kiel, Germany; educated Universities of Munich and Berlin; assistant professor of physics, Kiel 1885–9; professor of physics, Berlin 1889–1928; initiated the quantum theory 1900; awarded Nobel prize in physics 1918; elected to the Royal Society 1926; wrote several works in his field published between 1879 and 1933. Died 3 October 1947.

Platt, General Sir William. Soldier. Born 14 June 1885, Cheshire, England; educated Marlborough College; Royal Military College, Sandhurst; entered British army 1905; served in India 1908 and in the First World War; captain 1914; major 1924; lieutenant-colonel 1930; colonel 1933; major-general 1938; commandant, Sudan defence force 1938–41; commander-in-chief, East African command 1941–5; retired 1945; knighted 1941.

Pohl, Johannes Dreyer. Government official and diplomat. Born 10 April 1905, Burgersdorp, Cape Province, South Africa; educated Grey College, Bloemfontein; joined department of justice 1922; served as public prosecutor and magistrate in various posts; private secretary to General Smuts 1938–9; assistant secretary, then under-secretary, department of external affairs 1940–8; minister plenipotentiary to Portugal 1949, in Brazil 1951; ambassador to Belgium 1956, Italy 1958, Federal Republic of Germany 1961–5.

Polak, Henry Solomon Leon. Journalist and solicitor. Born 1882, Dover, England; educated in London; entered journalism and was assistant editor of the *Transvaal Critic*, Johannesburg when he met Gandhi (q.v.) in 1904 and became articled to him; editor of *Indian Opinion*; imprisoned with Gandhi after the latter led an illegal march of Indians into the Transvaal; returned to England 1914 and built up a large practice as solicitor; edited *India*, the organ of the British committee of the Indian National Congress; founded the Indian Overseas Association in London 1919; chairman, East and West Friendship Council 1949–56; co-author of a biography of Gandhi (1949) and of *The Indians of South Africa*. Died 1 February 1959.

Poole, Major-General William Henry Evered. Soldier and diplomat. Born 1902, Caledon, Cape Province, South Africa; educated St Andrew's College, Grahamstown; Diocesan College, Rondebosch; joined the Union defence force 1921; after training at the South African Military College commissioned in the permanent force 1923; commander, special service battalion 1934; as lieutenant-colonel trained with the brigade of Guards in England 1935; commandant, S.A. Military College 1939; general staff officer, second division 1940; commanded a brigade in East Africa and western desert 1941–2; as major-general commanded the 6th South African armoured division in north Africa and Italy 1943–5; head of the South African military mission in Berlin 1948; minister plenipotentiary to Italy, Greece, Egypt 1949–60; ambassador to Greece 1961–3 when he retired. Died 9 March 1969.

Poorten, Hein ter. Army officer. Born 21 November 1887, Buitenzorg, Java; lieutenant in the royal Netherlands East Indies army 1908; after study at the military college 1919–22 appointed to the general staff 1926; promoted major-general and inspector of artillery 1937; chief of the general staff 1939; lieutenant-general, army commander and chief of the war department 1941; commander-in-chief in the war against Japan; prisoner of war 1942–5; resigned 1946.

Potgieter, Andries Hendrik. Voortrekker leader. Born 19 December 1792, Graaff-Reinet district, Cape Province, South Africa; no formal education; by 1812 settled near Cradock where he became a successful farmer; led a trekker party north to the Sand river 1835, and a reconnaisance party to the Zoutpansberg which made contact with the Tregardt (q.v.) trek in June 1836 and crossed the Limpopo river; on his return gained a victory over the Matabele at Vegkop (now Heilbron); elected laager commandant of the first Trekker government, December 1836; led a commando in a punitive expedition against the Matabele January 1837 after which he moved with his followers to Winburg and then across the Vaal river; commanded a second expedition against the Matabele and defeated them at Mosega, November 1937; trekked to Natal and then, following dissension with other Trekker leaders about responsibility for a reverse at the hands of the Zulus, to the future site of Potchefstroom. After the British annexation of Natal Potgieter and his advisers declared Winburg-Potchefstroom an independent republic and framed a constitution (April 1844), which lapsed when Potgieter established a new settlement in the north-eastern Transvaal (Andries-Ohrigstad) with a new government (1845). His ruling authority was not recognized by the united Trekker government of the Transvaal set up in 1849 but he continued to exercise it until British recognition of an independent Transvaal in 1852. Died 16 December 1852.

Power, Sir John Cecil, first Baronet. Company director, politician and benefactor. Born 21 December 1870, Eldon, County Down, Ireland; entered export merchant firm of Power, Power and Co. in London; later engaged in real estate business; Conservative member of parliament 1924–45; founded Institute of Historical Research, London 1920; benefactor of Royal Institute of International Affairs of which he was honorary treasurer 1921–43; honorary treasurer, British Council; member, executive committee, League of Nations Union 1929–36; director, Royal Insurance Company 1934–49; created baronet 1924. Died 5 June 1950.

Rackham, Harris. Classicist. Born 22 December 1868, England; educated City of London School; Christ's College, Cambridge; lecturer in classics, Newnham College 1893–1910; classical tutor 1898–1914, 1919–23; in intelligence department, admiralty and the treasury 1917–19; university lecturer 1926–34; published a number of Greek and Latin translations. Died 20 March 1944.

Radhakrishnan, Sir Sarvepalli. Philosopher. Born 5 September 1888, Andhra Pradesh, India; educated Madras Christian College; Madras University; professor of philosophy, Presidency College, Madras 1911–17; at Mysore 1918–21; at Calcutta 1921–31, 1937–41; vice-chancellor, Andhra University, Waltair 1931–6 and Benares Hindu University 1939–48; professor of eastern religions, Oxford 1936–52; Indian ambassador to Russia 1949–52; vice-president, Republic of India 1952–62; president from 1962; member, committee on intellectual co-operation, League of Nations 1931–9; member, Indian constituent assembly 1947–9; leader, Indian delegation to Unesco 1946–52; chancellor, University of Delhi 1953–62; received honorary Order of Merit 1963; author of many books on eastern religion and philosophy; knighted 1931.

Radziwill, Princess Eugenie. Born 10 February 1910, Paris, daughter of Prince George of Greece (q.v.) and Princess Marie; married, in 1938, Prince Dominique Rainier Radziwill; divorced 1946; married, in 1949, Raymond, Prince of Torre and Tasso, second Duke of Castel Duino.

Ranjitsinhji, Kumar Shri, Maharaja Jamsaheb of Nawanagar. Indian prince and cricketer. Born 10 September 1872, Sarodar, Kathiawar province, India; educated Rajkumar College, Rajkote; Trinity College, Cambridge; joined Sussex cricket club 1895; head of county averages 1895–1902 and of England averages 1896, 1900; succeeded to the throne 1906; served in Europe in the First World War. Died 2 April 1933.

Rappard, William Emmanuel. Swiss economist and political scientist. Born 22 April 1883, New York; educated Universities of Geneva, Berlin, Harvard; assistant professor of economic history, University of Geneva 1910; assistant professor of economics, Harvard 1911–13; professor of economic history, University of Geneva from 1913; on diplomatic missions for Swiss government 1917–19; first director, mandates section, League of Nations 1920–4; member of League commissions 1925–8; founder and director, Graduate Institute of International Studies, Geneva

1928–55; member, Swiss delegation, assembly of League of Nations 1928–39; rector, University of Geneva 1926–8, 1936–8; president, international labour conference, Geneva 1951; author of works on international relations. Died 29 April 1958.

Rau, Sir Benegal Rama. Indian diplomat. Born 10 January 1889; educated Presidency College, Madras; King's College, Cambridge; joined Indian civil service 1913; under-secretary, government of Madras 1920; deputy-secretary 1922; deputy-secretary of finance, government of India 1926; financial adviser, Indian statutory commission 1928–30; joint secretary, industries department 1930–4; deputy high commissioner for India in London 1934–8; agent-general for India, then high commissioner in South Africa 1938–41; Indian ambassador to Japan 1947–8, to the United States of America 1948–9; governor, Reserve Bank of India 1949–57; knighted 1939.

Raven, Reverend Charles Earle. Theologian and university official. Born 4 July 1885, England; educated Uppingham School; Caius College, Cambridge; ordained 1909; lecturer in theology, Emmanuel College, Cambridge 1909–20; army chaplain 1917–18; canon of Liverpool 1924–32; professor of divinity, University of Cambridge 1932–50; master of Christ's College 1939–50; vice-chancellor, 1947–9; publications include *Christian Socialism*; *The Creator Spirit*; *Is War Obsolete?*; *Science, Religion and the Future*. Died 8 July 1964.

Reynolds, Lewis Frank. Politician and industrialist. Born 14 September 1898, England; educated Radley College; Christ Church, Oxford; served throughout the First World War; private secretary to General Smuts 1922–4; member of the Union parliament 1930–8; active in the sugar and other industries in Natal and Zululand. Died March 1940.

Rice, Elsie Garrett. Painter. Born 1869, Derbyshire, England; sister of Edmund Garrett (q.v. vol. IV); studied at the Slade School, London and in Florence; active in the suffragette movement; married Charles E. Rice 1898; went to South Africa 1933; became interested in the flora; illustrated *Wild Flowers of the Cape of Good Hope* by R. H. Compton from 250 water-colour paintings. Died 27 April 1959.

Richardson, Sir Lewis, first Baronet. Merchant. Born 2 February 1873, Birmingham, England; educated there; went to South Africa 1881; became an ostrich feather and wool merchant; established the firm of L. Richardson and Co. in Port Elizabeth; knighted 1921; created baronet 1924. Died 2 April 1934.

Roberts, Alexander William. Educationist and politician. Born 4 December 1857, Farr, Scotland; went to South Africa 1882 to work at the Lovedale mission school of which he later became acting principal; nominated member of the Union senate to represent Africans 1920–30; member, Native affairs commission 1920–35; amateur astronomer whose work gained international recognition. Died 27 January 1938.

Roberts, Alfred Adrian. Government and university official. Born 18 February 1890, Fauresmith, Orange Free State, South Africa; educated Trinity Hall, Cambridge; barrister of the Middle Temple; registrar, Transvaal University College 1919–29; law adviser to the Union government 1935–44; secretary for education 1944–9; high commissioner for the Union in Canada 1949–53; Union delegate to the United Nations 1950, 1952; author of legal works including *South African Legal Bibliography*. Died 7 April 1964.

Robertson, Donald Struan. Classicist. Born 28 June 1885, London; educated Westminster School; Trinity College, Cambridge where he was lecturer in classics 1913–28; regius professor of Greek, University of Cambridge 1928–50; vice-master, Trinity College 1947–51; held temporary commission in royal army service corps 1914–19; author of *A Handbook of Greek and Roman Architecture*; co-editor of the *Metamorphoses* of Apuleius. Died 5 October 1961.

Rockefeller, John Davison, junior. Industrialist and philanthropist. Born 29 January 1874, Cleveland, Ohio, United States of America; educated Brown University; associated with his father in the Standard Oil Company and various philanthropic foundations and directed these after 1911; founded Rockefeller Centre, New York City; donated site of the United Nations buildings. Died 11 May 1960.

Rogers, Arthur William. Geologist. Born 5 June 1872 near Taunton, Somerset, England; educated University of Cambridge; went to South Africa as member of the geological commission of the Cape Colony 1896; director, geological survey of South Africa 1916; president, international geological congress 1929; author of the first textbook of the Cape geology; retired 1932. Died 23 June 1946.

Rommel, Erwin. Army officer. Born 15 November 1891, Heidenheim, Württemberg, Germany; entered the army as a cadet 1910; served in the First World War; infantry officer and instructor 1919–38; commanded Hitler's bodyguard batallion 1939 and an armoured division in France 1940; German commander in Libya, Tunis and north Italy 1941–3; as field marshal commanded an army group in France 1944. Implicated in the attempt to assassinate Hitler, he was forced to commit suicide on 14 October 1944. His military writings were published in English as *The Rommel Papers.*

Romyn, Anton Christian. Attorney. Born 1860, Soest, the Netherlands; emigrated to the Transvaal 1882; served in the office of the state attorney 1882–9; became a financial agent and established a firm of attorneys in Pretoria; member of the Pretoria town council 1907 and later mayor; chairman, Pretoria Iron Mines Ltd.; first chairman, South African Iron and Steel Corporation 1920. Died 8 March 1923.

Rood, Karel. Politician, soldier, lawyer, chairman of companies. Born 15 October 1892, Vanrhynsdorp, Cape Province, South Africa; educated in law at the South African College, Cape Town; joined the army 1912; lieutenant in the Union defence force 1913; served in South West Africa 1915; qualified as captain, South African Military College 1922; commanding officer, Vereeniging commando 1924; promoted lieutenant-colonel; gave up legal practice and became director, then chairman of the Union Steel Corporation 1930–3; National party member of parliament 1929; member, Union defence council 1930; United party member of parliament 1933–49 when he resigned; chairman of a number of companies.

Roosevelt, Anna Eleanor. Journalist and publicist. Born 11 October 1884, New York City; educated by private tutors and at Allenswood School, England; married F. D. Roosevelt (q.v.) 1905; became known as a writer and speaker on public affairs; vice-principal and part owner of Todhunter private school for girls 1927–33; began her column *My Day* 1936; member of the United States delegation to United Nations assembly 1945; chairman, commission on human rights 1947–51; wrote children's books and an autobiography. Died 7 November 1962.

Roosevelt, Franklin Delano. President of the United States. Born 30 January 1882, Hyde Park, New York; educated Groton; Harvard; Columbia University law school; admitted to New York bar 1907; member of the senate for state of New York 1910–13; assistant secretary of the navy 1913–20; stricken with poliomyelitis 1921; resumed legal practice 1924; governor of New York 1929–33; inaugurated Democratic president of the United States March 1933; put into effect wide-ranging policies, known as the 'New Deal', to counter the grave economic crisis; re-elected in 1936 and for an unprecedented third term in 1940 and fourth term in 1944. Died 12 April 1945.

Rousseau, Izak Jozua. University lecturer. Born 7 January 1888, Paarl, Cape Province, South Africa; educated Paarl Boys' High School; South African College, Cape Town; became a schoolmaster 1908–15; served in the First World War 1917–19; read history at New College, Oxford 1919; appointed on probation to chair of history, Rhodes University College, Grahamstown 1920; further study at Institute for Historical Research, London and at Oxford 1922–3; senior lecturer at Rhodes 1925; lecturer, 1931; associate professor 1938; retired 1946. Died 27 January 1966.

Rowallan, Thomas Godfrey Polson Corbett, second Baron. Chief scout and administrator. Born 19 December 1895, Gourock, Renfrewshire, Scotland; educated

Eton; served in both World Wars; commanded a battalion of Royal Scots Fusiliers 1940–4; chief scout of the British Commonwealth and Empire 1945–59; governor National Bank of Scotland 1951–9; governor of Tasmania 1959–63; succeeded to the baronetcy 1933; knighted 1951.

Runciman, Walter, first Viscount, of Doxford. Statesman and ship-owner. Born 19 November 1870, South Shields, England; educated Trinity College, Cambridge; entered his father's shipping firm; Liberal member of parliament 1899–1900, 1902–18, 1924–37; parliamentary secretary, local government board 1905–7; financial secretary, treasury 1907–8; president, board of education 1908–11, board of agriculture 1911–14, board of trade 1914–16, 1931–7; lord president of the council 1938–9; headed British government mission to Czechoslovakia 1938; created viscount 1937. Died 14 November 1949.

Russell, Reginald James Kingston. Journalist. Born 12 March 1883, Wells, Somerset, England; went to South Africa soon after the Anglo-Boer War; on staff of *Natal Witness*; returned to England and joined editorial staff, *Birmingham Post*; news editor, *Daily News*; served in the First World War 1914–18; assistant editor, *Cape Times* 1920–6; editor, *Natal Mercury* 1926–36; founded and edited *The Forum* 1938. Died 11 May 1943.

Rutherford, Ernest, first Baron, of Nelson, New Zealand. Physicist. Born 30 August 1871, Nelson, New Zealand; educated Nelson College; Canterbury College; Universities of New Zealand and Cambridge; professor of physics at McGill University, Montreal 1898–1907, at Manchester University 1907–19, at Cambridge from 1919 where he made notable discoveries in nuclear physics; awarded Nobel prize for chemistry 1908, the Order of Merit 1925; president of the Royal Society 1925–30; knighted 1914; created baron 1931. Author of *Radioactivity*; *Radioactive Substances and their Radiations*; *The Newer Alchemy*. Died 19 October 1937.

Sachs, E. Solomon. Trade union leader. Born 3 November 1903, Svinsk, Latvia; went to South Africa as a child 1913; educated Newtown Government School, Johannesburg; read law and economics at University of the Witwatersrand 1927–8; acting secretary, Reef Shop Assistants' Union 1920; secretary, Witwatersrand Tailors' Association 1928; general secretary, South African Garment Workers' Union 1928–52; member, Communist party from which he was expelled 1930; workers' delegate, international labour conference 1946, 1950, 1951; restricted under Suppression of Communism Act 1952; went to Great Britain 1953; held research scholarships at University of Manchester and London School of Economics 1955–9.

Salisbury, Robert Arthur James Gascoyne-Cecil, fifth Marquess. See **Cranborne.**

Sanders, Sir Robert Arthur. See **Bayford.**

Sandys, Duncan Edwin. English politician. Born 24 January 1908; educated Eton; Magdalen College, Oxford; entered diplomatic service 1930; served in foreign office and British embassy, Berlin; Conservative member of parliament 1935–45, 1950 onwards; served in the Second World War 1940–1; financial secretary to war office 1941–3; parliamentary secretary, ministry of supply 1943–4; chairman of a war cabinet defence committee 1943–5; minister of works 1944–5; member, European consultative assembly at Strasbourg 1950–1 and since 1965; minister of supply 1951–4; minister of housing 1954–7; minister of defence 1957–9; minister of aviation 1959–60; secretary of state for Commonwealth relations and the colonies 1962–4.

Sastri, Valangiman Sankaranarayana Srinivasa. Indian educationalist and diplomat. Born 22 September 1869; educated Government College, Kumbakonam, Madras; teacher, then headmaster in Madras; joined Servants of India Society, Poona 1906; member, viceroy's legislative council 1916–20; elected to council of state 1920; represented India at League of Nations assembly, Washington conference, imperial conference 1921–2; mission to Australia, Canada, New Zealand on Indian disabilities 1922; agent for government of India in South Africa 1927–9; vice-chancellor, Annamalai University 1935–40. Died 17 April 1946.

Sauer, Paul Oliver. Politician and wine farmer. Born 1 January 1898, Wynberg, Cape Province, South Africa; only son of J. W. Sauer (q.v. vol. IV); educated South African College; University of Stellenbosch; National party member of the house of assembly since 1929; for many years chief whip of the party; minister of transport 1948–53; minister of lands 1953–64 when he retired from office; member of the senate 1964–70 when he retired from politics.

Schacht, Hjalmar Horace Greeley. Banker. Born 22 January 1877, Tingleff, Schleswig, Germany; educated at schools in the United States and at the Universities of Kiel, Berlin, Munich, Leipzig; employed in Dresdner Bank 1903–15 (assistant manager from 1908); financial administrator of occupied Belgium 1914–16; director, Nationalbank für Deutschland 1916; took leading part in reparation discussions after the First World War; as president of the Reichsbank (1923–30) stabilized the inflated currency and resigned in protest against the Young plan; Reichsbank president 1933–9 and minister for economic affairs 1934–7; dismissed by Hitler 1939; arrested July 1944 and sent to Dachau camp; tried at Nuremberg and acquitted 1946; sentenced to imprisonment by the German people's court at Stuttgart but released after a successful appeal against its verdict; senior partner, Privatbankhaus Schacht & Co., Düsseldorf since 1953; author of books on the German economy and an autobiography. Died 4 June 1970.

Schemm, Hans. Teacher and politician. Born 1891, Bayreuth, Bavaria, Germany; gauleiter, Bavarian Ostmark; founder, National-Socialist teachers' association; member, Bavarian landtag and of the reichstag. Died 1935.

Scherz, Ernst R. Archaeologist. Born 20 June 1906, Germany; educated Technische Hochschule, Berlin; went to South-West Africa 1933; engaged in work on the rock engravings and paintings of that region.

Schlesinger, Isidor William. Industrialist and financier. Born 1871, New York City; went to South Africa 1894; worked as an insurance agent; founded a real estate company 1902; the African Life Assurance Society 1904; the Colonial Banking and Trust Company 1910; the cinema company later known as African Consolidated Theatres 1914; established pineapple plantations near Grahamstown, fruit canneries in Port Elizabeth, huge orange orchards at Zebedelia, Transvaal; was a pioneer of film production and radio broadcasting in South Africa; chairman of over 100 companies. Died 11 March 1949.

Schofield, John Frank. Architect and archaeologist. Born 1886, Rugby, England; educated Coopers' Company School; articled to firm of architects, Woolwich; employed by architectural firms in London; served in France in the First World War; went to Salisbury, Southern Rhodesia, as assistant director of public works *c.* 1921; became authority on archaeology of Zimbabwe; chief building inspector to Durban Corporation *c.* 1926; invited by University of Pretoria to undertake archaeological work in northern Transvaal at Mapungubwe; author of *Primitive Pottery* and various reports and articles. Died 11 June 1956.

Schonland, Sir Basil Ferdinand Jamieson. Physicist. Born 5 February 1896, Grahamstown, Cape Province, South Africa; educated St Andrew's, Grahamstown; Rhodes University College; Gonville and Caius College, Cambridge; served in both World Wars; lecturer, then professor of physics, University of Cape Town 1922–36; director, Bernard Price Institute, University of the Witwatersrand 1938–54; superintendent, army operational research group 1941–4; scientific adviser to General Montgomery (q.v.) 1944; president, South African Council for Scientific and Industrial Research 1945–50; deputy director, then director, atomic energy research establishment at Harwell, England 1954–60; director, research group, United Kingdom Atomic Energy Authority 1960–1; chancellor, Rhodes University; knighted 1960; author of *The Flight of Thunderbolts*; *Atmospheric Electricity*; and articles on cathodes, cosmic rays, lighting, etc. Died 24 November 1972.

Schroeter, Carl. Swiss botanist. Born 19 December 1855, Esslingen, Württemberg, Germany; professor of botany, Huguenot Polytechnic and High School in Zürich 1883–1925; worked chiefly in the field of plant geography and the description of Alpine flora and vegetation; author of *Das Pflanzenleben der Alpen*. Died 17 February 1939.

Schuschnigg, Kurt von. Statesman and lawyer. Born 14 December 1897, Riva, South Tirol; served in the First World War and then practised law; member of parliament 1927; minister of justice 1932; minister of education 1933–4; after the assassination of Dolfuss (q.v.) became chancellor and minister of defence; in 1936 and 1938 entered into agreements with Hitler in the hope of preserving the independence of Austria; arrested and imprisoned in March 1938 when Austria was occupied by Germany; after liberation in 1945 emigrated to the United States; professor of political science at St Louis University 1948–67; author of books on the events of his chancellorship.

Scott, Lieutenant-Colonel Lord Francis George Montagu-Douglas. Soldier. Born 1 November 1879, sixth son of the sixth Duke of Buccleugh; educated Eton; Christ Church, Oxford; entered British army 1899; served in the Anglo-Boer War; aide-de-camp to the viceroy of India 1905–10; served in the First World War; retired 1920; rejoined army and served in East Africa 1941; member, executive council and legislative council of Kenya. Died 26 July 1952.

Senanayake, Dudley Shelton. Statesman. Born 19 June 1911, Colombo, Ceylon; educated St Thomas' College, Mount Lavinia, Ceylon; Corpus Christi College, Cambridge; barrister of the Middle Temple; practised in Ceylon from 1934; elected to state council 1936; elected to house of representatives 1947; minister of agriculture 1947; prime minister, minister of defence, minister of external affairs 1952–3, March–July 1960, since 1965; president, United National party 1958; leader of the opposition 1961–5.

Seward, Sir Albert Charles. Botanist. Born 9 October 1863, Lancaster, England; educated Lancaster Grammar School; St John's College, Cambridge; fellow and tutor, Emmanuel College 1899–1906; University lecturer in botany 1890–1906; master of Downing College, Cambridge 1915–36; vice-chancellor of Cambridge 1924–6; trustee of British Museum from 1938; knighted 1936; author of many botanical works, notably on fossil plants. Died 11 April 1941.

Shapley, Harlow. American astronomer. Born 2 November 1885; educated University of Missouri; Princeton University; astronomer, Mount Wilson observatory 1914–21; director, Harvard College observatory 1921–52; publications include *Star Clusters*; *Galaxies*; *Of Stars and Men*; *Climatic Changes*. Died 20 October 1972.

Sharpey-Schäfer, Sir Edward Albert. Physiologist. Born 2 June 1850, London; educated University College School; University College, London; assistant professor of physiology, University College, London 1874–83; Jodrell professor 1883–9; professor of physiology, University of Edinburgh 1899–1933; general secretary, British Association 1895–1900; knighted 1913; author of *Essentials of Histology*; *The Endocrine Organs*, etc. Died 29 March 1935.

Shearer, Vernon Lyall. Dental surgeon and politician. Born 1904, Durban, South Africa; educated Durban High School; George Watson's College, University of Edinburgh; member, Durban city council 1932–5, 1958–66; member of the Natal provincial council 1933–8; Dominion party member of the house of assembly 1938–9, United party member 1939–54, Conservative party member 1954–8; served in the South African medical corps in the Second World War; mayor of Durban 1964–6. Died 19 September 1968.

Shiels, Sir T. Drummond. Medical practitioner and politician. Born *c.* 1875, Edinburgh, Scotland; educated University of Edinburgh; served in the First World War; Labour member of parliament 1924–31; parliamentary under-secretary, India office 1929 and colonial office 1929–31; secretary, Commonwealth Association; member, Inter-parliamentary Union (British Group); knighted 1939. Died 1 January 1953.

Simpson, Sir John Hope. Government official. Born 23 July 1868, Liverpool, England; educated Liverpool College; Balliol College, Oxford; joined Indian civil service as assistant magistrate 1889; magistrate 1897; secretary, board of revenue, United Provinces 1902; president, municipal taxation committee, United Provinces 1908; acting chief commissioner, Andaman and Nicobar Islands 1914; retired 1916; Labour member of parliament 1922–4; vice-chairman, refugee settlement commission, Athens 1926–30; on special mission for British government to Palestine 1930; director, national flood relief commission, China 1931–2; member, commission of inquiry on Newfoundland 1934–6; director, refugee survey, Royal Institute of International Affairs 1937–9. Died 10 April 1961.

Skrzynski, Count Alexander. Diplomat and politician. Born 1882, Zagorzany, Poland; educated in Cracow, Munich, Vienna; entered diplomatic service 1906; ambassador to the Holy See 1910; secretary, Austro-Hungarian embassy in Paris 1914; Polish minister at Bucharest 1918–22; minister of foreign affairs 1922–3, 1924–5; Polish delegate to League of Nations 1923; prime minister and minister of foreign affairs 1925–6; in retirement after Pilsudski's *coup d'état*. Died 1931.

Smit, Douglas Laing. Government official and politician. Born 21 March 1885, Seymour, Cape Province, South Africa; educated Seymour public school; joined Cape civil service 1903; magistrate in various posts until 1933 when became under-secretary for justice; secretary for Native affairs 1934–45; member, Native affairs commission 1945–50; United party member of parliament 1948–61. Died 19 December 1961.

Smit, Jacobus Stephanus. Administrator and politician. Born 9 October 1878, near Pretoria, South Africa; barrister of the Middle Temple; practised as attorney at Klerksdorp; assistant magistrate at Pietersburg, Klerksdorp, Vereeniging 1909–15; National party member of parliament 1920–4; high commissioner for the Union in London 1925–9; Union delegate to League of Nations 1925–7; administrator of the Transvaal 1929–34; member, diamond board. Died 10 February 1960.

Smith, Sir Grafton Elliot. Anatomist and anthropologist. Born 15 August 1871, Grafton, New South Wales, Australia; educated University of Sydney; held clinical posts 1892–4; began research on the brain, chiefly at Cambridge 1896–1900; professor of anatomy in the government medical school, Cairo, where he took part in the archaeological survey of Nubia 1900–8; professor of anatomy, University of Manchester 1909–19, and University College, London 1919–36, when he retired; interpreted discoveries in relation to the early history of man; author of many books including *Human History* (1930) and *The Diffusion of Culture* (1933); knighted 1934. Died 1 January 1937.

Smith, John Alexander. Philosopher and classical scholar. Born 21 April 1863, Dingwall, Ross, Scotland; educated Inverness Academy; Collegiate School, Edinburgh; Edinburgh University; Balliol College, Oxford; assistant in Greek, Edinburgh University 1887–91; fellow of Balliol (1891) and lecturer in philosophy 1896–1909; professor of moral and metaphysical philosophy, University of Oxford 1910–36 when he retired; joint editor, *Works of Aristotle* (1908–12). Died 19 December 1939.

Soames, Arthur Christopher John. English soldier and politician. Born 12 October 1920; educated Eton; Royal Military College, Sandhurst; served in Middle East, Italy, France 1939–45; assistant military attaché, British embassy, Paris; Conservative member of parliament 1950–66; parliamentary private secretary to the prime minister 1952–5; parliamentary under-secretary, air ministry 1955–7; parliamentary and financial secretary, admiralty 1957–8; secretary of state for war 1958–60; minister of agriculture 1960–4.

Somerville, Admiral Sir James Fownes. Naval officer. Born 17 July 1882, Somerset, England; joined royal navy and commissioned lieutenant 1898; commander during the First World War; admiral 1937; commander-in-chief, East Indies 1938; invalided home 1939; in command of task force against the French fleet at Oran 1941; commander, British fleet in the Far East 1942–3; head of admiralty delegation in Washington 1944–5; admiral of the fleet 1945. Died 19 March 1949.

Sophie, Princess, of the Asturias. Born 2 November 1938 at Psychico Palace, Athens; eldest daughter of Paul I of the Hellenes and Queen Frederika (qq.v.);

educated at the school at Psychico and Salem School, Germany; married, in 1962, the Infante Don Juan Carlos, Prince of the Asturias, grandson of Alfonso XIII of Spain.

Spears, Major-General Sir Edward Louis, first Baronet. English soldier, politician, diplomat. Born 7 August 1886; educated privately; joined Kildare militia 1903; commissioned 1906; served in the First World War; head of military mission, Paris 1917–20; retired 1920; Conservative member of parliament 1922–4, 1931–45; headed mission to Syria and Lebanon 1941; minister to Syria and Lebanon 1942–4; chairman of companies; created baronet 1953; author of books on the First and Second World Wars.

Spilhaus, Karl. Merchant. Born 11 December 1876, Lisbon, Portugal, of German-Portuguese descent; educated in Lübeck, Germany; went to Cape Town 1895; joined his uncle's firm Wm. Spilhaus and Company, and later the Imperial Cold Storage; became chairman and managing director of Poppe, Schunhoff and Guttery Ltd.; commissioner of commerce for the Union of South Africa in Europe 1922–5; published his memoirs. Died 3 November 1968.

Stalin, Josif Vissarionovich (Dzhugashvili). Russian dictator. Born 21 December 1879, Gori, Georgia, Transcaucasia; educated Gori Ecclesiastical School; Tiflis Theological School; joined Tiflis Social Democratic (Marxist) party 1898; five times arrested for political activity, he escaped each time 1902–13; took part in party congresses in Stockholm and London 1906–7; joined the Bolsheviks and became a member of the central committee of that party 1912; editor of *Pravda* 1912; arrested and exiled 1913–17; commissar of nationalities in first Bolshevik government 1917–22; active in the civil war and the war against Poland 1918–21; appointed general secretary of the central committee, Communist party 1922; eliminated Trotsky from the party 1927; initiated and enforced intensive industrial and collective agricultural projects from 1928; eliminated political opponents by police action and 'purge' trials; secured adoption of a new constitution of the U.S.S.R. 1936; made agreement with Germany followed by joint partition of Poland 1939; supreme Russian commander in the war against Germany, becoming marshal (1943) and generalissimo (1945); attended Allied conferences at Teheran, Yalta and Potsdam; author of *Lenin and Leninism*; *Problems of Leninism*, and other Marxist works. Died 5 March 1953.

Stallard, Charles Frampton. Lawyer and politician. Born 4 June 1871, London; educated St Edward's School; Merton College, Oxford; barrister of Gray's Inn; served in the Anglo-Boer War 1900–2; practised as advocate in Johannesburg 1903–14; member of Transvaal provincial council 1910–14; served in South West Africa and Flanders 1914–18 attaining rank of lieutenant-colonel; resumed legal practice; South African party member of parliament 1929–33 in which year he formed the Dominion party; member of parliament 1933–8, 1939–48; minister of mines in the war cabinet 1939–45. Died 13 June 1971.

Stamfordham, Arthur John Bigge, first Baron. Court official. Born 18 June 1849; educated Rossall; Woolwich Academy; entered British army 1869; served in the Zulu War 1878–9; appointed to the royal household as assistant private secretary to Queen Victoria 1880–95; became her private secretary 1895–1901, then private secretary to the Prince of Wales 1901–10 and later to King George V (1910–31); knighted 1895; created baron 1911. Died 31 March 1931.

Stamp, Josiah Charles, first Baron, of Shortlands. Economist. Born 21 June 1880, London; educated University of London; assistant secretary, board of inland revenue 1916–19; secretary and director, Nobel's Industries Ltd. 1919–26; chairman of the L.M.S. Railway; director of the Bank of England 1928; British representative on Dawes committee 1924; joint secretary and editor, Royal Statistical Society 1920–30, president 1930–2; held various university appointments in economics; created baron 1938; published works include *The Fundamental Principles of Taxation*; *The National Income*; *Taxation During the War*; *Financial Aftermath of the War*. Died 16 April 1941.

Standley, Admiral William Harrison. Born 18 December 1872, Ukiah, California, United States of America; educated U.S. Naval Academy; served in training ships *Pensacola* and *Adams*; lieutenant 1904; commandant, navy yard, More Island, California 1911; commander, U.S.S. *Yorktown* 1914; captain 1919; in charge of war plans division, bureau of naval operations 1923–6; assistant chief of naval operations and rear-admiral 1928; special naval adviser to the president 1939; ambassador to the U.S.S.R. 1942. Died 25 October 1963.

Stanley, Oliver Frederick George. Statesman. Born 1896, a younger son of the seventeenth earl of Derby; educated Eton and Oxford; served in the First World War; called to the bar 1919; became a stockbroker; Conservative member of parliament 1924–51; parliamentary under-secretary, home office 1931–3; minister of transport 1933–4; minister of labour 1934–5; president, board of education 1935–7; president, board of trade 1937–40; secretary of state for war 1940; served as major in royal artillery 1940–1; secretary of state for the colonies 1942–5. Died 10 December 1951.

Stansgate, William Wedgwood Benn, first Viscount. British politician. Born 10 May 1877; educated University of London; Liberal member of parliament 1906–27, Labour member of parliament 1928–31; junior lord of the treasury 1910–18; served in the First World War; secretary of state for India 1929–31; secretary of state for air 1945–6; created viscount 1941. Died 17 November 1960.

Stapf, Otto. Botanist. Born 23 March 1857, Ischl, Austria; educated University of Vienna; *privat dozent* there 1887–91; assistant, Royal Botanic Gardens, Kew 1891–9; principal assistant 1899–1908; keeper of the herbarium and library; botanical secretary, Linnaean Society 1908–16; author of works on Oriental and African flora. Died 3 August 1933.

Steer, George, Lowther. Journalist. Born 2 November 1909, Cambridge, East London, South Africa; educated Winchester; Christ Church, Oxford; reporter for *Cape Argus* 1932–3; dramatic critic, *Yorkshire Post* 1933–5; war correspondent, *The Times*, in Addis Ababa 1935–6 and Spain 1936–7; special correspondent, *Daily Telegraph*, in Africa 1938–9; served on the British army intelligence staff in Burma in the Second World War; author of *The Tree of Guernica*; *Judgment on German Africa*, etc. Died 25 December 1944.

Stent, Vere Palgrave. Journalist. Born 1872, Queenstown, Cape Province, South Africa; educated St Andrew's College, Grahamstown; Whitgift's Grammar School, Croydon, England; joined De Beers Company as mining engineer but became reporter for *Diamond Fields Advertiser*; as correspondent of the *Cape Times* reported Matabele rebellion of 1896; during Anglo-Boer War was Reuter's correspondent at Mafeking; editor of the *Pretoria News c.* 1902–22; Reuter's correspondent in the 1914 rebellion and the East African campaign; resigned from active journalism in 1922; subsequently wrote press articles on South African politics and a number of books including *Some Incidents in the Life of Cecil Rhodes* and *The Great Safari*. Died 29 June 1941.

Stettinius, Edward Reilly. Statesman and industrialist. Born 22 October 1900, Chicago; educated Pomfret School, Connecticut; University of Virginia; held executive posts in General Motors 1926–34; chairman, U.S. Steel Corporation 1938–40; member, war resources board 1939; lease-lend administrator 1941–3; under-secretary of state 1943–4; secretary of state 1944–5; head of United States delegation to U.N.O. 1945–6; rector, University of Virginia 1946–9. Died 31 October 1949.

Steyn, Gladys Evelyn. Lawyer and politician. Born 12 December 1890, Bloemfontein, Orange Free State, South Africa; second daughter of President M. T. Steyn (q.v. vol. IV); educated Grey University College, Bloemfontein and in teachers' training institutions in Europe; teacher at Oranje Girls' School, Bloemfontein 1914–15 and principal 1916–19; barrister of the Middle Temple 1925; practised as advocate in the Orange Free State division of the supreme court of South Africa 1925–42; member, Orange Free State provincial council 1933–6, 1939–53;

member, social and economic planning council until its dissolution; a life vice-chairman, United party congress.

Stokoe, Thomas P. Mountaineer and botanist. Born 1868 in Yorkshire, England; at one time press photographer for the *Cape Times*; over a period of forty-seven years collected thousands of South African botanical specimens including mainly high altitude species previously unknown; of these about thirty have been named after him. Died 21 April 1959.

Stout, Sir Robert. Judge and statesman. Born 28 September 1844, Shetland Islands, Scotland; emigrated to New Zealand; admitted to the Dunedin bar 1871; lecturer in law, University of Otago 1873–5; member of the general assembly 1875–98; attorney-general and minister for lands 1878–9; prime minister 1884–7; chief justice 1899–1926; chancellor, University of New Zealand; knighted 1886. Died 19 July 1930.

Strabolgi, Joseph Montague Kenworthy, tenth Baron. Sailor, politician, author. Born 7 March 1886; educated Royal Naval Academy, Winchester; entered the royal navy 1902; retired 1920 with rank of lieutenant-commander; Liberal, later Labour, member of parliament 1919–31; succeeded to the peerage 1934 and became chief Labour whip in the house of lords 1938–42; author of books on politics and sea-power and the autobiographical *Statesmen and Others*. Died 8 October 1953.

Strakosch, Sir Henry. Banker and economist. Born 9 May 1971, Hohenhau, Austria; entered upon banking in London 1891; after 1895 associated with industrial and gold-mining houses in South Africa; represented the Union at various international conferences on finance and trade; advised Union government on the draft South African Currency and Banking Act of 1920; South African delegate, League of Nations assembly 1923–4; member of council of India 1930–7; member, financial committee, League of Nations 1920–37; adviser to secretary of state for India 1937–43; author of several works on monetary problems and policy. Died 30 October 1943.

Strauss, Jacobus Gideon Nel. Politician, lawyer, farmer. Born 17 December 1900, Calvinia, Cape Province, South Africa; educated Calvinia High School; University of Cape Town; private secretary to the prime minister 1923–4; practised at the Bloemfontein bar, then in Johannesburg from 1925; South African party member of parliament 1932–57; minister of agriculture 1943–8; leader of the United party 1950–6; retired from politics 1957 and became a farmer.

Stresemann, Gustav. Statesman. Born 10 May 1878, Berlin; educated Universities of Berlin and Leipzig; leading industrialist in Saxony 1902–18; National Liberal party member of reichstag 1906–12; leader of the German People's party 1918–29; chancellor and foreign minister 1923; withdrew as chancellor after three months but remained foreign minister until 1929; awarded Nobel peace prize 1926; author of books on post-war Germany. Died 3 October 1929.

Strijdom, Johannes Gerhardus. Statesman. Born 14 July 1893, Willowmore, Cape Province, South Africa; educated Fransch Hoek School; Universities of Stellenbosch and Pretoria; began practice as advocate 1918; National party member of parliament 1929–54; leader of his party in the Transvaal from 1934; minister of lands 1948–54; deputy prime minister 1953; prime minister 1954–8. Died 24 August 1958.

Struben, Robert Henry. Farmer and politician. Born *c.* 1880 in South Africa; educated Diocesan College, Cape Town; Wadham College, Oxford; farmed in the midlands of the Cape Province for some twenty years; co-founder, Cape Province Agricultural Association; served in the Anglo-Boer War with the British forces and in the First World War in the remount service in England; South African party member of parliament 1924–36 and Cape Province whip. Died 28 February 1936.

Stuart, Sir Campbell. Director of *The Times*. Born 1885, Montreal, Canada; educated College of William and Mary, Virginia, United States of America; University of

Melbourne; attaché, British embassy, Washington 1917; deputy director of propaganda in enemy countries 1918; managing director, *The Times* 1919–24 and director until 1960; chairman, advisory committee, ministry of information 1939; director of propaganda in enemy countries 1939–40; chairman, Hudson Bay Record Society 1938–59; knighted 1918; author of *Secrets of Crewe House*; *Opportunity Knocks Once*.

Sturman, Edward Albert. Government official. Born 1864, London; educated there; joined central telegraph office, British post office 1879; transferred to Cape Colony telegraph 1889; principal telegraph clerk 1902; served in Anglo-Boer War; director of posts and chief field censor during the First World War; postmaster-general of the Union of South Africa and first chairman, South African civil air board from 1921. Died 1932.

Sturrock, Frederick Claud. Politician and merchant. Born 25 May 1882, Newport, Scotland; educated Dundee High School and Technical College; bought a business in Johannesburg 1907; president, Johannesburg chamber of commerce 1918 and, later, of associated chambers of commerce of South Africa; South African party member of parliament 1929–50; minister without portfolio 1936–8 when he resigned from the cabinet; minister of railways 1939–47; minister of finance January–May 1948. Died 4 August 1958.

Stuttaford, Richard. Business man and politician. Born 13 June 1870, Cape Town; educated in Reading, England; entered the Cape Town firm of S. R. Stuttaford and Company 1892; chairman and managing director from 1898; member, Cape Town city council 1905; South African party member of parliament from 1924; commercial adviser of Union delegation, Ottawa conference 1932; minister without portfolio 1933; minister of the interior and of public health 1936; minister of commerce 1939–43 when he retired. Died 19 October 1945.

Sumner, John Andrew Hamilton, first Viscount, of Ibstone. Judge. Born 3 February 1859; educated Balliol College, Oxford; barrister of the Inner Temple; standing counsel to the University of Oxford 1906–9; judge of king's bench division of the high court 1909–12; lord justice of appeal 1912–13; lord of appeal in ordinary from 1913. Died 24 May 1934.

Swart, Charles Robberts. First president of the Republic of South Africa. Born 5 December 1894, Orange Free State; educated University College of the Orange Free State; Columbia University; lecturer in law, University of the Orange Free State 1917–18; practised as advocate 1919–48; organizing secretary of National party in Orange Free State 1919–28; member of federal council of the party 1930–59; member of parliament 1923–38, 1941–59; leader of his party in the Orange Free State 1940–59; minister of justice 1948–59; minister of education 1954–9; governor-general of the Union 1960; state president of the Republic of South Africa 1961–7; chancellor, University of the Orange Free State.

Swingler, George Henry. Engineer. Born 1884, Stamford, England; educated Stamford Grammar School; went to South Africa to join a Cape Town firm of building contractors 1902; superintendent of municipal power-station at Kalk Bay and electrical engineer 1905–13; joined Cape Town electricity department 1913; city electrical engineer, Cape Town 1918–44; seconded to represent director-general of war supplies on a mission to the United States of America 1940–3; local manager, Electricity Supply Commission 1924–46. Died 19 August 1946.

Talbot, Sir Edmund. See **Fitzalan-Howard.**

Talbot, Right Reverend Neville Stuart. Bishop. Born 21 August 1879, Oxford, England; educated Haileybury College; Christ Church, Oxford; Cuddesdon College, Oxford; served in the Anglo-Boer War 1899–1902; deacon 1908; ordained 1909; curate of St Bartholomew, Armley 1908–9; examining chaplain to the Archbishop of York 1909–10; tutor and chaplain, Balliol College, Oxford 1910–15; served as chaplain in France 1914–19; Bishop of Pretoria, Transvaal 1920–33; vicar of St Mary, Nottingham and rural dean of Nottingham 1933–43; author of books on religion. Died 3 April 1943.

Tallents, Sir Stephen George. Government official. Born 20 October 1884; educated Harrow; Balliol College, Oxford; entered board of trade 1909; ministry of munitions 1915–16; principal assistant secretary, ministry of food 1918–19; private secretary to Viscount Fitzalan (q.v.) 1921–2; imperial secretary, Northern Ireland 1922–6; secretary, Empire marketing board 1926–33; public relations officer, General Post Office 1933–5; controller (public relations), British Broadcasting Corporation 1935–41; principal assistant secretary, ministry of town and country planning 1943–6; knighted 1932; author of short stories and memoirs. Died 11 September 1958.

Tedder, Arthur William, first Baron, of Glenguin. Air marshal. Born 1890; educated Whitgift School; Magdalene College, Cambridge; entered the colonial service 1914; commissioned and served in France 1915; seconded to royal flying corps 1916; served in Egypt 1918–19; transferred to royal air force 1919; held various air training posts 1923–36; commander R.A.F., Far East 1936–8; commander-in-chief R.A.F., Middle East 1940–3; deputy supreme commander and chief of Allied air operations in western Europe 1943–5; chief of air staff 1946–50; knighted 1942; created baron 1946; chancellor of the University of Cambridge 1950; author of *Air Power in War* and memoirs. Died 3 June 1967.

Teichmann, Waldemar Robert Ferdinand. Farmer and politician. Born 20 November 1887, Pretoria district, South Africa; educated Staats Model School, Boys' High School, Pretoria; served in South West Africa 1915; member, Transvaal provincial council 1917–41, and chairman 1940–1; commissioner, South African railways and harbours board 1945–50; served on agricultural and educational bodies in the Transvaal; director, Nederlandse Bank 1951. Died 30 October 1954.

Teilhard de Chardin, Pierre. Scientist and philosopher. Born 1 May 1881, Orcine, Puy-de-Dome, France; educated at a Jesuit college and the University of Paris; joined the Society of Jesus 1899; taught physics and chemistry at Jesuit College in Cairo 1906–8 and Hastings 1909–12; ordained priest 1912; stretcher-bearer in a Zouave regiment during the First World War: doctorate in science, Paris, 1922; attached to geological division of the university in Peking where he studied palaeontology 1923–46; pursued this study in Ethiopia, northern India, Burma, Java, South Africa; returned to France 1946; worked under auspices of the Wenner-Gren Foundation in New York 1951–5; author of *The Phenomenon of Man*; *Le Milieu Divin*; *The Future of Man*; *Letters from a Traveller*. Died 10 April 1955.

Temperley, Harold William Vazeille. Historian. Born 20 April 1879, Cambridge, England; educated Sherborne School; King's College and Peterhouse, Cambridge; lecturer, University of Leeds 1904–5; Harvard 1911–12; served in the First World War at Gallipoli 1915; general staff officer 1918; military adviser at peace conference 1920; member, Albania frontiers commission 1921; University professor of modern history and master of Peterhouse, Cambridge; author of *The Foreign Policy of Canning*; *England and the Near East—The Crimea*; co-author of *Europe in the Nineteenth (and Twentieth) Century*, etc. Died 11 July 1939.

Templewood, Samuel John Gurney Hoare, first Viscount, of Chelsea. Politician and diplomat. Born 24 February 1880, England; educated Harrow; New College, Oxford; Conservative member of parliament 1910; served in military intelligence in the First World War; secretary of state for air 1923–9; secretary for India 1931–5; secretary of state for foreign affairs 1935; resigned following criticism of the Hoare–Laval agreement on Italian policy in Abyssinia; first lord of the admiralty 1936; home secretary 1937–9; lord privy seal 1939–40; ambassador to Spain 1940–4 when he resigned; created viscount 1944; chancellor of University of Reading 1935; author of books on penal reform and memoirs. Died 7 May 1959.

Tereshchenko, Mikhail Ivanovich. Politician and merchant. Born 18 March 1886, Kiev, Russia; educated there and at University of Leipzig; made a fortune as a sugar merchant; Liberal member of the Duma 1912; active in the organization of war industries; minister of finance in the Lvov government March 1917; minister of foreign affairs in the Kerensky cabinet August–November 1917; arrested by the Bolshevist government and escaped to Norway where he engaged in banking and trading with Mozambique; became well known in financial and commercial circles in London and other European capitals. Died 1 April 1956.

Te Water, Charles Theodore. Diplomat, politician, lawyer. Born 1887, Graaff-Reinet, Cape Province, South Africa; educated Normal College, Cape Town; George Watson's College, Edinburgh; University of Cambridge; barrister of the Inner Temple; practised as advocate in Pretoria 1910–29; National party member of parliament 1924–9; high commissioner for the Union of South Africa in London 1929–39; first delegate of the Union, League of Nations assembly 1929–39; ambassador-at-large for the Union 1948–50; director, South African Reserve Bank 1952–63; president, National Veld Trust 1948–64. Died 6 June 1964.

Theiler, Sir Arnold. Veterinary scientist. Born 26 March 1867, Frick, Switzerland; educated in Aarau, Berne, Zürich; went to South Africa 1891 as veterinary surgeon to the Johannesburg sanitary board; government veterinary surgeon 1896–1900; government veterinary bacteriologist 1900–10; founded Onderstepoort Institute of Veterinary Research 1908; head of veterinary branch, Union department of agriculture 1910; director of veterinary education and research 1920; professor of veterinary science, Transvaal University College; retired 1927; knighted 1914; author of books on tropical diseases of domesticated stock. Died 24 July 1936.

Thomas, James Henry. Politician. Born 3 October 1874, Newport, England; educated in council schools; became an engine-driver; general secretary, National Union of Railwaymen 1918–24, 1925–31; Labour member of parliament 1910–36; secretary of state for the colonies 1924, 1936; lord privy seal 1929–30; secretary of state for the Dominions 1930–5; resigned from office and parliament following unauthorized budget disclosures; author of *When Labour Rules*; *My Story*. Died 21 January 1949.

Thompson, Sir D'Arcy Wentworth. Zoologist. Born 1860, Galway, Eire; educated Edinburgh Academy; Trinity College, Cambridge; professor of natural history, University College, Dundee 1884–1916 and St Andrews University 1917; British delegate at various fisheries conferences; author of *Science and the Classics* and books on birds and fishes. Died 21 June 1948.

Thomson, Sir Francis Vernon, first Baronet. Director of shipping companies. Born 10 February 1881, Manchester, England; educated Glasgow; began his business career with the King line, London 1897; became director 1921, chairman 1931; director, Union-Castle line 1932, chairman 1939; assistant director, ship management branch, ministry of shipping 1918–21; chairman, documentary committee, chamber of shipping of the United Kingdom 1923–35; president of the chamber 1936–7; chief shipping adviser and controller of commercial shipping, ministry of shipping, later ministry of war transport 1939–46; member, committee of Lloyd's register of shipping since 1927; knighted 1921; created baronet 1938. Died 8 February 1953.

Thomson, Sir Joseph John. Physicist. Born 18 December 1856, Manchester, England; educated Owens College; Trinity College, Cambridge where he was lecturer 1883–4; Cavendish professor of experimental physics, Cambridge 1884–1919; professor of natural philosophy, Royal Institution, London 1905–20; master of Trinity College 1918–40; awarded Nobel prize for physics 1906; awarded the Order of Merit 1912; pioneer in the study of atomic physics; knighted 1908; author of *Application of Dynamics to Physics and Chemistry*; *The Electron in Chemistry*; and books on the theory of electricity. Died 30 August 1940.

Tilby, A. Wyatt. Journalist. Born 1880, Addiscombe, Surrey, England; educated privately and abroad; on editorial staff, *Globe* 1905–12, *Saturday Review* 1913–15; editor, *Evening Standard* 1915–16; editor, *Outlook* 1924–8; author of *The English People Overseas*; *The Evolution of Consciousness*; *The Quest of Reality*; *Lord John Russell*. Died 1 September 1948.

Tito, Josip Broz. President of Yugoslavia. Born 25 May 1892, Kumrovec, Croatia, of peasant stock; locksmith in Zagreb from 1910; served as private in the Austro-Hungarian army in the First World War and was prisoner of war in Russia; returned to Zagreb and joined Yugoslav Communist party 1920; imprisoned 1928; attended Lenin School in Moscow and became member of Yugoslav politburo 1934; secretary-general of Yugoslav Communist party 1937; organized a guerilla partisan army to resist Nazi invasion of Yugoslavia 1941 and received Allied support; became supreme commander and president of the national liberation committee 1943; the Communist victory at the election of 1945 was followed by the abdication of King Peter II and the proclamation of the Republic, Tito being prime minister and minister of defence until 1953 when he was elected president, chairman of the executive council and supreme commander of the armed forces.

Tregardt, Louis. Voortrekker leader. Born 10 August 1783 near the present town of Oudtshoorn, Cape Province; farmed in the districts of Graaff-Reinet and Uitenhage; became field-cornet 1825; with other Boer families settled beyond the eastern frontier 1834; trekked north 1835 reaching the region west of the Soutpansberg May 1936; after a ten months sojourn south of the mountains moved on over the Drakensberg to the east coast; reached Lourenço Marques 13 April 1838 with a party of fifty-two of whom twenty, including Tregardt, died there within a few months. His diary (July 1836 to August 1838) is extant. Died 25 October 1838.

Trichardt, Louis. See **Tregardt.**

Truman, Harry S. President of the United States. Born 8 May 1884, Lamarr, Missouri; educated Independence School; worked as bank clerk; later a farmer; served in the First World War in France as major; twice elected presiding judge of Jackson county court 1926–34; twice elected Democratic senator of Missouri 1934–44; vice-president 1944; succeeded to presidency on death of F. D. Roosevelt (q.v.) 1945; re-elected 1949; declined presidential candidature 1952. Died 26 December 1972.

Truscott, Lieutenant-General Lucian King. Soldier. Born 9 January 1895, Chatfield, Texas, United States of America; educated Norman School, Oklahoma; commissioned second lieutenant 1917; graduated from cavalry school, Fort Riley 1926; major 1936; brigadier-general 1942; organized an American ranger (commando) unit in England; served in north Africa and commanded an infantry division in Italy 1942–3; commander, sixth army corps, then commanding general, fifth army 1944–5; succeeded General Patton as commander of the third army and the eastern military district 1945. Died 12 September 1965.

Umberto, Crown Prince of Italy. Born 15 September 1904, only son of Victor Emmanuel III (q.v.) and Queen Elena; educated privately and at Royal Military Academy, Turin; married Princess Maria Jose of Belgium 1930; put in command of the army of the Alps with rank of general 1940; designated lieutenant-general of the realm when his father relinquished the royal powers June 1944; assumed the throne on the abdication of his father May 1946; went into exile when Italy became a republic June 1946.

Uys, Jacobus Johannes. Voortrekker leader. Born 26 June 1770, Wydgelegen, present district of Bredasdorp; farmed at Driefontein near his birthplace; moved with several members of his family to district of Uitenhage *c.* 1822; thence trekked to Natal as the leader of several families, many of them his relations, 1837. Died July 1838.

Uys, Petrus Lafras. Voortrekker leader. Born 10 July 1797, Potteberg in the present Heidelberg district, Cape Province; son of Jacobus Johannes Uys (q.v.); led a reconnoitring expedition to Natal 1834; left Uitenhage with the Uys party 1837; with A. H. Potgieter (q.v.) gained a decisive victory over the Matabele at Mosega, November 1837; chosen as the first commandant-general of the Trekkers. In the course of punitive operations against the Zulus Uys, his young son, and nine of his men were ambushed and killed at Italeni on 11 April 1838.

Van Boetzelaer van Asperen, Constant W. Baron. Diplomat. Born 22 June 1915, Batavia, Java; educated Gymnasium Utrecht Zeist; University of Utrecht; second ambassador for the Netherlands in Chungking 1945, Peking 1946–7, Nanking 1948, Batavia 1949; in ministry of foreign affairs 1949–50; first ambassador in Washington 1950–4; in Bonn 1954; counsellor in London 1958–63; minister plenipotentiary in London 1964–5; director of information, ministry of foreign affairs 1966.

Van Coller, Clifford Meyer. Politician and attorney. Born 13 June 1876, Humansdorp, Cape Province, South Africa; educated South African College, Cape Town; president, Cape Municipal Association 1923–4; South African party member of parliament 1929–53; chairman of committees 1943; Speaker of the house of assembly 1944–8; retired from political life 1953.

Van der Bijl, Hendrik Johannes. Engineer. Born 23 November 1887, Pretoria, South Africa; educated Victoria College, Stellenbosch; Universities of Halle, Leipzig, Chicago; instructor in physics, School of Technology, Dresden 1912–13; research physicist for American Telephone and Western Electric Companies, New York 1913–20; technical adviser to department of mines and industries of the Union of South Africa from 1920; organized the Electricity Supply Commission and the South African Iron and Steel Corporation; was director-general of war supplies during the Second World War; author of works on pure and applied physics. Died 2 December 1948.

Van der Byl, Major Pieter Voltelin Graham. South African soldier, farmer and politician. Born 21 February 1889; educated Diocesan College, Rondebosch; Pembroke College, Cambridge; on general staff, defence headquarters, Pretoria 1913; on General Botha's staff 1914; staff captain in South West Africa and East Africa campaigns 1914–17; served in royal air force in France 1918; aide-de-camp to Earl Haig (q.v. vol. IV) 1921; South African party member of parliament 1929–66; minister without portfolio 1939–43; minister for Native affairs 1943–8; retired from political life 1966; farmer at Caledon, Cape Province.

Van der Merwe, Nicolas Johannes. Minister of religion and politician. Born 17 February 1888, Senekal, Orange Free State, South Africa; educated Grey College School; Grey University College; Theological Seminary, Stellenbosch; University of Amsterdam; ordained 1915; Dutch Reformed (N.G. Kerk) minister at Wepener 1915, at Theunissen 1921–4; retired from ministry; National party member of parliament 1924–40; leader of the party in the Orange Free State 1934–40; biographer of President Steyn (q.v. vol. IV). Died 11 August 1940.

Van der Walt, Hendrik Stephanus. Government official. Born 31 May 1899, Philipstown, Cape Province, South Africa; educated in the United States; teacher at Gill College 1926–8; joined Cape provincial administration 1928; chief clerk, prime minister's office 1936; head of hospital administration, Transvaal Province 1939; transferred to Union department of education; secretary for education 1949; controller and auditor-general 1957–64.

Van Fleet, General James Alward. Soldier. Born 19 March 1892, Coytesville, New Jersey, United States of America; educated United States Military Academy; commanded machine gun battalion in France 1918 (rank of major); professor of military science and tactics, South Dakota State College, and University of Florida 1921–34; commanding officer (colonel), eighth infantry regiment of the fourth division 1935; led this regiment in invasion of France 1944; in command of army corps, first army, in the advance into Germany 1945; director of United States forces in Greece 1948 (rank of general); commander of United States forces in Korea 1948–50; became director of real estate and other companies.

Van Heerden, Anne Petronella. Medical practitioner. Born 26 April 1887, Bethlehem, Orange Free State, South Africa; educated Huguenot Seminary, Wellington; Victoria College, Stellenbosch; University of Amsterdam; in general practice at Harrismith 1917–21; practised as gynaecologist in Cape Town 1925–40; served in South African medical corps in the Second World War; became farmer in Harrismith; author of memoirs and a genealogy of the van Heerden family.

Van Niekerk, Christiaan Andries. Politician and farmer. Born 26 August 1874, Vegkop, Orange Free State, South Africa; educated Boys' High School, Wellington,

Cape; Victoria College, Stellenbosch; commandant of Kroonstad commando during Anglo-Boer War; delegate to Vereeniging peace conference; member of the legislative assembly of the Orange Free State 1907–10; member of the Union house of assembly 1915–24 and chief whip, National party; became senator 1924 and was president of the senate 1930–40, 1948–56; retired from political life 1960. Died 2 January 1966.

Van Rensburg, Johannes Frederik Janse. Government official and politician. Born 24 September 1898, Winburg, Orange Free State, South Africa; educated Universities of Stellenbosch and South Africa; entered civil service as private secretary to the minister of justice 1924; transferred to attorney-general's office and became a law adviser; under-secretary of the department of justice 1930, later secretary; administrator of the Orange Free State 1936; resigned in 1940 to become commandant-general of the *Ossewa-brandwag*, a Fascist organization, later absorbed by the National party; member of the group areas board 1953; retired from public life *c.* 1960; director of assurance and other companies. Died 25 September 1966.

Van Rensburg, Johannes Jacobus Janse. Voortrekker leader. Born 12 August 1779, district of Graaff-Reinet, Cape Province; lived in the region of the present towns of Beaufort West and Carnarvon from 1803; served as temporary field-cornet; trekked with other Boers to a settlement on the Caledon river 1830; after service in the Sixth Frontier War (1835), returned to the Caledon river but soon trekked north with the party of Tregardt (q.v.). After a quarrel the two leaders separated, van Rensburg's party going on to the Soutpansberg which they reached in May 1836. He then turned eastwards towards Delagoa Bay. His party was attacked and wiped out by a Zulu impi north of the junction of the Limpopo and Olifants rivers *c.* August 1836.

Van Ryneveld, General Sir Pierre. Soldier and farmer. Born 2 May 1891, Theunissen, Orange Free State, South Africa; educated Grey College, Bloemfontein; University of Cape Town; Imperial College of Science, London; joined the royal flying corps; in command of 45th squadron in France 1917–18; made, with Major Quinton Brand, a pioneer flight from England to South Africa 1920; started the South African air foice as director of air services 1920; commander of the military college and troops at Roberts Heights 1929; chief of the general staff 1933–49 when he retired and began farming in the Transvaal; knighted 1920. Died 1 December 1972.

Vansittart, Robert Gilbert, first Baron. Diplomat. Born 25 June 1881, Farnham, Surrey, England; educated Eton; entered diplomatic service as attaché 1902; third secretary 1905; second secretary 1908; assistant clerk, foreign office 1914; first secretary 1919; private secretary to Lord Curzon (q.v. vol. IV) 1920–4; head of the American department 1924–8; assistant under-secretary 1928; private secretary to Earl Baldwin (q.v.) and J. Ramsay MacDonald (q.v. vol. IV); permanent under-secretary 1930–8; chief diplomatic adviser to the foreign secretary 1938–41; author of novels, verses, plays. Died 14 February 1957.

Van Zyl, Carel Johannes. Attorney and farmer. Born 13 May 1869, Richmond, Cape Province, South Africa; educated there and at Victoria College, Stellenbosch; practised in Carnarvon, Cape; served in South West Africa in the First World War; senior commandant, defence force. Died 1937.

Van Zyl, Gideon Brand. Governor-General of the Union of South Africa. Born 3 June 1878, Cape Town; educated there at the Normal College School and the South African College; practised as attorney in Cape Town from 1898; served in the First World War attaining rank of major; South African party member of parliament 1916–42; administrator of the Cape Province 1942–5; first South African born governor-general of the Union 1945–50 when he retired. Died 1 November 1956.

Vermooten, Octavius Septimus. Attorney and politician. Born 8 September 1871, Colesberg, Cape Province, South Africa; educated at Venterstad; practised as attorney at Dordrecht from 1896; imprisoned on a charge of high treason 1900–3;

member of Cape legislative assembly 1907–10; National party member of parliament 1915–21, 1924–33 and leader of the party in the Cape Province; retired from political life 1933. Died 8 June 1943.

Victor Emmanuel III. King of Italy. Born 11 November 1869, Naples, only son of Umberto I and Margherita of Savoy; educated by private tutors and at the Military Academy, Turin; married Princess Elena of Montenegro 1896; succeeded to the throne 1900; offered Mussolini (q.v.) the premiership 1922; became emperor of Ethiopia (1936) and king of Albania (1939) after the conquests of those countries; opposed the entry of Italy into the Second World War on the side of Germany; dismissed Mussolini, appointed Marshal Badoglio prime minister and signed an armistice with the Allies July–September 1943; ceded the royal powers to his son, Umberto (q.v.) 1944 and abdicated 1946; went into exile in Alexandria when Italy became a republic. Died 28 December 1947.

Viljoen, Philippus Rudolf. Government official and veterinary scientist. Born 28 February 1889, near Krugersdorp, Transvaal, South Africa; educated South African College, Cape Town; Royal Veterinary College, London; fought with the Boer forces 1901–2 and in South West Africa 1914–15; bacteriologist, Onderstepoort veterinary research laboratories 1913–17; professor of veterinary science, Transvaal University College 1918–21; assistant director, veterinary research 1922–6; deputy director, veterinary services 1927–30; under-secretary, then secretary for agriculture 1931–45; high commissioner for the Union in Canada 1945–9, in Australia 1949–51. Died 3 June 1964.

Villiers, George Herbert Arthur Edward Hyde, Lord Hyde. Born 6 May 1906, only son of the sixth Earl of Clarendon (q.v.); educated Eton; Trinity College, Oxford. Died 27 April 1935 in a shooting accident, Kimberley, South Africa.

Vishinski, Andrei Yanuarievich. Jurist and politician. Born 10 December 1883, Odessa, Ukraine, Russia; educated University of Kiev; joined Social Democratic party 1902 and the Communist party 1920; member of the Soviet supreme court 1923; rector of Moscow University 1925; member, commissariat for education 1928–31; public prosecutor of the U.S.S.R. 1935–9; elected member of the central committee of the Communist party 1939; deputy commissar of foreign affairs 1940; minister of foreign affairs 1949; permanent Soviet representative, U.N.O. 1953; author of works on the Soviet legal system. Died 22 November 1954.

Visser, Thomas Christoffel. Medical practitioner and politician. Born 18 December 1871 near Fauresmith, Orange Free State, South Africa; educated Graaff-Reinet; Wellington; qualified in medicine in England; served with the Boer forces in charge of an ambulance unit in Natal 1899–1902; one of the founders of the National party; elected to the house of assembly in 1920, he later became a senator. Died 1 April 1943.

Von Bülow, Eduard Kurt George Victor. Business manager. Born 6 May 1893, district of New Hanover, Natal, South Africa; domiciled in South Africa since 1909; volunteer, Natal Mounted Rifles 1911–14; employed on farms and in business offices 1909–23; employee of Malcomess Ltd. from 1923 and manager of a subsidiary of Malcomess in Durban 1931–9; interned 1939–44; went to Germany in connection with a legacy 1944; interpreter for British military government 1945–7; returned to Natal 1946.

Von Kahr, Gustav. Government official and politician. Born 29 November 1862, Weissenburg, Bavaria, Germany; entered the Bavarian civil service 1890 and was in the department of the interior in 1919; premier of Bavaria March 1920–August 1921; governor-president of Upper Bavaria 1921–3; state commissioner of Bavaria with dictatorial powers September 1923 in which position he first supported, then opposed Hitler's *putsch*; president of the chief administrative tribunal, Munich 1924–30. Murdered during the Roehm purge, 30 June 1934.

Voroshilov, Kliment Efremovich. Army officer and politician. Born 4 February 1881, Verkhne, Dnepropetrovsk, Russia; worked from childhood in mines, ironworks and was a fitter at Alchevst 1896; joined the Bolshevik faction of the Social

Democratic party 1903; revolutionary leader, Lugansk 1903–7; delegate to party congresses 1906–7; experienced arrest, exile, escape 1907–14; member, Petrograd soviet 1917; military commander defending Tzaritsyn 1918–19; commander, Kharkov military district and of the 14th army 1919–20; member, central committee of the Communist party 1921; suppressed Kronstadt rising 1921; commander, north Caucasus area 1921–4, Moscow area 1924–5; commissar, military and naval affairs 1925–34; commissar for defence 1934–40; member of supreme soviet from 1937; commander-in-chief, north-western front 1941–5; chairman, allied control commission, Hungary 1945–7; vice-chairman, council of ministers of the U.S.S.R. 1946–53; president of the praesidium 1953–60, member from 1960; marshal of the U.S.S.R. from 1935; author of books on military science and history. Died 3 December 1969.

Wallace, Henry Agard. Journalist, politician, agriculturalist. Born 7 October 1888, Adair County, Iowa, United States of America; educated Iowa State College; associate editor, *Wallace's Farmer* 1910–24, editor 1929–33; breeder of high-yielding strains of maize 1913–33; secretary of agriculture 1933–40; vice-president of the United States 1941–5; secretary of commerce 1945–6; Progressive party presidential candidate 1948; author of books on agriculture and contemporary politics. Died 18 November 1965.

Wallas, Graham. Political philosopher. Born 31 May 1858, Sunderland, England; educated Shrewsbury School; Corpus Christi College, Oxford; schoolmaster 1881–90; university extension lecturer 1890–5; lecturer, London School of Economics 1895–1923; University of London professor of political science 1914–23; member of Fabian Society 1886–1904; member of London school board 1894–1904; member, London county council 1904–7 and of its education committee 1908–10; member of senate, University of London 1908–28; author of *Human Nature in Politics*; *The Great Society*, etc. Died 9 August 1932.

Walton, Edgar Brocas. Journalist and newspaper proprietor. Born 1880, Port Elizabeth, Cape Province, South Africa; educated Grey Institute, Port Elizabeth; served in the Anglo-Boer War and in South West and East Africa 1915–17; joined editorial staff, the *Eastern Province Herald* 1902; managing editor from 1906; editor 1923–38; succeeded his father as chairman of E. H. Walton and Co., proprietors of the *Eastern Province Herald* 1942; retired 1947. Died 18 July 1964.

Warburg, Max M. Banker. Born 5 June 1867, Hamburg; educated Gymnasium, Hamburg; Universities of Munich and Paris; head of the banking firm of M. M. Warburg 1893–1938; played a leading part in banking companies and chambers of commerce in Germany; financial adviser to Reichsbank 1924–33; director of the Hamburg-Amerika shipping line; served on the German financial commission in Paris 1919; left Germany 1939 and became a citizen of the United States of America 1944. Died 26 December 1946.

Waterson, Sydney Frank. Politician, diplomat and company director. Born 4 June 1896, Sydenham, Kent, England; his parents emigrated to South Africa 1897; educated in Johannesburg, at Walmer, Kent and Westminster School; served in Salonika and France 1915–19; returned to South Africa and entered commerce becoming director of J. Sedgwick and Co., wine merchants; South African party member of parliament 1929–38; minister plenipotentiary to France 1939; high commissioner in London 1939–42; United party member of parliament 1943–70; minister of economic development 1943–8; minister of mines 1945–8; minister of transport 1948; retired from political life 1970.

Watkins, Arnold Hirst. Medical practitioner; politician. Born 1851, Middlesex, England; educated University of Edinburgh; went to South Africa 1875; district surgeon, Victoria East 1875–8; practised at Boshof 1878–85 and Kimberley 1885–1910; Unionist party member of assembly 1910–21; senator 1922–7. Died 1927.

Watson, Herbert Gordon. Government official and administrator. Born 5 December 1874, Pietermaritzburg, Natal, South Africa; joined the Natal civil service; clerk in the office of the governor of Zululand 1895; transferred to civil service of the

Cape Colony 1901; chief clerk 1904; assistant clerk, executive council of the Union 1910; secretary to the prime minister 1916–27; accompanied General Hertzog to London as secretary of the Union delegation to the imperial conference 1926; administrator of Natal 1927–43 when he retired. Died 17 November 1948.

Watt, Alexander Strahan. Literary agent. Born 1869; educated privately in London and New York; senior partner of A. P. Watt and Son, literary agents. Died 30 December 1948.

Wauchope, General Sir Arthur Grenfell. Soldier. Born 1 March 1874, Edinburgh; educated Repton School; entered British army; served in Anglo-Boer War, rank of captain, and in the First World War as major; chief of British section, inter-Allied commission of control, Berlin 1924–7; commander, 44th home counties division 1927–9; high commissioner, Palestine and Transjordania 1931–8; knighted 1931; promoted general 1936. Died 14 September 1947.

Wavell, Archibald Percival, first Earl, of Cyrenaica. Soldier and administrator. Born 5 May 1883, Colchester, Essex, England; educated Winchester; Sandhurst; joined British army 1901; served in Anglo-Boer War, in France 1914–16, in the middle east under Allenby (q.v. vol. IV); general staff officer, war office 1923–6; commander, 6th infantry brigade, Aldershot 1930–4; then 2nd division 1935–7; commander in Palestine 1937–8; commander-in-chief, Middle East 1939–41; commander-in-chief, India 1941–3; viceroy of India 1943–7; created viscount 1943 and made a field marshal; created earl 1947; author of a biography of Allenby, essays on military science and other writings. Died 24 May 1950.

Waverley, John Anderson, first Viscount. Statesman. Born 8 July 1882, Esbank, Midlothian, Scotland; educated George Watson's College, Edinburgh, and Leipzig; permanent under-secretary, home office 1922–32; governor of Bengal 1932–7; lord privy seal 1938–9; home secretary 1939–40; lord president of the council 1940–3; chancellor of the exchequer 1943–5; member of the war cabinet 1940–5; created viscount 1952. Died 4 January 1958.

Weinthal, Leo. Journalist. Born 24 September 1865, Graaff-Reinet, Cape Province, South Africa; educated Grey Institute, Port Elizabeth; went to the Transvaal 1887; lithographer in the department of the surveyor-general 1889; editor of the *Press* in Pretoria; founded *Pretoria News* 1897; representative of *The Times*, the *Daily Telegraph* and Reuter's in the Transvaal 1888–97; settled in London 1900; founded *African World* 1900 of which he was editor; chief editor of *The Story of the Cape to Cairo Railway and River Route* (5 vols.); biographer of Sir Joseph Robinson. Died 4 June 1930.

Weizmann, Chaim. Chemist and Zionist leader. Born 27 November 1874, near Pinsk, Russia; educated Pinsk and Universities of Berlin and Freiburg; lecturer in chemistry, University of Geneva 1901; reader in bio-chemistry, University of Manchester 1904; became British citizen 1910; director, admiralty laboratories 1916; president, world Zionist organization 1921–31 and 1935–46; president, Jewish Agency for Palestine 1929; first president of the state of Israel 1948; chairman, Hebrew University in Jerusalem 1932; director, Weizmann Institute of Science; wrote an autobiography. Died 9 November 1952.

Welsh, William Thomson. Government official and politician. Born 1873, Bedford, Cape Province, South Africa; educated Dale College, King William's Town; joined Cape civil service 1892; held various posts in department of justice; appointed magistrate 1907, holding various posts as such until 1920; chief magistrate, Transkeian Territories and chairman of the general council 1920–33; member, Cape provincial council 1933–7; elected senator representing Transkeian Territories 1937–42; nominated senator representing Natives of the Union 1942–8; member of various commissions on Native affairs. Died 22 February 1954.

Weygand, General Maxime. Soldier. Born 21 January 1867, Brussels; educated Lycées Michelet, Henri IV, Louis-le-Grand; Saint-Cyr; officer in the French army 1887; chief of staff to Marshal Foch (q.v. vol. IV) 1914–23; promoted general

1916; high commissioner in Syria 1923–4; director, Centre for Military Education 1925; army inspector 1931–4; commander-in-chief of French forces in eastern Mediterranean 1939–40; supreme Allied commander 1940; minister of national defence under Pétain, June–September 1940; delegate-general to French Africa 1940–1; governor of Algeria 1941; imprisoned in Germany 1942–5; author of military biographies, a history of the French army and memoirs. Died 28 January 1965.

Wheeler, George Carlos. Biologist. Born 10 April 1897, Bonham, Texas, United States of America; educated Rice Institute, Houston; Harvard; instructor in zoology, Syracuse University 1921–4, then assistant professor of biology 1924–6; professor of biology, University of North Dakota 1926–63; co-author of *The Ants of North Dakota.*

Whitehead, Alfred North. Philosopher and mathematician. Born 15 February 1861, Ramsgate, England; educated Sherborne School; Trinity College, Cambridge; fellow and lecturer in mathematics, Trinity College 1885–1911; lecturer, applied mathematics and mechanics, University College, London 1911–14; professor of mathematics, University of London 1914–24; professor of philosophy, Harvard 1924–37; awarded the Order of Merit 1945; co-author, with Bertrand Russell, of *Principia Mathematica*; author of *Science and the Modern World*; *Process and Reality*; *Adventures of Ideas*; *Nature and Life*; and other works on mathematics and philosophy. Died 30 December 1947.

Wild, John Robert Francis (Frank). Explorer. Born 18 April 1873, Skelton, Yorkshire, England; entered merchant navy, then joined the royal navy in 1900; took part in the Antarctic expeditions of Scott 1901–4, Mawson 1911–13, and Shackleton 1907–9, 1914–17 and 1921–2; took over command on death of Shackleton in 1922; went to South Africa to grow cotton in Zululand 1924 but this venture failed; became hotel barman in Gollel, Zululand 1929 and later foreman of a slate mine in Klerksdorp, Transvaal; author of *Shackleton's Last Voyage.* Died 20 August 1939.

Wilhelm, (Friedrich Wilhelm Victor August Ernst von Hohenzollern). Crown Prince of Germany. Born 6 May 1882, Potsdam; eldest son of Kaiser Wilhelm II; educated Plön Cadet School; University of Bonn; commander of Hussar regiment 1905; seconded to general staff in Berlin 1913; given command of the fifth army 1914 and of the army group before Verdun 1915; fled to the Netherlands November 1918; renounced his rights of succession to the throne December 1918; permitted to return to Germany 1923; supported the Nazi movement; fled to Bavaria 1945 and was later captured by French forces. Died 20 July 1951.

Wilhelmina (Helena Paulina Maria). Queen of the Netherlands. Born 31 August 1880, The Hague; only child of William III and Emma of Waldeck-Pyrmont; succeeded to the throne 1890 under the regency of her mother; enthroned 1898; married Hendrik, Duke of Mecklenburg-Schwerin 1901; on the invasion of the Netherlands by Germany went with her family and her ministers to England 1940; returned to the Netherlands 1945; abdicated in favour of her daughter Juliana (q.v.) 4 September 1948; wrote memoirs *Eenzaam maar niet alleen.* Died 28 November 1962.

Wilkinson, James Alfred. Chemist. Born 1873, Manchester, England; educated Manchester Grammar School; Gonville and Caius College, Cambridge; science lecturer, Transvaal education department 1902; professor of chemistry, Transvaal Technical Institute, later Transvaal University College, later University of the Witwatersrand 1904–34; chairman, chemical section, South African engineering standards committee 1911–19. Died 1934.

Wilks, Edward Craven. Politician and business man. Born 12 July 1899, London; educated in Durban, Natal, South Africa; member of the Natal provincial council from 1930 and of the executive committee from 1945; honorary organizer of the United party in Natal up to 1949; vice-chairman 1949–51; honorary treasurer 1951–9.

Williams, Alpheus Fuller. Mining engineer. Born 21 June 1874, Oakland, California, United States of America; educated University of California; went to South Africa 1899 and joined staff of De Beers, Kimberley; assistant general manager 1900–4; general manager 1905–32; subsequently founded a firm of civil engineers; author of *The Genesis of the Diamond* and memoirs. Died 6 January 1953.

Willingdon, Freeman Freeman-Thomas, first Marquis. British administrator. Born 12 September 1866; educated Eton; Trinity College, Cambridge; Liberal member of parliament 1900–10 when he was made a peer; junior lord of the treasury 1905–12; governor of Bombay 1913–19; governor of Madras 1919–24; governor-general of Canada 1926–31; viceroy of India 1931–6; lord warden of the Cinque Ports; director of companies; created marquis 1936. Died 12 August 1941.

Willkie, Wendell Lewis. Politician and lawyer. Born 18 February 1892, Elwood, Indiana, United States of America; educated Culver Military Academy; University of Indiana; served in the First World War as artillery captain; member of the bar, New York City 1924; president, Southern and Commonwealth (electricity supply) Corporation 1933; opposed Roosevelt's 'New Deal' policies and was Republican candidate for the presidency in 1940 and 1944; advocated American support of the Allies; special representative of the United States in the Middle East, Russia and Nationalist China 1942; author of *One World*. Died 8 October 1944.

Wilson, Admiral Sir Arthur Knyvet. British naval officer. Born 4 March 1842; entered the royal navy; served in the Crimean War, the Chinese War and in Egypt; aide-de-camp to Queen Victoria 1892–5; rear-admiral 1895; lord commissioner of the admiralty 1897–1901; vice-admiral 1901; commanded Channel squadron 1901–3; commander-in-chief, home and Channel fleets 1903–7; admiral of the fleet 1907; first sea-lord, admiralty 1909–12 when he retired; awarded the Victoria Cross and the Order of Merit 1912; knighted 1902. Died 25 May 1921.

Wilson, Sir Henry Maitland, first Baron, of Libya and of Stowlangtoft. Soldier. Born 5 September 1881, Suffolk, England; educated Eton; joined the British army and served in Anglo-Boer War 1900–2; served in France and Flanders as brigade-major 1914–17; lieutenant-colonel serving with Australian forces 1918; commander, 1st battalion rifle brigade 1927–30; commander-in-chief of British troops in Egypt with rank of lieutenant-general 1939–41; commander-in-chief, Persia–Iraq 1942–3, Middle East 1943; made field marshal and supreme Allied commander, Mediterranean 1944; head of British staff mission in Washington 1945–7; created baron 1946; author of memoirs. Died 31 December 1964.

Winant, John Gilbert. Politician and diplomat. Born 23 February 1889, New York City; educated St Paul's School, Concord; Princeton University; teacher at St Paul's School 1912; enlisted as aviation private 1917 and became commander of an air squadron; senator of New Hampshire 1921; governor of New Hampshire 1925–6, 1931–4; assistant director, international labour office 1935, 1937–9 and director 1939–41; United States ambassador to Great Britain 1941–6; received honorary Order of Merit 1946. Died 3 November 1947.

Windsor, Duke of. See **Edward VIII.**

Wirth, Karl Joseph. Politician. Born 6 September 1879, Freiburg, Germany; educated University of Freiburg; teacher of mathematics, Freiburg Realgimnasium 1908–13; Centre party member of the reichstag 1914; finance minister of Baden November 1918–March 1920; finance minister of Germany March 1920–October 1921; chancellor May 1921–November 1922; minister for occupied zones 1929; minister of the interior 1930–1; lived in Switzerland 1933–48; founded the party *Union der Mitte* 1948; supporter of German–Russian collaboration after both World Wars; awarded Stalin peace prize 1955. Died 3 January 1956.

Wrey, Sir Philip Bourchier Sherard, twelfth Baronet. Mining engineer. Born 28 June 1858, England; educated as civil and mining engineer in Cornwall; went to Kimberley, South Africa, 1879; Cape government surveyor of Walvis Bay region 1883; practised as mining engineer on Witwatersrand from 1886; general manager,

Mashonaland Agency, an associate of the British South Africa Company from 1891; chairman of the Rhodesian chamber of mines 1923. Died 8 May 1936.

Wright, Robert Alderson, Baron, of Durley. British judge. Born 15 October 1869; educated Trinity College, Cambridge; barrister of the Inner Temple; bencher 1923; judge in king's bench division of the high court 1925–32; lord of appeal in ordinary 1932–5, 1937–47; master of the rolls 1935–7; created a life peer 1932. Died 27 June 1964.

Young, Sir Edward Hilton, See **Kennet.**

Younger, George, first Viscount. Industrialist; politician; company director. Born 13 October 1851, Scotland; educated Edinburgh Academy; chairman, George Younger and Son, brewers, Alloa; director, National Bank of Scotland, Lloyds Bank, Southern Railway, etc.; Unionist member of parliament 1906; chairman, Unionist party organization 1916–23, treasurer from 1923; created baronet 1911, viscount 1923. Died 29 April 1929.

Zimmern, Sir Alfred Eckhard. Politicial scientist. Born 1879, Surbiton, England; educated Winchester; New College, Oxford; lecturer in ancient history and tutor, New College 1903–9; inspector, board of education 1912–15; political intelligence department, foreign office 1918–19; professor of international politics, University College of Wales, Aberystwyth 1919–21; acting professor of political science, Cornell University 1922–3; director, Geneva School of International Studies 1925–39; professor of international relations, University of Oxford 1930–40; deputy director, research department, foreign office 1943–5; associated with Unesco 1945–50; author of *The Greek Commonwealth*; *The League of Nations and the Rule of Law*; *Spiritual Values and World Affairs*, etc.; knighted 1936. Died 24 November 1957.

INDEX

Bold figures refer to document numbers; ordinary figures refer to volume and page numbers
Document numbers are in all cases listed first.

Smuts, J. C., (2) letters (*cont.*)
July 1935, **382**; Spain; dictatorships; state of Europe, 7 September 1936, **407**; 'war is not imminent', 18 September 1937, **420**; replies to a request for his views on the international situation, 2 October 1937, **422**; state of Europe, pacifism and Nazism, 10 March 1939, **455**; the chances of peace, 17 August 1939, **470**; comments on 'unconditional surrender'; concern over future of Europe, 4 March 1945, **661**; democracies becoming lazy; Russia moving into a smashed Europe, 9 October 1945, **683**; Russia an enigma; J. H. Hofmeyr as his successor, 21 November 1945, **691**
to A. W. Gillett: 2 August 1920, **27**
to M. C. Gillett: taking up the premiership; state of Europe, 6 September 1919, **2**; beginnings as prime minister, 14 September 1919, **4**; political tour in north-west Cape; British railway strike, 4 October 1919, **7**; their friendship; world prospects dark, 30 December 1919, **16**; United States opposition to League of Nations, 19 January 1920, **20**; childhood recalled; human service, is it worthwhile? 26 July 1920, **26**; party fusion, the world scene is dark, 25 October 1920, **33**; the new South African party; Europe is sick, 1 November 1920, **34**; feels tired; the League and Wilson; women's suffrage, 26 December 1920, **40**; election tours; reads Einstein; his 1919 memorandum on war pensions, 3 January 1921, **41**; visits Sierra Leone; publication of his letter to De Valera, 20 August 1921, **63**; Ireland; the Washington conference, 6 December 1921, **66**; Witwatersrand strike; Anglo-French relations, 18 January 1922, **68**; Witwatersrand strike, 1 February 1922, **69**; Witwatersrand strike; Ireland; Lloyd George 'in a mess', 23 February 1922, **70**; Witwatersrand strike; British foreign and internal affairs; Ireland, 24 March 1922, **73**; making friends with the Rhodesians, 31 July 1922, **79**; political and economic conditions in South Africa are difficult; Germany seems to be going under, 30 August 1922, **80**; fall of Lloyd George's government, 25 October 1922, **82**; in a despondent mood; fears the madness of France; a last vestige of faith, 20 December 1922, **92**; speech on Table mountain; his reparation memorandum; French foreign policy, 1 March 1923, **95**; Europe plunging to destruction – can it be saved? 15 March 1923, **97**; the spirit of joy; out of tune with the British government, 30 March 1923, **101**; role of leaders in difficult world problems, 31 May 1923 **105**; his health; British foreign policy, 14 August 1923, **107**; his defeat, 24 June 1924, **149**; attitude to political defeat and assumption of leadership of the opposition, 9 July 1924, **152**; enjoying leisure, 17 September 1924, **153**; reading, riding, writing, 25 September 1924, **154**; climbs Klein Swartberg and is 'made one with nature', 11 May 1925, **164**; on holism and his book, 2 October 1925, **172**; profound unhappiness over colour bar and segregation legislation, 25 March 1926, **189**; riding in the bush; reading; Hertzog's Native bills farcical as a solution, 30 June 1926, **202**; A. N. Whitehead and holism, 17 November 1926, **211**; botany; Hertzog claims credit for 'sovereign status', 13 December 1926, **213**; efforts of himself and Botha to secure independence sneered at; lack of public interest in proposed Native bills; would leave politics without regrets, 5 January 1927, **218**; holism; Hertzog's Native bills; the flag question, 5 May 1927, **228**; holism and Bertrand Russell; state of Europe, 31 August 1927, **232**; wishes to retire from politics but future still uncertain, 30 November 1927, **235**; his new house in Cape Town; mountaineering; attitude on Hertzog's Native bills, 18 February 1928, **238**; has written his paper on 'The Nature of Life'; coming trip to East Africa; despairs of the Native question, 4 April 1929, **253**; the election campaign; British internal politics; Rhineland crisis and reparation problem, 22 April 1929, **255**; awaiting result of general election; Franchise Association makes difficulties, 11 June 1929, **258**; results of the general election; a new draft of 'The Nature of Life'; position of Great Britain is unsound, 19 June 1929, **259**; dissolution of the Union senate; his coming lectures in Great Britain, 9 August 1929, **263**; preparing his lectures; Hague reparation conference; clashes in Palestine, 28 August 1929, **264**; a day on Table mountain; Hertzog's Native bills in select committee, 28 February 1930, **275**; discouraged at reactionary legislation, 7 March 1930, **276**; the Native franchise question; reading Spinoza, 8 April 1930, **281**; Rooikop a dreamland, Native franchise impasse, 30 April 1930, **282**; his first duty to South Africa; Hertzog and imperial matters; preparing for his presidential address, 25 November 1930, **291**; on Winston Churchill; drought and depression, 4 December 1930, **292**; approves Hertzog's attitude

Smuts, J. C., (2) letters (*cont.*)
future of Christianity, 23 April 1939, **460**; reflections on religion; Danzig, 7 May 1939, **461**; resignations of J. H. Hofmeyr and L. Blackwell; negotiations with Russia, 27 May 1939, **464**; subversion in South Africa; his letters and papers; the Anglo-Russian negotiations, 3 August 1939, **469**; adventure on Table mountain; the Russo-German pact, 20 August 1939, **471**; special session of Union parliament; the Russo-German pact; neutrality issue, 28 August 1939, **473**; occupation of Poland; German and Nationalist attacks on him, 21 September 1939, **480**; the failure of fusion; grandchildren; labour on his farms; national roads, 30 October 1939, **483**; speech on futility of secession; naval engagements; Union aircraft for Finland, 19 December 1939, **487**; thoughts on a future international settlement; 'we are all soldiers', 24 January 1940, **490**; on 1 *Corinthians* xiii; War Measures Bill, 3 March 1940, **491**; the standstill war; trials of parliament, 4 April 1940, **492**; on personal immortality; invasion of Denmark and Norway, 7 April 1940, **493**; German successes; gift of a ciné set; extensions of holism, 9 May 1940, **494**; invasion of Holland and Belgium; moral significance of the war; Churchill as prime minister, 12 May 1940, **495**; surrender in Belgium and its consequences; all seems meaningless; seventieth birthday functions, 28 May 1940, **499**; fall of Paris; the rhythms of nature; 'still looking for the God within us', 14 June 1940, **502**; Franco-German armistice; refugee children; Nationalists and peace demand; confidence in British defence, 24 June 1940, **505**; course of the war; France; separate peace demand, 10 July 1940, **507**; Battle of Britain; attitude of the opposition; the session, 8 September 1940, **511**; visit to north Africa and flight over east Africa, 5 November 1940, **516**; march of motorized troops through the Union; Italy seems to be cracking, 8 December 1940, **518**; the United States and the war; Hertzog 'booted out', 30 December 1940, **522**; the war in north Africa; Germany must be tamed, 6 January 1941, **526**; visit to Egypt; flight over Kilimanjaro, 4 March 1941, **529**; course of the war; Vichy and the New Order; Native affairs, 18 May 1941, **537**; disarmament not the way to peace; South Africa and the war, 2 June 1941, **540**; the German invasion of Russia, 25 June 1941, **543**; thoughts on aspects of religion; troubles in India, 23 September 1941, **551**; Mozambique; Pauline mysticism, 29 October 1941, **553**; Japan and the United States in the war; advance in Libya, 13 December 1941, **554**; the war in the Far East and north Africa; his trusteeship speech; botany; New Testament reflections, 23 January 1942, **558**; South African expansion; reverses in the Far East and north Africa; on Churchill, 31 January 1942, **559**; course of the war; fifth column in South Africa; New Testament studies, 11 February 1942, **560**; course of the war; natural religion; gruelling days in parliament, 10 March 1942, **564**; Indian national movement; course of the war; the post-war world, 12 April 1942, **565**; war and native populations; pacifism, 7 June 1942, **568**; fall of Tobruk; Shakespeare studies; Jesus and Mary Magdalene, 23 June 1942, **569**; Jesus and the disciples; El Alamein, 10 July 1942, **572**; meeting with Churchill in Cairo; may visit London but avoids Moscow, 10 August 1942, **574**; his political opponents, 24 September 1942, **581**; flight from London via north Africa; course of the war; the opposition in South Africa, 29 November 1942, **586**; course of the war; the Abbé Breuil; Whitman, 14 December 1942, **587**; re-assessment of Whitman; the problem of good and evil, 26 December 1942, **588**; the coming general election; Native demands and wages, 13 January 1943, **591**; the bickering French leaders; premature preoccupation with social security, 19 January 1943, **594**; on Churchill; on Gandhi; Russian advances, 22 February 1943, **597**; his article on the British colonial empire; premature post-war plans, 27 February 1943, **598**; his burdens as prime minister; no time for long-range planning, 14 March 1943, **599**; the social service state; Indian question, 15 April 1943, **604**; victory in north Africa; South Africa's part; the modern tempo and the inner life, 14 May 1943, **607**; general election; the post-war world order; mankind must find its soul, 17 May 1943, **608**; Princess Frederica; supplies and civil aviation; coming invasion of Sicily, 9 June 1943, **611**; on death; merits of Left and Right; the war goes well, 21 July 1943, **615**; victory in the general election; fall of Mussolini; a triumph of faith in the invisible, 31 July 1943, **616**; the Russian alliance; Katyn; United party loyalty, 1 September 1943, **618**; activities in London, Tunis, Cairo, 24 December 1943, **628**;